D0936512

Yehuda Amichai

Yehuda Amichai

THE MAKING OF ISRAEL'S NATIONAL POET

Nili Scharf Gold

BRANDEIS UNIVERSITY PRESS

Waltham, Massachusetts

· Published by University Press of New England

Hanover and London

BRANDEIS UNIVERSITY PRESS

Published by University Press of New England,

One Court Street, Lebanon, NH 03766

www.upne.com

© 2008 by Brandeis University Press

Printed in the United States of America

5 4 3 2 1

Library of Congress Cataloging in Publication Data
Gold, Nili Scharf.
Yehuda Amichai : the making of Israel's national poet / Nili Scharf Gold. —
[1st ed.]
    p.   cm. — (The Tauber Institute for the Study of European Jewry series)
  Includes bibliographical references and index.
  ISBN 978-1-58465-733-0 (cloth : alk. paper)
  1. Amichai, Yehuda. 2. Poets, Israeli—Biography. 3. Amichai,
Yehuda—Criticism and interpretation. I. Title.
  PJ5054.A65Z686 2008
  892.4'16—dc22
  [B]   2008015514

This book was published with the support of the Lucius N. Littauer Foundation, Inc.

 University Press of New England is a member of the Green Press
Initiative. The paper used in this book meets their minimum
requirement for recycled paper.

To Billy, Doria, Avitai, and Jocelyn,

with all my love

And to the memory of my half-sister, Chana Scharf,

who perished during the Holocaust

Contents

Preface

An analytic study of Yehuda Amichai must address the conflict between the poet's German past and his new homeland. I have spent most of my adult life in the United States, far from my Hebrew mother tongue, and I knew the struggle inherent in linguistic double allegiance and the substitution of one landscape for another. I believed that despite Amichai's love for Israel and its language, he could not have rid himself of all traces of his childhood.

The persistence of Amichai's German birthplace and mother tongue in his creative process is manifest in the papers I scoured in the Beinecke Library at Yale University, the previously unknown documents I discovered, and interviews I conducted.

When I set out, I realized that the central thesis of the book would be provocative. Indeed, Yehuda Amichai is Israel's beloved unofficial national poet whose Hebrew works are seen by many as wholly and emblematically Israeli. The act of revealing his German origins may upset some of his admirers. As I show in this book, however, Yehuda Amichai, who was born Ludwig Pfeuffer, carried the sights, sounds, and experiences of his youth in Germany with him, and they contributed to making him the rich and layered poet we know today.

*   *   *

Over the course of my research, I had the unique privilege of meeting Ruth Z., the woman whom Amichai knew in Jerusalem from 1946 through 1947. The twenty-two-year-old Amichai, as seen through her eyes, and her spellbinding personal history, became integral to my narrative. In our many conversations, I not only learned about the poet as a young man, but also gained a new perspective on Jewish and Israeli history and the years of the struggle for independence. I am forever grateful to her for the documents she imparted to me, her incredible memory, and her clarity of vision. She made an unmatched contribution to this book and the field of Amichai studies as a whole.

I owe a tremendous debt to those who helped me reconstruct Amichai's German childhood, his hometown, and the life of its Jewish community that no longer exists. I interviewed Jewish children of Wuerzburg, survivors who were born or grew up there in the 1920s and 1930s. Most of them knew Amichai, attended the same school or synagogue, or sang with him in the boys' choir. I met them face to face and, in a few cases, conducted long-distance phone interviews. Together, they formed a virtual memory chain, each directing me to another Wuerzburgian who would enrich and color the portrait of the child Amichai in a different way. Norbert Hellmann, Amichai's classmate, and the son of Moritz Hellmann, who was both the last director of the school and the conductor of the synagogue choir, remembered the mischievous Ludwig. Hellmann guided me through the Jewish school day and curriculum, daily prayers, beloved rituals, choir rehearsals, and favorite romping grounds. Ludwig Bravman was also a classmate of Amichai's and a member of the same Orthodox circle. He provided incomparable testimony about their class, classmates, and teachers. Bravman tenderly and affectionately recalled the bright and spunky Ruth Hanover, Amichai's best friend and the rabbi's daughter. Ruth Kobliner (née Katzmann) was Amichai's distant cousin who spent summer vacations with him and his sister in their grandparents' village from the time they were all little children. When her father died, her mother married Rabbi Hanover and she became Ruth Hanover's stepsister. Kobliner's intimate depictions of her stepsister and of Amichai's family's household in Wuerzburg and Jerusalem were invaluable. Her portrayal of Amichai's father, Friedrich Pfeuffer, was an independent testament to this man's kindness. Like Kobliner, Mordechai Einsbacher spoke with admiration about this righteous man, a cornerstone in Amichai's poetry. Einsbacher also recalled fondly how Wuerzburg's children watched the trains and inhaled their smoke.

Henry (formerly Hans) Eschwege, the son of the cantor-mohel Ruben Eschwege, told me about his father's artistic designs for the mappot, the ribbons that tied Torah scrolls. Eschwege also drew a vivid picture of the synagogue milieu and of Rabbi Hanover, whom Amichai revered. Otto Schlame, the musical son of the violin teacher, was in the choir with Amichai, Bravman, Eschwege, and Hellman. He remembered how, on Simhat Torah, the choir boys watched jealously as the other children followed the Torah with bags, which the adults filled with sweets, when suddenly they were showered with candy, thrown from the synagogue's women's gallery. Schlame also shared with me the nickname for the devilish Ludwig—"Pfif." Elizabeth (formerly Ruth) Cecchetti (née Schwabacher) was younger, and therefore did not know

Amichai, but she could reconstruct her childish perception of the atmosphere in Wuerzburg and the scary walks to the Jewish school in the mid-1930s. She gave me a rare photograph of the second-grade classroom and recalled in detail the teachers, especially the caring Mr. Gruenfeld. She connected me to her older brother, Bill (formerly Wolfgang) Schwabacher, who, in Wuerzburg, tried to protect his sister on their long walks to school. Children of a Liberal, non-Orthodox family, the Schwabachers provided a somewhat different perspective on the school and the community. Finally, I would like to thank Yehudit Silber, Ruth Kobliner's daughter, for the precious photographs she generously sent me.

In addition to interviewing those who knew Amichai, I traveled to Germany in order to reconstruct Amichai's childhood accurately. I am grateful to Amichai's friends and current residents of Wuerzburg, Rosa and Otto Grimm. They learned about the poet's idiosyncratic childhood landmarks from conversations they had and excursions they took with Amichai when he visited Wuerzburg in the 1980s and 1990s. Among other things, the Grimms showed me the deep well that had frightened Amichai and the arched entrance to his father's notions store. They drove me to the villages of his grandparents and their local, rural cemeteries. Christian Leo, a German Amichai scholar, was the best tour guide to Wuerzburg anyone could have imagined. He is a native of the city and an expert in its art and history. Christian helped me follow Amichai's footsteps as depicted in Amichai's novel and continued to be a bountiful source of information about the German language, local cultural traditions and the materials in Wuerzburg's archives. Christian's kind assistance was instrumental from the initial stages of research all the way through to the book's completion.

Arnold Band—Arnie, my teacher and mentor—was not only the motivation for my scholarly interest in Amichai (my dissertation and then my Hebrew book on the poet), but also my support throughout the years. He and his wife, Ora, even led me to one of my first interviewees from Wuerzburg. Arnie has never ceased to believe in me and the importance of my research. In our meetings across the United States and over long, laborious phone calls he generously bestowed upon me his deep literary insight, vast historical knowledge, and editorial genius.

I am profoundly grateful to Yigal Schwartz. His vision of the Israeli literary political system was extremely significant for my description of Amichai's place within it. Yigal's loyal friendship helped me to overcome the various obstacles I met while writing this book.

Glenda Abramson's unique understanding of Amichai's person and writing proved invaluable to me at many crossroads. I thank James Shapiro for his encouragement and generosity of spirit.

I am indebted to my late teacher, Gershon Shaked, for his sage advice.

I thank my academic home, the University of Pennsylvania, and my colleagues there, and I am grateful to the Center for Advanced Judaic Studies, which was the midwife of the initial chapters. I would especially like to thank the chair of my department, Roger Allen, and my colleague, Jeffrey Tigay, for standing by me.

Maayan Harel, using her detective talent, gracefully and confidently made her way through the various labyrinths of Israeli archives and solved many bibliographic mysteries.

I appreciate the insight and hard work that my editors, Phyllis Deutsch and Sylvia Fuks-Fried, invested in their careful and insightful reading and commentary on the manuscript. I am pleased to have my book appear in both the Tauber Institute Series and the Schusterman Series in Israel Studies with Brandeis University Press. I benefited from the support of the Lucius N. Littauer Foundation Publishing Award, the Judah Goldin Research Fund Grant of the Near Eastern Languages and Civilizations Department at the University Pennsylvania, and the American-Israeli Cooperative Enterprise Publishing Grant.

Thanks go as well to Mark Anderson, Avis Berman, Julia Bloch, Miriam Hoffman, Tom Klein, Victor Kovner, Chana Landes, Hanaan Marwah, David Rosenthal, and Helen Wheeler for their editorial, technical, and investigative help at various stages. My deepest gratitude goes to Judy Bass, Jack Levy, Kiki Hadar, and Bathsheva Rifkin, for their steadfast friendship and unwavering support.

The writing of this book would have been impossible without Julia Holleman, my assistant and right hand. Her voice, her outstanding talent and style, and her integrity are intertwined with this book. She shared in its composition from her college graduation in 2005 until the submission of the manuscript in 2007. Julia never flinched at the massive quantities of raw material that had to be reined in and transformed into orderly computer files; she never lost her optimism and faith in me and in the project, even in the most difficult moments. For all that and more, I am eternally grateful.

This book is dedicated to my beloved family, who together helped me to bring it to life. Billy, my husband and cheerleader, was with me every step of the way. His love and devotion cushioned and shielded me and never let me fall. His inventiveness and ingenuity, and the deep bond we share, enabled me to realize this mission. My son, Avitai, who, like me, loves words, edited countless drafts. His enlightening comments on language and expression and his passionate readings are embedded in the book's various chapters. His unflagging encouragement was the engine behind my finishing this book. Jocelyn, my daughter (in-law), expressed her confidence in me in her elegant and understated way and allowed Avitai to spend his weekends reading drafts without losing her patience. My daughter, Doria, who knows what I intend to write before I even conceive it myself, helped me to weave all the threads of this book into a cohesive whole. Her astute psychological and literary insight, her identification with me, and her dedication are at the heart of this book. I thank the four of them with all my heart.

Amichai and the words he wrote will remain with me forever.

Yehuda Amichai

CAMOUFLAGE AS THE KEY TO THE
POETRY OF YEHUDA AMICHAI

One evening in 1997, I went to a university lecture in New York City with Yehuda Amichai, Israel's best-known poet. We sat in a back row at the end of a crowded hall and waited for the speaker to begin, when suddenly he touched my arm and said, almost in a whisper, "Do you see, three rows in front of us, near the aisle, a woman sits? Her name is Ruth Z. Do you remember the poem about the one who 'ran away to America'? I wrote it about her."

I knew the text. "The Rustle of History's Wings, as They Said Then" is a bitter poem from 1980 fraught with details about a bygone love during curfew in Jerusalem, a love that eventually ended with a betrayal.[1] I wanted to know more, yet something in the sound of the poet's voice prevented me from asking any questions. I wondered why he revealed the subject of the poem to me, but in our subsequent meetings before his death in 2000, I did not dare inquire about the woman we had seen in the lecture hall.

As fate would have it, two years after Amichai died, I sat face to face with the woman whose name and features were forever etched in my memory. A friend introduced me to her, saying, "You two have something in common. You both knew Amichai."

"I know," I said.

"How do you know?" asked Ruth, startled.

"Amichai told me who you were some years ago." I omitted Amichai's reference to the poem about the woman who had deserted Israel for America. Later, however, it became clear to me that Ruth Z. knew "History's Wings" very well. As a matter of fact, she alone knew the private history to which the poem's lines allude.

This time, I decided not to suppress the urge to investigate. "Would you be willing to tell me what happened between the two of you?"

"Yes. Come see me and I'll tell you."

A few months later, I went to Ruth's home in New York.

We sat in her apartment for many hours while she unveiled a story that had been kept hidden for half a century. As I listened to her, little by little a chapter opened in front of me about the love affair of Ruth Z. and Amichai, Amichai's emergence as a poet, and the history of Israel and its people. After we became closer, Ruth confided to me that she had a stack of letters from Amichai that she had not touched in almost sixty years.

The letters had been sealed in a dark tin box since April 1948.

When Ruth opened the box, my heart skipped a beat. In front of me lay over one hundred pages filled with cramped handwriting, as well as a faded blue, hand-bound notebook and a tiny booklet held together by a rusty safety pin. I knew that these papers, strewn on Ruth's coffee table, represented the earliest substantial body of Amichai's writings in existence and that I was the first to see them besides Ruth.

The magnitude of this finding overwhelmed me. I had spent the previous year at the Beinecke Rare Book and Manuscript Library at Yale University (where Amichai had deposited his papers shortly before his death), struggling to read tiny, ripped pads, and attempting to decipher lines that the poet had jotted to himself.[2] The earliest documents in the archive are dated 1954, when Amichai was already thirty years old and was about to publish his first book of poems.[3] And behold, there in Ruth's living room, dozens of pages in meticulous Hebrew script, written by the poet when he was twenty-three, were spread in front of my eyes. The letters are numbered, as though Amichai wanted to facilitate scholarly citation or to maintain control over the continuity of his narrative.[4] When Ruth and I started reading the densely written aerograms, I realized that they chronicled not only the days before the poet became a poet, but also the historical times before the State of Israel became a state.

Over the weeks that followed, I felt as if I were participating in a séance. I heard the tale of those momentous months in two intersecting voices: the feminine voice of Ruth Z. at the beginning of the twenty-first century, and the resurrected voice of Amichai, inscribed in blue ink on the face of lightweight paper, from the middle of the twentieth.

Amichai's love affair with Ruth Z. lasted from January 1947 to April 1948, and the poet's name still bears the mark of their love story. In the summer of 1947, after they had both graduated from the teachers' college in Jerusalem, they decided to build their life together in the port city of Haifa. The teaching position that Amichai found at the Geula Elementary School there required that he replace his German surname, "Pfeuffer," with a Hebrew one. The couple started looking for a Hebrew name that would melodically complement both "Yehuda" and "Ruth."[5] They had been trying unsuccessfully to find a nice-sounding name beginning with "P" to match "Pfeuffer" when Ruth finally called out, "Amichai! Yehuda Amichai!" She thought that the name "Amichai," which means "my nation is alive" (*ami*, my nation; *chai*, is alive), mirrored their patriotic hopes and feelings.

The young man hesitated. "Yehuda Amichai? Isn't it too bombastic?"

Ruth answered, "You want to be a great poet, right? Yehuda Amichai sounds like the name of a great poet." And so it came to pass.[6]

In the end, however, Ruth Z. did not move to Haifa, nor did she adopt the new, patriotic surname. On August 31, 1947, she boarded a ship for America, leaving Amichai longing for her and in total denial about the fact that she might never return to him. Her departure motivated an ardent correspondence that lasted for eight months. In the poem that he wrote about her thirty-three years later, Yehuda Amichai bemoans:

I paid five shillings and changed my ancestral name
from the Diaspora to a proud Hebrew name to match hers
. . . [she] fled to America. . .
and left me with my new name . . .[7]

With a "new name," a rented room, and a "teacher's paltry salary,"[8] Amichai began his life in Haifa. His letters to Ruth Z., he thought, would be the ideal repository for his observations, reflections, and lyrical musings. And, indeed, the forty-three aerograms he wrote from September through November 1947 document Amichai's poetic growth and his romantic image of himself as a poet writing to his beloved; but history soon reared its head. As the vote in the United Nations on the partition plan for Palestine approached, Amichai labored as a teacher and a poet under the shadow of escalating violence. After the resolution passed on November 29, 1947, and the conflict between Jews and Arabs intensified, he was drawn into military activities, ultimately becoming a teacher by day and a soldier by night. His life plan to be a poet and his national, patriotic duty pulled him in different directions. Yet through his grueling schedule, his fatigue, and the bloodshed that surrounded him, Amichai persevered in sending letters to Ruth. He stopped writing to her only after he found out that she was marrying another man; her "Dear John" letter arrived less than a month before the full eruption of the Israeli War of Independence.

In interviews he granted later in his life, Amichai rarely mentioned Ruth Z., and if he did so, it was only in passing, without saying her name. In these interviews, he also often left out the eight months he spent in Haifa, the time when he first blossomed as a poet.[9] An omission of this kind occurs in the only monograph dedicated to him.[10] In the list "Dates and Turning Points in Amichai's Life" at the end of that monograph, Yehudit Tzvik, the editor, disregards the poet's time in Haifa, lumping together his teaching there with the fifteen years that he taught at various schools in Jerusalem. Amichai, who was still living when this publication appeared, probably approved this biographical outline and decided to exclude that turbulent school year he spent in Haifa.[11] A more dramatic and deliberate erasure of his memories from that period is manifested in the fate of one early poem published in 1951, entitled "Other Evenings."[12]

Amichai's poems, which began trickling into newspapers in 1949, often retain the imprint of his distant beloved and his unmistakable longing for her. Especially heartrending are these lines from "Other Evenings": "Our love is embroidered on the room and on them, / and your blue dress and your red dress strewn with white dots."[13] Almost sixty years later, Ruth Z. pointed to a picture taken in Jerusalem in 1947; she was wearing the polka-dot dress that the poem so wistfully recalls. In Amichai's debut volume, *Now and in Other Days*, however, the dress was missing. Its polka dots were also absent from what is now considered Amichai's canonic collection, *Poems: 1948–1962*, where this first book was republished.[14] This particular early poem was excised from Amichai's representative corpus, and although the poet later reinstated a few poems he had initially passed over, "Other Evenings" remained one of the outcasts. This poem of yearning was not the only remnant of the relationship to disappear. The story of Amichai's love for Ruth Z., and, with it, the record of his first steps as a poet all but vanished. The self-censorship that Amichai exercised with regard to this single poem is symptomatic of the way he confined the memory of that time and much of its poetic legacy to the subtext of his canonic verse. Amichai's own biographical accounts and, more significantly, the lyrical works that established him as a poet cover up his personal saga during these crucial years.

Thanks to Ruth's cooperation and the discovery of the letters, this book is the first to expose the deep impression that Ruth Z. made on the poet's life and early work. Most consequential to the understanding of Amichai's oeuvre is the reinterpretation presented here of Amichai's flagship collection, *Poems: 1948–1962*, in light of these new findings. Furthermore, the content of the letters confirms that Amichai suppressed his artistic and emotional origins in his poetry.

The question, however, remains: Why would a poet who considered himself lyrical and autobiographical cover up this defining period of his life?[15] Was the pain of Ruth abandoning him so great that he was unable to approach the affair or even its temporal and geographical background? A review of Amichai's poetic oeuvre and his self-portrayals in interviews reveals that concealing the memory of Ruth Z. was not an isolated incident. In fact, the poetic suppression of this trauma is a microcosm of an overarching behavioral, psychological, and literary force at the heart of Amichai's verse. In 1984, I identified this poetic pattern and later devoted a chapter to it in my dissertation (although I did not name it "camouflage" at the time).[16] After reading an early draft of my dissertation, Amichai told me that I had made him aware of this behavior, and he tacitly acknowledges this admission in his 1989 poem, "What Did I Learn in the Wars."[17] Here, Amichai testifies that "camouflage" is a defense that has served him superbly in both art and life. Accordingly, in this book I refer to the underlying literary and psychological principle that determined so much of Amichai's poetry as "camouflage." Amichai's relationship with Ruth Z., then, was only one of a number of significant facets of his life that he chose to camouflage in his verse.

Other areas that Amichai buried deep in his poems belong to the world of his childhood. Amichai lived his early years as Ludwig Pfeuffer, far from the Israeli sites that formed the setting for his affair with Ruth Z. He grew up in Wuerzburg, Germany, the ancient capital of Franconia, whose arching bridges and cobblestone alleys are adorned with statues of saints and ornate fountains. In his beautiful hometown, in the region of Bavaria, Amichai knew another Ruth, whom everybody called "Little Ruth." The memory of her name undoubtedly resonated in his initial attraction to the striking Ruth Z. whom he met in Jerusalem in 1947. Little Ruth had blue eyes and chestnut hair; she was approximately the same age as Amichai and lived a few houses up the street. The two were so inseparable that the members of their community referred to them as "bride and groom." They had a unique friendship, deep and "completely platonic."[18]

Little Ruth was the daughter of the revered Rabbi Hanover, and Amichai's father was one of the beloved leaders of Wuerzburg's Orthodox Jewish community. During services, Little Ruth's father delivered oratorical sermons in

German, draped in his majestic robe, while Amichai's father coddled his son under his fuzzy prayer shawl.

The commanding synagogue was housed in the same building complex as the German-Jewish school the children attended. Little Ruth Hanover and Amichai had been classmates since kindergarten and, starting in second grade, Little Ruth would pick up Amichai from his house every morning.[19] The path to school took the children through Wuerzburg's most magnificent landmarks. Rennweg, the broad boulevard that stretches from the train tracks toward the center of town, led them to a pair of gigantic, intricate wrought-iron gates. These gates guard the Hofgarten, the elaborate, terraced garden surrounding Wuerzburg's grand palace, the Residenz.[20] Inside the garden, the two friends passed the baroque fountains, whose bubbling waters cascaded around copper statues of sensual nymphs and wild animals, but they could not stop there in the morning lest they be late for school.

Some of these scenes unfolded in front of my eyes when I visited Wuerzburg in 2001 and 2004 and walked in the footsteps of the two Jewish children on their way to school.

In his apartment in Washington Heights, Norbert Hellmann, an eighty-year-old classmate of the two friends, remembered that Little Ruth and Amichai were the brightest students in their class. She was studious and took school seriously, and, although Amichai was the class clown and loved to make people laugh, he was entranced by the stories and poems they read with their teachers.[21] Paralleling the study of Jewish texts, German language and culture formed the core of the secular curriculum that the Jewish school shared with the Bavarian system.[22] Its goal was to instill the students with a love of the German homeland, its language, literature, and culture.[23]

Even after the Nazis' rise to power in 1933, everyday life for the young students at the Jewish school continued with relative normalcy. In the winter of 1934, their main preoccupation was the school's traditional and highly celebrated Hanukkah play. On a snowy day, Little Ruth and Amichai got into a heated argument about the casting of the lead role of Judah Maccabee. During recess, the ten-year-old girl borrowed another boy's bike, rode off, and got into a life-threatening accident. Her leg had to be amputated, and she was bedridden for almost a year. Amichai visited her in the hospital, and when she recovered and had been fitted with a prosthesis, they again walked to school together, but their world had changed. By 1935, Nazi youths had begun assaulting students from the Jewish school. The hounded children learned to dodge stones and glue themselves to the walls of buildings, skipping from doorway to doorway, ready to hide from an attack. Walking to school had become dangerous and the crippled girl was now an easy target. The day that Little Ruth and Amichai were ambushed outside the gardens on the way to school remained branded in Amichai's memory for the rest of his life.[24] Not long after, Amichai's father, who was a volunteer at the Jewish burial society, was shaken by the sight of the corpses of two village Jews who had been beaten to death. He subsequently led an entire tribe of Pfeuffers in their flight to Palestine. Little Ruth's father, who felt responsible for his deteriorating congregation, decided to stay behind with his family. In July 1936, as the train pulled out of the station, Amichai waved goodbye to Little Ruth. The two friends never saw each other again.[25]

The horrific scenes that preceded the Pfeuffers' exodus and the emigration itself are virtually absent from Amichai's canonical verse. Missing, too, are the German language, the Bavarian landscape, and the little girl he loved. Synagogue Hebrew, however, prevailed in his writing, and quotations from the prayer book became his stylistic trademark. Jewish customs are woven into the fabric of his verse as well, while the monumental figure of his protective father towers above his entire poetic universe. Thus, Amichai did not repress the entirety of his childhood, but rather made certain elements fade away while allowing others to survive.

Despite the state of the Jews in Germany, on the whole, Amichai's early years were happy. He grew up the pride of a doting family in a picturesque medieval town nestled in verdant hills. When he left Wuerzburg, he was old enough for it to have made a profound impression on him. Nevertheless, Amichai left many scenes of his childhood out of his poetry, just as he suppressed his first adult love.

Like most modern Hebrew writers in the first half of the twentieth century, Amichai considered poetry to be the pinnacle of literary expression and wanted to make his name as a poet. Raised on the romantic tradition and an avid admirer of the poet Rilke, he believed that childhood was the source of artistic creation.[26] Why, then, would this lyrical and autobiographical poet efface his formative experiences from the genre he revered? What motivated Amichai to discard some memories but hold on to others? What was the threat posed by the German childhood and the adult love? What do they have in common and why did the poet "abandon" them? Are they really omitted from his verse? These questions have never been asked. The answers to them are intertwined with Amichai's poetic practice of camouflage. They are the key to understanding not only Amichai's poetry, but the man and his oeuvre as a whole.

Most critics have accepted the absence of these materials and periods from Amichai's verse without reservation. Indeed, historians and scholars of Amichai could not have imagined the scope of what he concealed. No one knows the details or the impact of the love affair with Ruth Z. or about the crucial time he spent writing poetry and teaching in Haifa. While all of the poet's biographical accounts acknowledge that he was born in Germany in 1924 and lived there until he was twelve, few scholars, if any, heed the artistic implications of these facts. Amichai's foreign roots are known, but they are typically glossed over by journalists and reviewers alike. In the Israeli tradition, both the poet and his critics emphasized his Israeliness and treated 1936, the year he arrived in Palestine, as though it were a second birth. *Poems: 1948–1962* was hailed as a revolutionary work. It deals almost entirely with the Israeli experience. Even though Amichai recounts parts of his childhood in *Not of This Time, Not of This Place*, a semi-autobiographical novel published in 1963, the critical literature, for the most part, dismisses it and does not apply its contents to the interpretation of his poetry.[27] No critical work has delved into the conflicts at the heart of Amichai's poetry and its biographical, psychological, and multilingual sources. Furthermore, no study has either examined the poet's early years or recognized their meaningful role in his poetry, in part because of Amichai's own efforts to marginalize them.

Historically, Amichai belongs to the group of writers who founded "Israeli literature" in the 1950s and early '60s. Scholars would later call its members the "Generation of the State," because they were the first authors to publish in the State of Israel after it was established. Their innovations radically transformed the way Hebrew literature was written.[28] Amichai and his peers rebelled against their predecessors' grandiose, ideological verse and proclaimed that "understatement" would be one of their guiding principles. Of his literary generation, only Amichai attained the unofficial status of "national poet."[29] In 1963, when he was thirty-nine years old, he published *Poems: 1948–1962*, the collection that would define him as a poet for the rest of his creative life (for a photograph of Amichai during this period, see image 15). It contains uncollected poems written between 1958 and 1962, as well as the three volumes he had published previously. *Poems: 1948–1962* epitomizes the ways Amichai's work severed ties with the old traditions and heralded a new one.[30] Critics often consider this collection as the embodiment of the poet's groundbreaking oeuvre, even though Amichai went on to publish two novels, a book of short stories, a collection of plays, and ten additional books of verse.

From the time that they first appeared in newspapers and periodicals, Amichai's poems overturned Hebrew poetry by lowering the linguistic register and deflating the pathos of the previous literary generation. His "rugged rhyme schemes"[31] shattered traditional meter, and his heterogeneous vocabulary reflects the drastic changes that had taken place in Hebrew during World War II and the War of Independence. Amichai's poems absorb and rework everyday materials, integrating them into a poetry that had hitherto avoided modern terms so as not to mar the beauty of classical Hebrew.[32] In Amichai's hands, airplanes, tanks, gasoline, iceboxes, legal contracts, and mathematical axioms became the building blocks of poems for the first time. He used unexpected metaphoric and linguistic combinations throughout his verse, pairing the high with the low, nature with technology, the emotional with the mechanical; storks flying over rural landscapes become jet planes and the eyes of a tired soldier close like the portholes of a tank.[33] A girl's weeping carries many sorrows, like a locomotive that pulls many train cars.[34] Under Amichai's command, literary, biblical, and liturgical Hebrew became flexible and vibrant as he playfully interwove modern concepts with fragments of prayers and ancient prophesies. For instance, he subverted the prophet Micah's pastoral vision of peace at the End of Days and transported it into the contemporary arena of war. In biblical times, a man sitting under a vine or a fig tree symbolized tranquility. In Amichai's poem "Sort of an Apocalypse," however, the "man under his vine" telephones the "man under his fig tree" to strategize their military defense.[35] This irreverent tone and the inclusive use of all layers of Hebrew remain signature traits of Amichai's writing, influencing generations of poets.

Amichai's poetry replaced the high diction, tone, and nationalist bent of his predecessors' poetry with prosaic verse that refuses to worship heroism. Although Amichai's speaker identifies with the national struggle, he challenges the sacrifices it demands.[36] He desires a home, a family, and normality, while subtly expressing feelings against the war that squelches such aspirations. This emphasis on the individual voice is one of Amichai's most significant contributions to Hebrew poetry. He shunned the collectivist "we" that had dominated through the War of Independence and forged a poetic "I," whose unmistakable Amichai-like traits are still emulated and venerated. In recognition of his literary contributions, Amichai was awarded the Israel Prize, the highest honor Israel bestows on its citizens.[37] But Amichai's humanist poetry reaches beyond the borders of Hebrew language and literature and touches people around the world. Ted Hughes, whose translations first introduced Amichai to English readers in the 1960s, said, "I, for one, return to these poems again and again, and always find myself shaken."[38] The esteemed British poet laureate was not alone in his admiration for his Israeli colleague. At the time of Amichai's death in September 2000, his poetry had been translated into over thirty-seven languages and Amichai was on the short list for the Nobel Prize. When he died, memorials were held for him across the globe; in Israel, thousands came to bid him a final farewell in front of Jerusalem's City Hall. Teachers and students, soldiers and generals, writers and housewives showed up, because Amichai's poems spoke for them all.

Israelis from all walks of life see Amichai as the quintessential Israeli. For them, he is inextricably linked to the country and its narrative, in part because the Hebrew readers conflate the man's representative biography and the poet's Israel-centric verse. The turning points in Amichai's life neatly parallel the turning points of twentieth-century Jewish history: he grew up in the shadow of the Third Reich and immigrated to the Land of Israel in 1936. During World War II, he enlisted in the British army and in 1948, as a member of the elite military Palmah, he fought in Israel's War of Independence. In numerous interviews, Amichai recounted how he began writing poetry to soothe himself in the midst of the famous battles in the Negev Desert. In both intra- and extrapoetic statements, he described his emergence as a poet as an unexpected "consecration" that took place at the atypically late age of twenty-four during the War of Independence.[39] Thus, even the first lines he set to paper seem tied to the land: in his personal mythology, Amichai the poet and Israel the state were born simultaneously. After the war, he became the voice of a generation that was weary of bloodshed. His poetry accompanied the State of Israel for the ensuing five decades, through subsequent wars and the intervals of calmness. For the most part, his poetry is local, its rich imagery connected to the land's topography and vegetation. It continually returns to the War of Independence and its formative battles, even when the subjects of the poems are distant from it.

Amichai's speaker walks through Jerusalem and the desert, his footsteps echoing the strides of his country. Viewed together, his poems seem to be the personal diary of an authentic "I" who is documenting his life in his writing. Amichai's biography and his image as the "poet-soldier" made him an Israeli icon; when the late prime minister Yitzhak Rabin received the Nobel Peace Prize, he asked Amichai to read one of his poems at the ceremony.[40] Amichai, too, believed in the kinship between himself and his country and wove it into his verse:

When I was young, the country was young too. My father
Was everybody's father. When I was happy, the country was happy, when I
    jumped
Upon her, she jumped under me. The grass that covered her in spring
Softened me too. Her soil in summer pained me
As parched skin in my soles. When I loved
Immensely, her independence was announced, when my hair
Waved, her banners waved. When I fought,
She fought. When I rose, she rose too, and when I declined
She began declining with me.[41]

These lines, published in 1977, frame Amichai's life entirely in terms of the State of Israel, implying an individual mythology that is typically Israeli. The youth of the speaker parallels that of the Land of Israel and the reciprocal motions of his body and her soil are erotically charged. His hair mirrors her flags and the Declaration of Independence, the climax of her existence, overlaps with his "great love." Sadly, the decline of the land reflects the aging of the speaker, her human image. This poem appeared when Amichai was fifty-three years old. In its theme and tone it evokes other ostensibly autobiographical poems that punctuate Amichai's poetic oeuvre.

A quarter of a century earlier, a twenty-eight-year-old Amichai published a poetic manifesto of sorts in the revolutionary literary periodical Likrat.[42] It was called "Autobiography 1952."[43] After a theatrical opening filled with birth-related imagery, the poem's speaker (who is exactly the same age as the poet) retells his life story. He recalls his "merry and small" hands at play when he was seven years old ("in '31"), but immediately afterwards leaps ahead to when he was seventeen and first learned to hold a gun ("And in '41 . . ."). The allusion to military activity at this age casts the speaker as a typical Israeli adolescent—army training for high school students was part of daily life for Jewish youth in the 1940s in Palestine. The poem intimates that its speaker fought bloody battles in the years that followed 1941; it concludes in spring 1952, when he has become a civilian family man. There is no hint in this chronological narrative, however, as to what transpired between 1931 and 1941. Although "Autobiography 1952" preceded the declaration "When I was young the country was young . . ."[44] by twenty-five years, the poems share a core belief: the parallel identification between Israel and the speaker. There is another similarity, however: neither poem discloses where the "child" or the "young one" came from.

Both poems reflect the prevailing generational conviction that the self begins with the Land of Israel and is entirely captured by its boundaries. The Zionist myth, which accompanied the development of society and culture in the Jewish settlement in Palestine and later in the State of Israel, was that the Land of Israel would redeem the Jews from the Diaspora. It would bring about a spiritual and social revival of the Jewish people.[45] In his magnum opus, *Hebrew Narrative Fiction*, Gershon Shaked wrote, "The terms 'exilic' and 'Israeli' became two poles that characterized the thinking of Israeli society, in which 'Israeli' signifies the new, healthy and erect, while the 'diasporic,'—the old, sick and bent-over."[46] He observed that "writers were called upon to identify with the strong, victorious, conquering [Israeli] hero."[47] According to this analysis, Amichai's self-presentation as a near-native and his attempt to hide his strong ties to Europe were not an individual or idiosyncratic phenomenon. Rather, his self-made persona fit the general belief that in order to create a new, free nation in Israel, one had to suppress the diasporic past, identify completely with the Zionist ideology, and immerse oneself, body and soul, in Zionist goals.

It is tempting to read Amichai's poetry as the unfolding narrative of a man's life from childhood through his wars, his loves, his partings, and his conflicts. Indeed, Amichai's Israel-centric self-portrayal misled many critics, who failed to see that beneath this picture lay another one, which the poet painted over. A careful reading of *Poems: 1948–1962* reveals that, contrary to common belief, Amichai's poems contain little concrete information from the poet's early life. As Glenda Abramson rightly notes in *The Writing of Yehuda Amichai*, "Amichai's poetry falls somewhere between both possibilities, autobiographical in appearance and mood rather than in substance."[48] Amichai may have replaced the collective "we" with an "I," but that "I" in his verse is quite amorphous. Like most Israelis, the speaker of Amichai's poems fights in wars and loses friends, falls in love and suffers heartbreak, is familiar with the Bible but has questioned God. Yet, many details are missing from this portrait. Absent are his childhood landscapes, their textures and smells, the sounds the child heard and the people who inhabited his world. Amichai's earliest impressions are almost always missing from his "autobiographical" poems, and in "Autobiography 1952" this absence is particularly conspicuous; in a poem that begins its biographical account in 1931, Amichai did not even hint at his experiences in Nazi Germany. This incomplete poetic autobiography has been unquestioningly accepted by Amichai's critics and welcomed by his readers, as it reflects their idealized image of their poet. The truth, however, lies somewhere between the repressed and the unveiled.

On a piece of lined paper, another poem entitled "Autobiography" was hiding.[49] Unlike the canonical "Autobiography 1952," it bears no date in its title. Its penciled letters were never typed or printed; its lines are neither published in a book nor read by Amichai's wide, adoring public. The unpublished poem does not begin with a child's "merry hands" and refrains from Israeli allusions. From between its short, hand-scribbled lines, a small, scared child emerges. Devoid of any decorative scenery, the poem captures the stark essence of a bygone nightmare. Its first line is simple and haunting: "I ran away from the Nazis." But this flight does not lead to the safe shores of Palestine. Although the Nazis are left behind, the speaker cannot truly escape them, and they continue chasing him. "They are now inside me," he confesses, and, as the poem continues, he depicts himself in schizophrenic terms: he forever remains both the guard and the captive, the assailant and the victim. The Hebrew alliteration *makeh / mukeh* underscores the bond between the "one who beats" (*makeh*), and "the one who is beaten" (*mukeh*). The poem does not divulge the cause of this duality. The speaker's declaration that he must be a "prison guard" of his own fears suggests the need to ensure that his weakness will never be visible. Perhaps Amichai dubs himself an eternal inmate in "concentration camps," because after coming face to face with the Nazis as a child, he will never feel completely free, even as an Israeli. Amichai never shared this tortured representation of himself with his readers, but he did not destroy the poem, either. After the poet's death, this pregnant scrap of paper made its way into his archives, where I found it in 2002.

Concealing the phantoms of a European childhood, however, was not unique to Amichai. In fact, he belongs to a fraternity of writers who grappled with their diasporic past. The negation of this past was an integral part of the Zionist construction of the national identity. According to the Zionist myth, the Land of Israel would redeem the stereotypically weak Jew and transform him physically and psychologically into a strong Hebrew man.[50] In the decades that preceded the establishment of the state and through the 1960s, writers and critics alike cooperated in the perpetuation of this myth, stifling anything that would undermine the Zionist ideal. Like other members of his generation who immigrated to Palestine at a young age, Amichai felt compelled to repress the earlier period of his life. It is not surprising, therefore, that scholars and readers welcomed the Israeli poetic persona that Amichai forged. Most critics ignore the inner conflicts inherent in his biography and fail to see how his poetry works to blur the traces of his foreign origins.

In the mid-1980s, far from Israel and Israeli scholarly preconceptions, I began working on a doctoral dissertation on Yehuda Amichai. Faced with the poetic corpus of this canonical yet popular poet, I was struck by the critical neglect of much of Amichai's later verse. Having deemed that later poetry uninventive and postcanonical, critics were biased in favor of studying his groundbreaking early poems. I approached Amichai's entire corpus from a different angle, attempting to uncover the underlying structures and patterns that define his poetic oeuvre as a whole. I posited an overarching thematic and formal principle, the essence of which was this: behind what we see hides another reality, and the truth is often covered by a deceptive façade.

At the time, Amichai had yet to write "What Did I Learn in the Wars," which declares the "wisdom of camouflage" to be the foremost lesson he learned during the wars.[51] Even without this text, I had already detected the substructure of camouflage in his poetry from the mid-1980s—the idea of a veiled, or camouflaged, truth is not limited to his later poems, however. In fact, it is present in an embryonic form even in his earliest ones. In "It Has Been a While since They Asked," he wrote, "A dead tree stands together with those that blossom, a dead tree. / It's an old mistake, an ancient misunderstanding."[52] Likewise, in "Poems for Rosh Hashanah III," there is this image: "the house that is partially demolished / is similar to the house that is not yet completed."[53] In both cases, the observer is unable to distinguish between opposites, for the dead and the living, the built and the destroyed, look exactly alike. As with many other images scattered throughout Amichai's oeuvre, the "tree" and the "house" suggest that reality is not to be taken at face value. Moreover, within this skeptical vision of the physical world there is an underlying metapoetic warning—that words (in this case, poetry) may say one thing, but mean another.

Although at that stage in my work I did not fully grasp the far-reaching ramifications of the poet's underlying purpose, I did realize its potential interpretative power as an indicator of Amichai's creative process. In much of Amichai's verse, the truth does not so much lie beneath the surface as it is consciously concealed:

And my yearnings are closed inside me
Like air pockets in a loaf of bread.
On the outside, I am smooth and quiet and brown.
The world loves me.
But my hair is sad as reeds in a drying swamp—
All the rare birds with beautiful plumage
Flee from me.[54]

Here, the poetic "I" covers his inner pain with a smooth, unified shell. Like the "tree" and the "house," this very early work may be read as a literary self-reflection: Amichai's desire to preserve the intactness of the "brown crust" dictates a way of writing that incorporates the "air pockets" of yearning without revealing them. Read metaphorically, the concept of the crusted bread can apply to all of Amichai's verse. Underneath the calm, comforting exterior of many of his poems, longings churn and regretful memories linger, but the source of these longings and memories remains buried.

As I continued my studies, I became increasingly intrigued by the disparity between inside and outside that passes through Amichai's poetry as a common thread. It became evident to me that this disparity is more than a mere poetic structure. Returning to the poems from his formative period, I set out to unearth the deeper implications of this phenomenon and determine whether it attests to inner truths that the poet had consciously camouflaged. As I was familiar with Amichai's biographical outline, I suspected that the motivation for avoiding certain materials in Poems: 1948–1962 was tied to his personal history. Contrary to the critical consensus on the autobiographical nature of his poetry, I observed that the volume that established him as an important poet actually reveals very little of his life. At the center of this lyrical collection stands the individual speaker, as befitting the work of a poet who deposed the collective voice of his predecessors and placed the "I" at the center of Hebrew poetry. Nevertheless, the poems that allude to the early years of the poetic "I" speak in generalities and leave out many of the particulars of their author's childhood and past. Cracks in the poetic façade intimate that this autobiographical veneer is hiding personal landmarks.

The combination of Amichai's European origins and my own life experiences pointed me to the loci of emotional turmoil in his poetry. Language, the poet's clay, the material in which he creates, was the first area I questioned. Having lived between two languages myself—Hebrew and English—I recognized that the poet's linguistic background was an issue. I wanted to know what happened to Amichai's German mother tongue on his way to becoming an Israeli Hebrew poet.

Admittedly, the loss of a mother tongue is not unique to Amichai. The twentieth-century revival of the ancient Hebrew language in Palestine played an integral part in the formation of the Zionist national entity. Like other immigrants, Amichai was expected to abandon his mother tongue and, consequently, he wrote an entire corpus in his acquired language, Hebrew. The absence of any trace of German from the poetry of the German-born Amichai was unconditionally accepted by Israeli critics and readers. In contrast, I strove to understand the ways Amichai metabolized the loss of the German language in his verse and maneuvered between the two languages and cultures. Following my investigation into the role of one's mother tongue in the psychological-literary realm, I hypothesized that the language of childhood continues living in the writing of the adult poets. I was convinced that works that are not written in the author's mother tongue still contain remnants of the sounds that he absorbed as an infant and internalized as a child. Amichai, who arrived in Palestine when he was twelve, could not have forgotten or completely abandoned the language in which he grew up. My premise was that although Amichai had to suppress the linguistic sources that nurtured him, these sources could not have disappeared completely.

I went to Amichai, who by then had become my friend, and he agreed to let me pry into the origins of his writing. In a day-long conversation at his home in Jerusalem in the summer of 1996, I tried to learn if and how the German language had affected his work. Acknowledging the foreign roots of many Israelis, he "diagnosed" schizophrenia as a normal Israeli condition. In his matter-of-fact, calm manner, he created a spontaneous simile: "A person has two souls, like he has two feet." Although he did not spell it out, I understood this metaphoric duality to apply to the function of the two languages, German and Hebrew, in his own psyche. I asked if he ever wrote poetry in his first language. He conceded that he could still hear the music of his childhood rabbi's German sermons, but insisted he had known Hebrew "from age zero" and firmly rejected any suggestion that he ever wrote German verse.[55]

This assertion was not true. A treasure trove of German phrases, stanzas, and even short poems in Amichai's handwriting attest to the poet's own "schizophrenia." Four years after our meeting in Jerusalem, Amichai died. His death gave my scholarly journey another motivation—the wish to pay him homage. I traveled to the Beinecke Library at Yale. Before they were even catalogued, I searched through the thirty-four heavy cardboard boxes brimming with newspaper clippings, final proofs of poems, and handwritten notes. It is fair to assume that Amichai also wrote in German before 1954, but that material is unfortunately not in the archive. What I did find was invaluable. A few boxes held miniscule notepads from 1954 to 1959, whose orange or gray covers are marked with the month and the year and whose pages are crammed with ideas and drafts of poems in large script. Other boxes contain larger notebooks from the 1960s onward. Leafing through all these documents showed me that Amichai's linguistic heritage had not, in fact, disappeared; German continues to simmer under the surface of his Hebrew publications. I found short poems in German; drafts of published Hebrew poems in which the key image or a stanza is jotted down in big, wild German letters; verse in German script dotted with Hebrew terms like Kineret Lake or Mount Gilboa; German and Hebrew mixed in the same sentence to form jarring metaphors. What's more, at times, clasped within the existing German lines are other phantoms from the poet's past.

On the back of an undated piece of stationery from the Hotel Helmhaus in Zurich, I found a German name, a proper noun whose letters encapsulate Amichai's entire childhood. This word, forcefully inscribed in the Latin alphabet and spelled with the proper umlaut, is the title of a handwritten Hebrew poem, "Würzburg."[56] Nowhere in Amichai's published oeuvre is this name written out. When he alludes to it in his poetry, it is "the city of my childhood," and in his semi-autobiographical novel he calls his hometown "Weinburg." In the archived papers, however, the name Würzburg crowns the following broken Hebrew lines: "Pass quickly / before the place / where you were born . . ." The disparity between title and text is clearer in the archive because they are written in two different alphabets, the German and the Hebrew. This distinction is lost when the poem is translated. Thus, when an English translation of this fragment appeared posthumously in the New York Times in 2004, there was no indication that the original is a bilingual text or that it is the first in a three-part sequence.[57] The two segments that follow "Würzburg" are entitled "Travels" and "Germany"; they recall the scenes that led to Amichai's flight from his former homeland. "The hand" that saluted Hitler is depicted under the title "Germany," and the Nazi greeting, "Heil," is the only German word embedded in this otherwise Hebrew stanza. Like the word "Würzburg," it is written in Latin script. "Würzburg," "Heil," and the hand saluting Hitler, however, remain buried. This bilingual poetic record of the poet's torment never reached Amichai's readership.

Single German words like "Würzburg" and longer German segments found in the archive show that German remained at Amichai's fingertips and evoked the trauma of persecution even after he was forty years old. More significantly, the German drafts document Amichai's creative process: he conceived and wrote poems in German only to translate them into Hebrew, and ultimately transplanted these translations into the local, Israeli milieu of his poems. These handwritten scraps and the poems they nourished are the embodiment of the underlying substructure of Amichai's poetry. They expose the German "truth" beneath the Hebrew façade, and the European landscape beneath the Israeli topography and history in some of Amichai's most frequently quoted poems. Because these foreign origins are camouflaged, the poems are perceived as exclusively Israeli. The German lines found only among Amichai's unpublished papers undermine that interpretation and endow the poems with new meaning.

Looking at the published Amichai and the hidden, archived Amichai side by side, I more clearly understood the motivation behind his monumental effort to suppress some of the most significant landmarks of his life. In striving to become an Israeli, Amichai had to repress his experiences as a child in Germany and his mother tongue, but in order to be a poet, he had to remember them. His idiosyncratic solution to this conflict was the practice of camouflage. Amichai hid "foreign" (that is, European) linguistic, cultural, and biographical residues of his past in the deepest layers of his texts. This enabled him simultaneously to conceal and preserve these materials in his verse. It is a strategy that served him throughout his entire creative life.

The roots of this poetic and psychological mechanism lie in Amichai's childhood and the rift that tore it apart: his community's persecution in Germany. Amichai, along with the other Jewish children of Wuerzburg, was routinely targeted by the Catholic school students. In interviews, his fellow pupils described how they were beaten up on the way to school if they were caught alone or were not fast enough to escape. They learned to avoid drawing attention to themselves. Like his peers, the young Amichai learned the "wisdom of camouflage" and internalized the protective strategy of blending into his surroundings. This lesson served him again over a decade later when he fought in the War of Independence. Like the Jewish child in Wuerzburg, the young soldier had to keep himself from being noticed—this time, to avoid enemy fire.

By the time he became a soldier, however, the scope of camouflage in his life had expanded drastically. It had become a method of social and cultural assimilation as well as a mechanism of physical self-preservation. After his migration to Palestine in his early adolescence, not sticking out became a way for Amichai to conform to the expectations placed on him. Assimilation was the rule for new immigrants and it seemed especially desirable to a twelve-year-old boy who just wanted to fit in. As a result of this social pressure, Amichai did not identify himself as an immigrant or a refugee, but instead as a member of the elite generation that struggled for Israel's independence.[58] Thus, Amichai's poetic theme of a façade that conceals the truth applies to how he formed his Israeli identity as well.

As the years passed, the strategy that protected him from bodily harm in childhood and served the drive to conform in adolescence became a psychological tool for the suppression of emotional turmoil. Amichai used camouflage to cope with both traumatic events from his childhood and betrayal by the woman he loved. Covering these painful aspects of his past enabled the construction of a strong Israeli identity. Camouflage became a mechanism that he used whenever the wholeness or integrity of his self was threatened. The cohesive Israeli persona was the protector of his fragile inner world, and Amichai guarded it with all his might.

Yet part of Amichai's personality conflicted with his Israeliness; this part, his past, he knew to be of vital importance for his creative self. By inventing the poetics of camouflage early in his career, Amichai learned to walk the thin line between his clashing identities. He became a model Israeli poet, rooted in the land, its landscape, its history, and its language, by hiding certain facets of his personal history and highlighting others. Camouflage allowed Amichai to minimize the psychological and poetic price of repression. It enabled him to forge a personal mythology that would befit a national poet without discarding his formative experiences. This book follows the making of Amichai as the national poet, uncovering and interpreting the abandoned landmarks of the past that survive, although veiled, in his corpus.

The theory of camouflage offered here illuminates the inner logic behind Amichai's work—why some biographical elements are hidden while others are revealed—and the literary and extraliterary methods the poet used to weave together the secret and the known. With this key to Amichai's poetics and inner life, it is possible to reread his entire corpus and understand it anew. "Camouflage" explains various textual phenomena that seem incongruous and answers all of the questions raised earlier in this chapter.

The identification of this strategy explains why Amichai abandoned important life landmarks—the love for Ruth Z. and much of his childhood—in his seemingly autobiographical verse. Wuerzburg, Little Ruth, the German language, and the experience of migration were all but barred from Amichai's published poetry lest they jeopardize his image as a quintessential Israeli and endanger the reception of his work. Although Ruth Z. was not part of his childhood, she could still damage the image of the consecrated Israeli poet Amichai had crafted: she knew about his pre-war literary ambition and had the proof of it in the letters. The method and the degree of camouflage varied with each of the landmarks, but the principle remained.

The fact that the poet openly included the prayer book, Biblical texts, and Jewish customs that he knew from his infancy, as well as his Orthodox father, is testimony to the selective logic of camouflage. After all, these elements reinforce, rather than challenge, his Israeli persona. Although Amichai rejected his father's faith, the language of that religion was intertwined with the love for the father and remains the solid bedrock of Amichai's first book, as well as the poetry that followed. In fact, the warm reception that Amichai's poetry received in Israel and its continuing popularity can be attributed partly to the presence of these particular elements from his childhood. The poetic use of camouflage is even more effective because Amichai does embrace these elements in his poetry, fooling many into believing it is wholly autobiographical. Critics have long considered the caring, worrying father and the liturgical and biblical language as the classic markers of the autobiographical nature of Amichai's poetry.[59]

Granted, Amichai was open about some traumatic and non-Israeli segments of his past in his oeuvre. He wrote short stories, radio skits, and a semi-autobiographical epic in which the Wuerzburg of his childhood and the experience of migration play a role. In addition, Little Ruth is a protagonist of his first novel, Not of This Time, Not of This Place, which is set in Wuerzburg and even contains a few German phrases. These disclosures in his prose and drama, however, are simply another facet of camouflage. Because Amichai hoped to make a name for himself as a national poet, he kept poetry, his canonical genre, almost entirely Israel-centric. As he could not keep these experiences permanently repressed, he allowed pieces of them to slip, barely masked, into his more marginal genres. Prose became Amichai's repository for the truth because he valued it less and, as such, it contains the emotional-psychological inspiration that his poetry conceals.[60] Nevertheless, certain secrets were even kept out of his prose, and he always remained aware of the possible negative effects that his revelations might have on his Israeli persona. Consequently, he did not publish his novel until after he had cemented his reputation as an Israeli poet with *Poems: 1948–1962*.

Orchestrations of this kind and the tweaking of significant biographical and literary dates were yet another form of camouflage. Through his autobiographical accounts in interviews and articles, Amichai minimized those parts of his life story that did not advance his persona as a national poet and exaggerated those that did. He "corrected" facts, as well as publication and biographical chronologies. A minor inconsistency in the year he immigrated to Israel may be a reflection of his attempt to reduce the time that he spent as a German child. The Wuerzburg city archives record his family as living in Wuerzburg until 1936; the Central Archives for the History of the Jewish People in Jerusalem, as well as the *Encyclopedia Judaica*, confirm 1936 as the year of his immigration. In early interviews, Amichai gave 1936 as the year he emigrated, but beginning in the late 1970s, he would often say that he left for Palestine one year earlier, in 1935.

Amichai also consistently minimized Wuerzburg's role as his hometown, especially in interviews he granted in Israel.[61] He referred to Jerusalem, not Wuerzburg, as the "landscape of [his] childhood"[62] and said that his "childhood" took place during the riots of 1936–39, even though he was no longer a "child" then, but a teenager.[63] When he did talk about Wuerzburg, he emphasized Hebrew over German and the synagogue over his school's German curriculum. He insisted that he had been called by the Hebrew name "Yehuda" in Wuerzburg, despite the fact that his surviving classmates remember that everyone called him "Ludwig," even in the Jewish school.[64] Although his classmates recall that they could not speak Hebrew when they left Germany, Amichai implied in his interviews that he was almost fluent in that language when he arrived in Israel.[65] Finally, Amichai claimed that the rise of the Nazis and the attacks on Jewish children by Nazi students "were not deep traumas."[66] Even though his family essentially fled Wuerzburg, he denied that they were "running away"[67] and described the trip as "a great happy event." Projecting Zionism onto the child's perspective, he said that he felt he was "going home," as opposed to leaving home.[68]

The discovery of another instance of Amichai's chronological camouflaging is tied to the discovery of Ruth Z.'s letters and has the greatest implication for the literary study of his development as a poet. Amichai camouflaged the personal side of his life between the springs of 1946 and 1948 in order to have the chronology of his writing chime with that of the country's history.[69] After the War of Independence, he subtly altered the timeline of his poetic career, synchronizing his creative naissance with the birth of Israel. In interviews, as well as in poems about his creative calling, Amichai stated or implied that he had never desired to be a poet—that, rather, the 1948 battles in the Negev caused him to start writing poetry spontaneously to comfort himself.[70]

From my interviews with Ruth Z. and from Amichai's letters to her, however, we know that by January 1948 Amichai had already been writing for at least two years and believed poetry was his life's mission. Throughout her relationship with Amichai, Ruth Z. read many of his poems. In his letters to her, he documented his total commitment to perfecting his craft and copied long segments of poems he had prepared for competitions. Ruth Z. was not passed over in his biographical accounts just because of the pain she caused him; rather, she was the sole intimate witness to a period of his life that he wished to reframe. Amichai had to camouflage Ruth Z. because his time with her contradicted the creative autobiography he had forged, which had him bursting forth as a poet because of, and in unison with, the establishment of the state.

The drastic difference between the levels of openness in Amichai's earlier and later poetics confirms how deep-rooted the camouflage had been. The hermetic, enigmatic nature of much of *Poems: 1948–1962* is due to the varied tactics of camouflage Amichai employed during that period. After publishing his canonical collection and his autobiographical novel, he gradually opened up. But it was not until two decades later that Amichai first began to allow the most problematic or painful materials he had buried to emerge. In 1980, he published *The Great Tranquility: Questions and Answers*, which contains the first poems that refer almost openly to his relationship with Ruth Z. and to his life as a teacher in Haifa. In 1989, in his penultimate book, *Even the Fist Was Once an Open Palm and Fingers*, he dedicated an entire poem to "Little Ruth" for the first time, using her nickname as its title.[71] In the same volume, he included the self-referential poem "What Did I Learn in the Wars,"[72] which exposes both the literary practice of camouflage and its experiential origins by describing the wisdom of war and the wisdom of poetry in the same words:

... above all, I learned the wisdom of camouflage,
Not to stand out, not to be recognized
Not to be apart from what's around me
. . . .
Let them think I am a bush or a lamb
A tree, a shadow of a tree. . .[73]

For Amichai, the same defensive strategy applied to both war and writing. The process of self-exposure culminated in 1998, in his final collection, *Open Closed Open* (for a photograph of Amichai in 1998, see image 16).[74] There, it becomes evident that his emotional life and his childhood were fully available to him as poetic materials.

This "relaxing" of camouflage occurred because, as Amichai grew older, he became increasingly secure with who he was and confident in his status as a national Israeli poet. Additionally, by the 1980s, the Israeli social climate had become more pluralistic, allowing foreign sensibilities into the Israeli milieu and diminishing the need for camouflage.[75] Nevertheless, certain aspects of Amichai's past, like the German language, never emerge from the subtext of his verse.

There is only one known place where much of Amichai's inner world is laid almost bare in writing—the letters to Ruth Z. In them, one can see the raw biographical and linguistic sources of Amichai's literary work, and the motivations for his poetics of camouflage. They are a rare, intimate reflection of the intersection between Amichai's passage from adolescence to maturity and his identification as a poet, and Israel's evolution from its prenation status into an independent state.

This temporal overlap generated an inner transformation: while Amichai, the fledgling poet, was spreading his literary wings, his patriotic conviction soared. The letters he mailed from Haifa to New York from 1947 to 1948 are perhaps the only record of the conflict between the creative and the national trajectories. They track Amichai's attempts to integrate his poetic self and its foreign heritage with his growing Israeliness. At this crossroads of identities, Amichai reached the emotional-psychological resolution that ultimately developed into the poetics of camouflage.

In the letters, therefore, one can find the primal scenes that Amichai would eventually hide. Among them are the longings for the snowfalls of his childhood and the clichéd frozen bird he was forced to include in his grade-school compositions about winter, the monogrammed sheets that his mother embroidered for her dowry in a small German village, and the ill-fated argument with Little Ruth.[76] Moreover, the letters reveal the strong attachment that remained between the poet and his mother tongue. Approximately a third of them contain poems in German or translations from that language. Despite his denials, this emerging Israeli drew inspiration from the language of his childhood. The letters encapsulate Amichai's attempts to fuse elements of the German literary tradition with his Israeli existence. Perhaps more than any of the others, one letter attests to Amichai's desire to combine his German past and his new identity as a soldier-poet.

It was dawn, February 28, 1948, when Amichai wrote to Ruth Z. He had just returned home after a fierce shoot-out that followed a night of lying in ambush "with the finger pressed to the trigger."[77] In vivid language, he describes his fear and the climactic moment of action when his fright turned to ecstasy. The letter moves seamlessly from the tensions of that wintry night in 1948 to an epic by Rilke set in medieval Europe.[78] From memory, Amichai describes how Rilke's hero was fighting his last battle alone in the enemy camp, disconnected from his soldiers. At the height of danger, as the enemies poured in from all directions, raising their rounded sabers, a playful joy came over the hero. The crooked swords suddenly seemed to the lone soldier like the jets of water that he remembered from the fountain of his father's glorious palace. At this point, the narrative of Amichai's letter returns in midsentence to the modern battle. It states that there is a limit to fear and that beyond this limit, fear evaporates and one can find the strength to pull the trigger of the machine gun.

This heroic story that Amichai told is an invaluable key to his art, not because of the identification with Rilke's epic, but, rather, because of Amichai's digressions from it. His version reveals the way he intertwined the classical text with his own psychological makeup, as well as how his childhood memories and the German poet Rilke became a source of strength for him in times of danger. While in both Rilke's epic and Amichai's retelling of it in the letter, the enemies' swords remind the hero of a fountain, Amichai adds the location of these arching streams of water: the splendid garden of his father's palace. The fountains in Rilke's original narrative are not from any particular place. With this supplement, Amichai conflates the German language of Rilke's epic and its European setting with the architecture of his own hometown, Wuerzburg. The palace's gardens find their way into Amichai's recollection of Rilke because for Amichai they recalled the Hofgarten, Wuerzburg's landmark. The jets of water in the epic triggered the memory of the elaborate fountains that adorned Wuerzburg's palace. Moreover, Amichai merges his beloved poet's spirit with the radiant figure of his own father. Together, they provide the young, scared soldier with courage. Amichai thus imports an early memory into Rilke's epic, which had nothing to do with childhood, and secures a place for a father where there is none. His letter transports Rilke's medieval European battlefield and the modern Middle Eastern gunfire to the town where Amichai grew up, the beloved son of a man who was his king. It is not far-fetched to assume that at the height of battle, and of fear, a composite of Rilke's epic, Amichai's own hometown, and his beloved father endowed Amichai with the strength needed to continue and survive the battle.

Rilke's German epic appears in the letter unmasked and affords a peek into Amichai's artistic process. Amichai's re-creation of the tale reveals how he used materials from his past like the work of the great German poet and the landscape of his hometown to help him in forming his new identity as a courageous Israeli fighter. These materials remained available to him for the rest of his career, but they never again appear in such an overt form as in the letter. In his verse, Amichai hides his strong bond to the German language and its culture, along with the fountains he remembered from the palace garden. Only in the letter are they on the surface of the text.

The letters are not only an essential intertext for much of Amichai's corpus, they are also the last (and only surviving) pieces of writing in which he makes no attempt to hide his past or the subjects of his poetry. Drawing on both Amichai's published oeuvre and these materials that were not previously available to scholarship, this book reconstructs a research-generated "bildungnarrative." It presents a biographical description of young Amichai's life from his birth in 1924, through his adolescence, to the time immediately before the establishment of the State of Israel in the spring of 1948 and his ultimate emergence as a poet. It uses the information gleaned from these personally and historically crucial periods as an apparatus to understand Amichai's writing as a whole. My portrayal of Amichai embraces that which the writer had self-censored. It looks beyond Amichai's literary persona as an Israeli national poet, to his diasporic past, and studies the ways in which this clandestine period manifests itself in his poetry.

Although Yehuda Amichai's hometown of Wuerzburg is masked by generalizations or anonymity in his poetry, its sites, sounds, and people remained in the poet's consciousness. An autobiographical novel, a few radio skits, short stories, and a long epic poem recall Wuerzburg, and while they distort the city, they are a testament to the writer's attachment to it. The following pages attempt to reconstruct Wuerzburg in the mid-1920s and 1930s and the early life of Amichai, its native son. Only a full knowledge of Amichai's childhood world can illuminate the hidden corners of his poetic work and thus demonstrate how much of this rich background he suppressed. In this narrative of the poet's first twelve years, from 1924 to 1936, he is referred to by his German name, Ludwig, because this name is bound up with the formation of his personality, the German language, and his geographical and traditional roots.[1]

In 1924, Wuerzburg, situated in the wide valley of the Main River, looked like a storybook illustration, with its ornate Catholic churches, narrow alleys, and ancient squares, monuments, and statues. The surrounding hills were covered with vineyards, and on their ridges one could see the onion-shaped spires of the Kaepele church, a destination for Christian pilgrimages.[2] Bridges lined with images of saints connected the dense center of town with its older section on the slope. The castle stood on top of a hill, crowning the cityscape of timber-framed houses and cobblestone streets (see images 1 and 2).[3]

At that time, Wuerzburg was a town of ninety thousand people, the capital of the Lower Franconia district of Bavaria, and the center of an area famous for producing wine.[4] It had its own university, which, like many of its buildings, dated back to the Middle Ages. The ruling prince-bishops commissioned Wuerzburg's famous baroque-rococo palace and gardens between 1719 and 1744. Their palace, the Residenz,[5] was located in the heart of the town, surrounded by the Hofgarten, with its manicured French- and English-style gardens.[6] These gardens embodied the baroque ideal of nature tamed to create a paradise, featuring shepherds in a pastoral landscape and sculpted angels.

At the time of Amichai's birth, Wuerzburg was the home of a venerable Jewish community of 2,600.[7] Fragments of a thousand tombstones, some inscribed with biblical and talmudic quotations, testify to the size and the learnedness of the town's medieval Jewish population.[8] But it was not until the nineteenth century that a new, vigorous community, with all its vital institutions, started to flourish.[9] This growth was due, in part, to the fact that Jews were finally officially permitted to live in Wuerzburg itself and were not relegated to the outskirts of the town.[10] Even as late as the 1920s, however, many Jewish cattle merchants were forced to live in the small surrounding villages.[11] In 1834, the decision to build a synagogue was approved, and the legendary Rabbi Seligmann Baer Bamberger was elected to the rabbinate in 1839. Under his leadership, a Jewish elementary school was established in 1856 and, eight years later, a teacher's institute (ILBA) was founded.[12] It was the only Jewish teachers college in Germany; it survived until 1938.

By World War I, Jews seemed to be almost completely accepted by other Germans. In his sermons, Nathan Bamberger, who was the rabbi in that period, encouraged financial contributions to the war effort. Four hundred Jews from Wuerzburg fought, and forty were killed.[13] Rabbi Zigmund Hanover, who succeeded Rabbi Bamberger in 1919, said nostalgically, "In the glorious days of 1914, the entire nation was united."[14] After Germany's defeat, however, many argued that the Jews had not contributed enough, and the rising antisemitism shattered the Jews' illusion of belonging. The Jewish community published statistics of Jewish soldiers in 1917,[15] but this attempt to counteract the accusations of inadequate patriotism failed. Antisemitism continued to fester, especially among embittered war veterans. Rabbi Hanover, who had been a chaplain in the army, tried to create a dialogue between Jews and Christians, and was even friendly with the Wuerzburgian bishop. He also promoted unity among different Jewish factions.[16]

Wuerzburg's congregation worshipped in one synagogue, which served the needs of both Orthodox and Liberal (less observant) Jews. It stood at the heart of the building complex that was the symbol of the community. Behind the synagogue, separated by a yard, was the three-story community building that contained the Volksschule (elementary school), an assembly hall, a mikve (ritual bath),[17] and a small stiebel (chapel).[18] One of Ludwig's boyhood friends, Norbert Hellmann, remembered that "[t]he yard surrounded the synagogue, and behind the synagogue, there was a yard for the children of the school. . . . That yard was the center of community life."[19]

Rabbi Hanover, who was renowned for his inspiring sermons and oratorical talent, conducted the Shabbat services.[20] The prayers were led in the German-Jewish Ashkenaz *Nusach*[21] by the cantor, Ruben Moses Eschwege, who also served as *mohel* (ritual circumciser) and secretary of the community.[22] The congregation was diverse, consisting of physicians, a dentist, and wine merchants. Jewish businesses included two bakeries, three butcher shops, a restaurant and grocery store, a drug store, and several department stores.[23]

By the 1930s, two Jewish kindergartens had been established in Wuerzburg, the newer one following the Montessori method. The Jewish-Bavarian elementary school was supported by the state and its secular curriculum followed that of the non-Jewish German schools.[24] There was also a modern Orthodox youth movement called Esra, which combined hiking, singing, and social activities with Jewish content.[25] Jewish Wuerzburg took great pride in its unity, traditions, and prestigious institutions. It was into this rich and bustling Jewish life that Ludwig Pfeuffer was born.

✳   ✳   ✳

On May 3, 1924, Friedrich Moritz Pfeuffer and Frieda Walhaus Pfeuffer registered their newborn son as Ludwig Pfeuffer.[26] Eight days later, the community celebrated as the cantor-mohel Eschwege performed the *brit mila*, the ritual circumcision. The boy was given the Hebrew name Yehuda; as in most Jewish families, it was chosen in memory of a deceased relative. The infant's mother, Frieda, was from Gersfeld, a small village in the Hesse region, whose Jewish cemetery still contains tombstones bearing her maiden name. On some of these stones, a lion-related first name—such as Leopold or Yehuda—is carved, suggesting that the boy's Hebrew name stemmed from the tradition of Frieda's family.[27] Jewish children in Germany, however, used their Hebrew names only in the synagogue, not in everyday life. While "Yehuda" would be used in Jewish rituals, the child would be known as "Ludwig" even during religious studies at the Jewish school.

The early months of Ludwig's life were blessed with beautiful spring and summer weather, and he was often taken outside in a baby carriage. Sometimes, Frieda would wheel him down the path that ran along the river between the nearby Saints Bridge and the Lions Bridge, which was farther down the river and guarded by iron lions. She pushed the carriage through "old, cozy alleys between ringing bells and bridges over the river Main."[28] When he looked up, he would have been able to see the sails of nearby boats. As he grew older, he would lie on the shore and look upward at the masts and reeds. The opening poem of Amichai's first volume would later recall these vistas: "When I was a child / Grasses and masts stood at the shore."[29] On her daily outings, Frieda often stopped at the nearby dry goods store.[30] Because of a postwar housing shortage, the widow Ricka Goldbach, who owned the store, and her unmarried niece, Henrietta, both shared living space at Sanct Augustinerstrasse with the Pfeuffers for a few years. Although they were not blood relatives, these two childless Jewish women were like aunts to young Ludwig and his sister, Rachel, and showered them with love even when they were no longer neighbors.[31] Toward the end of his life, when his childhood memories reemerged, Amichai commemorated these women in a poem, remembering how they would tickle him with their knitting needles.[32]

Ludwig's family lived at Sanct Augustinerstrasse 8 until he was nearly four years old.[33] (For a map of Wuerzburg, see appendix B.) The trolley line ran by the somewhat crowded apartment building and its frequent ringing blended with the bells of the many churches clustered in that part of town.[34] The house was close to the ancient town hall, built in 1766, and the main square, which was dominated by the rococo Vierroehren fountain (for photographs of this neighborhood, see images 3 and 4).[35] Around the corner was the ancient Saints Bridge, which connected the two oldest parts of town. The Virgin Mary, as the patron saint of Franconia, stood at the center of the bridge, along with Joseph and the baby Jesus.[36]

The Pfeuffer residence was also conveniently located near Domerschulstrasse, where the synagogue complex and the family's wholesale notions store, which sold supplies for seamstresses, were situated.[37] As soon as the child could toddle, his father would bring him to the synagogue on Saturdays. On their short walk, they would see the heavy gates of the university, the thickwalled monastery, and the cathedral, which gave the ancient street, Domerschulstrasse, its name. But once they entered the synagogue and were engulfed by the protective walls of the Jewish complex, the world of churches and monasteries seemed to fade away (for a photograph of the synagogue, see image 5). Little Ludwig became absorbed by the synagogue music; the chanting of the synagogue's chorus, in which boys sang the soprano parts, and the lull of Cantor Eschwege's Hebrew prayers probably put the toddler to sleep.[38] The voice of Rabbi Hanover delivering German sermons would accompany his slumber.

Like men in other synagogues, Ludwig's father would sometimes be called to the Torah during services, and he would hold the child in his arms as he stood on the *bimah*, the small platform with a table on which the Torah scrolls are opened in a synagogue. From there, Ludwig could see the scrolls up close. Men in prayer shawls took the scrolls out of the Holy Ark, which was guarded by twin carved lions. They undressed the long cylinders and laid them gently on the table. After the reading, Ludwig watched as the men wrapped the Torah scrolls with silk "dresses" and then covered them with velvet—dark, lush, and soft.[39] The Torah scrolls, now adorned with gold, silver, and little bells, were hugged and kissed and carried around the synagogue.

Even as a small child, Ludwig had already touched the Torah scrolls himself and, like other members of the congregation, had kissed them ceremoniously. When he turned three years old, his connection with these magical objects would be cemented symbolically in a communitywide celebration. His parents dressed him in festive clothes and took him to synagogue. There, little Ludwig and his father were called to the *bimah* together. The cloth, called a *wimpel*, which had been delicately painted by the cantor and saved since Ludwig's circumcision, was his offering.[40] His father lifted him, made the blessing, and then helped Ludwig wrap the rolled, undressed scroll with the ribbon that carried his Hebrew name. These and other icons from the synagogue infiltrate his nostalgic prose and lions persist in the imagery of his poems.[41]

Week after week, in an endless rhythm, the Saturday sounds of Shabbat would turn into Sunday's church bells, with their many sizes and rings. Every fifteen minutes, the chimes would sound, and every hour, bells tolled from every church, creating a continuous melody.[42] As the musically inclined boy grew, so did his fascination with the sounds of his town. He could identify each church by the sound of its bells and was moved by the Hallelujah Chorus that echoed from the churches. Once, he secretly entered a church when he thought no one was there and listened to the soft and lonely voice of the organ.[43]

On Sundays, the Pfeuffers walked to the parks and gardens that form a ring around Wuerzburg, away from the center of town. Kleine Nitze was a favorite because of its exotic flowers, little fountains, wide paths, and inner enclaves. As many Pfeuffer family photographs demonstrate (one shows Ludwig wearing a national Bavarian costume), this was a popular spot for taking pictures. Concerts were performed in Kleine Nitze and the palace gardens and, like many Wuerzburg families, the Pfeuffers went to the gardens to listen to the classical music.[44]

After the delight of weekends, Ludwig did not understand his father's long disappearances during the week, and would later write, "I didn't know when my father would come back."[45] As he grew older, he learned that his father was a traveling salesman. The connection between Ludwig and his father was stronger than the common bond between father and son. Amichai wrote that his father, "like a magician . . . pulled love out of his small body."[46] This father understood that even when his son would misbehave, "All the same, he is a good boy and full of love."[47] The image of Friedrich sadly leaving on Saturday or Sunday nights carrying a lamp remained with Ludwig until he welcomed him home on Friday. The child's longing for his father echoes in a note he wrote thirty years later, "What do you remember / from age two? . . . That my father left / afterwards, nothing."[48] Nevertheless, he was a happy child, and during the week he enjoyed spending time with his mother, sister, and the two loving "aunts." When he could just speak, his mother taught him the first prayers a Jewish child must know, the modeh ani and the bedtime prayer, which he dutifully recited each morning and night. His parents explained to him the meaning of the Hebrew words in German. Thus, even his first Hebrew words of worship were learned and understood through the German language. Once Ludwig began attending school, he learned the details and significance of the rituals and the full text of the prayers.[49]

In 1928,[50] the Pfeuffers moved to a newer part of town where many other Jews lived. Now their address was Alleestrasse 11, only a few houses away from Rabbi Hanover, who lived in Alleestrasse 20.[51] The Pfeuffers were neither rich nor poor; their new, larger apartment was standard, with five or six rooms, including a living room and dining room.[52] Their non-Jewish landlord, Professor Leininger, lived with his daughter on the same floor.[53] Some other non-Jews also lived in the building, but the Pfeuffers' relationships with them, although polite, were distant.[54]

Surrounded by wider avenues and parks, the family's new home was near the railroad tracks, the Jewish hospital, and the Jewish old-age home. The rhythm of the trains' chugging and whistling would come to be a beloved emblem of that neighborhood for the many children who lived there. For Ludwig, the trains' regularity became a metaphor for the cyclical nature of time. For instance, he later compared the inevitability of a birthday to that of the passing of an anticipated train.[55] Rabbi Hanover, whose wife Klara was related to Ludwig's mother, lived in the corner house at the top of the street's gentle hill. Their younger daughter, Ruth, was a few months older than Ludwig, and the two became best friends. They went on adventures together, sneaking into the nearby Christian cemetery through the back entrance and counting train cars while hiding in the bushes that bordered the railroad tracks.[56]

With the move to Alleestrasse, Ludwig's physical environment had changed significantly, but he continued to feel secure in the bosom of his family, in a warm home filled with books and music. Shabbat was a special day in this Orthodox Jewish household, and the God-fearing Friedrich never missed it, always returning home from his travels on Friday.[57] On Shabbat afternoons, together with other Jewish families, the Pfeuffers visited the elderly in the old-age home. Amichai recalled in an interview that while some of the residents at the home befriended him and others scared him, their varied life stories offered him his first glimpses into the outside world. When the children grew tired of staying inside, they would go out to watch the trains passing and inhale their warm fumes.[58]

While Shabbat was exclusively dedicated to religion in the eyes of Friedrich and Frieda, for the children there were some deviations; occasionally, the parents sent Rachel and Ludwig to the children's theater with their non-Jewish maid;[59] the siblings cherished each other and looked forward to these outings.[60] Frieda and Friedrich believed in exposing their children to the culture around them. They both loved music and were well-read,[61] even though they grew up in rural communities and their formal education barely lasted through high school.

Their ancestors on both sides had been cattle merchants—village Jews who had lived in the same area for generations.[62] They were proud and loyal subjects of the kaiser, who served their German homeland: men from both families fought in World War I. Amichai honored their memory in his poems. He wrote, "[M]y father fought four years in their war," and also described his mother's brother who was killed in action: "Uncle David fell in the war in the Carpathian Mountains."[63] The rural roots of the two families were in small villages not far from Wuerzburg. Frieda Wahlhaus Pfeuffer was born on April 6, 1895, in Gersfeld, some hundred miles away.[64] She grew up in a farmhouse and had a basic education in the village school. The Gersfeld Jewish community was close-knit, numbering around twenty to thirty families.[65] Many were Frieda's relatives, either Wahlhauses, like her father, or Katzmanns, like her mother. When it came time for Frieda to marry, it is likely that a matchmaker was enlisted to find a man whose family background and occupation were similar to hers. She was introduced to Friedrich Pfeuffer, the son of a cattle merchant. The wedding took place on July 12, 1920, and the couple moved to Wuerzburg soon after.[66]

Frieda had rarely left Gersfeld before her nuptials. Like most women of her era, she had few opportunities for a career and remained a housewife, which fit well with her down-to-earth manner[67] and concern for the household.[68]

Friedrich Moritz Pfeuffer was born closer to Wuerzburg in the larger town of Giebelstadt on November 13, 1888.[69] His father, David, had lost a leg in an accident while he was loading cattle onto a train. His mother, Klara, had been orphaned in childhood and was raised in Wuerzburg in the house of the renowned Rabbi Bamberger. Inspired by this cultured household, she educated herself while working there and became one of the most respected figures in the community. She loved literature and would always read German poetry to the grandchildren. Like Frieda's relatives in Gersfeld, David and Klara Pfeuffer were deeply Orthodox, but not scholarly, using Hebrew only as a language of prayer. They lived in both the German and Jewish worlds without feeling conflicted about their identity.[70]

As only one of the Pfeuffer sons could inherit the farm, however, the other two left Giebelstadt.[71] In early January 1906, Friedrich followed his oldest brother, Samuel, to Wuerzburg to work in his wholesale notions store,[72] thus becoming a seller of buttons instead of a merchant of cattle.[73] In 1914, he joined the military and fought in World War I for four years. He returned home decorated with medals, winning the *Eisernes Kreuz* (iron cross) at Verdun and the *Bayerisches Ritterkreuz* (Bavarian knight's cross) on the Isonzo.[74] The brothers' store was near the Volksschule and Ludwig frequently visited even when Friedrich was traveling, for he loved playing with the shiny buttons and zippers.

*   *   *

Friedrich was a sensitive and emotional person who cared deeply about his fellow men. For example, he knew the names of all the lonely people at the old-age home. As the elderly were not able to check whether or not he was telling them the truth, Friedrich would invent messages from relatives for each lonely person to make him or her happy.

One story in particular exemplifies Friedrich Pfeuffer's unique combination of humor and true righteousness. In the 1920s, *Ostjuden* (poor Jews from Eastern Europe) were ostracized by the German Jews. Unwelcome in the main synagogue, they were forced to pray in a former matzoth factory that had been converted into a one-room chapel. During the Jewish holiday of Purim, when it is customary to give to charity and play tricks, Friedrich went to one of his gentile friends, a barber with whom he had fought in World War I, and asked him to make him a long fake beard. Then, dressed in a typical Eastern European Jewish *kaftan* (coat) and *streimel* (hat), Friedrich disguised himself as a *shnorer* (beggar), a Polish Jew trying to collect money for charity. He approached many of the members of his community, but most rebuffed him, telling him to "go to work," to which he replied "today's Purim." Finally, he went to the welfare office to ask for help, and they kicked him out. He broke the window, and a clerk called the police. Only when the police arrived did he take off his beard. When his identity was revealed, there was an uproar, and people begged him not to disclose the names of those who had treated the needy man badly.[75] In this way, Friedrich Pfeuffer drew attention to the lot of the rejected *Ostjuden*.

Friedrich showed great tenderness for his family as well, especially his children. Although he was authoritarian and pedantic about fulfilling every Jewish commandment, he was also a loving father who enjoyed telling stories to his children. Ludwig marveled at his father's adventures during the "Big War."[76] While the child saw his mother as "God's housekeeper," his father was God himself. As Amichai explained in an interview, he took the prayer "our father, our King" literally: "I reached the naïve conclusion that if you can compare God with a father, my father could also be my God."[77]

Every summer and sometimes in the winter, Ludwig's parents would take their children to visit their grandparents, uncles, aunts, and cousins in their home villages. Ludwig and Rachel would visit Giebelstadt to play with the Pfeuffer clan. In Gersfeld, distant cousins from the vicinity would also come to visit their shared relatives. One of those cousins was Ruth Katzmann, who would eventually move to Wuerzburg with her mother, where she got to know Ludwig and Rachel even better. These trips to the country exposed the city-bred children to nature and brought them closer to their familial roots.[78]

The children loved spending time in the rural surroundings,[79] where their relatives had many animals and fields, fruit and vegetable gardens, horses and carts, and hired workers.[80] These trips revealed southern Germany's haunting beauty to Ludwig, with its lush forests, beautiful churches, and shimmering rivers.[81] As he grew older, the landscape that he saw on his excursions outside of Wuerzburg fed his imagination. In interviews he granted in Germany, Amichai revealed that Christian legends and German folktales were as important as Jewish ones in the stories he told himself as a child and they blended together in his imagination. For him, the green valley between Wuerzburg and Oxenford (near Giebelstadt) became the valley where David killed Goliath.[82]

After four years of a carefree life, Ludwig resisted being reigned in by nursery school. On his frightening first morning, he clung to the railing, refusing to enter the building. The school that Ludwig feared so much was the first Jewish Montessori kindergarten,[83] founded in 1929.[84] The 1920s were a decade of education reform in Germany, and this mixed Jewish and Christian kindergarten was known for its progressive approach.[85] Despite his initial apprehension, Ludwig grew to love the little school, and he recalled it fondly as an adult.

While Ludwig was in kindergarten, political developments began threatening the Jews of the region. On March 17, 1929, there was a blood libel in the neighboring village of Manau after a five-year-old German boy was found dead.[86] The Nazi newspaper *Der Stuermer* accused the Jews of ritual murder. Later that year, when he was still too young to understand what had happened, Ludwig experienced antisemitism viscerally for the first time: he was slapped in the face while watching an Easter parade because he had not removed his hat.[87] By the time Ludwig entered first grade in 1930, antisemitism in Wuerzburg had become more organized: although the Nazis were not yet in power, Hitler visited Wuerzburg and met with the leader of the Wuerzburg Nazi Party.[88]

Ludwig, however, was not fully aware of these events.[89] In contrast to his traumatic entrance into nursery school, he would cherish his first day of first grade as the most memorable day of his childhood.[90] That morning, his parents presented him with a large cone filled with candy to underscore the sweetness of learning.[91] A photograph documents him proudly holding his cone, ready for his new school, the Jewish-Bavarian Volksschule, which he would attend for the rest of his time in Wuerzburg.[92]

Now that the Pfeuffers lived on Alleestrasse, it was a twenty-minute walk to the school behind the synagogue (see appendix B). Ludwig's regular walking companion was his neighbor and best friend, Ruth Hanover. Ruth would stop in front of Ludwig's house every morning and the two then continued on to school, chatting the entire way. They often returned home for lunch, thus walking the same route together four times a day,[93] passing many of Wuerzburg's most beautiful landmarks.[94] The path to and from school took them along Rennweg, the city's wide, ancient entrance road, which stretched from the train tracks to the southern exit of the Residenz.[95] The Rennweg guided the children to the iron gates of the palace garden. Ludwig and his friend gazed at the ornate fountains, their waters cascading around copper statues of satyrs, sensual nymphs, and wild animals embodying the hedonism of the palace's former masters. Little stone cherubs, or putti, with chubby cheeks and fat legs flew whimsically over flowerpots or coveted clusters of stone grapes with their sculptured lips (for photographs of the Hofgarten, see images 7, 8, and 9). On their way back in the afternoons, the two children would linger and play among the statues in the magical garden.

Starting in May 1930, and for the next six years, Ludwig would make this walk to school and enter a classroom very much like the one captured in an extant photograph of a second-grade class (see image 10).[96] In that picture, boys and girls are sitting next to each other because they are still young (boys and girls were separated in the higher grades). A picture of a Holy Ark is prominently displayed, as though to remind all who entered of the school's Orthodox Jewish mission. The inscription at its top reads *"da lifne mi ata omed"* (know in front of whom you are standing) and a crown is drawn in the center, surrounded by the acronym for *keter Torah* (the crown of Torah). The children are seated in twos at wooden benches attached to old-fashioned desks with tops that open, a hole for the inkwell, and artfully carved legs. On his first day in the new classroom, Ludwig recognized a few familiar faces, among them Lore Kleemann, who lived on the other end of Alleestrasse.[97] He also met new schoolmates from different neighborhoods, such as Norbert Hellmann, the son of the principal.[98] And, of course, Ruth Hanover was there as well.

Although Ludwig knew how to read before entering school, the mischievous child had difficulty adjusting to structured studies. His day started with two hours of *limude kodesh* (religious studies): the prayer book, the Torah, and Hebrew.[99] This part of the curriculum also focused on everyday practices and rituals, Jewish holidays, and the texts relating to them.[100] The class was conducted in German and the teacher called Ludwig by his German name, even when the lessons revolved around readings in Hebrew, the ancient language that Ludwig recognized from synagogue but did not really understand. The method of instruction was traditional; the teacher would read in Hebrew, in the Ashkenazi pronunciation, and then translate the text, word for word, for the students. By the time they were in second grade, the students knew the Hebrew alphabet and vowel symbols and had started to read and translate from the Bible themselves. They did not learn Hebrew as a modern, spoken tongue.[101]

After two hours of religious studies and Hebrew texts, the all-German secular classes that followed seemed easy (though, certainly, the children still looked forward to noon and their two-hour lunch break).[102] Nonetheless, the German curriculum was extremely rigorous. In the first two years of school, Ludwig would not only learn how to read and write, but would come to know four alphabets in German alone: the Gothic and the Latin in print and in script.[103]

An important part of the curriculum at this Jewish school was the study of the German language and its culture.[104] In 1924,[105] books influenced by German Romanticism had been made an integral part of the Volksschule curriculum in an attempt to create a collective memory in the age of German nationalism.[106] According to an official list of the works printed in the German textbooks at the beginning of the 1930s, the Brothers Grimm's folktales and regional folk songs were at the center of the children's education.[107] The abundance of small songbooks from the 1930s confirms the enormous status that was afforded German music in the curriculum of that decade (see image 11); only a handful of the classical works that had been taught before remained as mandatory texts.

Ludwig fell under the spell of the Brothers Grimm and Hans Christian Andersen, whose stories the teachers read to the class, and he would remember these legends for years to come.[108] He internalized the tales about lovers and siblings who were torn from each other and left to wander in the woods, where magicians and sorcerers lurked and bad animals and witches seduced them. He read "Hansel and Gretel," "Brother and Sister," and "The Snow Queen" and would fantasize about going on such adventures with Rachel. Ludwig's heart would fill with pity for Andersen's little match girl, who knew that a star would fall whenever a person died, and Andersen's description of a celebrating city would forever epitomize a collective eruption of joy for him.[109] The narratives he studied were often laced with recurring metered rhymes, which acted as refrains and became etched in Ludwig's memory. Each time he heard the rhyme, the entire story would come to life.[110] He would never forget the name Falada, the loyal horse in "The Goose Maid," thanks to the old German rhyme, "*Oh du Falada, da du hangest | Oh Jungfer Koenigin, da du gangest!*" (Oh Falada, here you hang | Oh virgin queen, here you go!)[111]

The schoolchildren studied not only literature and folk culture, but also the history of Franconia and Bavaria. They focused on Wuerzburg's former glory and the significance of its landmarks. Ludwig's head was filled with the battles of local knights who had fought one another centuries earlier, and, like many little boys, he would reenact them with his friends.[112]

When he was ten, Ludwig was introduced to Goethe, Schiller, and Heine through the simple cadences of the poems in the fifth-grade curriculum.[113] Goethe's "Erlkoenig" ignited the child's imagination and, as he memorized the lines, he was haunted by their rhythm and scared by Erlkoenig, the Master of the Forest.[114] The singing of Heine's long-haired beauty, Lorelei, seduced him, as it had generations of sailors. These German classics would forever remain in his heart.

German cultural studies were not the only feature that the Jewish elementary school shared with German schools; the Jewish Volksschule also adopted their strict discipline, rigid teaching methods, and philosophy of education. While the new educational ideas that flourished during the Weimar Republic were used in Ludwig's Montessori kindergarten, they were not reflected in his Volksschule. But its general rigidity aside, the Jewish Volksschule of Wuerzburg was considered an excellent school overall.[115]

The instruction of composition likewise adhered to the old-fashioned framework. The teachers encouraged their pupils to use clichés and formulaic phrases like the snow "covered everything in shrouds"[116] in an attempt to teach them a literary, poetic German. In so doing, they discounted individual expression. Nonetheless, this dogmatic teaching style did not stifle Ludwig's creativity or prevent him from loving literature. He liked writing and treated his notebooks and pencils with care.[117] Together with Ruth Hanover, he earned the highest marks in the class and his academic achievements won him his friends' respect and his parents' pride.[118] While Ruth was a model student, however, Ludwig found it difficult to be obedient and sit still for the entire day because there were always jokes to tell and tricks to perform. He was quick to answer and would often get into trouble.[119]

Ludwig also participated in a variety of extracurricular activities, like the synagogue choir, which he joined when he was eight years old. Ever since he could remember, Ludwig had admired the musical dialogue between Cantor Eschwege's solos and the choir's response, and he had memorized the melodies of Jafet and Levandowsky when he strove to be one of the lucky choir boys.[120] Ludwig became an enthusiastic member of the choir, but he never lost his impish spark—once causing the strict choirmaster to break a violin bow over his head. The other boys nicknamed him "Pfif" (short for Pfiffiguss, "little devil" in German). Years later, long after he lost his boyish soprano, music continued to affect Amichai deeply. Before airing his radio skit Lekha Dodi, which commemorated this choir, Amichai spent hours with the producers finding the correct German-Jewish melodies, in an attempt to preserve the beloved traditions.[121]

Another cherished childhood pastime was the school's theater program. As the class clown and star of many imaginary battles,[122] Ludwig was naturally drawn to it and his innate talent meant that he often played leading roles. The program was open to all ages, and its holiday performances were the boast of the community, attracting adults as well as children.[123] The subjects of the plays varied widely, ranging from the German "Snow White" and "Little Red Riding Hood" (in which Ludwig played the wolf) to the Jewish "Hanna and her Seven Sons."[124] The jewel in the crown of this ambitious amateur theater was the Hanukkah performance, and all the boys coveted the role of Judah Maccabee. The teachers put a great deal of effort into each show: auditions were taken seriously, with all the ensuing competition and tension, and the productions were of an almost professional quality.

Less structured than the choir or the theater were the youth organizations to which most of Wuerzburg's Orthodox Jewish children belonged. Ludwig joined Esra, a coed youth movement, when he was seven.[125] Ruth Hanover, along with her sister, Rosi, and stepsister, Ruth Katzmann, were members of another Jewish cultural organization, Brith Halutzim Datiyim.[126] Ludwig and his friends followed the leadership of the local Jewish teachers' college students, who acted as both counselors and coaches.[127] Together, they hiked on the riverbanks and visited Steinbachtal, the nearby forest that surrounded the former mansion of Wuerzburg aristocrats.[128] Sometimes they would walk through the forest's thick autumn foliage alongside a deep stream, or camp out on the mountain.[129]

Although after-school activities were important to the fourth and fifth graders, it was the home and the synagogue that truly shaped their lives. The heart of synagogue life was Shabbat, the climax of the Jewish week; and for Ludwig, it was tied to his father. Even as Ludwig grew older, his longing for his father merged with his anticipation of the holy day. From the moment Friedrich left on his travels, Ludwig waited for him to return on Shabbat, for it was only then that they could spend precious time together.

On Shabbat morning, Ludwig and Friedrich went to schul (synagogue), sometimes with Frieda or Rachel. Ludwig knew the order of the morning prayers, and the rituals were familiar. His body had memorized the recurring movements, when to bend and when to cover his eyes during the Shema.[130] The Torah service was the core of Shabbat morning, and over the years he also came to understand the weekly Torah portions. Bar mitzvahs were celebrated during this part of the service; he waited for the time when he, too, would stand at the bottom of the stairs while Rabbi Hanover addressed him from the height of the pulpit.[131] The rabbi was famous for his oratory, and Ludwig absorbed the sound and rhythm of his German sermons before he actually understood their content.[132] When the Torah was returned to the Holy Ark in a long procession, the cantor chanted, "Bring us back and renew our days," one of Ludwig's most beloved prayers.[133]

While Shabbat regularly punctuated the life of the community, the holidays were the headlines, especially for the children: the high holidays in autumn, the festival of lights in winter, and Passover to announce the spring. The rhythms of the Bavarian world, its seasons, nature, and celebrations, underlined it all—winter snows and spring blossoms in the palace's garden, the tall weeds on the riverbanks, and the deep red berries of summer. Autumn in Wuerzburg was defined by the dances and frivolity that followed a successful harvest. The roads were full of vessels carrying wine grapes, and Ludwig could smell them fermenting from the cellar beneath his father's store.[134] The joyous local German traditions coincided with a time of introspection for the Jewish community. When the leaves of the Hofgarten trees changed colors and fell to the ground, the Jewish New Year celebration (Rosh Hashanah) and the Day of Atonement (Yom Kippur) drew near.[135]

For the two days of Rosh Hashanah, the melodic prayers echoed through the central hall of the synagogue, reminding members of the congregation that in heaven, destinies were being determined. At the same time, the music, the singing of the cantor and the choir, penetrated their hearts. As the Torah was returned to the ark on Rosh Hashanah, the choir enthusiastically sang, "Gates, raise your heads," and as Ludwig harmonized, he imagined the gates opening for the king of the universe.[136] Years later, in "The Travels of Benjamin the Last, of Tudela,"[137] Amichai would resurrect the blessing of the priests, the lions that adorned the ark, and the holiday routines and ritual movements of the worshippers during prayers.

On Yom Kippur, the child observed his strong father and the other men pale from fasting and wrapped in "shrouds" as is the custom on the holiest day of the Jewish calendar.[138] Friedrich would kneel and bow all the way to the ground, his forehead touching the floor, and come up effortfully, his face a deep red.[139] It was frightening for the child to see his father so weak. In Amichai's story "The Times My Father Died," this scene is described as a near-death experience for his father, depicting in vivid detail the child's worry that his father would never recover and get up.[140]

Compounding the ominous nature of Yom Kippur was the sad and mysterious memorial prayer for the dead, in which only those who had lost a parent participated. Ludwig and almost all the other children were made to leave the synagogue, only to return to find their parents with tear-stained faces. One of Ludwig's friends, the son of a widow, was the only child who was allowed to stay, arousing the other children's jealousy.[141]

As the holiest day of the Jewish year drew to a close, Ludwig witnessed the most dramatic moment of the holiday, the Ne'ila prayer. The ark was opened and everyone in the synagogue cried, "Open for us the gates in the hour of closing the gates, for the day is passing away."[142] Ludwig imagined that he was knocking on the gate of a besieged city as the gate closed slowly, but he could not see who was closing it.[143] After Ne'ila, one single, long shofar note was sounded, and the fast was over.[144]

When the holidays were over, it was time to return to school. Ludwig's teachers taught him and the other children to add the prayer for rain to their daily prayers. They recited it through the winter until the snow began to melt and little buds appeared.[145] The dissonance between the Jewish and European calendars was even more dramatic during the midwinter holiday Tu Bishvat, the "New Year" for trees, when everybody would eat fruits from Israel—dates, figs, oranges, and carobs—celebrating the birth of trees and their blossoms, while the ground was covered with snow.[146] When the spring came and the River Main began to overflow with water from the melting snow, Passover arrived; the Jewish community would begin praying for dew, a prayer more befitting the dry Israeli climate than the German one.

Ludwig learned that the most important holidays were the biblical ones: Rosh Hashanah, Yom Kippur, Sukkot, Passover,[147] and Shavuot. This, however, did not prevent Hanukkah from playing a major role in his fantasy world. He was fascinated by the Hanukkah candles that celebrated the miracle of oil and the victory of the Maccabees, and Judah Maccabee was his childhood hero.[148] Ludwig longed to play Judah Maccabee, the coveted lead role in the school's Hanukkah production. In his mind, the famous warrior had fought his wars in the snow-covered hills around Wuerzburg, not near Jerusalem.[149] The winter landscape seeped into Ludwig's pores; the falling snow, the white, and the cold colored his impression of the holiday.[150] The anticipation of Hanukkah and its wonders became intertwined with the magic of winter.

It was difficult to return to the school routine in January after the glorious holiday celebrations and the long vacation, to see the untouched carpet of snow turn to trampled slush. Walking with Ruth, Ludwig saw yesterday's celebrated Christmas trees become refuse, just as the ceremonial palm fronds did after

Sukkot. Ludwig spent the long evenings playing with the games he had received at Hanukkah. His father taught him how to play chess; on Shabbat afternoons, the two would be bent intently over the chessboard. Ludwig was also an avid reader, creating imaginary worlds based on stories he had read; the cowboys and Indians from Karl May's books dovetailed with Jewish author Max Lehmann's kings of Israel and the Jewish martyrs.[151]

Ludwig's imagination combined his theatrical tendencies with the scenery he saw around him. In the Catholic city of Wuerzburg, Christian symbols and icons were prevalent year-round in the architecture and sculpture. He learned about the binding of Isaac in school, and when he snuck into the Christian cemetery through its back entrance and saw a monument of Jesus on the Mount of Olives, the two coalesced in his mind.[152]

Although Ludwig's social world revolved around his male friends, the most significant relationship of his childhood was with Ruth Hanover. After he had grown up, he said that this friendship had determined his entire life.[153] Ruth was a beautiful girl, tall with brown hair and blue eyes. Bright, gifted, spunky, and strong-minded, she was the perfect foil for Ludwig from an early age.[154] They had a singular connection, both pure and profound.[155]

On May 28, 1932, when Ruth was eight years old, her mother, Klara, died of a stroke.[156] The family wanted Rabbi Hanover to remarry as quickly as possible because Ruth and her older sister, Rosi, were still very young, and so pressured him to marry Ernestina Katzmann, his sister-in-law, who was also recently widowed. After the marriage in 1933, Ernestina moved to Wuerzburg from Fulda with her own ten-year-old daughter, also named Ruth. To avoid confusion, Ruth Katzmann became "Big Ruth" and Ruth Hanover was henceforth called "Little Ruth." The nickname quickly stuck.[157] Despite the loss of her mother, Little Ruth kept her charm and amicability (see image 6).

While the children were absorbing the changes in their small circle, the outside world was evolving. The Nazis came to power on January 30, 1933. And in March 1933, Jews were arrested in Wuerzburg "for their own protection."[158] The children were old enough to grasp some of the implications of the situation. All the love of their parents, teachers, and community could not hide the reality from them. They saw the statue *Der Deutsche Michel* that had been erected to celebrate Aryan superiority.[159] Returning from school one day, Ludwig and Ruth heard the loud parade that announced the renaming of Theaterstrasse to Hitlerstrasse. The building of the *Fraenkisches Volksblatt*, Wuerzburg's central newspaper, was attacked because the paper had reported the existence of the concentration camp Dachau.[160] Even the mayor was forced to resign after refusing to hang the Nazi flag on the Rathaus (city hall). Suddenly, the square near the Jewish complex was covered with swastikas.[161]

Bedecked with Nazi symbols and monuments, Wuerzburg was altered visually; even the sounds of the city became hostile. The bands leading the parades that Ludwig used to follow began playing Nazi music, Hitler's voice blasted from radios, and the echoes of *"Jude Blutsauger"* (Jew bloodsucker) rang in his ears. The pleasant music of church bells that had enchanted Ludwig as a baby was now tainted. Like generations of Jews before him, Ludwig learned that the hourly chimes were the bearers of bad tidings, and he and his friends avoided passing near churches.[162]

On May 1, 1933, the Pfeuffers left the Christian-owned house at Alleestrasse 11 and moved to Alleestrasse 16.[163] At that time, many zealous landlords evicted their Jewish tenants, and the Jewish-owned houses near the old age home and the hospital filled with newcomers.[164] Even the name Alleestrasse changed; the Nazis renamed it Bertoldstrasse.[165] Standing on the street where he had lived for most of his life, Ludwig, with his older cousin, watched a gang of Nazi youths overturn a piled-up fruit cart and saw the produce roll down the street.[166]

One day, the Nazis noticed a red flag hanging from a window in the old-age home. It belonged to an old man who had been a communist in his youth. The ensuing uproar took a toll on the already-frayed nerves of the neighborhood's uneasy residents, the Pfeuffers among them.[167] As a child, however, Ludwig had not grasped the magnitude of the threat. Consequently, when he found a Nazi pin, he could not resist this symbol of power and brought it home. When his father heard about this, he immediately threw it out. The next morning at five o'clock, the SS pounded on the door, demanding the pin and accusing the Pfeuffers of defiling German honor. The scene was a nightmare for Ludwig; Frieda held him in one room while Friedrich faced the Nazis. He tried to convince them that the pin had been lost, but they arrested him anyway.[168] Luckily, he was released shortly thereafter. In the story "The Times My Father Died," this incident becomes one of the "times his father died."[169] Unlike his father's first "death," bowing on the synagogue floor, however, this particular metaphorical "death" could easily have turned into a real one.

Friedrich was in a vulnerable position not only as the head of his household, but also as a Jewish storeowner. Three weeks before the official boycott of Jewish stores on April 1, 1933, the local *Gauleiter* (Nazi district leader) incited a mob to force them to close.[170] The Pfeuffers' store was targeted a year later, in 1934.

Nazi bullies stood outside the shop to prevent it from opening. Ironically, they did this on a Saturday, when the store was closed anyway because of the owners' strict observance of the Sabbath.[171]

Despite these ordeals, Ludwig's parents did not share their growing alarm with their children. First, Nazi informers were rampant and children's chatter could endanger the entire community; second, they wanted to preserve a semblance of a normal life for their offspring.[172] As before, the parents allowed Ludwig and Ruth to walk unaccompanied to school. But as much as they tried, the parents could not hide the harsh reality from their children. Ruth and Ludwig sensed that the Hofgarten was no longer as safe as its pastoral design had promised. Now, the two friends hurried through their route to avoid any encounter with the brown-shirted bullies.

While history was closing in, chance still had its cruel role to play. On a snowy day in December 1934, Little Ruth and Ludwig got into an argument on the way to school; later, at recess, Ruth borrowed another boy's bicycle, and while riding on the icy main street, she was caught between two cars in a terrible accident. Ludwig never forgot this tragic event and continuously returned to it as an adult. For a few days, no one knew whether Ruth would live. She survived the accident, but one of her legs had to be amputated above the knee.[173] Ludwig visited her in the hospital almost every day. After long months convalescing, she used crutches and later wore a prosthesis. Because of the accident, she matured quickly, while Ludwig remained a mischievous boy, and their friendship suffered.[174]

Neither Ludwig's relationship with Ruth nor the other aspects of his life in Wuerzberg would ever return to normal.[175] During the year that his friend lay in the hospital, the Nazi political machine stepped up its activities. In 1935, the Nuremburg laws were passed; Jews lost their property rights and their right to practice their former professions.[176] Even the school environment changed: because of the imposed restrictions on the numbers of Jews in all educational institutions, Jewish students were forced to transfer to Jewish schools and both the elementary and high schools were expanded.[177] Ludwig's classroom was filled with new Jewish students who could not read Hebrew. ILBA (teachers' college) students began to serve as regular teachers to accommodate the school's sudden growth, but the relative stability they brought was shaken each time one of them disappeared. The children guessed that they fled to Palestine, but no one ever spoke about it.[178]

While sitting in the classroom still felt safe, the daily walk to and from home became perilous.[179] Despite precautions, as Ludwig and his schoolmates walked home, members of the Hitler Youth, wearing swastikas and ribbons on their shirts, attacked even the youngest among them.[180] They yelled names like Jude (Jew) or Saujuden (pig Jews),[181] threw stones, and chased the Jewish children.[182] Those who could not escape were beaten.[183] These incidents reminded Ludwig of the stories in his Jewish history classes about the few pitted against the many. On the streets of Wuerzburg, however, the few did not win.

One time when he was all alone, Ludwig heard the sounds of the SS military band and hid in a garden. In the midst of the horror, he imagined himself returning to his hometown as a conquering ruler, searching left and right for his former foes, then identifying and executing them.[184] The revenge plot of Not of This Time, Not of This Place, his 1963 novel, might have stemmed from this childhood fantasy. In 1935, however, the Nazi soldiers were the rulers, not the dreaming boy. They marched up and down the streets and the boy ran away when he saw their flag. While parents desperately sought exit visas, the children developed their own Nazi-dodging strategies.

Unfortunately, Nazi-dodging was not feasible for the crippled Little Ruth. In 1935, when she and Ludwig resumed walking to school together, the pair had become easy prey. One day, Little Ruth was walking slowly but erectly with Ludwig at her side when four Hitler Youths from a Catholic school attacked them.[185] They threw the two to the ground and held Ludwig down as they beat and kicked Ruth. The sound of their boots on her prosthetic leg continued ringing in his ears long after the kicking had stopped. Little Ruth's life and fate became a touchstone for his development as a man and an artist.[186]

A short time after this incident, Ludwig overheard his parents whispering anxiously late at night. Deeply distraught, Friedrich had witnessed a gruesome sight: the bodies of two village Jews who had been beaten to death.[187] After that, he resolved to leave Germany.

It took every ounce of Friedrich's might to carry out this resolution and he paid a heavy emotional toll, but he saved his family.[188] The day after the harrowing burials of the two men, Friedrich began liquidating his business. Within a few months, he had convinced all of his extended family members to follow their relatives who had already immigrated to Palestine.[189] Luckily, there was some fortune in this time of misfortune: the Pfeuffers had received a large inheritance from America;[190] they had kept most of it in their apartment for fear it would be confiscated by the Nazis. This money ensured them the coveted immigration certificates to enter British Mandatory Palestine.[191] Unlike refugees who left at a later date, they were allowed to take their property with them and ship their furniture and belongings to their new home.[192] In the summer of 1936, the Pfeuffers parted from their close friends at the railway station.[193] They boarded the train to Venice, fearful for those who stayed behind.[194]

In the years after the Pfeuffers left, the Jewish community in Wuerzburg dwindled further and lost most of its resources and rights. On Kristallnacht, the night of November 9, 1938, Rabbi Hanover and 130 other Jews were arrested and taken to Buchenwald. The synagogue was vandalized.[195] In September 1942, the few Jews who were left in Wuerzburg dressed in ceremonial clothes and brought a box containing twenty-five Torah scrolls to the Jewish cemetery, where they buried them because services were no longer being held.[196] Between 1941 and 1945, the 1,500 Jews who remained in Wuerzburg were deported.[197]

The Pfeuffers only heard about the fate of their beloved Jewish community from letters and from those lucky ones who arrived in Palestine before 1939. As the war progressed, fewer communications were allowed and the German Jews in Palestine were panicking about the world they left behind. From his bedroom in their Jerusalem apartment, Ludwig (now called Yehuda) overheard the adults' anxious voices and later wrote, "and inside, German was spoken of nearing danger" (literal translation).[198] The German that was spoken was that of his parents. "Inside," in the heart of Hebrew-speaking Jerusalem, they continued to share their fears and their hopes in the language of their former homeland.

A reader who scours Amichai's verse for traces of the world the poet left behind will find very few. Wuerzburg and the highlights of Amichai's childhood years are missing. The absence of the bad times is also striking: there is no sign of the Nazis' impact on him or his family. The memories of the friends who accompanied Amichai throughout his childhood, including Ruth Hanover, were suppressed almost entirely as well. Although *Poems: 1948–1962*, the canonic collection that brought Amichai to the consciousness of the Israeli reader, gives the reader the impression of being personal, even autobiographical,[1] in reality, it hides more of Amichai's life story than it reveals. In fact, it is almost devoid of the German world that formed the core of his being. Of the entire repository of past memories, a few elements remain, but their presence only underscores the absence of the rest. Significantly, the God-fearing father and his language, the Hebrew of the synagogue, are present, magically transformed by Amichai into a pliable medium, ideal for modern poetry.

The poetry that Amichai wrote and published from 1948 to 1962 (and even beyond) almost entirely suppresses the foreign elements of his background. The poet who ushered the voice of the individual into Israeli poetry was actually distant from his own childhood, the primary wellspring of his work. More than anything, Amichai wanted to be known as an authentic Hebrew, Israeli poet with local roots, whose childhood had taken place in Jerusalem during the British Mandate and whose youth had passed in preparation for the anticipated military service. In order to present himself as such a poet, he had to hide the exilic universe he carried inside him: an entire microcosm of beauty and culture, with its own fears and loves, friendships and hatreds. In the personal, biographical, Israeli mythology that he forged for himself in his creative work, there was no room for the child from Germany. But even with the understanding of the poet's motivation for concealing his past, the question remains: Where did the stuff of Amichai's rich childhood go? The following chapters excavate the remains of Amichai's early years, exposing them as the hidden, secret foundation of his verse.

Indeed, the canonic collection of poetry that Amichai published in 1963 includes some hints to the past, but they are generally camouflaged, murky, and distorted. Amichai disguised his memories ingeniously, slipping them under the Israeli landscape and enigmatic imagery. His use of genres was also deliberate. Amichai saw himself as a poet and wanted to be known as such first and foremost.[2] As a result, he tended to cover the German tracks in his verse while allowing himself to be more open in his fiction and drama—genres that he considered to be somewhat inferior to poetry. He relegated his foreign past almost exclusively to those venues that were not intended to take part in the construction of his public persona as a national poet.

In his 1963 novel, Not of This Time, Not of This Place, Amichai revealed more of his German past than he did anywhere else in his entire oeuvre, as though he was storing memories that he could no longer suppress within the novel's inaccessible, complex, and winding narrative.[3] Additional autobiographical elements are discernible in a handful of short stories and in a radio skit he published in the late 1950s and early 1960s.[4] The existence of these autobiographical materials in Amichai's nonpoetic work clearly demonstrates the pervasiveness of Wuerzburg in Amichai's psyche.

Behind this dichotomy between genres lies both Amichai's conflict as an artist and the split in his personality between the fully rooted Israeli he wanted to be and the German-born immigrant he was. Only after his status as a Hebrew, Israeli poet had been established and three volumes of his poetry had met with great acclaim could Amichai unveil the other side of himself within the pages of a novel; even then, however, the memories of Europe did not surface in his poetry. In the early 1960s, the cultural climate in Israel reflected the country's continued preoccupation with the creation of a monolithic, centralist Hebrew Zionist identity, and Amichai must have felt that it was still too early in his career as a poet to elaborate on his German past. The closest he came to revealing his roots in his poetry was in the epic "The Travels of Benjamin the Last, of Tudela," which was published in its entirety only in 1968, five years after the novel.[5] Thus, Amichai continued to store foreign materials in his less-accessible genres and disclosed these materials only after he had already achieved recognition.[6]

Although Amichai postponed writing any verse explicitly about his roots until he was in his forties, one can detect, even in his earliest poems, an inner struggle between the pull of his foreign past and the wish to appear Israeli by suppressing that very past. Indeed, the world of his childhood was not merely a psychologically meaningful source for Amichai, but also a creative force behind his writing. The intimate letters that he wrote in 1947 and 1948 to Ruth Z., the woman he met in Israel and planned to marry, confirm this notion.[7] They contain memories from Amichai's hometown, from his grandparents' villages, and from his Jewish-Bavarian elementary school. The prevalence of these memories in the letters, in which Amichai wrestles with the awareness of his calling as a poet, testifies to their lasting power in his consciousness and to their inherent link to the origin of his poetry.[8]

POEMS: 1948–1962

A reading aimed at finding remnants of childhood in Amichai's early and most camouflaged collection, Poems 1948–1962, will come up with occasional signs of the German past, but these are hidden by generalizations, metaphorical overabundance, hermetic language, and Israeli landscapes that blur their foreign origin.

Although Amichai might have been only partially aware of this underlying principle of his poetic practice of suppression, this creative "philosophy" emerges metaphorically in this collection. The emotional and poetic strategy of camouflage is evident in images scattered throughout the poems. Lines such as "And my yearnings closed inside me / Like bubbles in a loaf of bread. / On the outside, I am smooth and quiet and brown . . ."[9] suggest the disparity between outside appearances and an inner, turbulent reality. Similarly, in "Instructions for Her Voyage," Amichai's speaker lists rules to help his beloved on her trip that in fact lay out the essence of camouflage: "do not show the ticket / For inspection. Let no one know / Where you're going . . . / Do not / Show your identity."[10] It is not surprising that the laws of survival that Amichai's poem teaches apply to the traveler and the immigrant alike; these are laws that Amichai must have internalized when he was a refugee, and they seem synonymous with the principles that guided him, perhaps unconsciously, in his writing at that early stage.

Another poem that discloses Amichai's poetic thinking is entitled "Hakavana lemashehu aher" (something else is intended).[11] It comes closer than other poems to defining Amichai's strategy, both explicitly and through its imagery. The poem is structured as a catalogue of natural and social phenomena whose common thread is the gap between the perceived phenomenon and its true implications, or "intention." Thus, darkness lurks around the loud laughter of two lovers, and the seemingly sturdy mountain in the background is not truly stable, for it is constantly changing. The poem displays instances of similar inconsistencies in language and text. The goal of language is communication, but the poem lists instances in which the intention behind words is never conveyed. Amichai writes that a "draft" is left uncorrected and its mistakes then become permanent; in other words, the final text is a mere draft, forever flawed and incomplete. He continues with the observation that translations of words are imprecise; the translation is far from the original intention of the writer. Words are uttered, but disappear quickly in the shadows without conveying their message.

This poem, whose title and refrain are "something else is intended," hints at Amichai's awareness of his own practice of camouflage, of the gap between what he said or wrote and what he really meant. Indeed, the final stanza opens with an almost prosaic question, "shall I say everything that I think." This question, however, lacks a question mark at its end; its punctuation is testament to the fact that the answer is, No, I will not. . . . Not in life and also not in poetry.

Amichai's strategy of camouflage is also evident in the covering up of the landscapes and people that populated his German childhood; most notably absent are his birthplace, Wuerzburg, and the beloved girl whose memory is inextricably connected with it, Little Ruth. Amichai internalized Wuerzburg's landmarks, and their aesthetic deeply influenced his worldview. Because recalling these landmarks created conflict, when he intended to retrieve the scenes of Wuerzburg, he wrote about "something else," namely, Jerusalem or Paris. In a line in a private notebook from 1966, Amichai openly describes this tactic, saying that he used the name Jerusalem, but meant his "childhood in other cities."[12] This statement is especially true for *Poems: 1948–1962*. Wuerzburg only peeks out through a few scattered metaphors in the book's 360 pages, many of which contain two or three poems.

"When I Was a Child," the poem that opens both Amichai's first book, *Now and in Other Days*, and *Poems: 1948–1962*, is an apparent manifesto that seems to announce the lyrical and autobiographical tenor of the book. Yet even in this initial, declarative poem, the landscape of Wuerzburg is reflected as through a broken mirror. The poem contains two indicators of the European, German countryside: the river and the forest. The river is evoked in the first lines: "When I was a child / Grasses and masts stood at the shore."[13] The child's perspective, looking at the world while lying on his back near the shore, conflates structures that rise upward: weeds and masts. The shore itself remains unidentified. Upon further analysis, however, it becomes clear that the German landscape of Amichai's childhood is being evoked.

While in "When I Was a Child" the river's presence is implied by the shore and the masts, in "In Yemin Moshe"[14] the river becomes prominent by its absence; it appears as a conspicuous void within the cityscape of Jerusalem. In this love poem, Amichai emphasizes the authenticity of the Israeli landscape by including a prosaic explanation of the title in square brackets: "Yemin Moshe is an ancient neighborhood in Jerusalem outside the walls." The poem itself is studded with references to the biblical Song of Songs, whose love plot takes place in Jerusalem. Furthermore, its local components are unmistakable: the wall, small leaves of the indigenous olive trees, and the scorched earth of the no-man's-land near the pre-1967 Israeli-Jordanian border that passed next to Yemin Moshe. During the romantic evening, bells toll to the lovers. Although they are the bells of Jerusalem's churches, not Wuerzburg's, they evoke the longing for the city of the speaker's childhood: "we sat on the shore of our city / the *river-less* one" (emphasis added). By dubbing Jerusalem a "river-less city," Amichai implies that for him, a "true" city must have a river, bridges that stretch over it, and a shore. The poem transforms the couple into the river: "and we were instead of the river / and bridges were above us." With their bodies flowing with passion, the lovers provide what Jerusalem, the river-less city, lacks.

The desire to endow Jerusalem with Wuerzburg's river and bridges is found more explicitly in an unpublished entry in a journal from 1967. "Bridges calm me," Amichai wrote, adding, "In Jerusalem bridges should be built / even over dry / valleys."[15] The child who grew up near ancient bridges will always find comfort in them, even as an adult.

Like wide rivers, forests are prominent in European scenery but absent in Israel. In the few cases when Amichai included a forest in his verse, he necessarily drew upon the countryside of his birthplace. The word "forest" is thus a marker of that other, German world. The speaker of "When I Was a Child" wonders when his father would return because "there was another forest beyond the clearing."[16] An unaware Israeli reader might understand the forest as a storybook metaphor for the distances beyond which the beloved father disappears. With the knowledge of Amichai's boyhood, however, one may extract from the poem a fragment of a true experience. It is Amichai's memory of himself as a child and his anxious waiting for the return of his father, the traveling salesman, whose absences seemed like an eternity.[17] The tie between forest and father reverberates in another poem dedicated to the medieval poet, "Ibn Gabirol," in which Amichai portrays his father as a tree in a grove.[18] As in "When I

Was a Child," behind the arboreal image likely rests Amichai's authentically re-created childish perception that linked the European forest to his father.

The lush forests of southern Germany also give color to the portrayal of "A Girl Whose Name Is Sarah." The redness of Sarah's mouth is reminiscent of a raspberry or a wild strawberry, forest fruits that do not grow in Israel's Mediterranean climate: "her mouth has grown red on a bush / in the forest next to my childhood."[19] With this image, Amichai subtly recalls the hikes he took as a child in the forests surrounding Wuerzburg and his grandparents' villages, where he would collect wild berries. This poem locates the "forest," if not in place, then in time: "next to childhood." Indeed, while this reference to childhood is abstract, it is one of very few in this collection that openly associates the European scenery with Amichai's youth.

The significance of that amorphous place called "childhood" is acknowledged with even fewer identifying features in a short poem entitled "Advanced Training for Angels."[20] The "training" takes place at an imaginary shooting gallery at the end of the world, where angels begin their practice by hitting round targets with a bull's-eye at the center. The bull's-eye metaphor exposes the writer's awareness of the essence of his poetry: "In the middle, there is the black bull's eye of my childhood / where I am vulnerable." The speaker acknowledges that the core of his being, the heart of his entire life, remains his childhood. Immediately after this terse confession, however, the celestial trainees "advance" from shooting at targets to shooting at moving human cardboard figures, each representing different stages of a person's life. This poem's admission of the crucial role of childhood is intense and direct, but it still obeys the dictates of the poetics of camouflage in its brevity and in the use of the universal, nonspecific code word yalduti (my childhood). Moreover, the components and the semantic field of the poem's overarching metaphor are the Israeli military arena—that of soldiers at shooting practice—which signals the military service of the speaker and the Israeli environment in which his childhood is implied to be embedded.

While Amichai often used the Israeli milieu to obscure the location of his childhood at the "bull's-eye" of a poem, he allowed the suppressed landmarks of Wuerzburg to burst forth in detail when masquerading as those of another European city. In "Three Poems about the Autumn in Paris," Amichai used Paris to displace the city of his birth.[21] Indeed, the European climate of his childhood was more natural to him than the arid weather of his new homeland. Paris is a city with all the elements that Amichai missed: the gold and red of fallen leaves in autumn, an overflowing river, and stone statues. September in Paris with leaves on the ground evokes his hometown, as does the Seine, the "river that makes a vow quietly to the trees." Amichai's love of statues and monuments, a love that originated in ornate Wuerzburg, is also expressed through the Parisian cityscape. He depicts the French city's "stone heroes" riding horses or wrestling with one another. The speaker argues, "A man is recognized in stone." It is unclear whether this means that a man's character may be deduced from the stone statues that he loves and for which he longs, or from the kind of stone monument erected in his honor.[22] Whichever interpretation of the line is chosen, Amichai's fascination with the stone monuments of European capitals goes beyond that of an Israeli tourist for whom statues of humans are quite foreign. The intricate sculptures of the Hofgarten come back to the poet, who saw them regularly as a boy. Although the poem never divulges the connection between Paris and Wuerzburg, the yearning for the European cityscape contained in its verses cannot be denied. In the third, longest, and final part of "Three Poems about the Autumn in Paris," a specific statue prompts the speaker to identify himself as a centaur: "And I am a centaur: half me and half / galloping love . . . "[23] It seems that for Amichai, the lustful half men–half beasts of Paris recall the stone satyrs near Wuerzburg's palace.

Toward the end of this nostalgic triptych, against the backdrop of the urban vista and the man who contemplates it, a "newspaper-boy" sells papers dipped in blood. This unmistakably macabre image may symbolize the speaker's ambivalence toward Paris and, more importantly, toward his former hometown. Indeed, Europe's grandeur was marred by its history, especially during the Second World War; violence and danger were always lurking behind the cityscape of statues, fall colors, and rivers.

Amichai's admiration for European cities is thus an indirect way of expressing longing for Wuerzburg. One must emphasize that while foreign cities like Paris and Rome appear by name in *Poems: 1948–1962*, Wuerzburg never does. Its appearance and texture are spelled out only in the unpublished papers now in the Beinecke Library. Amichai literally expunged the name of Wuerzburg from his entire published oeuvre. In his poetry he calls it "the city of my childhood" or "the city in which I was born" and refers to its scenery only elusively.[24]

Even these oblique references, however, are scarce. Only once or twice in the entire volume may an alert reader encounter a specific visual detail from Wuerzburg preserved intact. Such an image hides in the seventeenth poem in the medieval-style cycle of quatrains entitled "Twenty New Quatrains": "the gate closed, whose wrought-iron flowers are like the patterns of your blood."[25] While the words "the gate closed" are highly evocative and may be understood metaphorically, the poem's literal, not symbolic, features are most important in interpreting it.[26] Unlike the poems set in Jerusalem, like "In Yemin Moshe," this poem does not name the gate's location. Nevertheless, one who has visited Wuerzburg can speculate that the poem refers to the immense, intricate, wrought-iron gates guarding the Hofgarten, which Amichai passed through countless times (for a photograph of the gates, see image 9). The connection between the patterns of the iron gate and the speaker's blood is physical and tangible. It is the link between the features of a city and the body of the person who grew up in it. The traces of the past, however, are hidden in enigmatic lines such as this one, which lead the reader to mistakenly relate to them only as metaphors rather than as concrete objects from Amichai's childhood.

Amichai's repression of his German past is underscored by his apparent favoritism to Israeli places. While only approximately fourteen allusions to European landscapes of any kind may be found in the three hundred and sixty pages of *Poems: 1948–1962*, the collection contains nearly one hundred references to Israeli topography. In contrast to the elusive hermetic language used to depict a childhood placed in a generic time and a nameless location, the allusions to Israel are drawn with great attention to detail. This descriptive specificity emphasizes the writer's Israeli identity and establishes the Israeli landscape as the backdrop for his life. Furthermore, in interviews, Amichai repeatedly used the phrase "in my childhood in Jerusalem," as if his experiences before his migration to Palestine had never occurred.[27]

Common Israeli flora and fauna appear frequently in the poems as background, subject, and metaphor: cypress trees, fig trees and figs, almond trees and thorns, oranges and watermelons, and especially olive trees, their leaves, and their coarse trunks. Israeli topography and weather are spelled out in the language of someone who has lived in them. Wadis, the Arabic term used in colloquial Hebrew for seasonal streambeds that are only full during periods of rainfall, feature prominently in many poems. Mountains, sands, rocky surfaces, stones, and dry land, and with them the climatological Hebrew terms that define the first and the last rains of the season, and *sharav*, the unique Hebrew word for a heat wave, appear often. The local geography and environment—a desert in the east and a sea in the west; such natural landmarks as the Sea of Galilee, the Valley of Olives, Mount Hermon, the Jordan River, and the Judean and Negev deserts; the cities of Jaffa, Tiberias, and Jericho; as well as historical sites like Kefar Nahum and Masada—grant the text an undeniably Israeli texture. Jerusalem towers above all these sites, with references to its name as well as to its neighborhoods and historical sites: the Old City and the wall, Mamila Garden and David's Tower, Yemin Moshe and the Valley of the Cross, Mount Zion, the Church of Maria, and the nearby Arab village, Abu Ghosh. This abundance of Israeli elements in Amichai's first collection throws into relief the vagueness of the language he chose to use in connection to his non-Israeli childhood, when he described it at all.

*　　*　　*

Poems: 1948–1962 is not monolithic in its Israeliness or in the extent to which it covers the past, however. Especially in its second half, which was written after 1958, more European residues rise to the surface, subverting the patriotic, local facade. Wuerzburg, the deleted city, emerges with the greatest force in the cycle of elegies that closes the entire collection. Yet the more the city of Amichai's youth creeps into the text, the greater the effort to conceal it; the more intense the memory and the pain it evokes, the more intricate the work of camouflage. As a result, the expressions of distant memories and the stress provoked by foreignness are buried deep beneath the elegies' Israeli landscape. For the reader who knows the poet's life story, however, the occasional acknowledgments of the past are the exceptions that prove the rule: they confirm the existence of invisible undercurrents, hidden yearnings for a faraway land.

Amichai's longing for that lost land is intertwined with his longing for his lost language. He often jotted notes to himself in German that clearly express how much he missed the place he left behind. Many of the German notes in the Beinecke archives capture the feeling of alienation or being lost and exude a sense of vulnerability and nostalgia for a European climate and nature.[28] On a piece of paper from the archive, two German words appear: "Bist verloren" (you are lost).[29] The Hebrew lines that accompany this German phrase are less direct. In them, Amichai laments that he is like a geographical map—he is but a faded copy of the true land. In the margins, he comments to himself, "more and more, I resemble a map." As time progresses and the memory of the exact characteristics of his former homeland fade, only its outline is preserved, like the lines on a map. They cannot capture colors, feelings, and sights, but, at the same time, they cannot be erased. Amichai put into poetry this tie between the place of childhood and its language; it is on a piece of yellow, lined paper in the archive that, judging by its size, is from the same period (the mid-1950s).

In it, the poet describes how he "translated" European landscapes into Israeli ones: "I translated the forests / of my childhood to bare rocks and acacias. . . . "[30] In other words, the move from one land to another is a translation of landscapes, not only of languages.

"ELEGY ON THE LOST CHILD"

Unlike these overt autobiographical admissions in the archives—cries of pain in the mother tongue—"Elegy on the Lost Child" hides the authentic, childlike sensation of being lost within an ambiguous narrative[31] (see appendix A). This 144-line poem, which closes *Poems: 1948–1962*, is a highly artistic amalgam of the Israeli terrain and the European landscape, and an elaborate metaphorical depiction of the sensation of being lost. At the end of 1957, Amichai took notes in both German and Hebrew before composing this hermetic masterpiece. Those handwritten notes alternate between the languages; they consist of short segments that contain preliminary ideas and individual lines. The connection between the notes and the published work is confirmed by the proximity of their dates and their shared title. The Hebrew words "Elegy on the Lost Child" are underlined at the head of the notes. Moreover, the last section of the elegy contains verses that are word-for-word translations of the notes' German lines.[32]

The identity of the child in the published version of "Elegy on the Lost Child" remains amorphous. Nevertheless, the speaker's identification with, or at least affection for, that child comes through. In one of his last letters to Ruth Z., on April 1, 1948, Amichai describes a recurring nightmare from his childhood: he sees a beloved person and calls out her name in vain. In the letter, Amichai interprets this haunting dream as an expression of the fear of separation. He then compares it to the fear of a little child who lost his mother on a busy street or in a large store. The prevalence of this theme in dreams, he explains, is proof of its universality, for there is no one who has not experienced it.[33] This letter supports an interpretation of the "lost child" in the published elegy as emerging from autobiographical and subconscious roots. In light of the letter, one sees that there is also a clear association between the lost child and a lost love.

"Elegy on the Lost Child," which tells the story of a search for a lost child, with concrete rescue missions, airplanes, and search dogs, may be read as a metaphorical quest for lost childhood.[34] Amichai's own, unpublished interpretations of his elegy insist that the death of childhood is adulthood. In two notes found in the Beinecke Archive, Amichai wrote, "[T]he child is no longer . . . because he grew up"[35] and "ran away to his adult life."[36] Even without seeing these notes, some of the elegy's interpreters have read it as a lament for the loss of childhood.[37] Shimon Sandbank contends that although the elegy is based on a concrete occurrence—and the mountains and olives trees are the true background for the police searches—the landscape is actually an emotional one, like the "land of lament" in Rilke's "Tenth Duino Elegy."[38] Indeed, Amichai, like Rilke, attributed human qualities to the land, but the lines of Amichai's elegy hide a large number of landscapes, both real and imaginary.

The elegy opens with a metaphor in which the speaker describes himself in terms of a dry wadi, as he questions the endurance of memory. Specifically, he wants to know what parts of his past remain in his body and soul: "how can I know what level / love reached inside me?"[39] Just as the watermark left on a wadi's sides indicates the highest point that the water had once reached, so too the speaker searches for a mark on his body and soul that could attest to emotional connections in and to the past.

The use of the wadi as a container analogous to the speaker is in itself a declaration that the structure of his body is similar to the geology of Israel, whose rivers flow only in the winter and dry up in the summer. In this arid Middle Eastern land, only a line of mud on the side of the wadis is left to mark the height that the water reaches in the rainy season. Despite the pronounced Israeliness of this picture, Amichai relates it to childhood through the imagery: the "congealed mud"[40] on the side of the wadi is compared to the white "moustache" of a child who has drunk a glass of milk. By means of this simile, the question with which the poem opens, "how can I know what level / love reached inside me?" is concerned not only with the boundaries of adult emotions, but also with childhood.[41] The identification of the speaker with a wadi, the river without its water, underscores the Israeli self who erased the memory of the bountiful river on whose shores he grew up.

According to the elegy's speaker, memory and love are bound to each other because the ideal of love is a rejection of that which preceded it: "Loving means having to forget the other love, / closing the other doors."[42] In other words, discarding former romantic ties is a precondition for the budding of a new love. Based on this opening, as well as on the poem's explicit allusions to love throughout and its frequent use of the first-person plural voice, some readers argue that the "lost child" symbolizes a lost love.[43] As suggested above, however, the object of the search cannot be merely love. The past and traces of the lost German childhood lurk in the language. The German expression, "to close the doors to the past," lies beneath this line. A reader unfamiliar with the idiom would recognize neither this faint mark of the poet's linguistic past, nor its implicit suggestion that the past is indelible. Indeed, closing the door to the past and turning one's back on the child one used to be is not an easy task.[44]

Interjected in the narrative of the search for the child are increasingly urgent reiterations of the crux of the elegy's quest: "but the child got lost";[45] "but the child disappeared";[46] "the child hasn't been found";[47] and finally, "but the child died."[48] The poem's speaker glides between recording the exterior plot (looking for the child among the dunes) and his inner stream of consciousness. In these musings, the speaker recalls specific Israeli spots—the Jordan River and the Kineret, Mount Arbel and Sussita—that testify to the locality of the events and his sense of belonging to Israel. In contrast, he also invokes "foreign cities and . . . lakes"[49] and a "foreign shore"[50] that are nameless, generic entities. The fact that the foreign places are nameless suggests that they are unknown or unfamiliar to the speaker. Indeed, the mere reference to "cities" in the plural camouflages the origin of the "lost child," Wuerzburg. In this way, Amichai includes non-Israeli landmarks, yet distances himself from them. Although the speaker declares that "names are not forgotten,"[51] in the elegy the names of the foreign people and foreign places remain unknown. Nevertheless, memories of them rise to the surface. Within the elegy's various landscapes, Amichai wove identifiable threads of his past and laced them into the explicit Israeli fabric so as not to betray their origin.

Amichai's German notes reveal his awareness of his process of substituting Israeli objects for German ones. On a small sheet from around the same time, he wrote in German that bushes of the desert are "relatives of" the trees of "my evil homeland." The sharp language of this note opens a window onto Amichai's poetic thinking and the conflict of identity that spurred it: the place of birth is at once beloved and evil.[52] For "homeland," Amichai even used the loaded word he learned in childhood, which was later adopted by the Nazis: "Heimat." The formula set forth in this phrase is similar to the archival note in which Amichai "translates" Germany's "forests" to Israel's "bare rocks and acacias."[53] He was continuously trying to find equivalents in his new homeland for the elements he cherished in his old one. While his notes divulge that process of substituting Hebrew for German, bushes for trees, and rocks for forests, the published poetry only has the rocks, the bushes, and the Hebrew language.

One childhood element that dovetails naturally with Israeli features is the "empty wells" among which the lost child wanders: "He came and went in the ringing of his toys among / empty wells, at the ends of holidays and within the terrible cycle of cries and silence. . . . "[54] Indeed, empty wells exist in Israel, as do the Jewish holidays, but the map of Wuerzburg and the map of Amichai's life within it point in another interpretative direction. The proximity of empty wells, festivals, and a "cycle of cries and silence" in the elegy's text is not a mere poetic chain of free associations.[55] Rather, it touches on distinct recollections of places within one or two square blocks of each other in old Wuerzburg: the empty, deep, and ominous well in the courtyard near his father's store was a stone's-throw away from the synagogue, the site of solemn holiday services and prayer "cycles" alternating between silence and loud, chanted prayers. Moreover, the fact that "the *ends* of the holidays" (emphasis added) are singled out in the published poem is also no coincidence. Because the Jewish day lasts from sunset to sunset, holidays end when it is dark outside. Amichai's childish fears of the empty well and of darkness, combined with memories of exiting the synagogue after the holidays' evening prayers, are evoked in this poetic lament for a child whose whereabouts are unknown.

Like the empty Israeli wells, Israeli stones become a hidden passageway to the speaker's childhood: "And the stones / chanted in the choir of black mouths, into the earth, / and only the child could hear them. . . . "[56] This choir of stones holds the voices of the boys of the Wuerzburg synagogue choir in which Amichai was a soprano. The black color of the mouths and the fact that they belong to stones instead of living children are a moving intimation of the bitter fate of most of the choir's young singers, whose bodies were burnt in the Nazi crematoria.[57] The image transforms the silenced boys into the muted voices of stones with black mouths, and so alludes to the Holocaust. An un-camouflaged version of this morbid image appears in a notebook from 1966. This time, the boys, not the stones, sing in the synagogue choir, their mouths open "like the memory of dead ones. . . . "[58]

The adult speaker of the published poem acknowledges that only the lost child can hear the choir from the past, thus implying the kinship between himself and the child whose experiences he records. In addition, when the child dies at the end of the poem, he is "chanted upon / in the psalm-books of the lands of the dead."[59] This may refer to the child that Amichai used to be, the child who sang in the doomed synagogue choir. These hermetic lines thus also conceal the connection between the Holocaust and the lost child. In the elegy, as in the entirety of *Poems: 1948–1962*, Amichai covered the tracks that would have hinted to the fate he would have encountered had he stayed in Germany. The entire elegy may be interpreted as mourning the metaphorical death of the choir boy, the death of the soprano who lost his singing voice along with his mother tongue. The German-Jewish boy's choir is now in the land of the dead.

The futility of the quest for the child becomes evident at the heart of the poem. The sophisticated rescue devices of spotlights and snares, police dogs and low-flying airplanes are failing. They all pass near the child without noticing him and do not save his life. As the search is winding down, the elegy describes the child as a part of the landscape: "the child remained and began resembling the mountains . . . and the olive tree trunks."[60] This is the last time that the child appears in the text before his death. His transformation into stones and trees is both a precursor of his demise and a hint at the reason behind it. His disappearance and ultimate death are results of his absorption into the countryside and his assimilation into his new environment. The German child died when he became Israeli. Moreover, the resemblance between the child and the Israeli terrain may be interpreted as a metapoetic disclosure, a description of Amichai's strategy of blending into the surroundings, of camouflage, in his life and his writing.

The final lines of the published version of the elegy are conspicuously unemotional and understated. A few people continue to search for the child, but the poem suggests that they are, in fact, only looking for feelings that would fit their outer expression, be it tears or laughter.[61] This segment of the elegy can be traced back to the 1957 draft, which speaks forlornly of a woman searching for an appropriate weeping between "pain and weeping" (*suchte sich ein passendes Weinen zwischen Schmerz und Weinen*).[62] Two Hebrew words follow this ambiguous but wrenching German description in the archives: "*shelo yir'u*" (lest they would see). These Hebrew words spell out Amichai's struggles with displaying emotion, as though weeping is unwelcome in his new, Israeli, Hebrew-speaking milieu.

The unpublished German draft acknowledges the intensity of the pain, while the published Hebrew poem preserves its outer expression alone: "they searched for a pain that would fit their tears, / for a joy that would fit their laughter. . . ."[63] Furthermore, while the German draft speaks of crying and pain, the final Hebrew version creates an equation: weeping is to pain as laughter is to joy. Thus, the potency of the pain is diluted. In the process of transforming the German draft into the publishable Hebrew version, Amichai covered more than language. The comparison between the draft and the published poem demonstrates that Amichai used three camouflage techniques: first, instead of highlighting pain, the published poem parallels pain and joy; second, in the draft, the feeling is paramount, but the published poem contains only its external expression; finally, while his draft speaks of a woman who was searching for an appropriate weeping, the elegy speaks of an indefinite "they" who are searching for a feeling. The last line of the elegy describes the complete dispersal of the search party. After the boy's death, each participant dispassionately goes in a different direction.

The enigmatic text of the elegy is structured as an arc. Its beginning and end are understated, with its emotional climax in the middle. Amichai concealed the evidence of his own loss, the loss of a twelve-year-old who had to shed his German-Jewish identity and adopt an Israeli one, at the climax of the poem. The most highly charged moment in this failed search, the fatal moment of the missed opportunity to find the child, is where the connection between the poem and Amichai's conflict of identity is hidden. In the published version, before the searchers blindly pass by the child, there is a description of new, modern houses with large glass panes. At the climactic point, the detectives do not see the child because he is hiding between those future Israeli buildings. "But they passed / the place and didn't see, for the child . . . / hid in the stones of tomorrow's houses . . ."[64] The German version of this line, written on an archival notepad, endows the entire text with new meanings. It starts, "*the child hides between the languages*"[65] (emphasis added). As is evident from the newly discovered line, the published version of "Elegy on the Lost Child" obscures the painful truth of the poet's life in Israel and denies his mother tongue. At this stage in his writing, in the late 1950s, Amichai was unable to reveal the pain of living between two languages and therefore preserved only a distorted translation of the German sentence in the published poem: "*the child hid, curled up / among the stones of tomorrow's houses*"[66] (emphasis added). This act of hiding perhaps causes the child's final disappearance, because anyone who "hides between the languages" is doomed to muteness, doomed to a condition in which he will not be able to speak in either language. Furthermore, the houses of tomorrow may be housing developments (*shikunim*), the Israeli buildings, but in Hebrew, the word *bayit* (house) also means a stanza. Thus, the German-speaking child may be hiding between the Hebrew stanzas that the adult poet would write, just as the poet himself is hiding behind the Hebrew lines that conceal his identity and the roots of the poem.

A tragic line closes the German draft. It states, "he quieted down slowly into his death."[67] Although this description is absent in the published poem, it sheds light on the elegy. Hiding between languages causes a type of death—silence.

NOT OF THIS TIME, NOT OF THIS PLACE

"Elegy on the Lost Child" may be read as a lament not only for the lost paradise of childhood, but also for the cache of childhood memories that remained submerged, distant landmarks that the adult Israeli poet was reluctant to visit in his verse. To a certain extent, when Amichai changed genres, the repression of *Poems: 1948–1962* was lifted. In his fiction, he was less reluctant to appear as an outsider haunted by memories and unveiled his European background. The lost child who vanished in the poetry was found, so to speak, in a novel, segments of which are unmistakably autobiographical. In fact, based on publication dates, drafts in the Beinecke Library, and records of Amichai's trip to Wuerzburg, the writing of the elegy appears to have been concurrent with his work on the novel, suggesting that the two texts share Amichai's hometown as the source of inspiration.

In 1959, at the age of thirty-five, Amichai traveled to Wuerzburg for the first time since he had left it in 1936. That visit spurred him to write his novel *Not of This Time, Not of This Place*, which he would publish after *Poems: 1948–1962*.[68] In the novel, German Wuerzburg makes its literary debut in Amichai's oeuvre. Amichai also rendered Jewish Wuerzburg, along with its people, prayers, and customs, with affection and nostalgia, alongside the horrors of the Holocaust that annihilated this flourishing community after he had emigrated. Despite the 1959 visit, the descriptions of his childhood in the novel are mostly based on early memories of Wuerzberg. The flood of details that characterizes the novel highlights more intensely the absence of this information in the poetry, making it difficult to assume Amichai omitted his hometown from his verse accidentally.

Many of the protagonist's descriptions in *Not of This Time* present an authentic documentation of Amichai's early years.[69] Indeed, the local Wuerzburgian scholars Christian Leo and Hans Steidele were able to draw the map of Wuerzburg in the 1930s and to identify its streets, buildings, and architectural landmarks by following the novel. Leo was even able to chart the route Amichai walked to school based on the narrative (see appendix B). The lushness of the novel illustrates how rich with stimuli Amichai's childhood was and, more significantly for this discussion, how much of that childhood Amichai remembered. Unfortunately, when the novel was translated into English, much of the detail of the German background was cut from the translation.[70]

In Not of This Time, Amichai confronts the "foreign self" he abandons in his verse. Indeed, the psychological structure that the critic Dan Miron developed to analyze the poetry of the classical Hebrew national poet, H. N. Bialik, is applicable to Amichai.[71] Miron argues that in order to return to writing poetry, Bialik, who suffered from writer's block, had to deal with autobiographical circumstances he had previously avoided. Similarly, Amichai could not eternally suppress parts of himself that threatened his Israeli poetic persona. He had to confront the German Jewish child he had been in order to continue to write poetry, so he returned to the place of primeval memories before resuming his poetic career. Amichai might not even have been conscious of this need; in an interview he granted in 1962 as he was finishing the novel, he admitted that he did not know what prompted him to return.[72] He faced Wuerzburg physically as well as creatively, and through writing the novel he reworked and metabolized the loss of the place, the people and even the language that he loved. In Amichai's words:[73]

> Pictures from childhood became primeval pictures of my life and I forgot their source. Places and landscapes that I thought were taken from my dreams I found here. . . . Terms and symbols like resurrection that were in my soul I discovered their source here.[74]

Not of This Time's style is at times ambiguous and its plot is hard to follow. Even within this somewhat revelatory narrative, Amichai continued the work of concealing the German to a certain extent; as the need to revisit his childhood was fraught with feelings of guilt and inner conflicts, repression still remains ingrained in the fabric of the novel. As Glenda Abramson observes in her book on Amichai, the novel is less concerned with maintaining an ordered plotline and developing believable characters than with dealing with the internal world while scrambling narrative, characters, and chronology.[75] The motivation for this challenging style may lie with Amichai's self-doubts about the revelations he makes in the novel. The often fantastical, poetic, and disjointed style, replete with dense language and loaded metaphors, serves to obscure some of the personal disclosures.

Amichai's physical and artistic return to the place of his childhood may have been triggered by a crisis in his romantic life. There were urgent psychological reasons that compelled the poet to go to his birthplace in 1959.[76] His first marriage was crumbling and his stormy extramarital affair with an American woman had just reached an excruciatingly painful end. The need to reclaim the child once was and to tell the story of his hometown and childhood arose at the same time that his personal life was unraveling. One might assume that Amichai wished to retrieve the memory of his early years—his emotional comfort zone—and draw strength from it.

Not of This Time's narrative mirrors the inner merging of various abandonments throughout the author's life. It intertwines the doomed love affair of an Israeli man in Jerusalem and his feelings of guilt toward his wife with the wish to avenge the death of his childhood sweetheart who was left to die in Europe.

The novel's opening scene is set in the Jerusalem house of the narrator's friend, in the throes of an orgiastic, wild party. Despite the bacchanalian atmosphere, Joel, the protagonist, seems to be on the verge of suicide: "He stood at the edge of the roof and his entire life was within him—all his memories, his childhood, his encounters, his conflicts. . . . "[77] The city of Jerusalem itself reflects Joel's self-destructive attitude—"the streets of Jerusalem are as empty as the veins of a man who has voluntarily let his blood."[78] Joel is looking for a purpose to his life[79] and declares that he is "at a crossroads . . . at an intersection, on the eve of a great decision, in crisis, before a great turning."[80] In order to overcome the crisis and save his lost soul, Joel signs a Faustian contract that compels him "to live a double life in order to fulfill all his longings and all his desires."[81] The two parallel plotlines that ensue from this point represent two alternative paths for the conflicted protagonist.

Joel then embarks on a winding journey into the depths of his consciousness, a journey that takes the form of a schizophrenically split narrative whose action alternates between Israel and Germany.[82] To the extent that any linear plot can transpire in two settings at once, the novel follows Joel simultaneously in two universes. The first is a sweeping, romantic love story (set in the Jerusalem of the early 1960s) between Joel and an American woman named Patricia (reminiscent of Amichai's own affair); the second is a detective / revenge tale that takes place in a German town, where the protagonist attempts to uncover Nazi crimes.[83] At the heart of this latter quest is Amichai's desire to reconstruct the last days in the life of his childhood sweetheart, Little Ruth, and avenge her death. This intricate, suspenseful story is set in the fictitious town of Wein-burg, obviously modeled after Wuerzburg. Just as Weinburg replicates Amichai's real hometown, so too Joel, the protagonist, is a close reflection of the author: "It began with a dream and grew with a great longing for a lost childhood. Now all these feelings have merged into a passion to avenge what they had done to Little Ruth."[84] Despite this call for revenge, however, the pas-sion for it slowly wanes and the narrator realizes, toward the end of his stay in Weinburg, that he had really traveled there to revisit his childhood. The strug-gle between the will to propel the detective / revenge action toward its denoue-ment, and the obsessive, seemingly aimless circling around the handful of places that sooth the pain of longing, drive both the protagonist's movements and the rhythm of the text. Moreover, it seems that the one-man effort to ex-pose hiding Nazis is a retroactive attempt to grant meaning, structure, and di-rection to the amorphous and chaotic yearnings for home that overcome him and are in conflict with his Israeli milieu.

Indeed, the revenge plot is a pretense from the outset, an artistic ruse to jus-tify the narrator's return to his birthplace within the context of the Zionist na-tional ideals. The protagonist (or the author) must affirm that he is not a weak, exilic Jew, but rather an Israeli who fought in the War of Independence, whose language is Hebrew, and whose city is Jerusalem. Before he arrives in the Ger-man city, the narrator gives himself the courage to face it by using military ter-minology to prove that he is a skilled warrior, not a victim.[85]

Joel, an archeologist by profession, tries to penetrate layers of time and de-struction and reveal the truth underneath. Symbolically, he is also an archeolo-gist of the soul, who strives to excavate the maze of the subconscious. The text subverts Joel's—and the reader's—archeological or psychoanalytical efforts by constructing narrative layers that cover the subterranean city of childhood. The topmost, visible layer for the reader (and the protagonist) is Weinberg of the present: a German city of the economic miracle of the late 1950s and early 1960s, described with both real and fictional details. Weinburg, while serving as the set of an American-made film about the Second World War, remains a haven for hiding Nazis and a breeding ground for neo-Nazis. Underneath this 1960s layer, another layer of the past is reconstructed by the author: the city as it was from the day the narrator left it in 1936 until the end of the war in 1945. The descriptions of that layer are partly fictional and partly historical, based on written records and photographs from the Gestapo archive that were available to Amichai. In the body of the novel, the narrator uses his imagination and the on-location American film to fill in the gaps and recreate the horrific fate of the remaining Jews during that period. Hiding behind the thick narrative smoke-screen of these two evocations of the city is the Weinburg of the narrator's childhood, the true core of the novel. Toward the end of his stay in his home-town, the narrator admits, "Sometimes I would close my eyes and see Wein-burg as I remembered it from childhood, *for it was this Weinburg that I had really returned to*" (emphasis added).[86] In other words, under the shelter of the com-plex narrative, stylistic, and structural mechanisms, Amichai allows himself to return to the places that forged his soul.

The narrative of *Not of this Time* elegantly glides—often in the same sen-tence—between the various layers: the new Weinburg that the narrator is visit-ing, its imagined appearance in the years 1936 to 1945, and the city of his child-hood. This constant shifting from one period to another, from one topographical map to another, is done with such subtlety that the picture created in the reader's mind is unified and given depth, like a scene observed through binoculars, in which the two separate images captured by each eye are subconsciously integrated. Yet the wholeness of the depiction of Weinburg in the novel is an illusion, the product of an artful work of composition that hides, or at least blurs, the connections between its separate parts. The schol-arly attempt to ignore modern-day "Weinburg" and distill the authentic experi-ences of the author's early years from the layers of fiction and historical recon-struction reveals that the "Weinburg" (and Wuerzburg) of the past is contained within a very small area—the world of a child.

The map of the core of Weinburg is comprised of a few focal landmarks that were etched in the young Amichai's mind and which often have little or no histori-cal significance. Their elevated status in the narrative hierarchy stems from their relative importance in the poet's memory. Amichai recreated the city of his child-hood through its sensory details, writing Wuerzburg, so to speak, through the body that remembered it. Wuerzburg of the late 1920s and early 1930s was com-posed of sounds, touches, and scents no less than it was composed of sights, events, and actions. His memories of the early years were deeply connected to the physical site. As a result, Amichai's recollection of events evoked the old land-scapes, and vice versa. When a corner of the remembered Weinburg / Wuerzburg is illuminated, its only significance is in the childhood experiences connected to it. Old Weinburg never serves as background, but rather, is intertwined with the plot. In this way, the present-day ringing of church bells, a prominent fixture of the Catholic city, triggers the memory of a children's guessing-game from bygone days:[87] "Church bells were ringing. . . . When I was a child, I knew how to differentiate between the churches by the sound of the ringing of their bells. This is Maria's church. This is the Dom [Wuerzburg's large cathedral]. . . . "[88] The acoustic landscape of Weinburg / Wuerzburg has not changed; the adult responds to it almost as the child he used to be would have responded.

Were Amichai free of internal and external inhibitors, he might have created a work that clearly focused on childhood and its emotionally significant people and places. He bluntly expresses the desire for such an undertaking in the body of the text: "I caused the earth to be empty of people and I left in it only myself as a child, and little Ruth and a few others from my childhood."[89] Alas, while his desire was to focus on select people and places, he ended up obscuring them by burying them under layers of extraneous details. The abundance of images and subplots, along with an entire intricate system of motifs, analogous characters, metaphors, symbols, and alternating chapters, serve to bury the heart of the novel. Fewer than 25 of the 619 pages in the Hebrew original contain verifiable childhood materials. Those faithfully describe the hometown as it was during the author's childhood, almost without deviation. Yet, the knowledge of this world's inevitable demise tints its image and interrupts the narrative's attempts to reconstruct the object of longing in its purest form.

> My eyes dimmed and I saw my teacher of many years ago as he used to come out of the cellar, many years before he was burned, arm in arm with his drinking companions.[90]

The description of the teacher is marred by the interjected allusion to the Holocaust: "many years before he was burned." The intrusion of the Holocaust prevents the narrator from wallowing in sweet nostalgia.

Similarly, as Joel picks up a bulletin board that he accidentally knocked off the wall of the old university, he sees his name:

> My fingers discovered my name scratched into the wall with the point of a nail, and I realized that in the past this had been the entrance to my father's store. As a child, I had scratched my name on the wall and it was still there. . . . I stepped over two stairs at once as I did then. . . . I found myself in a calm library. A girl lifted her head. . . . She began telling me about her father who was arrested for his actions in the concentration camp. . . . I sat next to a wall of books where the shelves of merchandise of my father had once stood. All the buttons and spools of thread and buckles and snaps and laces.[91]

While in some reminiscences, like the ones quoted above, the nostalgia is pricked with the dagger of the Holocaust, other episodes begin with the full recognition of reality, but the magic words "in my childhood" sweeten the associations.

Although they occupy a small space in the novel, only the sites within the map of the child's memory have a true emotional intensity, and, almost without exception, they are accompanied by the phrase "in my childhood," as if to emphasize that the relevant landmarks are those connected to the earliest events. When these places are reconstructed, they appear as chains of associations, both topographical and psychological. One may view those recollections as clusters around which the childhood narrative is organized. The vicinity of Augustine Street, where the narrator was born, is the kernel of such a cluster. Similarly, the child's route to school, stretching from his home through the Hofgarten to the Jewish complex, forms another.[92]

These narrative clusters are revisited numerous times throughout the novel; each recounting amplifies the description by focusing on the objects of interest with increasing specificity. For instance, in the narrator's first encounter with the Four Pipes fountain in the square near his first house, he concentrates only on the trolley that passes nearby. The second time he sees the fountain, he notices the neighboring city hall and envisions his teacher exiting the bar in its cellar.[93] Not until his third visit does he describe the fountain itself and the sculptures of four fish that spit out water, for which the fountain was named.[94] On that most revelatory visit, he also affectionately remembers Hayden's *Children's Symphony* and his violin teacher who played it.

The first station in this semi-autobiographical literary journey is, indeed, Augustine Street, the street on which Joel (and Amichai) was born (see appendix B). Time and again, he walks down that old central street and contemplates its highlights. Many of the child's early pleasures revolved around this old neighborhood. His two indulgent surrogate aunts lived there. The aunts' neighboring grocery store was a nexus of happiness. Decades later, the narrator remembers the smells of the sugar, cinnamon, and soap sold there. The scents of childhood still waft from the local bakery and pastry shop, where the adult narrator eats his sweet "childhood cake" and recalls the basket of poppy and caraway rolls that the baker's messenger would hang on their door every morning.[95] Near the bakery was his beloved father's store.[96] All the stimuli in this crossroads of memories near Augustine Street are sensory: sweet tastes and smells, music and sound.

Another emotional station in Joel's visit to Weinburg is the street where he lived since age four, after his family moved away from Augustine Street.[97] A new cluster of associations floods the narrator and as he walks up the hill, his legs remember the familiar ascent.[98] Unlike Augustine Street, which was located in the old town and which appears in the novel by its real name, this street (Alleestrasse) is only given the ambiguous title "the last street" and is never identified.[99] The moves from one residence to another along Alleestrasse that happened after 1933 are probably attributable to the Nazi directive that prohibited non-Jews from renting out their property to Jews. The novel glosses over these circumstances, perhaps because, as a child, Amichai was unaware of why his family changed dwellings. Amichai's motivation for dubbing Alleestrasse "the last street" may be its role in both the city's topography and the visitor's memory. It is "last," for it is quite far from the center of town, and, more significantly, it was the last street where Joel (and Amichai) lived before emigrating and therefore the last German home he had.

As he sits and sips a milkshake before he reaches the "last street," Joel describes the first apartment building his family occupied on Alleestrasse and reconstructs its façade in detail:

> The house was built early in the century and was a medley of styles. . . . It had big towers and strange little towers and pillars . . . and heads of women that supported balconies and other stone images and gargoyles and birds' heads and griffins, and more and still more projections and windows and grilles and niches, and patient giants with sad faces of beasts of burden supporting lintels.[100]

This exuberant architectural hodgepodge is resurrected entirely from memory, because the building was destroyed in the Allied bombings of Wuerzburg.[101]

The interior of the family's home is never described, but the experiences associated with it are recalled in detail and with much emotion. Faint music fills the narrator's ears as he walks down "the last street": "I was lying on my back and the sound of the piano gently lulled me to sleep."[102] The Christian landlord's beautiful daughter played the piano, practicing in the evenings until the young boy dozed off. While the calm piano music is long gone, the present-day smells of the "last street" still trigger scenes from the past. As Joel walks down the street, the vegetation that lines its sidewalks evokes the scent of the sukkah that his father built and covered with the branches of fir trees. The narrator also remembers the street's residents, especially Little Ruth.

Joel's chain of associations then leads him to yet another place near "the last street"—the old-age home where he spent many Shabbat afternoons visiting the elderly with his parents, playing in its garden, and waiting for the trains to chug by. Indeed, "the last street" is dotted with many attractions, sites that capture the attention of the man who had lived there as a child. The family home on that street was the point of departure from which Joel and Little Ruth used to set out to school every morning.[103] The route to school is a condensed narrative cluster that, like the surroundings of the family's former homes, recurs periodically in the novel. The recollections of it, which grow in intensity and detail with each iteration, refer to Joel and Little Ruth's walk through the Hofgarten— the magnificent garden surrounding the baroque palace, and the uncontested highlight of the route. And, yet, the visitor who has returned to the town of his childhood does not approach it. Instead, he often sees the Hofgarten from a distance or in his imagination.[104] The literary reworking of the Hofgarten distances it even further by painting it as a symbolic paradise from which the child was expelled when he left Weinburg. Although Joel refers to the Hofgarten almost obsessively and replays in his mind the childhood scenes that took place in it, he postpones his actual visit to the garden.

The ambivalence toward the palace garden prevents the narrator from facing it until the last hours of his stay in Weinburg.[105] Even without a direct encounter, Amichai's repeated references to the Hofgarten create memories of sorts for his readers. When his narrator finally enters the garden, the reader is familiar with it and almost shares in the climactic bliss that overwhelms the protagonist. At this point, the portrayal of the garden ceases to be symbolic and becomes painstakingly accurate. The adult renders the enchanted place of his childhood with endless love and with attention to every statuette, corner fountain, and stone cherub (see images 7, 8, and 9). The spell that the nymphs and putti of the garden cast over the child lasted a lifetime. The adoration of the adult protagonist for this beauty mirrors the awe that he felt for it in bygone days.

The Hofgarten's enormous iron gate is a more ominous wonder. Symbols of power—crosses and wild animals—are wrought into the gate's intricate pattern alongside flowers and laurels. They represent the southern German princes who had made this city their capital. This imposing gate was etched in the memory of the imaginative Jewish child, who internalized the elaborate black pattern he had seen every day and turned it into an emblem of the divine.[106]

This description of the Hofgarten gates reveals the interplay between German and Hebrew—and the Christian and the Jewish—in Amichai's psyche.

Indeed, the novel is the only piece in Amichai's entire oeuvre that affords a glimpse into the concrete sources of his imagery. From Jewish liturgy, Amichai knew of the Gates of Heaven that open on the Day of Atonement to accept the prayers for forgiveness and close at the end of the Ne'ila prayer, which is sung as the sun sets on the holiest of days.[107] The gates of the Hofgarten also shut at sunset. The bell that announced the garden's closing stirred up pleasurable memories for Amichai of playing there and toying with the idea of staying after the gates had closed.[108] Furthermore, if the Hofgarten is childhood's Garden of Eden, its closing gates are the symbol for the expulsion from that garden.[109] For Amichai, this gate became a prototype of all gates, real and literary, German and Hebrew, earthly and heavenly.

This pairing of landmarks was possible only in the mind of the Jewish child who lived in both Jewish and German Catholic worlds. Against the background of Christian architecture and iconography, as well as European nature, the novel's protagonist recalls Jewish practices, texts, and sites that, at least in childhood, did not seem to contradict the German ones. Amichai's poetry, however, almost completely deletes the German side of the coin, preserving only the Jewish one. Yet it is the duality of sources that endows Amichai's poetry with imaginative abundance. It is a poetry replete with visual imagery that stems from both the German monuments and icons and the Jewish articles of worship.

Wuerzburg's Jewish Life

Amichai's poetry camouflages more than the German Catholic city whose statuary and figures of saints decorated his childhood. Although his verse highlights generic Jewish elements disconnected from time and place, like Rosh Hashanah, the Holy Ark, and the shofar, it ignores the unique fabric of Jewish life in Wuerzburg. Universal Jewish elements are prominent in Amichai's poetry, but the Wuerzburg Jewish community is preserved only in the novel, where Amichai tries to document its particular customs, its functionaries, and its house of worship. The novel is, in fact, an attempt to erect a memorial for the world that disappeared by both retelling Amichai's personal experiences and painstakingly reconstructing the hometown of his Jewish community. The artistic manifestation of Amichai's deep connection to his hometown is his obsessive effort to write the history of Jewish Wuerzburg, its people, and institutions.

For example, in the novel Amichai refers to his old congregation with the traditional Hebrew acronym "KK," which stands for Kehila Kedosha (holy congregation). The "KK," which commonly precedes a reference to an individual

Jewish community, gains an ironic and somber overtone in this post-Holocaust narrative, and comes to mean a community that has been annihilated. For Amichai, the holy congregation consists of those who perished. His narrator is acutely aware of the fact that while the ancient monuments of Wuerzburg, destroyed by Allied bombs, were undergoing reconstruction, Jewish Wuerzburg has disappeared forever. It survives only in the memories of those who left it. Commemorating the holy congregation of Weinburg becomes one of the narrator's declared missions in his novel: "I have to write the history of KK Weinburg that was turned over with everything that was in it, all my childhood and all that should have been my future and Little Ruth and her home and everything in it."[110]

The principle that guides the novel's reconstruction of Weinburg in general applies to Jewish Weinburg as well. In both, Joel follows a map of the landmarks that carried special meaning for him as a child and sees them through the child's eyes. But there is a difference. In some instances, the Jewish childhood recollections seem to be motivated by the commitment to memorialize. Although they are connected to the child, they are recorded mostly for the sake of documentation. As a part of this resurrection of KK Weinburg, the narrator singles out the house that used to belong to "Rabbi Rosenheim," the "revered Rabbi of KK Weinburg."[111] Joel notes that his grandmother, who grew up as an orphan, had worked at this rabbi's house and so became learned in Judaism. This information identifies the fictional Rabbi Rosenheim as the historical Rabbi Bamberger, who was a luminary beyond the limits of southern Germany but died before Amichai was born.

In the novel, Amichai also describes two German Jewish folk traditions in detail: the *wimpel* cloth was placed under the newborn during circumcision, and later decorated and wrapped around the Torah when the child turned three. In the rowdy naming ceremony, the *Hollekreisch*, a group of children lifted the cradle and screamed the German name of the new baby.[112] These events are explicitly connected to his life as a child but it seems that Amichai did not rely solely on his memory for their portrayal. Rather, the tone and content of their descriptions suggest that he researched them, seeing it as his mission to record these customs exactly, so they would be preserved forever. Therefore, he announces the *Hollekreisch* and the *wimpel* with anthropological declarations like "one of the finest rituals practiced by German Jews."[113]

Most of the scenes that depict Jewish Weinburg, however, are founded less in historical documentation than in Amichai's longings for the Jewish context of his early life. The precision with which he recreates the synagogue and its architecture is matched only by the intensity with which he delineates the Hofgarten. Unlike the Hofgarten, the synagogue had been destroyed, and thus the desire to "copy" it into the narrative is driven by both his affection for it and a sense of responsibility. Norbert Hellmann, Otto Schlame, and Henry Eschwege were born in Wuerzburg around the same time as Amichai and were his schoolmates. Their independent, nonliterary accounts of Jewish Wuerzburg corroborate the accuracy and specificity of Amichai's reconstruction of the Jewish complex. Amichai remembered the synagogue's structure, the women's gallery, the choir's balcony, and the big clock. The Holy Ark, hiding behind the *parocheth* (its embroidered velvet curtain) and guarded by lions, is portrayed with reverence, as are the Torah scrolls, dressed in silk and adorned with silver bells: "I would look at the huge curtain over the Ark embroidered with gazelles fleeing before the lions that stood on the marble pillars on either side of the Ark."[114] Some of the protagonist's recollections of the synagogue are neither visual nor auditory, but physical—they preserve the motions of the body at prayer. He knew where he had stood with his father during services[115] and his body remembers the "steps" of the *Amidah* (the eighteen benedictions, recited standing), rising on tiptoe with the words "Holy, Holy, Holy," the bowing and then the kneeling.[116] All these continued existing in the mind of the writer, even when the religion they represented ceased to be relevant to him.

Amichai used creative ingenuity to transform the hollow space where the synagogue once stood into a concrete structure. In order for the narrator to recreate the physical sensation of moving between the levels of the building, he enlists a crane. The crane simultaneously serves as the facilitator of memory and as its destroyer. It lifts the man who had returned to the site of his childhood so he could be "moved here and there in the space which had once been the interior of the synagogue." With childlike joy, Joel exclaims, "Now we are on the level of the women's section; now on the level of the choir gallery where I sang as a child."[117] Even in its destruction, the synagogue in Wuerzburg is where he belongs. He knows its architecture by heart and can instantly transform himself into the child who sang soprano in its choir or ran to his mother in the women's gallery. In reality, though, once the crane, the enabler of memory, completes its construction job, the empty space will be occupied by a modern building, thus further erasing the memory of the synagogue.

The narrator's desire for accuracy is sometimes undermined by his wish to relive his childhood days. Even when the goal is to render the space objectively, the child's gaze intervenes, intertwining the documentary text with a nostalgic one. According to the child's emotional hierarchy, the choir has a unique status. The narrator therefore first draws the choir balcony, suspended on the western wall in the middle between the main sanctuary and the women's gallery and the clock. Despite the attempt at detached reportage, Joel cannot resist interjecting a personal story about the choir conductor who broke the bow over his head when he sang off-key.[118] The child's exclusive perspective also prevents the protagonist from describing Yizkor, the prayer for the dead. As a child, he was not allowed to remain in the synagogue when the adults were reciting the words of the Yizkor. Instead of the service itself, the narrator recalls his jealousy of the one child, an orphan, who shared the perceived secrets of the adults: "When I was a child, they used to chase us children out of the synagogue during the memorial service. Only Heinz, whom I loved, was permitted to remain, because his father was already among the dead. We envied him. . . . "[119]

Little Ruth

If the synagogue and the Hofgarten were the "Holy of Holies" in Amichai's childhood, Little Ruth was its queen. Until 1934, everybody referred to the two children as the "bride and groom" because they were almost inseparable. Naturally, then, Little Ruth is inextricably linked to the memories and landmarks of Wuerzburg. When Amichai recalls the alleys and parks of his birthplace, he simultaneously resurrects the little girl who was always by his side.[120]

Amichai reworked and transformed the factual underpinnings of Little Ruth's childhood and the tragic events that cut it short into one of the most important axes of Not of This Time, Not of This Place. The literary character is modeled after Amichai's best friend, Ruth Hanover. She was born in Wuerzburg in August 1923, the second daughter of Klara and Rabbi Zigmund Hanover. As Ruth and Amichai walked to school on the day before Hanukkah in 1934, they quarreled over the school's upcoming play. Amichai was competing for the coveted role of Judah Maccabee with the principal's son, and the two best friends were arguing over whether he should fight for the lead role or nobly give it up. They remained infuriated with each other the entire morning as the auditions slowly grew nearer.[121] Little Ruth tried to talk to her friend again at recess, but he wouldn't listen to her, so she turned away. As heavy snow fell, she borrowed another boy's bicycle and angrily pedaled off. She was crushed between two cars in front of the courthouse. One of her legs had to be amputated above the knee, and she spent a year in the hospital convalescing.

In the months that followed, Amichai visited her every day. He made his first trip to the hospital a week after her leg had been amputated. The adults prepared him for the visit and told him not to mention her leg, but he could not resist staring at the blanket that covered the missing limb. He tried to entertain his friend by suggesting games and talking about school until the nurse came and asked him to leave because she had to give Little Ruth a bath. Suddenly, Amichai realized that Little Ruth would have to see the stump, and he felt the full magnitude of her catastrophe.[122] While she would eventually get a prosthetic leg, her life would never be the same.

After Little Ruth was released from the hospital, their friendship waned, but the two still walked to school together. En route one horrible day in 1935, the children were attacked and beaten up by Hitler Youths. The next year, while Amichai and his family fled to Palestine, the Hanovers stayed behind: the rabbi wanted to continue leading his rapidly deteriorating community. In January 1939, Rabbi Hanover and his family left Wuerzburg for Holland in the hope of escaping the Nazis. While Rabbi Hanover and his wife received the coveted visas to Great Britain, their crippled daughter did not. The parents, nonetheless, continued to England on March 27, 1939, leaving Ruth with a foster family in Amsterdam. When the Nazis invaded, she went into hiding, only later to be found. She was deported with the last Jewish transport from Holland and perished.

The search for traces of Little Ruth dominates the novel's Weinburg plotline.[123] Most of the events of Ruth Hanover's life that occurred before 1936 are authentically documented in the novel. Amichai's recounting of the subsequent years, however, is largely fictional. Amichai was forced to resort to his imagination because he had not witnessed Little Ruth's life in the years after he emigrated. His deviations from the true story have deeper motivations, however. More than any other character from his childhood, Little Ruth and her terrible fate aroused complex feelings of guilt in Amichai. These feelings are reflected in the fictional retelling of her story and are at the heart of Amichai's effort to immortalize his childhood friend in the novel.[124]

From the moment that the novel's protagonist returns to his childhood in a dream, it is clear that Little Ruth is a driving force in the narrative. As his visit to Weinburg unfolds, the references to Little Ruth are incessantly woven into Joel's reconstruction of it. As in the portrait of Weinburg, different levels of time and consciousness overlap in the reconstruction of Little Ruth's story. She is the main character in each of Weinburg's layers of time: the distant past, as part of recollections of the twosome's friendship and its end; the conjured years of 1936 to 1945, as part of the misfortune of the Jewish community; and the present, as part of Joel's psyche. Little Ruth thus becomes a leitmotif of the novel; her physical, living presence during the narrator's childhood in Weinburg evolves into a permanent and dominant psychological presence for the narrator as an adult.

Joel's relationship with Little Ruth is also divided into two different eras: before and after Little Ruth's bicycle accident. The event irreversibly transformed the narrator's childhood and ushered in a new stage in his life. Accordingly, Joel's childhood years as a whole can be broken down into two periods. The first period was relatively idyllic, defined by Joel's playful but dedicated friendship with Little Ruth. The second phase begins on the day of the accident, immediately after the two friends had quarreled, and continues until the departure of Joel's family. Even within the seemingly disordered trains of thought represented in the novel, one can see that the narrator is aware of this inner division. He admits that he thought of two "Little Ruths"—"the one before the catastrophe, and the one after."[125]

Before depicting either of these young Little Ruths, however, the novel establishes the girl as a victim of the Holocaust and even as a martyr. When the narrator first arrives in Weinberg, Little Ruth is mentioned in passing, either by name[126] or qualified in general terms, such as the daughter of "Rabbi Dr. Manheim,"[127] "Little Ruth from my childhood," "Little Ruth who was burned in a crematorium,"[128] or "burned little Ruth."[129] The bicycle accident, the subsequent amputation of her leg, and the beating she suffered at the hands of the Nazi youths anoint her as a saint.[130] Only after Little Ruth has been sanctified as a Nazi victim does the reader encounter the "real" little girl whom the protagonist loved in his childhood.

As in his depiction of the landscape of Weinburg, Amichai tells the story of Little Ruth in narrative clusters that recur throughout the novel, each time in successively greater detail. But unlike the topographical associations that often guide the portrayal of the city's childhood landmarks, the scenes that capture Joel's childhood sweetheart are organized thematically.

The narrative clusters of the landscape and the story of Little Ruth differ in their developmental structure. The stations or landmarks of old Weinburg reach their literary climax toward the end of the novel, with Joel's visit to the Hofgarten. In contrast, the recollections of Little Ruth seem to follow a chaotic stream of consciousness with no discernable buildup. But this apparent randomness is a façade. The repetition of the Little Ruth scenes forms a spiral-like, obsessive crescendo toward the center of the novel. Once Amichai has told the full story of the quarrel that led to her accident (two thirds through the book), the length and intensity of the descriptions begin to decline and Little Ruth's story ultimately disappears entirely.[131] The revelation of the causal connection between the argument about the Hanukkah play and the fatal accident should thus be read as a "stone" dropped into the novel. The other episodes in Little Ruth's childhood and the shorter retellings of the tragic events can be read as its ripples. Furthermore, the contrasting developmental structures suggest that while Amichai's separation from childhood was emotionally completed, his farewell from Little Ruth was not. The placement of the catastrophic accident in the novel's center underscores the fact that this trauma remained at the heart of Amichai's being, never to be fully reworked, never reaching closure.

* * *

Despite the plethora of biographically accurate features and events in its plot, *Not of This Time* omits a crucial fact about Little Ruth: her mother's death. Curiously, although the novel paints the girl as a saint walking down her personal road of suffering, the first station on that path—the death of her mother when she was eight years old—is missing. When referring to the bicycle accident, Amichai writes that it was "the *first* time ever life hit Little Ruth in the winter on a snowy day" (emphasis added), implying that the accident was the first time that the girl had met with grave misfortune.[132] Furthermore, nowhere in Amichai's entire corpus does he allude to the fact that Ruth Hanover did not become "Little Ruth" due to the poet's own creative invention. The reality, as Amichai knew, is that the name "Little Ruth" contains the history of Ruth Hanover losing her mother at age eight and the presence in her home of "Big Ruth," her older stepsister.[133]

Amichai omitted that detail of Little Ruth's personal history purposefully. He thus appropriated Little Ruth for himself, painting an idealized picture of their pure childhood "romance" without any shadows. This perfect portrait is designed to become all the more heartbreaking when it is shattered by the accident and the events that follow. Had Little Ruth already suffered before her accident, the contrast between the two periods and the magnitude of the accident would not have been so pronounced.

Indeed, Amichai succeeded in sketching an idyllic portrait of the two friends and captured the beauty and idiosyncrasy of Little Ruth's personality. His depictions of Little Ruth match photographs taken of Ruth Hanover and descriptions given by her stepsister, cousin, and other acquaintances: "her delicate chin, her joyful braids, her pug nose, her freckles, and the way her hair was parted exactly in the middle in the manner of ballet dancers."[134] Even seventy years later, Ruth's former classmates recalled her as a sweet, beautiful, happy girl who was a gifted student. She was very popular, charismatic, and a leader among her friends.[135] In the novel, Joel wistfully recalls Little Ruth as an outspoken girl with a "well-developed sense of justice" who always held onto her principles.[136] Although Little Ruth never had a chance to apply her honorable values in the adult world, for Joel, her integrity remains an ideal for which to strive. He also reminisces about their boisterous playtimes, saying that sometimes he and Little Ruth made so much noise when they played inside that "Dr. Winniger would send the maid to quiet us down."[137] One of the friends' favorite pastimes was watching trains and becoming enveloped in their steam:[138]

> When the train went by, a warm, white steam would envelop us. We were almost suffocated and when the cloud was diffused, we saw each other anew and a sharp smell of locomotive smoke was in the air. The train would then disappear and we saw it and we would put our longings and our wishes on it until it was not seen. Sometimes we would say, "what if we jump and if we travel, what would they say? We will reach the sea and we will reach Paris."[139]

This nostalgic recollection bursts with the blissfulness of their time together. The children were transfixed by the trains' speed and noise and the breeze that almost threw them back as the cars rushed by. The best friends saw the trains as a springboard for their fantasies of travel to glamorous foreign places. A note that Amichai wrote in 1958 reveals the extent to which the sound of train engines was bound with his childhood, saying that it transforms "us into children."[140]

In contrast to these heartwarming episodes, most of the narrator's memories of Little Ruth are associated with trauma; they revolve around the story of her accident and its repercussions. Using a stream of consciousness technique, the narrator constantly jumps from one major event to another in Little Ruth's life, blurring the lines between cause and effect and ignoring temporal realities. Yet what seems to be a chaotic narrative of free association is in fact carefully constructed. It follows an individual emotional logic, consistently avoiding one excruciating sequence: the moment that links the fight between the two friends to the accident.

By the time this link is exposed, the gory details of the accident have already been spelled out, the fact that her leg was amputated has been painfully divulged, the deterioration of their friendship has been recounted, and the story of the Nazi youths kicking her has been told twice. The trigger for this tragic chain of events, the fight between Little Ruth and Joel, is the last piece in the autobiographical puzzle to appear in the novel, as though the narrator must gather strength to relate it. Furthermore, while the details of the argument are first revealed on page 299, the causal tie between it and the fatal accident is not established until much later, and even then, only in an obscure manner. This connection, which implicitly suggests that the boy bears responsibility for the girl's misfortune, fully emerges for the first time two-thirds into the novel (page 399). Indeed, this guilt would weigh on Amichai throughout the rest of his life.

Not of This Time provides two contradictory accounts of Little Ruth's advice to her friend during the argument. According to one version, she tells Joel to surrender the lead role of Judah Maccabee proudly and let the principal's son have it. In the other, she encourages him to fight for the part with all his might. Considering Little Ruth's character, both scenarios are plausible because both attest to the girl's sense of dignity, justice, and inner strength. The narrator, on the other hand, is portrayed in less favorable terms: in both versions, he refuses to listen to her, out of selfish desire for the part and cowardice, respectively. Even the extraliterary material contradicts itself.[141] In 1947, sixteen years before he published the novel, Amichai wrote about the incident in a letter to Ruth Z. While working as a teacher in Haifa to put on a Hanukkah play with his young pupils, the competition in Wuerzburg and its aftermath had come to mind. According to the letter's retelling of the fight, Little Ruth thought he should make a "noble gesture" and give up the role.[142] In 1990, Amichai wrote in a journal found in the archive that Little Ruth thought he should have fought harder for it.[143] Regardless of the sides taken by the two children, however, the tragic consequences were the same in the novel as in life.

While the novel's first recollection of the argument on page 299 does not establish a causal relationship between it and the accident, it is still ridden with guilt. In it, the ghost of Little Ruth takes the form of ivy climbing in a broken window. After she reiterates that he should fight harder for the role of Judah Maccabee, her spirit throws painful questions at the narrator, accusing him of betraying their love: "And if I were to appear, would you have married me with only one leg?" and "Why didn't you write to me?"[144] The second account of the argument on page 370 is again only abstractly associated with the snow and the "catastrophe."

> On the morning when the final decision was to be made, Ruth said to me, "Let them have it. Fling the role in their faces." "What?" I protested. "After I have memorized it all?" "You don't understand," she insisted. "You don't understand. Show them that you have character." "Character? What do you mean character?"
>
> This conversation took place in the morning as we walked to school through the Palace Park. It was a cold morning, and snow began falling, a bitter morning of misfortune.[145]

Amichai does not intimate until the third retelling of the argument on page 399 that, in his mind, his refusal to listen to Little Ruth caused the accident. Here, the minuteness of the details Amichai recalls artistically renders the emotional density of the experience. The narrator identifies the exact spot where he and Little Ruth parted in fury:

> On the eve of Hanukkah the misfortune occurred. That morning . . . near the wooden railing of the school . . . Ruth tried to persuade me for the last time to renounce my claim to the role, to fling it in their faces, and I refused. We quarreled *and to make me angry she rode off on Franz's bicycle.* It was snowing then and Ruth rode off in the snow. . . . [146] (emphasis added)

This is the most explicit revelation of the cause-and-effect relationship between the fight and the accident. Joel acknowledges one final element of guilt over one hundred pages later (page 558), in regard to the accident: when he first heard about the accident, he saw it as her punishment for being angry at him and was happy.

In the last reiteration of the argument, the reality of Ruth's death replaces the imagined recollections of the argument in earlier retellings, which repress her death. The narrator realizes the futility of his wish to correct past mistakes, and hints that the burden of Little Ruth will haunt him forever.[147] Returning to Weinburg—the place of danger—had been an attempt to reenact the old scenes and dialogues and change their outcome, but this unrealistic plan failed. Even if Joel had agreed to obey Little Ruth this time, it would not have brought her back to life.

The story of the fight and the subsequent accident is an open wound that continues to bleed throughout the novel. A closer analysis of the renderings of the repercussions of the fight, in the novel and elsewhere, affirms their emotional and artistic weight. In the exact middle of the book, on page 311, the accident is rendered graphically, with attention to every detail. The spot where Little Ruth was hit by the car is described with such precision that the Wuerzburg scholar Christian Leo was able to identify the building into which the injured Ruth Hanover was carried before the ambulance arrived.

Twenty-six years after the incident, the novel's dedication to conveying the exact location where the narrator is standing when he hears about the accident can be seen as a measure of his horror. As is often the case at a moment of extreme distress, the smallest aspects of a scene are noticed and imprinted in the memory. Immediately after Joel arrives on the scene of the accident, he "started to run home. I couldn't stand the sight of all the blood that was on the pavement. . . . I realized that the festivities would be canceled. There would be no Maccabees, no Judahs and no Matthias. Everything would be canceled."[148] The annulled Hanukkah is almost the first thought that crosses the child's mind when he hears of the catastrophe.

> All the Hanukkah festivities were canceled, the singing of the Hanukkah hymns in four parts was called off, for little Ruth was already in the hospital where they amputated her leg on that snowy Hanukkah evening. . . .
> At home we sang the Hanukkah hymn "Maoz Tzur" in weak and choked voices, and there were no games . . . or spinning tops, or bell and hammer.[149]

The narrator's pain is conveyed through the meticulous enumeration of the various celebratory activities that did not take place that year.

The story of the accident retroactively clarifies the multiple references to "Little Ruth whose leg was cut off in an accident,"[150] the time "when Little Ruth's leg was cut off,"[151] or Little Ruth, "for whom they made an artificial leg."[152] These allusions to the girl pepper the narrative almost from the outset, but as it progresses, the amputation becomes increasingly tangible and raw. Joel describes how "[t]he nerves in her [Ruth's] head then still pretended to feel the pain in the leg, but the leg was no longer there."[153]

Such concrete recollections of the actual amputation are few, yet subtle literary references to it pervade the novel. Little Ruth's mutilated body is often reflected in other characters and situations that testify to the emotional impact her physical suffering had on Amichai. One of the novel's fictional characters is a Holocaust survivor named Yosel, who tattooed the Little Mermaid on his arm.

The Little Mermaid is a figurative transformation of Little Ruth. In the famous fairy tale by Hans Christian Andersen, the Little Mermaid endured tremendous pain when her tail was cut in two and she had to walk on newly acquired feet. With each step she took, she felt as if she were walking on sharp knives. Amichai must have imagined that Little Ruth's absent leg hurt when she walked on it, the way the Little Mermaid's feet did.[154] Additionally, dancers and figure skaters, whose art relies on their ability to balance on one leg gracefully, abound in Not of This Time, metaphorically evoking the memory of Little Ruth and her amputated limb.[155]

The theme of amputation also surfaces in Amichai's archives. An unpublished German love poem recalls the way Little Ruth had to hop on one leg on crutches after the amputation. Even though the poem otherwise has nothing to do with the poet's childhood or his past, the line appears: "Ruth jumped on one leg."[156]

Amichai internalized Little Ruth's suffering and used amputation as a metaphor for the painful separation from a loved one. In his second letter to Ruth Z., written two days after she had left for America, he compared his excruciating longing for her to the pain that persists even after the limb has been amputated.[157] Although Amichai does not directly mention Little Ruth in that letter, it is as though the pain of separation from his adult love has intersected with the pain he witnessed Little Ruth suffer. Amichai, who felt he had abandoned his childhood sweetheart, is now feeling abandoned by the woman he loved.

In a love poem published in the 1970s, Amichai again speaks of the separation of lovers from each other as an amputation, covertly alluding to Little Ruth: "they amputated your thighs / off my hips. / As far as I'm concerned / they are all surgeons."[158] This poem was written in 1966, during the stormy love affair with the woman who later became his second wife. The prospect of losing her was captured by this vivid image of cut-off limbs.[159]

The retelling of Joel's first visit to Little Ruth following the accident is psychologically loaded. It finally appears on page 430 after the stories of the accident and the fight have been fully told; but even so, Joel approaches the memory of this encounter slowly. He begins outside the hospital, in the garden, and commences the story when Little Ruth is no longer bed-bound. The first image is an idealized, springtime portrayal of Little Ruth as a queen, ruling over the other children. As Joel draws closer to describing the core memory, he returns to the time of his first visit, the winter season of the accident.

Instead of leaping to the actual scene, however, the narrator digresses, retreating to comforting recollections unrelated to Little Ruth's misfortune—the synagogue and its customs, the choir, and the cantor—as though he is still incapable of unveiling the full story. Like the other highly charged autobiographical episodes, the novel's depiction of this particular visit is painfully precise. The sensitive young boy is upset and fearful, unsure of what to say to his injured friend: "I was told that she wanted to see me and I was terrified."[160] The narrator remembers how he stood outside the hospital, trying to gather the courage to enter. The white path leading to the hospital building and the gatekeeper who opens the door endow the description with the aura of a fairy tale, as though Joel were entering an enchanted castle "where Ruth had been bewitched." A nun leads him to the girl's hospital room and, finally, he enters it and sees Little Ruth's pale face on the pillow, framed by her dark hair. As instructed by the adults, Joel avoids the topic of the lost leg, but when he later realizes with horror that his friend will see the stump during her bath, Joel runs out of the hospital. The overwhelming guilt of a broken promise underlies the record of this visit. Here, on page 432, is the only time in the novel that the boy's vow never to abandon his beloved friend is divulged: "And only when I was outside the hospital wall did I stop [running], and I swore by the smoke of a passing train that I would never abandon Ruth, never."[161] The shame of having broken this vow is incorporated in the ambiguity of this line: swearing by the smoke of the train seems binding—it symbolizes the children's friendship, aspirations, and favorite pastime—yet smoke is fleeting and fickle, like the boy's loyalty to his poor friend.

In this disorderly narrative, the betrayal on page 232 precedes the actual vow of loyalty. The two friends have their last intimate conversation in the palace garden. Little Ruth asks, "How will things be in the future, do you think?"[162] In response, Joel points out appropriate professions for someone in her condition—a cripple. She interprets his answer as a rejection, for she had been implicitly asking whether he still loved her. Joel understands that he has disappointed her, but is not sure how, and writes, "From that day on she never talked about her disability and I dimly felt that something new had arisen between us." At this early point in the narrative, only Joel knows that at this moment, he broke the promise he made to himself in the hospital garden. Nevertheless, the reader understands that Joel has abandoned Little Ruth.[163] The descriptions of their devoted friendship therefore become tinged with sadness.

When the two distanced friends first resume their daily walk to school, Joel carries Little Ruth's schoolbooks for her, but as time progresses, the proud girl insists on holding them herself.[164] The memory of the Nazi students beating the two children on their way home is almost equal to the bicycle accident in both its traumatic impact and literary magnitude. The Nazi youths catch the crippled girl and her companion, holding him down while they kick her repeatedly. This attack is the first narrative cluster related to Little Ruth. As this beating is the single crime against Little Ruth that Joel (and Amichai) witnesses, it reaches monumental proportions in the novel and functions as the primary motivation for Joel's desire for revenge.

Amichai's first account of the story is terse, merely stating that the boys threw her to the ground: "Once, she and I were knocked down by Nazi boys. I will find the ones who knocked her down when they were boys. Perhaps they have been killed in the war, but if by a miracle they remained boys I will recognize them."[165] Joel glosses over the particulars of the attack, concerned solely with identifying the boys in order to carry out his retribution.

Details are added to this kernel of memory in an emotional crescendo. Before the experience is told a second time, the background for its dramatic effect is carefully drawn: the narrator emphasizes Little Ruth's prosthesis and the sounds of its wood and metal parts, thus preparing the reader for the chilling kicks that would follow: "[T]he amputation healed over and was ready for an artificial limb which squeaked and banged."[166] While the concreteness of the wood and metal arouse horror and pity, those feelings grow as the reader realizes their relevance to the second retelling of the attack. At its climax, Joel hears the boots hitting Ruth's artificial leg:

> Later a boy from the Hitler Youth kicked Ruth cruelly, and the echo of those kicks beats in my head and in my blood. Since that time, I have heard many violent collisions between bodies, iron striking earth, metal striking metal, iron striking stone, stone colliding with stone, steel with flesh, flesh with flesh. All those sounds dimmed in my memory. But the sound of the brown-shirted boy's foot striking Ruth's crippled body has grown stronger instead of dimming, until it has become the *thunder in my life*.[167] (emphasis added)

The "thunder" described by Amichai's narrator echoes as a refrain in many interviews in which the author himself talked about his friend. In these interviews, he would repeat that the attackers knew she was a cripple and how he "heard the sound of the beating of their shoes on her wooden leg and all the metallic sounds."[168] This sound remained with him "more than all the Auschwitz books."[169]

In the third telling of the assault, Amichai emphasized the nationality of the attackers by referring to them with the German words "*Hitler Jugend*" (albeit transliterated) instead of the Hebrew "*No'ar Hitlera'i*" (the equivalent of the English "Hitler Youth"). For the first time, he discloses the position from which he heard the kicks: "[W]e both lay on the ground, the boys of the Hitler Jugend holding me fast."[170] This explains the increased impact of the sound of the beating, as well as the religious terminology associated with the beaten girl. From his spot on the ground, the boy could only see her face: "Her face is the *eternal light* for my action and, like all eternal lights, her face is exerting a calming effect on me. . . . "(emphasis added).[171] The adult narrator turns to the central synagogue object—the eternal light—to convey both the lasting power of the experience and the radiance of the countenance that continued shining at him for the rest of his life.

The penultimate retelling takes place while Joel is in the Hofgarten. The beauty of the garden around him contrasts with the horror of the memory, and its presence metaphorically alludes to the role of the attack in the narrator's life. In the midst of his visit, the bell that announces the closing of the Hofgarten rings. In childhood, that bell simply signified the time of day. For the adult, it symbolized the expulsion from the paradise of his childhood. The proximity of the story of the beating to the ring of the bell associates the attack with Joel's forced departure from the world he loved. This intense recollection of the episode follows a recitation of the rhymes Joel has memorized for the Hanukkah play. Quoted verbatim, these lines evoke the first link in the tragic chain of events; namely, the friends' quarrel.

This retelling in the Hofgarten also contains more concrete incriminating evidence: the precise location of the beating and the number of the attackers. It adds that the victims' schoolbags were thrown and the textbooks fell out of them like the "guts spilling out of a killed soldier." It also captures the perspective of the young boy: "A person who sees terrible things when he is lying on the ground in his pain does not forget ever what he saw. . . . I saw then the trunks of the oak trees and the feet of the assailants and their white socks."[172] The vividness of these details reinforces the authenticity of the literary reconstruction.

This vignette is the climax not only of the narrator's retellings of the beating, but also of the entirety of his suffering at the hands of the Nazis. Immediately after he recalls this episode, Joel turns to the unrelated event that propelled his family's emigration. His father saw the mutilated bodies of two local Jews who had been beaten to death by Nazis. The father's experience and decision is appended to the story of the assault, underlining this overdetermined crossroads of childhood's end and the decree of fate: the boy would go on to live in Israel, while the girl would remain in Europe and ultimately perish. Amichai's guilt toward Little Ruth, first for not protecting her as she was being kicked, and then for abandoning her altogether, is unspoken in this retelling, yet clear through the appending of the stories.

The last time that the attack is mentioned, it loses the rawness and genuineness of the previous retelling. In a jarring departure from the premise of the novel, Joel miraculously finds Little Ruth alive in a convent. Because she is not dead, he no longer needs to hunt for her killers, and instead states a collective accusation directed toward all Nazis:

> Because Ruth is living, I will take revenge at least for the kick that they kicked her. I will look for the one who kicked, I will look for the one who bit, for the one who burnt, for the one who hit, for the one who whipped, and the one who ran over and the one who devoured and there will never be an end to my searches.[173]

In this rhythmical catalogue of cruel actions, Amichai is alluding to the Yom Kippur prayer *Unetaneh tokef*, which graphically describes alternate forms of violent deaths: "who by water, who by fire, who by suffocation. . . . " The prayer assures the believers that with proper repentance, one who has been destined to die in the coming year may reverse his fortune. Amichai's subtle allusion to this particular prayer evokes its mythological author, Rabbi Amnon, whose limbs were cut off when he refused to convert. His last words were said to be the haunting *Unetaneh tokef*. Like Little Ruth, he was martyred through the loss of his limbs.[174]

Hebrew prayers continue to reverberate in the final chapters of the novel, specifically, the *Ne'ila* prayer, which depicts the closing of heaven's gates at the end of Yom Kippur. The gates of the Hofgarten represent heaven's gates and thus symbolically carry Amichai's guilt about Little Ruth and his plea for forgiveness. After the conversation that marks Joel's betrayal of Little Ruth and the breaking of their bond, she walks toward the iron gate, offended.[175] The moment when their friendship is severed is conveyed through the gate and the girl's physical motion toward it. The narrator reflects on the exchange and confesses, "And I left everything. And Ruth too was not allowed into the park after a while. . . . "[176] Although there is a period separating the phrase "And I left everything" from "And Ruth too," it is clear that "I left everything" means "I abandoned Ruth too." Joel's abandoning her is also rendered through the vehicle of the gates: after his emigration, she was no longer allowed to enter the garden through the gates with which they were both so familiar.

The association between Little Ruth and the gates, however, predates the painful conversation and the prohibition against Jews entering the garden. The narrator reveals that he first heard the terrible news of Little Ruth's accident in the Hofgarten. Before reconstructing that moment of horror, Joel meanders through present-day Weinburg and notices that one of the Hofgarten entrances is under construction. The wing of one of the iron angels that decorate the gates was damaged.[177] Through the description of the damaged gate, the narrator prepares himself for reliving the moment of the terrible announcement. The broken angel reflects the perfect girl who had also been broken.

At the end of the novel, when Joel finally enters the Hofgarten, the gate is highlighted in all its glory and the intricate designs on it are enumerated for the first time.[178] The textual proximity of the illustration of the gate, its closing, and the news of Little Ruth's accident links the departure from the paradise of childhood to the separation from Ruth. The narrator is fully aware of this symbolic connection, stating, "The gate . . . was wide open. When it closes behind me, I will know that little Ruth is locked in this park of our childhood amid the fountains of death and the lawns of conflagration and beneath the clouds."[179]

The entire novel may be read as an attempt to alleviate the layers of guilt that surround Little Ruth. Amichai felt that she must have been upset by their quarrel and so did not concentrate as she was riding the bicycle on the busy, snowy street. That fateful bike ride led to the amputation of her leg and, ultimately, to her death in a concentration camp. Additionally, when Little Ruth and Amichai were attacked by the Hitler Youth, the Nazis only beat up Little Ruth. In an almost Christian outlook, perhaps inspired by Wuerzburg's iconography, Amichai felt that Little Ruth had suffered for him, as though she had, in some sense, sacrificed herself to save him. Although Amichai could not control his family's emigration and thus could not keep his promise to stay with Little Ruth forever, he did not do the only thing he could have: when she wrote to him in Palestine, he did not respond.

Amichai metabolized some of this guilt in one significant deviation from the true record of events in the story of Little Ruth. This departure is the only exception to the accurate reconstruction of the two early periods of the Weinburg chapters. It is important to ask why, in the text that most openly mirrors his childhood, Amichai chose to blur her true and tragic fate. In a short story of

Amichai's called "The Aswan Dam," the narrator imagines Little Ruth crouched in her hiding place in Holland; but in the novel, Little Ruth remains in Weinburg and is deported from there with her father and the rest of the community.[180] Indeed, the Jews of Wuerzburg were deported and most of them perished, but all the members of both the Pfeuffer family (Amichai's family) and the Hanover family (Little Ruth's family) left in the 1930s and were saved. Little Ruth, who was trapped in Holland, was the only member of either family to die in the Holocaust. Why then, is this historical fact omitted from the novel?

One can argue that the disparity between the fate of the real Ruth Hanover and that of the fictional character based on her has ideological roots: by having Little Ruth deported from Wuerzburg, the author accuses the Wuerzburg Germans who sent their Jews to death. This interpretation, however, while it may be partially valid, fails to capture Amichai's more profound motivation for this inaccuracy.[181] This departure from the actual events may be read on a deeper level as Amichai's artistic and psychological metabolism of his guilt. Fictionalizing the way Little Ruth met her fate in the novel was an implicit attempt on his part to clean his own conscience. If the novel had endowed the character of Little Ruth with the true fate of Ruth Hanover, who was unable to leave Holland solely because of her amputation, then the connection between Amichai's role in the accident and Little Ruth's death would be established. If, however, he placed her in Wuerzburg at the time of the Nazi deportations, then she died like all the other Jews of Wuerzburg, irrespective of her physical state. This kind of death, therefore, camouflages the direct guilt that Amichai felt. By making her part of the deported Wuerzburg Jewish community, she died not because she was a cripple, but because she was Jewish. Late in his life, Amichai transformed Little Ruth into a symbol for the Holocaust; in so doing, he covered the true source of his guilt with the widely accepted, collective guilt of the Holocaust survivor.

LITTLE RUTH IN AMICHAI'S POETRY

While Amichai cast Little Ruth as a protagonist in the novel, referred to her in his short stories and drama, and spoke quite openly about her in interviews throughout his life, his poetry almost completely avoids any allusion to her until quite late in his life. She is virtually absent from *Poems: 1948–1962*. Indeed, in the entire 360 pages of the collection, Amichai mentions her just once by name and obliquely alludes to her on only two other occasions.

Given the intensity of Amichai's relationship with Little Ruth as a child and her prevalence in his work in other genres, her absence from his poetry is particularly striking. Moreover, two of the three allusions to Little Ruth in the canonic collection ignore her role in his childhood and hint about her only in the context of the Holocaust. Even these allusions are so obscure that for a reader who does not already know about her, they are impossible to decipher. Only one poem, "Hanukkah," recalls Little Ruth as his childhood friend, but as is characteristic of *Poems: 1948–1962*, Amichai reveals this relationship in a radically camouflaged way. Covertly, the poem retrieves the accident that led to the amputation of her leg, and ultimately to her demise.[182]

The religious, national subject of "Hanukkah" hides the dense mass of personal memory. It is an anti-Hanukkah poem. In every line, the adult speaker announces his refusal to celebrate the holiday or perform its traditional ceremonies and customs; he proclaims that no candles will be lit, no blessings recited, and the miracles of God will be neither remembered nor praised. The speaker declares that he did not place the Hanukkah menorah on the windowsill, as is custom, nor did he observe the melting candles with childish wonder. The blessings "Blessed art Thou the Lord of the Universe who commanded us to light Hanukkah candles" and "Blessed art Thou the Lord of the Universe who performed miracles for our forefathers in those days at this time" are inverted one by one and in aggregate to form the nightmarish condition of a lost man.

The end of the poem continues the series of inversions and transforms it into an existential statement. To do that, Amichai exploits various derivations of one verb root, some of which relate to Hanukkah and others that do not. The last tradition the speaker breaks is spinning the dreidel (*sevivon*, in Hebrew), playing with various derivations of the verb root (S.B.B. / S.V.V.), from which the word *SeViVon* stems.[183] The same Hebrew root generates the term for spinning or "turning" the dreidel (*leSoVeV*), as well as the concept of wandering aimlessly (*lehiStoVeV*) and the word "cause" or "reason" (*SiBBa*). Through the outwardly amusing alliteration, the end of the poem reveals that the speaker did not spin the dreidel on this sad Hanukkah (lo SoVaVti SeViVon), but rather wandered in the streets (hiStoVaVti) for some specific reason (SiBBa) or reasons (SiBBot). ("*velo sovavti sevivon / vehistovavti barehovot ki / hayta li sibba / hayu li harbe sibbot*"). Though the true reason for the association between Hanukkah and pain is absent, one may guess that it is connected to the "love" mentioned briefly earlier in the poem—the "love" of the past who "sings with a burnt, black mouth."

The poem uses the traditional Hanukkah blessing, which states that God's miracles occurred "at this time in those days," to underscore the dichotomy between the ancient past and the miracleless present. The speaker contrasts his current apathy about the holiday with the joyous Hanukkahs of "those days." The wonder that had accompanied the child's celebrations of the holiday has disappeared, as has another element that had been indelibly linked to the speaker's childhood Hanukkahs: the falling snow. This evocation of the wintry scene from the distant Hanukkah transports the entire poem to Europe and reveals, even to a reader who does not know Amichai's life story, that the Hanukkahs of "those days" were spent elsewhere. "At this time" in the present, however, in the speaker's adulthood, both the candles and the snow are noticeably absent.

This seemingly simple poem hides the poet's deeply intimate connections to the holiday. "Hanukkah" was first published before the novel and its autobiographical roots were unavailable at that time to Amichai's readers. Only after the novel's appearance could a careful reader interpret the poem's title as a shorthand reference to particular associations with the holiday. That connection, however, remained unknown and unnoticed. No one thought to use the novel's revelations to interpret the nearly imperceptible traces in this poem that are bound up with one of the greatest traumas of Amichai's young life.

In his December letters to Ruth Z. about his work as a teacher in the Ge'ula school, Amichai wrote about how important it was for him that the Hanukkah play should take place despite the outbreak of violence. The letter refers to the cancelled Hanukkah in Wuerzburg, as if performing the current Hanukkah play in Haifa would atone for that lost Hanukkah and its victim, Little Ruth. The negation of Hanukkah in the poem implicitly echoes how it was both Hanukkah and not Hanukkah after Little Ruth's 1934 accident: it was mournful, without celebration, singing, or games. The accident, however, does not appear anywhere in the poem.

Two separate "testimonies" found in Amichai's archives reaffirm the hold that the 1934 Hanukkah had over him. The first is labeled "first Hanukkah candle" and reads like a journal entry that recalls Hanukkah in 1934, when "the accident of Little Ruth happened." This handwritten page from 1990 brings up the painful memory of the fateful quarrel about the role of Judah Maccabee.[184] The second, written in 1991, is the beginning of a poem that calls Little Ruth "my first love." According to this unpublished draft, Little Ruth is simultaneously distant and omnipresent. The speaker compares her to "an eternal Hanukkah.[185] One may assume that the memory of Little Ruth came up for Amichai every Hanukkah.

In the published "Hanukkah," the straightforward chain of negations of the holiday and memory is presented as a quotation from a letter addressed to a woman (her gender is indicated by the Hebrew feminine inflection). The speaker tells her that a great love grew for him at "this low time," meaning the present, as it did "in those days" when snow was falling. These lines indicate that there are two parallel loves—a present and a past one. The love of the present shares a strange quality with the love of the past; namely, they both sing with a "burnt, black mouth."

These ambiguous lines contrast with the rest of the poem, which is relatively straightforward. The enigmatic, hermetic nature of this image signals to the reader that its meaning is the heart of the text, but only extrapoetic material can unlock it; the poem itself does not contain the key. The great love of "those days," the days of childhood and snow, is without a doubt Little Ruth. In his mind, Amichai continues to hear her voice singing Hanukkah songs, as she did when they were children. Her mouth is not the red, sweet mouth of a little girl, however, but the burnt, black mouth of the dead. A boy's choir, singing with black mouths, recurs in Amichai's oeuvre as a marker of the children of Wuerzburg who perished. That mouth, then, is also a reference to Little Ruth's fate—her body was burnt in a crematorium during the Holocaust. The connection between the little girl and Hanukkah is macabrely overdetermined. Here, instead of the burning Hanukkah candles, is the burnt mouth, all that remains of Little Ruth. This association between the burning of the candles and the burning of Little Ruth's body is made more explicitly in Not of This Time. As the narrator wanders in his hometown, he confesses, "I thought again about the fire that ate her body in the oven, how the flame bent lovingly on her face until it was totally extinguished like the candles of Hanukkah on the windowsill."[186]

While the deepest associations with Hanukkah go back to 1934, there is another layer of loneliness, which relates to a separation from a present-day love. Although the date that the poem was written is unknown, it is almost certainly connected to Hanukkah in 1947. The two Hanukkahs—in 1934 and 1947—represent the two loves: the love from "those days," Little Ruth, and the love from "this low time," Ruth Z., to whom the letter in the first stanza is written. In December 1947, Amichai's beloved was in America. Lonely and longing for her, the depressed poet wandered the streets of Haifa, pining for the holiday the way it should be. In a letter from that time, Amichai relates the tragic events of

Hanukkah, 1934, to Ruth Z., enumerating all the elements that characterize the holiday in the poem. The letter also reveals what the poem covers up: the ill-fated competition for the school play and accident that followed.[187]

Nevertheless, while the connection between the "burnt, black mouth" and Little Ruth is understandable, it is hard to interpret why the mouth of the adult love is also burnt and black. In order to decipher this aspect of the image, one must resort to a German idiom, Sich den Mund verbrennen (to burn one's mouth).[188] The moral of this proverb is that he who has been burnt once will be careful the next time he eats hot soup (akin to the English idiom "once bitten, twice shy"). In that context, the burnt mouth belongs to the speaker, who was "burnt" because the woman he loved betrayed him. The speaker's reluctance to light candles and celebrate Hanukkah, as well as his aimless wanderings, may stem from both his disenchantment with his present love and the memories of 1934.

Many lines in "Hanukkah" obscurely reconstruct a specific time in Amichai's childhood that involved Little Ruth, even though her nickname is not cited, and the memory of her is blurred. In that, "Hanukkah" is unique, for it is the only poem in Poems: 1948–1962 that refers to her in childhood, before the Holocaust. The two other poems that reference Little Ruth in that 360-page collection define her solely by her tragic death, a decade after that Hanukkah. Amichai practically omitted the memory of his childhood love from the verse he published while he was making his name as a poet. A reader who is unaware of Little Ruth's profound psychological impression on Amichai could never deduce it from reading his canonic collection.

A LATE RETURN TO LITTLE RUTH

Amichai's work during the years in which his canon was formed reflects a murky image of his childhood, its landscapes, and its people. Indeed, Not of This Time stands out in its authentic reconstructions of Amichai's early years, but, as demonstrated, these accurate literary imitations constitute only a small part of its rich, inaccessible narrative. Furthermore, the novel is the exception that proves the rule of camouflage—it reveals the extent to which Amichai remembered his childhood and the depth of his connection to his childhood home. This revelation, however, is in a genre other than poetry, and Amichai delayed its publication until he was already thirty-nine years old and a well-known poet.

Amichai refrained almost entirely from addressing Little Ruth in particular and the topic of the Holocaust in general in his poetry before publishing Not of

This Time, and for twenty-five years after he completed it. He began working on the novel when the subject of the Holocaust was still taboo in the newly formed Zionist state. It is one of the earliest Hebrew literary attempts to openly and directly confront not only the fate of European Jews but also the issues of conscience, memory, survivors' guilt, and revenge. It was published not long after the Eichmann trial in 1961, the first time that the State of Israel dealt officially with issues of the Holocaust.[189]

In the novel, Little Ruth is both a symbol of the Holocaust and the protagonist's spirited childhood counterpart. Thus, the ties between the biography of Ruth Hanover and that of the fictional heroine that she inspired remain strong. By contrast, in Amichai's poetry, Little Ruth is an abstraction; in other words, Ruth Hanover is transformed from a girl of flesh and blood to a memory. This psychological entity becomes a literary symbol through an elaborate process of artistic reworking; it becomes an idiolectic sign that represents the Holocaust.[190] In the rare instances when the two words in the nickname "Little Ruth" appear in Amichai's verse, they signify the Holocaust, not the adored girl. Her name is an idiosyncratic emblem that Amichai created to represent mourning, pain, and guilt. The only poem he openly dedicated to her (in 1989), however, is more than an homage to those who perished in the Holocaust. There, almost indiscernably, Little Ruth is once more a lifelong object of longing.

By transforming Little Ruth into a representative of the Holocaust, Amichai distanced himself from the real causes of the guilt he felt toward her. Even late in life when he became fully aware of the internal artistic process that forged her as a poetic trope, he was still unaware of the psychological function of that transformation; namely, that it allowed him to cope with his guilt. Two years before he died, Amichai recorded the conversion of his emotions in a notebook. Under the heading "Metamorphoses," he wrote that when he heard Richard Strauss's musical work on the firebombing of Dresden, he transferred his sadness to Little Ruth. The fact that he was touched by the musical lament for Germans disturbed him, and he felt compelled to justify his sorrow by attaching it to a Jewish subject: Little Ruth "in an extermination camp."[191] Amichai articulated the artistic implications of his ability to reallocate feelings more explicitly in an interview with the German journalist Claudia Schulke. He told her that he was the "guardian of Ruth's life," suggesting that he must use that life as a voice for all those who perished. He added that Little Ruth was his "ambassador of the Holocaust."[192] This concept is echoed in a draft of an unpublished poem from 1992, in which Amichai expands upon the notion of individuals becoming "representatives" of ideas. He recalls a friend who had fallen in the War of Independence and says that, for him, his friend Dicky became "the representative" of all the soldiers who die in wars, just as Little Ruth became "my representative of the Holocaust." Thus, Little Ruth made the transition from a childhood friend to a generalized symbol.[193]

The first steps toward this process of symbolization can already be seen in *Poems: 1948–1962*. Her nickname appears only once in that entire collection, in the poem "The Clouds Are the First To Die." The words "little Ruth" appear in a catalogue of those who are hurt by the determination of others to carry out harmful, aggressive actions: "Machine guns of decisions . . . shoot . . . and hit dogs, / my hand, little Ruth, and also those / who are not marked with numbers. . . . "[194] These three violent lines are in the exact middle of the poem (the thirtieth, thirty-first, and thirty-second lines of a sixty-line poem). The oblique allusion to those "marked with numbers" hints at the Holocaust, where the Nazis tattooed numbers on the arms of concentration camp inmates.

While the strategic placement of the specific reference to Little Ruth points to how important she is to the poet, her nickname is buried as a single, unexplained item in a long list that camouflages the emotional weight her name carries for Amichai. In many poems, Amichai used catalogues to hide his past. It was a good strategy for obscuring the importance of a single item—when a fraught item is placed in a list, it does not draw attention to itself. Amichai hid the biographical aspects of the poem further, by removing its language from the foreign, German milieu of Little Ruth. Instead, unlike the poem "Hanukkah" with its snow, "The Clouds Are the First To Die" is set in an archetypal Israeli setting and topography filled with references to the native wildflower cyclamen and words like wadi (valley).

As its title indicates, "The Clouds Are the First To Die" is an inventory of those who died. A reference to clouds occurs only in the opening line, but the rainfall described in the first stanza may explain their "death": they disappear when they unload their water. According to this interpretation, the clouds themselves are the first to die, but their "death" is disconnected from the other fatalities that Amichai enumerates. If, however, one reads this poem with the aid of another, it is possible to see what the clouds really mean and how they relate to the center of the poem. The text that may be used to interpret "The Clouds Are the First To Die" is the third and last poem in *Poems: 1948–1962* that alludes to Little Ruth. Quatrain 46 in the cycle entitled "In a Right Angle" never identifies Little Ruth by name. She is called "the girl" and her death is described as "the cloud / of her burning. . . ."[195] Amichai makes the seemingly unrelated association between clouds and death in "The Clouds Are the First To Die" specifically applicable to Little Ruth. The cloud in the quatrain is a cloud of smoke; those burnt in the Nazi crematoria went up to the sky in a cloud. This prevalent image in Holocaust poetry has a particular significance here, for it connects two of the three poems in the volume that allude to Little Ruth.[196]

The presence of "Little Ruth" in the quatrain—like her appearance in "The Clouds Are the First To Die"—is oxymoronically camouflaged and emphasized through the strategic placement of the allusion to her image. In "Clouds," Amichai hides her in a catalogue, but does so precisely in the poem's center. In the cycle "In a Right Angle," she emerges in a nondescript place (the penultimate of forty-seven quatrains), but that quatrain is the one that carries the name of the entire cycle—its first words are "in the right angle":

In the right angle between a dead man and his mourner I'll start
living from now on, and wait there as it grows dark.
The woman sits with me, the girl in the cloud
of her burning rose into the sky, and into my wide-open heart.[197]

      ✶   ✶   ✶

In the years that followed the publishing of *Poems: 1948–1962*, Little Ruth's presence in Amichai's poems remained minimal and obscure. The phrase "little and dead Ruth," for instance, appears in one stanza in a long poetic cycle published in the 1971 collection, *Not to Remember*.[198] The title of this poetic cycle, "Poems of the Hot Wind," is borrowed from the Israeli climate and environment, creating a distance between the tragic events in Europe and their belated literary recollection.[199] As in "The Clouds Are the First To Die," specific Israeli plants (here, oleander, mint, and oranges) define the scenery. Only in the last of the six poems in that cycle does "little and dead Ruth" rise from her bed, covered with glass shards. This image clearly recalls Kristallnacht, the symbolic beginning of the Holocaust. On that night, the Hanovers' house was targeted by the Nazis, Little Ruth's bedroom window was shattered, and her father was arrested.

Amichai's late collection *The Great Tranquility: Questions and Answers*, which was published in 1980, marks a turn in Amichai's poetics.[200] It also diverges thematically from his earlier verse. By then, Amichai was already an established national poet, and he had a lesser need for repression. This 1980 collection conveys a greater affinity for more concrete events from the past; it contains poetic snapshots from Amichai's early years and openly admits to their autobiographical nature. Two of those allude to Little Ruth, but she remains the subject of neither, appearing only in a segment of a longer text. In "Spring Song," the speaker observes his life from the vantage point of a light surveillance airplane.[201] He "sees" the "smoke of / Burning leaven in the yard, the little girl who died afterwards." The proximity of the "burning leaven" to "the girl" is reminiscent of the quatrain, merging the girl's death with the rising smoke, thus depicting Little Ruth's fate.

The second poem that relates to Little Ruth in *Great Tranquility* is the only poem other than "Hanukkah" in Amichai's entire oeuvre that refers even allusively to Little Ruth as his childhood sweetheart, and not solely as a victim of the Holocaust. In this poem, "All These Make a Strange Dance Rhythm," Amichai describes an existing photograph of himself and Little Ruth seated under a pear tree, taken approximately one year before the accident.[202] In it, Amichai hugs Little Ruth and the two grin at each other affectionately.[203] The poem depicts neither the physical sensation of sitting next to Little Ruth while the picture was being taken, nor the memory of the living girl herself. By capturing the photograph rather than the girl, Amichai detaches himself and becomes an outside observer. Furthermore, the first line in the stanza dedicated to Little Ruth is "Some time ago I found an old photograph." Thus, the act of finding the photograph is presented not as a deliberate attempt to remember, but rather as an accident. Nevertheless, this is the first tangible detail about their relationship as children in Amichai's poetry; while "Hanukkah," published in 1962, is an abstract record, here there is the pear tree, a concrete embrace, and an admission of their actual relationship. The poem also depicts the girl's physical gesture in the photograph. One of her hands hugs her friend and the other is "free, reaching out from the dead / to me, now."[204] This poignant line confesses that the girl has a continuous hold over him. The last word in the stanza is "now," again signaling the eternal connection between the two subjects of the photograph.

In 1989 Amichai finally dedicated a poetic lament to his friend who did not escape the fate of the six million, and entitled it "Little Ruth" (see appendix A). The poem begins as follows:

Sometimes I remember you, little Ruth,
We were separated in our distant childhood and they burned you in the
    camps.
If you were alive now, you would be a woman of sixty-five,
A woman on the verge of old age. At twenty you were burned
And I don't know what happened to you in your short life
Since we separated.[205]

After its publication, Amichai would recite this poem in one poetry reading after another. In the question-and-answer period that followed, the listeners often inquired about it, as most of them had just heard about the little girl named Ruth for the first time. When he responded, Amichai never revealed the full significance of "Little Ruth" to his spellbound audience. With his calm and patient manner, he would retell the story of his own family's flight from Germany. He would explain that because none of his own relatives perished, Little Ruth had become the symbol of all Holocaust victims for him. Nearly five decades had passed since the high school student Yehuda Pfeuffer had tried to lead the life of a typical teenager in the Land of Israel, suppressing the concerns for those who, like Little Ruth, remained in Europe (for a photograph of Little Ruth at fifteen, see image 12).

Fifty years after she died, Amichai addressed his childhood sweetheart directly, trying to atone for his long oblivion: "I don't know what happened to you in your short life / since we separated," he wrote. In reality, he did know of his friend's suffering after they parted, although not in detail. After their escape from Germany in October 1938, Ruth's sister and stepsister frequently visited the Pfeuffer family in Jerusalem and shared what Rabbi Hanover, Little Ruth's father, wrote about her terrible predicament. It is also almost certain that Amichai knew of his own father's correspondence with Little Ruth and his desperate efforts to obtain an immigration certificate for her.[206]

Little Ruth wrote loving letters to the fourteen-year-old Amichai, but he ignored her longing and neglected to write back. In the 1989 poem, he describes himself as one who "wallowed in his forgetfulness" like a drunk who wallows in vomit. At the time that he was infatuated with a classmate in Jerusalem, Little Ruth was facing death. It is as though in surviving and falling in love he squandered treasures that belonged to her. In an interview Amichai granted to Aryeh Arad, he confessed that Little Ruth wrote to him that although her friends whispered behind her back about her boyfriend, she suspected that "this boyfriend is not interested in me any longer." Amichai expressed his awe at the maturity of the fourteen-year-old girl, and clearly regretted not having written to her. As though to repent, he claimed in that interview that he would have married her had she suddenly reappeared.[207]

The notes in the Beinecke archives and Amichai's prose shed light on the more obscure metaphors in the poem "Little Ruth." A catalogue of military or athletic honors springs out in the middle of the first stanza, as the speaker wonders whether the girl was awarded ranks and medals for her courage:

> What did you achieve, what insignia
> Did they put on your shoulders, your sleeves, your
> Brave soul, what shining stars
> Did they pin on you, what decorations for valor, what
> Medals for love hung around your neck. . . .

An excerpt from *Not of This Time, Not of This Place* illuminates these lines. The novel's narrator describes Little Ruth during the deportation: "[O]n the lapel of her coat was a star . . . on which it is written 'Jude.'"[208] The poem's "shining stars" thus refer ironically to the yellow star that Jews were forced to wear, as badges of honor. It transforms the ultimate sign of inferiority into an honorific symbol. Further explanation for these lines may be deduced from a brief mention of Little Ruth in the short story "The Aswan Dam," published in 1956, in which she is also figuratively awarded ranks: "in the hall sat soldiers . . . Poles, French and English, and each had different symbols of rank on the sleeve and shoulders. . . . little Ruth had many qualities on the narrow shoulders of her heart, but they were invisible."[209] It seems that a long time before writing "Little Ruth," Amichai toyed with the idea of Ruth's being a brave soldier who deserved to be granted honors. Additionally, an archival note about "Death" broad-jumping in the "Olympics" may be related to the image of Ruth, decorated with medals for jumping on one leg as she was deported[210] (it was a common practice for the Nazis to confiscate artificial limbs before deportation). In the novel, Amichai quotes the last letter Ruth sent. She had resigned herself to her fate, without blaming God or anyone else: "Today I am quiet. I reached the conclusion that has nothing beyond it. I always read our beautiful prayers. Soon I will go in the way of all."[211] Her nobility in the face of death is also recalled in the poem. The poem's allusion to the girl's "brave soul" is a reflection on her ability to face her fate with open eyes and with dignity.

The poem "Little Ruth" is divided into two stanzas, eighteen lines each. The numerical value of the word "alive" (hai) in Hebrew is eighteen (Hebrew letters also function as numbers). Doubled, it also signifies the thirty-six righteous people (akin to Christian saints) who, according to tradition, are alive at any given time. It is no coincidence that Amichai played with these traditionally magical numbers; he perceived Little Ruth as a saint of sorts. The first words in the second stanza are "you gave me your life," and, indeed, at that point, the poem switches focus, from her life to his. It is as though the speaker feels that he received extra years to live because she did not live her allotted lifespan and gave him the years that were meant for her. This echoes a Christian concept of a human sacrificial lamb that dies to atone for others' sins. The novel similarly describes Little Ruth as a saint and explicitly portrays her as a sacrificial lamb: "She had been brave to her last day. She had known that there is the fire and the knife, and also who was destined to be the lamb for the burnt offering."[212] It does not specify for whom Little Ruth was being sacrificed. In atypical directness, only the poem reveals that Amichai believes that she died for him. Furthermore, the draft in the archive entitled "First Love" implicitly associates Little Ruth with the biblical Isaac. Although in that unpublished poem the speaker is the blind Isaac, the mere allusion to him evokes the akedah—the binding of Isaac—at the center of which is the notion of sacrifice.

The final—and enduring—image of the poem is that of an unclaimed suitcase revolving endlessly on a conveyer belt. While the poem's image of the airport's automatic conveyer belt may seem far removed from the world of Little Ruth, one can trace its roots back to the Wuerzburg train station. In *Not of This Time*, the narrator imagines that the sign Little Ruth carried when she was deported was like "the numbered tag on my suitcase in the checkroom at the station."[213] Underneath this imagined scene is probably Amichai's memory of the day he left Wuerzburg, carrying suitcases and wishing he could carry with him the people he loved. The narrator's guilt-ridden questions, "Who claimed her after she died? Who came with a checking stub and claimed her ashes?" reflect his own guilt because he could not. Little Ruth is the quintessential "unclaimed suitcase"—no country allowed her to enter. She remained in Holland, waiting to be "claimed."

In many interviews, Amichai said that he felt that Ruth was always with him and that she lived inside him.[214] The final image of the poem "Little Ruth" is an indirect metapoetic statement: just as the suitcase appears and disappears but is always present, so is the vision of Little Ruth in his life and his writing:

Now and then, I remember you in times
Unbelievable. And in places not made for memory [. . .]
As in an airport [. . .]
And there is one suitcase that returns and disappears again
And returns again, ever so slowly, in the empty hall,
Again and again it passes.
This is how your quiet figure passes by me,
This is how I remember you until
The conveyor belt stands still. *And they stood still. Amen.*[215]

In the poem, her former friend, now an Israeli poet in his sixties, stands in the airport, almost hypnotized by the constant motion of pieces of luggage on the conveyor belt. As the poem draws to a close, the concrete image is transformed into a spiritual one. There is no longer a reference to the intoxication with life. Rather, the suitcase becomes a quiet, ephemeral entity that passes by the speaker. The final words of the original Hebrew poem resemble the closing of many psalms, ending with the untranslatable word "*sela.*"[216] This ominous line foreshadows the death of the speaker. When he dies, so will her memory. The conveyor belt will finally stop.

4 Hiding Between the Languages

THE GERMAN MOTHER TONGUE
IN AMICHAI'S UNIVERSE

A few German words, scrawled across the page in Amichai's elongated script, encapsulate the fate of the immigrant child: he "hides himself between the languages" (*"versteckt sich zwischen den Sprachen"*).[1] This phrase, which is found in a small, gray notepad marked "November–December 1957," forms only a single line in a draft of a substantial poem. Its succinct wording captures the bewilderment Amichai must have felt as he reached his new homeland. When he landed in Haifa in 1936, his ears were flooded with a cacophony of tongues; the sounds of languages he did not understand spurred his instinctive infantile response to "hide himself." Within a short time, however, his allegiance would be divided "between the languages," the familiar language of his past and the dominant one of his future. The vivid image of the child who hides in the space between two languages, as though they were concrete objects that could shelter him, is emblematic of Amichai's own struggle between his mother tongue and his adopted one. He existed between German and Hebrew, never wholly belonging to either. This duality, however, remained internal, its marks surviving mostly in handwritten notes in his archives. More than any other traces of his past, the German language was erased from the face of Amichai's work; while the footprints of the German landscape could be subtly camouflaged, remnants of the German language needed to be completely purged from his poetry for the sake of his career. In order to cement himself as an Israeli Hebrew poet, Amichai had to eradicate his German completely.

* * *

Although his parents held onto their native German language and related traditions in Palestine, Amichai immediately plunged into life in his new homeland; he ran barefoot in the sand dunes and soon spoke Hebrew almost like a native.[2] In the Land of Israel, there was no longer a need for Amichai (or, for that matter, anyone else) to separate religious and social identities. Ludwig, his German name, was never used—everyone called him Yehuda, the Hebrew name he had inherited from his maternal forefathers.[3] Two forces—Amichai's universal adolescent desire to belong, coupled with the omnipresent Zionist ideology in Israel in the 1930s—shaped his emerging personality; he adopted a new Hebrew national identity and turned his back on his mother tongue and European background.

The "betrayal" of the mother tongue was not unique to Amichai, but rather represented a behavior that was typical of his entire generation; many Jews of Palestine lived with the traces of a foreign mother tongue that they sought to erase. The waves of immigrant refugees who arrived on the shores of Palestine during the 1930s, spurred by the rise of the Nazis, were followed by waves of Holocaust survivors after the end of World War II. Amichai was one of those "young immigrants who joined the native-born Israelis."[4] The foreignness of these newcomers, however, clashed with the Zionist image of the ideal "Hebrew." For those writers who were born abroad, the obligation not only to live in but also to create their works in an acquired language presented an obstacle that often proved insurmountable. Many older writers who wrote in their mother tongues were ignored, while the younger authors who could successfully suppress their linguistic roots were greeted warmly by the public. The critic Gershon Shaked appropriated the phrase "born from the sea" (first used by the writer Moshe Shamir to describe his heroic brother) for his characterization of Amichai's Israeli-born contemporaries and those immigrants who had successfully assimilated into them. Shaked argued that the authors of that generation aspired to create themselves in the image of "New Hebrews," detached from their exilic European ancestry and born, so to speak, "from the sea." That phrase symbolized both the New Hebrews' aversion to the history of the Jewish people and their attempt to break their ties to the Diaspora, where Jews were discriminated against. To a great extent, this self-creation relied on the adoption of the Hebrew language as the sole means of expression.

Even before the 1930s, the majority of literary works in modern Hebrew were written after a long series of departures from mother tongues. Israeli literary critics, like most of the writers themselves, viewed writing in Hebrew as a validation of the national revival, a return to the Jewish people's ancient heritage, as well as to normalcy. It was also an expression of national solidarity with "the enterprise of the Jews in the Land of Israel."[5] Writing in Hebrew was a kind of linguistic "enlistment," a perceived "civic duty" and circumstantial necessity that often also served the deep emotional need to construct a new self.[6] The study of the linguistic struggle caused by immigration and bilingualism is thus at the heart of modern Hebrew literature. Not surprisingly, both the writers and the Hebrew literary critics have overlooked the issue of the abandoned mother tongue, mostly for these ideological reasons.[7] In their analyses of Hebrew literature, they have ignored the impact that the transition from one language to another might have on literary development.

Writers who abandon their mother tongues and subsequently write in an acquired language develop various solutions to their linguistic conflicts, and Amichai's linguistic trajectory was no exception. While forsaking the mother tongue has implications for everyone, its effects are most far-reaching for poets and authors, whose very identities are grounded in language. Literary works not written in the author's mother tongue contain traces of the sounds that the fetus heard before birth and that the infant suckled along with his mother's milk; they conceal—and perhaps repress—the notes and echoes of a different verbal past. Bringing these lost notes to the surface and acknowledging their existence leads to a more complex and complete reading of these works.[8]

While adopting a new language may help the individual forge an independent identity, severing all ties with the mother tongue may also be destructive. A writer who writes in an acquired language either out of necessity or choice must attach new signifiers to his signifieds, relinquishing that vital kinship of word and thing that is essential for the verbal creator. This issue strikes a deep chord in Hebrew literature. On the one hand, many writers struggled as they abandoned the language into which they were born. On the other, the new Hebrew language, which is so inextricably linked to Zionist ideology, enabled many of them to acquire a new voice and therefore, perhaps, a new, stronger self. Within the Zionist narrative, Hebrew represented a stronger, masculine side of the language, while other languages, especially Yiddish, were considered feminine. In the case of Amichai, as in the case of a number of Israeli writers, the relinquished mother tongue was the German language. I am keenly aware of the unbearably heavy shadow that the Holocaust casts over any discussion of the German language and that eradicating it became an ideological agenda and a form of rejection for some segments of Israeli society. This is not, however, my primary focus in this chapter. For a child like Amichai, who had grown up in a German-speaking Jewish home, this was, and continued to be, the mother tongue and his verbal home.[9]

When, in a private conversation in 1996, I asked Amichai directly about his winding passage between languages, he implicitly acknowledged how much of his past he still carried with him. He told me that the "most healthy person is a split person with a split soul" and that "the entire land of Israel is like that."[10] This statement may easily apply to Amichai's linguistic duality.

*   *   *

When Amichai and his family left Nazi-controlled Wuerzburg for Palestine in 1936, they brought over much more than the large wooden containers filled with their belongings. They carried a wealth of memories and, most significantly for this discussion, the German language.[11] Even after they settled in Palestine, the dominant language in the Pfeuffer household, as in the homes of most German-speaking immigrants, remained German. Amichai would speak it with his parents until they died.[12] Even after their passing, the poet's mother tongue continued to accompany him throughout the rest of his life.[13] While German and ancient Hebrew peacefully coexisted in Amichai's childhood, once he moved to Palestine, that harmony was shattered. Modern Hebrew threatened the German linguistic heritage.

Although Amichai's initial transition to Hebrew was quick and complete, it was neither painless nor simple.[14] In addition to the difficulty of leaving German behind, the ritual Hebrew that he had learned in the German-Jewish school differed drastically from the modern Israeli speech that bombarded him from the moment he stepped off the boat in Haifa. While he had heard Hebrew in synagogue from a tender age and recited its blessings from the moment he could speak, he had learned the holy tongue only in the European Ashkenazic pronunciation and never as a modern, spoken language. It surely took a large, conscious effort for Amichai to adopt modern Hebrew, slowly substituting the sounds of the old language with the fluent, everyday form of expression prevalent in Palestine.

In many of the interviews he granted throughout his career, Amichai routinely claimed that his transition to the Hebrew language was easy and natural[15] and that he had known spoken Hebrew as a child in Germany.[16] The testimonies of his schoolmates from Wuerzburg, however, contradict these assertions. They remember classes in which they studied Hebrew texts, but these were conducted entirely in German. They recall not knowing enough Hebrew to speak the language after getting off the boat.[17] Amichai, however, downplayed his relationship to his mother tongue in interviews, saying he lost touch with German almost entirely upon his arrival in Palestine.

Contrary to the impression Amichai wished to give in these autobiographical accounts, parting from the German language and assimilating into Hebrew had constituted an excruciating experience for him. The reverberations from his early life in Germany were too strong to be so easily discarded.[18] As a result, Amichai's relationship to German remained a conflicted, if not a painful, one.[19] One stanza that Amichai published almost three decades after his arrival in Palestine captures the essence of this pain. Its graphically cruel language is testament to the intensity of feeling surrounding Amichai's transition from one language to another.

> History is a eunuch,
> Looking for mine too
> To castrate, cut with paper sheets
> Sharper than any knife, to crush
> To block my mouth forever
> With whatever she cut,
> As a desecration of the war dead,
> So I sing only an impotent chirp,
> So I learn many languages
> And not one tongue of my own,
> So I am scattered and dispersed,
> Not a Tower of Babel rising to heaven.[20]

The brutality of these lines, as well as their bitterness, is uncharacteristic of Amichai. It is significant, then, that he used them to relay how he had to substitute one language for another, due to historical circumstances. According to this rare depiction of his experience as an immigrant, the transition to Hebrew was a form of linguistic atrocity for Amichai; giving up his mother tongue felt as though his mouth was being forcefully "blocked," as though he had been castrated.

Despite this initial trauma, Amichai quickly conformed to the Hebrew milieu. Both national and personal motivations drove this harrowing linguistic conversion. Years later, when Amichai realized poetry was his calling and decided to follow it, there was no doubt in his heart that he would write in his adopted language and become an Israeli *Hebrew* poet. In this, his chosen artistic path, the fact that he was so intimately versed in the language of the synagogue became an asset. His modern Israeli Hebrew poetry integrated the Hebrew of the Bible and the prayer book that he knew from childhood. In a unique reworking, Amichai transformed the biblical and liturgical Hebrew of his father into an elastic and playful "mother tongue."[21] He emerged as a writer in the patriotic climate of the mid to late 1940s, when his identity as an

Israeli was blossoming.[22] Amichai fought in the Israeli War of Independence; when it was over in 1949, he began to construct a literary persona that reflected his nationalist feelings and emphasized his biographical identification with the trajectory of his country. In this Israeli self-portrayal, Amichai had to repress his foreign roots. Any trace of a foreign language would not have been acceptable by the literary norms of the time.

It is implausible, however, that Amichai could have parted completely with the language in which he was loved as a baby, the language of the lullabies he heard before he fell asleep, the language of his prattling with Little Ruth. But where did the sounds go? What happened to the German that he discarded, but could never have forgotten?

Despite his insistence that he never wrote in German, a careful reading of Amichai's oeuvre reveals that he continued nursing from the distant breast of his German childhood. Those who remember Amichai's voice can easily recall his German accent.[23] Amichai's artistic voice is no different.[24] His writing is suffused with materials drawn from the German world he left behind, the sources that nurtured him in his formative years and became the forces behind his work.[25]

This chapter strives to retrieve the sunken remains of Amichai's mother tongue and to listen to the German sounds that dwell in the depths of his writing.[26] Such an investigation goes against the grain of dominant Israeli scholarly criticism, but this virtually uncharted territory in Amichai's creative universe is essential to a comprehensive understanding of his writing. Amichai muffled the echoes of German, repressing both its sounds and the associations bound with them, yet clues to his process of linguistic alchemy can be found in his books and archives.

*   *   *

There is no use of German in Amichai's canonical poetry. While there are some words in German in his marginal genres—namely, his prose and drama—the vital role German played in his creative and emotional world is only manifest in his unpublished writings. Thanks to the newly found letters and archival materials, it is possible to examine Amichai's oeuvre in its preparatory stages and to analyze the role of German in his creative process in both the years before he began writing poetry and the years during which he built his canonic Hebrew corpus. They openly show the important creative and emotional role German continued to play in Amichai's life. Drawing from this awareness, the analysis of the published works gains new dimensions. Amichai's verse is read in this book together with its unpublished, foreign "shadow" side, the side the great Hebrew poet felt he had to camouflage, and even bury completely, in the process of attaining his national status.

THE LETTERS

Before Amichai was shaped as a poet and before camouflage became an overarching force in his life, he wrote his letters to Ruth Z. in New York. They are not only Amichai's earliest body of writing available to scholarship now, but also the most revelatory. The letters lay bare the inner workings of his creative process and how vital German was in its development. Because Amichai addressed his beloved who shared some of his cultural and linguistic background, he felt no need to cover up his roots. The letters offer unparalleled insight into the artist's linguistic universe during the years 1947–1948, when he began forging his identity as a poet. They allow us to observe Amichai's unguarded, natural relationship with his German mother tongue at a time when he lived far from his German-speaking parents and when his social and professional life was conducted exclusively in Hebrew.[27]

Amichai's love letters to Ruth Z. reflect the transition in his attitude toward his mother tongue: over the eight months of the correspondence, Amichai's use of German declined while his sense of himself as an Israeli patriot grew. The letters reveal how many of the early linguistic experiences survived in his consciousness. They are peppered with German poetry, references to German texts, and expressions from the artist's childhood and interlaced with children's songs, folktales, and stories. In fact, certain lines from Amichai's poems—even those that were written over half a century after he attended German elementary school—can be fully understood only through the letters and the texts they recall.

In a rare admission on Amichai's part, he described the emotional role his mother tongue played in his psyche, saying: "German was for me a kind of language of the soul." Starting in eleventh grade, Amichai kept a diary in German. At the time, he was in love with a girl who had just arrived in Palestine from Germany "and did not know a word in Hebrew, so this love was conducted mostly in German."[28] While this adolescent diary has probably been lost, the enduring hold of German on Amichai persisted, as it was the language that best expressed his strongest emotions and, as such, would become the language woven into the fabric of his first adult love relationship, with Ruth Z. Indeed, the fact that he and Ruth shared a mother tongue may have increased his attraction to her. He spoke German with her parents and admired their library full of German books. Amichai and Ruth spoke Hebrew to each other, but Ruth stated that during that time Amichai showed her poems that he had written in German.[29] Their eight-month-long correspondence reveals the emotive power of that language. Although the letters themselves are written in a rich and fluid Hebrew, German is integrated into them with perfect ease.

The multitude of German love poems in the letters is one of the strongest indicators of the connection between Amichai and his mother tongue. Although Amichai expressed his love for Ruth through his original Hebrew poems, all the other love poems quoted in the letters are taken from German literature. In the body of the aerograms, all written in Hebrew, Amichai copied or referenced eleven specific works by German poets, most having to do with love. German seems to be the only language he trusted to faithfully express his feelings.[30] For her birthday, he even sent her a collection of Heine's poems.[31] It is important to note that not one love poem written by a Hebrew or English poet is ever mentioned in the entire correspondence. Amichai sent love poems by the Romantic poet Christian Morgenstern (e.g., "Nun wollen wir uns still die Haende geben" [Now we calmly hold hands]),[32] Johann Wolfgang Goethe (e.g., "Naehe des Geliebten" [Nearness of the Beloved]),[33] and Rainer Marie Rilke (e.g., "Liebeslied" [Love Song]),[34] as if he believed that these established, German-language poets could best convey his longings. Even when he grew tired or ran out of space on the aerogram, Amichai would promise the next installment of the poem in the following letter and would dutifully copy down the rest of it for her the next time he wrote.[35]

"The Prayer of Separated Lovers to Each Other" by Morgenstern was the first German poem Amichai sent to Ruth.[36] He included it in his fifth letter to her, which he mailed on September 7, 1947, only a week after she had left. He told her he had translated Morgenstern's poem into Hebrew, yet copied it in the original German. As he would do in other letters that contained poetry, he added his own comments. He remarked that the rhythm of "The Prayer of Separated Lovers," exuded "calmness and mutual security." The sensual, irreplaceable power of the mother tongue is evident in Amichai's request that Ruth not only read the poem for its content, but also "recite" it out loud with her "low voice." He was confident that when she did this, she would "feel its strength" in her very body.[37] Even a reader not fluent in German can hear the rhythm of the lines: "*Wohne in mir wie das Licht in der Luft. | Auf daß ich ganz dein sei— | Auf daß du ganz mein seist*" (Dwell in me like the light in the air / So that I would be totally yours—So that you would be totally mine). Although Morgenstern never reached the literary status of Heinrich Heine, Goethe, or Rilke, his sentimental tone clearly fit Amichai's mood in the early months of fall 1947, and Amichai included three of Morgenstern's poems in the letters.[38]

As the correspondence continued, Amichai shared with Ruth literary associations that often reveal his complex relationship with German works. His treatment of Richard Beer-Hofmann's "Lullaby for Miriam" demonstrates how he imbued the German text with his ambivalent longings for European nature and scenery. In a letter from October 2, Amichai quoted the second and third lines of the poem's last stanza. Beer-Hofmann's lines suggest that the blood of their Jewish ancestors flows through the Jews alive today, toward future generations, thus implying the eternity of the Jewish people: "*Ufer nur sind wir und tief in uns rinnt / Blut von Gewesnen*" (We are but banks of a river and the blood of our past flows wildly through us).[39]

Amichai, however, gave the image a new meaning. Before mentioning Beer-Hofmann, he opened his letter with an inventive metaphorical rendering that portrays his inner world as a picture of colorful leaves in an autumn forest, along the floor of which flows a powerful stream. With this intersection of European nature and his own inner world, he glided into Beer-Hofmann's famous lullaby for his daughter Miriam. Amichai took the dark stream from Beer-Hofmann's poem and situated it in a northern forest, the formative European landscape of his own childhood. Through his reading of the German poem, he describes the landscape of his soul.

Appropriating the German lines, Amichai's ecstatic epistolary interpretation blurs the boundaries between Beer-Hofmann's figurative stream and his own outpouring of emotion. Furthermore, while Amichai copied the lines in German verbatim from Beer-Hofmann's poem, he also translated them into Hebrew. In doing so, he transformed the nationalist image of blood flowing like a river through generations into a passionate declaration of his love for Ruth. Amichai exclaimed: "Our blood already flows together in one gorge" and likened their union to that of ancient nations who drank each other's blood as a sign of allegiance.[40]

The reworking of the German poem reaches its climax as the letter closes. The dark stream from Beer-Hofmann's poem is "transported" from the European forest to the Carmel Mountain in Israel. There, Amichai, like most Mediterraneans, anxiously anticipates the rain that will fill the narrow valleys, hoping for the stormy waters to quench the thirst of the dry land. The letter thus moves from the inner to the outer, from blood to water, and from the lush forests of Germany to the dry terrain of Israel. In this letter, therefore, Amichai reinterprets the German source to fit his new life, translating Beer-Hofmann's love for his daughter Miriam into his own romantic love for Ruth, and substituting the German landscapes for the Israeli one. This early intimate piece, the product of Amichai's imagination, predates the poetics of camouflage. Nevertheless, it anticipates the transformation Amichai would later make as a poet. While he did not yet cover his tracks, the young Amichai began to invent the way he would rework his foreign early roots into his Hebrew oeuvre, translating the German to the Hebrew and Israeli.

The letters contain more than a record of the way Amichai metabolized the loss of the German language and landscapes; they also expose some of the greatest influences on his writing. Not surprisingly, the poet Amichai revered most of all was a German-language poet, Rilke. Amichai was first introduced to this poetic giant by his high school teacher, and he continued to read Rilke's poetry throughout his life.[41] In later years, he spoke openly about his admiration for him. Rilke's influence touches many corners of Amichai's writing of that time, an inspiration that was later recognized by critics of his verse.[42] The letters, however, reveal the personal and creative kinship Amichai felt with Rilke, which surpassed his emotional connection with any other writer, at least during the period in which he was making his initial strides in verse. Rilke is the most frequently mentioned poet in Amichai's letters to Ruth, and his significance goes far beyond poetic inspiration. Rilke held the status of an older soulmate; Amichai spoke of him as his idol, calling him "my beloved poet."[43] Amichai identified so closely with Rilke that he sometimes internalized his work without realizing to what extent he emulated the older poet. Rilke's power over Amichai stemmed not only from his art, but also from the language in which this art was executed and the German landscape and experience that motivated it.[44] It is hard to imagine that Amichai would have responded so intensely to poetry written in a language other than his German mother tongue.

The letters show that Rilke served as a catalyst for Amichai, enabling him to access and use comforting European memories. In mid-December 1947, Amichai describes to Ruth Z. his joy upon receiving a letter from her. For the romantic Amichai, receiving an envelope containing a letter from Ruth made him feel like a child receiving a beautifully wrapped gift, the rustling paper magnifying the anticipation of opening the present. Carried by his associations, Amichai then wrote about the intensity of early memories and the role of childhood in determining a person's emotional state throughout life. Yet it is not Freud whom Amichai quoted to bolster his argument but, rather, Rilke, saying, "great people like Rilke" perceived childhood as the "key and the source" of creation.[45] That idea, especially in connection with Rilke, returns in the letters like a refrain.

In his commentary on Rilke, Amichai ignored the great disparities in their environment and life circumstances, and highlighted only the similarities. When he read Rilke's poem "Autumn," Amichai recognized in it the elements of loneliness, alienation, and homelessness that reflected the condition of his beloved Ruth as she took her first steps on the sidewalks of New York.[46] It was not Ruth's experience, however, but his own that made him copy Rilke's poem for her. Its last stanza, the one that Amichai believed mirrored her situation, speaks of loneliness in terms reminiscent of Amichai's descriptions of himself at that time: sitting alone in his room, reading, and writing long letters into the evening. It is as if Rilke were depicting both the lover and his beloved at once. Although Amichai may have deromanticized Rilke's classics in his later poetry,[47] as suggested by the critic Shimon Sandbank, in the letters and his verse of that time, Amichai emulates the German poet's romanticism. Amichai never published his own Hebrew poem entitled "Autumn," which he wrote for Ruth and included in one of his first letters to her. In it, he mourns Ruth's departure and refers to autumn in melancholic, European terms redolent of Rilke. Following both his own German past and his poetic idol, Amichai ignored the lush, blossoming Israeli autumn that surrounded him on the green slopes of the Carmel Mountain and instead wrote about the barren fall, the quintessential season of European loneliness.[48]

Amichai often blurred the lines between Rilke and himself, unconsciously changing one to fit the other. His treatment—both poetically and in the letters—of the poem "Liebeslied" (Love Song) by Rilke is emblematic of the way he was influenced by and connected to his favorite poet. Rilke's poem depicts the male speaker's struggle to shield himself from the quaking of his beloved's stormy soul and ends with a striking final image: lovers as two strings strung on the same violin, producing a sweet song together—the love song—as they are played by an otherworldly hand with an invisible bow. That mysterious hand may be the hand of God, implying that an inexorable fate dictates the fortuitous meeting of the two souls. When Amichai quoted the image of lovers as two strings on one musical instrument to Ruth, he exclaimed: "Only an artist like Rilke could express such a strong picture!"[49] Through the process of translating this German love poem into Hebrew, Amichai made it his own, weaving together his passion for Ruth with his love for the German language.

A careful reading shows how Rilke's "Love Song" affects the prose of Amichai's letters as well as his later published poetry. Moreover, the prose of those letters suggests that some of the poetry Amichai published in 1959 was in fact written in the period that preceded the 1948 war. In a letter from early January, Amichai paints for Ruth the violent, everyday reality of bloody shootings on the streets of Haifa. Against that harrowing and precarious background, his work as a teacher became more meaningful and demanding. He compares his attentiveness to the children to a musician strumming on instruments whose "strings are pure and tuned." From children, he turned to adults, wondering if they were also "musical instruments," albeit instruments that were "more complex and out of tune."⁵⁰

This same image later serves Amichai in a much more tragic context. In a long and heart-wrenching letter about the effects of the rampant violence on his school, and on the land in general, Amichai told Ruth about a newspaper piece on the defenders (*meginim*) of a kibbutz who were killed during an attack. Due to an inadvertent error, instead of using the word *meginim* (defenders), the article uses a similar-sounding word, *menagnim* (musicians). The typographical error impelled Amichai to write a poem that takes advantage of the unintended pun *meginim / menagnim*. In the poem, they become defenders of music and of musical instruments, while their falling turns into "the falling of two heavy hands" on a piano. Although the poem includes the piano, the violin, the harp, and the trumpet, and Amichai reported that the pictures came to him "in free association," it is quite plausible that one of the sources of its imagery was Rilke's metaphor of people as musical instruments played by divine hands.⁵¹

In fact, Rilke's "Love Song" ultimately spurred one of the central images in Amichai's fifty-segment modernist epic, "In the Public Garden." The music of the violin intermittently plays throughout this fragmented epic and soothes the fear and bitterness of its speaker. The violin is the antithesis of the cynicism, loneliness, and blunt sexuality that dominate the rest of the poem. Although Amichai did not publish "In the Public Garden" until 1959, he undoubtedly created sections of this work in 1947, during his correspondence with Ruth and while he was under the spell of Rilke's "Love Song." He copied the last quarter of "In the Public Garden" into a letter from January 1948, and it is likely that when Amichai wrote it in the last month of 1947, he was nourished by Rilke's portrayal of two lovers as strings on a violin.[52]

Amichai shared this primeval experience of love with Ruth Z. and throughout the correspondence he enlisted their common German upbringing to reawaken her ties to him and to help her understand the scenes that he was describing. The connection to the German texts was a part of their shared past and Amichai wished to stir up that association in his letters to Ruth. Folktales from Amichai's childhood, like "The Snow Queen" and "The Fir Tree," appear often in his letters.[53] The presence of nursery rhymes and folktales in the correspondence shows the bond between Amichai and the German language through the texts of his childhood, as well as the emotional bonding power that he attributed to that language. Amichai remembered the *Grimm Brothers Collection of Folktales* from his school days in Wuerzburg.[54] Together with stories by Hans Christian Andersen that had been translated into German, they were frequently read in the Volksschule. Both Grimm and Andersen were well known to Ruth, for she was raised on German children's books and culture in a German-Jewish home. Unlike the songs and poetic verses, which Amichai often quoted verbatim, however, his references to the folktales from his childhood are thematic. In his letters to Ruth, Amichai often turned these tales' plots and characters into a private code.[55] Andersen had an added personal meaning for the lovers.[56] When Ruth's parents prepared to immigrate to Palestine, they packed an illustrated German edition of Hans Christian Andersen's stories in the trunkful of German books for their children.[57] Amichai and Ruth, both over twenty years old at the time, would sit together in her room in Jerusalem and read these stories to each other out loud, in their common mother tongue.

Again and again in his letters, Amichai evoked the stories he and Ruth had read in German together, saying "do you remember . . . ?" When they were separated, he wanted to resurrect those intimate moments, and he used Andersen's stories to reestablish their closeness and bridge the gap between their lives.[58] Although he refers to "the stories," there is no doubt that the language in which they were shared played a part in the emotional weight they carried. While the beautiful language and fantastic plots of these tales allowed Amichai to distance himself from the violent reality in Palestine, he also used them in an attempt to evoke the empathy of his beloved and to help her identify with the grief that surrounded him.[59]

In a series of stormy letters from October 1947, Amichai told Ruth about his first face-to-face encounter with death. The bus he was riding was attacked in an ambush on the Carmel slope, and the young man who sat in the seat behind him had been killed. Amichai used Andersen's story "The Little Match Girl" to draw Ruth into the scene of the funeral of the twenty-year-old, but also to process the events that were unfolding in front of him. As the mourners lined up to follow the hearse, Amichai looked out at the sea and saw one boat separated from the rest, sailing forward quickly and leaving a long, white trail of foam behind it. He recalled Andersen's match girl, who knew that whenever a person died, a star would fall. In Haifa, he thought, when someone dies, a white boat sails away and disappears over the horizon.[60] Andersen's imagery thus triggered Amichai's own lyrical musings and helped him to endow with meaning a death that otherwise felt senseless.

Months later, in January 1948, when tension was growing in Palestine, Amichai again resorted to Andersen's stories to transform the horror into beauty. On their way to rescue a besieged Jewish settlement, thirty-five exceptional young volunteers were killed. Among them was Danny Mas, a young man who had shared Ruth Z.'s desk in elementary school. The letter that bore the terrible news to Ruth in America alludes to "The Mother," a tale from Ruth's illustrated book of Andersen stories. "The Mother" is about a young mother who travels to the Land of Death in an attempt to bring her dead child back to life. Death lets her choose between two flowers, one of whom is her child and the other is a child with a great future ahead of him; the flower she picks will die. She refuses to choose. Amichai associates the "flowers" with the lives and futures that were wasted and the desperate mothers who tried in vain to retrieve the irretrievable.[61]

Andersen's imagery enabled Amichai to express not only sadness, but also great joy. In his ecstatic letter written on November 29, after the UN vote for the partition of Palestine and the creation of a Jewish state, Amichai tried to transport Ruth from New York to the wild party on the streets of Haifa by capturing one of Andersen's rejoicing cities. He wrote that the festivities resembled Andersen's depictions of an exuberant celebration after the birth of a prince or a royal marriage: "the candy-sellers give for free and the king turns somersaults in the air." Amichai's German mother tongue springs out from the letter at the most emotional moment. Although the outpouring of joy is told in Hebrew, at its climax, the word for the king's somersaults is uttered in German: "Purzelbaeume."[62]

Amichai's letters to his beloved recall not only the German reading they shared, but also other texts from his childhood in Wuerzburg. In the lower grades in Amichai's school in Wuerzburg, songbooks were a lynchpin of the curriculum. The journey of one of these songs through Amichai's writing is a prime example of how the sounds of his early life were ingrained in him for years to come. A simple nursery rhyme that Amichai knew from grade school found its way into the intimate correspondence between Amichai and Ruth. It imitates the "ticktock" of large clocks and the "ticktock-ticktock" of small ones. In a letter from March 21, 1948, Amichai recalled how, as a child, he and his classmates sang, "*Grosse Uhren machen* **tick tack** / *Kleine Uhren machen* **tick tack tick tack** / *Und die Allerkleinsten* **tick!**" (emphasis added).[63] The German lines appear in the letter in their original language, but the meaning attributed to them in 1948 is far removed from the Wuerzburg classroom. Amichai, the junior teacher, describes how his nerve-racked young pupils in Haifa, like their German peers, imitated in song the loud and soft sounds they heard around them. In 1948 Haifa, however, the sounds were not a ticktock made by clocks. Instead, the children chanted the "boom boom" and "ba-bi ba-bi" of the midsized and lightweight machine guns, the Bren and the Sten. As the violence in Haifa increased, Amichai might have found some comfort in remembering the old German rhyme.

Almost twenty years after the clock-gun connection was first made in the artist's mind and recorded in a letter, it resurfaces as a poetic image. It appears camouflaged within Amichai's autobiographical epic, "The Travels of Benjamin the Last, of Tudela." One of the central scenes of the epic is an apocalyptic, psychedelic vision that combines sexualized body parts and fabrics, articles from the poet's Jewish childhood, and the sounds of war: dynamite, hand grenades, and gunshots. Slipped in between all these associations is the line, "cannon barrels climbing like ivy, shooting / cuckoo shells every fifteen minutes: cuckoo / boom-boom."[64] The shelling sounds like a cuckoo clock; and the origin of the association between these two noises is in the letter.

There is no equivalent to this kind of continuous "narrative" of Amichai's internal world after April 1948, when Amichai mailed his last letter to Ruth Z. It seems that none of his private papers from April 1948 to 1953 have survived. Indeed, other than a handful of letters written in Hebrew and German to Ruth Z. in the early 1950s, the earliest papers available to scholars are from 1954 (the year that Amichai's personal writings begin in the Beinecke archive). By 1954, Amichai was thirty years old, had published poetry in newspapers and journals, and was about to publish his first book. Additionally, these archival materials are of an entirely different nature than the letters because they are comprised of notes and drafts that Amichai wrote for himself, not to another person, and therefore are much more fragmented. But even this limited source confirms that Amichai's connection to the German language persisted in the years that followed and that German remained a strong, creative force while Amichai was making his name as a definitive Hebrew poet.

AMICHAI'S WRITINGS FROM 1948 TO 1962

Although the archive and the letters clearly demonstrate German's presence, there is no overt German in Amichai's entire poetic corpus—only modern Hebrew, laced with the Hebrew of the ancient Scriptures. Nevertheless, faint traces of the mother tongue did survive in Amichai's idiosyncratic use of sound, syntax, and imagery. One may think of the German language as the "subconscious" of Amichai's verse and the remnants of it as the scattered pieces that break through the mask of repression. In fact, segments of Amichai's poems can only be fully understood and appreciated when translated into German. A meticulous reading of the verses in *Poems: 1948–1962* uncovers traces of the other tongue, some that were left in his writing unintentionally and some of which Amichai might have been aware and therefore carefully camouflaged.

Amichai covered German with layers of Hebrew and countless mentions of the Israeli landscape. While Jerusalem, Tiberias, the Jordan River, and Mount Hermon all are referred to by their names, the names of parallel German sites are absent: there is no trace of the Main River, the city Wuerzburg, or the country Germany. Rather, the foreign places are called by generic names, like "the city of my childhood" or "a river." Even the word "Europe" appears only once in the entire 360-page book;[65] only once did he call the German language by its name, and, even then, without any further elaboration.[66] In other places, generic phrases like "a foreign language" and "a mother tongue" conceal the German identity of those references.[67] Finally, the word "Gothic" emerges as an adjective, in "Gothic smiles."[68] There are no other explicit references to Germany, its culture, or its language in the collection that established Amichai as a leading Israeli Hebrew poet.

While explicit references to German are almost nonexistent, *Poems: 1948–1962* does contain some hints of a linguistic barrier, the effort required to learn a language, and the frustration of always having to translate one's thoughts (while still being misunderstood): "everybody needs to learn languages / under the rock, a cyclamen screamed / nobody understands cyclamens. . . . "[69] Amichai here implies that the Israeli flower, the cyclamen, shares an immigrant's fate—even when it raises its voice, it cannot convey its thoughts and desires.

The cyclamen's distress goes unnoticed by those who cannot understand it. Another such reference is to "the foreign language of fish."[70] This ironic remark underscores the similarity between a fish and an immigrant: neither can speak—the fish, because of its nature; the immigrant, because all he knows is a foreign language (and thus must be as silent as a fish). Similarly, in the line "we are simple, easy to learn, as words in an elementary language textbook," the language learner is constrained by his vocabulary and becomes "simple."[71] Such allusions to the condition of those who cannot speak the language of the land are rare, however. On the few occasions in which they do appear, they are vague and hidden within metaphors or catalogues. The reader of these lines, therefore, is often misled into thinking that they are mere images, marginal to the poem's core meaning.

The lasting power of the mother tongue is confirmed by the poet's unpublished papers. In the years 1954 through approximately 1960, Amichai wrote in tiny, pocket-sized pads, with faded cardboard covers of orange or gray. According to a letter to Ruth Z., he began the practice of using these pads as early as September 1947, when he bought a tiny notepad on which to write all of his thoughts and ideas: "I have a small pad, a tiny, tiny pad, and there I write everything that comes to my mind, all that I see and absorb . . ."[72] Reading into the semiotics of notepads, it is evident that as the years went by and his reputation and perhaps self-assurance grew, so did the notebooks.

The two-by-three-inch pages are filled with scribbled notes and drafts of poems in different stages of completion. Despite Amichai's firm denial that he had ever written poems in German,[73] there are long series of uninterrupted lines in German that can be read as complete poems. Frequently, though, Hebrew and German are interwoven, and entire lines alternate between the two. At other times, a line starts in one language and ends in another; or, in several instances, a single German word, like *Erinnerung* (memory) or *Tod* (death), might punctuate (and illuminate) an otherwise Hebrew text.[74] Thus, the perception of Amichai as an exclusively Hebrew poet becomes untenable. German played a complex and multifaceted role in Amichai's creative process and in his emotional life.

Unlike the meticulous script that fills the aerograms to Ruth Z., the pads present a sometimes insurmountable challenge to the reader. Amichai's handwriting in both the Hebrew and German alphabets is almost illegible, with long and tall letters that lack the required curves. Often, the notepads seem to have served as a place to jot down isolated thoughts and metaphors as opposed to continuous texts. The contents of the pads thus reflect Amichai's feelings at the time and can be seen be as preparatory sketches for the poems in *Poems: 1948–1962*. Furthermore, Amichai's process of translation is clearly visible in the archival drafts. For instance, the image of a flower holding a man's hand—"*die kleine Blume | haelt meine | Hand*" (the small flower held my hand)—first appears in German in a notepad, dated April 1957, and shows up in Hebrew over a year later, in a notepad from August 1958. Additionally, many of the lines in the archive seem to be first drafts, replete with crossed-out words and alternatives in the margins. Occasionally, the title or a segment of a well-known published poem springs out. In fact, the infant stages of some of Amichai's most famous poems are hidden in these pads—a number of them originally written in his mother tongue.[75] The discussion that follows focuses solely on the legacy of the repressed mother tongue as it is expressed in Amichai's canonic collection *Poems: 1948–1962* and on poems from that collection that touch upon German in one way or another.

One of the manifestations of Amichai's need to resort to German and his artistic connection to that language is his frequent use of the word "translation." No one exists between two languages to the extent that translators do. Only those who are fluent in two languages are able to move freely from one linguistic realm to another; but the price of this freedom is often high. The translator surrenders the intimate linguistic bond of those who live exclusively in their mother tongue. One can therefore conclude that Amichai identified with the figure of the translator. He camouflaged the linguistic conflicts behind that figure and endowed the concept of translation with a metaphorical dimension. In both his published poetry and his private notes, he enlisted the idea of translation to describe matters other than the actual translation of languages.[76] This metaphor lends itself easily to depicting his creative process, the verbal communication between individuals, the pain of living in a foreign language, and even romantic love.[77]

A relatively long poem written mostly in German with scattered words in Hebrew shows how Amichai used German when he was in love. It opens with a poignant image: longing ("*eine Sehnsucht*") passes through the words of his beloved ("*deine Worte*") like the wind passes through leaves.[78] The poem continues with an association between romantic love and language. The metaphor that connects the two encapsulates the tragedy of an immigrant: his beloved feels to him like a "translated language" ("*uebersetzte Sprache*"); she is "mine and yet foreign." The woman belongs to the poem's speaker because he can understand her, but she is "foreign" because he can never fully grasp her essence.

This connection between romantic love and language surfaces more covertly in an uncollected poem entitled "Onot" (Seasons), published in 1956. As in all of Amichai's published verse, any German traces have been deleted, and therefore the connection between love and language is less blatant than in the mostly German poem discussed above. The published poem uses the concept of translation to speak of lovers who remain in the pocket of a cold winter, unable to bloom in the spring. The unfulfilled love is told in terms of linguistic miscommunication: "it was difficult to translate us / we remained in our language, not understood, among blooming trees."[79] Although this poem ostensibly speaks only of romantic love, it is also about the hardship of abandoning one's native tongue. The lovers remain separated from the joyous spring around them by a linguistic barrier—they cannot be translated, and so they cannot be understood. The fact that Amichai did not include this poem in the volume that he intended to become his canon also suggests the possibility that he saw it as too revealing of his foreign roots.

Unlike "Seasons," the poem "And We Shall Not Get Excited" was included in *Poems: 1948–1962*. It is a uniquely explicit example of the role of language for Amichai.[80] By focusing in its title and refrain on the Talmudic guideline for translators "not to get excited," this enigmatic poem alludes to the legal domain. The translator, the "*turgeman*" who appears in the second line, is traditionally ordered by the court to remain neutral and not to "get excited" by the testimonies he must translate. This calm behavior implicitly becomes a model for the poet. He defines his job as quietly transmitting words from one person to another, like an uninvolved "mediator." He is simply a link in the chain of a poetic tradition.

The poem camouflages the contemporariness of its subject by using the Aramaic phrase *de'ika birshuti udela ika birshuti* ([any leaven] that is in my possession and that is not in my possession) from the Passover Haggadah as a smokescreen. This phrase is provided as an example of the translator's original occupation—in Talmudic times, he would translate the scholars' Hebrew message into Aramaic for the masses.[81] Both the rare Talmudic term for translator, *turgeman* (instead of the more common *metargem*), and the quotation in Aramaic give the poem a traditional, ancient patina, thus distancing it from Amichai's Germanic roots.[82]

The common occupation of a translator as someone who translates words from one language to another is avoided in this text. Instead, the poem says that the translator transmits the words from one language to another pair of lips. In order to camouflage his preoccupation with the conflict between German and Hebrew, Amichai introduces the erotic domain by exploiting a pun: the word *safa* means both "language" and "lip" in Hebrew. The transmission of words in the poem is therefore a cross between translating and kissing. Furthermore, according to the poem's speaker, transferring words is an unconscious, involuntary action, like passing genes from parent to child.

This claim that the job is involuntary is dubious. As the poem progresses to its third, penultimate, and longest stanza, it seems that the translator himself is the one who has committed a crime and is therefore on trial. His crime may be that of silence: he has omitted words or pleas that were entrusted to his hands without transmitting them, he let them "slip out." Words have fallen by the wayside because of the translator's negligence. Without his services, no one will know of the despair these words convey. The idiom "silence is an admission," which is quoted in the poem, suggests an admission of this wrongdoing. Indeed, a translator's silence is a sin—he has neglected his job. This failure to accomplish his mission results in a harsh verdict, the severing of the chain: "And no more shall we tell what we were told / to other tellers."[83] The translator will no longer transmit to others the words that were spoken to him.

The hermetic nature of the poem reflects the inner turmoil it hides. While there is no explicit linguistic tension between languages here, the mere presence of a "translator" at the center of this poem implies it. The identity of the two languages that the translator knows is not revealed, but the centrality of translation signals the rivalry between Amichai's mother tongue and Hebrew, the language into which he must translate. Furthermore, the poem's refrain that the "translator does not get excited," suggests that the acquired tongue forever lacks the libidinal power of the language of origin. For this additional reason, the translator "does not get excited"—much gets lost in translation.

Even though "And We Shall Not Get Excited" raises the issue of living in two languages more openly than any other poems in the collection, it still hides the main part of the struggle. The shadow side of the "translator's" existence is most explicitly recorded in a draft of this very poem. First, and unsurprisingly, part of this poem was originally written in German and these German lines are less abstract.[84] They describe the pain of the translator who is never able to use his own words or his own language. Like the published poem, the March 1959 draft contains the translator's obligation to be quiet, in effect voiceless, because he is "Merely a mediator,"[85] but the words that were erased from the published version are testament to the inner struggle.

While the published poem takes place entirely in the realm of adults, the final lines of the draft make the connection between translating and leaving the world of childhood. In the draft, the speaker is a child who grew up in one place, had to leave it, and upon returning, discovers that it is smaller than he remembered. These archival lines unveil the proximity between the two longings—for another place and for another language. The draft states that a translation is a faded version of the original, like the landscape one visits as an adult after years of absence. In other words, the translated words are like the diminished version of the beloved place. It is no wonder that these lines, ghosts of the past, were erased and never reached the surface of the poet's oeuvre, for they undermine its Hebrew character by suggesting that it is a struggle for the poet to express himself in Hebrew.

Another poem, "I Write from Right to Left," published in the literary journal *Moznayim* in 1960, confesses more explicitly to the writer's foreignness and his struggle to write in the acquired language.[86] This poem was excluded from *Poems: 1948–1962*, presumably because it was too revealing to become part of his canon. Like "And We Shall Not Get Excited," "I Write from Right to Left" avoids any explicit allusions to the clash in the poet's psyche between German, which is written from left to right, and Hebrew, which is written from right to left. This poem, however, is less vague in conveying its underlying anguish. In fact, its seemingly straightforward title concretely reveals the conflict at the core of the poem and its body subtly suggests the parallel in belonging to the landscape and belonging to the language of the place. Even though Amichai knew how to read Hebrew from first grade, changing the direction of his writing from left to right must have felt unnatural. Those whose first language is written from right to left take that fact for granted; the author's awareness of the language's direction proves that he does not. Furthermore, although the speaker does not admit openly that he would prefer the Latin alphabet, he confesses, "I write from right to left, yearn from left / to right. . . . "[87] While writing in Hebrew, his soul continues longing in the opposite direction—that of its mother tongue. The speaker admits that although he lives in a scorching, dry climate, his emotions resemble those of people who live in the landscape of his childhood, namely Europe. He loves in the style of those who live "among the forests and along brimming rivers."

Indeed, while the speaker dubs Hebrew "my language," using it to describe "pain" and "love" is a necessity, not a choice: "and in the hard and square words of my language / I must say my pain, / And describe the love that . . . / I inherited from my forefathers." The speaker inherited these feelings from his ancestors, who came "from far away." His inner world, his deepest emotions, and the way his psyche is constructed are all European and the demand to articulate pain and love in the acquired language is experienced as a straightjacket.[88]

The state of longing for one language while living and creating in another is expressed in Amichai's archival notes. They reveal the reality of his role as a translator and provide clear evidence of the suffering caused by the loss of the mother tongue.[89] In a little pad from 1956, under the Hebrew title "A Poem about Zafet," Amichai mixed German and Hebrew in a description of a "school of pine trees."[90] The bluntness of the conclusion of this unpublished poem is unparalleled in any of Amichai's published works. Its final words—"without a language of my own"—encapsulate the frustration of a poet who does not feel as though he completely owns either language—the one he left or the one he acquired. Unlike the rest of the text, which is written in blue ink in mixed German and Hebrew, this last line is written in red, in Hebrew, indicating that he revisited the draft and added this line. In this revision, he revealed his secret, the painful truth that was not uttered when the draft for the poem was first written.

In a small gray notepad marked "January 1958," under the title "Survivors," Amichai wrote that "we the refugees," like "coins," have a number of different "exchange rates," referring, perhaps, to the need to "exchange" languages. Nowhere in his entire published oeuvre or public interviews and speeches did Amichai ever refer to himself as a refugee or survivor. The word "translation" appears a few lines later, not only in relation to language, but also to one's life as a whole: "we . . . / translate / childhood into. . . . "[91] This fragmented phrase summarizes the poet's undertaking: all he does is transmit the treasures of childhood into his poetry. This transmission is not dubbed "translation" by coincidence. For Amichai, childhood occurred in another language and therefore had to be translated. In fact, Amichai saw the entire process of writing as translation, and many lines from his works were literally translated from German.[92]

The marks of forced translation may be seen in his published Hebrew poetry. Even without the verifications provided by the archival material, it is plausible to assume that many lines were first conceived and perhaps even written in German and only later turned into Hebrew verse. While the use of certain words (like "Europe," "German," and "Gothic") is deliberate, some of the traces of German in Poems: 1948–1962 are simple, basic "mistakes" that underscore the persistence of the mother tongue in the language of the adult artist. More than once, the poems in Amichai's first collection contain mistakes in syntax, the gender of a noun, or the placement of an adjective or verb. For example, he incorrectly uses the noun *sade* (field) in the feminine in two separate poems. In modern Hebrew, the word for field is in the masculine, while in German it is neutral, neither masculine nor feminine.[93] Amichai's mistake therefore derives from a remnant of his native tongue, in which the gender of "field" is different from its gender in Hebrew. Likewise, "stones" is a feminine noun in Hebrew, but masculine in German. Amichai confuses the two.[94] At times, an awkward or incorrect Hebrew phrasing hides a southern German dialect. For example, in a poem entitled "On Every High Hill," the kindness of summer days is given to a pair of lovers "*temurat lo khlum*," meaning "for free," without charge.[95] While *temurat lo khlum* sounds wrong in Hebrew, its southern German equivalent, *fuer ohne* is a common peasant expression that Amichai almost certainly heard as a child.

Many lines in the collection that sound awkward or overly poeticized in Hebrew make perfect sense when they are translated into German. For example, German word order appears in "Now, When the Water Presses Hard." The lovers in the poem live in a time of war, but are described oxymoronically with images of a pastoral landscape: "Now, when the white storks, the returning ones / become in the middle of the firmament flocks of jet planes."[96] The order of words in the metaphor of storks as jet planes is foreign to Hebrew, as it is to English. When translated into German, the structure becomes completely natural: *Wenn die weissen Stoerche, die zurueckkehrenden / zu Flugzeugen werden.*

Many lines in *Poems: 1948–1962* resemble each other in their German structure and they often recall common German idioms, sometimes revealing a German poetic sensibility or a connection to German nature and landscape. In some cases, translating the Hebrew poems to German or retrieving their German inspiration brings them back to their origin and reveals deeper layers of meaning.

Amichai's tendency to use German constructions and idioms is apparent to the alerted reader in a poem entitled "And After All This—the Rain."[97] At its conclusion, the speaker compares himself and his beloved to the rain. These lines and the image they describe are even more awkward in Hebrew than in the Harshavs' English translation: ". . . we too / are rained together / into the one who receives us and doesn't remember / The spring earth."[98] Yet when these lines are translated into German, they gain a new meaning: *Wir / Tropfen zusammen herab / in diejenige, die uns immer empfaengt ohne sich zu erinnern / in die Fruehlingserde.* It becomes clear that Amichai compares the lovers to raindrops that drip to the earth, which is a common image in German love poems. While pairing the verb *mekabelet* (receiving) with *adama* (earth) seems forced in Hebrew, in German the combination of *Erde* (earth) and *empfaengt* (absorbs/welcomes) is idiomatic. Moreover, the syntactical construction in which the object is preceded by its description (i.e., "one who receives and does not remember" precedes "the spring earth") is strange in Hebrew, yet is entirely correct in German. When German is evoked, images from childhood that are inextricably linked to it often appear as well, even when the subject of the poem is not childhood. Thus, in addition to the linguistic reverberations of the German mother tongue, this poem echoes the European landscape. The words "the spring earth" that seal the Hebrew poem derive from a non-Israeli environment. The fertile earth in Israel is the winter earth. In Europe, where winter is synonymous with snow and ice, the earth becomes ready to absorb the water only at springtime.

A particularly striking example of a Hebrew poem with German roots is found upon the careful examination of one of Amichai's most frequently quoted poems, "Half the People in the World." This is the poem that he recited at the Nobel Peace Prize ceremony for Israeli prime minister Yizhak Rabin. The setting of this poem seems characteristically Israeli, as it includes olive trees, white housing projects, and sands, but the poem's language and imagery hide its German origins. The syntax of "Half the People in the World" is, in fact, German. The poem opens with an axiomatic declaration: "Half the people in the world / Love the other half, / Half the people in the world / hate the other half." This axiom is followed by a series of questions.[99] The speaker asks if he is required to perform a variety of actions because of this divided reality: "is it because of those [who love and hate] . . . / That I must . . . endlessly . . . ?" He wonders, "[must I endlessly] wander," "[must I endlessly] change," "[must I endlessly] hear," etc. The interrogative syntactical construction "*ha'im biglal ele alay*" is rare in Hebrew. (Literally, it means "is it that because of those it is upon me to incessantly. . . .") When translated into German, however, the awkwardness disappears, for the phrasing is a German, and specifically southern German, idiom: *Muss ich* (must I).

The German phrasing *Muss ich* is but the tip of the iceberg. A German draft of "Half the People in the World" is a monument to the frustration Amichai must have felt with the final version of this poem, which lacks the draft's unity of sound and content. In a notepad from September 1957, a few lines of plain, idiomatic German form the embryo of this poem.[100] They begin with the poem's core question: "*Muss ich nicht dauernd . . .*" (Must I endlessly. . .). The

German lines ask if the speaker must search under olive trees and whether walls must conceal "songs" ("*Lieder*") made of "old stones" ("*aus alten Steinen*"). The only Hebrew words in this entire poetic segment are "*atse zayit.*" (olive trees). The German is full of alliteration, which got lost in translation. The question that is found only in the archive, "*muessen dauernd Mauern. . . ?*" (must walls endlessly. . . ?), is very musical, but could never be duplicated in Hebrew. The published poem attempts to replicate the syntax and preserve the style of the rhetorical question, along with the images of walls, houses, beams, and shelters that appear in the German notes. The German foundation of the poem, however, is much more potent than the published Hebrew. It testifies to Amichai's talent in the German language through his attention to musicality and powerful alliteration.[101]

Written a few years after "Half the People in the World," the four elegies that close *Poems: 1948–1962* are a prime example of poems that have their roots in the German notations in the archive. The elegy, by definition, is a lyrical lament for the past. It is therefore logical that Amichai's elegies, more than the other poems in the collection, reveal the poet's reliance on his early sources. Moreover, Amichai's affinity with Rilke, who favored this genre, adds another link between the elegiac form and the poet's mother tongue.[102]

A German expression is implicitly evoked in the heart of the first elegy, "Don't Prepare for Tomorrow." The title's instruction not to prepare for the future hints at its wish to remain static. The poem consists of a series of authoritative commands that the speaker makes either to himself or to someone else to remain silent, not to move forward, not to erase the names of the dead, and to confirm that everything stays and does not pass—in effect, to stay in the present or return to the past. The elegy's enigmatic images recall scenes of childhood such as narrow alleys or the mumblings of prayers. The fifth and penultimate stanza reverses the common German saying "closing the doors" (*die Tueren verschliessen*),[103] which is a symbol of shutting out the past. While the German folk wisdom is to aim toward the future by leaving the past behind and "closing the doors," the poem demands the opposite. It repeatedly commands the addressee to prevent the "terrible doors" from closing, even if keeping them open causes pain. Here, the German syntax, in which the description of the noun precedes the noun itself, again peeks out; a literal translation of these lines would read, "and to the ones closing on you, slowly, / to the terrible doors, don't let them / close on you." Furthermore, when translated into German, the lines contain an alliteration which does not exist in the published original

Hebrew poem. Perhaps these lines were first drafted in German, for in that language their sound onomatopoetically underscores their message: "*und zu denjenigen, die* **sich** *vor dir* **langsam schliessen,** / *die* **schrecklichen** *Tueren,* **lasse** *sie nicht / vor dir* **schliessen** . . ."[104] The artful fusion of sound and meaning exists only when the Hebrew lines are translated into German. Presumably, Amichai's "inner ear" could hear the music of the German even as he wrote in Hebrew.

Because the German language and landscape are far more assiduously covered up in the published poems, the archival drafts (when they exist) are often crucial to opening up many of Amichai's dense lines. One such German draft proves beyond a shadow of a doubt that the roots of one of Amichai's most important poems lie in the German language, and it reveals the role Amichai's native tongue played in his creative process. It is the draft of the third elegy in *Poems: 1948–1962*, "Elegy on an Abandoned Village" (see appendix A).

This elegy retains more of its German draft than any other work whose German draft is in the Beinecke archives. The close tie of the text to its German origin may be interpreted as a form of a suppressed lament for the hometown and also as an expression of the inner conflict between the languages. The German draft contains references to a nautical journey that ends on the shores of Israel and to the difficulties of the newcomers. Amichai ended up translating only two or three lines from his German draft into the Hebrew poem he published. Yet even in the Hebrew version, and for that matter in the English translation of it, these lines poignantly preserve the essence of alienation and foreignness: "And like some stranger / in a strange city, who reads in a book of addresses and names, / I stand and choose a hotel: here."[105] As dictated by the poetics of camouflage, however, the stranger's origins are absent from the published elegy, as well as the fact, so clearly inscribed in the German draft, that he is an immigrant.

Amichai was so haunted by the visceral emotion in these lines that they reverberate in other poems in the latter part of *Poems: 1948–1962* and become a refrain of sorts.[106] The closing lines of the poem "From a Letter," for example, echo the elegy's depiction of a stranger: "And this is my address: a street and its number and my temporary name."[107] As in the elegy and its German draft, the temporariness and the preoccupation with finding a place for the night capture the experience of the recent immigrant. The point of view of the refugee is camouflaged in the opening of "From a Letter," contained in isolated sentence fragments and nouns that are supposedly "from a letter." This latter poem deals with longing for another place, but that place and its language are camouflaged almost beyond recognition: "I will always have to go back to the places / that were not understood, and explain them again." The line may easily be interpreted as a return to either a physical place or to a portion of a difficult text in order to understand it better. Amichai used the expression "return to a place" to both signify and hide the power that the distant place and its tongue have over him; the misunderstanding of a place overlaps with not understanding its language.

While the middle stanza of "From a Letter" specifies "here is Jerusalem," and the last highlights the gray thorns of Israel's summer and the green of its winter, the poem's title and opening betray another frame of reference. The seemingly generic details that follow "the date and the address of the recipient" in the opening line are more allusive than they seem. The apparently metaphorical "Road of Runners / Messengers," in the poem's second line, is in fact a Hebrew translation of "Rennweg" (runners road), the name of Wuerzburg's wide boulevard, down which Amichai walked to school every day. Amichai even hints at this interpretation, for while the second line says the "Road of Runners," the third line states "name of a street." The association between the German site and the poem's opening lines is confirmed understatedly by a potentially morbid Hebrew pun. The Hebrew poem refers to Rennweg as "derekh hashlihim," literally, "road of the messengers." (As in English, the Hebrew term for runner, rats, is a somewhat archaic synonym of shaliah, messenger). Amichai's choice of synonym is deliberate, for the poem's "derekh hashlihim" (Road of Messengers) is immediately followed by the "kivrey hanishlahim" (graves of the deported)—a passive form of shlihim (messenger) is nishlahim (deported, sent away). By translating Rennweg as "Road of Messengers" rather than "Road of Runners" Amichai creates a pun alluding to the Jews of his hometown, who began the sad journey of their deportation on Rennweg. The mention of "ancestors" and "generations" in this context fosters these lines' connection to the poet's hometown. This poem's opening, then, is likely an homage to the letters sent by Jews to and from Wuerzburg after the Pfeuffer family had already immigrated to Palestine. The letters "received" from the people who were later deported are "eternal" ("the eternity of the received"), but they are all that remain.

THE EMOTIONAL ROLE OF GERMAN FOR AMICHAI

While the main concern of this chapter is the period that coincides with Amichai's composition of *Poems: 1948–1962*, a glimpse of the poet's papers from subsequent years allows us to see beyond the creative role of the German language in Amichai's life to its emotional one. Because German had the power to bring back memories of events and sensations with a single word, it was also the best expression of primeval emotions, particularly pain, loneliness, and alienation. As a result, Amichai frequently resorted to the German language in times when he felt displaced. His mother tongue brought him back to a place where he felt comfortable and protected. It was the one treasure from his German past that he always carried with him, and it was easy to access when he felt vulnerable.

German's emotional role can be seen in the elegies and some of the poems from Poems: 1948–1962. There is, however, a remarkable resurgence of German in the archival notepads from the 1960s, a time when Amichai wrote that he felt like "an immigrant all over again."[108] During this period, Amichai met Hanna Sokolov, the woman who would become his second wife. The 1960s were a time of great emotional turmoil for him, when he contemplated leaving his first wife, Tamar Horn, and their four-year-old son. This crossroads of torment must have awoken the memory of another time of wandering and abandonment in Amichai's life. Indeed, in a notebook from this period, Amichai even writes in large, frantic letters that he wants to go to the "city where I was born."[109]

The echoes of this time reverberate through the tortuous lines of Amichai's autobiographical "The Travels of Benjamin the Last, of Tudela." The city of Tudela was the origin of a medieval Jewish traveler, Benjamin, yet his modern double, the "I" in this epic, alludes to an additional "Tudela." The Jerusalem home of Amichai and his first wife stood on the street named for the adventurous Benjamin, but Jerusalemites call the street "Mitudela" (of Tudela) for short. The "travels" in Amichai's epic, therefore, also signify the poet's migration from his home, wife, and child: "My child's first memory is the day / when I left his home, my home. . . . "[110]

In light of the agony described in the notebooks from the 1960s, it is plausible to suggest that at a time of terrible loneliness and vulnerability, Amichai regressed to the language in which he felt safest: his mother tongue. The confessions in these journals show that at the height of his torment, Amichai reverted to the German language. Although the Israeli-born Hanna was of Eastern European descent and did not speak any German, Amichai jotted down love poetry for her in German. The discussion below refers to the materials in those classified notebooks, but focuses only on their artistic and linguistic aspects.[111]

In otherwise Hebrew drafts, German words often spring out and expose the pain at the heart of the poem. German embodies Amichai's feelings of alienation and loneliness in the first line of a poem with the Hebrew title "Geometry Exercises." The central axiom of this Hebrew poem about Jerusalem appears succinctly in German: "*Einsamkeit ist / in der Mitte*" (loneliness is in the middle).[112] The roles of Hebrew and German in the poem mirror their roles in Amichai's life and psyche. As in the poem, the rest of his world is in Hebrew, but the aching, empty space in the middle is German.

Even a single word in German sometimes exposes the wound beneath the written lines. In a notebook from 1965, whose cover reads "in my hotel in Jerusalem," Amichai describes his depression when he had to say goodbye to his son. The pain of leaving his son is compared to death. *Tod* (death), the word that embodies the extent of his agony, is the only German word on the page.[113] At that moment, it seems that the German word for death was more powerful and evocative than the Hebrew one (*mavet*). In fact, the word *Tod*, along with the word *Schmerz* (pain), frequently appear isolated within a Hebrew text throughout Amichai's writing of that tormented period.[114]

That same year, Amichai wrote what seems to be a poem about the end of a love affair, on the back of a test that says, "the teacher is Hanna Sokolov." This text is thus connected to the crossroads of the 1960s because of its medium as well as its timing and theme. In it, Amichai likens the attempt to hold onto memories to a frustrating hunt: "remembering is a hunt." He writes that at the end of the hunt for memories, when the trumpets and guns are gone, all that is left is a small rabbit. In other words, when love is over, all that remains is the meager sweetness of recalling it. The smallness of the memory of love is pathetic and almost hurtful when compared with the intensity of the experience. And yet that memory is the one precious thing that remains. The German word "*Erinnerung*" (memory / remembering) holds in it the longing for the beloved as well as memory's inability to revive her. It punctures the Hebrew, revealing the core pain of the poem.[115]

In a notebook from 1966, Amichai wrote a German poem entitled, in Hebrew, "First Snow."[116] The speaker expresses his longing for "preparations for winter" and recalls his "forefathers," the peasants who knew how to weather storms. Significantly, while the climate of the European villages is captured in German, the poem's single Hebrew line highlights the impoverished existence of the speaker, who dwells among the arid deserts, presumably in Israel. The strong bond between the language and the environment from which it stems is thus fully visible in this poem.

The exact text of the 1966 "First Snow" reappears in a notebook from 1980 without the title, this time translated from German into Hebrew.[117] Even though neither draft was published, the act of translating a full poem from German to Hebrew twenty years after it was written is a covert admission by Amichai that he was camouflaging German in his work. This finding is rare in its comprehensiveness, but it must have been a part of a wider phenomenon, suggesting that translation from German to Hebrew was an integral part of Amichai's poetic practice. A line added to the 1980 Hebrew text may be read as a lament for the language of his forefathers: "words bring up the dead and the dead bring up words." The words spoken by the dead are most likely German: his European "forefathers" are deceased and German was their language. Through this line, the Hebrew version tries to diminish the role of German. It is no longer the speaker's language, but merely the language of "the dead."

Even in the late 1970s, after Amichai's personal life stabilized and the number of people with whom he spoke German diminished, his mother tongue continued to be a powerful source of comfort. In a 1977 archival poem, Amichai included three German words that he linked with the memory of his beloved father. The linguistic traces of Amichai's early years are frequently associated with the caring father who spoke words of love to his young son.[118] An echo of the father's ability to comfort his child may be found in these three words, traditionally sung to a child who had fallen down and gotten hurt: "Heile, heile, Segen" (healing, healing, blessing).[119] Immediately after this tender German refrain is the Hebrew word for "my father" and then the German "Du! Du! Du!" (You! You! You!). It is likely that, perhaps in times of stress, Amichai remembered how his father soothed him with this song, and drew upon the language in which he was first loved to capture this memory.

The Hebrew words that follow "Heile, heile, Segen" reflect the adult poet's thought process. While he revisits his feelings as a child in his mother tongue, the insight of the adult is formulated in Hebrew. After mentioning his father, Amichai added in Hebrew, "[I]t is as if this man gave us back our lost honor." This acknowledgment, a quarter of a century after his father's death, encapsulates the son's gratitude for the father who lifted him up every time he fell and supported him when he felt humiliated. Through Amichai's memory of the German words his father uttered, the father continued to support his fifty-three-year-old son. The adult poet commented in his notebook that these seemingly small, kind gestures were everything—all a father can do for his child is to say "calming words." Amichai explained that even though the son hears these gentle words less and less frequently as he grows up and moves away, they stay with him forever.

While Amichai's poetry appropriates the liturgical Hebrew words of the father, it suppresses his German legacy. That legacy survives to a certain extent in Amichai's novel, Not of This Time, Not of This Place.[120] This book contains the most intentional and clear expressions of the power of the German language in Amichai's published oeuvre,[121] partly because he used it to commemorate his foreign childhood as well as to retrieve the melody of its language. Although the novel is written almost entirely in Hebrew, it is plain that the characters in the Weinburg chapters speak to each other in German; for example, the narrator often remarks that he is speaking German to the locals. Accordingly, the cracks in the Hebrew surface are wider here than anywhere else in Amichai's corpus. In allowing the German language and milieu even a restricted presence, Amichai went against the Israeli literary and cultural climate of the 1960s. He performed this subversive creative task subtly, weaving transliterations or translations of German into the fabric of the book. The Hebrew text, then, is inlaid with German words and sentences spelled out phonetically in the Hebrew alphabet. German phrases appear in their proper Latin alphabet only twice in the 619 pages of the Hebrew volume. Nevertheless, even this limited glimpse of the foreign mother tongue was a bold action on Amichai's part, given the dominance of the purist Hebrew literary norms during that period.

My conversations with Amichai and with Dan Miron, the editor of his novel, show that there is, in fact, more German behind the novel than the published version reveals, and that a number of the novel's Weinburg chapters were originally written in German. Both author and editor said that when the novel's manuscript was edited in the 1960s, a hundred or so pages containing entire German passages were cut out.[122] Perhaps, given the literary and national climate of Israel in the early sixties, they felt that those segments would negatively affect the book's reception. Yet despite the heavy editing, and perhaps due to the sheer quantity of German in the initial draft, the novel retains more German than any other of his published genres.

The lasting power of childhood sounds is captured on many pages in Not of This Time, and their strength is shown through the intensity of the memories they evoke. Amichai's novel is his only published work to disclose, even implicitly, the grasp that the mother tongue had on his subconscious. A particularly striking example of this occurs during an otherwise unremarkable experience: riding a train. Like Amichai's father, Friedrich Pfeuffer, the father of the novel's protagonist, Joel, was a traveling salesman. When Joel's father (and Amichai's) returned home on Fridays, he would embellish his experiences for his son, re-telling them as a chain of humorous adventures, each taking place in a differ-ent town. As Joel travels back to Germany by train, the conductor announces the names of the train stations that he remembered from his father's stories. The mere sound of the words, which is engraved in his psyche, revives the memory of his father: the train stations' "names rose up from inside me as if they were also names of my father."[123]

This emotional bond with the German language is visible, and not just pho-netic. Twice in the entire novel, the German phrases appear untransliterated (i.e. not in the square letters of the Hebrew alphabet but, rather, in the letters of the original German alphabet). They are uttered at the rawest and most vulner-able points in the novel, when the author returns to the places from which some of his most loving memories of childhood derive. Accompanied by a little local girl, the adult Joel returns to the street where his father's store, the synagogue, and the entire Jewish complex had been. Seeing that all that remained of the once-impressive structure is one outer wall, Joel is suffocated with tears. At this point in the narrative, the German language emerges, unmasked by Hebrew letters and without any translation, even in the footnotes. It turns out that Sybil, the local girl who had joined him, has missed her ballet lesson. Joel offers to intervene with her instructor on her behalf. When he volunteers to do this, the little girl with braids mutters twice in German, "*Sie sind ein so netter Mensch*" (You are a very nice person).[124] Sybil is a double of Little Ruth. Thus, when she speaks to Joel, her words of affection are neither translated nor altered, for they must maintain a degree of the primeval connection to Jewish Wuerzburg and the little girl he loved there.

In his attempt to avenge the death of Little Ruth, Joel repeatedly encounters girls who remind him of her and serve as her doubles. It may not be a coinci-dence that the only other appearance of untouched German in the novel is also associated with a young girl, this time Leonora. Joel thinks of the last letter that Little Ruth sent before she perished and her courage in the face of her inevita-ble death. While Joel is lost in thought, Leonora bumps into him. Her face is covered with water, and she immediately insists that she has not been crying, that her face is wet from the rain outside. Because he was just remembering an-other brave young girl, Joel is "filled with great love towards the courageous girl, and I told her suddenly in German, '*Komm, Kleine. Komm her*'" (Come, little one. Come here).[125] The language erupts unexpectedly, speech welling up from some unknown internal source. When the narrator is overwhelmed with love, he bursts out in un-Hebraized German, the language of his heart.

Although German appears only twice in the novel in the Latin alphabet, various linguistic and cultural German references are rampant in the Weinburg chapters. The German texts that Amichai learned in childhood lie beneath the novel's surface and often express pain and longing that Hebrew, the acquired tongue, cannot adequately capture. It is important to note that in his reconstruction of his hometown, Amichai turned to the texts that were part of the repertoire of a child who grew up in Germany, and not later literary influences. As we have seen, many of Amichai's letters to Ruth Z. also recall the folktales he remembered from his childhood and use them as springboards for his musings. The letters contain his associations with the folktales in their rawest form, while in the novel, Amichai calls upon those simple texts, reworking them in highly intricate ways and deriving pleasure from the utterance of the familiar stories.[126] These idiosyncratic retellings interweave German and Hebrew, creating a tapestry that is haunting and at times even tragic. In some cases, Amichai exploits the gruesome aspects of the original Grimm folktales in order to give the novel's revenge plot its visceral potency. One such elaboration is the story of Lore Kleemann, who lived on Amichai's street and was a classmate of his in elementary school. Unlike other characters in the novel, she appears with her real name and her father, Mr. Kleemann, is given his true occupation, a stable owner.[127] The knowledge that this girl perished in a concentration camp must have affected Amichai deeply; in the novel he endowed the story of her death with almost mythological dimensions. As if his own retelling could not adequately capture the horror of the story, Amichai recreated it by orchestrating intertexts from various sources, including the Brothers Grimm, and invented an eyewitness to recount it.

Amichai used a folktale to color the narrator's encounter in a stable with a Christian man who used to work for Mr. Kleemann. As the man begins to divulge the details of the Kleemann family's demise, a horse's head appears next to his and the old man affectionately introduces the animal, "This is the mare, Falada."[128] The Brothers Grimm folktale, "The Goose Maid," which Amichai had read as a child in elementary school, enters the novel through the horse's name. Like other Brothers Grimm folktales that Amichai knew, "The Goose Maid" is peppered with repetitive rhymes that helped the children who had to learn it by heart to remember its plot. For instance, whenever the princess passes under the decapitated head of her faithful horse, she says, "*Oh du Falada, da du hangest"* (Oh, Falada, here you hang), to which the horse's head replies, *"Oh Jungfer Koenigin, da du gangest! Wenn das deine Mutter wuesste | das Herz taet'ihr zerpringen"*[129] (Oh virgin queen, here you go! If your mother only knew, her heart would explode). The plot of the folktale is not told in the novel. It is contained only within the parentheses, which represent Joel's consciousness.

The dialogue between the narrator and the stable owner integrates the rhythm of the folktale with the main narrative of the novel: "'Oh Falada, Falada, what happened to Mr. Kleemann?' As I said this, the old man began to weep bitterly."[130] By referencing Falada only obliquely, Amichai imitated a stream of consciousness. The details of the Grimm story are irrelevant to the novel and therefore remain untold. Only the morbidity of the folktale's plot remains embedded in the memorized, rhythmic refrains. Both the real Lore Kleemann and her fictional counterpart met with catastrophe, but unlike in the case of the folktale's princess, no magical force saved them.

The old man's account of the fate of his young mistress, "Fraeulein Lore," evokes another text—that of King David's rebellious son, Absalom. The German folktales and biblical narratives that Amichai absorbed as a pupil in Wuerzburg merge in one of the novel's most horror-filled scenes. Absalom fell prey to his enemy when his long, beautiful hair was caught in the branches of an oak as he was riding. In the novel, the old German owner of the mare Falada recalls how two SS soldiers burst into the stables and killed Mr. Kleemann. Lore mounted a wild horse and drove it into the killers, hitting one between the legs. She then rode out of the stable, but her hair got caught in the lintel, while the horse kept galloping. The second SS soldier emptied his revolver into her and ordered the old man to leave her body hanging, bleeding in the doorway. At the conclusion of Lore's tragic story, Amichai quotes verbatim two 1930s Nazi expressions in the Hebrew alphabet, and he immediately translates each of them into Hebrew in the body of the text: *"Blut und Boden,* blood and soil!" and *"Kraft durch Freude,* virility through pleasure!"[131] He twists these Nazi phrases (and his sexualized translation of them, especially the second) to mock the emasculation of the SS soldier who had been kicked in the groin.

The German cultural and linguistic references in this entire episode hold the innocence and tenderness that Amichai associated with "The Goose Maid," the terror caused by the Nazis, and Amichai's residual conflicted feelings toward the German language. The German name "Falada" from "The Goose Maid" thus became a code denoting pain for Amichai. It preserved the bond with his childhood texts, but at the same time served to eulogize the deaths of the class-mates with whom he learned those texts.

The memory of Lore Kleemann clearly haunted Amichai. Her name appears outside the novel in a small, grey notepad from January 1958, in the Beinecke archives. This was the period during which Amichai wrote the elegies, before he went to Wuerzburg to prepare for the novel. The text found in the notepad, however, makes no reference to a prose narrative. It is a poem, with clear line divisions, written mostly in German. In the first line, the poem's speaker declares his wish to publicize Lore's death. As in the novel, her memory is associated with horses. She is adorned with them, wearing horses like jewelry, but simultaneously buried beneath them. The central image of this poem is of "valleys full of shards."[132] Consistent with his poetic strategy of camouflage, the poet kept Lore Kleemann's death and her road of suffering on "valleys of shards" out of his published poetry. This poem's heartbreaking, metaphorical expression of mourning never appeared in print, not even translated into Hebrew.

The novel is full of young female characters, some based on real people, like Lore Kleemann and Ruth Hanover; some fictional; and some metaphorical, representatives of the German literary tradition. The most central—and most encoded—German text in the novel is the song "The Lorelei," considered by Germans to be an authentic representation of the German soul.[133] It is a poem by Heinrich Heine, based on an ancient Germanic folktale, which was later put to music. Heine, who was born near the source of the Rhine River, in Duesseldorf, converted to Christianity but wrote on Jewish themes. He is considered the father of German-Jewish poetry. "The Lorelei" was published in *Book of Songs* in 1827, four years before Heine was exiled to Paris.[134] The legend on which the poem is based is a tale of a beautiful maiden whose father would not let her marry the man she loved. He left Lorelei to die on a rock near the river Rhine, her blond hair blowing in the wind. Her spirit still hovers on the rocks, combing her hair and eternally singing her siren song. Generations of fishermen who saw her and heard her song would forget to steer, crash their boats into the rocks, and drown. The poem was hailed as the "spirit of Germany" and a monument for Lorelei was even erected in the town of St. Goar. (Ironically, "The Lorelei" was so ingrained in the German cultural vocabulary and national psyche that despite the fact that Heine was born Jewish, the Nazis were forced to appropriate it, and included it in their songbooks for soldiers. The song's byline, however, was false—"author unknown.") The first two lines of "The Lorelei" were also adopted by German Jews to express their longing for the homeland that betrayed them: "*Ich weiß nicht was soll es bedeuten, / Daß ich so traurig bin*" (I wonder what it presages — / I am so sad at heart).[135] The beloved "The Lorelei" was part of a section entitled "Homecoming" in Heine's *Book of Songs*, and came to represent the theme of *Heimweh*, a German compound of *Heim* (home) and *Weh* (pain). Bound together, they express the longing for one's homeland.

Lorelei's image, accompanied by quotations from the poem, serves as one of the leitmotifs of the Weinburg chapters in Amichai's novel.[136] Amichai knew it well — he had had to memorize it in the fifth grade.[137] Although he mentions Lorelei in *Not of This Time* only once by name ,[138] her presence and the feeling of *Heimweh* permeate the novel. The identification of German Jews with the underlying, inexplicable sadness of "The Lorelei" is never mentioned in the novel, but many of the novel's self-reflective paragraphs confess that sadness is a dominant force in the narrator's psyche. He quotes the poem's opening lines virtually verbatim when he laments that he feels "a deep sorrow that I don't know what it means."[139] He repeatedly states that his soul is made of joy and sadness, heroism and sadness, confusion and sadness, thus pairing sadness with various emotions or attributes. The constant presence of sadness, I believe, refers back to the sorrow and longing for home that pervades "The Lorelei."

Unlike innocuous German words like *bitte* (please) and *komm* (come), which appear in the novel transliterated, or spelled out in Hebrew letters, Amichai never includes the German word *Heimweh* in the novel, in either the Hebrew or German alphabet. Its absence speaks loudly, for without knowledge of German literature, most Hebrew readers would think that "The Lorelei" was simply a romantic story and would miss its association with Amichai's longing for his former homeland or language. Amichai thus camouflaged the full significance of using "The Lorelei" as a leitmotif in the novel, but hinted to his knowing readers of his longing for Wuerzburg.

There is no Hebrew equivalent for the word *Heimweh*, but Amichai translated it literally as "pain of home," which sounds foreign and awkward in Hebrew, as in English. The reference to "pain of home" triggers a pseudophilological discussion. Indeed, on more than one occasion the exercise of analyzing and etymologizing German words in the body of the novel's Hebrew text was a way for Amichai to subtly express his love for the German language.[140] Not surprisingly, one of these explications is devoted to the word *Heimweh*. Yet, the longing for the German homeland remains masked: toward the end of Joel's stay in Germany, the old aunt, Henrietta, asks him whether he misses his home, meaning Jerusalem. The object of the "pain of home," then, is Israel.

Henrietta's speech mirrors the German language through the foreign construction of her Hebrew sentence. She says, "Don't you have pain of home?"
Instead of a direct answer, her question is followed by a parenthetical sentence
(representing Joel's consciousness). Here, the parentheses offer an extremely
specific, and figurative, deconstruction of the term: "(When a person is in a
foreign land, his home hurts him like a tooth, as if the home is a part of his
body.)"[141] The visceral pain of longing takes on the tangibility of a physical
ache. While the declared object of longing in this exchange is the new homeland, Israel, the elaborations on the German term, the foreign syntax of the
paragraph, and the distant echoes of Heine's "Lorelei" point in the opposite direction: to the longing for the old hometown and its melody and language.

Amichai preserved the feel and sound of Wuerzburg and made the music of
German tangible by weaving German proper nouns into the fabric of the Hebrew text. Names of characters such as Henrietta, Heinz, Weininger, Hein-
rele,[142] and Siegfried, and places such as Bachfeld, Oberbach, and Parade-Platz
(Parade Square)[143] are transliterated in the Hebrew alphabet, thus preserving
their phonetics. Even when proper nouns are translated into Hebrew, they
maintain their German flavor.[144] Additionally, words and idioms transliterated
into the Hebrew alphabet and interspersed within the otherwise Hebrew work
evoke the melody of Germany.[145] Dubious terms of endearment like "Kleines Ju-
denkind" (little Jewish boy),[146] administrative terms like "Memorbuch," (memory
book),[147] and everyday expressions like "Wunderbar," "Oncle,"[148] "Herrlich" and
"Guten Tag,"[148] bring to life the streets of the author's hometown and help forge
its cast of characters. For example, the word Memorbuch captures not only the
meaning of the word, but also the person it represents. The Memorbuch is associated with "the cantor who remembered everything and used to write down . . .
every birth and every wedding and every death."[150] It is the record of the members of the Jewish community; it literally contains their memory. In that, it becomes a monument to their lives, synonymous with the man who devotedly recorded them in his beautiful handwriting.

In the novel's descriptions of Joel's return to St. Augustine Street, where he
was born, Amichai seems to have made a deliberate effort to reconstruct early
sensations while still writing in Hebrew. Unlike English, both Hebrew and German are gendered languages and nouns are arbitrarily either masculine or feminine. The word for street in German is the feminine Strasse. In Hebrew, that
same word, rehov, is masculine. The first time that Augustine Street appears in
the novel, however, Amichai refers to it in the feminine, as he would if he were

writing it in German.[151] Amichai clearly knew the correct gender of this common noun,[152] but in this case, the German mother tongue overrode the laws of Hebrew grammar. The connection between the writer and the place where he was born was subconsciously connected to the feminine gender; the German "street" is an extension of the author's mother, or, at a minimum, of his mother tongue.

This was by no means a typographical error or a careless mistake, but rather an intentional slip that attests to the content of Amichai's psyche. Dan Miron, the original editor of Amichai's book, insisted that this "mistake" was actually identified by the proofreader, who wanted to correct it.[153] When it was brought to Amichai's attention, however, he refused to change it. Amichai's decision to hold onto the "mistake" is another symptom of the author's attachment to his mother tongue and his desire to preserve hidden traces of it in his writing.

The feel of German is not only transmitted through German words and grammatical "mistakes," but also conveyed through syntax. Sometimes the structure of Amichai's Hebrew sentences mirrors the German, so that although the vocabulary is entirely Hebrew, the syntax is not. In the novel, these glimpses of German burst forth in numerous instances in which the adjective precedes the noun, and not the reverse. (For instance, to be syntactically correct in Hebrew, one sentence ought to read, "Where is Mrs. Minster the good?" but the novel reads, "Where is the good Mrs. Minster?")[154]

Amichai's language also preserves the tastes of childhood, almost like the Proustian madeleine. The novel speaks of an unidentifiable "ugat lev" (heart cake), also calling it an "ugat hayim" (cake of life). It takes a knowledge of German and, more specifically, the traditions of southern Germany to decode the Hebrew names given to this pastry. They represent the traditional southern German cookie, Lebkuchen, which comes in a variety of shapes and flavors. Every child who grew up in Germany had eaten these cookies. They were so inherent to the area that even Jewish children, and probably Amichai among them, were treated to a kosher version of the Christmastime delicacy.[155] Amichai used both the Hebrew names, ugat lev and ugat hayim, to capture the name Lebkuchen. For ugat lev, the German leb became the Hebrew lev, which means "heart" (in Hebrew, b at the end of a word is always pronounced v, so the two words are pronounced the same). Furthermore, the meaning of leb in Lebkuchen is "life." To preserve in Hebrew both the sound and the meaning of the name of the cookie one can assume he coveted as a child, he dubbed it both the "heart cake" and the "cake of life." The author's attempt at linguistic precision in identifying the baked sweet in the acquired language testifies both to the perseverance of sensual childhood memory and to the way those early pleasures are embedded in the mother tongue.

The German texture of the Hebrew text of Amichai's novel is artistically achieved in a variety of ways, but the struggle to translate the untranslatable is rarely discussed. The expression *Ewig nie* (forever never) is an important exception. Amichai seems to have attempted to transmit the meaning of this phrase without quoting it in German, movingly using this attempt to capture his relationship with both languages. Toward the novel's close, after the climactic visit to the Hofgarten, the protagonist is about to bid his final farewell to his hometown. He enters the destroyed Jewish hospital and suddenly breaks down, saying "[S]eeing this, a host of . . . words flooded me, words like 'forever,' 'forever and ever,' 'never again,' 'till eternity.'" Joel continues by describing how the words fell "like leaves without meaning and without any connection to other words."[156] The words "'forever,' 'forever and ever,' 'never again,' and 'till eternity,'" symbolize both his decision never to return to his hometown (and the void that will always exist inside him as a result) and the recognition that Jewish Weinburg will be gone for the rest of eternity. In this segment Amichai enlists all the possible synonyms of "never" in Hebrew, but his narrator fails to express the excruciating feeling that seizes him at that moment of final separation. Joel's emphasis that the words fell like leaves, without meaning and detached from any context, shows Amichai's awareness that these words emerged from the depths of his subconscious: they carry meaning not through an ordered syntax or a logical idea, but rather as an amorphous gut feeling. The phrase *Ewig nie* must have entered Amichai's mind in German, yet the novel does not record it even in transliteration, perhaps because of the enormous pain that it elicits. Instead, he records its imperfect Hebrew translation, which can only express fainter variations of that pain because it is disconnected from the original German source.[157]

The words *Ewig nie*, in both their untranslatability and finality, seemed to haunt Amichai. They appear in a notebook from the 1960s, when Amichai attempted to articulate another uncontainable pain, again connected to abandonment. He expressed the fear of separating from his beloved with the same words he used in the novel while leaving his hometown. The German words *Ewig nie* follow the Hebrew words "they separated us" in this draft for a love poem that tries to make peace with the lovers' final separation. At the bottom are Amichai's futile attempts to translate this German concept. Additionally, in the margins he analyzes *Ewig nie*, saying that it is "eternity through the negative." His comment suggests that when he loses his beloved, he can only experience eternity through the everlasting loss of her, as "never" and not "always."[158]

While Amichai often tried to capture German concepts in the Hebrew of the novel, sometimes the original German is too horrific, or too redolent of the events. When this is the case, Amichai hid the phrase and its meaning even deeper beneath the Hebrew, resorting to an enigmatic, unexplained reference in Hebrew, which can only be understood by meticulously scraping away the linguistic layers to get to the remaining relic of German. The translation of *Muss i denn*, (I therefore must), one of the novel's refrains, first occurs early in the novel, when the narrator turns to Little Ruth and says, "Beloved, beloved, I am leaving you here."[159] This refrain appears again when, in his search for Nazis, the narrator enumerates their sins: "the one who had kicked Ruth, and the one who had taken her artificial leg, and the one who had laughed, and the one who was silent, and the one who took snapshots of the last Jews, and the one who sang, 'Now I must / Now I must leave my native town / But you, my girl, are staying here.'"[160] Toward the end of the novel, the plot becomes increasingly surrealistic, and the narrator is brought to tears as he hears about the fate of the deported, Little Ruth among them. The dead Little Ruth tells Joel how no one pitied her as she limped toward her demise and the orchestra played the song "I must leave town, my beloved."[161] This song, quoted twice in two slightly varied Hebrew translations, but referenced more often, does not give away the painful story behind it.

When the novel was translated into German, this song was plainly identified as the popular, lighthearted Franconian folksong "*Muss i denn.*"[162] It is a parting song in which the man says, "I must leave town and you, my dear, must stay here." Amichai would have heard this song often as a child in Germany and probably knew its simple lyrics. There is, however, a morbid history to the song. On a photograph of one of the deportations from Wuerzburg that Amichai later saw, a Gestapo soldier had written lines from it: "*Muss i denn zum Staedtele hinaus*" (I therefore must leave town).[163] He was mocking the deported Jews in the photograph by putting the parting words "I must leave" in their mouths.

This piece of information made its way into the novel in a camouflaged form: the German words that would have been so clearly identifiable are merely translated, and their phonetic value is lost. Additionally, unlike many of the songs in the novel, this one is printed in a prose format, in a nonindented line. Most importantly, Amichai's narrative does not divulge the connection between the folk song and the handwritten remark on the Gestapo photograph, thus making it impossible for most readers to either identify the song or guess its function.[164]

Thirty years after the original publication, the novel was translated into German under Amichai's close watch.[165] In it, the folk song is quoted, verbatim, in the Franconian dialect. One can consequently argue that the novel, or at least some segments of it, can only be fully understood in the German translation. While the sound of the Hebrew original is unremarkable, the German translation identifies the source and the significance of the lines.[166] The Hebrew text is thus "returned" to its "original" only in the German version.

Amichai's treatment of the German language also reveals the deeply conflicted relationship he had with his mother tongue. The mission of the novel's Weinburg chapters is described as "closing the door to the past." While in Hebrew, as in English, "closing the door to the past" sounds poetic, as mentioned before, it is a preexisting idiom in German.[167] Through this idiom, the German language encapsulates the complex relationship Amichai had with German: in order to separate himself from his German past, Joel must "close the door," thus using an expression from the very language that he wishes to abandon.[168] Nowhere in the novel is the connection between the German expression and the novel's goal explained. In the German roots of this phrase, however, lies the recognition that closing the door to the past is indeed impossible. The narrator is only partially successful in his attempt to leave his past behind and liberate himself from loaded memories.

At the end of the novel, when the narrator enters the Hofgarten, the holy of holies of his childhood, the door is still open, but is about to be closed forever. Here, the idiom "close the door to the past" is transformed into "closing the gates" and is given biblical dimensions. Instead of a closing door, an elaborate iron gate is shut as the protagonist is expelled eternally from the Garden of Eden, his childhood paradise. The entire city shrinks until it is contained within the Hofgarten; for Joel, the closing gates to the Hofgarten symbolize the closing door to his hometown and his past.

An outcome of Amichai's expulsion from his hometown is his conflicted attitude toward its language. This comes to a head in Amichai's treatment of the word "heil." This word, with which one might assume he would have unequivocally negative connotations, also held great positive connotations for Amichai. One can imagine that as a young child, he first heard the sound of this word, without understanding its meaning, in Rabbi Hanover's sermons.

As he grew older, he learned the spiritual meaning of *heil* (salvation), but in 1933 to 1936 he also heard Nazis shouting, *"Heil Hitler."* The handwritten material found in the Beinecke archives reflects Amichai's inner linguistic conflict, dramatically embodied in his two contradictory associations with the word *heil*. One fragment includes the word *heil*, written in the German alphabet, referring to the haunting Nazi salute, while other notes mention it in the context of *"Ewiges Heil,"* the "eternal salvation" of Rabbi Hanover's sermons.[169]

Amichai's narrator acts out the conflicted attitude toward the German language by going to Zurich before returning to his hometown: "I decided to come first to Zurich in order to get used slowly to hearing the German language from the mouths of a nation that did not persecute Jews. . . . "[170] In other words, he must ease himself into the German language. This ambivalence is also evident in the protagonist's occasional attempt to speak German with a foreign accent in order to disassociate himself from Weinburg and Germany.[171] The author's ear is attuned to the variations in the German speech, a sensitivity that stems not only from his innate musical talent, but also from being a native. Furthermore, the novel's persistent use of German words characteristic of the Nazi vocabulary do not let the negative associations with German rest. They encapsulate the major trauma in the narrator's life: his exile from childhood. *"Herr Gauleiter,"* *"Sturmfuehrer,"* and *"Saujuden"*[172] are all words left over from the Nazi regime. With the exception of one or two incidents, however, the German of the Nazi years is portrayed in the novel as something the narrator did not experience, but rather heard about secondhand. This distancing from the negative associations with his mother tongue demonstrates that Amichai had not yet reconciled with their existence.

Throughout the novel, however, the majority of Amichai's associations with the sounds of his childhood language are tender. Joel's quest for the lost sermons of his beloved childhood rabbi drives one of the subplots of the Weinburg chapters. *Not of This Time* endows Rabbi Manheim, the father of Little Ruth, with almost divine qualities through the narrator's nostalgic depictions of the tall figure at whom both children (Joel and Little Ruth) looked with awe.

Through the narrator's search for the sermons, the novel hints at the emotional bond between its author and these German texts.[173] This search constitutes an indirect admission that Amichai was pursuing a similar quest to gather the sounds of his German childhood: "That is why I came here . . . to hear again the sounds of childhood. . . ."[174] These sounds were embodied by the heightened rhythms of the sermons delivered by the rabbi of the

Wuerzburg synagogue, the great orator. Although the sermons do not appear in German (not even transliterated into the Hebrew alphabet), they constitute the most impressive monument to the German sources of Amichai's writing in the novel. Although Joel translates the sermons into Hebrew when he quotes them in the body of the text, he always remarks that they were delivered in fluid, elegant German. The rabbi translated the ancient Hebrew phrases, such as *hamtse yeshu'a* (grant salvation) or *rofe holim* (healer of the sick) into German. Though the language of these sermons in the novel is Amichaian in that it is mostly modern Hebrew, it resonates with the elevated tone, rhythm, and syntax of the rabbi's original German sermons. This resemblance is fitting, as it was the German music of the rabbi's speeches that forever echoed in Amichai's ears—not the Hebrew original—and it was this music that he wished to reconstruct in his Hebrew oeuvre. By attributing such a central role to the rabbi's speeches and presenting the process of remembering them as the transformation from German to Hebrew, Amichai unintentionally reveals a secret: his Hebrew poetry was in some way a translation from the language he had absorbed as a child. Nevertheless, the novel does not tell the reader the important role the sermons played in Amichai's creative life. This disclosure would have to wait until he wrote the poem "Summer Rest and Words," published in 1989.

The traceable footprints that Amichai actively uncovered in the novel remained hidden for a much longer period of time in his poetry. It took thirty-five years for the rabbi to spring up in "Summer Rest and Words." The poem refers to the rabbi as "the rabbi in my childhood"; his sermons are etched in the mind of the speaker and eventually became Hebrew poetry through Amichaian recycling. This poetic model is revealed in a sort of ars-poetical confession:

I shut my eyes
And return to the words of the rabbi in my childhood
On the *bimah* of the synagogue . . . He changed
The words of the prayer a little, he did not sing and did not trill and did not
    sob . . . But said his words with a quiet defiance, demanded of God
In a calm voice that accompanied me all my life.[175]

Like the rabbi, the poet changes the words of Hebrew Scripture and prayer in his poetry; like him, Amichai does not trill and does not sob. The rhythm of the prayer, delivered by the rabbi, clearly continued reverberating with the child who listened to it every Shabbat.

Amichai's archival writings and my 1996 interview with him confirmed his deep and abiding relationship with the sermons he heard in his childhood. In my interview, I asked him about the rabbi in "Summer Rest and Words," and he told me that his name was Zigmund Hanover; that he had preached in German and the rhythm of his sermons came not from rhyme and verse, but from the phrases themselves.[176] Amichai said that he could still remember the inner cadences of Rabbi Hanover's expressions, his sentences, and the music of his words. Rabbi Hanover, Amichai told me, brought the music of Hebrew into German; "I," he said of himself, "am returning that music to its origins." In this interview, however, he continued to emphasize the Judaism of his childhood and the Hebraism of his writing. Even when he quoted the German of the rabbi, it was in order to restore the mutilated Hebrew to the proper original.

Although Amichai readily told me the name of his childhood rabbi in 1996, he omitted Rabbi Hanover's name from the 1989 published poem. This may have been due to his continued wish to camouflage overt German traces in his poetry, such as the rabbi's German name. Early drafts of the poem written from January 1987 to June 1987, however, mention Rabbi Hanover by name: "I want to return to the words of Dr. Hanover."[177] Moreover, on the back of one of the drafts of "Summer Rest and Words," Amichai scrawled the word "Eschwege," the name of the cantor at the Wuerzburg synagogue, in huge letters.[178] On yet another piece of paper, Amichai wrote, "then I return to Rabbi Hanover / eternal salvation to those who go to their world. . . . "[179] Furthermore, Amichai repeatedly evoked and wrote down from memory fragments of the sermons, most notably the words "*Ewiges heil*" (eternal salvation).[180] Finally, in a draft of a poem found on a large, torn piece of paper, he attributes his ability to write poetry to the rabbi's sermons: "Words of / the dead rabbi of my childhood / . . . / . . . allow me / now to sing praise. . . . "[181] This admission of the direct line between the voices from childhood and his present-day verse remain buried in the draft. Indeed, it is the only place where he lets the full beauty of the German come to the surface—both "Summer Rest and Words" and the novel translate the rabbi's words into Hebrew.

The rabbi's language continued to reverberate for the rest of Amichai's life. In a notebook marked "September 1991," Amichai quoted the blessing he remembered from 1936, when the rabbi bid farewell to the members of the congregation who were leaving for Israel, Amichai's family among them. The note in Amichai's archives preserves the rabbi's old, ceremonial German, with its rhythmical repetitions, as he wished the departing Jews good luck: ". . . *und neues Leben / und neue Heimat / und neue Hoffnung*" (. . . and a new life / and a new homeland / and a new hope).[182] It is as though Amichai carried the rabbi's wish inside him from age twelve to age sixty-seven.

THE CONFLUENCE OF SOURCES

Amichai's unique diction is an idiosyncratic blend of modern literary Hebrew, spoken Israeli Hebrew, and the ancient Hebrew of the Scriptures. The Hebraic façade hides its German roots, which are equally textured and heterogeneous. This invisible diction is drawn from the colloquial, spoken German Amichai heard and spoke at home, the classical German texts he read and learned as a child, Rabbi Hanover's oratorical style, and the colorful southern German dialect. The merging of these diverse Hebrew and German sources in Amichai's imagination produced the inimitable work known to his readers.

Two words in Amichai's handwriting capture this dual foundation of the poet's inspiration. They appear in large script in the two alphabets that he knew, and contain within them a code, a key to Amichai's world. A German word and a Hebrew one are connected by a mathematical symbol to form the simple equation "Erlkoenig = *akedah*."[183] The first word is the title of a famous classical German ballad by Goethe, while the second refers in Hebrew to the biblical story of the binding of Isaac. Both were formative texts that Amichai learned in grade school and whose themes and rhythms he internalized; both resonated with his personal life and both reappeared in variations in his work.

Goethe's ballad tells the tale of the evil Erlkoenig, the king of the forest, a supernatural being who tries to lure, and then intimidate, a sick young boy who is being held in his father's arms. The father is riding through the nighttime forest in a desperate attempt to save his child's life. In the course of Goethe's poem, the reader hears a melodic yet chilling dialogue between the father and his dying son: "My son, wherefore seek'st thou thy face thus to hide?" And then, twice, the son relates to his father the seductive invitation. "My father, my father, and dost thou not hear / The words that the Erl-King now breathes in mine ear?" and later, "My father, my father, and dost thou not see, / How the Erl-King his daughters has brought here for me?"[184] The ballad ends with a pieta-like scene in which the father carries the dead body of his son in his arms as though it were an offering. "Der Erlkoenig" was a part of the fifth-grade curriculum in Amichai's German-Jewish school in Wuerzburg; the children had to learn it by heart.[185]

When I interviewed Amichai in 1996, I asked him about the place that the German mother tongue occupied in his poetry. His first response was "Der Erlkoenig." He immediately mentioned Goethe and quoted the last line of the "Der Erlkoenig" in German: "*In seinen Armen das Kind war tot*" (in his arms, the child was dead). Amichai reminded me that three decades earlier he had openly integrated that line into his epic "The Travels of Benjamin the Last, of Tudela." He then elaborated on the historical and biographical context of the episode in the epic that alludes to Goethe's ballad. He said that it recalls a traumatic experience from a definitive battle in the War of Independence and explained, "There were all kinds of volunteers who joined the Negev Brigade. . . . As we retreated across the sands, I carried someone on my back. Only upon arriving did we realize that he was dead." The association Amichai made between himself and the father in Goethe's ballad is clear. They each carried someone a long distance, trying to save his life, but upon arrival, learned that he was dead:

> . . . In the first
> light of retreat and dawn he died. "In his arms
> he was dead." Just as in the poem by Goethe. . .[186]

Without specifying the allusion to Goethe, Amichai used this dramatic image in a 1961 article he wrote for *Bamahane*. He recalled the battle in Ashdod: "I was looking for the railroad passage in the sand. In that passage, many were wounded and killed. In those pale hours of dawn I carried then a friend on my shoulders. Only . . . after the retreat, I found out from the doctor that he was already dead."[187] The ballad's ending, "in his arms the child was dead," resounds in the article, seven years before it made its way into the epic poem. Amichai transported the Gothic forest where the father frantically rode with his son into the Israeli reality of 1948. The German text Amichai memorized in childhood had provided him with the framework that would help him deal with his war experience. He metabolized the trauma caused by the 1948 battle through the rhythmical lines that played inside him in the music of his mother tongue.

These lines from "Der Erlkoenig" also reverberate through *Not of This Time* and function as a frame of sorts. As the novel begins, Joel accompanies his friend, who is secretly committing his wife to a mental institution. Joel recites Goethe's poem from memory: "[H]e will arrive to the yard at the last minute, in his arms, the dead child."[188] This first reference to "Der Erlkoenig" in the novel likens the husband who brings his sick wife to the hospital to the father who brings his dead child back home.

At the end of the novel, "Der Erlkoenig" reappears in a longer quotation, but, as in the beginning of the novel, the scene described has little to do with the content of Goethe's poem. The narrator is sitting in the old-age home after Henrietta, the old woman whom he loved in his childhood, has died:

> Suddenly I thought of a poem I learned as a child, a poem by Goethe about Der Erlkoenig, the wizard king of the trees, and a sick child whom his father held before him on the saddle on the way home. The trees, the wizard's daughters, wanted to play with him, and the feverish child said to his father again and again: "Father, don't you hear? Father, don't you see?" The father tried to calm him, saying that it was only the rustling of the branches. Finally they reached home, the child dead in his father's arms. . . . [189]

Sitting there, in his city of birth, but already planning his departure, the narrator clings to the old ballad. It relates only loosely to the dead woman, yet its plot is retold with great accuracy. As the narrator mourns Henrietta, Goethe's poem is a source of comfort for him.[190] He replays it in his mind at a time of utter loss, when his journey of return has nearly ended. The healing power of the ballad for Amichai stemmed from its origins and from its music. He recalls its closing line, "In his arms, the child was dead," a few times in the novel, and perhaps implies that while he himself grew to be an adult, the child that he used to be in Germany died.

Although he quoted openly from Goethe's poem[191] in his semi-autobiographical works (the 1963 novel and the 1968 epic), the full significance of "Der Erlkoenig" for Amichai remained hidden. Neither the novel nor the epic dwell on the crucial figure of the father. Goethe's ballad had a special allure for Amichai because it speaks of a father's love for his son. The special bond between Amichai and his father inspired many of his works and was also highlighted in interviews with people who knew them both.

A seemingly unrelated yet touching document found in the Beinecke archives sheds more light on their relationship. It is a handwritten essay about a Hebrew poet from the Middle Ages that the student Yehuda Amichai wrote and submitted to his professor, an eminent scholar of medieval poetry, Professor Shirman at Hebrew University. Its topic is the poetry of Samuel Hanagid, the Jewish medieval warrior-poet, but at the heart of the paper is young Amichai's analysis of the loving connection and correspondence between the eleventh-century hero and his son. In the essay, written on a blue-covered notebook that Amichai handed to his teacher, he calls the poet's son "the light of [his father's] eyes" and says that the son was the source of security for his father. Amichai compares King David's love for Absalom to that of Hanagid for his son and argues that his "testimony" of the "love of a father for his son" is unparalleled in Hebrew literature. Professor Shirman praised the sharpness of his student's "psychological insight."[192]

As a young adult, Amichai responded to Hanagid in the same way that he had reacted to "Der Erlkoenig," and the same theme motivated his identification with each of the texts. Both are exemplary works about fathers and sons. Amichai's early published references to the line from Goethe's poem do not touch on the true allure that this poem had for him, but the spell of "Der Erlkoenig" ultimately seeps into his poetry. Indeed, a close reading of one of his later works demonstrates the ballad's lasting influence and reveals the deepest layer of Amichai's connection to Goethe's ballad. "Der Erlkoenig" reverberates in Amichai's poem "A Meeting with My Father," published in 1980.[193] The poem opens with the straightforward recollection, "my father came to me during one of the intermissions / between two wars or between two loves." The poem accompanies the son and his father to a Haifa café and finally closes with a generational declaration: "And we didn't know then that I'd be called 'the *tashah* [1947–1948] generation.' / And I played chess with my father, *tashah*-mate." The phrase "*tashah*-mate" is a pun in Hebrew. The year 1947–1948 in the Hebrew calendar was *tashah* (Tav-Shin-Het). In Hebrew, *shah* means "chess" and "*shah*-mate" is "checkmate." Thus, the phrase *tashah*-mate holds both the nickname for the heroic generation and the implication of an inevitable death. Saying that he did not know he would be part of "the *tashah* generation" also means that he did not know that this would be the generation destined to be sacrificed.

Between the intimate father-son encounter that opens the poem and the quintessential generational Israeli self-identification that closes it, hides a remnant of the German milieu. In the midst of the prosaic account of the father's visit to the Hadar HaCarmel neighborhood, the speaker calls out: "my father, my father, before me you surely begot / cherries that you loved . . . / My brothers, my brothers, the sweet cherries from that other world."[194] The European fruits, cherries, are an evocation of the sweetness of childhood, but also a symbol for the speaker's latent wish that he could have stayed in his German homeland to fulfill his father's yearning for a son who is not a soldier. The syntax of "that you have loved" recalls the central myth of the War of Independence, the sacrifice of young men on the altar of their homeland. The idea of sacrifice was associated in the thinking and writing of this period with the *ake-dah*, or the Binding of Isaac.[195] The poem's line reflects the phrase, "Take thy son, thine only son, whom thou lovest."[196]

For Amichai, however, the father was different from Abraham, who was willing to sacrifice his son. A poem from the archive gives the *akedah* a nontraditional interpretation: the father and son "play" a game of *akedah*.[197] The father, however, is the one who dies. Amichai implicitly suggests that his own life was spared because of his father's early death, as though Amichai's father sacrificed his life to save his son. He could not grasp a father who would willingly sacrifice his son. For him, the *akedah* is more reminiscent of Goethe's ballad than the biblical story: a father who would give his last breath so that his son might live.

It is now that we return to the cryptogram from the archive: "Erlkoenig = *akedah*."[198] The equal sign is as revelatory as the actual words—it gives the same value to the German and Hebrew. This equation is emblematic of the merging of the German and the Jewish in Amichai's mind, with each text shedding light on the other. It contains the poet's universe: the German ballad of childhood, the love of the father, and the biblical sacrifice demanded of an entire generation. "*Mein Vater, mein Vater*," the ballad's child calls to his father, who holds him in his arms, unable to save him, and "my father my father" cries Amichai's adult speaker as he remembers meeting with his father in October 1947.[199]

German was the language that reverberated in Amichai's ears when he was still in the womb, the language in which he said his first words, the language of the lullabies that put him to sleep. When Amichai grew up and became a poet, these first sounds remained in the seabed of his soul. Even if Amichai had wanted to integrate his mother tongue with his career as a poet, such an endeavor probably would have been a recipe for failure. Moreover, as Amichai did not study in a German school after fifth grade, there is no doubt that the Hebrew in which he lived and continued studying became richer and more accessible to him than the German of his childhood. He wrote beautiful Hebrew poetry and is a preeminent Israeli poet, one who occupies a central role in the history and development of Israeli poetry. Yet inside him, the sounds of childhood always remained, connected to the European sights, tastes, and sensations that had accompanied his mother tongue. Indeed, as late as the 1990s, both those who translated his work into German and his interviewers in the German media remarked on his fluid, sometimes poetic, spoken German.[200]

One interviewer even commented that Amichai spoke German as if he had never left his hometown.[201] Clearly, German did not disappear from Amichai's psyche, but continued to dwell inside him, emerging in moments of inspiration when he first envisioned the pictures he would later transform into poetic imagery. The materials in the Beinecke archives confirm that Amichai's mother tongue was an important creative engine for him, but they also establish that German played an equally crucial emotional role in alleviating his pain in times of overwhelming stress. In times of sadness and despair, loss and helplessness, Amichai returned to the language of the soul; his deepest sorrows, cries of pain, and pleas for help are all expressed in German. He regressed to German in the manner that a person in emotional or physical pain crawls back into a fetal position.

Amichai buried his mother tongue in his creative work, especially in his poetry; in order to hear the voice of the poet in full, one must also listen to the music that was muted. Throughout this chapter, I have tried to show the winding path of the mother tongue, how it was preserved relatively openly in his communications with Ruth Z., how it was then pushed underground during the years of writing *Poems: 1948–1962*, and how it was given various opportunities to surface in *Not of This Time, Not of This Place*. One could argue that Amichai's assimilation of German into his writing, as urged here, somehow detracts from his Israeli persona. I believe, however, that the artistic means by which he subtly incorporated his German universe into his works is precisely what renders him a poetic genius. This Amichai is by no means less Israeli, but rather a richer and more multifaceted poet.

5 Growing Up in Palestine

Ludwig clutched the rucksack with his most precious keepsakes to his chest. From the train window, he bid farewell to the rivers, forests, and church spires of his childhood.[1] At the border post between Switzerland and Italy, the Pfeuffers waited anxiously among the trunks and packages that held all that remained of their lives in Wuerzburg. They need not have worried—the Italian police let them cross, and the family of four stopped in Venice for a few days to pick up the necessary immigration documents from the British consulate. Ludwig's father, Friedrich, spent those days frantically running between travel agencies and the British consulate, trying to get the capitalist certificate that would allow the family to enter Palestine.[2] After two days of stress, Friedrich got the papers, and the Pfeuffers arrived in Trieste in time to catch their boat. The two wooden, room-sized crates filled with their belongings had already been sent to Trieste, where their ship, the *Gerusalemme*, was anchored.[3] The *Gerusalemme* was full of young pioneers who would be the Pfeuffers' traveling companions on the five-day journey to the port of Haifa. These men and women passed the time dancing and singing Zionist songs that Ludwig and his sister Rachel recognized from school.[4] The two siblings watched the young pioneers' celebrations on the ship's deck and anticipated the arrival in Palestine with a mixture of joy and anxiety. The boat trip was a time of suspended calm, a protected existence that would end when the family set foot on the shores of Palestine.[5]

When the Pfeuffers disembarked in Haifa, their papers and their capitalist certificate to farm in Petah Tikva were checked by British soldiers who indifferently observed how Ludwig's parents, Friedrich and Frieda, knelt to kiss the gray cement of the Holy Land.[6] As he looked around at the strange, new world, Ludwig sensed that his life was about to change dramatically. At this juncture, he would forever shed a part of his German identity: his name. From now on he would be called by his given Hebrew name, Yehuda. The family gathered its belongings and boarded the train for Petah Tikva, where their relatives had already settled, along with other German Jews.[7] The Pfeuffers' travails were not over yet, however. On the final leg of the trip, the stretch from Jaffa to Petah Tikva, their train was attacked by Arabs. As the sound of the gunshots echoed through the air, the frightened passengers threw themselves to the floor of the train car. As he lay on his stomach, hoping the firing would stop, Yehuda tried to calm himself by imagining that it was all a game of cowboys and Indians, as in his favorite Karl May adventure books.[8] He eased his nerves by thinking about how he would have something exciting to write about to his friends in Germany when it was over.[9]

Finally, they arrived in the quiet, agricultural settlement of Petah Tikva.[10] An unpaved, sand-covered road led to their house, nestled among citrus groves. Everything was very different from their urban life in Wuerzburg. None of their neighbors locked their doors.[11] The nights were filled with the sound of water pumps throbbing, the wail of jackals, and the chirping of cicadas.[12] As the Arab disturbances began, the crack of rifle shots became a part of the familiar music of the night. Most of the settlers in Petah Tikva had come from Eastern and Central Europe to settle and work. Like the Pfeuffers, they were middle-class people attempting to perform unfamiliar manual labor like planting, building houses, and paving roads.[13] As many of their neighbors did, the Pfeuffers bought a little black donkey to carry the shopping and a piece of land to cultivate. Although he had grown up on a homestead, Friedrich Pfeuffer did not prove to be a successful farmer. When his attempt at farming failed, he opened a small salami factory with his nephew and remained sanguine.[14] Even though the customs of the land were foreign to him, he was able to incorporate the local elements and habits into his practical jokes. At one point he fooled the Jewish settlers by dressing up as an Arab in a kaffiyeh (a cloth headdress) and riding the family's new donkey.

Yehuda felt intoxicated by the smell of oranges that wafted from the endless green groves. He enjoyed the palm and eucalyptus trees swaying in the breeze[15] and the freedom of the wide, open spaces.[16] It was vastly different from the vineyards and rococo architecture of Wuerzburg: few roads were paved, and the children climbed trees and ran barefoot in the sand.[17] Yehuda would walk with his new friends between the groves and the sea all the way to Tel Aviv.[18]

The unbridled environment of Petah Tikva was far from the Wuerzburg "ghetto" and seemed non-Jewish to young Yehuda.[19] Nevertheless, it contained remnants of his old life. Yehuda's knowledge of the Bible and Hebrew prayer eased his transition into the new linguistic milieu,[20] and his father tried to preserve the German linguistic environment that was precious to him. Friedrich was among the founders of a German-Jewish synagogue in an old colonial building, where they continued praying in the *deutsch-juedischer ritus* (the German-Jewish custom), and the rabbi delivered his sermons in German.[21] The Hebrew babble of children at play could be heard from outside while Yehuda sat inside next to his father and listened to the German prayer service.[22] The rabbi even wrote Yehuda's bar mitzvah speech, in which he discussed *tazri'a metsora*, his bar mitzvah portion, in German.[23] For a year or two after his bar mitzvah, Yehuda was still devotedly Orthodox because he "wanted to be like his father."[24] He was now occasionally allowed to chant the weekly Torah portion from the pulpit (and would later recall with disdain those in the congregation who would wait for the reader to stumble).[25] Slowly, Hebrew and German switched roles in Yehuda's life: German grew to represent the soul and Judaism, while Hebrew became a secular street language.[26]

Upon their arrival in Palestine, Yehuda's parents registered their children in the local religious school, Netsah Israel, where Hebrew was the language of instruction.[27] This presented hardships for the new immigrant children. The ancient Hebrew that they had learned in the German Jewish school was not sufficient to let them participate fully in classes and school activities.[28] At first, it was easier for Yehuda to function in the Petah Tikva synagogue than at school, because the services echoed those of the synagogue in Wuerzburg, in both their liturgical Hebrew and German sermons.

The Palestinian school was worlds away from its German counterpart. Unlike the strict German Volksschule, Netsah Israel was almost completely devoid of discipline. Bad students were left back, so when Yehuda entered sixth grade, some of his older classmates were already sporting moustaches.[29] Children constantly broke the rules, threw things at teachers, and ran away from classes.[30] Once, a boy in Yehuda's class refused to leave the classroom, and the teacher and the janitor had to pull him out the door while he kicked and screamed.[31] The mischievous Yehuda drew attention to himself in the schoolyard soon after he arrived by parodying the first prophesy in the biblical book of Isaiah. His sister Rachel cried because he was embarrassing her, but for him it was a way to fit in quickly with the new school's rowdy environment.[32]

The troubles in the school were not hidden from the eyes of Yehuda's father. Friedrich wanted his children to receive a better education and grow up in a more European, Orthodox Jewish atmosphere.[33] It was no wonder, then, that with the eventual failure of the salami factory, the family left Petah Tikva. In

1937, the Pfeuffers moved again, this time to Jerusalem, where they would live for the rest of their lives.

A multitude of autobiographical sources elaborate on this period in the poet's life. In interviews he granted, Amichai nostalgically described running in the sands in Petah Tikva and playing in the olive groves in Jerusalem. As the years went by, these times seemed retroactively to be applied to earlier years. For instance, when remembering his adolescence in Jerusalem, he described it as his "childhood."[34]

Yehuda's first impression of Jerusalem was of an underdeveloped, small town, "a noisy hubbub of sand and exotic commotion, void of any streets or municipal structures, which was wonderful for us kids."[35] In 1938 the Pfeuffers bought an ivy-covered house in the neighborhood of Neve Betsalel, which was sandwiched between a Sephardic neighborhood and a religious one.[36] The nearby Valley of the Cross, with scattered olive trees that framed the lone monastery at its heart, became the children's playground,[37] as did the streets of Jerusalem. The teenagers would chase after the poet Elsa Lasker-Schueler as she walked down the street, because she had a reputation as a madwoman.[38]

Thanks to his inheritance from America, Friedrich did not have to be regularly employed.[39] His sense of humor, kindness, and devotion to his family and community continued unabated; in order not to offend a refugee from Germany by giving him charity, Friedrich paid him for Torah lessons that he did not really need.[40] He also demonstrated the same open-mindedness in Jerusalem that he had shown in Wuerzburg—he would sometimes take Yehuda to pray at the Yemenite synagogue, whose customs were unfamiliar to them.[41] At the same time, Friedrich still longed for the style of worship he knew; together with Rabbi Una from Mannheim, he founded a German synagogue.[42] Gradually, Yehuda started praying elsewhere or skipped services altogether.[43] As his attendance at services waned, Friedrich would lament, "Woe to the hunting dog that must be pushed to hunt."[44] Years later, Amichai wrote "A Song of Lies on Sabbath Eve," in which he admits that he had lied to his father when he claimed to have gone to "another synagogue."[45]

Friedrich's ties with his roots were not limited to his building a German synagogue in Jerusalem; he also stayed in contact with those who remained in Germany. Friedrich fondly remembered the less fortunate Rabbi Hanover from Wuerzburg and his family and faithfully corresponded with them. The rabbi had felt that it was his duty to support his congregation, and thus the Hanovers remained in Germany.[46] At first, Yehuda wrote to Little Ruth Hanover, but after he moved to Jerusalem and adolescence began, he lost interest.[47]

While Little Ruth stayed in Wuerzburg, the older girls of the Hanover household, Ruth Katzmann and Rosi Hanover, arrived in Palestine with the Youth Aliyah[48] on October 26, 1938; the Pfeuffers helped them find a foothold in Jerusalem.[49] Rosi Hanover stayed with the Pfeuffers when she first arrived, saying: "It is hard to describe how wonderful it is here, or how wonderful it could have been if not for my worries."[50] Every Friday night and Saturday lunch, the Pfeuffers invited the sisters and other recent immigrants to eat with them, and Friedrich bought the girls tickets for every play and movie that he could. Ruth Katzmann, Little Ruth's older stepsister, testified, "It was our home."[51] About a month after the girls arrived, news of Kristallnacht reached Palestine and they learned that Rabbi Hanover had been sent to Buchenwald.[52] He was later released, but the Nazis gave him an ultimatum: he had to leave the country with his family before January 1939. The letters from Germany were censored, but even though the descriptions of desperate attempts to get visas to flee were disguised as preparations for a vacation, the Pfeuffers knew what the euphemisms meant and understood the magnitude of their dear friends' situation.[53] When the girls visited the Pfeuffers on Friday nights, the worry for the Hanovers and the others who remained in Germany cast a pall upon the conversations.

The specter of antisemitic Wuerzburg followed the immigrants on the streets of Jerusalem as well: violence spread throughout Palestine, lead by the Grand Mufti of Jerusalem.[54] The shots they had heard at night in Petah Tikva had only been the beginning. Many lost their lives during the Arab revolt of 1936–1939, to which the Jewish settlement in Palestine referred as "riots." Yehuda experienced it firsthand: Arabs threw stones at him and his father when they walked to the Western Wall to pray.[55] The father and son used to take a detour through the Armenian quarter to avoid the stones.[56] Despite the tensions, the Pfeuffers maintained their traditional routines. They still invited guests for every Friday night dinner, opening their home to Wuerzburgians who knew no one in Palestine.[57] They also tried to help those who were left behind.

Like many German Jews in Jerusalem, Friedrich spent hours in the offices of the Zionist organizations in desperate attempts to obtain certificates for friends and relatives still in Germany.[58] His was an uphill battle, for he was trying to help Little Ruth Hanover. The rabbi and his wife had been able to flee to London in the summer of 1939, but had to leave Little Ruth behind in Amsterdam;[59] because she was disabled, the authorities were reluctant to grant her a certificate.[60] The Hanovers had hoped to send for her later, but when the war broke out in September 1939, her slim chances of leaving Holland diminished to almost nothing.[61] Yehuda witnessed his father's frustration as his attempts to obtain an entry visa for Little Ruth were thwarted again and again. Although by then Yehuda had completely lost touch with his childhood friend, his father and Rosi Hanover told him that she had left for Holland in January 1939 and was hiding in the Dutch underground.[62] To the teenage boy in Jerusalem, however, her fate felt very distant from his own.

Almost every Jew in Palestine had relatives in Europe and was able to comprehend—even though it was impossible to foresee the future—the danger that their loved ones faced. The fifteen-year-old Yehuda, however, was not fully aware of the gravity of the situation; he was still trying to maneuver in the tricky waters of adolescence.[63] Like other immigrant children, Yehuda was ready to shed his past and the qualities that differentiated him. Despite his eagerness to be a part of the Hebrew youth scene in Jerusalem, however, Yehuda refused to join any of the popular youth movements. He tried the religious youth movement Bnei Akiba for ten days, but resented its rigid discipline and quit.[64] He remembered all too well his dangerous childish identification with the Nazi youth,[65] and now he was suspicious of any structured organization with an all-encompassing ideology,[66] a distrust he had inherited from his father.[67]

While Friedrich accepted the authority of Judaism fully and obeyed its commandments without questioning them, Yehuda did not. He applied his father's skepticism of organizations to religion as well.[68] When he was fifteen or sixteen years old, the rules and rituals that had enchanted him in his childhood began to confine and bore him, and the once-magical prayers seemed like "endless repetitious chanting."[69] He wore berets to school because he didn't want to be identified as Orthodox, and only changed into his yarmulke when he arrived in class.[70] He did not want to limit his independence for a religion that was no longer relevant to him and argued that because he could not perceive God's justice, there was no reason for him to obey God's laws.[71] Along with many of his classmates,[72] he rebelled.[73] Friedrich begged him repeatedly to return to synagogue,[74] but despite Yehuda's great love and respect for his father, and the guilt he felt at betraying him, he felt he could not.[75] When he himself was the father of teenagers, the poet would reflect melancholically on this time, "My father was sad from it. . . . I tried not to hurt him. He tried not to hurt me."[76] Even though he was no longer observant, however, Yehuda continued studying at the religious school he attended.[77]

World War II broke out when Yehuda was fifteen, and his studies in the religious Ma'aleh High School continued under the war's shadow. Ma'aleh was an Orthodox but coeducational institution[78] with no political affiliation.[79] The classroom in which he studied was Arab in character, its windows arched and its walls thick. The principal was Dr. Katznelbogen, who had taught at the prestigious Reali School in Haifa and brought its commitment to academic rigor and discipline with him.[80] The study of the Bible was intense, with required memorization and frequent competitions organized by the math teacher.[81] The curriculum also focused on the Talmud and "general education," with less emphasis on modern Hebrew literature.[82] They studied English literature, but works written after the nineteenth century were absent from the curriculum.[83]

The faculty of Ma'aleh was made up of progressive religious intellectuals who had escaped from a hostile Europe to Palestine,[84] many of whom would later become university professors.[85] These refugee teachers introduced Amichai and his classmates to the works of Franz Kafka, Rainer Maria Rilke, and Elsa Lasker-Schueler.[86] Yehuda's most important mentor was his homeroom teacher throughout high school, Dr. Blumenthal. Dr. Blumenthal created a bond among the students in his class; together they read journals, discussed problems, and went on organized trips, thereby rendering youth movements superfluous.[87] This Orthodox, tolerant, and cultured man introduced his students to Leo Tolstoy and Kafka, and, more importantly, he taught them skepticism and independent thinking.[88]

Although Yehuda revered some of his teachers, he had not lost his mischievous edge and mercilessly mocked others. He teased his Hebrew literature teacher, the writer and radio host Feivel Meltzer, about his sentimentality.[89] Once, his Bible teacher, Dr. Brandt, lamented the fact that there was no epic like the *Odyssey* about the Land of Israel. In response, Yehuda asked, "Dr. Brandt, can I write an epic instead of homework?" As if it were a curse, Brandt decreed: "You, sir, you're going to remain a clown your entire life."[90]

When Yehuda reached eleventh grade, however, infatuation replaced taunting teachers: he fell in love. The girl was a recent immigrant from Germany who spoke only German. For the two teenagers, this became the language of love. Yehuda even started writing a diary in German; it was then the language of his soul:[91]

I waited many months and only at the end of the eleventh grade, she asked me for a book. I went to her house and I put my hand in hers and my head inside her hair. From that time on, we would stand every evening at the entrance to the house.[92]

In 1942, while Yehuda was immersed in his love affair, Rommel's Panzer Division was moving toward Egypt.[93] Yehuda heard the fright in his parents' whispers, reminiscent of their last year in Wuerzburg. Jerusalem was filled with the black news of deportations and the extermination of Jews:[94] if the Germans were to reach Palestine, their fate would be sealed. Meanwhile, Friedrich wrote to Ruth Hanover for as long as he could and continued his tireless efforts to obtain a Palestinian visa for her. He finally got her an immigration certificate number, but it was too late. He wrote to her in her hiding place, but never got a response.[95]

The war accelerated graduation that year.[96] Thousands of high school seniors gathered in Kibbutz Tel Yosef to volunteer in the Palmah or the British army and hear Eliyahu Golomb, commander of the Hagana, speak.[97] Against the backdrop of Jezreel Valley's biblical landscape, the boys and girls talked about their uncertain future. Committees determined where each student was assigned, with no regard to the student's preference, and they sent Yehuda to the hastily assembled British coast guard.[98] Yehuda completed some of his training in Sarafand;[99] he was then stationed near Atlit[100] to protect against a potential attack from the sea, with only a broken Italian revolver as a weapon.[101] On the handle of the gun, someone had carved a woman's name.[102] Standing on the sand near the Mediterranean, he grew to love the shore of Israel.[103] As a British soldier, Yehuda Pfeuffer did not take part in battle, but saw his name in print under a poem for the first time. His sonnet was published in the section named "Of the Poetry of Our Soldiers" in the military newspaper *Hagilgal*, which was issued by the British Mandate.[104]

From the Palestinian coast, he was transferred to the desert near Cairo,[105] facing the pyramids.[106] He joined the Department of Maps, lead by the geographer Amiran, in the engineering corps of the British army.[107] As the Second World War drew to a close, immigrants started arriving from all over Europe, bringing the Holocaust to the consciousness of the soldiers.[108] The engineering corps did not see much combat, but in 1945–1946, it sent stolen British munitions and dynamite to the Hagana for the upcoming struggle against the British.[109] The corps also began smuggling illegal immigrants from the Halutz movement of Cairo, at one point dressing the refugees in scout uniforms to evade the British:[110] "Seventy scouts, with Yehuda Amichai as scoutmaster, marched out of Cairo, telling the British officer they were Egyptian boy scouts making a pilgrimage to the holy city. They changed their clothes to pretend to be British soldiers in order to get on the train. . . . "[111] During this stay in Egypt, Yehuda discovered the library in the Club for the Hebrew Soldier, and read almost every book in its collection.[112] He encountered the poets of the 1930s and 1940s, and immersed himself in C. S. Lewis, T. S. Eliot, Dylan Thomas, and especially W. H. Auden.[113] He also learned to appreciate Hebrew fiction for the first time and read it incessantly.[114] His greatest discovery was the writing of S. Y. Agnon, who soon became his favorite Hebrew author.[115] After months of smuggling and reading, Yehuda was discharged from the British army in the middle of 1946 and returned to his parents' home in Jerusalem.[116]

6 "And the Migration of My Parents Has Not Subsided in Me"

Amichai, who was unwillingly forced out of the land of childhood, always carried with him the trauma of that passage.[1] As an adult, however, he insisted that the experience of immigration was "a joyous event"[2] and that there was "nothing traumatic" about it.[3] When he identified the place where he grew up, he named Jerusalem. Although he immigrated with his family on August 24, 1936, in many interviews he granted later in his life Amichai insisted that he arrived in Palestine in 1935, when he was eleven years old instead of twelve. This distortion of his biography is an indication of an inner conflict. He thought that it would strengthen his image as an Israeli if his readers perceived him as one who came to the new land younger rather than older.[4] The years that he spent as a youth in Jerusalem became a second childhood, a childhood whose backdrop he did not need to hide in the Zionist ideological context of the formation of Israel, which rejected the diasporic past.[5] The road that led him from Wuerzburg to Palestine, the long journey by train and ship from Europe to the port of Haifa, ostensibly left few marks on his poetic oeuvre.[6] Likewise, the hardships of being a new pupil in school, adopting a new language, and adjusting to unfamiliar landscapes barely reached the surface of his seemingly personal verse. Yet Amichai never forgot this turning point of his childhood; rather, he artistically disguised its influence.

Only the story "Venice–Three Times," published in 1963, retrieves any tangible scenes from that transitional period, recalling the family's train ride across the German border to Italy and the stop in Venice.[7] His autobiographical novel, Not of This Time, Not of This Place, allots only a few sentences to the days preceding his father's decision to emigrate, while the events that followed are not recalled at all.[8] A poignant and subtle lyrical disclosure of Amichai's poetic strategy is found in "As for the World."[9] In the middle of this poem, the speaker compares himself to Venice: unlike regular cities, dark streams flow through him instead of streets, as in Venice. This metaphor implies not only the opacity of the speaker's character, but also Amichai's affinity for Venice, the place where he stopped on the way to Palestine. Its connection to his migration, how-ever, remains hidden.

The poetics of camouflage, which blurs the footprints of Wuerzburg and erases the echoes of the German language in Amichai's poetry, also deletes the memory of the journey and the first footsteps in the new land. Nevertheless, being a refugee was an important formative experience for the poet and it sub-tly colored the work that he would ultimately produce. Thus, the idea of migra-tion plays a pivotal role, even in a poetic oeuvre that rarely mentions it.

*   *   *

In Amichai's home in Jerusalem, I saw a large black-and-white photograph of a long luxury car with its roof rolled back, ready to leave. The seated passen-gers are impeccably dressed in light suits and white hats. This, I thought, must be a snapshot of wealthy Europeans about to embark on a voyage. But a closer look revealed a different story. Not a single passenger is smiling. The travelers' expressions all resemble that of someone who has mistakenly bitten into a piece of unripe fruit. In the second row sits a solemn-faced, stocky man. On his lap rests a boy with fright in his eyes—it is the twelve-year-old Amichai. The photo was most probably taken in Venice, before the family boarded the ship from Trieste to Palestine. It captures the fateful crossroads in Amichai's life, after which nothing was permanent or certain.[10]

Only two works in Amichai's verse address the period of his migration expli-citly. The first, "And the Migration of My Parents," is an almost hermetic poem that appears in Poems: 1948–1962 (see appendix A). The second, the epic poem "The Travels of Benjamin the Last, of Tudela,"[11] is included in Now in the Storm: Poems 1963–1968, published a few years after his first novel. Amichai confined the experience of migration to the margins of his verse by openly dedicating just one poem to it, and burying the subject later in a less accessible genre. Just as Wuerzburg is exposed to the greatest extent in the genre of the novel, so, too, the experience of migration is most substantially revealed in the epic.

The apparent neglect of this subject in Amichai's oeuvre should not be inter-preted as a consequence of its insignificant status in the poet's psyche. In fact, Amichai's struggle with the issue of his own migration was not confined to the two texts that explicitly relate to it; the traumatic experience of the flight from Europe and the details of this journey are reworked throughout his verse. Cam-ouflaged, they form the foundation of Amichai's idiolectic vocabulary, his unique language of pain.[12] For Amichai, the initial migration journey tied travel—particularly sailing and ships—to the trauma of parting. Through the poetics of camouflage, he forged this landmark event into a poetic trope. Though Amichai rarely mentions migration by name, ships in his oeuvre are always harbingers of separation and sorrow. He obliquely acknowledges the connection between ships and sadness in a quatrain published in 1958: "Deep within the black ships, under the grief."[13] His unpublished materials make this association more explicit. In a letter to Ruth Z., he admits that the sound of a ship's horn "saddens me always."[14] Moreover, in a later fragment from the archive, he expresses the wish that this sound would cease to mean separation.[15]

The excruciating bond between ships and parting is hidden in Amichai's published verse. In the whimsical poetic cycle "The Visit of the Queen of Sheba," for example, Amichai covertly uses the biblically inspired Jewish legends about the Queen of Sheba's visit to King Solomon's palace to process artistically his trip to Israel.[16] According to tradition, the Queen of Sheba traveled by boat for three years to reach Israel and test King Solomon's wisdom. After he proved his superiority, they had a passionate love affair. This story, which in its ancient form considers a lengthy voyage at sea and the barriers of language, allows Amichai to speak about his own unforgettable journey by ship, which must have seemed interminable to him at the time; moreover, he must have identified with the experience of docking in the port of a foreign land whose language is incomprehensible. Although "The Visit of the Queen of Sheba" is about the sexual relationship between a man and a woman, Amichai dwells on the details of the voyage by sea, from the smell of the salt water to "woolly packing materials." In fact, four out of the poem's eight subtitles are about traveling by boat: "Preparations for the Journey," "The Ship Waits," "Setting Sail," and "The Journey on the Red Sea." The pain of immigration and the memories of a traumatic voyage underlie all these segments. For Amichai, ships are always associated with longings, both suppressed and expressed: "A ship in the harbor / . . . with a cargo of yearnings, / some folded and some taking wing . . ."[17] The description of the silk flags of the ship reveals the danger and suffering inherent in such a journey: the flags are made of dead migrating birds who could not reach the land of their destination.[18] Migrating birds are the quintessential wanderers and, like immigrants, not all of them survive the journey to the new land. The avian metaphor about the perils of migration indicates the pain at the poem's core. In another death, this time an emotional one, the anthropomorphized ship itself is "without a subconscious." The lack of a subconscious implies an inability to dream.

Thus, Amichai suggests that a successful migration is one that culminates in forgetting the port of origin; successful immigrants no longer dream of the places they left. Amichai, however, never forgot—only repressed.

While Amichai's efforts of concealment are present in his earliest two volumes, they are particularly prevalent throughout the second part of *Poems: 1948–1962*, which is given the somewhat enigmatic title, "The Place Where I Never Was." Leafing through the twenty-eight poems that comprise "The Place Where I Never Was" reveals a common thread: beneath their unrelated surfaces lies the subject of parting, which occupies the speaker in many of these texts. Undoubtedly, the poet's memories of the initial nautical journey overlapped with the pain he felt during subsequent separations. One may guess that the departure of the woman he intended to marry was especially excruciating. In 1947, Ruth Z. sailed away on a large ship from the port of Haifa, and although Amichai did not know that she would never return, waving goodbye to her from the shore must have evoked his first trip overseas as a child. This composite of separations likely triggered titles such as "A Man Near the Window," "Farewell," "A Last Night in the Boulevard," "Leaving," "The [trains'] Time-Table," "A Room in the Hotel," "From a Letter," and "Instructions for Her Voyage."[19] The semantic field of travel influences not only the titles, but also the content of most of these works.

The fusion of different forms of parting that dominates "The Place Where I Never Was" is presaged by the cycle of quatrains in *Two Hopes Away*. Quatrain 14, for example, merges the sadness of separated lovers with the sadness of migration. In it, the speaker's life is represented by the image of journeying birds. As a parting couple is etched on an antique box, this image of his life is etched on an abstract surface—"mourning." In other words, his life is a life of migration—and for the speaker, migration, parting, and mourning are inextricably linked. The emotional implication of these hermetic lines is stunning. Instead of a rebirth, he sees migration in terms of death: leaving one's home is something that should be lamented.

A poignant variation on this connection is found in an archival note in which the speaker's tear ducts are transformed into canals that connect distant places. This unpublished poem implies that passage by sea from one place to another is carved in the speaker's body—in his tear ducts, the canals of pain.[20] Similarly, Quatrain 27 says that the speaker's heart is about to migrate far away to the love of another woman. As a seasoned traveler, the speaker knows that preparations for a trip take the entire summer. Slowly, he prepares "provisions" for his heart as though in preparation for a long trip: letters of recommendation; "a passport"; and blood that has an "exchange rate." The insertion of the words "heart" and "blood" into the list of items needed for the trip expresses the heavy-heartedness with which he approaches travel. This conflation of the end of a relationship and migration is even found on scraps of notes in the archive. When Amichai tried to describe the most extreme state of distress, when he was fearful of losing the woman he loved, he expressed the pain through another immigration metaphor. The peak of despair and loss was akin to standing "at the seaside without a port"[21]—trapped, wanting, but unable, to depart.

Amichai's letters to Ruth Z. provide a glimpse into his interior life, and expose his first artistic reworking of the association between travel and eternal parting. In one of the first love letters, Amichai reported a nightmare he had in which the door of the wardrobe in her room swung open and revealed the emptiness inside.[22] This dream generated a short poem of longing, with the darkness inside the wardrobe as its central image.[23] One of the hangers in the poem's wardrobe trembles, as if Ruth had just taken a dress off of it. Amichai referred in his letter to the symbolism of his own dream. An armoire from which all the clothes have been removed and packed for transport is the embodiment of an extended departure.

This love poem was never published, but it nurtured those that were, like "Hayi shalom" (Farewell). In fact, many of the letters to Ruth end with this rare phrase, which later became Amichai's poetic signature, "Hayi shalom"; literally, "fare thee well." The published poem "Hayi shalom" echoes the sadness of the poem about the empty armoire, listing things like "threads" and "feathers" that remain after packing an entire closet: "Farewell, death's bundles, suitcase packed with waiting. / Threads, feathers . . ."[24] The following lines go further and equate packing with death. The roots of this morbid association lie in the tense weeks leading up to Amichai's departure from Wuerzburg and the joyless preparations for the trip, in which children were forced to sort through their belongings and pack only the most precious and essential items. He kept this immigrant mentality and later wrote to Ruth Z. that it was best to have only a few treasured possessions so that one could move easily.

On the surface, the termination of a love affair alone seems to motivate many of the poems in "The Place Where I Never Was." The presence of a feminine addressee is evident through specific references ("woman," "nipples") as well as through verb conjugations and noun inflections inherent in the Hebrew language. ("Shimshekh," [your sun], for example, is inflected in the feminine.)

And indeed, monumental poems like "Such as Sorrow" and "Farewell" feature a parting from a once-beloved woman:

> . . .
> We were exchanged like briefcases, like a raincoat
> In the stations . . .
> . . . .
> Now all that's left from your sun is the pallid moon.
> Trivial words that may comfort today or tomorrow:
> Such as, give me rest. Such as, let it all go and be gone.
> Such as, come and hand me my last hour. Such as, sorrow.[26]

Or:

> . . .
> For what we did not understand, we sang together.
> Of generations, of the dark, the face of change.
> No more my own, for me no more deciphered,
> Nipples, buckle, mouths, screws—all closed and strange.
> . . .
> Fare thee well, the packs, the valises of death
> The strings, the mess of living. . . .[27]

Lines like these, which mourn the estrangement of one-time lovers, are abundant in Amichai's verse. The building blocks of these portraits of separation tend to include images of packing: suitcases, closed buckles, bundles, and string. While it is entirely plausible to associate the loss of a loved one with images of departure, the somber nature of the action has deep roots. The initial parting from his homeland radiates its despair on all the separations that are so movingly delineated throughout his creative corpus. The pain of migration—the first separation—is evoked and reconstructed in the psyche each time there is a new loss. It may also be that because his first adult love ended with a journey across the sea, the connection between separation and migration was solidified. Clearly, these partings merged for Amichai, both poetically and psychologically, and the lines between them blurred; the subject of parting in love artistically appropriated the experience of migration. Because Amichai's migration did not fit the Israeli persona that he wanted to exude, he transferred its heavy emotional weight to a separation in the context of romance. The work of camouflage thus preserves the intensity of the experience while attributing it to a less fraught subject.

"And the Migration of My Parents" is the seventh of the twenty-eight poems gathered under the title "The Place Where I Never Was." Many of the poems in this section skirt the subject of migration but allude to it through their imagery and figurative language, providing an interpretive context for "And the Migration of My Parents." In contrast to the poems that surround it, this poem calls migration by its name and openly addresses the experience of the poet's family; yet despite its blunt title, it only obliquely deals with the traumatic circumstances of the emigration. Nevertheless, a careful reading of "And the Migration of My Parents"—considering some later works by Amichai—illustrates how the migration experience became the poet's original template of "parting" against which all other partings were compared.

AND THE MIGRATION OF MY PARENTS

And the migration of my parents
Has not subsided in me. My blood goes on sloshing
Between my ribs, long after the vessel has come to rest.
And the migration of my parents has not subsided in me.
Winds of long time over stones. Earth
Forgets the steps of those who trod her.
Terrible fate. Patches of a conversation after midnight.
Progress and retreat. Night makes one recall and day makes one forget.
My eyes looked long into a vast desert
And were calmed a bit. A woman. Rules of a game
I was not taught. Laws of pain and gravity.
Even now my heart barely ekes out the bread
Of its daily love. My parents in their very own migration.
On the crossroad, where I'm always an orphan.
Too young to die, too old to play.
The weariness of a hewer and the emptiness of a quarry in one body.
Archaeology of the future, repositories
Of what was not. And the migration of my parents
Has not subsided in me. From bitter nations I have learned
Bitter tongues for my silence
Among these houses, which are always like ships.
And my veins and my sinews, a thicket
Of ropes I cannot unravel. And then
My death and an end to the migration of my parents.[28]

The original Hebrew title and the opening line are almost onomatopoeic: Vahagirat Horay: *Vahagirat horay lo nirge'a bi* [emphasis added]; literally, "And the Migration of My Parents: And the migration of my parents has not calmed down in me." *Hagirat* is the construct state of the noun *hagira*, "migration of," similar to the English possessive form. The repeated sound *gr, gr* echoes the imaginary "sloshing" of fluids in a tightly sealed vessel. This sound continues to reverberate six times throughout the poem, until it ultimately "seals" it. It is as though migration causes the inner fluid (blood) of the speaker to shake restlessly between the walls of the "vessel" (his body). (In Hebrew "*leshakshek bedofnatoy*," translated as "sloshing between my ribs," literally means to "shake," "make noise," "splash," "rattle between my walls.") The memory of the boy's travel by ship is echoed in the poem's sounds. The *gr, gr* sloshing and gurgling recalls the slap of the Mediterranean's waters against the hull of the ship; these salty waters seem to have merged with the blood sloshing inside the body-vessel. In the letters to Ruth Z. and in his archives, Amichai recalled the strong, physical memory of the trip itself, the bodily state of floating in a vessel that constantly hummed and trembled and shook under his feet.[29]

This image is a variant of a deep structure in Amichai's writing: he perceived the self as a closed box, and the body as a fluid-containing vessel in danger of cracking or breaking. The critic Shimon Sandbank, who initially identified a variant of this structure in Amichai's work, attributed it to Rilke's influence on him.[30] Later, Dan Miron suggested that this image stems from Amichai's military involvement; a soldier's greatest fear, Miron argued, is the perforation of the body-box, a wound that would cause fatal bleeding.[31] But another vessel is just as strongly at play here. The refugee child on board a ship must have been scared of holes in the hull. The child's fear of a breach that would cause the ship to sink and drown the passengers preceded the soldier's attempt to protect the wholeness of his body-box in battle. The identification of the traveler with the vessel that bears him, with the container, already exists in very early poems by Amichai, as well as in those that were never published.

In a short poem Amichai sent to Ruth Z. on October 8, 1947, entitled "Go to the Port, My Girl," he says that his body is a boat, anchored at midnight in the port, waiting. Its oil is his blood, its light is his light, and the humming that comes out of its belly is his poetry. The basic rhythm and rhyme of the poem are reminiscent of a children's song. Despite its simplicity, one can clearly observe in it the creation of Amichai's artistic perception of himself as a vessel, and, specifically, as a ship.[32]

A similar self-perception appears in "Mashakht oti kemo sefina" (You Pulled Me Like a Ship), a poem Amichai published in *Likrat* in the summer of 1952.[33] This poem shares its female addressee, its simple structure and sound, and the identification of the speaker with the boat, with the unpublished "Go to the Port, My Girl." The 1952 poem was not included in a book, however, until almost two decades later.[34] The two published versions (in 1952 and 1970) are not identical, and the difference between them is telling: the word Amichai used for ship in 1952 is the medieval word "*oni.*" He chose this rare synonym because the words *oni* (ship) and *ani* (I) look virtually identical in Hebrew, for they are spelled exactly the same way.[35] The written reference to a ship as *oni* highlights its resemblance to *ani,* thus emphasizing the affinity between the ship and the self. While the later version deletes that word game by using the more common word for a ship, *sefina,* it maintains the identification between the speaker and the ship—"You pulled me like a ship / Into the port of your secret."

Elsewhere in his poetry, Amichai uses the concept of ships as embodiments of the self and the body to capture other traumatic separations. Fragments of the jarring, traumatic voyage resurface in other painful junctures in the poet's lyrical accounts. An early poem, "Autobiography 1952," portrays Amichai's emergence as a young man. This pseudo-autobiographical poem avoids any explicit mention of Amichai's escape from Germany and camouflages the passage from one land to another. The trauma of migration, however, peeks through in its figurative vocabulary; the excruciating parting from a beloved father is told in this lyrical poem in the language of ships and sea travel: "My father built over me a worry, big as a shipyard / and I left it once, before I was finished, / and he remained there . . ."[36] The autobiographical narrator of this poem has become an unfinished ship leaving its dock, bidding farewell to its beloved builder.

It is possible that the poem's opening, the journey by sea that followed the detachment from the worried father, covers the pain of the journey that followed the abrupt exodus from the homeland. While separation from one's father is a universal process of maturation and therefore legitimate in the patriotic mood of the time, the departure from Germany had to be camouflaged. Furthermore, although Amichai's father immigrated to the Land of Israel with Amichai, the journey of migration overlapped with the poet's emotional distancing from the European father and his world.

The connection between Amichai's departure from Germany and the separation from his father is confirmed by a later poem entitled "These Are Preparations for a Trip," a German draft of which is found in the Beinecke archives.[37]

The word "*Reisevorbereitungen*" (preparations for a trip) appears twice, and the act itself is characterized by a series of negatives: to prepare for a trip is "not to eat, not / to go," and, notably, "not to stand together." The fact that the draft is written in German and involves restrictions rather than the excitement of embarking on a journey signals that it is about the departure from Germany. An excruciating line written in Hebrew in the draft describes the father after his death, "imprisoned in the holy ark" and weeping as he never had before. For both father and son, then, breaking away from Germany was a painful period that encompassed leaving their homeland as well as ending their shared worship in their beloved synagogue. Amichai's story "The Times My Father Died" describes the events that surrounded the departure from Germany as a series of his father's "deaths." All this charged material, which made its way into Amichai's published poetry much later, is condensed in the opening lines of "Autobiography 1952," about an unfinished ship leaving a shipyard.[38]

The poem subsequently likens the arduous movement of the young man's life away from his father to "the movement of many slaves rowing a ship." This text finally ascends toward an optimistic future and a pregnant woman, but it remains fraught with anxiety:

> And the twentieth century was the blood in my veins,
> Blood that wanted to go out to many wars,
> Through many openings.
> It pounds on my head from inside
> And moves in angry waves to my heart.[39]

From the lines quoted here, it becomes evident that the image of the blood sloshing inside closed vessels served Amichai to portray both the fear of being wounded in battle and the inner turmoil that overwhelms the speaker in 1952, three years after the end of the War of Independence.

The primary experiential source of the body / vessel image, however, is not suggested until the poem "And the Migration of My Parents." In that poem, blood sloshes between the walls of the vessel, the veins entangle, and houses are not fixed in their place but, rather, move like boats. Amichai's childhood experience of migration thus becomes interwoven with unrelated subjects through the figurative language and is used in the artistic rendition of later traumas, like war.

Violence and suffering are wrought by images of sailing and of an endangered body / container in yet another poem from the early fifties, "Yehuda Ha-Levi." This portrait of Yehuda Ha-Levi, the medieval poet, mirrors Amichai's own torments surrounding both migration and creativity. According to legend, Yehuda Ha-Levi's nautical pilgrimage from Spain to the Holy Land ended tragically under the hooves of an Arab rider in Jerusalem.

> His forehead: a sail, his arms: oars
> to carry the soul inside his body to Jerusalem.
>
> But in the white fist of his brain
> he holds the black seeds of his happy childhood.
>
> When he reaches the beloved, bone dry land –
> he will sow.[40]

At the journey's end lies the rupture, the broken skull that symbolizes both the fertility of writing and the dangers of moving away from the place of one's "happy childhood." Memories of the speaker's childhood, the raw material of poetry, are kept in the brain's sealed box. Opening that box would enrich the beloved land with seeds, but would cost the poet his life. Fragments from Amichai's own migration are scattered in this short poem; it begins with sea travel and progresses to the knowledge that the self, the brain filled with kernels of childhood, may burst open as a result of the journey. By displacing the trip to the medieval arena, Amichai camouflaged the authentic, personal resonance of the poem.

Sea travel and the danger to the integrity of the self, however, are not the only images associated with the experience of migration. Another element from the semantic field of travel in this poem is packing: travelers who carry all that is dear to them in such sealed "containers" as their bodies, their skulls, and their coffers frequent Amichai's verse. The aforementioned poem "Farewell" transports the image of luggage to the arena of love. As the lovers depart, they seem to fasten the buckles on themselves. "No more my own, for me no more deciphered, / Nipples, buckle, mouths, screws—all closed and strange."[41] As discussed in chapter 3, the image of the beloved as a suitcase made its way to a much later (1989) poem, "Little Ruth."

Amichai's initial nautical journey survived in his verse through the very words he chose as well as his imagery. In "And the Migration of My Parents," the gurgling, repeated consonants g and r carry meaning through their etymology. Two unrelated Hebrew verb roots—Gur, to fear, and Gur, to dwell—contain both consonants. Both these meanings are implied in the poem. While fear (Gur 1) is a constant undertone in the life of a refugee, the quest for a new residence (Gur 2) is the goal of new immigrants. Furthermore, the biblically recorded migration of the Hebrews to Egypt, or, as it is called, the experience of "having been a ger [stranger, foreigner]," has been imprinted in the Hebrews' collective memory and has motivated some of their ethical code. The commandment to be kind to temporary residents, migrants of sorts, derives from national history: "for you were strangers [gerim] in the land of Egypt."[42]

While the term ger is over two millennia old, the poem's original Hebrew title, "hagira" (which could be translated as "migration," "immigration," or "emigration"), is a neologism derived from Arabic. And yet, the modern word carries with it primeval fears, the anxiety of homelessness, and the sound of the twelve-year-old boy's blood sloshing. In the poem, the proximity of the word "hagira" to the word "dami" (my blood) brings to mind the noun hagara as well: the act of pouring out liquid, especially blood (from the verb root N.G.R., to pour out). One may then imagine the migration of the parents as their figurative pouring-out of the child himself, or of the child's living fluids, from one vessel to another, one country to another.

Hagarat dam is also the Hebrew equivalent of the shedding of blood. Through its soundscape, the text may then imply that migration is closely associated with the violent spilling of blood. The passage from the German home to the new land is thus laden with potential violence, not a far-fetched implication in the case of Jewish immigration to British Mandatory Palestine from Nazi Germany in 1936.

The overdetermination in Amichai's choice of words is evident not only in the onomatopoeic sounds g, r, with their various echoes; in the biblical reverberations of the roots gur (dwell) and gur (fear); and in the association with hagarat dam (bloodshed), but also in the term hagira itself, which reveals a clear ideological bias. While the Zionist perception of Jews coming to the Land of Israel is one of "ascent," or aliya, the poem's speaker tells of a "migration," a word devoid of any national connotations. Jews who arrived there during that period were called ma`apilim (climbers) and later olim (ascenders). The quasi-derogatory word mehagrim (imm / emigrants) was reserved for those rootless wanderers who searched for a place in which to reside, without any ideological motivation. This word choice is particularly curious when one takes into account the background of the speaker, who is reporting an autobiographical event. His Orthodox Jewish family deliberately chose to come to the Land of Israel, as opposed to America or Australia.

Amichai's choice of the word "migration" to identify his family's move from Germany to Palestine allows the reader a peek into the otherwise-camouflaged experience of the child refugee, for whom the move from one land to another felt like a "migration," not an ascent. It is but one of the cracks in the collection's smooth Israeli surface.

Furthermore, the phrase "the migration of *my parents*" (emphasis added) distances the speaker from the experience. It is as though the child who accompanied his mother and father on their journey was either absent from the scene or objected to it. The detached perspective of the twelve-year-old, which is merely implied here, is more explicitly divulged in "The Travels of Benjamin the Last, of Tudela." This 1968 epic refers to the child's entry into Israel in three separate verses: "—the earth that I didn't kiss when I was brought to it / as a child";[43] "[Richard the Lionhearted] He too was brought / with the traveling circus to the Holy Land";[44] "I didn't kiss the ground / When they brought me as a little boy / to this land."[45] The rare, passive voice of the verb *bo'* (to come), is employed in all three references to the arrival in Israel. The first-person narrator, then, is a pawn who was involuntarily moved from Germany to Palestine. In addition to the use of the passive voice, the speaker's reluctance is manifest in his insistence to not kiss the ground, a traditional symbolic act of gratitude for reaching the Holy Land. This defiance peaks in equating the child immigrant to the Crusader King, for they were both brought with a "traveling circus" to a glorified place (for the poem's speaker, glorified unjustifiably).

At the same time, the reference to "migration" as the parents' affair (rather than the child's) may hide a completely different awareness; i.e., a feeling of compassion for the adults' struggle. In the very middle of the twenty-four-line-long text, an ungrammatical phrase appears: "My parents in their very own migration." That broken phrase is framed by the preceding "My heart barely ekes out the bread / Of its daily love" and is followed by: "On the crossroad, where I'm always an orphan." In other words, the parents' migration is compared to their death. They are no longer able to protect their child, or even love him in the same way that they did before the crisis. As a result of migration, the child must struggle to obtain his "daily love" and is forever standing at a crossroad. He is an eternal orphan of parents who lost not only their home, but also their omnipotent status.

Following the powerful opening, "And the Migration of My Parents" continues with a succession of short, disconnected, at times incomplete, sentences and ambiguous phrases. It finally closes with forthright lines that echo the bold opening. There is no chronological or logical order to the images, actions, and objects. Inner tumult and a feeling of being lost are manifest in the syntax and grammar as well as in the content. At the heart of this less coherent middle section of the poem, an inner battle seems to be raging between remembering and forgetting, between a painful past and attempts to rebuild. "Night recalls and day causes to forget." The series of lines, reminiscent of a stream of consciousness, seems to present morsels of old conversations, fragments of memories that have escaped from under the lid of repression, and traumatic events disguised by ambiguous language. Staccato phrases such as "Terrible fate," "Patches of a conversation after midnight," and "Progress and retreat" contribute to the chaotic nature of the text. These phrases recall the broken voices of adults' anxious conversations that the child heard from his bedroom. The reader can almost hear a parent's retelling of someone's "terrible fate" and guess the fear surrounding a child who overhears the terror in his parents' voices. The "terrible fate" spoken about "after midnight" may even conceal the specific incident that hastened the migration: Amichai's father's seeing the corpses of two Jews who had been beaten to death. The poem "Through Two Points Only One Straight Line Can Pass," contains the only other reference to the child's perception of the Nazi period's horror and of the family's preparations to leave Wuerzburg. In it, he discloses that "inside, they spoke German about imminent danger."[46] These faint echoes, isolated from any context, are the only remnants of that terror in Amichai's poetry.

A tiny notepad from November 1958 confirms the association between the poem "And the Migration of My Parents" and actual exchanges Amichai remembered from his childhood.[47] The notepad includes the published poem's first line, followed by a line in which the speaker says that his parents "spoke to me about the events." This sentence was not included in the published version; it is most likely the uncamouflaged precursor of the phrase "patches of a conversation after midnight." In his revisions, Amichai made this line more abstract and placed it later in the text, thus scrambling the chronological causal connection.

In the published poem, he separated the migration from the parents' pivotal conversation that led to it, using lines that grapple with the relationship between a place and the people who live in it: "the earth forgets the steps of those who trod her." It is as though the land betrayed those who naively thought it was their home. The force that helped erase their footprints from the ground hides in an untranslatable pun, "Winds of long time." "Wind" (ru'ah) in Hebrew also means "spirit," so the "wind of time" (*ru'ah hazman*) is also the "spirit of time," and, therefore, the equivalent of the German Zeitgeist. The conflict between the human product, Zeitgeist, and the land is perhaps the essence of Jewish emigration. Germany's earth forgot the Jews, people who were her children, who had helped to form her spirit. The Zeitgeist of Germany in the 1930s was the "spirit" or the "wind" of time that blew the Jews away.

The poem is written as one continuous text, without stanzas, as though the migration is an undifferentiated mass of unrest. The word "*hagira*" in the poem's title is appropriately translated as "migration," thus preserving the Hebrew word's directional neutrality: it does not specify emigration or immigration. Nevertheless, every migration has two parts—leaving one country and entering another. The poem does not mark that divide structurally, but its first seven or eight lines address the cruelty of the homeland while the remainder of the poem confronts the torment of trying to assimilate into the new land. After the "patches of conversation," the poem moves into a no-man's-land of memory and forgetfulness, which serves as an understated divide between the two sections.

The latter segment introduces the Israeli landscape into the poem with the word "desert" and hints at the new immigrants' confusion in the face of unfamiliar norms: "Rules of a game / I was not taught." Contributing to this confusion is the immigrant's inability to speak the local language. Amichai accentuates this frustration in the poem by placing it after the last full repetition of the refrain, "And the migration of my parents has not subsided in me":[48] "And from bitter nations I learned / Bitter languages for my silence / Among the houses, which are always like ships." He whose footsteps were forgotten by the ground on which he first walked will always be a mute of sorts. Languages become bitter in his mouth because none of them are fully his own.

A second archival draft of "And the Migration of My Parents"[49] from September 1958 contains two variations on the phrase "From bitter nations I learned. . . ." In one variation, the line appears as it was later published. In the other, it is not the "I" who "learned from bitter nations," but rather "the dead" who are arriving on the shores. This second, unpublished, and more morbid variation implicitly compares refugees to dead people, suggesting that by the time they arrive on the new shores, they are mere ghosts of who they used to be.

Amichai did not allow the full graphic depiction of the struggle to acquire the "bitter languages" to appear in verse until six years after the publication of "And the Migration of My Parents." It is "The Travels of Benjamin the Last, of

Tudela" that portrays the cruel "education" provided by history as a form of castration:[50]

> History is a eunuch,
> Looking for mine too
> To castrate, cut with paper sheets
>
> . . .
>
> To block my mouth forever
> With whatever she cut,
>
> . . .
>
> So I sing only an impotent chirp,
> *So I learn many languages*
> *And not one tongue of my own. . .*[51]

(Emphasis added.) Throughout the epic, the individual is completely vulnerable, and history abuses him without pity, physically as well as mentally. The castration here is a symbol of both the speaker's helplessness in the face of history and his muteness. In this segment, the penis is equaled to the tongue; it is the place of masculine potency, while the tongue is the place of creative potency. History can strip a man of his masculinity and a writer of his tongue.

The last two lines of the above-quoted segment of the epic illuminate their hermetic counterparts in "And the Migration of My Parents": "I learned / Bitter languages for my silence." In "The Travels of Benjamin the Last, of Tudela," Amichai writes that history forced his migration, and thus forced him to learn many languages. As a result, he will never speak any of these languages well— no language will be his own. And so, learning many "bitter languages" makes him a mute, with no language in which he can fully express himself.

The "bitter languages" that do not belong to him in "And the Migration of My Parents" are echoed in the houses that are never real homes. The houses "are always like ships"—they are adrift, never fully belonging to one land, just as the speaker never has a home or a language of his own. In these two lines, the desire for a mother tongue and a motherland overlap. Whereas the opening of the poem suggests the existence of a ship only through the *gr, gr* sloshing sound of waters, at its close, houses become ships, and the speaker's veins and sinews are like "a thicket / of ropes I cannot unravel." The memory of the 1936 formative voyage is summoned through ships and sea, sails, ropes, and waves. This image recalls Amichai's portrayal of the medieval poet and traveler Yehuda Ha-Levi, his "forehead: a sail; his arms: oars."[52]

While "ropes" are associated with ships, the word "thicket," in both Hebrew and English, is a clear marker (for the reader familiar with the Bible) of the binding of Isaac: "And Abraham lifted up his eyes, and looked, and behold behind him a ram caught in the thicket by his horns."[53] The proximity of the "thicket" to the idea of being entangled, as well as the inability to untangle the knots, evokes the quintessential story of sacrifice. The Land of Israel to which Amichai migrated, or rather, "was brought," as a child became an arena for wars in which he was made to fight, thus being offered up as a sacrifice. Although this reference is merely insinuated here, the perception of the young men of Amichai's generation as sacrificial lambs in the new Land of Israel is evident in Amichai's poetry as well as in the poetry of other members of his generation.[54]

The poem's final words echo its title, but what was open and restless at the beginning comes to rest at the end. The only dénouement possible for the emigrants' child is death: "And afterwards / my death and an end to the migration of my parents." Only with his death will the memory and the trauma of migration be over.

Through the cracks, the refugee experience creeps up almost in every one of the twenty-eight poems under the inner-title "The Place Where I Never Was." Hidden by imagery and ambiguity, the turmoil of Amichai's flight from his hometown in Germany continues to churn. It finds expression in words or phrases from the semantic field of journeys, such as "road," "exit," "outskirts," "old letter," "going home," "map," "hotel room," and "the whistle of a ship." The twenty-eight poems use this language in similes and metaphors: a painful deliberation before an action is described as a Cain-like wandering;[55] when a man standing by a window questions the direction of his life, his "thoughts sail around him like ships." Amichai also describes this man's turmoil in terms of packing: "Fold for him his suit, his atonement, in a suitcase."[56] In another poem, the parting of lovers transforms them into articles of travel: "Like two bags we were interchanged for each other, like a raincoat / in the stations. Now I am no longer I, and you are not you."[57] The "antiheroes" portrayed in "The Tired People" are clearly immigrants, though not declared as such.[58] They return to their houses after work, when "Night is open like a sea. They will not sail. [. . .] They belong to somebody, to something. / And they dream in their faraway mother tongue." Other poems in the same sequence contain even more of Amichai's idiolectic vocabulary of wandering. Most notably, the title poem, "The Place Where I Never Was," is full of characteristic travel words.

In the place where I never was
I never shall be. The place where I was, as if
I never was there. Human beings wander away
Far from the place of their birth
And far from the words their own
Mouth uttered,
[. . .]
And what I shall never return
To see, I must love forever.
Only a stranger will return to my place. But I shall
Inscribe the words again, like Moses,
After breaking the first tablets.[59]

Although it is less personal than "And the Migration of My Parents," this poem touches the raw experience of the refugee-poet. The schematic nature of the opening lines belies the pain beneath them: the speaker will never revisit the places he roamed as a child. He longs for the land he has left, but the land behaves as though he "never was there," bringing to mind the line "Earth / forgets the steps of those who trod her" from "And the Migration of My Parents." "The Place I Never Was" equates the yearning for the place with the yearning for the language: "Human beings wander away / Far from the place of their birth / And far from the words their own / Mouth uttered. . . . "[60]

A more wrenching expression of new immigrants' painful struggle to learn the local language is found in a poem scribbled on a small pad marked "September 1957," under the Hebrew title "New Immigrants."[61] As though to demonstrate the process of learning and constantly changing languages, the poem alternates between Hebrew and German. The Hebrew sentence "the woman learns the language" is framed by blood; the lines preceding it recall "red trees" near "the slaughterhouse" and a few lines below, the earth looks like an "execution wall." By placing the weeping woman who is learning the language in this context, Amichai endows the scene of language acquisition with an aura of wounds and trauma. These images also recall elements of the poet's biographical background. The bloody earth likely alludes to the salami factory that Amichai's father opened and ran for a short time in Petah Tikva. The reference to a slaughterhouse thus dates the scene to the first year of Amichai and his family's migration; this is where they settled when they first arrived from Germany.

* * *

Such archival materials tangibly retrieve the feelings that were suppressed and denied in both Amichai's poetry and his public interviews. His decision not to publish them and, in many cases, not to translate them into Hebrew, must be interpreted as an active decision to keep the pain associated with his status as an immigrant from his wide readership. The papers in the archive openly group together travel, the difficulties of adjusting, and longing, sometimes in the same line and often in the same poem. One particularly telling scrap describes the process of assimilation in terms of travel. In it, the speaker envies the sea and the mountains, for they never have to wander. Unlike him, they are permanent and, therefore, have a memory. He, however, is crumbling and forgetful because he has no roots.[62] Another image from the archives encompasses the entire experience of migration and its lasting effects. Amichai wrote that the conductor punched his ticket, and through the hole in that ticket, he looked at the world. One can imagine the young boy on the train ride to Italy trying to amuse himself by peering through the hole in the ticket at his family and the foreign landscape speeding by. The adult's recollection of that image, however, captures the metaphorical significance of this game: for the rest of his life, he would see the world through the hole of a train ticket—from the point of view of a traveler and an immigrant.[63]

Wandering and exile rarely surface as subjects in Amichai's verse, but they lie beneath much of his writing and are brought to light through his poetic imagery. "And the Migration of My Parents" is unique in Amichai's corpus in that it is a concentrated, direct rendering of his own traumatic migration.[64] Homelessness, the vulnerability to violence, loneliness, the absence of language and orphanhood, all associated with migration, are all embodied in this poem. Yet even this singular text is highly ambiguous. It holds such a compact mass of camouflaged pain, that it requires an analysis of the poems that surround it, other published works, and archival materials, in order to understand all of its layers.

In the poet's published and unpublished works, traces remain of his initial journey from Germany to Palestine, from Ludwig Pfeuffer to the national poet Yehuda Amichai. For Amichai, the vocabulary of travel became the vocabulary of pain; migration, the blueprint for loss.

1. Wuerzburg and the Saints Bridge, located near Amichai's first home.
Seen across the River Main. Photograph courtesy of Dr. Christian Leo.

2. View of the castle and the Saints Bridge from Wuerzburg proper.
Copyright Bayerisches Landesamt für Denkmalpflege, München.

3. The old City Hall and Vierroehrenbrunnen (four pipes fountain) in Amichai's early childhood neighborhood (1897). Copyright Bayerisches Landesamt für Denkmalpflege, München.

4. An alley intersecting the street where Amichai was born, Augustine Street (1910).
Copyright Bayerisches Landesamt für Denkmalpflege, München.

5. The interior of the Wuerzburg synagogue that Amichai and his family attended. Rabbi Zigmund Hanover was the officiant. Photograph courtesy of Dr. Christian Leo.

6. Rabbi Hanover and his family. *Top (from the left):* Ruth Katzmann, Ruth Hanover. *Bottom (from the left):* Rosi Hanover, Rabbi Sigmund Hanover, Ernestina Hanover (née Deutsch). Photograph courtesy of Judith Silber (Kobliner).

7. A contemporary photograph of the Residenz and the Hofgarten (Wuerzburg's palace and gardens). Amichai and Ruth Hanover passed through the Hofgarten every day on their way to school. Photograph courtesy of Dr. Christian Leo.

8. Statues of putti in the Hofgarten (1906). Copyright Bayerisches Landesamt für Denkmalpflege, München.

9. The gates of the Hofgarten in Wuerzburg (1911). Reproduced by permission of the Anne and Jerome Fisher Fine Arts Library, University of Pennsylvania.

10. A second-grade classroom in the Volksschule Amichai attended (similar to the one he would have sat in), circa 1934. Photograph courtesy of Elizabeth Cecchetti.

11. A picture from a 1927 songbook used in the Volksschule while Amichai was a pupil.

12. Ruth Hanover ("Little Ruth"), Amichai's best friend, age 15 (1938). Photograph courtesy of Yehudit Silber.

13. Amichai, age 23, portrait photo. Amichai mailed it to Ruth Z. on November 24, 1947. Photograph courtesy of Ruth Z.

14. Amichai and his students during a gym class he taught in the Geula Elementary School yard in Haifa. Amichai mailed it to Ruth Z. on November 24, 1947. Photograph courtesy of Ruth Z.

15. Amichai, age 38. This photograph was taken the year his canonic collection *Poems: 1948–1962* was completed (1962). Reproduced by permission of the Government Press Office of the State of Israel and photographer Fritz Cohen.

16. Amichai, age 74 (1998). This photograph appeared on the commemorative stamp issued on the anniversary of the poet's death in 2001. Reproduced by permission of photographer Dan Porges.

7 The Love Story

As the new veteran Yehuda Pfeuffer climbed the stairs of the Bet Hakerem Teachers Seminary[1] in Jerusalem on a bright Sunday in June 1946, he did not know that at the top was the woman who would eternalize for him the connection between ships and sadness. The crash course from which they would both graduate was already well underway. It was a special class, made up of twenty-two men and four women, all recently discharged from the British army and in need of a profession. On the Friday before his first day of classes, Yehuda was invited to a party in the Kiriyat-Shmuel neighborhood. At midnight, after the party ended, twenty of the guests walked down the middle of the empty street, chatting all the way back toward Rehavia, where many of them lived. The conversation of those who had just been discharged revolved around their experiences in the military and their plans for a civilian future.

Yehuda was attracted to a woman in a green silk dress, and started walking by her side. Her name was Ruth and, sixty years later, she still remembers the details of that conversation.

"I overheard that you are at the teachers' college," he began. "I was just discharged and I registered for the course, but I am afraid that I missed important material."

To his surprise, Ruth gave him her address on Ramban Street and said, "I can lend you my notebooks."[2]

"You don't mind if I copy your notes?" he asked. "Many people don't like to share."[3]

He stopped by her home the next day, a Saturday, to borrow her notebooks, thanked her politely, and returned them on Sunday. He may have known that he would go back to the house on Ramban Street.

This encounter marked the beginning of a time of tentative peace both in Amichai's life and in the life of his country, Israel. Despite the intermittent violent clashes with the Arabs and the growing tension with the British, which peaked with the bombing of the British headquarters in the King David Hotel by the militant Jewish underground, Israelis would later call this interval in history "the time between the wars." The Second World War had ended and looming in the unknown future was the end of the British Mandate in Palestine and the ensuing eruption of Israel's War of Independence in 1948. The poet himself, in a handful of works that evoke this lull between the wars, dubbed it the time "before the fateful days."[4]

This tranquil period spent as a student in Bet Hakerem preceded almost any known literary activity on Amichai's part,[5] yet during that time he absorbed stimuli that would nurture his future literary creations and educated himself in the craft of poetry. Despite the significance of this time in his creative development, neither his published poetry nor the numerous interviews that he would eventually grant elaborated on the life he led between his discharge from the British coast guard and the second time he was called to arms.[6] As part of his effort to portray his emergence as a poet as an exact parallel to the establishment of the State of Israel, Amichai tried to camouflage the importance of this period. Nevertheless, understanding the personal and emotional development of the young Yehuda Pfeuffer during this period is crucial, because it reveals the process by which he became the poet known as Yehuda Amichai. The following pages attempt to fill in the gaps in the poet's self-description and offset the absence of detail about the days from mid-1946 to early 1948.

For Amichai, this period was defined by his courtship of Ruth Z. and their ensuing relationship. They were together for seven months before Ruth went to study in America, and they corresponded for eight more months thereafter.[7] Amichai's letters record the couple's love affair with an almost obsessive precision. Each time he wrote the date at the top of a letter, it evoked a specific memory of their time together. Many of the letters celebrate the anniversary of an individual event—a concert, a party, a hike—that took place on exactly that date in the previous year. Even after six intervening decades, Ruth's recollections are astonishingly detailed, capturing specific conversations and anecdotes. She offered a reserved point of view, devoid of the nostalgia that sometimes surfaces in Amichai's letters. The intimate chronology of the pair's courtship and liaison is retold here against the backdrop of the historical events that coincided with them and, in the succeeding chapters, with the poetry that this love inspired.

Ruth Z., the first woman the adult Amichai loved, was born to a German-speaking Jewish family; her parents met in the Zionist office in Berlin, where Ruth's father, who had studied at the University of Prague, worked as a newspaper editor with Zalman Shazar.[8] When the League of Nations selected Britain as the temporary mandatory of Palestine, the leadership of the Zionist office moved to England. Consequently, Ruth and her younger brother were both born in London, though her older sister had been born in Berlin. Although they lived in Britain and learned the English language, the family continued to speak German in private; it was Ruth's first language. In 1927, the family emigrated to Palestine,[9] taking with it a large trunk full of German and English children's books. Bringing this trove proved to be a wise decision, for during an entire year after their arrival, Ruth suffered from chronic ear infections and was unable to attend school. That year, her mother read the first volume of the Doctor Doolittle series to her in German; by the time she was five, Ruth had read the other nine volumes in German on her own. The family settled in Jerusalem, where its secular Zionist home quickly became a meeting place for writers and political leaders. In 1929, while her father was attending the Zionist Congress in Zurich, her mother took Ruth and her siblings to visit relatives in what was then Czechoslovakia. When news of riots near the Wailing Wall in Old Jerusalem and the slaughter of the Jews in nearby Hebron reached them, her father returned to Palestine, while the rest of the family went to Berlin, where Ruth was enrolled in school for a brief period.

Upon their return, Ruth attended school in Talpiyot, a neighborhood at the outskirts of Jerusalem, where she was treated as an outsider; both the children and the teachers often teased her as the foreign newcomer. The family then moved closer to the center of town, and Ruth completed her studies at the famous Hebrew Gymnasia in nearby Rehavia.

On June 4, 1942, after a year at Hebrew University, Ruth enlisted in the army. Like Amichai and many of the Jewish youth of Palestine, she decided that joining the British to defeat the Nazis took precedence over the national Zionist struggle for independence. For the majority of her four years of military service, she was stationed in Egypt; first in Alexandria, during the pivotal El-Alamein offensive, and then in Tel el-Kabir, a desert camp between Cairo and Ismailiya. She drove a truck and had to contend with rigid British commanders and soldiers. They expressed their resentment of the female recruits from Palestine by assigning them difficult manual labor; the Jewish recruits repaired trucks disabled in battle, and sometimes had to push them to the repair shop by hand. The conditions were fierce: twenty-four women in one room, cold showers at eleven o'clock at night, and no contact with the outside world. Because of her initiative and her fluency in English, however, Ruth impressed the British major and was permanently transferred to work for him at the men's camp.

Once every three months, Ruth made the long trip home from Egypt, some-times hitching a ride on a coal train. On her third vacation in Jerusalem, in the spring of 1943, she received a phone call. It was from Avraham, a handsome young man nine years her senior with whom she had become infatuated at a party three years earlier, when she was seventeen years old. It was as though she had been waiting for this phone call. When Avraham picked her up, she knew she had already fallen in love with the stranger. Three weeks later, when she was back at her base in Egypt, she received an eighteen-page letter from Avraham. From that point on, she spent all of her leaves from the British army with him. But the initial harmony between the two did not last long. Avraham, who had strong right-wing affiliations, hated the British, hated Ruth's uniform, and wanted her to leave the army. After Japan surrendered to the allied forces on Au-gust 15, 1945, the British army transferred Ruth to Jerusalem, where she became the driver for the head of the female military police. Living in the same city exac-erbated the widening ideological gap between Ruth and Avraham. Ultimately, they separated because of Avraham's nationalist views and underground activi-ties. To this day, however, Ruth refers to Avraham as the love of her life.

In late May 1946, the British released Ruth from the army. Unwilling to be a secretary, she decided to enroll in the teachers' course that had begun a couple of months earlier. Yehuda Pfeuffer, a soldier who had been discharged from the British army a month later than Ruth, also signed up for that course. He was a conscientious student who worried about the material he had missed and wished to borrow notebooks. Fortunately, she loaned him her own.

Six decades later, only Ruth's memories, a few published poems, and a tin box full of love letters remain to tell the story of the would-be national poet as a young man in love.

$*$ $*$ $*$

For Yehuda, the name "Ruth" stirred up memories of Ruth Hanover, and this resonance increased his attraction to his new acquaintance.[10] As soon as he set foot in her parents' home, he realized that he and Ruth shared German as their mother tongue. Although he spoke Hebrew with her, Yehuda quickly learned that they both had the German language and culture at the root of their upbringing and had grown up with some of the same children's stories and songs. He later discovered that although Ruth arrived in Palestine at a younger age than he did, she also had stinging memories of trying to integrate into the Jewish-Palestinian milieu.

Yehuda soon became infatuated with the beautiful, charismatic, and self-confident young woman and pursued her in his gentle manner. Despite his unassuming demeanor, she could tell that he was attracted to her because he sprang up at her side at every opportunity. After her breakup with Avraham, however, Ruth was reluctant to become involved with another man. She did not find Yehuda attractive, and, as far as she was concerned, there was nothing about him that stood out—"he was not brilliant and not an athlete." One day, their class hiked from Jerusalem to the Dead Sea on a path that, according to their teacher, followed the escape route of the Judean King Zidkiyahu. Yehuda helped her down the rocks and walked by her side all the way to Jericho, but disappeared shyly once they reached the city. As the course continued, he became more daring. When they went to donate blood for an injured teacher, he flirtatiously told her she was "too delicate" to do it. Repelling Yehuda's advances as she often did, Ruth retorted, "I was just discharged from the army, where I drove a truck."

Some time later, Yehuda asked Ruth how old she was. "I was born in January, 1923," she replied. Instead of telling her his true age, Yehuda lied and said he had been born in May 1922. Although she believed him, she thought that he behaved younger than his declared age, so she asked him, "How did you finish high school a year after me if you're older than I am?" Without missing a beat, he replied, "I was left back because I didn't know Hebrew when I first arrived in Palestine." Later, Ruth found out that Yehuda had misled her because he assumed that she would not consider dating him if she knew that he was younger than her. He need not have worried about being younger than Ruth, however, because around this time, her interest in him began to grow. She loved his sense of humor and his tall tales made her laugh.

By December 1946, Yehuda was completely smitten with Ruth. He attended a Hanukkah celebration at her home; a year later, he still remembered the dark dress she had been wearing, the holiday concert they attended on Ben-Yehuda Street, and the words to the Hanukkah songs they learned from Mr. Lempel in their seminar. For him, Hanukkah marked the beginning of their "legend."[11]

Immediately after Hanukkah, the class started preparing for the comprehensive Bible proficiency examination. On their way home from Bet Hakerem, as they were hanging onto the straps in the crowded bus, Yehuda asked Ruth if she would like to study for the exam with him. She agreed, but not without including a third party, Uri Twerski, who was standing nearby. It did not take long before their routine was set in stone: they would first study in her room from four to six o'clock, then relocate to one of the nearby cafés. The smell of coffee and the background noise became their preferred milieu and brought them closer together.[12]

After two months of studying as a trio, Yehuda found the courage to invite Ruth to a concert in an elegant Arab stone house in Talbiye, near Rehavia. Ironically, it was her indifference to music that would become the catalyst for their relationship and would show her that the man whom she had considered nondescript did, in fact, stand out. While they were sitting in a café on Gaza Street after the concert, the violinist, who happened to be Yehuda's friend, invited her to his next concert, but she refused the invitation.[13] After he left, Yehuda asked her why and she replied, "The world of musical notes is not my world." Yehuda wanted to know which world *was* hers, and she replied, "The world of letters." That evening, he half-jokingly asked her if she could ever marry a writer, and with equal humor, she answered, "Yes."[14]

The following day, Yehuda brought Ruth a story he had written about a kite that had gotten caught in the electric lines. When she finished reading it, she recalled thinking to herself, "This young man is not just anyone," and she began to surrender to his wooing. When she saw Yehuda in school the next day, she told him that the story was fantastic. He was incredulous, "You're only saying that. Do you mean it? Really?" Ruth assured him that she did, and asked if he had written anything else.

He told her he had, and from that day on, Yehuda frequently brought Ruth his writing. After their friendship deepened, she asked him why he was studying to be a teacher. He replied, "This profession will give me time to do what I want to do."

"And what is that?"

"To be a poet." He then confessed to her that he had sent some poems to various newspapers, only to be consistently rejected.

*   *   *

As time went by, Ruth and Yehuda no longer needed the excuse of studying to visit the neighborhood cafés. Their favorite was Café Atara, where they had a regular table. Ruth was a member of the Hagana, and she and Yehuda would meet at 9:30 in the evening after her weekly two-and-a-half-hour practice. Yehuda's father would not let him join the Hagana and, accordingly, Yehuda regularly waited at the café for Ruth. After going to the movies, they also automatically turned toward their café. The waiter and the regulars at Atara knew them and smiled at them.[15] While they were hanging out, they amused themselves by doing "crazy things," like loudly deliberating about absurd purchases. "Shall we buy the Cadillac or the Rolls Royce?" he asked on one occasion.

"It doesn't matter, as long as it's red," she retorted. They loved the attention of other patrons in the café, who grew quiet and listened to their mock conversations.

One rainy afternoon, the entire class went to Haifa.[16] Yehuda wore a rumpled brown-leather jacket, and Ruth poked fun at him, saying he looked like a kibbutznik.[17] The students from the teachers' college were assigned to different schools throughout the city. Most, like Ruth, were assigned to classes at the prestigious Reali School, where they acted as student-teachers. All the teachers-in-training stayed in Bet Rutenberg, a study center used for supplementary education, on Mount Carmel. One day, the class went on a hike up the mountain. As Ruth and Yehuda climbed up the steep, rocky trail, Ruth suddenly began to cry because she was conflicted about her yearnings for Avraham and her growing friendship with Yehuda.[18] They discussed the tension between chance and fate and the coincidence of them finding each other when they each needed a shoulder on which to lean.[19] Strolling down Haifa's famous Panorama Street, they admired the blue-green landscape and the ridge of the Carmel, which embraces the bay. When evening fell, Ruth and Yehuda found a small café and sipped cocoa. They felt as though the weight of Jerusalem had been lifted from their shoulders. Although they still defined their relationship merely as a close friendship, Yehuda sensed that Ruth had begun to harbor romantic feelings for him.[20]

He turned out to be right. A short time later, back in Jerusalem, his hopes were fulfilled and he kissed her for the first time.

"You don't know how to kiss," she said.

"Teach me," he replied.

*   *   *

Winters in Jerusalem are temperamental, so whenever the sun came out on a Shabbat, Ruth and Yehuda wallowed in it, taking long strolls through the city's streets. A favored route was toward the Valley of the Cross, where they could lean on the rocks and bask in the winter sun.[21] Another was to the Old City. One Shabbat morning, Yehuda picked Ruth up at her house; she was wearing a gray suit and a wide-brimmed, brown hat. They walked through Mamila Street all the way to the Tower of David, taking pictures of each other. These pictures of him are still in Ruth's album, his profile against the background of the Old City. They entered the tower, and there Ruth impulsively turned to him and said, "I love you a little bit today."[22]

On weekdays, they wandered around downtown Jerusalem, and Ruth remembered Yehuda's playful quirks from these strolls. Sometimes when they were walking behind a pretty woman on the street, he would stop Ruth and say, "Wait a minute, I must see her face." He would run ahead, steal a glance at the woman, and then return to Ruth. One of their private jokes involved a store on Ben Yehuda Street called "Ruthie." It overflowed with toys, dolls, stuffed cats, and elementary school textbooks; every time they passed, they laughed because the storeowner always seemed to be sitting outside, as if there were no room for him in his crowded store.[23]

Their life settled into a blithe routine. Each day they went to school, returning home afterwards on the crowded bus. Yehuda noticed every detail of the advertisements on the walls of the bus. Girdles and bras, cleansers and kosher sausages—nothing escaped his perceptive gaze. On occasion, Ruth and Yehuda managed to find a seat, and their friends would pile their schoolbags loaded with books onto their knees. Under the cover of the heavy bags, they would sometimes hold hands.[24]

Although times were relatively quiet, tension was increasing between the British and the Jews; their cooperation during World War II had been forgotten, partly due to pressure from the Arabs to block the influx of Jews into Palestine. There were still a quarter of a million Jews in displaced-persons camps in Germany after the Holocaust. Nevertheless, the British, under the leadership of Foreign Secretary Ernest Bevin, continued to follow the policy outlined in the White Paper and refused to allow the refugees to immigrate to Palestine. The Jews—most notably, the semiofficial organization the Hagana and its military arm, the Palmah—found illegal ways to dodge the coastal blockade the British imposed on Palestine, and brought the refugees safely to shore. Other, more militant underground organizations like the Irgun responded to the decrees of the White Paper with terrorist attacks. In an attempt to curb both the violence and the illegal immigration, the British routinely imposed curfews, which became so frequent that Jerusalemites referred to their town as "Bevingrad" out of contempt for the British foreign minister.[25]

For Ruth and Yehuda, it was impossible to go out on nights when there was a curfew. But while curfew sometimes cut short their evenings together, it also occasionally made them longer and more enchanting. They were required to be at their respective homes before dark, and if Yehuda lingered too late at her apartment, he would have to stay over. The couple imagined that they were imprisoned together, as they lay quietly in Ruth's room, listening to the footsteps of the British guards whose post was in the ground floor of Ruth's building.[26]

Ruth rarely visited Yehuda's home, but he often visited hers; they spoke German in both places, as it was the household language. Thanks to their study sessions, Yehuda already knew the route to Ruth's home. As he approached her building, he would look up from the street, searching for her balcony. He memorized the window in the front door to her apartment and the flight of steps that led up to it. Ruth's parents knew Yehuda well. When their daughter started seeing him regularly, they happily approved; he had been brought up in a nice German home and they liked his polite manners. Yehuda became especially fond of her father, whose extensive library he admired. On the crowded bookshelves, Yehuda recognized the German volumes of Der Jude as well as authors like Kafka and Herzl.[27]

Yehuda loved every detail of Ruth's room: the large, dark armoire; the poplar trees standing erect outside the window;[28] and the pug-nosed, stuffed koala bear that sat on the windowsill, even though its owner had already turned twenty-four.[29] Ruth had an illustrated German edition of Hans Christian Andersen's stories, and the two would sit together, taking turns reading them out loud. When it was time for Yehuda to go, they would say goodbye near the garden gate of her house.[30]

Although both families were German-speaking and Zionist, the atmosphere in their respective homes differed significantly. Ruth's parents were secular and liberal, while Yehuda's were Orthodox and more traditional and may have had some misgivings about Yehuda's dating anyone before marriage. Yehuda's parents were rarely home when Ruth came over, and even when they were, they did not speak to her. Regardless, the young pair conversed in German in the presence of Yehuda's parents, in an effort to be polite.

Alone in Yehuda's room, the couple switched back to Hebrew and they would choose a book from Yehuda's overloaded bookshelf and read it together. When evening fell, he would close the shutters. Whenever the wind rattled them, she would jump and Yehuda often teased her about her skittishness. Outside his window, she could see a torn kite that was perpetually stuck in the electric lines. Though months passed, the kite never completely disintegrated—the paper tore off, but the wooden frame remained. The sight always reminded her of the first story that he had ever showed her, about the kite stuck in the electric lines.[31]

Even though they spent much of their time together, the specter of Avraham still haunted Ruth. She would not let Yehuda embrace her when they took a shortcut through a public garden in Rehavia because she still remembered walking there with Avraham.[32] The turning point came one day when she asked Yehuda to accompany her to Avraham's house in the religious neighborhood of Mekor Baruch. She wanted to return the last of the belongings he had left in her house. Once she was there, Ruth stayed a while to talk with Avraham. Yehuda stood at the threshold of the building, conflicted about whether or not to leave. In the end, he waited for her, and, to his relief, Ruth returned to him. Afterwards, they strolled down the narrow path in the public garden, illuminated on either end by tall streetlamps—but now they held each other tightly. The long garden had benches on either side, and stretched from Ramban Street, where Ruth lived, to Ibn Gabirol Street.[33] At the end of it, they had to let go of each other and walk single file because of a barbed wire fence. In describing their nocturnal route, both Yehuda in his letters and Ruth in her interviews identified the small park (or, as he would call it, *hagina hatsiburit*, the public garden) by the prominent figures who inhabited the houses around it, Dov Yosef and Ben-Zvi.[34] The significance of that public garden, however, goes beyond the love story of Yehuda and Ruth and beyond Yehuda's rivalry with Avraham.[35] Their familiar park became a literary trope that played a monumental role in Amichai's oeuvre in particular and in modern Hebrew poetry in general.

*   *   *

While the poem "In the Public Garden" is known to Amichai's readers,[36] the poems that he wrote about Binyamina, the small settlement not far from Haifa, never gained exposure. Binyamina was the site of the other crossroads in their relationship. In this book, the content of the Binyamina poems is brought to light for the first time, publicly immortalizing the peak of the love affair. Many months after Yehuda wrote those poems, when Ruth was far away in America, his letters tirelessly return to that period. In March 1948, when the school in which he taught in Haifa was destroyed by an explosion, he escaped to the sweet memories of the previous March. When the world around him collapsed, Yehuda would resurrect Binyamina—its train tracks, its school, and its green fields—and recall it longingly.

A week after Ruth descended the stairs from Avraham's apartment into Yehuda's arms, the pair was assigned to Binyamina to complete their practical training for the teachers' course.[37] The educational goal of this trip was to build upon the participants' previous student-teaching experience in the Haifa schools, but in a more independent, challenging setting. All twenty-six teachers-in-training were divided into groups of twos and threes and were scattered throughout the country in a range of elementary schools, where they taught for two weeks.[38] Their professor, Binyamin Brenner,[39] traveled to the various schools to supervise the students.

For different reasons, later accounts by both Yehuda and Ruth tend to understate the romantic intensity of the time spent in Binyamina. In only a couple of the many interviews Amichai would grant over the years did he mention Binyamina at all, even briefly; Ruth, for her part, despite her usually outstanding memory, did not elaborate on that episode of sixty years ago.[40] Their subsequent denials notwithstanding, a sweet love story can be reconstructed using testimonies written closer to the events—the Binyamina poems that Yehuda gave to Ruth but never published, and his reminiscences in the letters he wrote to her after she left for New York. Yehuda would idealize the two weeks in the little settlement as a time of absolute bliss, where the foundation of their relationship was laid.[41]

Binyamina was an old, well-established agricultural settlement situated alongside the railroad tracks south of Haifa.[42] Before heading there together from Jerusalem for their student-teaching duty, Ruth and Yehuda asked one of their classmates to arrange housing for them. The classmate found two rooms at Mr. and Mrs. Kaiser's house.[43] The Kaisers were a divorced couple who still lived together, using a chalk line drawn through the living room to partition the house. Yehuda was given an inner room, while Ruth's faced the garden. On the first night, as they were settling in—Ruth had just washed her hair and put it in pink curlers—the calm of the Binyamina night was rudely interrupted. She heard a noise and saw dozens of soldiers surrounding the house, with their guns aimed through the windows. They barged into the young woman's room and demanded her papers. It turned out that the British had heard that a young man and woman had recently arrived from Jerusalem, and thought that they were members of the Irgun.[44] Ruth told them that she had served in the British army and had recently been discharged. She presented both a civilian document and her British pay-book as proof. The soldiers realized they had made a mistake, but insisted upon searching Ruth's room and opening her suitcases before turning to Yehuda. It was eleven o'clock at night when the intruders finally left, but Mrs. Kaiser felt the urge to wash the floors, perhaps attempting to erase the traces that the British soldiers left behind. Yehuda comforted Ruth; later, they laughed about the entire incident together.[45]

The next morning, to Yehuda's disappointment, Ruth ran into Shimon Hakohen, an acquaintance of her parents, who pressured her into leaving the Kaisers' home and staying with his widowed mother instead.[46] But the rough beginning of their fortnight in Binyamina only strengthened the bond between them, and Ruth and Yehuda felt as if they existed in a world of their own. The pair taught in the elementary school every day. They had their morning tea in a small restaurant across from the school, where they sat facing each other, tossing affectionate comments back and forth over breakfast. At noon, they ate with the students in the school's small dining room, sitting on children's chairs at children's tables, eating tiny portions from tiny plates.[47] In the afternoons, Ruth would accompany Mrs. Hakohen to the cemetery, and then the couple would shop for groceries at the local store and read Tolstoy.[48]

One Shabbat, they climbed a hill and sat under an old fig tree with a split trunk. Yehuda tried to teach Ruth how to play the recorder, but suddenly the spring sky clouded, and a downpour surprised them. It was an unseasonable shower—Ruth still could recall that it fell after the local newspapers had already officially announced that the last rain of the year (the malkosh) had fallen. The rainstorm drove the two from the hill, and they ran down laughing, looking for shelter. They found a room-sized wooden shed—one of the containers, or "lifts," that were common in Palestine at the time. Initially, immigrants used these to move their belongings from Europe, but with the housing shortage, many lifts had been converted into homes. There was no door on the lift, and every piece of furniture was made from empty orange crates, even the bed. Ruth guessed that its inhabitant was a woman because it was so neatly arranged. For a short time, this poor dwelling became a small paradise for the two as they waited for the downpour to stop.[49]

Even Avraham's short visit to Binyamina could not dull their happiness. It was spring; the air was full of bees and butterflies. As they were sitting outside on their last day, Yehuda drew Ruth as she was reading.[50] The drawings were probably lost, but the couple's stay in Binyamina was immortalized in another art form—poetry. In her tin box, Ruth had saved a tiny booklet held together by a rusty safety pin, which contained a playful love poem. She also kept a more serious poetic cycle, on faded blue construction paper, bound with string, which Yehuda gave her after their trip to Binyamina. On the cover is a simple title: "Binyamina, 1947." That notebook contains a cycle of six sonnets that predates even the letters.

*   *   *

After their trip to Binyamina, Yehuda and Ruth matured both as teachers and as a couple. The school year was nearing its end, and the students began to discuss their plans for the future. While they enjoyed attending parties in Jerusalem, they also spent time visiting friends together. One of Yehuda's closest friends was Herbert, a sculptor who had narrowly escaped the Holocaust in Europe and arrived in Palestine as an illegal immigrant with nothing except the clothes on his back.[51] Yehuda and Ruth spent long afternoons with Herbert, his wife Ruth, and their young daughter. Yehuda loved children; while the adults were talking, he would play with little blonde Yael.[52]

Yehuda was so in love that he thought everyone else was in love with him and with Ruth, as well. They sat in cafés and went to concerts and movies. They both loved Charlie Chaplin. Ruth and Yehuda had a small ritual before each film started: she would take out her glasses and he would clean them. From his recollection of their trips to the movies in the letters, it is clear that he looked forward to the scary parts because he knew this was when she would hold him tightly. When a movie was sad, she would cry, and his heart would go out to her.[53]

When Ruth visited his house, he enjoyed preparing meals for her. They would set the table with a tablecloth and a vase of flowers in the middle. He would ceremoniously prepare an omelet for the two of them and serve it on nice dishes, she would pour the instant coffee into wide china cups, and they would sit together enjoying the moment.[54]

Yehuda loved to take care of Ruth and pampered her in every way possible. There was something motherly about his attentiveness.[55] Once, when she was sick, Yehuda visited her before a concert, left to listen to a Schubert quartet, and returned to take care of her.[56] He had strong opinions about her wardrobe and had picked two of her dresses as his favorites; one was blue and the other was red with white polka dots and a square, décolleté neckline.[57] He also saved her from missing a final examination. As part of their requirements for graduation, the junior teachers had to take both an oral test on the Bible and give a model lesson in one of the Jerusalem schools. Ruth was to give her lesson at her alma mater, the Gymnasia Rehavia, but just as she was about to start teaching, the school secretary called her out of the classroom. Yehuda had phoned to tell her that her oral Bible exam was scheduled at the same time. She made it back to the college in time for her examination and got the highest marks in the class.

Yehuda and Ruth completed their studies at the teacher's college in July 1947. In a photograph taken of the entire class standing in front of the seminar, Ruth is wearing one of Yehuda's favorite dresses—the red one with white polka dots.[58] Throughout the summer after they graduated, the British turned back shiploads of refugees from Europe. Many were transported to displaced-persons camps in Cyprus, while others entered the country illegally, often after clashes with the British soldiers who guarded the border. Despite occasional outbreaks of violence with both the Arabs and the British, the atmosphere was one of anticipation. Far away, at the temporary home of the United Nations, a committee had been discussing a document that would give the Jewish settlement in Palestine a degree of autonomy. The young graduates were full of optimism. There were many new children in the schools, many new classes had opened, and teachers were needed everywhere.

Starting when the classes at the teachers' college were still in session, Ruth and Yehuda used their weekends to travel around the country. To escape the summer heat, the playful couple traveled to cool, shady Tel el-Kadi in the north of the country.[59] They were both tired and thirsty when they reached the waterfalls. As he was about to drink the water, Yehuda jokingly quoted from a German folktale they both knew from childhood, in which a bewitched stream turns those who drink from it into animals. A thirsty boy is tempted to take a sip, even though he would be transformed into a lion if he did. Looking at the cool water, Yehuda roared to Ruth, "Now I will turn into a lion!" and they both laughed.

The couple spent as much time as possible away from Jerusalem, a practice that Yehuda's traditional parents found objectionable. Rather than confronting them, Yehuda simply made up stories. When they visited Ruth's older sister and her family in the kibbutz in the Beth She'an Valley, Yehuda would tell his parents he was going somewhere else, because he knew they would not approve of the liberal environment at the kibbutz.

Ruth was attached to her sister and Yehuda quickly befriended her husband, who was also from a religious German family and spoke with an accent similar to Yehuda's. (Ruth's brother-in-law was later killed in the defense of kibbutz Degania during the War of Independence.)[60] When Ruth's sister went away on a two-week vacation that summer, she asked Ruth to watch over her three- and eight-year-old sons at the kibbutz. Yehuda went back and forth between his home in Jerusalem and Ruth at the kibbutz. Following the kibbutz practice in those days, Ruth's little nephews did not live with their parents, but rather stayed with the other children in the "children's house." Yehuda liked blending in with the parents who were putting their children to bed. He loved children and they, in turn, were drawn to him and returned his affection. During the sweltering summer days in Bet She'an, the swimming pool was the favorite refuge. Ruth and Yehuda held Ruth's nephews by the hands and splashed around in the water to amuse them.[61]

Like Ruth, Yehuda also had an older sister. Rachel lived in Tel Aviv with her husband, Benjamin, and their daughter, Hanna'le.[62] It was the perfect weekend trip. Not only was Tel Aviv closer than the kibbutz, but it also lay on the sea; Yehuda and Ruth both loved to swim. Rachel's sunny home in Tel Aviv became a respite for the young Jerusalemites. In the mornings, they sat on the balcony in their pajamas, eating a leisurely breakfast and laughing constantly. In the shining bathroom, they would make faces at each other in front of the mirror.[63]

In two separate photographs, Yehuda and Ruth sit on the sand in Tel Aviv, with beach chairs in the background. Neither of them is wearing a bathing suit, and Ruth's dress is femininely arranged around her. Only their profiles are visible because they are gazing at each other so intently.[64] In addition to going to the beach, they played with mischievous Hanna'le, who called her young uncle "Oodale." A shorter version of that name would become Ruth's nickname for Yehuda; the letters he later wrote to her were all signed by that nickname, "Ood." In turn, he invented a name for Ruth. Yehuda transformed the Hebrew word *motek* (sweetie) into "Teki" or "Tekile."[65]

As the summer progressed, their relationship became more intimate. Yehuda was deeply in love with her, and longed for children of his own. He asked Ruth to marry him. The idea was a bit frightening to her. Although Yehuda intimated that his father would support them, she hesitated. Ruth wanted to be financially independent before she married. Ignoring her misgivings, he assumed that it was only a matter of time before they would be husband and wife. Yehuda asked "Where should we live?" Ruth replied, "Our parents are in Jerusalem, we love swimming, we don't like Tel Aviv, so let's go to Haifa."[66]

Indeed, Tel Aviv did not appeal to him, either. Haifa is on the sea, and they both remembered the wonderful time they had spent there as part of their training to be teachers. Yehuda thought that the slope of the Carmel would be an ideal location for their new home. Together they decided to look for a first teaching position in Haifa, where they would one day build their future. Yehuda went for an interview with Mr. Haklay, the vice principal at the Geula Elementary School in Haifa. When he returned, he told Ruth, "The principal accepted me, but told me that he hopes that I will change my name." Mr. Haklay's request was not unreasonable, as it was common at this period of heightened national feelings for people to "Hebraize" foreign surnames, thus rejecting their diasporic heritage. The couple started looking for a last name that would melodically complement "Ruth" and "Yehuda."[67] They sat in a café and tried to think of Hebrew surnames that started with P, for Pfeuffer. One was Pilpel (pepper), but Yehuda rejected it, saying, "They're going to call me 'Falafel.'"[68]

After exhausting all the names that started with P, Ruth had a suggestion. "Amichai. Yehuda Amichai." The name Amichai, meaning "my nation [ami] is alive [chai]," mirrored the times—after six million Jews had perished in the Holocaust, it spelled hope. Yehuda tried the new creation out loud, "Yehuda Amichai," and asked, "Isn't it too bombastic?"

She answered, "You want to be a great poet, right? Yehuda Amichai sounds like the name of a great poet."

*   *   *

Earlier that year, Ruth had seen an advertisement that the Jewish Theological Seminary of America was looking for students and was giving preference to teachers and veterans. She applied; in spring 1947, she learned that she had received a visa to come to New York City and study at the seminary. Although they had already agreed on a common surname and a place to live, the opportunity to travel to America was difficult to forego. Yehuda recognized the value of studying abroad and, consistent with his considerate nature, encouraged Ruth to embark on her journey.

In preparation for her departure, Ruth bequeathed her journals, which she had kept from the time she was ten years old, to Yehuda. At her parents' apartment, she did not have a cabinet with a key, and she did not want her parents to find them; Yehuda already had a private room in Haifa. She gave him her diaries, assuming that he would take them with him; she also gave him sole permission to read them. Yehuda felt that he was now the guardian of her innermost thoughts. He treasured her gift; to him, it was a promise that she would return.[69] The diaries, however, were not enough to bring Ruth back. They stayed in Yehuda's possession for a few years and ultimately disappeared. Echoes of his regret for that loss are found in a poem whose topic is the transmission of words from one person to another. "My beloved," the speaker says, "gave me a few words before she left." The poem does not divulge that the "words" were actual diaries or to what distances his beloved traveled, but it admits guilt for not transmitting the message.[70]

When she left, Ruth did not know that she would never return. Traveling abroad, however, was more than an educational opportunity for her; it was a way to postpone making a permanent commitment to Yehuda. Even though she loved him dearly as a friend, she worried that her passion for him was less than what she had felt for Avraham. She also had some doubts about their relationship in general. She knew that he occasionally suppressed the truth in order to avoid uncomfortable situations and feared that he would be capable of lying or being unfaithful to her. She also knew he liked to look at pretty girls who passed by. While she could ignore it when they were dating, she wondered what would happen after they were married. She would say to him, "You're going to leave me and you're going to cheat on me. You will not be satisfied with one love in your life." Ruth was tempted to test him. If he could stay faithful to her while she was so far away, perhaps she would be able to trust him.

Despite these fears, Ruth was not yet prepared to lose him. She thought they would get along as husband and wife. She recognized her great influence over him and the fact that he would do anything to please her. Leaving for America would put off the decision about marriage for a year and allow her to remain in a relationship with him without making the ultimate commitment.

How could she have known that historical and financial upheavals would make it a one-way trip?[71] How could she have known, in the summer of 1947, what would happen after she left? July and August were relatively quiet. The United Nations Special Committee on Palestine had started to deliberate on the fate of the Jewish settlement in Palestine in May. There were talks about the partition plan, but no one imagined that it would be approved as early as November, and that six months later the British Mandate would have ended, war would be raging throughout the country, Jerusalem would be under siege, and travel to Palestine would become all but impossible.

She spent her last day and night in Palestine in Yehuda's newly rented room on Emek Hazetim Street in Haifa. They went for a stroll through a pine grove on the Carmel, feeling as if they were getting lost in an enchanted forest.[72] Most of the time, however, they stayed inside. Ruth gave him a farewell present—a calendar with pictures of children and Israeli landscapes.[73] Although they knew that the alarm clock was set for the early hour of her departure, it was a restless night. The two could not fall asleep and kept asking each other what time it was. This night would later be immortalized in Amichai's epic "In the Public Garden":

And at two o'clock,
two
are whispering
. . . .
"Morning comes soon."
"What time is it, beloved?"
"What?"[74]

On the morning of August 31, 1947, the same day that the United Nations
committee reached its decision to partition Palestine, Ruth and Yehuda met
Ruth's parents and brother at the Haifa port. After she boarded the ship, the
four of them could only wave to her as she stood high above them on its deck.
Yehuda was struck by the great distance between the people standing on the
pier and those on the deck. Although in reality only a few yards separated Ruth
and Yehuda, an entire ocean had, in effect, already divided them. Amichai stood
with Ruth's family on the dock until they could not see her yellow straw hat any-
more, and she disappeared in the thick cloud of smoke that rose from the
ship's smokestack. Yehuda brought her parents and brother to a small restaurant he knew from his days in the British coast guard. At first, they could not
talk, but after a while, they began to discuss the future. As the family boarded
the express bus to Jerusalem, Yehuda saw tears in Ruth's mother's eyes.[75] On
the walk back to his house, Yehuda had to put on his sunglasses so that no one
would see that he, too, was crying. To console himself, he stopped in a store
and bought fifteen aerograms,[76] then returned to his room and wrote a letter to
Ruth. At the top of the page, he wrote the number "1" and circled it.[77] From that
day on, three times a week, for almost eight months, Yehuda, now Yehuda Amichai, would fill every square centimeter of those pages.

Ruth Z. did not take many belongings with her when she left Haifa, but tucked deep in her bag, she did carry the hand-bound blue notebook on whose cover the words "Binyamina, 1947" were inscribed. The six sonnets in this notebook depict the light-filled, blissful days that she and Yehuda had spent together in Binyamina. While for Ruth Z. the sonnets capture specific, personal memories, for a scholar of Amichai's work, they are essential to understanding the poet. Knowing about the events that happened during that fortnight enables the critic to connect Amichai's life with his poetry in an eye-opening new way and to compare the precamouflage period in Amichai's writing with what he would eventually publish.

"BINYAMINA, 1947"

"Binyamina, 1947" is a cycle of six tender love sonnets—a poetic "diary" of groundbreaking scholarly significance.[1] According to Ruth Z., Amichai regularly composed poetry from the summer of 1946 through August 1947.[2] "Binyamina, 1947," however, is the only piece that remains intact. Written around Amichai's twenty-third birthday, it is the earliest piece of his poetry known to date, and the only complete, unpublished sequence of poems found from any period of his life.[3] "Binyamina, 1947" never appeared in print, piecemeal or otherwise. Only the phrase "We loved here," from the first line of Sonnet I, survived. Seven years later, Amichai would use it as the title of his canonic twenty-three-sonnet cycle, now a classic of Hebrew literature.[4] Were it not for the discovery of Ruth Z.'s collection of the poet's letters and other papers, this earlier cycle would have been lost entirely.

Amichai made no effort to camouflage the events that the Binyamina sonnets chronicle and recorded the experience just as he saw it. As truthful as they are, though, the sonnets are also colored by a strong bias toward idealization, which highlights their playful and ecstatic nature. Any negative experiences during the two-week stay in Binyamina are glossed over entirely. For example, neither Amichai nor Ruth ever forgot their first dramatic night in Binyamina and the British soldiers' invasion of Mrs. Kaiser's house, but the "Binyamina, 1947" sonnets completely ignore it.[5] It is clear, therefore, that the sonnets are not an accurate record of their stay, but rather Amichai's attempt to idealize the couple's time there. Amichai's underlying agenda in the sonnets is to preserve what happened in his own memory and to monumentalize that memory. The sonnets strive to establish the stay in Binyamina as a private myth—an island of existence undisturbed by the outside world.

Amichai's choice of the sonnet for "Binyamina, 1947" is logical, as it is the traditional genre of love poetry, but it also betrays his literary sensibility.[6] In writing "Binyamina, 1947," Amichai emulated the romantic German texts he had discovered in high school.[7] His idol, Rilke, favored the Petrarchan sonnet, and it is not surprising that Amichai was drawn to it. In fact, Amichai's published sonnets share a number of qualities with the German poet's.[8] Finally, the poems that Yehuda gave Ruth as a remembrance are not independent sonnets, but rather a sonnet sequence, the form Rilke used to write his masterpiece, *Sonnets to Orpheus*.

As the norm of sonnet cycles dictates, Amichai arranged the sonnets according to an intellectual order, with an overall integrity that is both topical and chronological. Woven around the subject of love, the poems contain a strong narrative thread that follows the couple's escapades. The work is neatly balanced and the web of interconnections among the sonnets allows them to be broken up in both symmetrical and asymmetrical ways. Each of the six sonnets that make up "Binyamina, 1947" is titled with a roman numeral, and each relates to a different aspect of Ruth and Yehuda's trip to Binyamina. Even though the cycle was written by a novice, it captures the atmosphere and the mood of the fortnight. Indeed, while Amichai's letters and Ruth's recollections allow for a reconstruction of particular events (as related in the previous chapter), the poetic lens of the sonnets enriches the portrait of the small town called Binyamina with colors, scents, sounds, and touch.

Sonnet I

The first line of "Binyamina, 1947" declares "we loved here," and exclaims that everything and everybody loved "us," the couple. The first sonnet goes on to paint a pastoral tableau in which couples, peasants, and children love a natural, spontaneous love: ". . . everybody loved us / The peasants, tombstones, cypress trees, children." In the midst of this intoxication, the quintessential Israeli landscape merges with Amichai's early memories, and idyllic images that stem from the baroque atmosphere of Wuerzburg enter the poem.[9] The man and woman in the Binyamina scene are idealized archetypes: their laughter, the sparkle in their eyes, and even the groceries they buy all cause everyone to love them.

Beginning in the first line, the first-person plural "we" dominates the cycle. At the time that Amichai wrote "Binyamina, 1947," this voice was used throughout Hebrew literature as a way of invoking the collective. Amichai used it differently. The "we" in the poems refers only to the two lovers, not to an entire generation. The repetition of the sound nu (as in "*ahavnu*," **we** loved) is used to reinforce the oneness of the lovers and their voices. The sound nu appears throughout Sonnet I (as well as the other five sonnets) as both an end rhyme and an internal rhyme. In Hebrew, the sound is inextricably connected to the first-person plural; it is the last syllable of the Hebrew word for "we" (*anahnu*). When one conjugates a verb in the past tense, the suffix nu indicates that the subject of the verb is "we." This usage of the suffix applies to nouns as well. (For example, the word *rosh* (head), inflected as *roshenu* means "our head.") Amichai takes advantage of this grammatical characteristic of Hebrew, appending nu to all possible parts of speech throughout the sonnets. Sonnet III, for instance, uses nu ten times: "*yadenu*" (our hands), "*sihaknu*" (we played), "*shelanu*" (ours), and so on.[10] The exceptions to the ubiquitous "we" in "Binyamina, 1947" are found in Sonnets II and III, in which the male speaker initially addresses his female counterpart in the second-person singular. Nevertheless, both sonnets slip back into the first-person plural after a few lines. Through the reiteration of this unambiguous sound, Amichai attempts to emphasize the lovers' unity.

Even though they were private poems meant for Ruth's eyes alone, the Binyamina sonnets contain one of the most famous trademarks of Amichai's writing: the introduction of the mundane into the lofty language of poetry.[11] While the beginning of Sonnet I draws on the baroque and rococo romantic aesthetic, the last stanza, by contrast, highlights the purportedly unpoetic, shopping for groceries: "buying butter, eggs, sugar, and tea."[12] Low language is likewise interjected into each of the sonnets in this cycle. This recurring dissonance between the idyllic and the everyday may be indicative of different literary and aesthetic ideals clashing inside the young Amichai or the gap between his romantic dreams and reality. More importantly, the existence of these elements in the body of such an early work establishes "Binyamina, 1947" as a precursor to Amichai's most recognized innovation, one that ultimately changed the face of Hebrew Israeli poetry.

Sonnet II

While Sonnet I draws an overall picture of the reciprocal love between the couple ("we") and the locus of their love ("here"), Sonnet II focuses on a sliver of the local landscape. As the poem opens, the two protagonists are standing on either side of the railroad tracks, just as a train passes by. They are engaged in a fantastical game of peek-a-boo in which they can only see each other in lightninglike flashes through the spaces between the cars.[13] As the train speeds by between the lovers, the speaker muses about the fates of the travelers, wondering in what directions their lives will lead them. Thus, by honing in on Binyamina's railroad station, the sonnet merges this whimsical, fleeting moment with weightier questions of destiny.

At the beginning of the sonnet, the lovers' cheerful voices seem to bounce back and forth over the passing train, and the poem uses the singular "I" and "you" instead of the "we" that dominates Sonnet I. The absence of the "we" allows the fear of a permanent separation to penetrate momentarily in spite of the stanza's cheerful mood. As the sonnet progresses, the singular voice is muted and the ringing of the sound *nu* (we) reappears to emphasize the couple's closeness. The abstract fear lingers, however, and is concretized by the description of the train and the individuals in it. The cars, overburdened with other people's lives, become a moving wall between the lovers: "Entire worlds pass then between us. . . ."[14] In a manner that foreshadows the older Amichai, the poem's speaker remains conscious of other people even when he is consumed by his own love. While describing the train as the mass that separates the lovers, Amichai also focuses on the passengers, "hundreds of . . . people" who have their own destinies. The second stanza is devoted entirely to the emotional cargo of the train. The crowded cars become carriers of the passengers' "thoughts and dreams," and the weight of these inner worlds makes the barrier between the lovers that much greater. The "train," then, both represents the intrusion of the outside world into the world of the lovers and acknowledges the value of that world.

In its description of the passengers, Sonnet II contains the kernel of a literary formulation that Amichai would later develop in a published poem. In both, he transformed the abstract notion of "thoughts and dreams" into a thick, tangible substance, an insulation that can either divide people from each other or protect them. In the 1947 sonnet, the "thoughts and dreams" of other people serve as a partition between lovers standing on opposite sides of a train track. In the later poem, "Look: Thoughts and Dreams," these thoughts and dreams turn into a "wide camouflage-net" that hides the intentions of the lovers from surveillance planes and from God.[15]

Despite some understated doubts, the tone of the first two stanzas is generally playful. Only after the volta (the classical sonnet's turning point, after the first eight lines), when the chugging of the train ceases and the lovers are left alone, does the imagery reflect the speaker's growing anxiety. Amichai introduces harshness into the soft landscape by interjecting a foreign, technical term into the lyrical language of the sonnet: the word "semaphore" ("*semafor*").[16] Although *semafor* is used in Hebrew, it is also recognizably foreign to a Hebrew reader. Amichai produces linguistic dissonance by inserting a mechanical, originally foreign term into the otherwise pure, literary Hebrew context of Sonnet II. While the lower diction in Sonnet I describes an everyday activity (shopping), in Sonnet II, the technical word "semaphore" is paradoxically used to elevate the scene, not to lower it. The prosaic is heightened by its linguistic and thematic surroundings: the arm of the semaphore is described as a "hard arm." While this is a metonym for the train controller, it also evokes a superior power: the word "*zero'a*" (arm) alludes to God's "outstretched arm" and, with it, the power of destiny.[17] With its typically Amichaian combination of technical, foreign associations, discordant sound, and biblical allusions, the "arm" of the semaphore destroys the bucolic setting. The tracks disappear "in the green curve," implying the lovers' inability to know the future. In the sonnet's last and ambiguous line, the speaker oscillates between "peace," and "no peace," reflecting the uncertainty about the future and foreshadowing the age-old ritual of "she loves me, she loves me not," invoked in Sonnet III.

Sonnet III

Harmony between man and nature pervades Sonnet III, as it does Sonnet I. Its first two stanzas are a mischievous call to play together, and love itself is portrayed as a masquerade in which the lovers pretend to blend in with the local farmers and their customs, the clouds, cypress trees, and sunsets. This joyful time is followed by the game of "she loves me, she loves me not" and, finally, a guessing game but in which the speaker tries to predict the future based on the layout of the landscape.

The speaker's repeated call to his beloved gives the octave of Sonnet III its intimate tone. Three of its eight lines open with the call, "Come, let's play!"[18] After each call to "come," the plural *nu* floods the melodic soundscape, appearing nine times in the first two stanzas. By contrast, after the volta, the *nu* sound disappears; it is absent in the entire sestet, signifying the switch to a more solemn tone. The concluding lines of the second stanza herald a turn away from the lighthearted mood: "Let's play . . . / as with flower petals, yes, no, yes."[19] It alludes to the "she loves me, she loves me not" ritual, in which tearing off petals predicts the couple's fate.

The fear that the affair will end, implied in the line quoted above, intensifies after the volta. The stakes of the bet become higher and more specific. Here, "she loves me, she loves me not" is no longer a universal ritual, but a personal, and local guessing game, whose rules are invented by the speaker and whose outcome will determine the fate of the lovers. If the "tracks and road" meet "beyond the hill," the lovers will stay together; if road and tracks separate, so will they. The three letters of the Hebrew verb root P.R.D. (separation) in the last line add to the poem's sense of fatalism.[20] As the sonnet nears its end and the cycle nears its midpoint, the dread of parting reaches its peak.

Sonnet IV

This moment of deep insecurity is completely inverted in Sonnet IV, which opens the second half of the cycle with a flood of gaiety and intense passion. It represses the worries expressed in Sonnets II and III and instead mirrors the carefree tone of the cycle's opening lines. Like the second sonnet, which is set near the train tracks, Sonnet IV takes place in a specific site in Binyamina: a hill and a nearby shed. The two lovers are lying on the hill when a rainstorm suddenly surprises them. They run into the shack for shelter, and for a moment it becomes their personal paradise. The sonnet highlights the couple's elation and is full of imagery that alludes to enchantment and intoxication: "The valley shook us drunk between fields and footpaths. . . ."[21] The sonnet's opening, however, also hints at an imminent turn of events: the hill throws off those who were sitting on top of it. This unlikely and bold image is explained seven lines later, when a sudden storm breaks—clouds, thunder, lightning, and hail. Laughing with excitement, the two look for shelter, and a hut appears through the deluge. The unbridled ecstasy of this sonnet is rare in Amichai's writing and is, perhaps, never matched again. Twice, he suggests that "madness" overcame them: "We tired, went mad, weeds, forest. . . ."[22] It is as though the energy released by the storm and the clouds unloading their heavy contents is paralleled by the release of the enormous erotic tension that pervades the sonnet. The calm after the storm is almost predictable, but its setting is a surprise.

Sonnet V

The fifth sonnet takes place in Binyamina's old cemetery. The lovers lie among the tombstones amid the lush vegetation and amuse themselves by reading the inscriptions. It is as though, after the passion of the fourth sonnet, there must be a shift to rest; in this case, to death. More than the other sonnets in the cycle, Sonnets IV and V form a pair, corresponding to the classical dichotomy of eros (the drive toward love and life) and thanatos (the desire for the state of death or nothingness). These sonnets are also connected by their focus on vignettes from Ruth and Yehuda's stay in Binyamina—both Amichai's letters to Ruth Z. and her interviews include recollections of the rainstorm as well as their visits to the cemetery.[23]

Although Sonnet V describes actual visits to the cemetery, its imagery is abstract, contemplating the proximity between love and death. It opens with the Hebrew phrase "*Po Nah*" (here lies), the traditional heading for Jewish gravestones. Commonly, only the acronym appears on tombstones, the Hebrew letters *Pe* and *Nun*, not the entire phrase (the acronym could also stand for a synonym of *Po Nah*, such as *Po Nitman* or *Po Nikbar* [here is buried]). The first line of Sonnet V begins with the words "here lies" and transforms them from an inscription on a tombstone into a depiction of the lovers' physical position: "we lay." The young lovers not only spend time in a graveyard, the domain of the dead, they also resemble the dead: both lovers and the dead forget the world; the bodies of both leave an indentation in the ground; grass covers and rises above both of them. Amichai's portrayal of the cemetery is blatantly cheerful, ignoring the solemnity of the location: "From grave to grave, a light stride and pause."[24] This gay tone prevails throughout the sonnet and reaches its climax at the end, when the lightheartedness of the couple becomes literal. The sonnet's closing lines liken tombstones to leaves; the stones fall from the lovers' hearts the way leaves fall from a tree,[25] making their hearts light in both weight and attitude: ". . . these tombstones fell off our hearts."[26] As the two leave the cemetery, they feel liberated from death.

Although Sonnet V dovetails perfectly with the structure of the cycle, it has some idiosyncratic features that demand further discussion. A close reading of the sonnet, combined with the knowledge of Amichai's childhood, uncovers the experiential sources behind its imagery and its irreverent attitude toward death. While the Binyamina cycle seems to be rooted in the here and now, visual remnants of the poet's early years enter it as well. In their covert quotations from the past, the sonnets are similar to Amichai's later works. This may represent a form of unconscious denial (as opposed to his later, more deliberate, camouflaging)—the repressed remnants of childhood surface in the young man's verse, but their roots may have been unknown even to him.[27] The baroque pastoral descriptions of the lovers in Sonnet I, for example, draw upon visual memories from Wuerzburg. Likewise, Sonnet V returns to the childhood landscape, but in even greater detail. In the first stanza, the scene is described from a particular visual perspective, as though the speaker is lying on his back, looking upwards. The blades of grass and the flowers seem to tower above his head. This point of view is attributed expressly to the lovers and the dead: "the dead and the lovers . . . both lie and the grass covers them."[28] A similar description of a scene, from the same physical position, is found in "When I Was a Child,"[29] which opens Amichai's first volume, *Now and in Other Days*. It describes childhood as a time when

> Grass and masts stood at the shore.
> When I lay there,
> They all rose above me to the skies,
> I couldn't tell them apart.[30]

The shore, the masts, and the grass probably refer to the riverside landscape as it was imprinted in Amichai's memory, from the time he spent as a child in Germany. This landscape is seen through the eyes of a child lying on his back. The physical position of the lovers in the graveyard is reminiscent of Amichai's lyrical self in "When I Was a Child." The similarity of images and visual perspective suggests a link between lovers and children in the poet's mind. This connection is confirmed by an early published poem, "God Has Pity on Kindergarten Children," in which children and lovers are singled out as the sole recipients of God's mercy.[31]

Another little-known feature of Amichai's early life appears in Sonnet V. Wuerzburg's Christian cemetery was located near his childhood home, its back entrance only a five-minute walk away. Amichai and his friends often played there, likely fascinated by the elaborate marble tombstones. Thus, for the young Amichai, cemeteries functioned almost as playgrounds. Additionally, not far from his maternal grandmother's village of Gersfeld, which he often visited, there was a modest Jewish cemetery where the names on some headstones seemed to have been scratched with a nail. It may be that when he was confronted with similar simple, hand-carved tombstones in Binyamina, they evoked for him these childhood memories. It is no accident then that there was nothing disturbing for him about Binyamina's rural cemetery and that the "nail-scratched" concrete tombstones of the poor in Binyamina made their way into this sonnet.

Sonnet VI

Unlike the illusion of the lovers' immortality that predominates in Sonnet V, the sixth and closing sonnet is explicitly aware of the inevitability of the end— the possibility of separation becomes overwhelming on the day the pair leaves their paradise. The mood of Sonnet VI parallels that of the third sonnet, but while insecurity takes the shape of a game of chance at the midpoint of the cycle, it is devoid of playfulness by its end. This last sonnet of parting summarizes the entire cycle. The sensory pleasures of the place are recalled, but are tempered by the knowledge that the idyllic weeks in Binyamina have passed: "We stored the landscape's colors in our hearts."[32] The sonnet laments that the two lovers did not make an enduring mark on the local landscape to prove they had been there. They did not erect a tombstone; they did not plant a tree. No one in that area will remember their stay. This absence awakens old fears—if there is no concrete evidence of their fortnight together, perhaps the entire love affair, or even life itself, will disappear. The only comfort that appears in Sonnet VI is the thought that the memories will remain: the lovers will be able to carry with them orchards and light, colors and sun.

By writing that they had not even planted a tree in Binyamina, Amichai alludes to the famous poem "To My Land" (1926) by the Zionist pioneer poet, Rahel (Bluwstein). Her ideological verse states, with false humility, "I did not sing to you, my country . . . only a tree my hands planted."[33] Much later in his writing, Amichai would return to the same lines.[34] In her poem, Rahel refers to planting a tree as a humble contribution to her land. Amichai subverted her Zionist-patriotic vein in "Binyamina, 1947" and appropriated its image for the lovers, thus undoing the collective agenda and adapting it to the individual. Unlike Rahel's speaker, the lovers did not plant a tree. Even if they had, it would have been to immortalize their love, not glorify the Land of Israel.

The idea of leaving a mark on the places he had been seems to have occupied the young Amichai. His concern about a person's ties to a place is never abandoned in his poetry. In "Binyamina, 1947," this anxiety is perhaps triggered by a latent but gnawing doubt about the future of his love. The roots of this anxiety, however, formed earlier: the young man who was forced to leave Wuerzburg, a city that immediately forgot him, must wonder about the permanence of human footprints on the earth.[35] The final sonnet in the Binyamina cycle is a precursor of what is to come in Amichai's work, not only in its subject, but also in the way this subject is treated. Although the trauma of migration is attributed to the parents in "And the Migration of My Parents," that poem contains a succinct expression of the same anxiety, stating that "Earth / forgets the steps of those who trod [on] her."[36] More than ten years before he wrote "And the Migration of My Parents," the young lover of the Binyamina cycle lamented that "we did not leave here any trace."[37] Even at this early stage, the parting from his homeland has penetrated Amichai's writing, surfacing whenever he writes about separation. A heavy note thus permeates the last sestet of the cycle: the couple is leaving paradise, having made no decisions about their future. As their bus drives away and Binyamina recedes into the horizon, the speaker wonders if their happiness will also fade into nothing.

*   *   *

As a whole, "Binyamina, 1947" reflects enduring influences on Amichai's writing, and predicts significant features that defined his work in the decades to follow. The sonnets are flooded with colors, shapes, and light. While visual imagery is neither exclusive to Amichai nor to modern poetry, it is a dominant quality of Amichai's published and unpublished oeuvre.[38] Furthermore, although they are seemingly traditional and amateurish, the sonnets from the spring of 1947 contain the revolutionary blueprint for the later Amichai,[39] the poet who inhaled the smell of gasoline in a love poem[40] and would compare the memory of his father to a sandwich.[41] The form of the sonnet cycle, with its traditional structure and obedience to literary dictates, is deceptively conformist. Under its unassuming surface lie the qualities that would separate Amichai from his contemporaries and endow him with his monumental status in Hebrew literature. Unafraid of defiling the aristocratic sonnet genre with ordinary words, the would-be-famous poet took historic poetic steps in the private verse he wrote for his beloved.

In the decade after Amichai wrote "Binyamina, 1947" for Ruth, he continued to write sonnets, which grew in complexity and maturity.[42] The importance of the Binyamina sonnets as a benchmark for and predictor of Amichai's future poetry is tremendous. A comparison to "Ahavnu kan" ("We Loved Here"), the long sonnet cycle that was published approximately eight years later in 1955, underscores both Amichai's poetic development and the deep emotional upheaval into which he was thrown after his separation from Ruth. Indeed, a number of the sonnets in "We Loved Here" can be seen as the dark side of the naïve Binyamina sonnets.

THE TWENTY-THREE SONNETS OF "WE LOVED HERE"

In the period that elapsed between Amichai's writing the Binyamina sonnets and the publication of "Ahavnu kan" ("We Loved Here"), his entire world was shattered and rebuilt. Exactly a year after the carefree stay in Binyamina, Ruth Z. married another man, the State of Israel was established, and the War of Independence erupted, in whose fierce battles Amichai fought. He eventually fell in love again, got married in 1949, and ultimately became disillusioned with the new state, and, perhaps, also with his new love and marriage.

A quarter of Amichai's 1955 debut volume, *Now and in Other Days*, consists of the sonnet cycle "We Loved Here." Its twenty-three poems are the only sonnets in Amichai's first collection, and the cycle is placed in a strategically important spot at the end of the book. In titling this cycle "We Loved Here," the phrase he originally coined in the handwritten love sonnets that he wrote for Ruth in 1947, Amichai transported his private expression of love for a specific woman into the public sphere.

The two sonnet cycles, the private and the published, differ in almost every respect, except their shared general subject, love. In fact, the published cycle as a whole can be perceived as the antithesis of the uncomplicated "Binyamina, 1947." Ruth Z. is present in both sequences, but while the Binyamina poems are overtly dedicated to her, the published cycle camouflages all recognizable evidence of her existence and the wounds that she inflicted. While we know exactly when "Binyamina, 1947" was written, it is not clear when "We Loved Here" was initially created. Isolated sonnets from the later cycle were published as early as 1949, but "We Loved Here" did not appear in its entirety until six years later. Nevertheless, Amichai's letters to Ruth Z. prove that, at the very least, he wrote drafts for parts of "We Loved Here" in 1947 and 1948. The bitter tone of the celebrated cycle of poems and their emphasis on the inevitability of separation can thus be interpreted anew in light of the letters, "Binyamina, 1947," and the love story itself. The very fact that Amichai did not discard the opening phrase of Sonnet I, but rather chose to recycle it and use it as the title for his momentous work, calls for a reading of the canonic sonnet sequence in the context of the unpublished one.

The phrase *ahavnu kan* seems simple and straightforward, but it is actually multivalent. Each of its two components (*ahavnu*, [we loved] and *kan*, [here]) has an overdetermined function. Due to the economy of the Hebrew language, the first word in the phrase is a distilled description of an experience. In Hebrew, one word can convey several pieces of information. In this vein, *ahavnu* articulates the fact that the action was in the past (tense), that it happened to "us" (the first-person plural: we), and that it was love (sense, type of action). Combining the trisyllabic, informative word *ahavnu* with the laconic *kan* creates an imbalance of meaning as well as of sound. The pronunciation of *ahavnu* is drawn out, the second syllable long and emphasized, while *kan* is terse; as a result, the prolonged feeling or action of love, *ahavnu*, is almost halted by the brief *kan* that follows it. Moreover, Amichai's choice of *kan* for "here" instead of its equally short equivalent, *po*, is significant. *Po* ends with an open sound, a vowel, while *kan* ends with a consonant and therefore sounds more finite.

Unlike "Binyamina, 1947," "We Loved Here" does not easily lend itself to a consistent thematic interpretation. This published sequence of twenty-three numbered sonnets is a fractured narrative told by a soldier who fought in Israel's War of Independence, fell in love, and had to face the anticlimactic postwar reality. The object of its speaker's infatuation is ambiguous, as the sonnets address more than one woman; some poems allude to a past love and some to a present one. Critics' attempts to understand this cycle as a cohesive unit have failed by and large because they tried to impose one narrative or a single psychological thread on it.[44] Some attributed the cycle's enigmatic nature to Amichai's struggle with the sonnet form, but it may, in fact, be a result of his attempt to conceal the identity of its female protagonist.[45] In 1978, more than two decades after the publication of "We Loved Here," Amichai declared that the entirety of the cycle was a birthday present for his wife at the time, Tamar (née Horn).[46] This expansive claim is questionable. The title was undoubtedly written in reference to Ruth Z., and some of the sonnets can be definitively linked to her. Amichai's revisionist dedication of the cycle to Tamar may be seen as part of his effort to camouflage its autobiographical sources and detach the cycle from its roots in his affair with Ruth Z. Now, with the discovery of the Binyamina cycle, the ambiguity of the love interest in "We Loved Here" can finally be explained.

The intratextual relationship between the two sonnet cycles is reciprocal.[47] Only by reading "Binyamina, 1947" and knowing the story behind it can "We Loved Here" be fully understood and its fragmentary nature justified. In return, with the awareness of how iconic its opening words, "We loved here," became, we can grasp the significance of "Binyamina, 1947" in Amichai's poetic development. The discussion of "We Loved Here" that follows will concentrate solely on the portions of it that were inspired by the love affair between Amichai and Ruth Z. It thus offers a new interpretation that uses previously unknown biographical information to augment an innovative close reading of the text.

During the epochal years that elapsed between writing the Binyamina sonnets and composing "We Loved Here," Amichai took the poetic sequence he had conceived in 1947 and reworked it almost beyond recognition. When he compiled the twenty-three sonnets that would make up "We Loved Here" for publication, he erased indicators of locality, chronology, and identity. He also shuffled the order of the sonnets and, in so doing, hid the sequence of the events they depict. This way, he actively prevented the reader from discovering one of the cycle's narrative arcs, the story of the lovers. The cycle's inclusion of this story is a manifestation of the insistence of the repressed: despite Amichai's tremendous efforts to erase Ruth, her presence persists.

* * *

Although the only explicit remnant from the "Binyamina, 1947" cycle is its opening phrase, pictorial, linguistic, and thematic echoes of it are scattered throughout "We Loved Here." The latter work often twists these residual elements until they are almost unrecognizable as descendants of their naïve ancestors. Nevertheless, Amichai did preserve one core stylistic trait that made its first appearance in "Binyamina, 1947"—the mundane. One of the most notable ways in which "We Loved Here" draws on its predecessor is in the unusual interweaving of everyday objects and technical language into the sonnet form. The Binyamina sonnets may therefore be seen as the incubator for what is now considered one of Amichai's greatest poetic innovations and contributions to Israeli poetry.[48] Mundane objects and images pepper the entire published cycle. Words like "water pipes" (Sonnet 4), "electricity" (8), "germs" (11), "tea" (20), "taxes" (21), and the "crippled and unemployed" (22) parallel the list of groceries, the nails, and the wires in "Binyamina, 1947."[49] Similarly, Amichai's use of non-Hebrew words like "patrol" (3) and foreign, technical words like "benzene" (10) and "antenna" (13) echo his use of the word "semaphore" in Sonnet II.

The structure of "We Loved Here" may be described broadly as a circle within a circle within a circle. The five sonnets at the beginning of the cycle (Sonnets 1–5) and the five sonnets at its end (Sonnets 19–23) will be designated the "framing sonnets." These roughly portray the war and the postwar world, respectively. Sonnets 1–5 unfurl a war narrative that begins with the oft-quoted words, "My father fought four years in their war" (World War I) and ends with the son's climactic war, the War of Independence, and its aftermath, thus spanning from 1914 to 1948. Sonnets 19–23 soberly depict the new, independent state and the consequences of war: soldiers who have returned when many of their comrades have not, and the new, dull life that has begun to emerge from the rubble. These final poems portray a dreary reality of unemployment and taxes, although the very end of the cycle expresses hope. While a few of these framing sonnets contain passing allusions to love—the mention of couples, the phrase "my girl"—the vocabulary of war permeates their lines. The remaining thirteen sonnets that form the "inner circle" of this long sequence (Sonnets 6–18) do include poems that may be described as love sonnets and will be referred to in this discussion as such. Furthermore, within these love sonnets sits a core of three emotionally dense poems (Sonnets 14–16), which will be called the core sonnets. They revolve around Ruth and Amichai's last night together. This organizational structure of a circle within a circle allows Amichai to set the love story against the backdrop of history. The passion and heartbreak of romantic love in "We Loved Here" subtly parallel the intense emotional state of a nation during the crucial war that would determine its fate. Thus, the last line of the first sonnet—"To all my wars it's I who have to go"[50]—refers not only to military wars in which the speaker is forced to fight, but to the battles of life, including those of love.

The extent of personal documentation in the love sonnets (Sonnets 6–18) is vastly different from that in "Binyamina, 1947." While in the Binyamina cycle the identity of the lovers is known and there is a firm sense of time and place, the setting and chronology of the love sonnets in the published cycle are often deliberately vague. Although the sites of some of the sonnets are geographically identifiable, the love sonnets of "We Loved Here" make jarring leaps among locations. They never fully establish any given setting and avoid any clear progression of time. Amichai intentionally upset the order of events in Sonnets 6–18 to conceal their underlying narrative.

The most striking difference between "Binyamina, 1947" and the love sonnets in "We Loved Here," however, is in the enormous change in outlook and mood. Reading both cycles side by side, one is struck by the romanticization of the world in the first and by the cynicism in the second. The 1947 sonnets were written in the midst of a love affair. They introduce the possibility of the relationship ending, but only as a generalized angst, not an imminent threat. In contrast, separation is inevitable in most of the thirteen love sonnets in "We Loved Here." These sonnets deal either with parting or with memories of a love that no longer exists. The disillusionment with love that Amichai felt while he was compiling "We Loved Here" for publication is manifested in the tempestuous mixture of disappointments and hopes that characterizes the cycle.

The Use of the Past Tense in the Title and in Sonnet 20

Capitalizing on the compact title phrase, Amichai uses the word *ahavnu* to play with different nuances of the past tense and their implications. His European linguistic background may have made him more sensitive to the imprecise concept of time in Hebrew grammar and enabled him to take advantage of it.[51] Depending on the context, *ahavnu* may mean "we loved," "we have loved," or "we had loved." While in the short cycle, *ahavnu* captures a couple's brief, blissful stay in Binyamina (perhaps indicating "we have loved here, and now we continue loving elsewhere"), the same word in the later cycle becomes a memorial for a past love that has already ended ("we used to love here, before our love ended"). In the Binyamina sonnets, therefore, *ahavnu* might be translated as a continuous action, "we have loved," but in the later sequence, published in 1955, it would be more final—"we loved" or even "we had loved."

This interpretation of the title phrase is supported by the context of its only recurrence in the cycle, in the opening of Sonnet 20.[52] Perhaps more than any other sonnet in the published cycle, Sonnet 20 and its monumental opening exemplify the disparity in the poet's attitudes before and after the war, before and after his farewell to Ruth Z. As in Sonnet I in "Binyamina, 1947," the first words of Sonnet 20 are followed by a period that divides the line in half. "Binyamina, 1947" opens with, "We loved here. Everybody loved us," while Sonnet 20 begins, "We loved here. Reality was different." The second half of each line describes the environment surrounding the lovers ("everybody"; "reality"), yet the implications are significantly different. In the later sonnet, the line not only suggests that the love has ended, but also that the sympathetic reality that had enabled it to flourish has vanished, as if to say, "We loved here [when] reality was different [but in the new reality, love is no longer possible]." After their first lines, both cycles elaborate on the world that surrounds the couple. While in Binyamina, "everybody" was enamored with the two lovers and nurtured their romance, the "reality" in the 1955 sonnet is callous and prosaic, a dog-eat-dog world filled with brigades of dead soldiers. Nevertheless, it is impossible to say definitively whether Amichai's "here" in the line "We loved here. Reality was different" alludes to Binyamina (and Ruth) or to the battlefields of the War of Independence (and Tamar). The only certainty is that the disillusioned, post-war existence depicted in Sonnet 20 is harsh and painfully unromantic. Like the high hopes for a perfect state, the hopes for a great love were not fulfilled.

Allusions to Ruth Z.: Sonnet 17

The phrase "We loved here" is not the only allusion to the affair embedded in the cycle. Ruth and Yehuda's relationship is the subject of a number of stanzas, and more particularly, a cluster of three sonnets (14–16) that revolves around the day Ruth left for America. These three sonnets form the emotional core of the cycle. In addition, hints about Yehuda's first adult love are scattered un-systematically throughout the ten other love sonnets. The allusions to the affair vary in their tone and level of abstraction, ranging from concrete recollections of nights together in Jerusalem to elusive images of letters, from recognizable romantic getaways, to lonely, sleepless nights. The apparent absence of an organizing principle that arranges these clues, however, is not coincidental; it is a part of the poetics of camouflage.

The beginning of Yehuda's affair with Ruth in Jerusalem—the earliest moment in their relationship that is specifically portrayed in "We Loved Here"—is not recalled until the cycle's end. Sonnet 17 begins with a young, hopeful love, but ends with harsh disenchantment.[53] Its opening line, "it was curfew then," is a reference to the lovers' time in Jerusalem, when the curfew imposed by the British played a dominant role in their love story. Ruth affirmed this association with confidence, saying, "every time he mentions curfew, it's me."[54] The association was confirmed by Amichai himself when he identified her as the subject of the 1980 poem, "The Rustle of History's Wings, as They Said Then."[55] Even in this angry poem, Amichai affectionately recalls their "sweet union" during the "curfew on the city."[56]

Curfews were extraordinarily romantic for Ruth and Yehuda, "forcing" them to spend more time indoors together after dark; in one case, Yehuda lingered at Ruth's house so late that he had to stay overnight. The curfew therefore hastened their intimacy in the early stages of their love. In Sonnet 17, this unexpected leap forward in the relationship is reflected metaphorically in the lovers' rapid growth from "unripe" to "mature." According to the speaker, the "curfew scene" took place "when we felt what un-ripeness was." In the following line, however, the lovers have already "matured."

The poem's figurative language exposes the romantic connotations that curfew bore for Amichai. The footsteps of soldiers, the sound that accompanied the curfew and which usually aroused fear, become the background music for the couple's enchanted evening: the rhythm of the guards' marching "back-and-forth" mirrors the beating of "the heart." Indeed, a British guard post was stationed in the ground floor of Ruth's apartment building in Jerusalem and the guards could be heard walking back and forth in front of it.[57] For the knowledgeable reader, this information explicitly identifies the sonnet's setting and context. It is about Ruth and Yehuda in her room in Jerusalem listening to British guards pace outside. These guards continue marching in the poem "History's Wings," although by 1980 the middle-aged poet no longer needed the protection of camouflage and so would remember "sweet love in a room / guarded by well-armed soldiers."[58]

Nostalgic musings notwithstanding, the overarching disillusionment that dominates all the sonnets connected to Ruth is present in Sonnet 17, as well. The "small hope" that "blossomed" in the "flower pot" is quickly replaced by dreams that grow up and "leave." In Sonnet 17, Amichai equated the romantic hope that accompanied the budding of their love with the hope for a "bloodless" transition to a Jewish state, for which he wished in the letters. Both hopes were unrealistic, and neither was fulfilled.

Chronological Scrambling in Sonnets 8, 9 and 11

Amichai's decision to place the memory of curfew in Sonnet 17 is an example of his effort to conceal autobiographical traces in "We Loved Here." In this instance, he does so through chronological scrambling. The budding love between Ruth Z. and Yehuda in January 1947 is not depicted until *after* the retelling of the couple's last night together, which occurred in August 1947. Furthermore, fragmented references to their unfulfilling correspondence, which began in September 1947, and their eventual breakup appear earlier in five sonnets—Sonnets 8, 9, 11, 12, and 13.

Reading these five sonnets alongside Amichai's letters to Ruth, it is clear that the figurative sources of these sonnets were developed during the correspondence.

Letter writing, the stuff upon which overseas romances are built, appeared in Amichai's poems even after the ill-fated correspondence had become a distant memory. The unambiguous image of letters that have failed to reach their destination appears in Sonnets 9 and 11. While undelivered letters may be read as a metaphor for unattainability, in the context of the affair's sad ending, they also become a signifier of Yehuda's loss of Ruth. Few of Yehuda's letters to Ruth were actually lost, but he felt as though they were, because she was often slow to respond and ultimately did not heed his message of love. He wrote to Ruth that he felt as though his letters vanished "in the mouth of the abyss" and that he was not sure if they ever reached her.[59]

It is no accident, then, that the letter remained a symbol of loneliness for Amichai. Indeed, Sonnet 9, a poem suffused with melancholy and a sense of loss, features a letter at its heart. It begins with the lines "The boathouse is without a boat, / Water laps at its walls like sad weeping . . ."[60] and continues with a letter that "Did not want" ("*Lo ratsa*"), which is floating in the water, "dripping with writing."[61] It is not clear what the letter "did not want" — to sink? To be forgotten? To be mailed? To be read? The scene, alternately concrete and ethereal, continues with steps leading down from the boathouse, not to the ground, but rather, to a "passing memory." The idea of an unfinished path appears yet again at the end of the octave, in the metaphor of a chain at the end of which there is nothing:

> A ring holds a rusty chain
> With nothing at its end. Like the empty hand
> Of Tantalus that didn't know
> That nothing's there . . . but holds on. . .[62]

And so, the steps that lead nowhere parallel both the letter that is not going anywhere and a "chain" with nothing at its end.

These inanimate objects imply a deep sense of emptiness and frustration, at the heart of which is the letter whose words are erased. The depiction of the letter floating on the water recalls the fact that Yehuda's letters had to cross the Atlantic Ocean to reach Ruth. The "weeping" ("water laps at its walls like sad weeping") and the unfulfilled desire symbolized by Tantalus's hand summon up Yehuda's unrewarded wait for a note from Ruth. The letter "dripping with writing," then, may be a subtle memorial to the aerograms that he sent to her in America.

Yehuda's last aerogram to Ruth helps to decipher even further the enigmatic image of the dripping letter. When he responded to Ruth's announcement of her engagement to another man in April 1948, the devastated Yehuda described his refusal to believe the shattering news in an image jarringly reminiscent of the sonnet: "as drops of water on oily cloth, so drip the words from me."[63] Thus, the "dripping writing" on a "floating letter" has its textual and figurative roots in the most painful moment of this love story.

The publication date of Sonnet 9 also ties it to that moment. It appeared in print immediately after the War of Independence. It was the first noteworthy poem that Amichai published. Although fifteen months had elapsed between the breakup and the appearance of Sonnet 9, these months were spent in battle. We have no way of knowing when the poem was completed, but it was likely conceived around April 1948, when his and Ruth's love ended and the war began.

Moreover, the publication history of Sonnet 9 embodies Amichai's gradual, retrospective attempt to camouflage its figurative and experiential roots. It first appeared with two other sonnets under the collective title "From the Poems of Tiberias" ("Mishirey Tveriya") in 1949, in the newspaper Al Hamishmar. In this initial publication, a trace of the relationship with Ruth survives in the name "Tiberias," the city where Yehuda and Ruth traveled together and swam in the Sea of Galilee. Ultimately, the first of these three poems became Sonnet 9, the second became Sonnet 8, and the third was eliminated.[64] In the canonic 1955 cycle, the name "Tiberias" was omitted, thus expunging the explicit reference to the poems' setting and erasing the initial connection between Sonnets 8 and 9. Mount Hermon, which appears in Sonnet 8, locates the poem's scenery; Sonnet 9, however, lacks any geographical specificity. Placed in the middle of a twenty-three-sonnet cycle, the geographical and biographical sources of these two sonnets are blurred.

Indeed, "From the Poems of Tiberias" may have alluded to an excursion with Tamar, Amichai's first wife, and not Ruth; Tiberias is, after all, a common vacation site. Yet oblique clues to Ruth's imprint on the poems remain. The lovers in Sonnet 8, for example, read German folktales about Til Eulenspiegel under an electric light. Reading aloud German children's books from Ruth's collection was one of the couple's favorite pastimes. Thus, while the sonnets may allude to trips he took with Tamar, they also reflect the persistence of Ruth in his memory. The floating letter that "did not want" in Sonnet 9 may also represent the lingering yearning for Ruth that refused to sink or to disappear long after the affair had ended.

References to letters appear twice in the cycle, and both times the descriptions are negative. In Sonnet 9, the letter "did not want"; in Sonnet 11, the lost letter represents the inevitability of love's end. Sonnet 11 depicts the frantic desire of lovers as "hot," boiling blood, doomed to get lost like "letters without an address."[65] Amichai's letter to Ruth from September, 1947, reveals a possible source of the imagery and language of Sonnet 11, as well as its gnawing anxiety. In this letter, Amichai described a nightmare in which he had forgotten to write Ruth's address on an envelope. In retelling his dream, he identified strongly with the "poor" letter "without an address" and its fate: "I suffered the suffering of the envelope that never reaches its destination."[66] Amichai's fear that his words would never reach his beloved is encapsulated by the image of the "lost letter." It is an overdetermined image, motivated by a variety of poetic and emotional considerations. The letters in Sonnet 11 are contrasted with the couple's love—while the letters are lost and disappear, the love "grows like germs." As idiosyncratic as this grouping of ardent love, "boiling blood," letters, and germs is, it appears in both Sonnet 11 and Amichai's letter from November 11, 1947, suggesting that a draft of the poem was conceived at that time.[67] That letter contains a copy of a different poem that associates letters, love, and germs growing in a Petri dish. In addition, the letter's prose likens the rhythm of Ruth's letters to the rhythm of "foaming," "stormy" blood. The letter from the still-optimistic autumn of 1947 associates the rhythm of flowing blood and letters with love's energy and passion; the sonnet, while making the same association, implies that when letters get lost, the blood, and perhaps love, does as well. Furthermore, by comparing lost letters to blood in a sonnet that appears in the textual context of war, Amichai evokes the idea of death due to the loss of blood (through a wound).[68] While too much "lost" blood causes corporeal death, lost letters are the sign of an emotional death. By linking the lost letters to lost blood, Amichai endows the comparison with both national-historical and personal implications.

Sonnets 12 and 13: Love and War

In "We Loved Here," Amichai translated the fact that he received Ruth's "Dear John" letter as he was going off to war into a poetic sequence that intertwines the national and the personal. Indeed, the overlapping of these two realms is one of the underlying themes of the entire cycle. Amichai saw his relationship with Ruth as entangled with the period that included both the UN vote on the Partition of Palestine on November 29, 1947, and the charged anticipation of May 15, 1948, when the British would depart and the War of Independence would erupt in full. In his response to her final letter, as he prepared to leave for combat, he wrote, "This is how this period ended in every way."[69]

The first lines in the cycle that may allude to either the UN vote or the Declaration of Independence appear in Sonnets 12 and 13.[70] There is no record of when these two sonnets were first written or if they were meant to be a pair. They do, however, contain a number of notable similarities, such as metaphorical references to historical events in the context of the couple's breakup, as well as linguistic and poetic correlations with "Binyamina, 1947." Regardless of the author's conscious intentions, these sonnets can thus be considered together as a discrete unit.

The metaphor that closes the first stanza of Sonnet 12 implicitly equates moments of great love with national celebrations. Rearranged to accommodate the English syntax, the lines would read "the event, which lifted our lives to the peak of a newspaper like a headline, has already happened."[71] In its Hebrew original, this metaphor seems simple, both structurally and syntactically. The Hebrew word used for "event," me'ora, frequently alludes to historical or political occurrences and is therefore semantically closer to the idea of newspaper headlines than the word "event" is in English. This makes it difficult to untangle the tenor of the metaphor (the event) from the vehicle (the headline), because both come from the same semantic realm of momentous, newsworthy incidents.[72]

Moreover, the climactic "event" in these lines could refer to either the establishment of the state or a life-altering private incident. This entanglement of public and private lends the image its ambiguity and allows the poet to blur the boundary between the personal and the national. Even if it is as private as the height of love, or a wedding,[73] the poem's peak "event" is tightly bound to the public sphere, the substance of newspaper headlines. The sonnet's language reflects the speaker's awareness of the historic time in which he lives. This awareness colors even the smallest details of everyday life with a dramatic hue. In his letters to Ruth, Amichai described the same feeling, albeit in simpler language: "every moment in my life is a peak," and in another, "every hour of my life is a great drama."[74]

An examination of Amichai's vocabulary in Sonnet 12 reveals further intricacies in the metaphor of the headline "event." The word "koteret" (title or headline) appears at an intersection between the personal and the national. Because koteret can mean "title" as well as "headline," it may be Amichai's nod to his sonnet cycle's own title, "We Loved Here." According to this reading, the life-altering "event" would be the stay in Binyamina. In his letters to Ruth Z., Amichai always referred to the weeks in Binyamina as the "peak" of their love story. They are also undoubtedly the inspiration for the title phrase "We Loved Here." The stay in Binyamina was thus the event that "raised our lives to the *koteret*"—the title of this cycle—but is now over.[75]

Whether the life-changing "event" was private or public, its glamour has faded and has been followed by disappointment; the dull life without love or patriotic enthusiasm is portrayed as a life of silence and shadows. The image in Sonnet 13 of a people roused "after an important declaration" plays a similar metaphorical role to that of the climactic "event" in Sonnet 12. Although, like the event, the "declaration" is mentioned only briefly, it anchors the poem in history and underscores the gap between the past heightened days of glory and the mediocre present that followed in their wake.

Sonnets 12 and 13 both concern an unspecified couple whose discontent and frustration are conveyed through fragmented but decipherable metaphors. Amichai buried allusions to Ruth deep in the textual subconscious of this pair of sonnets, but some memories of Binyamina are discernible. The textual interrelation between the Binyamina sonnets and "We Loved Here" is especially striking in two instances: the metaphorical use of roads, and the color palette. In both Sonnet 12 in "We Loved Here" and Sonnet III in "Binyamina, 1947," the speaker turns to his beloved, says, "look . . . ," and directs her gaze to the asphalt roads, comparing them to the lovers. In Sonnet III, the couple's future hangs in the balance. The asphalt road and the railroad tracks represent the man and the woman; if the tracks and the road meet behind the hill, the two will stay together. By contrast, the sentiment in the published sonnet is one of complete resignation. The once "wild," passionate roads will be tamed, and perhaps even broken in. Their domestication reflects the couple's lost passion.

Indeed, the free, untamed roads of Binyamina seem to have been "harnessed" and the colors of their background have faded in "We Loved Here." The initial, vivacious impetus behind the colors of the early cycle has been subverted. In "Binyamina, 1947," the color green denotes the couple's ecstatic vitality.[76] Weeds, grass, fields, forests, trees, and orchards make up its palette, creating a connection between Ruth and the color green. Though Amichai revived the association between verdant flora and euphoria in Sonnet 13, the euphoria no longer belongs to the lovers. The phrase "green days of happiness," which recalls the bygone Binyamina period visually as well as linguistically, is cut off from any romantic musings. Here, "green . . . happiness" is awarded to the grass, which is starkly contrasted with the lovers: while it was granted "two [more] green days of happiness" by the rain, the couple was not. Nature no longer favors them. While the sudden, unseasonable downpour in Binyamina generated the Dionysian description of a frolicking couple, Sonnet 13 is a bitter parody of that early, innocent joy. The older, more sober speaker laments, "only for us / the window of opportunity has closed." The former bond between the lovers, the green grass, and the rain has been annulled.[77]

Forsaking the memory of Binyamina's green fields, Sonnet 13 ends in a barren, urban setting. In their antenna-crowned houses, the couple ("we") sails aimlessly over a raging, "salty sleep."[78] Thus, the city's houses become ships, their antennae become masts, and their inhabitants drift over the surface of tortured sleep. The adjectives "salty" and "raging," used to describe the slumber, evoke a stormy sea and tears, as well as feelings of inner pain, turmoil, and anger. Although the "restless sea" that appears earlier in the octave of Sonnet 13 is a metaphor for the psychological state of the speaker, a concrete detail in its description lends this abstracted sea corporality: it is "raging" "near the shore." In using the sea both figuratively and as part of the scenery, Amichai's separate, fragmented brushstrokes merge into a picture of a person standing near the shore, gripped by emotion, bidding farewell to someone who is being borne away on a ship. Thus, the landscape of Haifa subtly begins to penetrate the cycle, and the stage is set for the climactic moment that is portrayed in the next three sonnets: the hours before, during, and after Ruth's departure on a ship from the port of Haifa. If Sonnets 12 and 13 allude to the distant bliss and splendor of Binyamina, they also set the stage for the three sonnets that follow this hidden plot to its sad conclusion.

The Core Sonnets: Sonnets 14, 15, and 16

Yehuda and Ruth's last night together is at the heart of the discontinuous narrative unit formed by Sonnets 14, 15 and 16. These core sonnets reflect Amichai's anguished recognition that their love affair is over, and can therefore be read as his poetic reconstruction of their farewell.

Sonnet 14: Parting

A bell strikes in the opening line of Sonnet 14, beginning the countdown to Ruth's departure: "and a bell began, slowly, to count us." Although the combination of the noun "bell" and the verb "count" with the direct object "us" is strange and ungrammatical in nature (in Hebrew as well as in English),[79] the significance of this word combination is made clear by its proximity to the word "la'azov" (to leave, abandon), which appears twice in the first stanza.[80] In the midst of a scene of a final parting and an empty room that has recently been vacated, the verb "to leave" appears in the third line, "we left everything . . ." and the fourth, "like a room that is left behind. . . ." It is as though the bell is counting the minutes until the two lovers part: when the counting stops, the speaker's beloved will abandon him.

Their imminent separation is prefigured by the structure of the sestet: each of its stanzas is exclusively devoted to one of the two lovers, thus already dividing them. The first stanza depicts a deserted boulevard. The emptiness of the boulevard becomes a reflection of the void inside the speaker. His loneliness is augmented by the awkward phrase in the third line: "*ehad yagi'a rak. hashe'ar bakvish*" (One will arrive only. The rest are on the road). The alienation of the "one" who will finally "arrive" is emphasized by the line's distorted grammar and punctuation: it is the single line in this sonnet that is split in two by a period. Additionally, the period follows the word "*rak*" (only), a word that never closes a sentence in Hebrew. It brings the reader to an abrupt stop, as if to suggest that not only the sentence, but also, perhaps, a relationship, was broken off midway and only one survived it. Thus, both the stanza's form and its content isolate that "one" from the "rest."

Amichai infuses the sestet with the anticipation of the separation through the idiosyncratic syntax of its first stanza as well as the classical structure of the sonnet, the division between the two parts of the sestet. While the dominant image in the first half of the sestet is one of emptiness, in the second, it is one of fullness. The first stanza may represent the male speaker's perception of himself through the empty, hollow landscape that surrounds him, while the second depicts a woman as an element in an imagined, urban setting: "a bank in the evening." Although the woman addressed in the second stanza is alone, she does not resemble the desolate boulevard; rather, she is similar to a bank: full of gold. The gold may be an indicator that, to the speaker, she is an unattainable treasure. At the same time, the "bank" may be a surreptitious criticism of the materialistic America toward which Ruth headed. Sonnet 14 ends with a night dubbed "the night of forgetting," which foretells not only Ruth and Yehuda's last night together (depicted in the following sonnet), but also the lovers' inevitable fate: the night when they will forget each other. The direct address to the woman continues into Sonnet 15, the only sonnet entirely "spoken" to a female companion by the male speaker,[81] as though he has seized this chance to talk to her because he knows that it will be his last.

Sonnet 15: The Last Morning

The chronological narrative begun in Sonnet 14 reaches its heartrending climax in Sonnet 15, which opens with the couple's last morning together. The first words of Sonnet 15 simply tell the exact time: "A quarter of six." Given the context, it is likely to be 5:45 in the morning.[82] The temporal connections between Sonnets 14 and 15 stretch beyond the progression of night into day. The opening lines of these two sonnets parallel each other. The bell that opened Sonnet 14 is echoed by the telling of time in Sonnet 15. The counting of the bell, then, may also be the ringing of an alarm clock that wakes up the lovers at 5:45. The precision of time embodies a sense of the finality of that moment and hides a wound that never healed—the memory of the exact hour when the man and woman had to tear themselves from sleep and from their dreams. Interpreted in light of Ruth and Yehuda's last night together, the early rising hour is enforced by the boat's early departure. In an interview, Ruth Z. recalled, "It was very early in the morning and we were both afraid that we would not wake up in time, even though the alarm clock was set."[83]

Repeating the loaded and ungrammatical punctuation of the eleventh line of Sonnet 14 (". . . only."), the first line of Sonnet 15 is also divided into two sections by a period. While the first part tells the time in a matter-of-fact manner, the meaning of the second part is ambiguous: "the dreams restrained" ("*hahalomot hivligu*"). A possible reading of the line might be that in order for the person to wake up, the dreams must restrain themselves or cease to exist. This interpretation fails, however, because it illogically endows dreams with a voluntary action. Furthermore, the phrase seems incomplete; in Hebrew the verb "to restrain" usually requires an indirect object.[84] Amichai's word choice, then, may also be playing with additional, more allusive meanings. The Hebrew word *hivligu* is phonetically close to *hifligu*, which means "sailed away" and is used in modern Hebrew exclusively in reference to ships and boats. The verb *hifligu* appears in the well-known romantic literary cliché, *lehaflig bahalomot*—to sail away or exaggerate in dreams. A classical example of this phrase is in the poem "At Twilight," H. N. Bialik's famous work, which develops this "dead metaphor" to describe how the dreams of two lovers sail away to unknown desolate islands, where they become lost.[85] Although there is no doubt that Amichai was familiar with this masterpiece of Hebrew poetry, the interpretation of his line does not depend on it. Whether or not the dreams of Amichai's sonnet make an intertextual reference to Bialik's "sailed-away dreams," the word *hivligu* (restrained) must be interpreted in its relation to *hifligu* (sailed away). The dreams in Amichai's sonnet not only sail away into the distance in the idiomatic, romantic way, but also literally sailed away on the boat that Ruth boarded that morning. This interpretation is confirmed by the sonnet's references to water in three out of four lines in the second stanza. These references to water, combined with the biographical background of the poem (Ruth sailing away) and the geographical markers (Haifa, New York, and the water separating them) almost demand the reading of *hivligu* as *hifligu*.

While the dreams can be interpreted either as restraining themselves or sailing away, they must also be read in the context of their punctuation. The "restrained dreams" appear in the same sentence as the "flower of forgetting" in the second line. The sentence suggests figuratively that in order for the flower of forgetting to blossom, the dreams must be suppressed, or held back. Additionally, the flower of forgetting echoes the "night of forgetting" from the end of Sonnet 14, as though the process of forgetting will commence as soon as that night ends. With underlying sarcasm, Amichai uses the blossoming flower to signify the slow fading of the memory of love. His invented phrase replaces clichés like the "flower of love" and negates the forget-me-not flower by removing the "me-not."[86] This unusual image is also tied to the sentimentalized flower in "Binyamina, 1947," which was used by the lovers in the ritual "she loves me, she loves me not." Here, however, the flower is no longer part of the lovers' playful game. Instead, it is a sign of alienation, for it blossoms only in the head of the speaker while his beloved is absent. The singular inflection ("*kodkodi*," my head) replaces the "we" of the Binyamina sonnets.

The stanza continues with images of vegetation, but in place of a flower, the days that follow are likened to fruit. The description of a woman as a fruit first appears in a letter in which Amichai gained solace by imagining that he would eventually "receive the fruit of [Ruth's] femininity."[87] The author of the sonnet, however, already knows that he will not, and reverses the hopeful image. The sonnet's speaker turns to his beloved and says, "the grapes of my round days became sweet / in your cluster—but not with me."[88] The departing woman has carried off the luscious days that the lovers spent together. Those days ripen in her and "become sweet" when she is already far away from the speaker. The image suggests that the experiences she collected with him have matured her and that she has used them to become a woman, but someone else will reap the benefit of her femininity.[89]

Departing from the voice of the first stanza, the speaker stops addressing the woman directly in the second stanza of Sonnet 15. Thus, removing himself from the situation. Instead, he looks at the landscape from a physical and temporal distance, as though he is standing far away, observing his past. Consequently, the text of this stanza constitutes a choppy, fragmented description that can only be deciphered using biographical details.

While the first stanza of Sonnet 15 ends with the words "not with me," the following stanza begins with the impersonal allusion to "the tall towers," perhaps inferring that the "tall towers" are the place where she matured without him: ". . . my round days became sweet / in your cluster—but not with me. // The tall towers are still silent. . . ."[90] Interpreted biographically, the "towers" might be the skyscrapers of New York City. On the day of Ruth's departure, which the core sonnets reconstruct, the "towers" have "not yet spoken" because Ruth has not yet seen them.

"Towers" can also be read as part of another, Israeli, landscape. Subtle clues scattered throughout the stanza (the silent towers, unbridgeable bodies of water, and the confusing word *shover* [breaker]) suggest that, here, Amichai confronts the site of his pain: the port of Haifa, the locus of the couple's final separation. Considering the vista of Haifa, "towers" may recall the overbearing presence of the tallest buildings in the Haifa bay area, which were, and still are, the oil refineries. Alternately, the referent of the towers may lie in the Hebrew word *migdal* (tower) itself. In Hebrew, while *migdal* is a tower, *migdalor* is a lighthouse, a fixture of any harbor, Haifa's included. The word "*migdal*" in the sonnet thus implies a seaport through its derivative, *migdalor*, while "water" and "bridge" in the subsequent lines explicitly evoke a seascape.

Read as lighthouses (*migdalorim*), the towers, which are supposed to warn ships of rocks, have failed. The silence of the poem's towers ("*migdalim*") implies the threat of a disaster against which there was no warning. The fact that the lighthouses are mute on the morning of the beloved's departure bodes ill for the speaker because "silent" lighthouses cause shipwrecks. The lighthouses' absent signals may be understood as either someone's failure to warn the speaker about the emotional crash looming ahead or as his own blindness to the imminent heartbreak.

This "heartbreak" is articulated in the line that follows, through the repetition of the root Sh.B.R. (break), which reads: ". . . the broken one did not yet know of the breaker" ("*velo yada nishbar od al shover*"). Despite the ambiguity of the alliterative language, both words, "*nishbar*" (is broken) and "*shover*" (breaker), seem to denote a future emotional calamity (in Hebrew, hearts "break" just as they do in English; *lev nishbar* is a broken heart). The nature of the breaker and the broken one, however, is not spelled out in this line. To a reader who knows how Ruth and Yehuda's relationship ended, it may be read as "the one who is about to be broken [the man] does not yet know the identity of the person who will break him [his beloved]." The broken one (*nishbar*) remains unidentified throughout the stanza; only the suffix *nu* (we/us) in the last line reveals that it might be the couple. Ironically, here, Amichai uses the sound *nu*, which is usually a sign of togetherness, to express parting ("*yavdil benenu*," literally, "will separate between us").

The connection between "heartbreak" and "break" does not capture all the nuances of the root Sh.B.R. explored in that stanza. Because it is used as a noun in the stanza's geographical context, *shover* may also refer to a prominent element of Haifa's landscape. A familiar feature of this port city is the long stone wall extending from one end of the bay to the other, the breakwater that separates the calm water of the bay from the waves of the open sea. In Haifa, it is called a *shover galim* (literally, "wave breaker"). In the sonnet, the breakwater is the wall between the waters of Haifa, where the speaker is staying, and the waters of the Atlantic Ocean, on which his beloved has sailed away. Thus, Haifa's landscape—its bay, the breakwater, and possibly the lighthouses—provide the setting for sorrow.

The sense of a vast distance is heightened through a garbled biblical reference that portrays an expanse of water without end that separates the lovers. Amichai quotes almost verbatim from Genesis 1:6, which reads, "divide **the waters from the waters**" ("*mavdil ben mayim lamayim*"), although Amichai's line reads "enlarged **the waters from the waters**" ("*higdil ben mayim uven mayim*"). The phrasing of "the waters from the waters" is a clear signal to this verse. Furthermore, the verb "enlarge" in this context is as awkward in Hebrew as it is in English. In addition to playing with "the waters," Amichai exploits the similarity between the verb root B.D.L. (separate) and G.D.L. (enlarge). The switching of the sounds *g* and *b* notwithstanding, the Hebrew reader would immediately identify the source of the phrase and automatically invert the letters. Through this reference to Genesis, Amichai implies that a divine power is involved in the separation of the couple. Moreover, by substituting the root G.D.L. for B.D.L., he grants mythical dimensions to the poem's bodies of water. God has not only separated the lovers, but widened the distance between them. He has enlarged the bodies of water to ensure that no bridge will ever connect the two, "*beli gasher*" (without bridging). In Genesis, the ability to separate is a positive, creative power, but in the sonnet, it is a destructive one, a "breaker" that parts the lovers. The role of God as the separator of waters also connects Him to a concrete element of the landscape. Like God, the *shover galim* (breakwater), divides water from water: the water of the bay from the water of the sea.

After the volta of Sonnet 15, references to water are replaced by references to fire. The lovers' hands and faces are spotlighted through two sets of binary oppositions: burn / extinguish and open / close. The lines of the sestet alternate between a woman's two pleas. In one, she asks the man to "extinguish" her "lit" and "burning" hands. He does not, and her hands continue to burn. Lifting her face to him, she also entreats the man to "close" her "open" face, but again, he refuses. The last, and lasting, image of the fifteenth sonnet is "your two hands—burning." The continuous burning of the pleading hands symbolizes an unyielding, unrequited passion. In this surreal scene, the speaker seems to recall a real or imagined moment of belated regret on her part. It happened when he had already detached himself from her, so while her face is still "open" to him, his face is "closed."

This arresting image of a woman's burning hands that must be extinguished appears elsewhere in Amichai's oeuvre, in the 1959 epic, "In the Public Garden."[91] The content of Amichai's letters to Ruth Z. removes any doubt that this epic was written almost entirely about her. Amichai completed a draft of it in December 1947 and sent the concluding segment to Ruth as a birthday present in January 1948. A comparative reading of Sonnet 15, the draft of "In the Public Garden" as it appears in the letter, and the published version of the epic reveals the intratextual relationship among these works, as well as their affiliation with Ruth. The image of burning hands is almost identical in all three. The lines "extinguish her hands / and the fire" appear in both the unpublished and published versions of the epic,[92] while "your two lit hands—for me to extinguish" and "your two hands—burning" appear in Sonnet 15. Amichai did not publish "In the Public Garden" until more than ten years later, but he did extract this image and plant it in "We Loved Here," unintentionally revealing that the sonnets, like "In the Public Garden," are connected to Ruth.

An elaborate linguistic and figurative web ties the fire imagery in the sestet of Sonnet 15 to the water of its octave. The wrenching images of separation and the dichotomy of water and fire are connected by an intricate textual and religious allusion: the Saturday night Jewish ritual of havdalah (literally, "division" or "separation"). The religious ritual of havdalah marks the end of the holy Sabbath and the beginning of the work week. Havdalah includes a blessing over the creation of fire as well as a blessing over God's power to separate elements from each other: "Blessed art thou . . . who creates the illuminations of the fire," and "Blessed art thou . . . who separates between the holy and secular, between light and darkness. . . ." The verse in Genesis ("divide the waters from the waters") is the linguistic and theological foundation for the havdalah: He who divided waters from waters also divided day and night, heaven and earth, the Sabbath and the workdays. The images of the sestet (extinguishing a flame, hands, face) and its vocabulary of fire, then, are connected to both the personal theme of the separation of two people and the havdalah, the theological concept and ritual of separation.

The physical performance of the ritual of havdalah involves lighting a multiwicked candle and then extinguishing it with wine. As they recite the blessings, participants in the ritual encircle the sole source of light in the room, the flame of the large candle. It shines on their faces alone, but when they reach the verse "The Creator of illuminations of fire," they extend their hands toward the flame as though to inspect them in the light. Like the faces and hands of Orthodox Jews at the end of the Sabbath, only those body parts of the man and the woman in the poem are "visible." Amichai, then, takes this memory from his religious youth and transforms it into a synecdoche. While recalling a religious tradition about separation, he also captures the essence of isolation via metaphors that highlight disjointed body parts.

Sonnet 16: A Final Farewell and the Book of Love

Until this point, the core sonnets have acted as a biographical narrative unit that progresses through time at a somewhat consistent rate. After the volta of the fifteenth sonnet, however, Amichai abandoned the underlying chronology of the past two sonnets. The narrative begins to fracture, and the moment in time becomes deliberately vague, as if the pain of the breakup could not be confined to one specific time period. The final image of the woman's "open" face in Sonnet 15 could have taken place at any time, as could the first stanza of Sonnet 16. While the couple's separation is final by Sonnet 16, its first stanza could refer to either of two crucial moments: Yehuda walking away from the dock and the wretched hours immediately after Ruth embarked for America, or the moment eight months later when he realized that she would never return.

Following the agonizing yet enigmatic depictions of the breakup in Sonnet 15 is a gloomy series of the actions that the lone speaker takes in Sonnet 16: "I walked . . ."; "I walked sadly . . ."; "I covered your face . . ."; "I exited calmly . . .". These activities are all intended to help the speaker forget his beloved. He walked away from his memory of her "without turning back" and "without eyes." In the first letter Amichai wrote to Ruth after she left, he told her that as he was walking away from the port, he had to cover his eyes with sunglasses lest his tears be visible. The image of a man walking away "without eyes" may refer to this moment.[93] Even though he is without eyes, the open face of the speaker's beloved, portrayed in the preceding sonnet, continues to haunt him. Her face is so etched in his mind that he must actively "cover" it in order to leave and stay "calm." While the openness of the woman's face in the fifteenth sonnet implies her vulnerability, in the first stanza of the sixteenth, her face no longer reflects her yearning for him, but rather his inability to forget her.

The second stanza of Sonnet 16 fractures the chronology of the core sonnets further. It is even more removed from the excruciating moment of her departure, and may occur years later. All that remains of the affair is the story of their love. The speaker no longer mourns the relationship that ended, but rather laments their "book," which has been abandoned. The book is open, exposed to the elements, and the wind "leafs" through its pages. The use of the phrase "our book" to describe "our love" could be a metaphor, associated with either the Jewish concept of the book of life or the speaker's occupation as a writer. The line "Through our abandoned book, the wind was leafing" ("*Betokh sifrenu hamufkar il'el haru'ah*"), however, is additional proof that this sonnet is bound to Ruth.

In seven separate letters dating from September 1947 to January 1948, Yehuda spoke of their affair, past and present, as a book.[94] He developed this metaphor in varied ways, at times their lives are the book, at other times the book is the literary rendering of their love. The letters contain phrases that are almost identical to the line in Sonnet 16: "the book about the two of us";[95] "If our lives were a book, it would say . . .";[96] "Our book . . . is written";[97] "Our story continues to be written";[98] "our book continues being written";[99] "Our book is being written . . . the writer . . . turns the pages."[100] The difference, of course, is that in the love letters their book is still being created, while in the sonnet it has been forsaken. Analogously, in the letters written while their love is still alive, Yehuda is the writer who flips through the pages, but in the sonnet only the wind leafs through the pages of an "ownerless" ("*mufkar*") book. The speaker in this sonnet clearly knows that their book does not have a happy ending and feels that its imaginary pages are prey to the wind.

Amichai's letters also reveal connections between images that seem unrelated in the text of the sonnets; principally, the hands and faces in Sonnet 15 and the book in Sonnet 16. In a letter written in December 1947, Yehuda includes a third-person portrait of himself as their book's author: "his face is burning and his white hands. . . ."[101] Only the author's disconnected "burning face" and "white hands" are visible as he writes. This image is reminiscent of the "burning hands" and "open face" of the rejected beloved in Sonnet 15. Thus, figuratively, the woman's "burning hands" (in the sonnet) formerly "belonged" to the writer of the lovers' book (in the letter), the same book that became "ownerless" in Sonnet 16. Discovering the commonality of imagery between the letter and the two sonnets contributes to the understanding of these sonnets in three ways. First, it reinforces the sonnet cycle's biographical link to Ruth; second, it demonstrates that the letters are a crucial intertext of the poetry. Finally, this commonality suggests that these sonnets were written, at least in draft form, as early as 1947.

Sonnet 16 builds upon the imagery of Sonnet 15 by further connecting the experience of separation to a body of water. While in Sonnet 15 the separation between waters parallels the separation of the lovers, in Sonnet 16 the water brings them together. The shallow water that the speaker can see near the shore (the Mediterranean) is an extension of the water that is "not from here"—the deep Atlantic Ocean that is near Ruth.[102] This metaphorical mixing of waters is an expression of longing for the woman who now dwells across the ocean, but also recalls Amichai's later love poems in which "to lie with you, water within water"[103] has erotic undertones. Similarly, sexual imagery appears in the sestet of Sonnet 16 when the male body is emptied of fluid. This sonnet's image, however, does not remain solely in the erotic sphere, but rather fuses with the national-historical realm. The speaker tells his beloved to look at his body, which is emptying like a vacant street after a large, festive gathering. This metaphor may convey the void caused by Ruth's absence, but the comparison of the male body to a street that empties "and then becomes silent" also has both erotic and national implications. The physical orgasm or climax mirrors the national one—the establishment of the state. As in Sonnets 12 and 13, the "celebratory gathering" may refer to the large celebrations of November 29, 1947, after the vote for the partition plan and creation of a Jewish State in the UN, and of May 15, 1948, after the Declaration of Independence. Both occurred during Amichai's slow and painful realization that his relationship with Ruth was over. Moreover, Amichai's description of the celebrations of November 29 in the letters captures an orgasmic euphoria as well.[104]

With the speaker's recognition of the irrevocability of the breakup, the arc of the core sonnets begins its sad descent in Sonnet 16. The denouement is reflected in the evolution of the image of hands from Sonnet 15. The "hands" that represented the woman now merely describe clouds: "clouds pass over me like a hand [passing] over cloth." The memory of the flesh and blood hands of the woman has evaporated. Furthermore, the *pair* of hands that appeared in Sonnet 15 has been replaced by one disconnected, ownerless hand. It is as though even the hand has lost its companion and is now isolated. At the sonnet's conclusion, the lonely hand "remembers" the past, then "cries," "remembers" again, "and forgets."

This line is yet another echo of Amichai's letters to Ruth. It refers to the words he wrote to her upon learning of her engagement. The distraught young man told her of packing his suitcases and learning to "*remember* a little bit and *forget*"[105] (emphasis added). In both the letter and the sonnet, Amichai is acutely aware of how quickly remembering can turn into forgetting and formulates the fluidity between them similarly: in each, only a minute separates the two.

*   *   *

With the exception of Sonnet 17, about a budding love during curfew, the cycle "We Loved Here" abandons the story of Ruth and Yehuda after the conclusion of the core sonnets (14, 15, and 16). The remaining sonnets are dominated by allusions to another love during the war and the disillusionment that followed. Not until the final sonnet (23) is there a reaffirmation of love and hope. Against the background of the poems that precede it, however, that faith in the future seems quite fragile.

We cannot know with absolute certainty exactly when and about whom the sonnets of "We Loved Here" were written, yet Amichai's declaration that they were all dedicated to Tamar remains suspect. The roots of "We Loved Here" lie in the amateur work written in the spring of 1947. The comparison of the two cycles allows the reader to follow the migration of Ruth and Yehuda's story from its humble beginnings in "Binyamina, 1947" and to see the ways in which it was reworked and artistically metabolized in the mature cycle. In addition, "Binyamina, 1947" may be seen as the incubator for the poetic revolution that would reach the public eight years later in *Now and in Other Days*. Reading the cycles side by side allows one to discover the poetic seeds that ultimately blossomed in Amichai's later works and reveals the significant developments in his poetry during the period between 1947 and the publication of his first volume.

The most dramatic illumination of the later cycle, however, comes from Ruth's memories and her documents of the love affair, which were meant neither as poetry nor for publication. Amichai's letters dramatically alter the reading of the oft-misunderstood canonic cycle. They supply concrete evidence that the sonnets draw upon language, images, and themes that Amichai conceived in 1947 and associated with his relationship and breakup with Ruth. They lend the segments of the "We Loved Here" cycle a cohesion that its previous interpretations seem to lack. Reading the letters as an intertext of "We Loved Here" exposes the buried emotional and autobiographical origins of Amichai's work, as well as its linguistic and figurative roots. The connections between the unguarded letters and the abstruse sonnets in "We Loved Here" establish Ruth Z. as the protagonist of Amichai's poetic narrative, even though all overt references to her are suppressed. They show the impossibility of discussing Amichai's life and creative work without also discussing Ruth Z.

Amichai deployed his entire arsenal of camouflaging techniques to erase the memory of Ruth from the surface of the poems. The pain she left was no doubt a part of the reason behind his cover-up, but his wish to preserve a chronology that would coincide with his desired status as a national poet was also a motivating factor. He constructed the persona of a national poet in part by linking his emergence as a poet to the heroic days of the War of Independence. He invented a personal mythology in which the first battles of the War of Independence unexpectedly "consecrated" him as a poet. If his poetic achievements of 1947 had been publicly known, they would have undermined the authenticity of this image. The "wisdom of camouflage" and the chronological scrambling that he employed in "We Loved Here" were repeated in another misinterpreted work, the epic "In the Public Garden." He not only camouflaged identities and content in this epic, but actually kept it from publication for over a decade, never revealing when it was written, so as not to endanger his national poetic persona.

A small booklet entitled *Bagina hatsiburit* (In the Public Garden) was published by the Akhshav publishing house shortly after the appearance of Amichai's second volume, *Two Hopes Away*.[1] This sequence is preserved in Amichai's first collected volume, *Poems: 1948–1962*, in which the poems are arranged according to the dates of each book's initial publication. Thus, the poems that comprise the long, lyrical cycle "In the Public Garden" (1959) succeed the poems of the previous collections, *Now and in Other Days* (1955) and *Two Hopes Away* (1958).[2] Amichai participated in the editing of the volume, so it is likely that he preferred this order. Naturally, critics have assumed that the atypical poetic sequence "In the Public Garden" was written close to the time that it was published, and the few who have addressed it analyzed it accordingly.[3] In fact, little has been written about "In the Public Garden"; its scant reviewers have had mixed reactions and found it difficult to interpret.

Comparing it to Amichai's first two volumes and contemporary works by other poets, several critics dubbed "In the Public Garden" a true revolution in Hebrew poetry. Gabriel Moked, for example, asserted that while *Now and in Other Days* merely swerved from the main road of Hebrew literature ("*derekh hamelekh*"), "In the Public Garden" was a genuine turning point, which enriched modern Hebrew poetry with an "innovative genre."[4] Others saw it simply as a poem about a garden of dreams or a place for pantheistic worship. Maxim Gilan suggested that it was a story of a hidden love between a man (the poet) and a woman who is married to someone else. He also wrote that he preferred "In the Public Garden" to *Two Hopes Away* because it was less rational. Gilan welcomed the collection's exuberance, which he saw as the similarity between "In the Public Garden" and *Now and in Other Days*.[5]

Most critics who wrote about it, however, had a more negative opinion. Indeed, the initial publication of "In the Public Garden" evoked sharp controversy at the time, because it was perceived as a brazen departure from poetic tradition and conservative social values. Critics who preferred the understated

Amichai saw the poem as a caprice, "a temporary stumble."[6] They believed that it was Amichai's misguided attempt to copy his peers, and that the poem's eroticism was mere pornography.[7] Nathan Zach, a proponent of modernism, defended "In the Public Garden" by saying that it followed the style of a modern epic and therefore used mood and repetition as a unifying principle, instead of a plot. Even so, Zach argued that the work was too arbitrary and anecdotal.[8]

Critics continued to misread the work and misunderstand its fragmentary structure through the 1980s. Even Boaz Arpali, in his exhaustive study of Amichai's early poetry, viewed "In the Public Garden" as individual "poems" that portray the "deeds and lives of simple people . . . whose happiness is trampled by collective ideologies." He described it as a catalogue of situations, scenes, and characters that together build an image of "public loneliness," in which the public garden is a "topographical common denominator."[9] Amichai's critics did not know, either in 1959 or in 1986, about his love for Ruth Z. Only with that history in mind, plus the texts of his letters to her, does "In the Public Garden" surrender to interpretation and its inner logic emerge.

From Amichai's letters to Ruth it is apparent that between September and December 1947, he worked on two long pieces, "Hada'aya" (Amichai's original term for a kite) and "In the Public Garden."[10] While "Hada'aya" was never published nor, indeed, ever found in full, "In the Public Garden" resurfaced in its entirety in 1959. Twelve years before critics thought that a capricious Amichai was trying to adapt himself to the innovative methods employed by his peers,[11] a twenty-three-year-old teacher in Haifa was writing a poetically revolutionary work about his relationship with a woman in Jerusalem during the previous year. At that early stage of his career as a poet, before he had published anything,[12] Amichai was confident that the work he had just completed was a new and original form of writing. In his letter, he told Ruth that he wrote the poem from "instinct" and that it was composed of individual pictures and "free associations."[13] Thus, the fragmentation of the work was, in fact, deliberate. As though he foresaw the criticism that would greet "In the Public Garden" twelve years later, Amichai explained to Ruth that the seemingly haphazard style was intentional. The fractured nature of the work and its truly groundbreaking structure, mood, and tone are more remarkable when we realize that the young poet consciously overturned everything that preceded him in Hebrew poetry even before he became known for what was thought to be his earliest work.

"In the Public Garden" is the only one of Amichai's works to have survived both in the letters and in print. It is also the only published work that can be un-questionably traced to the story of the poet's first adult love. On December 7, 1947, Amichai proudly told Ruth that he had finished "In the Public Garden," his new poem, the night before.[14] Despite her entreaties to read the poem, he withheld it for a special occasion: on January 14, 1948, he copied the concluding portion of "In the Public Garden" into an aerogram as a present for her birth-day, on January 22.[15]

The section of "In the Public Garden" that is contained in the January 14, 1948, letter is referred to herein as the "birthday poem." Although Amichai de-scribed the full "In the Public Garden" as "a poem" in 1947 (implying that it was one continuous text), when he published it in 1959, he divided it into fifty short segments. In the January 14 letter, however, there is no indication of a plan to divide the text. Yet, one significant structural detail remains: in both the 1947 and 1959 versions, Amichai designated the same portion of text to close his nontraditional work—the section he copied as a birthday present for Ruth.[16] Accordingly, the birthday poem roughly corresponds to the last thir-teen segments in the published work.

By postponing the poem's publication for almost a dozen years, Amichai camouflaged its autobiographical connection and may have sought to preserve his self-imposed ideological timeline. His decision not to throw "In the Public Garden" into the literary arena earlier in his career might also have been driven by more than a professional concern that its stunningly innovative form would be rejected. He might have feared that rewriting the poem too soon would re-awaken painful memories of his tender moments with Ruth or thrust him back into the emotional turmoil that followed the breakup. The critic Gilan may have sensed the emotional core of the poem that Amichai himself tried to hide; namely, that it was about a beloved woman who no longer belonged to him. There may have been another motivation for this deferral, however. Amichai al-ways publicly asserted that he never aspired to be a poet, and only began writing poetry to cope with battles during the War of Independence in 1948, thus forg-ing the connection between his nationalism and his poetry. Revealing the year when he actually composed "In the Public Garden" would undermine this ideo-logically motivated timeline. Even in 1963, when preparing Poems: 1948–1962 for publication, he retained this false chronology.

With the connection between the love story of Amichai and Ruth Z. and "In the Public Garden" exposed, it is apparent that the work is linked to Ruth geographically, biographically, and textually. At the heart of "In the Public Garden" is a particular small park in Jerusalem and a specific woman whose name is Ruth. In its final form, the epic lacks any indication of the public garden's true location, and it only fleetingly names its heroine. These omissions can be attributed in significant part to the author's attempt to veil the feelings and events behind the words. Moreover, the published poem as a whole is extremely enigmatic, perhaps as part of Amichai's attempt to camouflage its sources even more deeply. The text of "In the Public Garden" is so hermetic, in fact, that even when Ruth's name appears overtly within it, it is so wholly decontextualized that few would recognize its importance.

AN OVERVIEW OF "IN THE PUBLIC GARDEN"

Unlike the structurally autonomous texts that constitute the majority of the poems in Amichai's two first published volumes, "In the Public Garden" is a continuum that Amichai cut into fifty short, interdependent, unnumbered, individually titled segments.[17] This unusual structure, however, is not the only quality that separates "In the Public Garden" from its predecessors. Its genre is hard to define. It is reminiscent of a lighthearted poetic skit, a lyrical piecemeal narrative, or a series of snapshots. Amichai himself was aware that his creation did not fit within the mold of any existing genre. When he enthusiastically announced to Ruth that he had completed "In the Public Garden," Amichai dubbed the work "diklum shirim," a group of poems meant to be recited out loud.[18] With these words, he defined a new genre, one that straddles the line between poetry and drama. Its style is laconic, its lines are extremely short, and the scenes portrayed in its various segments are fragmented. These scenes highlight two unspecified but identifiable characters, a man and a woman who reappear periodically in alternating stanzas. There is additional ambiguity with respect to the woman: it is unclear if the work portrays one or more female protagonists.

The only consistency within the work is its location. The poem's fifty segments lend themselves to the interpretation that they are related to the public garden, and some may be perceived as pieces in the larger collage that makes up the garden. The fragmented narrative presented in this poetic sequence adheres to a plausible time frame and moves from daytime to nighttime. The latter dominates the work and seems to preoccupy the author. The title phrase "In the Public Garden," which recurs in five of the segments, together with the occasional and unpredictable appearances of death[19] serves as a refrain of sorts and grants the work some sense of unity of place and atmosphere.[20] The feeling of despair evoked by the darkness and the presence of death, however, is undermined by the whimsical, witty, and nonsensical linguistic and figurative combinations strewn throughout the work.

Beyond this general outline, it is difficult to determine a clear plotline or chronology. The central consciousness in this chain of poems, the "I" or "he," is portrayed as a forlorn, barren ("ariri") man who is longing for a certain woman.[21] As early as the second segment, curiously entitled "The End" (2), the speaker divulges that the object of his desire is a woman who is married to another man. Although she is gone, her ghost, together with the phantom of the man from the time they were a couple, hovers over the garden.[22] Other "characters" that inhabit this enigmatic work are regulars in a public garden: toddlers and their mothers,[23] part-time census takers and clerks,[24] along with a teenage girl posing for a photograph.[25] Accompanying the tableaux is a violin whose music emerges sporadically throughout the segments and that the speaker addresses directly.[26] In the latter part of the work, the setting becomes increasingly dark: while some of its segments recall nursery rhymes first introduced during "daytime," others echo typically nocturnal sounds. The garden turns into a dwelling place for lovers, for homeless people who sleep on benches,[27] for a "night butterfly,"[28] and for isolated objects lit by a street lamp.[29] Only a telephone ring pierces the quietness of the night.[30] Against this background, one "hears" a "conversation," the first to be recorded in this poetic sequence. It takes place at midnight.[31] From that point on, there is a progression toward two o'clock in the morning, when the second and final exchange, entitled "Last Conversation in a Whisper" (50), closes the poem.

THE PROSE OF THE LETTERS AS A KEY

While there is no question of when the birthday poem that comprises the latter part of "In the Public Garden" was written, an in-depth reading of the segments that precede it in the published work reveals that they, too, must have been written either in the fall of 1947, or soon after, inspired by the breakup. A textual analysis of the germane letters, as well as outside information provided by Ruth Z., confirms that a large portion of the work dates from that period. The letters from September to December 1947 shed light on the experiential sources for this revolutionary work, as well as on the laborious creative investment Amichai made in its preparatory stages.

A sequence of images from three segments is textually linked to "Liebeslied" ("Love Song"), a poem by Rainer Maria Rilke that Amichai included and praised in his letters to Ruth: the violin whose music accompanies the speaker, and the image of God playing lovers as instruments.[32] The striking final image of Rilke's poem depicts lovers as two strings strung on the same violin, producing a sweet song together—the love song—as they are played by an otherworldly hand with an invisible bow. The violin first appears in "In the Public Garden," in Segment 9, entitled "The Accompanying Violin." It moves closer to the speaker as he sleeps, into the range of "sweet hearing," reminiscent, perhaps, of the "sweet song" that closes Rilke's poem. The music may be that of a distant love whose sweetness softly returns to the speaker at quiet moments during the night. Violin-related imagery returns halfway through the epic, in "What's Your Name What's His Name" (26), which refers to the end of "Liebeslied" more directly. In it, the bow and the violin converse, asking each other why they are connected at their hips. As in Rilke's work, this intimate connection is not necessarily a voluntary one—a greater power has brought them together and is playing them. Finally, in Segment 33, the greater power appears. Rilke's poem asks "who is the violinist in whose hands we are," and the title of Amichai's Segment 33, "The Great Player," seems to answer that question: perhaps it is God.[33] Like the violin in Segment 9, the player comes to the speaker at night. Moreover, he arrives "on the feet of violins," which connects him directly to the imagery of the previous two segments.

These three segments are linked to Rilke, the letters, and Ruth in yet another way. While Amichai was living in Haifa, he brought his violin with him, keeping it in the corner of his room.[34] Echoing the conversation between the bow and the violin in "What's Your Name What's His Name" (26), he anthropomorphized the violin in the letters, along with the other objects in his room, imagining them coming to life.[35] In this, Amichai had clearly internalized not only Rilke's poetry, but also his way of looking at the world. One letter in particular reads as a variation on Rilke's worldview.[36] Amichai observed himself writing to Ruth and conducted an imaginary conversation with the electric lamp. He portrayed "her," the lamp, as bending down, peeking into the letter. He then told Ruth that as a result of his fatigue, he was like a "child" who hears "dead objects," like the violin or the lamp, speaking.[37]

While the violin plays a relatively minor part in "In the Public Garden," the most prominent element in the poem, the public garden itself, points most directly and unequivocally to Ruth. Although the public garden in the published version is a generic, universal urban topos, the letters, as well as Ruth's recollections, specify a place in the Jerusalem neighborhood of Rehavia, where the two used to regularly walk. The actual garden had benches on either side and stretched from Ramban Street, where Ruth lived, to Ibn Gabirol Street.[38] In describing their nocturnal route, both Amichai in his letters and Ruth in the interviews identified the "public garden" ("*hagina hatsiburit*," as he called it)[39] as the area where Dov Joseph and Ben-Zvi lived.[40]

This garden does not appear in Amichai's poem merely because he used to walk there with Ruth, but rather because the garden was the site of a defining moment in their relationship. When they first began to walk through it, Ruth would not let Amichai put his arm around her because she remembered walking there with her previous love, Avraham.[41] Amichai knew he had reclaimed the garden (and Ruth) from Avraham when she finally allowed him to hold her as they strolled down the narrow path illuminated on either end by tall street lamps.[42] In setting the poem in the Jerusalem garden haunted by the ghost of another man, Amichai showed an awareness of the fragility of their relationship. Although he tried to ignore the signs, it seems that even in the fall of 1947, long before he received Ruth's Dear-John letter, he subconsciously knew that she would not return.

That the work springs from a specific, local public garden and Amichai's relationship with Ruth is not only proven by the presence of the words "*hagina hatsiburit*" in the letters, but by the choice of the phrase as the poem's title and its appearance in the first line of five of its segments.[43] At the heart of the epic is a segment entitled "Avraham and I and Ruth" (22). Its four closing lines, "each one is barren [*ariri*] / and apart / Avraham and I / and Ruth," appear exactly at the middle of the work, on the twelfth out of twenty-three pages. The second and fourth of these lines contain only one word, "*u'lehud*" (and apart) and "*veRut*" (and Ruth), respectively. In the Hebrew, the word *lehud* (the *u* is pronounced *oo*) is an oblique rhyme with the word *veRut*. The rhyme implies the association between the name Ruth and separation (or being apart), and the shortness of these lines underscores the strong sense of barrenness. After reading the letters, the rhyme *lehud* and *veRut* accrues even greater significance. It echoes Ruth's intimate nickname for him, "Ood," the name he signed at the end of each letter. In this way, Amichai inserted their private term of endearment into the text, defined his state as separate, *lehud*, and identified himself as one of the triangle—Avraham, Ruth, and Ood. The overt mention of Ruth's name in connection with Avraham's at this strategic point of the epic points to the heart of the work. From its central position, it radiates loneliness and despair into the segments that surround it. The fact that "Avraham and I" appears in the same line underscores the shared fate of the two men: Ruth abandoned both of them.

As dramatic as the accurate identification of (the epic's) "Avraham" and "his" involvement with Ruth and the public garden may be, when one refers to the letters, the segment "Avraham and I and Ruth" (22) reveals additional new facts. The lines "Night . . . / . . . / There is no connection, / . . . / Between the things. / Each one is barren / And apart / . . ." point to the exact time that the poem was written. Late at night on October 30, 1947, approximately a month before the deadline for the competition for which he was preparing "In the Public Garden," Amichai wrote to Ruth. He had just returned from an evening stroll through the empty streets of Haifa. His impressions in the letter are formulated in language almost identical to the segment. In the letter he observed that ". . . at night . . . each one of the things was apart, separate. . . ."[44] And a few lines below, he wrote again, "each thing apart." While the language and the observations overlap, the conclusion put forth by the author of the poem is diametrically opposed to that in the letter. The poem exudes desperate barrenness, but the letter to the beloved highlights the night as the time for merging bodies and souls. The still-optimistic Amichai told Ruth that against the background of isolated objects at night, lovers can create the ultimate unity.

The October 30 letter is very long and contains what can be read as a parallel version not only of the very revelatory "Avraham and I and Ruth" (22), but also of other nighttime segments in "In the Public Garden." In the published poem, immediately following "Avraham and I and Ruth" (22), is a segment entitled "The Cat Thinks" (23). In it, Amichai enters the mind of a cat, a man, and a tree: "The cat thinks: / tree, house, man. / . . ." This construction is also used to reflect the thoughts of the man: "cat, tree, house." Unlike the man and the cat, the tree notices only the man in the darkness. In the poem, each subject ultimately recognizes its disconnectedness from the others. In the letter, the identical construction and thought process are attributed to the tree, as to the man and the cat: "The tree thinks: man, cat, house." Although the descriptions of the cat and the man are identical to the lines that would eventually become "The Cat Thinks" (23), the letter presents the musings of the cat, man, and tree as a treatise on the nature of objects at night, and not as poetic lines.

This letter contains both finished poetic lines that were put down on paper (possibly not for the first time) on October 30, 1947, and raw materials that made their way into the published poem in a revised form. Amichai wrote to Ruth that on his way home, he passed a dry-cleaning store; despite the late hour, someone was standing there, ironing. He then slipped into a lyrical description of the Haifa landscape: the night and the bay, he said, are smooth, "without wrinkles." The segment in the published poem entitled "An Ironing Shop" (28) echoes the evening impressions from the letter. The poem transforms the drycleaners into "an ironing shop" and combines two images from the letter: instead of smoothing trousers, the poem's worker irons "the sky."

The acoustics of the night portrayed at the end of the same letter appear in the poem immediately after "An Ironing Shop" (28). "A Phone Rings" (29) recalls the sound that pierced the quiet night while Amichai wrote the October 30 letter: a telephone that rang in the doctor's apartment above Amichai's head. The segment announces this detail, repeating twice, "A phone rings in the doctor's house." But while the segment ends with an innocuous statement about bittersweet life, the letter, like a dream, associates the ring with longing for Ruth. As he was writing the letter, the ringing reminded Amichai of his visits to her house, where the ring of the phone would be followed by her mother's call, "Ruthie, telephone!" While the memory of Ruth was cut out of the published segment, "A Phone Rings," many lines and complex segments, scattered throughout the epic, retain her specter.[45]

The Specter of Ruth

"The End," the second segment in "In the Public Garden," is simultaneously connected to the end of the relationship between Ruth Z. and Amichai and to Ruth's engagement to another man. This segment parodies signs posted in parks that forbid stepping on the grass and picking flowers. The repetition of the word "forbidden" ("asur"), which commonly appears on these signs, triggers a leap to another, more ceremonial intertext. The announcement that the married woman "is forbidden" (asura) to others from the moment she marries is part of Jewish wedding vows. In the poem, the prohibition is transformed into the lines "It is forbidden to approach . . . / It is forbidden to go overboard / because you are married." The segment is written with the impersonal language of commands, "It is forbidden to. . . ." Only at the conclusion of the segment does the speaker appear and speak in the first person, resigning himself to the fact that she is married, "And not to me. / To me not."[46]

The segment that follows "The End" records an event that chronologically preceded the marriage in "The End." This third segment, "They Saw You, They Saw You," is an excruciating reworking of Amichai's reply to Ruth's Dear-John letter. It imagines the people who stood by and watched as Ruth wrote that letter. "They saw you," says the speaker, "writing a letter . . ." and "they saw me, negotiating with my death." The imagined observer watched both her writing the letter of farewell and the speaker receiving it. Amichai's final, unnumbered letter to Ruth spends many pages saying what the poem presents in a very condensed form. In that heartrending letter, he describes how he had to remind himself constantly that Ruth was marrying someone else. The poem's succinct line about his "negotiation with death" is expressed more elaborately in the letter, which contemplates a military suicidal mission.[47] Like the letter, the poem also picks at the open wound. In it, the speaker compulsively imagines the preparations for her nuptials: her "veil," and how everybody "whispered about a wedding."[48] In the letter, Amichai torments himself by asking for information about the man whom she chose over him. The reverse order of the three opening segments exemplifies Amichai's technique of scrambling the chronology to disguise the underlying plot. The third segment speaks of the first step in the conclusion of their affair, the writing and receiving of the Dear-John letter. The second describes her after she has already married the other man, while the first chronicles the subsequent excruciating loneliness of the speaker.

Unlike Segment 3, which refers to Ruth's betrothal to another man, Segment 19, "Woman in a Dress of Sails," speaks of a wedding that never took place, the one between Amichai and Ruth. As in a few other segments, the speaker here is a woman. Dubbed the "Woman in a Dress of Sails," she is a lyrical abstraction of Ruth, who sailed away on a ship. The ship is emphasized in this segment by the redundant phrase "sails of ships." In the midst of "In the Public Garden," this segment is a reworking of the trauma of parting and betrayal. The female speaker declares that she will never be her male addressee's bride: "A bride / I will never be able to be."[49] Her tone is confident, for she knows that the man she has left will continue dreaming about her, even though she is not wearing a wedding gown, but a dress made of sails. The segment begins and ends with a description of the sailcloth dress, underscoring the notion that it "suits her body." This synecdoche casts the woman as a ship that sailed away. She is incapable of becoming his bride because she left him. Ruth is not called by name, and her trip to America is not specified; the details of the love story, the separation at the port, Ruth's long nautical journey from Palestine to New York, and her ultimate rejection of Amichai are rendered here in metaphors.

A safe distance from "Woman in a Dress of Sails" (19), the blatantly sexual segment "Who Am I?" (31) also has a ship at its center. By separating segments that evoke Ruth's memory, Amichai obscured the connection between them.[50] A careful reading, however, suggests that "Who Am I?" is a counterpart to "Woman in a Dress of Sails," the only other segment that refers to a ship. Like its predecessor, "Who Am I?" associates the ship with a desired woman, but while Segment 19 is about the man's unrequited love, "Who Am I?" is about lovemaking: the woman's head quietly sails over the curls on the man's chest. The chronology is confused, for in reality, lovemaking precedes the separation, yet the breakup is foreshadowed within the sexual encounter: the woman's hair is strewn "like the blood of a sacrifice" over the man's stomach.[51]

This intense sexual encounter recalls the erotically suggestive "Night Butterfly" (20) and "The Death of the Butterfly" (21).[52] These segments allude to the penis as a moth that becomes entangled in the pubic hair of the woman and dies there. So while these two segments do not provide explicit or implicit references to Ruth, they are linked to her through their location in the poem. They are placed between "Woman in a Dress of Sails" (19), which alludes to Ruth through the sailing metaphor and the cancelled wedding, and "Avraham and I and Ruth" (22), which calls her by name. The "sweet death" of the moth between the woman's legs at the conclusion of "The Death of the Butterfly" serves as the foreshadowing of the calamity expressed in the next segment, "Avraham and I and Ruth." In that segment, Ruth has already broken up with the two men who loved her. Pain, barrenness, and alienation mark this segment's total despair. Thus, these central segments of the epic (19, 20, 21, and 22) form a climactic cluster of sorts, a short sequence of passion and disappointment.

Toward the poem's conclusion, the first of two "conversation" segments appears, "Conversation at Midnight." This segment's chronological location is identifiable from its placement (it is Segment 34) and the time at which it occurs (midnight). In light of both the title of the final segment, "Last Conversation in a Whisper" (50), and the fact that it takes place at "two o'clock" in the morning, the midnight exchange in Segment 34 may be read as the precursor of the lovers' parting. The bits of conversation and fragmented narrative that span from midnight to two in the morning form an interrupted chain, echoing the couple's last night together.

At midnight, the couple is making love, but also planning a family together ("build me your home soon"). Although the sexuality of this conversation segment is understated, its reference to "Night Butterfly" strongly evokes a sexual encounter. A biographical interpretation might suggest that "Conversation at Midnight" refers to the bittersweet memory of sleeping together for the last time. The second stanza of this segment finds the female protagonist lying in a dark box, like a photograph that is being developed. This second part is an enigmatic reference to what Amichai learned only months after Ruth left; namely, all that would remain of their last night together or their relationship were the "developed negatives" of the pictures taken when they were still together. While a literal interpretation is possible—namely, that nothing but photographs of the couple remains after they break up—the image may carry a meta-poetic meaning. Just as it takes time to develop a photograph, memories can only be "developed" into artistic works months or years after the experience has ended. The unpublished ars-poetica poem "Hada'aya," from one of the letters, asserts that the work of the poet parallels that of the photographer: he absorbs impressions and only later prints them.[53] The scene described in "Conversation at Midnight" is played out while the woman was still innocent, ignorant of the world and of intimacy: "What does she know about the world / and about togetherness?"[54] The question of whether Ruth knew in advance that she would betray him must have preoccupied Amichai in the months after their relationship ended.

"The Empty Lot"

There is at least one other poetic segment in the published "In the Public Garden" that Amichai wrote during the correspondence, but he did not send it to Ruth until months after he sent her the birthday poem; it is found in the first part of this work.[55] Even a superficial reading of that segment shows why Amichai waited until April 1948 to send it to her, instead of including it with the rest of the poem in January. The distilled question posed in the first stanza of this segment, "The Empty Lot" (11), is reiterated almost verbatim in Segment 24, also entitled "The Empty Lot."[56] The placement of the second "The Empty Lot" is strategically significant because it splits the epic in two and is in close proximity to the segment "Avraham and I and Ruth" (22) and the four other segments that capture the devastation accompanying the breakup. Between "Avraham and I and Ruth" (22) and "The Empty Lot" (24), Amichai inserted the seemingly benign segment "The Cat Thinks" (23), possibly in an attempt to disassociate the two segments that are inextricably connected to Ruth. This maneuver conceals the fact that Ruth, whose name closes "Avraham and I and Ruth," is the addressee in "The Empty Lot" (24). The second half of "The Cat Thinks," however, contains a code for deciphering the message. It answers the blunt question posed in "The Empty Lot" (24): "The entire question is simple: / Will you cross the empty lot in order / To reach me, / Or are you afraid." The end of "The Cat Thinks" answers this question before it is asked: "We will never again / go from one to the other." The reversal of the order, the answer that precedes the question, is a part of the poet covering his biographical tracks.

In "The Empty Lot," the crucial question, "Will you cross the empty lot. . . ?" opens and closes the stanza. Clearly, Amichai initially posed the question to Ruth and therefore began and ended the segment with identical lines. The published version, however, alters the gender of the addressee; in it, the last line is delivered to a man. The main discrepancy between the version in the letter and the published versions, however, occurs in the third stanza. While in the published version, winds will blow "paper from another lot" and "scents and rain from another winter," in the version copied in the letter, the winds will bring rains that carry "scents and memories from another winter." By removing the loaded word "memories," Amichai distanced the published segment from the vivid recollection of the "other winter," the winter he and Ruth spent together in Jerusalem.

Although Amichai sent it to Ruth much later, "The Empty Lot" was probably written around the same time as the birthday poem. The poem itself reveals the approximate time of its writing, probably in the late autumn, for it relates to the wintry month of Tevet in the future tense: "And in Tevet there will be winds / And the winds will bring . . . rain. . . ." Tevet is often the parallel month to January. Nevertheless, Amichai waited until April to send "The Empty Lot" to Ruth. That letter, number 97, was the last he wrote to Ruth before she broke up with him. Amichai surely was aware of this poem's aggressive tone; but in the same letter, perhaps to counter the bluntness of the question, he called Ruth "my wife" and told her about a reasonably priced "cute apartment" of "a room and a half" that they could purchase together. Thus, it seems that while Amichai's letters continued to assume that Ruth would return, his poems knew better. This poem, which offers an ultimatum, was written in the fall of 1947, over six months before he gathered the courage to send it. He probably did not include it in the birthday poem because at that stage he feared confrontation. He must have recognized that if he forced the question, she would say no. Even as late as April, when he finally sent the poem, Amichai tried to soften its message by saying, "This is a strange one [poem], the last one, isn't it?"

Three months before the inevitable breakup, Amichai sent Ruth the birthday poem,[57] the draft for the final segments of the published "In the Public Garden."[58] The differences between the closing section of the published version and the excerpt copied in the January letter are not coincidental; the tone of the segments added to the published version is more depressed than that of those Amichai sent to Ruth. It is unclear whether the missing stanzas were written in 1947 and omitted from the birthday poem, or written after January, either when Amichai felt that the relationship was deteriorating or later, after the couple's final separation. Many of the disparities between the two versions may be explained by the poet's attempt to make his language more hermetic in the published poem, while others are testimony to the change in Amichai's mood after the end of the relationship.

The literary significance of the letter that Amichai wrote on January 14, 1948, goes beyond the accurate dating of "In the Public Garden." Its prose is also revelatory, for in explaining the poem to Ruth, he provided a guide to his reader, revealing the unifying principle of the entire work, which was previously thought to have none. He told her that he intended the poem to be a kind of lullaby, a "bedtime prayer" ("tefila al hamita"), recited after everyone had gone to sleep. Consequently, the various units of the birthday poem can be read as the ritual of going to bed—first the prayer, followed by going to sleep, and then night itself. The theme of a bedtime prayer is present in the published version of the work: Amichai transformed the prose introduction that he wrote for the entire birthday poem in his letter, into the title of the published segment, "The Great Prayer" (38).[59]

Amichai's comments on the birthday poem prove that although the printed version labels the segment "The Great Prayer" (38) alone as a prayer, it is, in fact, an interpretive title in the context of which the work's eleven concluding segments must be read. Moreover, while the published poem refers to God only once, in Segment 38, the birthday poem mentions God twice (in what would become the thirty-eighth and forty-first segments) and explicitly suggests that the mode of prayer is a guide to reading the work as a whole. A close reading of the published version shows that, although they do not name God, ten of the concluding poetic segments of the published poem (38–47) use the mode of prayer.

The traditional way to address God in Hebrew is by using the masculine singular imperative form to express requests. Following "The Great Prayer," almost all the segments use the imperative in both their titles and the body of their texts. These verbs express wishes and desires with varying degrees of directness. For example, Segment 39, "Dry!" pleads for the drying of tears; Segment 40, "Receive!" asks God to receive lost letters; and Segment 43 exclaims, "Connect!" begging for both phone lines and separated lovers to be reunited. The imperative verbs, however, are not the only linguistic remnants of prayer found in both the letter and the published poem.

"In the Public Garden" shows how Amichai used the bedtime prayer that he recited every night from the time he was a child to soothe himself during the long months of waiting for Ruth and dealing with loneliness and danger. His newly crafted "prayer" is a literary elaboration on the comforting ritual of childhood. The tone of the birthday poem is melancholic; in it, the familiar words of the prayer recited before sleep lay the groundwork for the poignant poetic reconstruction of his last night together with Ruth.

The birthday poem is uttered at bedtime, when the "rustling of trees" seems to disturb the speaker. He turns to God, asking Him to silence it, to place the rustling "in his pocket" and to "close the trees" to stop the rustling noise. In the published version, "closing the trees" is replaced by "closing the window shutter." This may be a covert allusion to an intimate association with the shutters on the window of Amichai's room in Jerusalem; one of the letters affectionately mentions Ruth's fear every time she heard them banging.[60]

The birthday poem, with the original, powerful image of "closing the trees" in its third line, has an interpretative potential beyond the arena of love in general and "In the Public Garden" in particular. That line, which was cut from the published version when Amichai replaced the trees with a shutter, springs up elsewhere. The intimate image is extracted from the personal sphere and inserted in the national, apocalyptic one. In one of Amichai's better-known poems, entitled "Sort of an Apocalypse," the action of "closing" trees (or "shutting them off") is associated with the preparations for war—"closing the trees" becomes a way to elude the enemy by keeping quiet.[61] The interchangeability in Amichai's mind between closing trees and closing shutters suggests a further correlation. In "Sort of an Apocalypse," "closing the trees" becomes associated with the mandatory blackouts for civilian houses during times of war. The idea remains of "closing the tree" as a way to stave off calamity. As the image was originally generated in a prayer for lovers, it is clear that Amichai initially tried to push away the personal apocalypse by "closing the trees" to shut out the rustling of his heart.

The connection between "In the Public Garden" in both its draft and published forms and "Sort of an Apocalypse" may be further demonstrated by the proximity of images. While in the short poem "Sort of an Apocalypse," both leaves and tree come in the same line ("fortify the leaves, close the tree"), in "In the Public Garden," the two are broken up. The phrase "close the shutter / trees" is in one stanza of the segment, and "forbid the leaves" is in another. In both instances, however, these are actions that are taken to protect oneself against an approaching disaster, be it a bombing during war or the loss of a beloved. Nighttime is perceived as a time of danger in all three texts (the traditional Hebrew bedtime prayer, "In the Public Garden," and "Sort of an Apocalypse"). But if "Sort of an Apocalypse" leaves humans to defend themselves, the prayer and "In the Public Garden" seek protection from God. Although in November 1947, when he wrote the birthday poem, Amichai was no longer religious, fearing that Ruth would not return, he regressed to the bedtime ritual that used to comfort him when he was a child: the prayer and the lullaby.

In the published poem, Amichai transformed the birthday poem speaker's request for God to "calm the souls" into a more abstract wish. Amichai replaced "souls" with a word he invented: "*bakhuy*" (that which is cried), and he calls upon God to dry what is cried—in other words, the tears. The theme of God's soothing role persists in both the birthday and published poems in the prayer's request that God "extinguish" both "her hands" and "the fire." This appeal implies that both "her hands" and "the fire" are burning.[62] It is not clear whether it is the fire of the woman's passion that needs to be extinguished or, perhaps more likely, the fire of destruction.

Immediately following the segment "Dry!" is another segment whose association with Ruth is painfully apparent. Its title and defining verb is the imperative "Receive!" (40). "Receive!" captures Amichai's daily reality during that period, the way his life, emotions, and routine revolved around whether or not a letter had arrived. In one letter, Amichai vividly described how returning from his work at school, his legs nearly gave way when his neighbor told him a letter had finally arrived.[63] In another, he painted the scene of waiting for her letter as though waiting for a guest—cleaning up his room in its honor.[64] When he went to Jerusalem for a vacation, he became restless thinking about the letters that might be waiting for him in his mailbox in Haifa.[65] This suspended, anxious existence described in the body of the letters was transformed into six lines in the birthday poem that are almost identical to those eventually published in "Receive!"

At the heart of these lines is a great empathy for those who write and wait for letters. God becomes a merciful recipient of—and container for—all the letters that never reach their destination. God is asked not only to collect them, but also to nurture them and bring them back to life, "Collect them into a womb." Metaphorically, the ill-fated letters are like aborted fetuses. Only within the walls of a divine womb will they grow anew. It is worth noting that God, to whom Amichai and Jewish tradition allude as being a male, receives a female body part—a womb.

This desire to give a home to lost letters has its roots in an early letter to Ruth. In it, Amichai recounted a nightmare he had in which he forgot to write Ruth's address on the envelope in addition to her name and "suffered the suffering of the envelope that never reaches its destination."[66] Given this pity for the plight of lost letters, it is understandable that Amichai seeks to give them a caring home in this segment. The desire for the letters to be granted a new life may thus convey the despair of a writer who writes in vain: "The fate of my letters is perhaps like the fate of yours, disappearing in the maw of the chaos. It is possible that I am writing to you a letter and in fact, I am only writing notes to myself, to my journal, because I am not sure any longer that my letters arrive."[67]

The mood of the subsequent segments grows darker even in the optimistic and understated birthday poem, and more so in the final, printed work. In the earlier poem, the loneliness of living as a boarder in a single, rented room is embodied by folding tables, Murphy beds, and umbrellas. The transience of the author's reality is communicated through this collapsible furniture: a person who has a stable, permanent home is likely to have heavy, sturdy furniture; only he who plans to move frequently needs furniture that is easily transportable.

In the birthday poem, God is asked to show compassion for the lonely people not only by making their beds, but also by "folding" their longings.[68] The printed version transforms the longings of the young men and women in the birthday poem into an abstract, impersonal "fresh longing" ("erga triya"). In this line, the individuals who are yearning and their genders are missing. Additionally, the published segment entitled "Fold!" (41)[69] transforms the birthday poem's plural "folding beds" and tables and its many lonely people, into the singular—there is one folding bed, one folding table, and one lonely man. The word Amichai used to denote this man is "boded," which means "single" as well as "lonely" and is usually used as an adjective or a verb, not a noun. The grammatically awkward noun boded is in the oxymoronic title of the first segment of the published work: "Boded tsiburi" (public lonely). The boded is the main protagonist, a "public" *boded* whose memories fill the public garden. Clearly, the disparities between the two versions stem from the change in Amichai's perception: the birthday poem was written when both Amichai and Ruth were poor boarders. While he was in Haifa and she was in New York, this "in between" existence still united them. Amichai assumed that his loneliness was parallel to Ruth's; therefore, he presented both the lonely men and women sympathetically. In hindsight, Amichai realized that when he sent Ruth the birthday poem in January 1948, she was already with the man she would marry. Thus, when he wrote of poor boarders, he bitterly revised the picture to include only one man. The use of the masculine singular in the published segments versus the plural in the letter underscores the excruciating loneliness and disappointment of the epic's male protagonist. Thus, this seemingly small grammatical change hides a deep emotional void.

Furthermore, "Fold!" replaces the hopeful parts of the birthday poem with depressed ones: in the published segment, God is asked to delete the name of the *boded* from the sign on the door, as is done when the resident of an apartment dies. The second stanza of "Fold!" elaborates on the purpose of that deletion. With the name erased, no one will ring his bell any longer. The image of erasing the name on the door is connected to a humorous (but self-pitying) poem that Amichai sent to Ruth in September 1947, which describes how the speaker continuously changes the sign on his door in an attempt to make it more inviting to potential visitors.[70] After each change, he waits hopefully, but no one rings his doorbell. Finally, he simply erases everything from the sign but his name. "Fold!" gives this story line a morbid twist by erasing the name itself.

The charged tone of the subsequent segment, "Collect!" (42), reflects the author's knowledge of the breakup.[71] "Collect!" is much shorter than the corresponding lines in the birthday poem, which in a hopeful manner ask God for energy, purpose, courage, the will to live and even to err. In contrast, the printed version stops abruptly and simply confesses to fatigue: "we are too tired to change." Both versions of the poem, however, express a wish to end eternity. This wish most likely refers to Amichai's long period of waiting: one can imagine him counting the days until Ruth returns or until her next letter arrives. Accordingly, in the poem, Amichai calls upon God to intervene and stop his endless misery. While the birthday poem speaks of God's limiting eternity by providing a "frame" to pictures, the printed version is almost brutal. The speaker in the published poem pleads with God to mark the end of eternity with "her body" ("*hatve li begufa sof lanetsah*"): this could mean either that her body will show him where the end is or that her body is the surface in which the end will be carved. This implies a wish to forget her body, thus ending the eternal waiting and longing for her. The despair and weariness of the printed version is an expression of the bleak outlook of the speaker, who wants to know when his tortured waiting will cease. The words *"veshehakol neda"* (so we would know it all), which express the speaker's urgent need to "know" if she still loves him and thus put an end to his waiting, appear only in the published segment. In January 1948, when Amichai first sent the poem to Ruth, he was still reluctant to press her for an exact date of her return. Thus, the lines that he copied for her are more ambiguous and do not present the question directly.

In a line not used in the published poem, the speaker in the birthday poem makes a request for some unidentified people (an anonymous "them") to be placed in an "envelope," "sealed with a red seal," and mailed to someone who is dreaming. The "them" are the lonely or separated ones, representatives of Amichai, who sent three or four letters to America every week. Longing for Ruth, he must have fantasized about being folded into one of the aerograms that sailed overseas. By the time the poem was published, the correspondence was over, and this fantasy was no longer relevant.

After this unrealistic vision in the birthday poem comes a more direct plea to God to "connect" (*"haber"*) torn phone lines and people who are separated. This logical and optimistic wish to connect exists in both the letter and in the 1959 work, but at this point the disparity between the two texts is the most apparent. The published version contains a series of six short segments, only one of which appears in the 1947 birthday poem. The dominant sound in these segments is the word *"ten"* (give), a short, succinct request often directed at God. The speaker asks God to give the "separated ones" both materials and emotions (i.e., clothes, food, love). The series of commands to "give" culminates with the segment entitled "Ten" ("Give!" [47]), the one segment in this series that is common to both texts.

The images in "Give!" lie on the border between the chilling and the grotesque.[72] God is encouraged to serve "them" as a warm meal in nice dishes and to prepare "them" for life as one prepares children for a *bikkurim* celebration. This concrete image of people as an offered meal, combined with the explicit reference to *bikkurim*, strongly suggests a form of human sacrifice. The festival of *bikkurim* is the religious ritual of presenting God with the first crops of the year. In ancient times, farmers would bring the first fruits and vegetables as an offering to the Holy Temple in Jerusalem. Now, however, the ritual has evolved; young children dress in festive white clothes with wreaths of fresh flowers in their hair and carry baskets with the fruits of the earth to symbolize the offering. This scene is evoked in the poem, but here people, not fruits, seem to be the offering. Furthermore, the imagery draws a dichotomy between the innocent children and the harsh futures that await them by suggesting that when they grow up, they will be "sacrificed" to life. God is asked to "prepare" the children for their lives, but at the same time to "serve them up" for consumption.

The kindergarten girl who is dressed up for the holiday in the birthday poem is transformed into a boy in the printed version, reflecting both the published poem's shift away from Ruth as a protagonist and Amichai's postwar, disappointed view of himself as the one anxiously facing life. The tenderness of the birthday poem, which details the nice clothing and the parents' proud smiles and their "loving pat," is replaced with the harsher "good words" and "a light push in the back" in "Give!" The birthday poem's depiction of the girl is more reminiscent of a real bikkurim celebration, whereas the published segment is less bound to the reality of kindergarten parties and more concerned with the allegorical or metaphorical implications of the ritual.

By momentarily ignoring the darker undertones of the allusion to the bikkurim offering in the published segment, a more biographical reading is possible: the birthday poem tenderly portrays a girl before she makes her first steps in life. When he originally wrote it, Amichai was probably thinking of Ruth arriving in New York City. When he later rewrote the poem and changed the gender of the child, Ruth had already left him and started a new life. Thus, as he completed "In the Public Garden," Amichai might have focused on his own needs and desire for a fresh start.

While the segments of "In the Public Garden" consistently defy any chronology or coherent plot development, the work's final segment is strikingly simple. Entitled "Last Conversation in a Whisper" (50), it quotes, almost verbatim, the concluding lines of the poem that Amichai copied into his letter of January 14, 1948. Only one line deviates from the 1947 version, and the changes made to it are not significant. From the segment's title, it is difficult to discern if the poem is a "last conversation" before the two lovers fall asleep or the last conversation before they separate forever.

The tone of this exchange at two in the morning is intimate and almost banal: "Are you cold"; "Take the blanket"; "What time is it?" The benign fragments of the whispered conversation, however, hide the sadness. Amichai rendered the anxiety of parting by the punctuation of the last three lines of this nineteen-line segment. One of the two says matter-of-factly, "Morning comes soon" ("*boker ba od me'at*"), but the fact that the approaching morning is ominous is suppressed. The closing lines are two consecutive questions: "What time is it, beloved?" and "What?" Neither is answered. The question marks seem to hang in the air above the sleeping lovers.

It is unclear whether neither person answers the other's question simply because they fall asleep or because saying the time is a painful reminder of how few hours they have left together. Although the time, two o'clock in the morning, is stated in the first line, the lovers are unaware of it. The availability of this knowledge suggests that the question "What time is it?" is willfully ignorant, almost as if the lovers had a clock in the room, but refused to look at it. Similarly, while the title of the segment implies that it is the last time the two will speak, the poem itself shies away from that knowledge. The gap between the title and the scene described in the segment is an indication of Amichai's reluctance to accept that Ruth had abandoned him.

Finally, Amichai added the title "Last Conversation in a Whisper" to the text in its published form. The letter to Ruth simply states, ". . . and at two / two are whispering," without labeling the conversation their "last." When Amichai finished writing "In the Public Garden" on December 6, 1947, he still hoped, of course, that Ruth would come back. "Last Conversation in a Whisper" is, indeed, the last conversation of Ruth and Amichai's relationship, as Ruth confirmed in an interview after reading the poem in 2005.[73] It is not surprising, then, that Amichai had to wait eleven or twelve years from the time he wrote this ode to his love for Ruth, to the time he published it.

While its title echoes the earlier segment "Conversation at Midnight" (34), the tone of this last poem is foreign to the remainder of "In the Public Garden." There is no trace of irony or cynicism, no alienation or bitterness, no realization in the text itself (outside of the title) that this is a monumental moment in the lives of the people who whisper in bed. The intimacy, the low voices, the staccato rhythm, and the mutual concern all contrast acutely with what precedes this segment.

When Amichai proudly told Ruth that he had finished "In the Public Garden" on December 7, he described it as "pictures, pictures and free associations."[74] Although he did not mention T. S. Eliot by name, his influence is evident both in the way Amichai spoke of his own verse and in the verse itself. "Last Conversation in a Whisper" echoes Eliot's modernist epic *The Waste Land*, or, to be exact, lines 111–14, in style and in the use of fragments of conversations: "'My nerves are bad to-night. Yes, bad. Stay with me. / 'Speak to me. Why do you never speak? Speak. / 'What are you thinking of? What thinking? What? / 'I never know what you are thinking. Think.'"[75] Even the repetition of the word "what" reinforces the affinity between the texts. Amichai's kind, gentle tone, however, is entirely his own. The tenderness of "Last Conversation in a Whisper" retrospectively radiates through the entire poem, showing it in a warmer light and giving meaning to the final third by underscoring its ritual series of pleas to God and its prayerlike nature. Indeed, the last thirteen segments are a sincere prayer for love, uttered at bedtime, before the lovers fall asleep together for the last time.

After speaking with Ruth and reading Amichai's impassioned letters to her, his literary achievement, manifest in "In the Public Garden," seems even greater. Amichai wrote this revolutionary poem with its extraordinary innovations a year before the battles of 1948 and almost two years before his poems started appearing regularly in journals. When he finally published "In the Public Garden" in 1959, no one suspected that the established poet had written it when he was still a fledgling and romantic writer, industriously preparing one of his first long works for a competition that would never take place—a competition ultimately terminated by the War of Independence.

＊　＊　＊

When Gershon Shaked, a scholar of Hebrew literature and Amichai's friend, lectured at the conference in honor of Amichai in the spring of 1994, he had no way of knowing about Ruth Z. or the literary legacy that Amichai's love for her inspired. He delivered his lecture at Oxford University, where a group of scholars from Israel, the United States, and Europe, all well-versed in Amichai's work, gathered to celebrate the poet's seventieth birthday by presenting papers on his oeuvre. The conference was held under Oxford's auspices, and its organizer, the Amichai expert Glenda Abramson, created an unforgettable forum for study. Amichai himself listened attentively and humbly as literary scholars spoke of the historic revolution he led in Hebrew literature, his status as a national poet, and the development of his poetry. Neither his expression nor his words betrayed his feelings, but those who knew him could tell that he was elated.

In a dramatic gesture, Shaked presented a photocopied sheet on which Amichai's earliest known poems were copied. The sheet itself was testimony to the symbiosis and shared history of Shaked the critic, Amichai the poet, and the Israeli literature that they embodied; it included Amichai's first published, amateurish sonnet from the 1944 British soldiers pamphlet, which Shaked dubbed "the first swallow that did not bring the spring," and other uncollected works. Amichai's first three important poems from 1949 appeared in their original newspaper font, as did two poems from 1951 and 1953. The format of the poem from 1952 attested to its mimeographed, typewritten origins. While he acknowledged the significance of the three sonnets from 1949 as the first building blocks of "We Loved Here," Shaked devoted much of his insightful analysis to another, little-known poem entitled "Aravim aherim" ("Other Evenings"). He demonstrated how Amichai's innovative poetic "genotype" existed and was identifiable even in that early poem. Shaked enumerated the characteristics of the prototypical Amichaian poem and said that "the abandonment of meter, open rhyme-schemes, an almost prosaic register . . . the utilization of the effects of repetition as an emotive element and a poetic, heterogeneous and catalogue-like language . . . that enlists unexpected combinations" were all evident in the long-lined free-verse stanzas of the love poem "Other Evenings" from 1951. He argued that "Amichai differed right from the start (in 1951) from the majority of both generations of his contemporaries."[76] In other words, he saw "Other Evenings" as the precursor of Amichai's literary revolution.

Today, after reading the letters Amichai wrote to Ruth Z. in 1947–1948, which include the original segments from "In the Public Garden," I wonder what Amichai thought of Shaked's bestowing upon "Other Evenings" the undue honor of being the first poem to introduce his innovations. He might have smiled to himself, knowing that he actually created that Amichaian "genotype" in a rented room in Haifa in 1947. He may have also remembered Ruth Z.'s "red dress strewn with white dots" that "Other Evenings" so tenderly features. But he never said a word.

We know now that Amichai had planned to send "In the Public Garden" to the competition that he hoped would make his name as a modernist poet. After the war and the breakup with Ruth Z., he chose to shelve this dramatically radical work and instead presented himself to the public with the more conservative sonnets that appeared in 1949, and later with the free verse of "Other Evenings" (1951) and "Autobiography 1952" (1952).

Judging by the reception of his work in the first decade of his career, Amichai was right to delay the debut of his genotype. He carefully orchestrated his initial exposure to critics and readers. Instead of introducing himself with the avant-garde "In the Public Garden," Amichai put forward the relatively conservative poems that he included in his 1955 debut volume. These poems struck a delicate balance between the familiar and the innovative. The letters to Ruth Z. demonstrate, however, that the order in which his works were published was a product of design, motivated by literary, emotional, and national agendas. In fact, parts of Amichai's genotype existed earlier than anyone could have imagined—at the very beginning of his self-identification as a poet. Characteristics that Shaked laid out as Amichai's genotype existed in an embryonic form in the Binyamina sonnets. It is clear that by the summer and fall of 1947, Amichai was consciously determined to make his verse different from the other poems of the time. The letters prove that before the War of Independence, this genius was already consciously and devotedly forging his unique art.

THE MAKING OF AN ISRAELI

Thirteen years had passed between August 24, 1936, when Amichai first saw the Carmel ridge from the deck of the *Gerusalemme*, the ship that brought him to Palestine, and his return to the city on the slopes of the Carmel as a temporary home. Although Haifa is almost completely absent from Amichai's poems, the footprints of the dramatic personal changes that occurred during the eight stormy months that he spent there were never erased. The letters that he wrote to Ruth Z. during that period bear witness to how his world was changing. Against the backdrop of September 1947–April 1948 in Haifa, the young man culminated his transformation from the immigrant child, Ludwig Pfeuffer, into the Israeli patriot, Yehuda Amichai. As the War of Independence shook the country and devastated the city of Haifa, Amichai consciously began to identify himself as an Israeli whose individual fate was synonymous with that of the new nation and its people. Indeed, Amichai's letters to Ruth are a unique record in this respect. They open a window into his daily life, his feelings, thoughts, and opinions during the period when he took his first steps as a poet and his worldview as an adult was being forged.

Amichai's letters are a testimony to his evolution from an impressionable young man in love, a neophyte teacher, and a categorically lyrical poet into an Israeli man whose poetry contained the history of his people and their land. During this liminal period, the psychological and linguistic experiences that Amichai brought with him from Europe were not covered up and are detectable in his correspondence with Ruth Z. to a degree that would never be matched in his public writing. During their correspondence, however, Amichai's identification with the Israeli reality grew and his notion of what it meant to be a poet went through a transformation. As the violence in Palestine escalated and Amichai's patriotic identity solidified, the values espoused by his poetic destiny and his national duties collided. Although Amichai still believed that a poet must draw on his childhood, his developing national identity dictated that his diasporic past—his foreign childhood—had to be repressed. After the war, as a mature poet, he would find a creative solution for the dichotomy between his two selves: not to delete, but rather to cloak that past with his newly acquired self-identification as an Israeli. During these tumultuous months, Amichai developed into a poet who was both personal and national, a poet whose voice was that of the middle-of-the-road Israeli man. This was precisely the voice that would make him "the people's poet," the only canonic poet whose works are read by the Israeli masses.[1]

Years later, Amichai insisted that he had not planned to become a poet, but rather began writing poetry around age twenty-five as a coping mechanism during the fierce battles in the Negev: "That one, decisive year spent at war in the desert had a great impact on my life and actually made me a poet."[2] As we have seen, however, the letters that he wrote to Ruth Z. reveal that he knew poetry was the essence of his being for a year or two before Israel's War of Independence. It is possible that his denial of his early aspirations stemmed from an effort to erase his ill-fated romance with Ruth and her mark on his poetry from that period. It is also possible that by delaying the date of his initiation as a poet until the period of the battles, Amichai intended to imply a stronger, more inherent connection between his patriotic side and his creative one.

*   *   *

When Ruth Z. arrived in New York, some of Amichai's letters were already waiting for her. These were the first of ninety-eight aerograms that he would mail in the months that followed. Ninety-four of them reached their destination, where Ruth read them before carefully placing them in a tin box.[3] With endless patience, exemplary order, and meticulous detail, Amichai told Ruth about his life. Underlying these descriptions is the writer's desire to share his new experiences with the woman he loved. He wanted to arouse her longings for the Land of Israel and for him, the man who was waiting for her and planning their future together.[4] The text of the letters can be seen as a form of unpremeditated epistolary bildung-narrative: a reflection of the artist Yehuda Amichai as a young man.

Amichai's first letters, written in the autumn of 1947, are inlaid with poetry, written by both himself and others, copied down in neat handwriting. These letters record Amichai's early steps as a poet and hint at what would come in *Poems: 1948–1962*. Even Amichai's epistolary prose is lyrical; full of poetic sketches of nature and unexpected analogies, it easily demonstrates the author's literary gift.[5]

Indeed, Amichai's belief in his destiny as a poet was the dominant force in his life at the start of the correspondence, but as time went on and his reality was shaken by the imminent war, he felt compelled to integrate collective, national, and military components into his artistic agenda. Amichai's work as a teacher played a unique role in the burgeoning of his national feeling; through his attempts to endow his students with patriotic values, Amichai himself evolved. He shifted from perceiving his military duties as detrimental to his poetic calling to viewing them as part of his identity and even as inspiration for his art. This strong personal element never disappeared from Amichai's work—instead, it merged with his national sensibility. This initial overlapping of the lyrical and the national developed into the Israeli persona that he would cultivate and solidify after the War of Independence. It is no surprise, then, that in Amichai's letters to Ruth Z. one can trace the growth of his identification with the Israeli national cause and the development of his poetry. The letters also preserve the origins of some of his famous works, which were being forged in 1947.

BECOMING A TEACHER AND A POET

The mere dates on the letters to Ruth would electrify any Amichai scholar, any historian of the State of Israel, or, for that matter, almost any Israeli. Their historical significance runs deep in the collective consciousness of the Jewish people. The letters correspond to the months that preceded November 29, 1947, the historic UN vote that recognized the right of Jews to a sovereign state in Palestine, and span the period between that vote and Israel's declaration of independence.[6] Technically, before the state was established, there could be no such thing as an "Israeli identity," as there was just a promise of a Jewish state within the land of Palestine. At the time, the entire Jewish population in British Mandatory Palestine, the Yishuv, was going through the simultaneously exhilarating and painful process of becoming an independent nation.[7] The decades-long Zionist objective of leaving behind the identity of the Jew from the diaspora—the weak, submissive "old Jew"—and adopting that of a strong "new Hebrew" reached its peak during this period. Moreover, the assumption of the identity of a "true Israeli" meant forgetting one's exilic past. Many, like Amichai, changed their European names to Hebrew ones, either by choice or due to professional obligation.

It is against this backdrop that the sensitive young man who saw himself as a poet even then, gradually had to abandon his pen in favor of the gun. In order to become a total Israeli, he needed to suppress his diasporic childhood—the wellspring of his literary creation—which caused an inner conflict. More important than the military activities that slowly encroached upon his life was the inner process by which the teacher/poet-in-love became a patriot committed to his national duty.

In the fall of 1947, Amichai often wrote to Ruth Z. of his wanderings through Haifa. One can hear in his letters how he, a Jerusalemite who had never lived near the sea, was hypnotized by the vista of the bay and the port. He wrote that the arch of Haifa's bay reminded him of the back of a cat and that the steaming boats were like pots in a busy kitchen.[8] He hiked on Mount Carmel with his fellow teachers and picked pink cyclamens to put in a vase (for a portrait of Amichai during this period, see image 13).[9]

The letters show how protective Amichai was of his world, composed of teaching, writing, and love for Ruth.[10] He often mused at length on the color of his pupils' eyes and hair, the way their games changed with the seasons, the articles in his rented room, the streets of Haifa, and the teachers' meetings. Although Amichai occasionally reflected on the still-abstract possibility of the partition plan taking effect,[11] and commented on his disdain for extremist organizations,[12] he was preoccupied mostly with his first steps as a teacher and his poetic experiments.

When he did raise national or collective issues, they were generally subordinate to personal and literary concerns. In a letter from September 7, 1947, for example, he quoted David Ben Gurion's famous lines, "We must assist the British in the war [WWII] as if there were no White Paper and we must resist the White Paper as if there were no war."[13] Instead of applying this speech to the current political situation in Palestine, Amichai transferred Ben Gurion's idea to him and Ruth, saying that they ought to gather their impressions of the world while they were far apart, but still remain united through their "common future as if the sea did not separate [them]."[14] Similarly, when he saw the site of a bombed-out police building in mid-October 1947, he noted that all the clocks showed the exact time that the bomb went off: "All the clocks stopped at 6 o'clock," and then added, "This could be the name of a novel."[15] He couched the bombing in artistic terms, glossing over its political implications.

Amichai was a fourth-grade homeroom teacher who had to teach Hebrew, Bible, and social studies, but as one of his former students, Rina Reznikov Ofek, recalled, he shone when he taught Hebrew literature. In a long telephone interview she granted nearly six decades after she sat in Amichai's classroom,

Rina emphasized "how excellent his Hebrew was in contrast to his German accent."[16] Although her teacher did not let on that she was his favorite, he mentioned her by name in the letters, recorded their conversations, and lovingly described her dimples and black hair to Ruth.[17] Amichai was deeply devoted to his students, and spent much of the early letters telling Ruth about them. He wrote humorously about the gym class with "forty-two children . . . in their white uniforms and Amichai the teacher standing in front of them."[18] A month later, he sent Ruth "a special edition letter"—so called because it contained three photographs of his pupils (for the photograph of the gym class, see image 14). He told Ruth of the children's reactions when they realized they were being photographed, and exclaimed, "Aren't they sweet?"[19] Rina remembered that even though he never once raised his voice, all the children listened to him and added, "He was handsome, but like a nerd."[20]

Rina remembered thinking that he had been a Holocaust survivor, in part because he was European, gaunt, and often seemed sad.[21] She sensed that her beloved teacher was, somehow, an outsider, although she could not have known that the latter two characteristics were in part due to his longing for Ruth. Rina, however, was not the only pupil for whom Amichai cared. He always managed to say something personal to each student, even though his class size was extremely large from the influx of immigrants who had flooded Haifa's classrooms.[22] His pupils, in turn, adored him, and the words of the letter from November 28, 1947, convey how he glowed when another teacher told him "your students love you very much."[23]

Teaching at the Geula School involved more than literature, gym class, and attention to individual students' needs. The school environment forced Amichai to focus on collective issues in a way that the surrounding events of fall 1947 had not yet mandated. On September 9, 1947, Amichai reported that the principal of the Geula School had instructed all the teachers to discuss in class the strike held by the entire Yishuv. They were protesting against the actions of the British. ships with Holocaust survivors were being turned away from the Israeli shores and directed to Hamburg. Amichai struggled to find a way to present this national crisis to the children in a manner that would be relevant to them. Luckily, that day one of the girls had brought a praying mantis in a cardboard box to class. The children fed the insect excitedly and crowded around the box in which the teacher had punctured holes for air. Amichai told his curious pupils that the refugees were like the praying mantis: in captivity, they were supplied with food and air, yet they still longed to go out to the sun and the

grass; they wanted to be free. The children understood the metaphor. Rina recalled that "whenever something happened," Amichai allowed the class "to
talk about it."[24] Indeed, after a heated discussion, the students decided enthusiastically to free the insect. Amichai proudly quoted the comment of one
child—"if the British were like us, they would free the refugees."[25] This episode also affected the teacher, who, through teaching, identified even more
with the national cause.

Amichai's ability to draw analogies between unrelated concepts, between a
shoebox and a ship full of immigrants, is in fact a signature trait of his poetry.
Decades later, this quality drew criticism,[26] but in the fall of 1947, this gift enabled the children to empathize with the stranded refugees. Amichai also applied this effective and concrete method with respect to other ideological matters. When he promoted the consumption of Yishuv-made products, he
personalized the issue for his students. For instance, if members of the Yishuv
bought "metal instruments" from abroad, he said, Rina's father "would be
fired." Rina's father worked in the Vulcan factory near Haifa that produced
metal appliances.[27]

Growing Unrest

When the situation in Haifa was relatively calm, Amichai concentrated on his art
and enjoyed a forceful creative burst in his poetry. On November 11, 1947, for example, he wrote that despite his packed schedule, he found joyful leisure hours
of reading and writing his poems.[28] As the days drew closer to the UN vote,
however, the tension rose in Haifa as well as in the letters describing the situation. In mid-November, a somewhat complacent and optimistic Amichai faced
death for the first time. While the newspaper dispassionately recorded the event
("shots were fired at four o'clock in the afternoon from a machine gun")[29] the
letters written after this experience vividly relate it in horrifying detail. Indeed,
the poet's pen is recognizable even when he writes about his terror.

On a Friday, Amichai and his friend and fellow teacher, Orah Haklay, took a
bus up the mountain to a party in the home of a colleague in the Merkaz HaCarmel neighborhood. In his November 16, 1947, letter, Amichai described the few
other passengers and reconstructed how he and Orah boarded the bus. Nine
people (including the driver) were on the bus when it was attacked with volleys
of shots from an ambush. Writing to Ruth about it, Amichai credited himself
with saving Orah by pulling her to the floor of the bus when he heard the shots.
As Orah Hadas (née Haklay) recalled in 2004, "When I heard the sounds, he

pulled me down. Perhaps he saved my life."[30] Sadly, those who were sitting nearby were not as lucky. The young man who was seated with his girlfriend in the seat immediately in front of Amichai was killed by a bullet to the head. An acquaintance of Amichai's from the army, who was sitting in the seat behind him, was shot in the stomach. The bus sped to the maternity hospital Molada, where his wounded friend was treated and where the body of Hayim Goldman, the dead passenger, lay motionless.[31]

Despite the political implications of the incident, Amichai described his first brush with death without reference to any national agenda. Instead, he framed his account in literary terms. As he often did in the letters, he referred to his love with Ruth Z. as "a book" that was being written, imagining himself as both the writer and the hero of this book. The threat to his life, therefore, was translated into a sudden halt in the writing of "[their] book." He said that "the hand" of the author stopped for a moment because it thought that one of the "protagonists of our story was hurt." His effort to remain in the intimate domain, removed from politics, is evident. It is visible even on the physical surface of the aerogram: the only allusion to the national situation is relegated to the margins, where Amichai noted the rumor that the attack was a "revenge action by the British."[32] In contrast, Orah could still go into the political details of the incident years later: "After the Irgun had hung British soldiers, the British plotted against the bus."[33] The conclusion that the young Amichai draws from the event, however, is that life is sweet, and he set out to absorb it with renewed intensity.[34]

The surviving passengers, Amichai among them, attended Hayim Goldman's funeral a few days later. In the letter, Amichai lingered on the glorious day, the blossoms of flowers, and the sunrays. As with the attack, he formulated the funeral in literary, not political, terms. He compared those who attended the funeral to characters in Hamlet.[35] The four letters that revolve around Amichai's encounter with death are symptomatic of his state of mind. He made no attempt to understand the political or military ramifications of the event, although he did mention that the victim was an active member of the Jewish underground, the Hagana. Amichai then described Hayim Goldman's Hagana friends, who joined the funeral procession on noisy motorcycles. He called their forceful appearance and the noise they made on their motorcycles a part of the "demonstration of life"[36] (and in the next letter, referred to them as "life itself"),[37] but related to them simply as an object for his observation. They occupy a mere four lines within the densely written four aerograms that linger over the autumn flowers in Haifa, the stylized depiction of the bus ride, and the subsequent funeral. In a particularly telling sentence, Amichai portrayed himself at the entrance to the morgue, watching the mustachioed, virile members of the Hagana, and said, "I am standing on the side." He compared his artistic attempt to fit the funeral into the landscape to a child who puts together "a jigsaw puzzle."[38] Here, Amichai implicitly adopted the role of an outsider, of a writer who is not a part of the scene, who feels and mourns but does not take an active role in the national struggle. Furthermore, Amichai wrote that the experiences in Palestine had made him into a "philosopher." He used the word "philosopher" in this letter as a synonym for the artist—one who absorbs the stimuli and reworks them into art.[39]

As part of this artistic process, though, Amichai also placed the killing he witnessed in the traditional Jewish context of martyrdom and sacrifice. He acknowledged that the funeral ritual was a part of "our tortured land,"[40] and a week later referred to Goldman's death in ancient literary terms, as the "akedah that was accepted."[41] The akedah, the binding of Isaac, would later become a mythical symbol of the young men of the Yishuv who were expected to offer their lives as sacrifice for the nation.[42] In mid-November 1947, this analogy between the sacrifice of Isaac and the struggle for national independence was not yet prevalent, but Amichai's imagination had already connected the two. Thirty-three years later, Amichai would write about his mindset in October 1947: "We did not know yet that we would be called the generation of [sacrifice]."[43]

One week after the Goldman funeral, Amichai began training unenthusiastically for the Hagana. There is no indication in the letters if his decision to join was inspired by the incident or whether the Hagana began recruiting more aggressively in preparation for the upcoming vote on the partition plan. In any event, he set out for his first full day of military training, lamenting, "Shabbat is spoiled," but ended up enjoying it. Amichai wrote about this first duty lightly, portraying himself as a high school student in an agricultural center. Furthermore, instead of using the military term "enlisted" to describe why he was participating in the training, he simply wrote, "[T]hey told me to go for an outing for a day. . . ." While he mentioned "jumping, running, and crawling," he focused not on military goals, but on the plowed fields of the Jezreel Valley and poetically painted the abundant light behind the mountains as "the Hallelujah singing in Catholic churches." He told Ruth how he derived pleasure from the intense physical activity, socializing with friends, and the admiring glances from passing girls. He then added, "It was good to play [lesahek] the role that day" and that he "played it to the last minute." In other words, he did not yet see himself as a soldier; he was merely filling the role of one. Nevertheless, this letter is the beginning of the shift in Amichai's priorities. He admitted that "in the last week" he had begun inquiring about the proposed borders. Indeed, the letter was written on November 23, 1947, one week before the vote in the UN. The mere fact that Amichai waited so long to study the subject is proof of his removed stance. On November 23, 1947, however, he included an explanation for Ruth regarding the drawbacks of the partition plan. Even so, he voiced the overly optimistic conviction that war would be unnecessary and that economic cooperation and a nonviolent solution would prevail.[44]

On November 28, 1947—the eve of the vote on the proposal to partition Palestine into two states—Amichai acknowledged, perhaps for the first time, that the destiny of the individual and that of the nation were interdependent. "Our fate," he wrote to Ruth, would be determined the following day. He went on to clarify that "our fate" meant that of both society and the individual.[45]

Amichai's letter from the morning after the UN vote in favor of creating a Jewish state (side-by-side with an Arab one) is an exuberant and palpable depiction of the collective intoxication on the streets of Haifa. Fearing that his beloved in New York could not imagine the magnitude of the joy, Amichai alluded to the descriptions of royal celebrations in Hans Christian Andersen's stories to capture the enthusiasm of the Yishuv.[46]

The ecstatic patriotism and the infectious joy of the letter from November 29, 1947, spilled into the aerograms that followed, but reality had also struck. Amichai chronicled the Arab strike, the riots in response to the vote, and the Arab sabotage of the convoys carrying supplies to Jewish Jerusalem. He also told of his first assignments to guard duty. He recalled the violence that swept Palestine in the years 1936–1939, saying that, then, "we were not prepared for defense," but he was confident that "[t]oday, we are prepared." He added that in 1936–1939, the Yishuv had "no determined goal," while "today, there is."[47] Although Amichai was still reluctant to declare a full identification with the collective, saying, "I'm not a nationalist," the divisions between the personal and the national gradually erode in the letters. "It is good to live now in the land," he admitted, "you feel history. . . ."[48]

The first day of December 1947 was a symbolic emotional and historical crossroad in Amichai's life. In fact, the entire correspondence may be divided into two parts: September 1 to December 1, 1947, and January to April 1948, with the month of December as a period of transition. While the fall months are characterized by the dominance of poetry in Amichai's life, the months that followed mark a decline in the amount of free time and mental energy he had for writing because of military and professional demands.

As December 1947 arrived, Amichai was attuned to his inner world and continued his creative development. Childhood memories remained a strong presence in his psyche and he made no attempt to suppress them. Yet his mood did change, and the level of his anxiety rose. After rereading one of his own letters, he observed that "some nervousness . . ." had entered his writing. Amichai also shared with Ruth the wisdom that he learned as a refugee, without mentioning how he acquired it: "When one feels a little danger, it is good . . . [to have] few possessions. A couple of knapsacks . . . [in order to] move easily."[49] He was well aware of the fact that everything in his life was transient, history was in the making, and that the tremors of the earthquake had only just begun.

Despite the unrest, the subject of Hanukkah dominates the aerograms in December. Amichai had written a play for the schoolchildren and was adamant about not canceling the performance and celebrations, as two other schools had done.[50] He was haunted by the memory of that sad Hanukkah in Wuerzburg when his friend Ruth Hanover had been injured after they had quarreled, and he was determined that this time nothing would mar the holiday. In his December 7, 1947 letter, he wrote to Ruth Z. about the cancelled Hanukkah play in Wuerzburg's Jewish school and the audition for the theatrical role of Judah Maccabee that never took place. He told her that he had shared this story with his pupils to show them how a silly competition for a role could turn into a disaster, and he felt that they had understood him. Amichai's dedication to the performance completely overshadowed the serious circumstances of the time. He proudly filled the letters with descriptions of his role as "playwright, director, tailor, prompter, usher, janitor and orchestra."[51]

Amichai continued teaching at the Geula School in December, but other aspects of his life were rapidly changing. Nevertheless, he perceived his life as a rich tapestry of "love, childhood memories, responsibility, children, our future and twenty other things."[52] His December letters intertwine the school Hanukkah play, his nighttime guard duty on the line that divided the Arab and Jewish neighborhoods of Haifa, and the longing for the December snows of his childhood in Wuerzburg. He imagined Ruth Z. walking through a city adorned with Christmas decorations like those in his hometown, pined for her, and dreamt of the rosy future they would build. His newest creative achievement was the most meaningful of all. He had just completed "In the Public Garden" and had great hopes for its chances in the literary competition to which he sent it.

While he proclaimed that he still merely "played" the role of a soldier (as opposed to actually being one), Amichai struggled to absorb his increasing military duties into his self-image as poet. Before going on guard duty, he stuffed his bag full of poetry books and explained to Ruth that he was "faithful to the idea of the educated knights" adding the English words, "arms and letters."[53] With this image, he attempted to create the persona of a medieval knight errant, grafting this romantic ideal onto the mundane reality of guard duty.

Although Amichai had been a soldier in the British army, he had never seen combat. On December 11, 1947, for the first time in his life, Amichai went through his "baptism by fire."[54] He disclosed that he "not only guarded but also attacked,"[55] yet he still expressed his contempt for war and admitted that he was scared but felt that he had to fulfill his duty. In the letters, Amichai continued to portray himself as one who sits next to his table, like "medieval copper engravers," trying to capture reality in his art.[56] That reality soon became the dramatic events and the dire condition of the land. In a letter dated December 14, 1947, he reported on hiding from bullets in an entryway on the street, but in the same breath, asked Ruth to send him *Poetry*, the Chicago-based journal for modern poetry.[57]

Transition: The Eve of 1948

After Hanukkah, Amichai's letters become shorter and shorter. The handwriting testifies to the fatigue of the writer who worked as a teacher by day and as a soldier by night. Even though the British had slowed the printing of aerograms and stamps, he continued to send three every week; but while the letters from the autumn are laced with poetry, the letters from the subsequent months are filled with the brutal reality of war.[58] Concurrently, the letters from Ruth became more infrequent. Although Amichai refused to see the "writing on the wall" and blamed the postal service, underlying anxiety about their relationship crept into his love letters. Orah still remembered his excruciating wait for Ruth and his refusal to let go of his hope that she would return to him.[59]

From the end of December onward, the letters record the bloody crescendo of war that would reach a climax with the Declaration of Independence on May 14, 1948. Amichai attempted a delicate balancing act: he strove to document his life accurately without scaring Ruth. At the same time, he wished to encourage her to return to him, even if it meant telling her about the dangers he had to face. In early December 1947, Amichai still sent poems he had just completed to literary competitions.[60] By the end of the month, however, he told Ruth of a woman who was shot while hanging the diapers of her two-month-old baby.[61] His former student Rina recalled that, by this time, "the trauma of the war was evident in the classroom."[62] The Geula School had become a shelter for Jewish refugees who had fled from the mixed Arab-Jewish neighborhoods in the lower parts of Haifa, and the first-aid station, Magen David Adom, was housed opposite the school.[63] Amichai's colorful tableau included the refugees' laundry on one floor of the school, a military draft station covered with flags and slogans on another, and buses unloading wounded civilians across the street.[64] Amichai contrasted his pupils' distressing compositions about their Hanukkah vacation with the compositions he used to write as a child. While he had written about a frozen bird in the snow as a child in Wuerzburg, his pupils suffered the first effects of the war. They wrote about curfew or the British knocking on the door, trying to arrest family members.[65]

As he attempted to see reality through the children's eyes, Amichai experienced a second childhood—one of a native, local Israeli. By listening to his students and reading their essays, Amichai entered their worlds; it seems that his "Israeliness" increased through his identification with his pupils. Beginning in September 1947, the letters document how he invented Israeli parallels to his own childhood memories. For example, he transformed the tragic fate of discarded Christmas trees that he remembered from Wuerzburg into a subject for his students' compositions. He replaced the fir trees with the discarded myrtle and palm fronds from the Jewish holiday of Sukkot and asked his pupils to imagine the feelings of the rejected symbolic, inanimate objects.[66] In later months, when the children of Haifa were caught in the midst of gunshots and bombs, he equated the children's expertise in the rhythm of machine guns to a German nursery rhyme about cuckoo clocks.[67] This way, and likely without being aware of it, Amichai internalized his students' experiences. He translated them, so to speak, into the vocabulary of his own childhood, thus granting himself a rebirth of sorts as an Israeli elementary school pupil.

When writing to Ruth about military activity, Amichai still clung to lyrical images. Under his wand, the sand around an abandoned kibbutz became as white and fine as snow, an object of beauty; the rust and decay that were slowly "conquering" the empty houses took on a romantic hue. The pages upon pages that he wrote to Ruth remained for him segments of the book of their love. He viewed himself as the author of this book, and described his "white hands" and the "dark curl" falling on his forehead—the countenance of an author, not a soldier.[68] At the same time, he knew that he was depositing his art in Ruth's hands for safekeeping lest something should happen to him.[69]

The balance between poetry and love, on the one hand, and Amichai's military duty, on the other, was tipping: while all three still existed, Amichai admitted that his life was now dominated by the national needs and woes. On the eve of 1948, he wrote that his world was a triangular one: poetry and his love for Ruth were lumped into one category, school constituted the second category, and the "noisy work of the collective" was the third. Furthermore, the brutality of the situation in Palestine prevented him from retreating into his literary world. After "provocateurs threw hand grenades" at Arab workers near the oil refineries, two thousand Arab workers attacked the four hundred Jewish co-workers and "murdered forty-two of them . . . with keys, screws, hammers . . ." while the British security guards watched "without lifting a finger. . . ." The brush of an artist is still evident in this vivid depiction, but the sad recognition of an end to creative output, at least temporarily, seeps through the words: "Forgive me, once I dreamt of beautiful letters . . . and now I have to write about other things."[70] While he did not wish to write about the political landscape, there was no way to avoid it. On January 7, Amichai acknowledged for the first time that Palestine was in a state of war.[71] In the midst of the chaos, however, he still tried to cling to the dream of being a poet and to the small wonders of everyday life—his landlords' classical record collection, the caring stepmother of one of his students, and the children he observed in the nursery school near his house.

Nevertheless, history had begun to affect the essence of Amichai's verse as well as the content of his letters. The three poems that he wrote and sent to Ruth in 1948 were all responses to the violence or national feelings of the time.[72] This was symptomatic of the shift in Amichai's poetic preference from introspective lyricism to an engagement with the nation (albeit from an idiosyncratic point of view). He no longer fought the effect of outside events on his inner world, but rather embraced it. The first of these poems to be included in a letter was "From Chance to Fate." This unpublished work alludes to a conversation Amichai and Ruth had in the spring of 1947. But while that conversation dealt with romantic choices, the poem written in the winter of 1948 is about the role of fate in determining who would be killed, who would be wounded, and who would remain unscathed.[73] While the notion of chance and fate is raised in the letters in relation to an artistic career and love, Amichai's transference of it into the realm of war is significant, because in January 1948 fate seemed to determine much in the lives of the inhabitants of Palestine. The situation was deteriorating. On January 16, 1948, Amichai wrote that there were shortages of food and supplies and that Haifa had become "a war front."[74] The military demands on Amichai grew; but while he was willing to give up all his free time for fighting, he rejected a higher military post. Even under the shadow of war, and despite his strong sense of duty, he still insisted that his "life's path" did not allow him to pursue any career other than that of a poet.[75] The concept of a "hero perforce" (gibor hova), which Amichai would later develop, began germinating at this early stage. This concept would eventually define Amichai's trademark national voice, the voice of the simple soldier who was not born to be a "hero," but became one due to circumstance.[76]

Be that as it may, Amichai told Ruth of his "new masculinity," his transition from being solely a thinker to being an actor as well. At this crossroads, Hamlet again appears in Amichai's letters, as it had after Hayim Goldman's tragic death in November. In mid-January, however, the "performance" was no longer limited to the local stage of Mount Carmel, with individual heroes or characters. Amichai referred instead to the entire land "as a great drama" in which everybody played a role: there were those who only think, like Hamlet, and others who merely act, like Fortinbras.[77]

Amichai, who previously depicted himself as a philosopher and a poet, now saw himself as standing in the middle, between Fortinbras and Hamlet; not fully an actor, but no longer a mere thinker.[78] The national predicament had transformed Amichai's self-image. His brand of a "new masculinity" meant standing "in the middle"—no longer on the sidelines—a place he would often occupy in his published poetry. Although he believed that "[i]f times were normal" his poetry would have enjoyed "a great blossoming," he accepted the postponement of his aspirations as a writer without bitterness.[79]

Perhaps Amichai's philosophizing about Hamlet and Fortinbras was a method of stalling, a way to withhold bad news from Ruth a little longer in order to spare her the pain it would cause. Thirty-five young men on their way to help small, besieged Jewish settlements near Hebron had been caught in an ambush and killed.[80] A number of them were Ruth's classmates from Jerusalem, including their commander, Danny Mas, who had shared her desk at school.[81]

Violence

From February onward, almost every letter bore news of another bout of violence, the perfidy of the British, or details of the military actions in which

Amichai took part. Amichai's concern for the fate of Jerusalem (in general) and that of his parents (in particular) heightened. His hatred for the British grew, as did his disdain for the traitorous United States, which had essentially retreated from the partition plan; and his affinity for the former Soviet Union, which remained committed to it.[82] Perhaps his yearnings added to his anger toward the United States—the land on whose streets he imagined Ruth walking in a "black fur coat."[83] After he heard that a hand grenade thrown from a passing train had killed a driver in Binyamina, he lamented that his and Ruth's "past was wounded." He said that, like everything else in "this land," their past was painted with "human blood."[84] By coloring "everything" in red, Amichai surrendered to the dictates of the collective; it was as though the war or the color of blood erased the differences between individuals. Personal memories and longings had to be suppressed. When Amichai wrote these lines on February 4, 1948, he also reported the national news: Syrian forces had penetrated Palestine while the British were busy disarming Jews, and all Jewish men under the age of thirty-five had been drafted.[85]

In a letter he wrote two days later, Amichai articulated the bond between his personal history and the history of the land, a connection that he would formulate poetically in the years to come. He confessed that, unlike heroes in plays and novels who are torn between love and duty, he experienced no conflict because duty had already won. Furthermore, he declared that, at this time, the plans of each individual and the plans of the society had become synonymous.[86]

Amichai also discovered that the behavior of the Yishuv was more dignified and restrained than what he had expected of "Jews" and recorded how the "weak" character of the Jew was changing. He watched himself and his nation being transformed through this struggle, from those who were "easily excitable" and would "quickly despair," into erect, strong, and calm new people.[87] On February 18, 1948, Amichai observed his "nation" as it was evolving into one, and integrated the Zionist ideals into his observations. The forming Israeli nation showed its true strengths in the composure and staying power of its people.[88] When heavy loss of life became a daily occurrence (seventy-four Jews were killed on the day the February 18 letter was written), he praised this unity of the Jewish inhabitants of Palestine. He stated that because the Yishuv was so small, the absence of each fallen person was genuinely and acutely felt; there was no concept of an "anonymous soldier."[89]

Though Amichai did not stop writing poetry, guns and bullets had entered his lines. One poem, sent on February 8, 1948, voices a clichéd collectivist perspective, stating, "we'll . . . lend our shoulder to the effort. . . ."[90] Amichai was aware of the change that this poem reflected, and compared himself to a car shifting gears.[91] He reported on a "new tone" that had penetrated his poems, and described it as "fuller and [more] mature," but admitted that this tone did not feel authentic, as if it were "not [his] voice."[92]

The naïve and self-absorbed poet who watched his own white hands writing under an electric light became infused with faith and patriotism, but he still struggled to find a balance between his inner world and the carnage around him. A printer's error in a newspaper story about soldiers killed defending a Jewish settlement afforded a momentary poetic solution. The Hebrew word "musicians" (menagnim) was mistakenly switched with the Hebrew word "defenders" (meginim). The article wrongly reported that "musicians," not "defenders," had died. The February 20, 1948, article inspired Amichai to combine battle, death, and music in a poem.[93] While the tone of Amichai's poem is lyrical, its content displays the shift in focus: music becomes a vehicle for describing the outcome of a battle. The poem opens with a melody played by trumpets and violins. As the lines progress, however, the music fades away and the dominant sound is that of falling—the hands on keyboards, the head on the chest, and, finally, the musicians themselves. Amichai's symbol of loss—bereaved mothers—concludes the poem, leaving the reader with the unambiguous reality of war. The national is no longer an external duty in conflict with poetic aspirations, but, rather, the stuff of poetry. Amichai began to allow "history" to play a role in his inner world and his artistic universe. Yet, in his letter, he called Ruth's attention to the original poetic technique that he employed, glossing over his new subject matter—death in war.

Unlike the fallen defenders whose death Amichai sublimated in a poem, the terrorist bombing perpetrated on February 22, 1948, by a British gang was bluntly conveyed to Ruth in what Amichai called his "saddest letter." Five major buildings on Ben Yehuda Street, in the heart of Jerusalem, had been demolished. Amichai's visceral reaction to the news was as though "some spring [had] disconnected" in him. That corner in Jerusalem had been his favorite haunt, where he and Ruth used to walk together. He described the scattered pieces of bones and live flesh, pots and pans, hats and toys. This bombing had a symbolic meaning for Amichai: the world that had belonged to him and Ruth had been destroyed. Nevertheless, Amichai had been transformed since he last strolled with Ruth on Ben Yehuda Street. "I have a new truth of my own," he said, and confirmed that he knew the purpose of his life and "for what I'm fighting."[94] As Amichai faced these brutalities, his military mission became a source of solace for him, while poetry had to remain dormant.

On February 25, 1948, Amichai disappointedly informed Ruth that the literary competitions had been cancelled because of the conflict.[95] This is a tangible confirmation of the state of his poetic career at the time; but, by the end of February 1948, the hierarchy of his priorities had altered. The intensifying battles and the pervasive bloodshed had changed him.

In March and April of 1948, the autumn months of 1947 seemed light-years behind. Instead of his fear of death, which he confessed after his "baptism by fire" (in December 1947),[96] Amichai now wrote about the thrill and joy of active battle after the long, quiet hours of waiting in ambush "with the finger on the trigger."[97] In a letter from March 14, 1948, he proudly told Ruth how onlookers stared admiringly at him and the other fighters as they went past, their weapons loaded and ready.[98] While his early letters focused on romantic depictions of his surroundings, the letters from March and April were replete with such details as the number of grenades he kept in his belt and the number of bullets he had in his gun.[99]

Perhaps to arouse jealousy in Ruth, Amichai also outlined the dynamics within the male and female paramilitary group. When describing the row of men advancing toward the target, he told of his affection for the man who marched right in front and the man right behind him. He wrote about the girls who waited with hot tea and "smiling eyes" when the mission was accomplished.[100] He captured his missions with dramatic accuracy: the rocky ground and the pebbles that rolled down the hill as the small unit inched hair-raisingly close to the enemy camp. He described how they suddenly caught sight of the Arab force on its way to attack; they had to send warning, but the radios did not function, then they had to make their way back to the front post quickly, without being noticed by the would-be attackers. Amichai's small unit managed to call for reinforcements in time to prevent a calamity. They then returned to the base, where they took part in the ritual of hot tea, cake, and alcohol that the girls had ready for them.[101] On another mission, they shot at cars that carried Arab gang members. Engulfed in a cloud of smoke, Amichai could think of nothing but the command "fire!" At dawn, there were again hot tea and the girls.[102] The letters from March and April elaborate on army life and emphasize the camaraderie among the fighters, but their style is still poetic. Nonetheless, Amichai noted that he sensed a new harshness in himself. He felt "quiet readiness";[103] he became sure of himself and reported that he had confidence in the justice of the cause.

Hamerkaz School

Like a leitmotif in a consciously constructed narrative, the theme of Amichai's last months of teaching in Haifa recurs in the letters from January onward. In them, Amichai drew a dramatic picture of his new school, an emblem for the "blood dance" that swept the city and the country at large.[104] At the end of January 1948, Amichai left the relatively stable Geula School in the Jewish neighborhood of Hadar for the Hamerkaz School in the diverse and volatile lower part of Haifa. He was called upon to substitute for a pregnant teacher who was afraid to stay there and also to coordinate the actions of the Hagana in that strategically located school.[105] In a poignant depiction of the goodbye to his pupils at the Geula School, he compared himself to a gardener who knows each flower in his garden. On the last day, he taught as usual, and waited until the last ten minutes to bid farewell.[106]

The Hamerkaz School was like a little, besieged fortress. Amichai no longer had the luxury of gym classes in the yard or watching children at recess. Most of the Jewish inhabitants of this quarter had already left; the only children who remained were those from low-income homes, whose parents worked in the port and in the commercial center. When Amichai arrived, there were 120 students, 6 teachers, 6 classrooms, and sandbags on all of the windows.[107] Through the cracks, the new teacher could see the Arab street, as the school bordered the Arab neighborhood. An army post was located on the roof of the school; the guards marched back and forth during school hours and throughout the day. There were holiday posters on the walls, but a machine gun lay by the teacher's desk, next to the colored chalk. In addition to conventional subjects, Amichai had to teach the children how to respond when they heard the sirens.

In the first week that Amichai took up his new post, gunfire erupted near the school, forcing the children to throw themselves to the ground. Within a month, as the fighting in the neighborhood intensified, the number of students dropped from 120 to 40, and the fourth grade was ultimately reduced to 8 frightened children scattered among the desks.[108] In mid-February, the cooking teacher was wounded, and teaching was no longer the most important activity in school; Amichai tried to keep the children safe and to establish some comforting order in "their chaotic lives."[109] That week, Amichai's class moved to an alternate room that had thicker walls.[110] The father of one of his pupils was killed in front of his own house, and the distraught teacher mourned him and his orphans ruefully.[111]

On March 2, 1948, a huge crash rocked the school, followed by gunfire. The glass shattered in the windowpanes and the children screamed, but, like little drilled veterans, they dropped to the floor. The teachers and their pupils were stranded in the classrooms for four-and-a-half hours. No one was hurt, but the children were scared and hungry. In the letter that Amichai wrote to Ruth that evening, he described the "special scent" of children's fear: "sweat and . . . wool wet with urine."[112] Forty-eight hours after this harrowing ordeal, the entire city shook with "the sound of a huge explosion, as a car bomb was detonated during the night in an attempt to destroy the commercial center in the lower part of Haifa. The bomb reduced the school building to rubble. The next day, Amichai returned to the ravaged building to salvage what he could; in his letter to Ruth, he depicted the sad image of the few children who came to the wreckage of their old school, searching in the debris "like dogs in the garbage."[113] Two days later, the brave Hamerkaz School teachers found a new place with boarded-up windows to hold classes. Fewer and fewer children attended school and any instruction became nearly impossible.[114] A Jewish man was killed near the school, and the children saw his "intestines" spilled across the sidewalk. Soon after, volleys of gunshots and bombs forced the children to descend into the inner courtyard by ladders. A shell entered their sheltered space, but luckily did not explode; afterwards, the teachers had to return the children home in armored cars, as was often the case.[115]

Throughout this entire period at the Hamerkaz School, Amichai went on military assignments almost every evening and was, in fact, living the life of a hero—teaching in perilous conditions by day and fighting at night. He patrolled and exchanged fire with Arab gangs, returning to the classroom after only two hours of sleep. A blood covenant was being forged between Amichai and his country, but also with his little pupils at the Hamerkaz School. His drive to protect them added another dimension to his sense of duty as a defender of the land. Working around the clock, however, had begun to take its toll. Food was scarce, and the burdened teacher admitted that he was tired. "Sometimes," he wrote to Ruth, "I feel weakness from lack of food."[116]

In mid-March the school again trembled from an explosion. Some girls burst into tears and others laughed hysterically. Someone announced that a building on the nearby Hanamal Street had exploded. No'a, the girl who lived there, asked only for colored crayons. As he watched her draw, the teacher Amichai wondered how she would remember the war in the years to come, if she survived it.[117] They later found out that No'a's apartment had been damaged and her mother wounded. Toward the end of March, a British soldier was gunned down by an Arab at the school's door. When they left the school, the children saw the blood on the doorposts and one remarked that it looked exactly like the blood of the Jew. The challenge of comforting children whose school was practically in a battlefield was enormous. Amichai remained as sensitive and empathic as he had been before, but there was little he could do for his class. He mourned that "our little wounded school is dying."[118] Indeed, in mid-April 1948, on the Passover break, the Hamerkaz School was finally shut down and Amichai was drafted. He was now required to be a full-time soldier.[119]

The Dear-John letter that arrived in April thus marked, in a poignant and ironic coincidence, the end of any shade of normality in other areas of Amichai's life. In April 1948, he wrote his ninety-eighth and last aerogram. He did not number this letter, which contains his painful resignation to the idea that a chapter in his life had ended, as a teacher and as a lover. He wrote, "[T]his is how one learns to pack things . . . put camphor and remember a little bit and forget."[120] In his confused and embittered letter to Ruth, he mentioned the upcoming battles twice. He told her not to be afraid; that his despair would not lead him to "volunteer for suicide missions." By raising the subject of suicide missions in this situation, Amichai was in fact hinting that he had considered them.[121] But her engagement to another man would "not destroy" him, because he knew what he was "destined for."[122]

I DON'T WANT TO BE A HERO

Just as Amichai's poetic destiny was the engine of his salvation when he lost Ruth, so, too, would it dictate the course of his military career. The letters suggest that his refusal to accept the high positions that the army offered him was driven not only by his nonviolent, unmilitaristic character, but also by a deep, early awareness of his artistic calling.[123] It was like the needle of a compass, always pointing him in the right direction.

Amichai was never a rabid patriot: his nationalism was always tempered by his unmilitaristic nature and his literary aspirations. The roots of the then-revolutionary worldview reflected in the 1958 poem "Ani rotse lamut al mitati" (literally, I want to die in my bed)[124] can be traced back to the poet's transformative months in Haifa (see appendix A).

One of Amichai's letters from December 1947 reflects the exact sentiment expressed in the poem. Written four days after the UN vote for the partition plan, the letter contains Amichai's realization that he might have to resign as a teacher and "again play a soldier." He bluntly confessed that he did not want it to happen. "I hate," he said, "all that is connected to it." Nevertheless, he acknowledged that "it is the duty of the hour."[125] For the word "duty," he uses the word "hova," the same word that would appear in the poem over a decade later in the expression "gibor hova," "hero perforce" or, literally, "compulsory hero." He expressed this sentiment forcefully whenever the pressure grew to intensify his military involvement.[126] In fact, it dominates a January 1948 letter as a refrain in the way that the refrain "I want to die in my bed" dominates the poem. In the letter, this antiheroic assertion escalates in intensity: first, "I have no ambition"; then, "I don't want to be like that"; then, "This does not suit me"; and, finally, the culminating, "I don't want to be a general."[127]

The letter, written on December 11, 1947, documents Amichai's first battle, which included blowing up Arab houses from which people had fired on Jewish buses. In contrast to his peers' excitement, Amichai conceded, "I am not a big hero." The disconnection between Amichai's perception and the prevalent sentiments of that war-crazed period is epitomized by this confession. Amichai did not like to boast, and even admitted to being afraid. He saw fighting as an obligation, repeatedly using the phrase "I hate" or "I deathly hate" for anything involving military bravado. He mocked and rejected heroic vanity and "gallows humor," telling Ruth that as soon as a battle was over, he liked to retreat from his fellow soldiers, become a civilian again, and "talk about good and simple and silly things."[128]

The poem "I Want to Die in My Own Bed" portrays a speaker who resists society's expectations of him as a man, which are to be a hero and aggressively pursue a life of action. The line "I want to die in my own bed," which serves as the poem's title and refrain, is implicitly juxtaposed with the patriotic ideal of dying for one's country. Each of the poem's five stanzas ends with this refrain, which is often preceded by a reference to a different famous biblical battle. Samson is singled out as the direct antithesis of the speaker (Judges 14–16). Samson's heroic powers lay in his hair; when his hair was cut off, so was his strength. In contrast, the speaker became a soldier, a "hero" (albeit a compulsory one), only when his hair was shaved off in a crew cut. Samson demonstrated his might by tearing a lion to pieces, while the speaker's power is in cushioning the nest, in turning the lion's mouth into a home: ". . . you could live and furnish. . . / even a lion's maw, if you've got no other place. . . ."[129]

"I Want to Die in My Own Bed" was not published until 1958, yet its thematic origins are readily apparent in Amichai's letters to Ruth a decade earlier. The poem does not mirror the letters' vocabulary and imagery as other published poems do, but it reflects the letters' underlying attitude toward war. Although "I Want to Die in My Own Bed" became an anthem for a generation of Israelis weary of war, it is not a pacifist poem, nor does it promote conscientious objection. The speaker, like the poet, *did* go to war. He was not a hero, but he voluntarily participated in battles. Like Amichai, who claimed in a letter from January 1948 that his sensibility lay somewhere between Hamlet and Fortinbras, the speaker in the poem also embodies this "middle ground."[130] He is not swayed by nationalist propaganda and knows that war is ugly and dangerous. At the same time, he believes—just as Amichai believed at the time of his correspondence with Ruth—that it is his duty to fight. Both the letters and the poem that echoes them highlight the conflict between the fear of battle and hatred of war, and the awareness that war is necessary for survival.

A REBIRTH AT WAR

For Amichai, the crescendo of violence that led up to the full-blown War of Independence also had deep psychological meaning. His letters from that time are a living testimony to the national frame of mind: a mixture of grief, caused by the many casualties, with an unparalleled courage and resilience. Amichai's occasional references to "anyone who would survive this period . . ."[131] reveal how aware he was of the threat of death that hovered over fighters and civilians alike. Yet this assertion often continued with ". . . will have witnessed the most awe-inspiring period in the life of the nation."[132] Indeed, almost every member of the Yishuv in 1948 recognized the magnitude of those times. As a writer, Amichai was able to convey the intensity of the national drama with the same imaginative powers of depiction that he lavished on autumn sunsets on the Carmel. His awareness of being part of the collective fate was all-encompassing; like most of the Jewish population in Palestine, he deeply identified with the creation of the Israeli nationhood. Concurrently, Amichai suspended his identity as a poet who drew from the wellspring of his early years for his verse.

The process that began upon his arrival in Palestine twelve years earlier reached its peak as he shed the persisting remnants of his diasporic past and recreated himself as a full Israeli. A poignant assertion he made thirteen years after the war suggests this inner shift. When, in 1961, the army weekly *Bamahane* urged him to revisit the Negev, where he fought in 1948, and to publish his impressions, he confessed, "It was a very personal journey of memory. . . . [I]n this way a person returns sometimes to the city of his childhood. . . ."[133] In other words, the battles provided him with a second birth—a new birthplace and a new identity.

The process of this transference is amply documented in Amichai's correspondence with Ruth Z. On the border between 1947 and 1948, Amichai made the inner decision to identify as and be a complete Israeli, whether consciously or unconsciously. The poetic "I," who is by nature an outsider—even more so when his origins are foreign—was temporarily suppressed. When this poetic "I" reemerged in 1949 after the war, its foreign roots had been unrecognizably camouflaged, not only so that his readership would welcome him, but also to help him maintain a sense of wholeness, an integrated self.

For six decades, Ruth Z. has been the guardian not merely of a collection of love letters or a record of national events, but of historical literary documents that encapsulate Amichai's maturation as a poet. These letters are also a work of literature in their own right. They weave an intimate narrative, at the core of which is the young man's desire to write and his conviction that poetry is his destiny. It is likely that during those dangerous times in the Land of Israel, Amichai sent his work to Ruth in the United States not only as a means of communication with his beloved, but also as a way of recording his artistic trajectory and ensuring its survival. Having been a refugee at the age of twelve, he understood that homes could be destroyed. Amichai thus preserved his art by sending it to a faraway land.[1] His poetry was the essence of his being, and even when Ruth had abandoned him four weeks before full-blown war erupted, Amichai still declared that the power of his art would "soften the blow."[2]

THE LETTERS: REVEALING THE FOUNDATION
The letters' verse and prose coalesce to form the portrait of the artist as a young man and paint his inner struggles against the backdrop of his nation's dramatic conflict. The correspondence that lasted from September 1947 to April 1948 is testimony to a life obsessed with writing, in which almost every experience was seen as a potential building block for a poem.[3] Almost a third of the letters that Amichai wrote to Ruth Z. in those months employ poetry in one form or another. Fifteen of the ninety-four letters in Ruth's possession contain original poems by Amichai—most of which have never been published[4]—while many others include works by Goethe or Rilke, either in the original German or in Amichai's translations into Hebrew.[5] This concentration of verse is a deliberate poetic signature, a mark of the primacy of creative writing in Amichai's life and his devotion to his vocation. Indeed, even the prose of the letters is touched by a poet's hand: it is elegant and rich with imagery. Plainly, Amichai used some of his letters as literary exercises to practice new strategies

for future poetry or fiction. In the later months of the correspondence, the proximity of war and the fear of a permanent separation from his beloved gave Amichai's writing a desperate tone that rarely appears in such a dark form in his later, published works.

Amichai's lyrical letters to Ruth Z. were born out of a time of emotional upheaval. In addition to their crucial role in the study of Amichai's verse, "letters" became a central trope for the poet. Correspondence, that is, the writing, sealing, mailing, and receiving of letters, is endowed with mythological dimensions in Amichai's later oeuvre. Both of the published works most closely associated with Ruth, "We Loved Here" and "In the Public Garden," are branded by the long months that the young Amichai spent writing letters to and waiting for letters from the United States. As late as his last volume, published in 1998, letters are endowed with a divine power.

The text of the letters reveals the deepest foundations of Amichai's work. During the period of the correspondence, Amichai thought a lot about his childhood. "I bring up many pictures from then," he wrote to Ruth. The letters are dotted with those pictures, many of which would never again appear in Amichai's writing. He told Ruth that childhood was an unfailing "source of . . . distilled experience" for him, and used Rilke to validate this connection between childhood and art.[6] Amichai referred to Rilke's advice in *Letters to a Young Poet*: "[A] young poet must go back and think of his childhood."[7] As shown in chapter 4, the young Hebrew poet identified with the German master, and their shared culture and mother tongue undoubtedly deepened that attachment.[8]

The letters reveal the heart of Amichai's intricate, multifaceted connection to Rilke's works.[9] While the intertextual relationship between Amichai's and Rilke's poetry has been established in critical works and by Amichai himself, its emotional foundation is exposed solely in the letters.[10] Rilke's belief in the power of childhood and his indirect way of drawing from it taught Amichai how to rely on his own youthful experiences as inspiration without explicitly depicting them.

The discussion below follows the making of Amichai as a poet, as reflected in the letters to Ruth Z. It highlights Amichai's strong belief in his poetic calling and the tremendous effort he invested in his vocation. It examines the practicalities of writing as they are detailed in the letters, from the writing utensils the poet used to the actual literary "sketches" or "studies" he copied into the aerograms. Most importantly, this analysis tracks Amichai's self-critique as a poet. It reveals the precepts he adopted as good poetry, such as innovation, imagery, musicality, and authenticity. In the letters, Amichai disclosed his admiration for Rilke and T. S. Eliot, who validated his artistic inclinations and the way he saw the world. The letters reveal the lyrical roots of some of Amichai's printed poems, providing a new reading of them, and sometimes deciphering hermetic lines. They cast Amichai's poetic development during the correspondence into relief.

Destined to Be a Poet

As early as the summer of 1946, when he decided to become a teacher because it would allow him time to write, Amichai was already writing poetry and was determined to follow it as his calling.[11] Poetry was his "life's path,"[12] his "great plan,"[13] his "road that was destined for me,"[14] and his "fate."[15] He was confident that in his life "poetry will not cease"[16] and attributed his sense of self-assurance and good mood to this "new truth."[17] Amichai believed that being a poet would retroactively make the ostensible coincidences of his past into the integral pieces of a predetermined fate. The process of creating art meant fusing accidental details into destiny, or, in his own words, "mak[ing] everything that is chance" in his life "fateful."[18] Accordingly, writing represented both Amichai's future and a way to endow his past with meaning.

★   ★   ★

Poetry was more than a destiny or a path Amichai had chosen; it was also an innate part of his physical makeup, an irrepressible compulsion. When Ruth sent him a poem she had written, Amichai saw it as a way to merge their blood, and likened their sharing of poetry to a covenant between ancient nations for whom drinking each other's blood was a sign of loyalty.[19] Poetry was as essential as blood for Amichai. Thus, to him, the act of exchanging poems was akin to sharing bodily fluids.

The notion of writing poetry as a bodily function resurfaces often in the letters, independently of the couple's relationship. For Amichai, creation involved a phase of gathering sensations and experiences and then "physically" absorbing them. In two letters, he wrote that images or sounds "enter [his] blood."[20] These raw materials were like food that not only would be digested and then reshaped into poetry, but also would nourish him.[21] After he read a new poem, he felt it "in all my body" and observed how it contributed to his "growing in strength. . . ." The materials he absorbed would later "grow" inside him and ultimately be born as complete pieces of art.[22]

As early as his second letter, Amichai coined the metaphor "filling his barns,"[23] which he used to describe his process of gathering and storing materials for his poems.[24] The idea of full barns as a symbol of prosperity appears in the Bible in the books of Proverbs and Deuteronomy.[25] Amichai appropriated this national, biblical image to capture his personal artistic behavior. He compared both his solitary hours and the times he spent with others to fertile ground from which his "poems grow," again implying that poems are as tangible as wheat or fruit.[26]

Throughout the entire correspondence, Amichai's letters communicate the exhilarating experience of internal creation with such lines as "the poems are many in me"[27] or "the creation inside me blossomed."[28] The power of poetry persisted even when the fighting in Palestine increased and he was not physically writing. While he lamented that "if times were normal," he would publish his first volume, his resolve to write continued even in the face of raging violence.[29] Yet sometimes even the generally optimistic Amichai surrendered to the horrors that besieged him. That experience, too, was expressed in physical terms. In the bloody, final months of the British Mandate, he worried that his "gathering" of materials would be in vain, and confided to Ruth that poems conceived in times of war were similar to aborted fetuses: most would never be "born" and those that were would be "born to a life of paleness."[30]

As the months progressed, Amichai became increasingly conscious of the way in which he internalized the world around him and transformed it into words, images, and rhythms.[31] He declared that each item in his field of vision was absorbed, even if it did not immediately become concrete poetic output. He was confident that the absorbed materials would eventually be metabolized and burst forth when the time was right. In one of the last letters to Ruth, written on April 1, 1948, he explained this creative process methodologically. While his focus in this example was on the creative "metabolism" of the experience, the subject at hand was preparing for battle. Amichai shared with Ruth how the impressions from a night patrol had penetrated his "consciousness" and become a part of his psyche, where they lay "like a rock inside [his] heart." In the future, he predicted, these images would sprout and "push themselves into words," even though he might have forgotten the initial inspiration for them because they had lain so deep in his subconscious for so long.[32]

Even in earlier letters, Amichai echoed the Surrealist belief that poetry emanates directly from the subconscious. In one such letter, he remarked in the margins of the aerogram that the "pictures" in a poem he had written had come to him unintentionally.[33] In another, he outlined this process in more explicit fashion, asserting that events that he had repressed into the "black cabinet" of his subconscious would periodically—and miraculously—break the surface and then vanish.[34]

The Letters As Narrative "Studies" or Literary Sketches

Ironically, Ruth's departure for New York kindled a renewed sense of purpose in her partner's writing. When they were together, Amichai never had to record his observations for Ruth; he simply told her about them. After she left, Amichai invented a new means of sharing his life with her: he began to walk around with a "tiny, tiny pad" in his pocket, pulling it out whenever he saw something that attracted his attention.[35] This was a groundbreaking moment in the making of Amichai as a poet, because he was transformed from a person who communicated intimately by talking into one who interpreted the world for his beloved exclusively through writing.

Long after the relationship with Ruth ended, the technique he invented because of her survived. Using small notepads became a hallmark of Amichai's creative process until his death; the pads that survive now reside in the Beinecke Library archives, full of fragments of conversations, phone numbers, and random thoughts. Unfortunately, the collection of papers that Amichai deposited at the Beinecke Library lacks his pre-1954 notepads, but the letters contain some of what he included in them. On September 17, 1947, Amichai revealed to Ruth the full import of the letters, saying that he looked to his notepads on which he jotted down ideas to inspire both his poems and his letters to her. He said that he wrote down "everything" in the notepads and later used some "words" from them for his poems. Additionally, most of these notes served as "building blocks" for his letters. With this confession, Amichai exposed the porous wall between his epistolary writing and his lyrical creations.[36]

Amichai's laborious effort to transform scattered words and ideas that he had jotted down on notepads into poetry is echoed in the technical details of his working routine, schedule, and writing utensils. The simple act of putting pen to paper "calmed" him in times of hardship,[37] enabled him to shut out his surroundings, and strengthened him when he despaired.[38] During the fall months, he toiled "days and nights"[39] on two long poems that he was preparing for separate literary competitions. The letters are suffused with his ambition, and record how he industriously copied and recopied those two poems for submission.[40] The letters also convey how proud Amichai was every time he finished a new poem. On November 9, 1947, for example, he boasted of his productivity because he had written four poems and translated three.[41] Amichai excitedly pointed out the "progress" he was making[42] or his "growth"[43] as a poet. Furthermore, he imparted his conviction that, regardless of the outcome of any competition he entered, he would continue on his path, perfecting his poetic craft.[44]

Amichai invited Ruth to witness the nuts and bolts of creating these poems by including her in the painstaking choices he made in the composition of lines and sentences. Amichai's admonition to Ruth that she should get an English thesaurus in order to enrich her English seems to be more a reflection of his own continuous search for the correct word than a genuine suggestion for her to follow.[45] Amichai's search for synonyms received lyrical expression in a November 28, 1947 letter, which he began with six different variations on the theme of longing. A sense of yearning is, indeed, the essence of any love letter, but the exploration of linguistic synonyms is what made the lover a poet.[46]

Amichai was fully aware of the role of the letters in his creative life. He openly admitted that, in addition to their emotional and communicative function, the letters served him as exercises. They were the ideal arena for him to experiment with translating the world around him into "words and sentences." They trained him to be "exact in my language" and sharpened his observation skills.[47] Thus, as painful as it was for him to rely on the postal service in order to communicate with Ruth, Amichai knew well that the letters had a creative silver lining.

An exercise in narrative and drama is at the center of a sad letter from October 12, 1947, in which Amichai told Ruth about a meeting with the wife of their friend, Herbert.[48] Herbert's wife had separated from him and decided to move to the United States, taking their little daughter with her.[49] Amichai's narrative is fraught with references to the process of packing, the Haifa port, the sea, and the sailing of the boat, all elements that recall the still-fresh memory of his parting from Ruth.

Yet despite its personal content, Amichai told the story of his meeting with Herbert's wife in the third person, and with a clear artistic agenda. He opened the letter with a lyrical depiction of a "white terrace" with two "blood-red" chairs overlooking a grove. With painstaking patience, Amichai described the body language of a man and a woman sitting and talking, as though they were protagonists in a novel. Only later in the narrative does he reveal that the two are Herbert's wife and himself. After describing the scene, Amichai invited

Ruth into his veritable private workshop. He paused to reflect on his own writing, asserting that any story may be told "in different ways" because real life is disorderly; stories are woven one into the other, their beginnings and endings unknown. He then shared with Ruth the possibilities among which he had to choose: the story could have been told chronologically, beginning with Herbert's wife applying for a visa, packing, and traveling from Jerusalem to Haifa. It could have also been told from a "bird's-eye" perspective, in which all events (packing, parting, and sailing) happen at once. Ultimately, however, Amichai disclosed that he began his narrative at an arbitrary point, one that he "simply chose." The point of departure notwithstanding, his diligence as a writer is evident in his meticulous search for the proper tone and structure for his story.

A similar confluence of a sad plot and literary deliberations appears in a series of letters written a month later, in mid-November. As recounted in the previous chapter, on November 14, 1947, the bus on which Amichai was riding was ambushed, and a young man sitting in front of him was killed. After the initial shock, the writer in Amichai became preoccupied with the intricacies of rendering the heartbreaking story in words.[50] The letters about the fatal bus ride are written with a clear literary consciousness. On November 18, 1947, one day after the funeral of Hayim Goldman (the only fatality of the attack), Amichai rhetorically called to his addressee, "Come with me."[51] Following this invocation is a carefully wrought documentation of the funeral, with specific allusions to *Hamlet*.[52] Amichai dubbed the funeral the "last act" of a play that had begun the previous Friday. Every one of the passengers who survived the shooting was present at the ceremony. In Amichai's depiction, each became a character in the play, complete with a costume and a role: the "courageous" bus driver with his cap, the "pregnant woman," Amichai's colleague Orah in a light summer dress, and others. The writer described himself as one who "stands on the sidelines" in an attempt to fit "the funeral into the landscape." The "play" was set on a beautiful, sunny, springlike day in Haifa, with "gay, small clouds" over the bay, blossoming flowers, and ships in the port. After repeating his invocation, Amichai moved from the visual background to the sounds, contrasting the mourners' "screams" and "prayers" with the everyday noises of "cars," "brakes," and "orders." Only after the stage had been set did the main characters step into the spotlight. The first to appear was the victim's girlfriend. The "lovely and poor" girl, her innocence and childlike disorientation, reminded Amichai of a "distracted" Ophelia appearing in the court after she was driven to madness.[53] As he watched the motions of the distraught young woman, Shakespeare's heroine became a model for him in the physical representation of grief. He then incorporated that notion into his narrative by attributing Ophelia's physicality to the girlfriend—her "light and heavy" steps, her disheveled hair. After this description, Amichai halted. His teaching duties created an intermission in the "performance." He had to stop telling his story in the aerogram to go to school, but continued the saga in a subsequent letter.

Amichai began that letter with, "[W]e see our Ophelia," thus immediately ushering his addressee into the audience of the live performance.[54] His portrayal of "Ophelia" is full of pity, but his most intense response was to the tragic figure of the victim's mother. For her, Amichai wrote, the death of her son was "the last scene of a play." The different aspects of the funeral, like the hearse and the cantor's voice, seem to accelerate the buildup of the drama. When the mother "jumps towards" the hearse, screaming her son's name when she sees the coffin, "the play," wrote Amichai, "reached its climax." After the tension had been released and everybody began to leave, Amichai bid a last farewell to "our little Ophelia."

The letters about Hayim Goldman are a testimony to Amichai's development and inspirations as an author. In the years to come, he published a volume of radio skits and plays, an interest that may have found its first expression in the theatrical depiction of the funeral. Furthermore, a poem he published in 1980 ("A Meeting with My Father") looks back at the autumn of 1947 using similar theatrical terminology (for example, his father comes to visit him "in one of the intermissions . . . as if to an actor resting backstage").[55] The portrayal of the funeral as a variation on a scene from *Hamlet* is the first of seven references to Shakespeare in the letters. Amichai looked to him for prototypes of personalities and conflicts and sought validation for his own insights.

Poetic Ideals
September through December 1947 marked great poetic strides and unprecedented literary productivity on Amichai's part.[56] In addition to the love poems for Ruth and the writing exercises in the letters, Amichai spent those four months preparing two long works for literary competitions. While the first work, "In the Public Garden," was preserved, only a segment of the other, "Hada'aya," exists. (It is unknown whether it was lost or discarded.) We do not know exactly when "Hada'aya" was written, but on September 9, 1947, Amichai told Ruth of a manuscript that he intended to submit to a literary competition

conducted by a publication he called *Ha'otobiyografya hahofshit* (*The Free Autobiog-raphy*).⁵⁷ It is clear that Ruth had read at least a draft or a portion of this work before she left, for Amichai said plainly, "[Y]ou know it . . . it is the one with the kite."⁵⁸ This chronicle of Amichai's writing is proof that he began preparing his innovative work for a competition and viewed himself as a poet at least a year before the 1948 date that he commonly gave as his "initiation."

A series of subsequent letters from September and October 1947 documents the laborious yet satisfying process of neatly copying down "Hada'aya" for this competition.⁵⁹ Amichai stayed up late every night, drawing pleasure from watching the sheets of white paper lying in front of him gradually fill with let-ters written in blue ink.⁶⁰ He insisted that even if he were rejected, it would not deter him from pursuing his goal.⁶¹ From the segment of "Hada'aya" that sur-vives, it is apparent that Amichai intended it to include an ars-poetica statement that would link him to modernist poets and would revolutionize the Hebrew poetry of the time. Only the final portion of this long poetic work and the title "Hada'aya" survive, and only because they were included in his November 11, 1947, letter to Ruth Z.⁶² Although the root of the word *da'aya* (*ha* is the definite article "the") is comprised of the letters *Dalet Alef He* (an existing Hebrew root that means "gliding"), the noun *da'aya* itself does not appear in the dictionary. While Amichai stated the title in his letter, he did not define the word. Ruth, however, was easily able to interpret the word that Amichai almost certainly in-vented. *Da'aya*, she said, was a kite.⁶³

The process of creating "Hada'aya" (as recorded in the letters) is a perfect example of how Amichai's inner workshop functioned: he recalled a visual fragment of reality, or, in his words, "gathered" an image, and, months later, used it in a poem. Amichai told Ruth that "Hada'aya" was about a kite stuck in the electric lines; according to both his letters and Ruth's oral testimony, the image of that kite preoccupied Amichai at the time.⁶⁴ In one of his letters, he described a kite that had become entangled in the tree next to his window in Jerusalem. He saw it each time he opened and closed the shutters and asso-ciated it with the intimate times that he and Ruth had shared in his room.⁶⁵ Furthermore, the first work that Amichai ever asked Ruth to read—the piece that ignited their love affair—was a short story about a kite.⁶⁶ Neither the story nor the poem, however, was ever published. The story has almost certainly since been lost; and the literary competition for which "Hada'aya" was in-tended never took place because of the war.⁶⁷ The absence of "Hada'aya" in its entirety is detrimental to the study of Amichai's poetic development, as even the short extant segment (which does not include a reference to a kite) and the prose of the November 11 letter into which it was copied expose an Amichai unknown to readers and scholars.

The view of literature that Amichai expressed in the November 11, 1947, letter and the poem inside it are truly revelatory. With unparalleled candor, the poem spells out Amichai's perception of the practical work of the poet and his mission. It is the only ars-poetica poem to be included in the letters. Moreover, this kind of self-referential writing is rare in Amichai's published corpus. It is especially astonishing that the principles that guided Amichai in "Hada'aya" clearly persist into his final collections.

Because all that remains of "Hada'aya" is the excerpt included in the November 1947 letter, it is hard to deduce the poem's overall theme, especially as there is no mention of a kite or the word *da'aya* in that segment. The first six lines can be read as love-verse, for the speaker describes walking away from a woman but singing her song. After the sixth line, however, the speaker begins a catalogue—an element familiar to the reader of Amichai's published oeuvre, but also to the reader of the letters themselves. The device of the catalogue is in fact an early expression of a characteristic trait of Amichai's poetry. Moreover, it is associated with one of Amichai's views on art. Art, according to a letter written on October 20, 1947, is finding the "common denominator" of all that exists.[68] The various catalogues in this early ars-poetica poem reflect Amichai's mode of thinking, which finds unusual connections between seemingly unrelated articles or phenomena. Many years later, this would become a poetic guideline for which Amichai would be criticized, one which critics called "an analogical net in which everything is compared to everything."[69] Amichai's statement in October 1947, combined with his early use of the catalogue in his poetry (and the prose of his letters), demonstrates that this technique or principle—disparaged as intellectual laziness—was a component of a well-thought-out treatise on the relationship between art and life.

The catalogue in "Hada'aya" enumerates a series of activities, all of which may be interpreted as allusions to the work of creating poetic verse: photographer, peddler of used merchandise, music recorder, and archeologist.[70] A number of synonyms of the verb "collect" appear, followed by the various items to be collected. These include "torn letters," "flowers" pulled out of "garbage cans," as well as used "clothes." The "collector" is the poetic "I," an artist who presents his outlook on poetry. Art, in this poet's eyes, is the art of collage. In fact, according to this segment of "Hada'aya," the speaker not only "gathers," but also "glues" leftover pieces together. In some cases, however, the collage is not the final step. This "creator" continues to grow some of his most precious collectibles like "microbes in a laboratory." The image of the collage is then replaced by that of the artist as a photographer who obtains "hidden negatives" of the lives of others and turns them into "photographs."[71] The very end of the segment is addressed to a collective plural "you" (atem). The atem are both the subjects of poetry and its readers. The speaker describes how he "engraves" their secret words in his heart "like on a music record." He then compares his work as a poet to that of an archaeologist who learns about ancient history by piecing together "pot-shards"; like the archeologist, he knows about people's lives from the fragments he finds. The "archeologist" resembles the "collector," but the attempt to unveil people's secrets and to penetrate the lives of others also dictates the actions of the "photographer" and "engraver," both of whom bring to light hidden, intimate aspects of people's existences.

"Hada'aya" metaphorically and systematically conveys poetic strategies and ideals, some of which remained the basis of Amichai's verse in later years. The poem comments on the work of gathering and collage, on the importance of the mundane, and on the inclusion of unheroic aspects of reality as subjects of poetry.[72] The remarks that accompany it fill in what the ars-poetica poem does not divulge explicitly. Furthermore, this is not the only letter that contains Amichai's views on poetry; he lays out many of his artistic ideals throughout the entire body of the correspondence.

Underneath almost every original poem that he copied into the letters, Amichai either asked for Ruth's opinion of it, evaluated the work himself, or both.[73] As an established poet, Amichai rarely spoke abstractly about his views on poetry. The self-evaluations that appear in the letters, therefore, offer an extremely rare peek into what he considered to be a good poem at this early point in his life. Amichai's beloved recipient of his letters became a silent partner in his creative searches and was privy to the construction of his writing. Amichai revealed to her his poetic ideals and values as well as the literary influences that bolstered them, especially Rilke and Eliot. Amichai's self-critique is a poignant and authentic record of the way he judged both poetry as an art form in general and his own brand of writing in particular. He evaluated the quality of a poem, and sometimes apologized for its simplicity or lack of innovation. At other times, he praised its melodiousness or, as he became more self-assured, the poetic maturity it reflected.[74] It is astounding both that he was able to create such verse so early in his career and that he was aware of its strengths and able to criticize its shortcomings. Through these short, consistent lines of reflection, one can see how Amichai's self-analysis guided him in his development as a poet.

* * *

The letters that discuss Amichai's entries to the two literary competitions become a treatise on his artistic beliefs; they clearly differentiate the poems he intended for publication from the love poems he addressed to Ruth. When he sent "Hada'aya" to her in November 1947, he accompanied the work with comments that communicate his sense of accomplishment. The poem had structure and images that were "very novel," he wrote, and an untraditional "inner rhythm."[75] This evaluation is very indicative of Amichai's poetic goals at the time. Before he applied any other measure, Amichai judged a poem on its degree of innovation in figurative language, musicality, rhythm, rhyme, line breaks, or theme. The only two works in the letters that were declaratively written for publication differ greatly in their artistic achievement. When Ruth asked why he had chosen to submit "Hada'aya" instead of another poem she had read, Amichai gave an extremely enlightening answer. He replied that although the other poem was personally meaningful, it did not "innovate," and swore that he would never publish anything that was not truly "innovative" and original.[76] He remained faithful to this overarching principle, and after he completed "In the Public Garden" for the second competition, he proudly noted that it was "very original" as well as "free."[77]

* * *

In the poems he valued most, Amichai applied his aspiration for innovation to the realm of a poem's meter—the unconventional meter of "Hada'aya" was an important asset.[78] In fact, the image in "Hada'aya" of the poet engraving people's conversations into his poetry like music on a record suggests that Amichai viewed the craft of writing poetry as transforming speech into music. Likewise, "In the Public Garden" was not only original in its structure and images, but also in its musicality. In his letter, Amichai declared, "[I]t just sings."[79] He even implied that sometimes, even before he knew the words of a poem, he could feel the "melody" playing inside him and it would fill him with joy.[80]

Amichai's ear was finely attuned; although he stopped playing the violin at a young age, he loved classical music. He described the effect of classical music on him in visual and physical terms and had an almost personal relationship with the various instruments in the orchestra. The closure of Hayden's Farewell Symphony, for example, was for him "a lonely, desolate song." The faint melody of the violin, he wrote, resembled "life leaving a body."[81] As a poet, he was enamored with the melodic elements of language. When he was especially pleased with the sonority of one of his works, he wrote that it "bounce[d] like a swing."[82] He often requested that Ruth read out loud a poem he had sent her, so as not to miss its musicality; once, he asked that she recite a love poem by Morgenstern in her "low voice," so as to feel its "power in [her] body."[83] Morgenstern, who was inspired by English nonsense rhymes, was known for his rhythmical, melodic verse; his lines were often quoted by German speakers. Although Amichai copied and translated Morgenstern's love poems into the letters primarily for their romantic value, he was also affected by their beautiful sound.

✳   ✳   ✳

More than musicality, the visual image is one of Amichai's foremost poetic ideals. Concrete pictures remained a dominant feature in his oeuvre throughout his career. On September 9, 1947, he even described Haifa, his new city, as a spellbinding "book" that he could read, and whose "illustrations" he internalized.[84] As he noted the progress of his writing, he proudly emphasized that his new achievements were poems constructed of pictures inspired by free associations.[85] Amichai happily used the words "pictures, pictures" to describe one of his own poems, and this sentiment reverberates in variation in a number of his letters.[86] This characteristic derives primarily from the way Amichai perceived the world. He had the eye of an artist and it was only natural that when using words to depict inner or outer reality, he used the expression to "paint" or to "draw." As a matter of fact, in the Beinecke Library archives one can find a number of drawings by Amichai that confirm his aptitude and his affinity for the visual.

Amichai's innate power of observation undoubtedly played a part in the remarkable closeness he felt toward Rilke,[87] and his admiration for Rilke in turn contributed to the centrality of the picture in his own poetics.[88] The concept of a Bild (picture) is essential in Rilke's verse; his affinity for modern art and his experience of the concreteness of nature contributed to the importance of the visual in his poetry. In his letters, Amichai quoted, paraphrased, and translated from Rilke's volume, *Das Buch der Bilder* (literally, the book of pictures).

Amichai's attachment to Rilke is apparent even in his vocabulary. When he wrote to Ruth about his ideal of pictorial representations of reality, he chose the concrete Hebrew word "*temuna*" (picture), which is a translation of the Rilkean term *Bild*, instead of the more abstract word "image," which is often used in Hebrew (as it is in English). For Rilke, *Bild* could designate a picture, portrait, or image that acted as a metaphor.[89] Likewise, in Amichai's letters, *temuna* could be either a concrete object or a metaphor. This emphasis on the picture is also explained philosophically in the letters, in which Amichai hailed poetry that is comprised of the tangible components of life and rejected verse devoted to abstract "feelings and ideas."

*   *   *

Throughout their correspondence, Amichai strove to paint a "clear picture" of himself for his beloved; the text of his letters is a collection of many episodes and fleeting impressions, as Amichai documented the minute details of his life.[90] His love verse was, in fact, less concerned with originality and more with the faithful expression of feeling. When he addressed his beloved in his poetry, Amichai had a separate, private language. In those love poems, Amichai dwelt on the yearning and the loneliness he felt. Barely six weeks after Ruth set sail for America, Amichai had already written her eighteen letters, seven of which contain love poems, including "On the Day You Left" (September 6, 1947),[91] "Autumn" (September 14, 1947),[92] and "Go to the Port, My Girl" (October 8, 1947).[93] Despite their deeply sincere tone, it is no surprise that Amichai never published these poems, as they foreshadow neither the innovations nor the wealth of images in Amichai's later poetry. Although he clearly viewed these poems as inferior to his experimental works, their saving grace was, in his words, their "sincerity."[94] "Truth" compensated for their other shortcomings.[95]

The function Amichai expected his letters to fill reflects his artistic goals as well. He spoke of his letters to Ruth as he spoke of pieces of art, hoping that they would "mirror" his "soul" and paint a "clear picture" of his thoughts.[96] A telling image that he used both in the letters and in his ars-poetica poem is that of a photographer. The ideal, then, was to reflect reality exactly as it is, as a photographer can. He repeatedly emphasized the great effort he invested in capturing the constantly changing life in Palestine.[97]

This emphasis on faithfully recording real life in his poetry motivated many of the innovative techniques Amichai used in his verse. Indeed, this ideal spawned his preference for concrete images over abstract themes, and the perception of life as a mosaic made up of small details that "wait" for the artist to observe and "collect" them. Since Amichai wanted his poetry to reflect life, his verse echoes that worldview.

*   *   *

One of the most significant innovations that Amichai introduced into Hebrew poetry is connected to his attempt to capture reality: the "lowering" not only of poetic diction, but also of poetic subjects and contents. The letters to Ruth document Amichai's fascination with, and idealization of, everyday life, and the fact that he saw it as the ultimate stuff of poetry. His first letter may be read as an ode to the mundane. He told Ruth that the rhythm of life soothed him in the first hours after her departure, and asked her to love what he called "the daily pulse." For him, this pulse was the Haifian motion of people who ascended from the lower parts of the city to the mountain in the morning and then descended at twilight and vice versa.[98] When Amichai received the first, very gloomy, letter from Ruth, in his reply, he tried to console her by telling her to "listen to the rhythm of life," as embodied by the people who "go to work" and "return in the evening."[99] Furthermore, Amichai turned to the "everyday" for comfort in times of danger and desperation. In January, when the streets of Haifa were filled with sounds of machine guns and his pupils had to seek cover in the school basement, Amichai told Ruth that his eyes "remained open" to all the little things and to the beauty of the daily routines.[100]

Although Amichai's formulation suggests that the "everyday" is the "great poetry" of our lives, one can understand his statement in reverse; namely, that great poetry captures the essence of the mundane rather than the heroic.[101] Amichai glorified the mundane and spoke of daily life as "a great epic," arguing that it, not one dramatic experience, "forges" people's characters out of hundreds of routine activities. When he proudly described "In the Public Garden" to Ruth, one of its best qualities in his eyes was that "all of life"[102] is at its core. In many other poems that he wrote after the war, Amichai followed this principle.

The Mosaic and T. S. Eliot

For Amichai, reality was a "mosaic" constructed of "fragments, images and incidents," and he argued that good poetry must reflect this nature of reality.[103] "Pictures" and fragments of conversations planted in his poems are but one aspect of Amichai's wish to incorporate fragments of reality in his art. His love for the quotidian found its innovative outlet in his attempts to capture this fragmented reality and create his own mosaics. For Amichai, a mosaic was not a sequence of pieces that added up to a cohesive whole. Instead, it was a belief that reality was made up of separate shards from which the whole can occasionally be deduced.

In two letters, both written in March 1948, Amichai revealed one of his inspirations for the poetry of mosaics. Amichai had discovered T. S. Eliot during his military service in the British army; and although he did not mention him in his letters until March, Eliot's influence is present in Amichai's innovative poems (like "In the Public Garden"), in the prose of the letters, and in his theoretical discussions of poetry. Amichai clearly sought poetic idols to emulate, yet, despite the fact that he had studied Hebrew poetry in school, he ignored the masters of Hebrew literature, determined to compete with his peers in Europe and the United States. The letters reveal that Amichai wanted to bring Hebrew literature into the twentieth century, to revolutionize it. Eliot's brand of modernism struck a chord with Amichai and, as time went on, he internalized the ideas Eliot espoused. In the March 1948 letters, Amichai acknowledged that Eliot's "way of writing" had affected him, applauded his originality, and dissected the technique of the more established poet.[104]

Principles that he had expressed spontaneously in September 1947, such as constructing poems through pictures and fragments of reality, became formulated in an orderly dissertation, suggesting that Amichai had read some theoretical writings in addition to poetry. He no longer spoke of art in general, but rather about modern art, opening his March 25, 1948, letter with what reads like a lecture about living "the life of the twentieth century." A man of the twentieth century, according to Amichai, ought to be exposed to modern art, and realize that it is comprised of spots of different "colors," not of full figures of objects or people. He argued that the true reflection of life is in patches of "conversations," "dangers," and "experiences."[105]

Amichai's use of the catalogue and mosaic structures as well as his emphasis on the mundane may be attributed, at least in part, to the influence of some of Eliot's lines in The Waste Land, such as: "Her drying combinations touched by the sun's last rays / . . . / Stockings, slippers, camisoles, and stays."[106] Although the role of the quotidian is different in the verse of Eliot and Amichai, the mere inclusion of it as a legitimate part of poetry was vastly unorthodox in early-twentieth-century British and American poetry, and certainly in Hebrew poetry well into the 1950s.

Although Amichai did not credit Eliot with his perception of the world as a mosaic, the influence is clear. One of Eliot's trademarks, which became the quintessence of modern poetry (and, indeed, of most forms of modern art), is a pervasive sense of disintegration. Eliot's fragmentation is not only his view of reality, but also a formal principle. He juxtaposed pieces of pictures, or fragments of reality, and presented them without transitions. The techniques that Amichai adopted in 1947, like listening to fragments of conversations and writing them down in his little notepads, were conducive to this mosaic style of writing. Amichai told Ruth that Eliot never wrote about a woman in general terms or abstractions. Rather, he would depict her in mosaics whose tiles are "her room," a sentence she uttered, or "her dress."[107] He concluded his summary of Eliot's strategy by stating that the sum of those parts creates an accurate reflection of the subject. Amichai alluded, perhaps, to Eliot's lines, "She smoothes her hair with automatic hand / And puts a record on the gramophone," which present a fragmented portrait of a woman in The Waste Land.[108]

Without attributing it to Eliot's influence, Gershon Shaked noted a similar trait in Amichai's poems published in 1951. He wrote of the Amichaian tendency to forge a "character . . . by its environment," dubbing it a component of the Amichai "genotype."[109] The discovery of the letters confirms that Amichai consciously adopted this technique, learned from Eliot, and that he did so two years before his official "debut" as a poet.

Although it is very different from The Waste Land, Amichai's disjointed poem "In the Public Garden" seems to follow Eliot's mosaic model, particularly in the way it records fragments of communication. As noted in chapter 9, the similarity between the lovers' conversation in "In the Public Garden" and the lines in The Waste Land is striking. Eliot's lines read, "'What are you thinking of? What thinking? What? / I never know what you're thinking. Think.' / . . . / 'What is that noise now? What is the wind doing?'"[110] The last lines of "In the Public Garden" are "'you take the blanket'. . . 'Morning comes / soon' / 'what time is it, / beloved' / 'what?'"[111] More than three months elapsed between the completion of the December 6, 1947, version of "In the Public Garden" and Amichai's explicit reference to Eliot in March 1948, but Amichai's poetic practices, as recorded in the letters, point to a strong Eliotian influence in the fall.

In addition to Eliot's poetic structures, Amichai was also clearly attracted to his powerful imagery. Inspired perhaps by the spring, Amichai quoted the famous opening lines of The Waste Land in his March 14, 1948, letter to Ruth. Without acknowledging the disparity between climates, he moved from the "fertility and sprouting" of the Israeli earth at the end of winter, to Eliot's depiction of a European spring in which the earth was still hard and frozen:[112]

"April is the cruelest month, breeding / Lilacs out of the dead land, mixing / Memory and desire, stirring / Dull roots with spring rain." Thus, in the middle of rainy, warm March in Israel, Amichai recalled the European climate. He then exclaimed, "Wonderful picture!" clearly identifying with Eliot's evocation. Like Eliot, he endowed the spring with emotion, implicitly attaching the older poet's "April" to the Israeli reality of war through the adjective "cruel."[113] One may assume, then, that in addition to their lyrical beauty, Eliot's lines affected Amichai because of the harshness that they contain as well as the landscapes and climate that they evoke. In 1948 Palestine, as everyone awaited the end of the British Mandate at the beginning of May, Eliot's line "April is the cruelest month" turned into a prophecy. In the midst of the bloody March of 1948, when Jerusalem was besieged and Amichai was participating in live combat almost every night, he anticipated an April that would be crueler still. The nature described in Eliot's lines is undeniably European, but for Amichai, the tension and violence in them was local and Israeli.

THE ROOTS OF "NOT LIKE A CYPRESS" IN THE LETTERS

While Amichai's letters demonstrate the poetic sensibilities already at work in the young writer, many also reveal the linguistic and thematic sources for some of his most recognized published works. Judging by the meticulous handwriting and absence of erasures in the letters themselves, it is likely that Amichai prepared drafts for a number of letters, especially in the fall of 1947. In the 1950s, when he composed his poems, it is likely that he still had access to various materials that preceded the War of Independence (at least the notepads that inspired the letters, if not the drafts of the letters themselves). The letters are now the only existing proof of the connection between the experiences and observations that he made in 1947–1948 and the poems he published a decade later.

Amichai feared that the poems created inside him while he was in military actions would never see the light, that they would be "aborted" by the fighting that surrounded him. Reading his published oeuvre in light of the letters, however, proves otherwise. Indeed, the letters contain "fetuses" of poems, but those were not aborted. They simply required a longer gestation in order to mature into finished verse. The internalized experiences and emotions related in the letters were born in poems that were published after the war. A number of poems from Poems: 1948–1962 can be traced back to the texts of the letters.[114] Amichai's oft-quoted poem "Not Like a Cypress" is a prime example of this connection.

＊　＊　＊

"Not Like a Cypress"[115] (appendix A) was published in 1958, the same year as the famous "I Want to Die in My Own Bed."[116] Like the latter poem, it, too, portrays a speaker who resists, and arguably resents, the role society requires him to play. As a young man during a national struggle, Amichai was expected to be a hero and to pursue aggressively a leadership position in the army. While "I Want to Die in My Own Bed" focuses on the military aspects of those expectations, the speaker of "Not Like a Cypress" relates in more general terms his reluctance to surrender to societal demands. "Not Like a Cypress" advocates an understated, restrained way of life and expresses a desire not to stand out.

Much of the imagery found in "Not Like a Cypress" has its roots in a series of letters written to Ruth Z. in October–November 1947. Given the high correlation of the imagery, it seems probable that Amichai wrote at least a draft of "Not Like a Cypress" at this time. In this way, the letters can be read as an early version not only of the poem's vocabulary, but also of the philosophies at its heart.

In both "Not Like a Cypress" and "I Want to Die in My Own Bed," the denial of the heroic ideal is articulated principally through a rejection of traits that are stereotypically considered "masculine" in favor of those that are conventionally perceived as "feminine."[117] The speaker's preference for the antiheroic, and therefore for what is customarily considered feminine, lends "Not Like a Cypress" its figurative language. Amichai's own identification with these traits is documented in the letters from October 1947 onward, especially in the way he viewed himself in relation to Ruth. This feminine strain was a deep-seated part of his personality expressed in his romantic relationship.

In the letter of November 11, 1947, as in the opening stanza of "Not Like a Cypress," Amichai used the imagery of vegetation and implicitly rejected the masculine role dictated to him by societal convention.[118] The speaker of the poem sees himself as spread out like grass, while the cypress shoots skyward. "Not like a cypress, / . . .but like the grass, in thousands of cautious green exits."[119] In the letter, Amichai said that he was the one who puts down roots; the woman he loved was seen in more masculine terms—"the strong branch" that emerges and stretches upwards. The proximity and juxtaposition of roots and branches in *The Waste Land* may have inspired Amichai's imagery in this letter: "What are the roots that clutch, what branches grow / Out of this stony rubbish?"[120] In his March 1948 letter, Amichai's image of "thousands of tender sprouts"[121]—his own, tender description of spring, juxtaposed with Eliot's harsh one—resembles the line from "Not Like a Cypress" that describes the grass as "thousands of cautious green exits."[122] The line, published in the poem in 1958, is likely a variation on notes that Amichai took a decade earlier and recorded in the March 1948 letter to Ruth.

In the November 11, 1947, letter, Amichai used another reversed masculine / feminine dichotomy—he not only referred to Ruth as an upward branch, but also characterized her as a fast boat, speeding forward. He then promised her that he would supply "the calm forms" into which she would pour her wealth of impressions.[123] As in the case of the rooted plant versus the strong branch, the fast boat charging forward is a masculine image, while Amichai is the feminine container, the form that will absorb the experiences of his beloved. The perceptions expressed metaphorically in the October–November 1947 letters, such as this idiosyncratic notion of gender roles, persist in Amichai's poems and become a recognizable characteristic in his writing.[124]

"Not Like a Cypress" is built on three metaphorical dichotomies: cypress tree / grass, king / raindrops, and sharp ring / heartbeats. These three "pairs" correspond to the traditional masculine / feminine categories. The poem outlines a life strategy at whose core is a refugee's wisdom merged with stereotypically feminine endurance: it is preferable to be unobtrusive, to be the one who does not charge forward and draw attention. In the traditional imagination, a man's power is swift and vertical, while the woman gives of herself and is physically associated with a wide plain or the earth. Some of the stereotypical masculine / feminine dichotomies with which Amichai plays are indeed active / passive, aggressive / nurturing, and linear / circular.[125] The first pair (cypress tree / grass) reflects the contrast between vertical and horizontal; the second (king / raindrops) alludes to the difference between aggression and nurture; and the third (piercing ring / heartbeats) refers to the tension between the sudden, singular event and the reliable or constant. Each of these dualities represents the dominating, masculine role that the poem's speaker is expected to adopt versus the more submissive, or more feminine, one that he desires. The wish to differ from the protruding cypress tree reflects a feminine sensibility:[126] the phallic cypress tree is like a spear point, shooting upward in one stroke, whereas the blades of grass and spring blossoms (with which the speaker identifies) are spread out across the plain. In a parallel fashion, the biblical, national hero King Saul is tall, broad shouldered, and conspicuous; the speaker longs to blend into his environment and be absorbed into the thirsty earth like raindrops. Instead of emulating the urgent, sharp ring, the speaker seeks to sound like the reassuring rhythm of heartbeats. In addition to integrating the "feminine" into his figurative language, Amichai wove it into his grammar. All the verbs that express the speaker's aspirations are in the stereotypically feminine, passive voice: "to be absorbed," "to be drunk," "to be breathed in," and "to be scattered."

At the poem's conclusion, beyond these existential dichotomies, lies resignation. Death is "a quiet exit," without the ceremonial ram's-horn-blast (teru'a) that accompanied biblical battles.[127] This image has its roots in a striking oxymoron from one of the January 1948 letters, in which Amichai described himself as walking with a "quiet, subdued teru'a."[128] In "Not Like a Cypress," Amichai deconstructs this synesthetic image, formulating it as two oppositions, the "quiet exit" and the "teru'a." The letter contains a restrained energy and optimism, but the poem ends with a surrender. The final wish in "Not Like a Cypress" is for a peaceful, nonheroic, unmilitary death, echoing "I Want to Die in My Own Bed," which places the desire for a peaceful death at its center.

Further evidence that "Not Like a Cypress" was drafted in the fall of 1947 lies in another letter from that period that uses similar concepts and linguistic expressions. Much of Amichai's letter from November 13, 1947, may be read as an ode to the quotidian.[129] In "Not Like a Cypress," Amichai's perception of the everyday versus the heroic is connected to his preference for the scattered, small multitude over the sudden or singular. In the letter, Amichai describes being "rooted" in Haifa with "thousands of . . . tiny and invisible roots," which were his day-to-day interactions. When he went to the office of the workers' union (Histadrut), to which he belonged as a school teacher, he told Ruth that the "thousands of little cards" gave him a sense of security. He believed that becoming a part of the social fabric occurred through "thousands of habits," and not by one great deed. He also described himself as tied to Israel with thousands "of small threads," which together are stronger than "one thick rope." A final variation on this theme is his interpretation of the everyday as the "miraculous" entity that gradually forges the self. He suggested that people's personalities are not cast "all at once" like a "bronze statue," but are built from "thousands of small pebbles."[130] Amichai consistently juxtaposed the unique (and often phallic) object (be it a statue or a thick rope) with the multitude (be it thousands of pebbles, small roots, or index cards). This is the psychological and poetic substructure of "Not Like a Cypress."

The mark of Amichai's life in Haifa on "Not Like a Cypress" is demonstrated through yet another image; in a letter from October 30, 1947, Amichai used the phrase, "a sharp ring," which would make its way into the published poem intact.[131] The "sharp ring" in the poem is the third and last of the entities with which the speaker does not identify. It is a variation on the previous two negative models, the cypress tree and King Saul, each of whom burst forth with one thrust. The ring is sudden and forceful, yet it is less tangible than the first two. The flawed logic of the series "cypress tree," "tall king," and "sharp ring" conceals a personal experience. The words "the sharp ring" ("hatsiltsul hahad") appear in the October 30, 1947 letter at the culmination of his description of a nocturnal scene. In the letter, Amichai compared the "naked finality" of the night with the "living body" that contains thoughts and feelings hidden in "thousands of various vessels." This phrase is reminiscent of the "thousands of green exits" attributed to grass in the first stanza of "Not Like a Cypress." When Amichai came home from this nightly walk, he sat down to write the letter. The sharp ring of the telephone cut through the silence of the night. In Israel of the late 1940s, telephones were limited to the very wealthy, high officials, and physicians. When Amichai heard the ring, he knew that it came from the apartment of the physician who lived upstairs. "Not Like a Cypress" repeats the words "sharp ring" from the letter, and also specifies that the ring heralds a night visit to a doctor. The ring's implicit urgency must have interrupted Amichai's tranquility as he wrote his love letter and poems in the quiet of the night.

"Not Like a Cypress" does not mention military life overtly, but it implies wisdom gained through persecution or war. The rejection of stereotypically masculine elements in its verses potentially reflects Amichai's aversion to being a military hero. In January 1948, Amichai wrote to Ruth that even though he had "no ambitions in military life," he had been offered a position equivalent to that of a colonel. Although he expressed readiness to do his "duty," he was opposed to a "military career," stating simply, "I don't want to be like that." Instead, he wanted to serve like other young men, and not stand out. In the letter, he used words like "summit" or "treetop" to indicate the high military positions in which he had no interest.[132] Both words are reminiscent of the language he had used to describe the "unique" in previous letters, and the cypress tree that he would later reject in "Not Like a Cypress."

If read as a metapoetic piece, "Not Like a Cypress" embodies the poetic strategy of camouflage in its rejection of conspicuousness and in its implicit desire to assimilate. In order to establish himself as an Israeli poet, Amichai had to blend into the local environment and camouflage the remnants of his past. The entire poem is about not sticking out from the crowd. Indeed, in "Not

Like a Cypress," one of the speaker's wishes is even "to be hidden like . . . children in a game [of hide-and-seek]."[133] This philosophy, as well as the poetic strategy, presumably derives from Amichai's life experience. In order to survive, either under persecution or in war, one must disappear into the environment.

*   *   *

Amichai told Ruth that if he were writing in times of peace, he would have experienced a "great blossoming" as a poet.[134] Indeed, the War of Independence severed the "blossoming" tree of Amichai's lyrical poetry in its early stages of growth and imprinted itself on his verse. Instead of allowing his poetry to die, however, Amichai grafted on a divergent branch: the voice of the Israeli national.

Once he was recognized as a national Israeli poet, Amichai maintained that it had been the war that had made him a poet in the first place. He created a time line that camouflaged the elements of his biography that would have contradicted the war's role as an impetus for his creative writing. Although Amichai maintained that he began writing in the battlefields, his letters to Ruth confirm otherwise. They expose the fact that he wanted to be a poet before—and entirely independently of—the war. Therefore, Ruth, who was the sole witness to his quiet transformation, remained Amichai's secret. He rarely mentioned their romance and never betrayed the existence of his letters to her.

Amichai revealed the secret of Ruth's identity to me when he was seventy-three years old, and no longer afraid to confront this part of his past. He did not tell me about the letters, the treasure that he had created semi-intentionally fifty years earlier when he diligently mailed his writings to the United States for safekeeping. But perhaps he wanted me to discover them. The letters that Ruth preserved are a time capsule that transports us back to the true history of the poet's art.

12 Conclusion

The discoveries and analyses presented in this book demand a sea change in the interpretation of Amichai's oeuvre from this point forward. Indeed, in order to fully appreciate his wondrous poetry, it is essential to look toward the true subtexts of his work: the German language, the landscapes of his childhood, his memories of migration, and the redemptive, but labored, absorption into the land of Israel and its language. While Amichai suppressed them in his corpus, remnants of these potent landmarks survive. The archival papers and the letters to Ruth Z. prove that his past churns beneath the surface of his work and thus indirectly offer evidence of Amichai's art of camouflage. Until now, this phenomenon could only be surmised through an exhaustive excavational reading of his verse. Unveiling these biographical elements allows a reading of Amichai that displays the depth and complexity of his oeuvre and renders comprehensible many of his most hermetic texts and images.

The reinterpretation of Amichai's verse in the context of his foreign origins sheds light not only on his own writings but also on the works of immigrant authors around the world who have betrayed their mother tongues. E. M. Cioran, a Romanian exile in Paris for almost sixty years, articulated this bond: "A man who repudiates his language for another changes his identity. He breaks with his memories and, to a certain point, with himself."[1] While similar, the Israeli context is also unique. Writing in Hebrew was an expression of national revival, a return to the Jewish people's ancient heritage, as well as to normalcy. Amichai's experience is thus particularly paradigmatic of an entire generation of Israeli Hebrew writers for whom the acquired tongue was both constricting and liberating. Amichai can—and should—be read as a case study of their creative struggle.

The treasures I found in the archives and the letters transformed my understanding of Amichai, both as a man and a poet. The archives show that Amichai repressed or camouflaged traumatic events in his verse, regardless of their origins, and that the deepest traumas in his life were all related to abandonment.

The letters to Ruth Z. expose the birth of poetic tropes and techniques that would characterize Amichai's verse for his entire creative life. Most significantly, the letters disclose precisely how early in his life Amichai found his calling as a poet and the colossal effort he exerted in fulfilling this destiny. They also revolutionize the dating of his canonic poetry and his groundbreaking innovations; thus, this revised chronology must be applied to any reading of *Poems: 1948–1962*. As a whole, the body of unpublished material highlights the centrality of abandonment for Amichai and the various ways in which he artistically reworked it, revelations that enlighten the reading of his entire oeuvre, early and late.

The process of writing this book taught me how to perform the detective work that would identify the layers of the poet's past and undo the camouflage in which he cloaked his poetry. The foregoing pages flesh out those areas in his biography that he submerged and raise them to the surface. Each chapter highlights a different camouflaged aspect of Amichai's life and work: the texture of his days in Wuerzburg amid the congregation that embraced him; the conflicts and pain he faced as a refugee and newcomer to the land; and the first year in which he adopted the name and identity of "Amichai," when he created himself as a poet and an organic part of his nation.

Weaving these individual strands of interpretation into the reading of one monumental poem succinctly illustrates how the understanding of Amichai's poetry grows with the knowledge gleaned from his biography, the archives, and the letters. The long poem "Elegya al kefar natush" ("Elegy on an Abandoned Village") is a microcosm of these forces at work, a masterpiece that was collectively forged by all of the aspects of Amichai's past. The analysis of "Elegy on an Abandoned Village" not only unearths the persistence of Amichai's foreignness and the significance of the transformative years of 1947–1948, but demonstrates how the varied camouflaged intertexts of his poetry dovetail beneath the surface. The chapters' varied interpretative strategies thus join to shed light on this heretofore barely decipherable poem. The discussion of the elegy below provides a concrete example of how the ideas put forward in the previous chapters can be applied to the reading of Amichai and represents the culmination of the analytical effort of this book.

*   *   *

"Elegy on an Abandoned Village" is the consummate example of Amichai's intricate act of creation (see appendix A).[2] First published in a journal in 1961 under the title "Shirim al kefar natush" (Poems on an Abandoned Village)[3] and later collected in *Poems: 1948–1962*, the kernels of this poem were planted or, to use the term Amichai coined in his letters, "gathered" long before its initial publication. The elegy bears the mark of Amichai's mother tongue as well as the landscapes of and experiences in his German hometown. It also retrieves events from Amichai's life in the winter of 1947–1948 and alludes to literary models whose influence is laid bare in the letters from that time. A reading of this poem in light of the findings presented separately in the previous chapters reveals that the elegy draws from Amichai's inner and outer sources, most of which were unknown until now. Contrary to its accepted interpretation, rereading the elegy in this new context shows that it laments a number of abandoned landmarks in the life of the poet: topographical, human, and linguistic. As is true in much of his work, Amichai's abandoned village is in fact a composite of many distinct elements of his past: an empty Arab village that Amichai visited in 1948, a Jewish settlement in the Negev whose evacuation in 1947 preceded any expulsion of Arabs, and Jewish Wuerzburg, the community that was abandoned by both people and God.[4]

The language of "Elegy on an Abandoned Village" is ambiguous and highly figurative. Its lines describe a village, emptied of its inhabitants, dominated by the winds, and haunted by the ghosts of those who used to populate its homes, streets, and schools. The speaker, whose relationship to the place is not clear, alternates between first-person singular and plural and questions God's justice. Other than this broad summary of situation and atmosphere, it is difficult to discern a chronological narrative or even an apparent structure in the elegy.

"Elegy on an Abandoned Village" has commonly been interpreted as a lament for an evacuated Arab hamlet. The title words "*kefar*" (village) and "*natush*" (abandoned) led critics to identify it as such. In the 1950s, the word *kefar* was almost exclusively used to describe Arab settlements—small Jewish communities were dubbed *kibbutz*, *moshav*, or *moshava*. Moreover, Amichai's choice of the word *natush* recalls the term's post–War of Independence usage in the expression *rekhush natush*, which denoted property that had been abandoned by Arabs who had either escaped the country or been driven away. When interviewed in 1989, in an attempt to prove his political correctness, Amichai himself boasted that in the 1950s he wrote "[a]nti-war poems on abandoned villages."[5] Additionally, certain elements in the body of the poem support the elegy's association with an Arab village; for instance, the fig tree, a classic feature of a Middle Eastern environment, and the blue-painted walls, which recall the blue traditionally used by Arabs to ward off the "evil eye." Such characteristics lead the reader to believe that the trauma of the abandoned village is an Arab one.

The discovery of Amichai's letters to Ruth Z. situates the origins of the elegy in an earlier time, ties it to Amichai's "baptism by fire,"[6] and exposes its reliance on classical texts. Thanks to them, we know that hidden beneath the pain of the Arab village is another trauma. A series of letters written on the cusp between the fateful years 1947 and 1948 (December 25, 29, and 31, 1947, and January 7, 1948)[7] contains references to Amichai's first battle and uses astonishingly similar vocabulary, materials, and figures to those of the poem. Although it is difficult to determine exactly when "Elegy on an Abandoned Village" was written, Amichai likely jotted down a draft of it as early as January 1948. In the letter he wrote as he packed his bag on December 25, 1947, Amichai told Ruth Z. that he had been called for a longer mission than usual and would be forced to miss teaching days. In a subsequent letter dated December 29, 1947, written upon his return from action, he said that he and his fellow soldiers had stayed in a kibbutz that had been "left" by its inhabitants the week before. The soldiers turned the nameless kibbutz into an army base. He described how they slept in the children's house of the kibbutz, and reported on the difficult conditions and "many dangers."[8] The adjective he used in the letter to describe the houses of the kibbutz later resurfaced in the elegy's title: "abandoned" ("batim netushim"). In this series of letters, the kibbutz is referred to as "kibbutz natush" (a kibbutz that was abandoned) or "kibbutz ne'ezav" (a kibbutz that was left). The word "abandoned" creates an intratextual connection between the letters and the poem. Far from being a reflection of the terminology of the 1950s, it is clear that the poem's title, "Abandoned Village" ("kefar natush") echoes the language that Amichai used in relation to a kibbutz in 1947–1948. In the fifteen years that elapsed between when the budding poet Amichai was "filling his barns" and the poem's publication, the abandoned kibbutz from the letters was transformed into a "village."

Thus, memories of the abandoned kibbutz became the building blocks for "Elegy on an Abandoned Village." In Amichai's famous early war poems, "Two Poems about the First Battles," the experience of sleeping in a space recently occupied by children is recalled in more concrete terms than in the elegy: "On the road to the front, we slept in a kindergarten / . . . And in my head there were big and small memories . . . they made dreams in it"[9] (emphasis added). While the elegy presents a highly reworked version of the experience, the overt resemblance between the letter from December 29, 1947, and the above-quoted poem is striking. The letter depicts the scattered toys in the children's house and uses the words "memories" and "dreams" in the same sequence as the poem.[10] Unlike the generic "memories" in "Two Poems," however, the letter divulges what specific recollections were triggered for the soldier Amichai by the children's house. The letter recalls a visit he and Ruth Z. made to the northern kibbutz where Ruth's sister lived. The letter lingers sentimentally on the bustling children's house where Ruth's nephew slept and on its miniscule showers. For Amichai, sleeping in the abandoned children's house evoked the idyllic, peaceful times he had spent with his beloved as well as the kibbutz children in the Negev who were evacuated because of the battles. The speaker of both "Two Poems" and the elegy is haunted by those absent children, but the former, romantic connection to the children's house never made it into either poem.

"Elegy on an Abandoned Village," the later and more complex poem, contains only abstract references to children, zooming in on other elements of the encounter with the empty kibbutz. The language that illustrates the devastation of the abandoned kibbutz / village is common to both the letters and the poem. The lines "Listen as the tin / gradually matures in its rust . . ."[11] is reminiscent of the "rust" that Amichai perceived as a symbol of an abandoned house's slow death in the letter from December 29. Additionally, the poem, like this letter, refers to exposed boards as signs of destruction and decay. The poem's speaker, like the author of the letters, witnesses the victory of nature and oblivion over structures whose inhabitants have left. Wind, stones, rust, bare wood, and the absence of children all come together in portraying the abandoned settlement. Facing the silence of the forsaken place, the speaker in the elegy listens intently to voices of phantom children, which burst into the heavens because the ceilings of the homes had collapsed. He observes phantom girls hidden between the quiet ruins and summons a scream that shatters the silence of the vacant place.

The scream that rends the elegy's landscape is a loaded, intertextual reference that confirms the bond between the elegy and the letters that preceded its publication by twelve years. Two of the letters about the abandoned kibbutz quote the line from Hamlet to which the elegy alludes: "[T]he rest is silence."[12] Amichai's preoccupation with Hamlet and its examination of death is evident in his fall letters, but the line in question seems to be associated with the more volatile time of his stay at the abandoned kibbutz and the violent days that followed.[13] It is possible that the line uttered by Shakespeare's hero before he dies remained connected in Amichai's mind with his own near-death encounter. Years later, when he transported this traumatic experience into the elegy, he preserved this literary association. In fact, nowhere else in Amichai's ninety or so letters or in the poems he wrote in the interim (1947–1962) is this line ever recalled.

The letter from January 7, 1948, explicitly relates Hamlet's line to the four-day assignment in the abandoned kibbutz-turned-army-base. Amichai quoted it to capture the depressive atmosphere in the kibbutz, and then said, "As the words in *Hamlet*." It is worth noting that Amichai's own translation of Shakespeare's English into Hebrew fluctuates; in this letter, "silence" is translated as "*demama*," which means stillness, a total absence of any sound, human or otherwise. The word *demama* is distant from an active or passive human expression and therefore appropriate for the description of the empty kibbutz and the stillness of the nature that surrounded it.[14]

Two days after his return from the abandoned kibbutz, Amichai again used the line "the rest is silence" as a response to unspeakable horror. This time, however, he was not describing a firsthand experience. In the letter from December 31, 1947, Amichai told Ruth of forty-two Jewish workers who had just been murdered by their Arab coworkers at the oil refineries. He described the absolute shock that struck Haifa, with a different rendering of Hamlet's words. In this letter, he translated the word "silence" as "*shetika*," the term used for silence as opposed to speech, in order to convey the ineptness of language in the face of inhuman cruelty.

In the elegy, as well, the word "silence" in Shakespeare's line is translated as *shetika* (speechlessness), not *demama*, to denote the inadequacy of words to express outrage. Amichai's elegy, however, negates Hamlet's statement, saying: "*hayeter eno shetika. hayeter tse'aka*" (The rest is *not* silence. The rest is a scream) (emphasis added).[15] In other words, faced with horror, Amichai demanded a loud, vocal cry. This outspoken response is atypical for the understated Amichai; it is a cry that rises against injustice.

The ties between the letters and the elegy go beyond their common references to *Hamlet*, descriptions of decay, and their significant uses of the word *natush*. All the surfaces in the abandoned kibbutz, as depicted in the letters, are covered with a thin layer of white sand. A sign of neglect, it penetrates every corner. Its whiteness, however, stirs in the young soldier pleasant memories of snow. The letter from December 29, 1947, thus explains the elegy's seemingly illogical evocation of snow in the midst of the Middle Eastern landscape. In the letter, Amichai explicitly stated that around the abandoned kibbutz, "the sand was like snow."[16] Over a decade later, he transformed this reference to snowlike sand into the hermetic line "the enormous snow was set down far away."[17] As the line in the elegy continues, the letter can be of further interpretative value: "The enormous snow was set down far away. Sometimes / I must use my love as the only way to describe it. . . ." These lines bear a hidden association with Ruth Z., whom Amichai called a "snow queen."[18] In his January 2, 1948, letter, he stated that although she lived "in many colors," from the perspective of her lover, she was white, reminiscent of the white path in the "abandoned kibbutz."[19] Ruth, who was in wintry New York at that time, merged in Amichai's imagination and in his letters with the distant snowy grounds that he remembered from his childhood. The elegy's lines thus indicate that only with the aid of his love can the Israeli speaker retrieve the snow in order to describe it in his poem. The reconstruction of Amichai's love affair with Ruth exposes further ties with her. Before alluding to the "distant snow," the speaker's heart beats in unison with the footsteps of guards. This metaphor recalls the rapturous night during curfew when Amichai slept over in Ruth's apartment, listening to the British soldiers pace back and forth on the street below.[20]

The image of the beloved against the snowy background is a loaded one because it not only draws on romantic longings, but also on Amichai's joyful memories of Wuerzburg. By placing the snow far away, Amichai subtly used the abandoned village to recall the distant locale of his childhood.

The allusion to the German winter also contains the sounds of Amichai's German mother tongue, which can only be fully heard by finding their acoustic brethren in the archive. The poem's association of the snow with the wailing wind is a subtle expression of how Amichai intertwined the longing for the landscape of Germany with the longing for his mother tongue. Immediately after the poem notes that the "snow was set down far away," the speaker alludes to his inarticulateness by declaring that he must "hire the wind to demonstrate the wailing of women" (emphasis added), as though he is unable to capture their cries himself.[21] The following stanza again implies that the wind carries weeping by comparing the wind's voices to those of an infant: "the wind brought voices from far away, *like an infant* / in her arms" (emphasis added).[22] The need to enlist the wind to imitate the sound of crying (like the need to call upon the love to describe the snow) is an understated allusion to the speaker's inadequate command of language. The poem, therefore, is a lament not only for an abandoned place, but also for the loss of language. This lament for the lost mother tongue is somewhat muted in the published Hebrew text. While the elegy expresses the wind's empathy with the suffering of the abandoned village and underscores the village's emptiness by using the wind that blows through it, the onomatopoeic value of the howling of the wind is missing from its Hebrew lines.

The wailing sound of the wind, however, is recorded in a German poem from the Beinecke archives. In that poem about learning a new language, Amichai used the wind in order to depict an uncontrollable weeping.[23] The German words *Weinen* (crying), *wie Hunde* (like dogs), and *wie Winde* (like winds) reverberate with the sound of sobbing through the repetition of the *v* and *n* sounds (in German, *w* is pronounced as the English *v*): "**Weinen** . . . erst **wie** Hunde dann **wie Winde**" (the weeping [attacked us], first like dogs and then like winds).[24] This German poem reveals that Amichai's repeated association between wind and crying stems from the alliterative properties of the words *Winde* and *Weinen* in German. These sounds, of course, are lost in translation.[25]

While the evocation of snow and the echoes of German alliterations understatedly hint at Wuerzburg, the reconstruction of Amichai's life there reveals the significance of a more specific and loaded detail of the German town: the train that cuts through the elegy. All three point at Wuerzburg as a component of the abandoned village. Although Wuerzburg was never abandoned, Jewish Wuerzburg and its institutions were deserted and destroyed. The departure and deportation of Jews from Wuerzburg left only their dwellings to memorialize them: "wooden beams stuck out / from the life of forgotten people."[26] The exiled or annihilated former Jewish residents of Wuerzburg were forgotten by others, but the elegy's speaker is still haunted by them and by the houses they were forced to leave behind.

The link to Nazi brutality is reinforced by the speaker's cynical allusion to the famous biblical story of Sodom: "Should I wait here for God's voice, or for the cry of / a train in its stress / between the hard-pressing hills?"[27] The Sodomites' horrific sins caused their victims to cry out to God so loudly that He descended to earth to see if the sins of Sodom were as terrible as the screams indicated: "And the Lord said, Because the cry of Sodom and Gomorrah is great, and because their sin is very grievous; I will go down now, and see whether they have done altogether according to the cry of it, which is come unto me; and if not, I will know" (Genesis 18:20–21). The first component of this story that is reflected in Amichai's lines is the reference to God ("Should I wait for God's voice"); the second is a reference to a scream or a cry;

and the third is grammatical. Amichai inflected the word mu'aka (stress) in the rare biblical grammatical form with which the similar-sounding word tse'aka (cry / scream) is inflected in Genesis. The biblical haketsa'**akata** (is it as bad as its cry) turns into bemu'**akata** (in its stress) in the poem (emphasis added). The proximity of the word "cry" to the poet's archaic inflection of "stress," as well as the words' acoustic similarity, clearly connect God and the train to the death of innocents: "Should I wait here for God's voice or for the cry of / a train . . . ?" Unlike the cries of the victims in Sodom and Gomorrah, the cries of those who were deported from Jewish Wuerzburg were not heeded by God.

Even the whistle of the train itself is a covert reference to Wuerzburg. Amichai's hometown is a railroad hub for trains that crisscross southern Germany; their chugging and whistling is almost as ubiquitous as the sound of church bells. Those who were children in Wuerzburg nostalgically remembered standing on the bridge near the old-age home (not far from Amichai's house), waiting to hear the whistle of the train. In this poem, however, the trains have a sinister connotation; the sweet childhood memory is tied to the cargo trains that carried the Jews to their deaths in the concentration camps. Significantly, Amichai's rhetorical question does not discriminate between God's voice and that of the train's. The answer to "Should I wait here for God's voice, or for the cry of / a train in its stress / between the hard-pressing hills?" is "No!"[28] There is no reason to wait for God or for the trains—they are equally devoid of mercy. The beloved landscape of childhood is as traitorous as the God of childhood. Neither had pity on those who were forced to abandon their hometown.

Subtle allusions to the remote childhood scenery, like the trains and the snow, create visible cracks in the seemingly Israeli locale of the poem. These cracks are widened by the alliterative German lines found in the archive, but the German archival drafts of the elegy allow the interpreter to penetrate its depths even further.[29] "Elegy on an Abandoned Village" retains more of its German draft than any other work whose draft has been found. Indeed, this draft reveals the German world that is repressed in the published poem. The fact that Amichai's lament for the abandoned village was conceived and partly written in the language of Amichai's old homeland suggests that the poet also mourned the home he left behind. The familiar German mother tongue at the foundation of this elegy comforted the poet when he was surrounded by the sounds of the language of his new homeland.

The German archival draft exposes the last experiential layer that was camouflaged in the elegy; namely, the author's migration. Amichai translated verbatim only two or three lines from his German draft into the Hebrew poem he published. These German lines that break through the lid of suppression capture the essence of foreignness. Even in English, they retain their power: "And like some stranger / in a strange city, who reads in a book of addresses and names, / I stand and choose a hotel: here. //"[30] While the Hebrew text says nothing of the "stranger's" origins or why he feels alienated, the long German draft does: the "stranger" is an immigrant. One of a handful of Hebrew words that dot this German draft of the elegy is "*mehagrim*" (immigrants), as though the writer is looking at himself through the eyes of a native. The handwritten German lines depict a colorful Israeli afternoon of valleys and fields, but these images are slowly supplanted by a seascape—a "white port," sands on the beach, and a ship steered toward "mountain peaks." All these belong to the semantic field of nautical travel and therefore are markers of the immigration from Europe. At the time, most immigrants, Amichai included, arrived in Israel by boat; the peaks of the Carmel were the first Israeli vistas they saw from the deck. In addition to its more explicit, revelatory setting, the German draft also reaches a level of pathos never attained by its Hebrew progeny: its speaker longs for sadness to overcome his body. In the published poem, he merely admits, "we were almost sad."[31]

The German draft is also the only place where the new immigrant's painful attempt at communication is preserved: "all my questions are hesitant with / 'excuse me' [*seliha*]." While this entire line is written in German, the term "excuse me" appears in Hebrew. Significantly, the polite apology appears in the new language in which it would have been haltingly spoken. This portrayal of Amichai's refugee past, so movingly captured in the German draft, is nowhere to be found in the published poem. In a typical Amichaian manner, the landscape of "Elegy on an Abandoned Village" is "Israelized" and the German translated into Hebrew.[32]

*   *   *

At the end of Amichai's poem about the migration from Germany to Palestine, he foretells: "And then / my death and an end to the migration of my parents."[33] Indeed, with the poet's death in 2000, the migration ended. The interpretation of the ripples it caused, however, is at the heart of this book. Weaving together his life story with his verse, newly discovered documents, and histories, along with his published poetry, the readings presented here retrieve the abandoned landmarks of Amichai's work and secure their status in the scholarly discourse of Israeli literature. Sixty-three years after he left his traitorous homeland and was reborn in the Land of Israel, Amichai died a much-beloved Israeli national poet. The study of his well-wrought and layered oeuvre, however, will forever evolve.

Appendix A

TEXTS OF POEMS DISCUSSED
IN THEIR ENTIRETY

I can see by their mark how high the waters reached
last winter; but how can I know what level
love reached inside me? And perhaps it overflowed by banks.
For what remained in the wadi?—just congealed mud.
What remained on my face?—not even a thin white line,   5
as above the lips of the child who was drinking milk
and put down the glass, with a click, on the kitchen table.
What remained? Perhaps a leaf in the small
stone that was placed on the windowsill, to watch over us
like an angel when we were inside. And to love means not   10
to remain; means not to leave a trace, but to change
utterly. To be forgotten. And to understand means to bloom.
Spring understands. To remember the belovèd means to
forget the many belongings that piled up.
Loving means having to forget the other love,   15
closing the other doors. Look, we saved a seat,
we put down a coat or a book on the empty chair
next to us, perhaps empty forever. And how long
could we keep it for ourselves? After all, someone will come,
a stranger will sit beside you. And you turn around,   20
impatient, to the door with the red sign over it, you look
at your watch; that too is a habit of prayer, like bowing
and kissing. And outside they always invent new thoughts
and these too are placed on the tired faces of people,
like colored lights in the street. Or look at the child, whose   25
thoughts are painted upon him like a pattern upon
an ancient urn, for others to see, he still isn't
thinking them for himself. The earth wanders, passes
beneath the soles of our shoes, like a moving stage,
like your face which I thought was mine and wasn't. But the child 30
got lost. The last scion of his games, the Benjamin
of colored paper, the grandson of his ancient hiding-places.

He came and went in the ringing of his toys among
empty wells, at the ends of holidays and within
the terrible cycle of cries and silence, in the process   35
of hope and death and hope. Everyone searched,
they were happy to look for some thing in the land of forgetting:
voices and a plane flying low like thoughts, police dogs
with philosophers' faces, question-words hopping on thin legs
in the grass that gets drier and drier, before our very   40
eyes. Words worn out from prayers and talk and newspapers,
prophecies of Jeremiah down on all fours.

And in the big cities, protesters blocked the roads like
a blocked heart, whose master will die. And the dead were already
hung out like fruit, for eternal ripening within   45
the history of the world. They searched for the child; and found
pairs of lovers, hidden; found ancient urns;
found everything that sought *not* to be revealed. For love
was too short and didn't cover them all, like a too-short
blanket. A head or two feet stuck out in the wind   50
when the cold night came. Or they found a short-cut of sharp
brief pain instead of the long, oblivion-causing
streets of joy and of satiation. And at night
the names of the world, of foreign cities and dark
lakes and peoples long vanished. And all the names   55
are like my belovèd's name. She lifted her head
to listen. She had the feeling that she had been called,
and she wasn't the one we meant. But the child disappeared
and the paths in the distant mountain emerged. Not much time.
The olives spoke hard stones. In the enormous fear   60
between heaven and earth, new houses arose and the glass
of windowpanes cooled the burning forehead of night.
The hot wind pounced upon us from a thicket of dry grass,
the distraction of mutual need erected high bridges
in the wasteland. Traps were set, spotlights turned on,   65
and nets of woven hair were spread out. But they passed
the place, and didn't see, for the child bent over
and hid in the stones of tomorrow's houses. Eternal

paper rustled between the feet of the searchers.
Printed and unprinted. The orders were clearly heard. 70
Exact numbers: not ten or fifty or a hundred.
But twenty-seven, thirty-one, forty-three, so that they would believe us.

And in the morning the search was renewed: quick, here!
I saw him among the toys of his wells, the games
of his stones, the tools of his olive trees. I heard his heartbeat 75
under the rock. He's there. He's here. And the tree
stirs. Did you all see? And new calls, like an ancient
sea bringing new ships with loud calls to the foreign shore.
We returned to our cities, where a great sorrow is divided among them
at appropriate intervals, like mailboxes, so that we can drop ours 80
into them: name and address, times of pickup. And the stones
chanted in the choir of black mouths, into the earth,
and only the child could hear them; we couldn't. For he stayed
longer than we did, pretending from the clouds and already
known by heart to the children of olive trees, 85
familiar and changing and not leaving a trace, as in love,
and belonged to them completely, without a remnant.
For to love means not to remain. To be forgotten. But God
remembers, like a man who returns to the place he once left
to reclaim a memory he needed. Thus God returns to 90
our small room, so that he can remember how much he wanted
to build his creation with love. And he didn't forget
our names. Names aren't forgotten. We call a shirt
shirt: even when it's used as a dustrag, it's still called shirt,
perhaps the old shirt. And how long will we go on like this? 95
For we are changing. But the name remains. And what right
do we have to be called by our names, or to call the Jordan
Jordan after it has passed through the Sea of Galilee
and has come out at Zemach. Who is it? Is it still the one
that entered at Capernaum? Who are we after we pass through 100
the terrible love? Who is the Jordan? Who
remembers? Rowboats have emerged. The mountains are mute:
Susita, Hermon, the terrifying Arbel, painful Tiberias.

We all turn our backs on names, the rules of the game,
the hollow calls. An hour passes, hair is cut off   105
in the barbershop. The door is opened. What remains is for
the broom and the street. And the barber's watch ticking close to
your ear as he bends over you. This too is time.
Time's end, perhaps. The child hasn't been found.
The results of rain are seen even now when it's summer.   110
Aloud the trees are talking from the sleep of the earth.
Voices made out of tin are ringing in the wind
as it wakes up. We lay together. I walked away:
the belovèd's eyes stayed wide open in fear. She sat up
in bed for a while, leaning on her elbows. The sheet   115
was white like the day of judgment, and she couldn't stay
alone in the house, she went out into the world
that began with the stairs near the door. But the child remained
and began to resemble the mountains and the winds and the trunks
of olive trees. A family resemblance: as the face of a young man   120
who fell in the Negev arises in the face of his cousin
born in New York. The fracture of a mountain in the Aravah
reappears in the face of the shattered friend. Mountain range
and night, resemblance and tradition. Night's custom that turned
into the law of lovers. Temporary precautions   125
became permanent. The police, the calls outside, the speaking
inside the bodies. And the fire-engines don't wail when they come from
the fire. Silently they return from embers and ashes.
Silently we returned from the valley after love and searching
in retrospect: not being paid attention to. But a few of us   130
continued to listen. It seemed as if someone was calling.
We extended the outer ear with the palm of a hand,
we extended the area of the heart with a further love
in order to hear more clearly, in order to forget.

      But the child died in the night   135
clean and well groomed. Neat and licked by the tongues
of God and night. "When we got here, it was still daylight.
Now darkness has come." Clean and white like a sheet of

paper in an envelope closed and chanted upon
in the psalm-books of the lands of the dead. A few went on searching,   140
or perhaps they searched for a pain that would fit their tears,
for a joy that would fit their laughter, though nothing can fit
anything else. Even hands are from a different body.
But it seemed to us that something had fallen. We heard
a ringing, like a coin that fell. We stood for a moment.   145
We turned around. We bent down. We didn't find
anything, and we went on walking. Each to his own.

The Selected Poetry of Yehuda Amichai, translated by Chana Bloch and Stephen Mitchell
(Berkeley and Los Angeles: University of California Press, 1996), pp. 43–47.

הָאֶלֶגְיָה עַל הַיֶּלֶד שֶׁאָבַד

אֲנִי יוֹדֵעַ עַד הֵיכָן הִגִּיעוּ הַמַּיִם
בַּחֹרֶף הָאַחֲרוֹן; אַךְ אֵינֶנִּי יוֹדֵעַ עַד הֵיכָן
הִגִּיעָה בִּי הָאַהֲבָה. וְאוּלַי עָבְרָה עַל גְּדוֹתַי. כִּי
מַה נִּשְׁאַר בְּדַפְנוֹת הָנָּאדִי? - רַק רֶפֶשׁ קָרוּשׁ.
וּמָה עַל פָּנַי? - אַף לֹא קַו דַּק וְלָבָן,
כְּפִי שֶׁהוּא עַל שִׂפְתֵי הַיֶּלֶד שֶׁשָּׁתָה חָלָב
וְהֶעֱמִיד אֶת הַכּוֹס עַל הַשַּׁיִשׁ הַבָּהִיר בִּנְקִישָׁה.
מַה נִּשְׁאַר. אוּלַי עָלֶה בָּאֶבֶן הַקְּטַנָּה,
אֲשֶׁר הוּשְׁמָה עַל אֶדֶן הַחַלּוֹן לִשְׁמֹר עָלֵינוּ
כְּמַלְאָךְ, כְּשֶׁהָיִינוּ בִּפְנִים. וְלֶאֱהֹב הוּא
לֹא לְהִשְׁתַּיֵּר וְלֹא לְהַשְׁאִיר סִימָן, אֶלָּא לְהִשְׁתַּנּוֹת
כָּלִיל. לְהִשָּׁכַח. לְהָבִין הוּא לִפְרֹחַ. הָאָבִיב מֵבִין.
לִזְכֹּר אֶת הָאֲהוּבָה, הוּא לִשְׁכֹּחַ אֶת כָּל הָרְכוּשׁ
שֶׁנִּצְטַבֵּר. לֶאֱהֹב הוּא לִשְׁכֹּחַ אֶת הָאַהֲבָה הָאַחֶרֶת,
לִסְגֹּר דְּלָתוֹת אֲחֵרוֹת. רְאִי, תָּפַסְנוּ מָקוֹם,
שַׂמְנוּ מְעִיל אוֹ סֵפֶר עַל הַכִּסֵּא הַפָּנוּי
לְיָדֵינוּ, אוּלַי פָּנוּי לָעַד. וּלְכַמָּה זְמַן
נוּכַל לִשְׁמֹרוֹ לָנוּ? הֲרֵי יָבוֹאוּ,
זָר יֵשֵׁב לְיָדְךָ. וְאַתָּה פוֹנֶה לַאֲחוֹרֶיךָ, בְּקֹצֶר רוּחַ,
אֶל הַדֶּלֶת שֶׁבָּה הַכְּתֹבֶת הָאֲדֻמָּה, תַּבִּיט בִּשְׁעוֹנְךָ,
גַּם זֶה הֶרְגֵּל שֶׁל תְּפִלָּה, כְּקִדָּה וּכְנַשִׁיקָה.
וּבַחוּץ תָּמִיד מַמְצִיאִים מַחֲשָׁבוֹת חֲדָשׁוֹת שֶׁגַּם הֵן
מוּשָׂמוֹת עַל פְּנֵיהֶם הָעֲיֵפִים שֶׁל בְּנֵי אָדָם,
כְּאוֹר צִבְעוֹנִי בָּרְחוֹב. אוֹ רְאִי אֶת הַיֶּלֶד, אֲשֶׁר
מַחְשְׁבוֹתָיו מְצֻיָּרוֹת עָלָיו כְּקִשּׁוּט עַל כַּד
לָרַאֲוָה בִּשְׁבִיל אֲחֵרִים, הוּא עוֹד אֵינֶנּוּ חוֹשֵׁב
אוֹתָן בְּעַצְמוֹ. הָאָרֶץ נוֹדֶדֶת, עוֹבֶרֶת תַּחַת סֻלְיוֹתֵינוּ,
כְּמוֹ בָּמָה מִסְתּוֹבֶבֶת, כְּמוֹ פָנֶיךָ, שֶׁנִּדְמָה
הָיָה לִי שֶׁהֵן שֶׁלִּי וְלֹא הָיוּ. אֲבָל הַיֶּלֶד
אָבַד. נֵצֶר אַחֲרוֹן שֶׁל מִשְׂחָקָיו, בֶּן זְקוּנִים
שֶׁל נְיָר צִבְעוֹנִי, נֶכֶד מַחֲבוֹאָיו הָעַתִּיקִים,
יָצָא וּבָא בְּצִלְצְלֵי צַעֲצוּעָיו אֶל בֵּין בְּאֵרוֹת רֵיקוֹת, בְּמוֹצָאֵי
הַחַגִּים וּבַמַּחֲזוֹר הַנּוֹרָא שֶׁל קְרִיאוֹת וָאֵלֶם,

בַּתַּהֲלִיךְ שֶׁל תִּקְנָה וּמָוֶת וְתִקְוָה. הַכֹּל
חָפְשׂוּ, שְׂמֵחִים הָיוּ לַחֲפֵשׂ דָּבָר
בְּאֶרֶץ הַשִּׁכְחָה: קוֹלוֹת וַאֲוִירוֹן
מַנְמִיךְ טוּס כַּמַּחֲשָׁבוֹת, כַּלְבֵי מִשְׁטָרָה שֶׁלָּהֶם
פְּנֵי פִילוֹסוֹפִים, מִלּוֹת שְׁאֵלָה הַמְּנֻתָּרוֹת
עַל רַגְלַיִם דַּקּוֹת בָּעֵשֶׂב הַמִּתְיַבֵּשׁ וְהוֹלֵךְ
תַּחַת עֵינֵינוּ. מִלִּים מְשֻׁמָּשׁוֹת בִּתְפִלּוֹת
וּבִשְׂיחוֹת וּבְעִתּוֹן, נְבוּאוֹת יְרְמְיָהוּ עַל אַרְבַּע.

וּבֶעָרִים נִסְתְּמוּ רְחוֹבוֹת בְּהַפְגָּנוֹת, כְּמוֹ לֵב
שֶׁנִּסְתַּם וַאֲדוֹנִי יָמוּת. וְהַמֵּתִים כְּבָר נִתְלוּ כְּפֵרוֹת
לִבְשִׁילַת־עַד בְּתוֹךְ תּוֹלְדוֹת הָעוֹלָם.
חִפְּשׂוּ אֶת הַיֶּלֶד וּמָצְאוּ זְגוּגוֹת אוֹהֲבִים חֲבוּיִים,
מָצְאוּ כַּדִּים עַתִּיקִים וּמָצְאוּ אֶת כָּל שֶׁבִּקֵּשׁ
לֹא לְהִגָּלוֹת. הָאַהֲבָה הָיְתָה קְצָרָה מִדַּי וְלֹא
כִּסְּתָה אֶת כֻּלָּם, כִּשְׂמִיכָה קְצָרָה מִדַּי. רֹאשׁ
אוֹ רַגְלַיִם בָּלְטוּ בָּרוּחַ כְּשֶׁבָּא הַלַּיְלָה הַקַּר.
אוֹ, כִּי מָצְאוּ דֶרֶךְ קַפֶּנְדַּרְיָה שֶׁל כְּאֵב חַד
וְקָצָר בִּמְקוֹם הָרְחוֹבוֹת הָאֲרֻכִּים וְהַמַּשְׁכִּיחִים שֶׁל
שִׂמְחָה וּשְׁבִיעָה מְמֻשֶּׁכֶת. וּבַלַּיְלָה
הָיוּ שְׁמוֹת כָּל הָעוֹלָם, שְׁמוֹת עָרִים זָרוֹת וַאֲגַמִּים
אֲפֵלִים וְעַמִּים שֶׁמִּזְּמַן עָבְרוּ מִן הָעוֹלָם. וְכָל הַשֵּׁמוֹת
דוֹמִים לְשֵׁם אֲהוּבָתִי. הִיא הֵרִימָה אֶת רֹאשָׁהּ
לְהַקְשִׁיב. נִדְמֶה הָיָה לָהּ שֶׁקָּרְאוּ לָהּ, וְלֹא
אֵלֶיהָ הִתְכַּוַּנּוּ. אַךְ הַיֶּלֶד נֶעְלַם
וְנִרְאוּ הַשְּׁבִילִים בָּהָר הָרָחוֹק. מְעַט זְמָן נוֹתָר.
הַזֵּיתִים דִּבְּרוּ אֲבָנִים קָשׁוֹת. בַּפַּחַד הַגָּדוֹל
בֵּין שָׁמַיִם וָאֶרֶץ הִתְרוֹמְמוּ בָּתִּים חֲדָשִׁים וּזְכוּכִית
הַחַלּוֹנוֹת הִצְנָה אֶת הַמֵּצַח הַלּוֹהֵט שֶׁל לֵיל שָׂרָב.
הָרוּחַ הֵגִיחָה מִתּוֹךְ סְבַךְ עֵשֶׂב יָבֵשׁ כְּחַיּוֹת טֶרֶף,
הֵסַח הַדַּעַת שֶׁל הַזְּדַקְקוּת הֲדָדִית הֶעֶלְתָה
גְּשָׁרִים גְּבוֹהִים בַּיְּשִׁימוֹן. מַלְכֻּדוֹת הוּשְׁמוּ, זַרְקוֹרִים
הֻפְעֲלוּ וְנִפְרְשׂוּ רְשָׁתוֹת שֶׁל שַׁעַר שְׁתֵּי נָעֶרֶב. אַךְ הֵם עָבְרוּ
בַּמָּקוֹם וְלֹא רָאוּ, כִּי הַיֶּלֶד הִתְחַבֵּא וְהִתְקַפֵּל
בֵּין אַבְנֵי בָּתֵּי מָחָר. נְיָר נִצְחִי רִשְׁרֵשׁ בֵּין רַגְלֵי
הַמְחַפְּשִׂים. מֻדְפָּס וְשֶׁאֵינוֹ מֻדְפָּס. הַפְּקֻדוֹת
נִשְׁמְעוּ בְּבֵרוּר. מְסֻפָּרִים הָיוּ מְדֻיָּקִים: לֹא עֶשֶׂר

אוֹ חֲמִשִּׁים אוֹ מֵאָה. אֶלָּא, עֶשְׂרִים וָשֶׁבַע,
שְׁלֹשִׁים וְאַחַת, אַרְבָּעִים וְשָׁלֹשׁ, כְּדֵי שֶׁיַּאֲמִינוּ לָנוּ.

וּבַבֹּקֶר הִתְחַדְּשׁוּ הַחִפּוּשִׂים: מַהֵר, מַהֵר, הִנֵּה!
רָאִיתִי אוֹתוֹ בֵּין צַעֲצוּעַי בְּאֲרוֹתַי, מִשְׂחֲקֵי אֲבָנַי,
כְּלֵי זֵיתָיו. שָׁמַעְתִּי אֶת הֶלֶם לִבּוֹ מִתַּחַת
לַסֶּלַע. הוּא שָׁם. הוּא כָּאן. הָעֵץ זָע מְעַט. הֲרְאִיתֶם?
וּקְרִיאוֹת חֲדָשׁוֹת, כְּמוֹ יָם עַתִּיק הַמֵּבִיא אֳנִיּוֹת
חֲדָשׁוֹת, בִּקְרִיאוֹת רָמוֹת לַחוֹף הַזָּר. וַאֲנַחְנוּ חָזַרְנוּ
אֶל עֲרֵינוּ, אֲשֶׁר תּוּגָה גְּדוֹלָה
מְחַלֶּקֶת בְּכֻלָּן, בִּרְוָחִים מַתְאִימִים, כְּמוֹ תֵּבוֹת
מִכְתָּבִים, כְּדֵי שֶׁנּוּכַל לְהָטִיל בָּהֶן אֶת שֶׁלָּנוּ: שֵׁם וּכְתֹבֶת
שְׁעוֹת הַהֲרָקָה. וְהָאֲבָנִים זִמְּרוּ בְּמַקְהֵלַת פִּיּוֹת
שְׁחוֹרִים לְתוֹךְ הָאֲדָמָה וְרַק הַיֶּלֶד שָׁמַע אוֹתָן,
לֹא אֲנַחְנוּ. כִּי הוּא הָיָה שׁוֹהֶה יוֹתֵר מֵאִתָּנוּ,
מַעֲמִיד פָּנִים מִן הֶעֲנָנִים וּכְבָר לָמוּד וְשָׁנוּן
עַל בְּנֵי זֵיתִים, שָׁגוּר וּמִשְׁתַּנֶּה בְּלִי לְהַשְׁאִיר סִימָן,
כְּמוֹ בְּאַהֲבָה וְשַׁיָּךְ לָהֶם בְּלִי שְׁאֵרִית.
כִּי לֶאֱהֹב הוּא לֹא לְהִשָּׁאֵר. לְהַשָּׁכַח. אֲבָל
אֱלֹהִים נִזְכָּר, כְּמוֹ אָדָם הַחוֹזֵר לִמְקוֹם מוֹצָאוֹ
לְהִזָּכֵר בְּמַה שֶׁהוּא שָׁכַח, אֱלֹהִים חוֹזֵר אֶל
חַדְרֵנוּ הַקָּטָן, כְּדֵי לְהִזָּכֵר אֵיךְ הוּא רָצָה
לִבְנוֹת אֶת עוֹלָמוֹ בְּאַהֲבָה. וְאֶת שְׁמוֹתֵינוּ לֹא שָׁכַח.
שֵׁמוֹת אֵינָם נִשְׁכָּחִים. גַּם כִּי יָמִים רַבִּים
נִקְרָא לַחֲלָצָה, חֲלָצָה - וּכְבָר מְנֻגָּבִים בָּהּ אֵין וָעָגֶן -
הִיא עֲדַיִן נִקְרֵאת חֲלָצָה, אוּלַי, הַחֲלָצָה הַיְשָׁנָה. וְכַמָּה זְמַן
נַמְשִׁיךְ כָּךְ? כִּי אָנוּ מִשְׁתַּנִּים. הַשֵּׁם נִשְׁאָר.
וּמַהִי זְכוּתֵנוּ לְהִקָּרֵא בִּשְׁמוֹתֵינוּ, אוֹ לִקְרֹא לַיַּרְדֵּן,
יַרְדֵּן, אַחַר שֶׁעָבַר דֶּרֶךְ מֵי הַכִּנֶּרֶת וְיוֹצֵא בְּצֶמַח.
מִי הוּא? הַאִם עוֹדֶנּוּ זֶה שֶׁנִּכְנַס בִּכְפַר נַחוּם?
מִי אֲנַחְנוּ אַחַר שֶׁעָבַרְנוּ בְּאַהֲבָה הַנּוֹרָאָה? מִי
הַיַּרְדֵּן? מִי זוֹכֵר? סִירוֹת מְטַיְּלִים יָצְאוּ. הֶהָרִים הֵם
אִלְּמִים: סוּסִיתָא, חֶרְמוֹן, הָאַרְבֶּל הַנּוֹרָא, טְבֶרְיָה הַמַּכְאִיבָה.

הַכֹּל מִתְנַכְּרִים לַשֵּׁמוֹת, לִכְלָלֵי הַמִּשְׂחָק, לַקְּרִיאוֹת
הַחֲלוּלוֹת. שָׁעָה עוֹבֶרֶת, שֵׂעָר נִגְזָז בַּמִּסְפָּרָה.
הַדֶּלֶת נִפְתַּחַת. הַשְּׁאָר לַמְטַאטֵא וְלָרְחוֹב.

וּשְׁעוֹן הַסַּפָּר קָרוֹב לְאָזְנְךָ, בְּעֵת הוּא נִרְכָּן מֵעָלֶיךָ.
גַּם זֶה זְמַן. סוֹף זְמַן, אוּלַי. וְהַיֶּלֶד לֹא נִמְצָא.
תּוֹצְאוֹת הַגֶּשֶׁם נִרְאוֹת גַּם כְּשֶׁקְיָ
עַכְשָׁו. בְּקוֹל רָם יְדַבְּרוּ הָאִילָנוֹת מִתּוֹךְ
שְׁנַת הָאֲדָמָה. קוֹלוֹת עֲשׂוּיֵי פַּח מְצֻלְצָלִים בָּרוּחַ
הַמִּתְעוֹרֶרֶת. שָׁכַבְנוּ יַחְדָּו. הָלַכְתִּי: עֵינֵי הָאֲהוּבָה
נִשְׁאֲרוּ פְּעוּרוֹת בְּפַחַד. מְעַט הִתְרוֹמְמָה בְּמִטָּתָהּ,
נִשְׁעֲנָה עַל מַרְפְּקֶיהָ. הַסָּדִין הָיָה לָבָן
כְּמוֹ יוֹם הַדִּין, וְהִיא לֹא יָכְלָה לְהִשָּׁאֵר
לְבַדָּהּ בְּבֵיתָהּ וְיָצְאָה אֶל הָעוֹלָם שֶׁהֵחֵל בַּמַּדְרֵגוֹת לְיַד
הַפֶּתַח. אַךְ הַיֶּלֶד נִשְׁאַר וְהֵחֵל לְהִדָּמוֹת לֶהָרִים
וְלָרוּחוֹת וּלְגִזְעֵי הַזֵּיתִים. דִּמְיוֹן כְּמוֹ
בִּקְרוֹבֵי מִשְׁפָּחָה: פְּנֵי נַעַר שֶׁנָּפַל בַּנֶּגֶב
עוֹלִים בִּפְנֵי בֶּן דּוֹדוֹ הַנּוֹלָד בְּנְיוּ-יוֹרְק. שֶׁבֶר
הַר בָּעֲרָבָה נִכָּר בִּפְנֵי הַיָּדִיד הַשָּׁבוּר. רֶכֶס
נַעֲלָה, דִּמְיוֹן וּמָסֹרֶת. מִנְהָג שֶׁל לַיְלָה
שֶׁהָפַךְ לִהְיוֹת חֹק אוֹהֲבִים. אֶמְצָעֵי הַזְּהִירוּת הַזְּמַנִּיִּים
הָיוּ לְקֶבַע. הַמִּשְׁטָרָה, הַקְּרִיאוֹת בַּחוּץ,
הַדִּבּוּרִים בְּתוֹךְ הַגּוּפִים. וּמְכוֹנִיּוֹת מְכַבֵּי
אֵשׁ אֵינָן מַשְׁמִיעוֹת יְלָלָה כְּשֶׁהֵן בָּאוֹת
מִן הַשְּׂרֵפָה. בְּשֶׁקֶט הֵם שָׁבִים מְאֹד וּמֵאֵפֶר.
בְּשֶׁקֶט שַׁבְנוּ מִן הָעֵמֶק אַחַר אַהֲבָה וְחִפּוּשׂ
בְּדִיעֲבַד: לֹא מוּשָׂמִים אֶל לֵב. אֲבָל אֲחָדִים
הִמְשִׁיכוּ לְהַאֲזִין. נִדְמָה הָיָה, כִּי מִישֶׁהוּ קָרָא.
הִגְדַּלְנוּ אֶת אַפַּרְכֶּסֶת הָאֹזֶן בְּכַף יָד,
הִגְדַּלְנוּ אֶת שֶׁטַח הַלֵּב בְּאַהֲבָה נוֹסֶפֶת
כְּדֵי לְהֵיטִיב שְׁמֹעַ וּלְהֵיטִיב שְׁכֹחַ.

אַךְ הַיֶּלֶד מֵת בַּלַּיְלָה
נָקִי וּמְסֹרָק לְמִשְׁעִי. מְטֻפָּל וּמְלֻקָּק בִּלְשׁוֹנוֹת
אֵל וָלַיְלָה. "כְּשֶׁהִגַּעְנוּ הֵנָּה, הָיָה עוֹד אוֹר
עַכְשָׁו בָּא הַחֹשֶׁךְ". נָקִי וְלָבָן כְּגִלָּיוֹן
נְיָר בְּמַעֲטָפָה וְסָגוּר וּמְזֻמָּר
בְּסִפְרֵי תְהִלִּים שֶׁל אַדְמוֹת מֵתִים.

אֲחָדִים הִמְשִׁיכוּ לְחַפֵּשׂ, אוֹ כִּי חָפְשׂוּ כְּאֵב
מַתְאִים לְבְכָיִם אוֹ שִׂמְחָה מַתְאִימָה לְצְחוֹקָם,
הַכֹּל אֵינוֹ מַתְאִים לַכֹּל. אֲפִילוּ הַיָּדַיִם הֵן
שֶׁל גּוּף אַחֵר. אֲבָל נִדְמֶה הָיָה לָנוּ, כִּי
מַשֶּׁהוּ נָפַל: שָׁמַעְנוּ צְלְצוּל, כְּמוֹ
מַטְבֵּעַ שֶׁנָּפָלָה. עָמַדְנוּ. הִסְתּוֹבַבְנוּ. הִתְכּוֹפַפְנוּ.
לֹא מָצָאנוּ וְהִמְשַׁכְנוּ לָלֶכֶת. אִישׁ אִישׁ אֶל שֶׁלּוֹ.

Yehuda Amichai, Shirim: 1948–1962 (Jerusalem and Tel Aviv: Schocken, [1963] 2002),
pp. 366–71.

LITTLE RUTH

Sometimes I remember you, little Ruth,
We were separated in our distant childhood and they burned you in the
    camps.
If you were alive now, you would be a woman of sixty-five,
A woman on the verge of old age. At twenty you were burned
And I don't know what happened to you in your short life
Since we separated. What did you achieve, what insignia
Did they put on your shoulders, your sleeves, your
Brave soul, what shining stars
Did they pin on you, what decorations for valor, what
Medals for love hung around your neck,
What peace upon you, *peace unto you.*
And what happened to the unused years of your life?
Are they still packed away in pretty bundles,
Were they added to my life? Did you turn me
Into your bank of love like the banks in Switzerland
Where assets are preserved even after their owners are dead?
Will I leave all this to my children
Whom you never saw?

You gave your life to me, like a wine dealer
Who remains sober himself.
You sober in death, lucid in the dark
For me, drunk on life, wallowing in my forgetfulness.
Now and then, I remember you in times
Unbelievable. And in places not made for memory
But for the transient, the passing that does not remain.
As in an airport, when the arriving travelers
Stand tired at the revolving conveyor belt
That brings their suitcases and packages,
And they identify theirs with cries of joy
As at a resurrection and go out into their lives;
And there is one suitcase that returns and disappears again

And returns again, ever so slowly, in the empty hall,
Again and again it passes.
This is how your quiet figure passes by me,
This is how I remember you until
The conveyer belt stands still. *And they stood still. Amen.*

Yehuda Amichai: A Life of Poetry, edited and translated by Benjamin Harshav and Barbara Harshav (New York: HarperCollins, 1994), pp. 431–32.

רוּת הַקְּטַנָּה

לִפְעָמִים אֲנִי זוֹכֵר אוֹתָךְ רוּת הַקְּטַנָּה,
שֶׁנִּפְרַדְנוּ בְּיַלְדוּת רְחוֹקָה, שֶׁשָּׂרְפוּ אוֹתָךְ בַּמַּחֲנוֹת.
אִלּוּ חָיִית עַכְשָׁיו, הָיִית אִשָּׁה בַּת שִׁשִּׁים וְחָמֵשׁ,
אִשָּׁה עַל סַף זִקְנָה. בַּת עֶשְׂרִים נִשְׂרַפְתְּ,
וְאֵינֶנִּי יוֹדֵעַ מַה קָּרָה לָךְ בְּחַיַּיִךְ הַקְּצָרִים
מֵאָז נִפְרַדְנוּ. לְמַה הִגַּעַתְּ, אֵילוּ סִימָנֵי דַּרְגָּה
הֶעֱנִיקוּ לָךְ עַל כְּתֵפַיִךְ, עַל שַׁרְווּלַיִךְ, עַל
נַפְשֵׁךְ הָאַמִּיצָה, אֵילוּ כּוֹכָבִים מַבְרִיקִים
הִדְבִּיקוּ לָךְ, אֵילוּ אוֹתוֹת גְּבוּרָה, אֵילוּ
מֶדַלְיוֹת אַהֲבָה תָּלוּ עַל צַוָּארֵךְ,
אֵיזֶה שָׁלוֹם עָלַיִךְ, עָלַיִךְ הַשָּׁלוֹם.
וּמַה קָּרָה לִשְׁנוֹת חַיַּיִךְ הֲלֹא מְשֻׁמָּשׁוֹת?
הַאִם הֵן עֲדַיִן אֲרוּזוֹת כַּחֲבִילוֹת יָפוֹת,
הַאִם נוֹסְפוּ לְחַיַּי? הַאִם הָפַכְתְּ אוֹתִי
בַּנְק הָאַהֲבָה שֶׁלָּךְ כְּמוֹ הַבַּנְקִים בִּשְׁוַיְץ
שֶׁהַמַּטְמוֹן נִשְׁמָר בָּהֶם גַּם אַחֲרֵי מוֹת בְּעָלָיו?
הַאִם אוֹרִישׁ אֶת כָּל אֵלֶּה לִילָדַי
שֶׁלֹּא רָאִית אוֹתָם מֵעוֹלָם?

נָתַתְּ לִי אֶת חַיַּיִךְ, כְּמוֹ מוֹכֵר יַיִן
מְשֻׁכָּר שֶׁהוּא עַצְמוֹ נִשְׁאָר מְפֻכָּח,
מְפֻכַּחַת מָוֶת כָּמוֹךְ, וּצְלוּלַת שְׁאוֹל
לִשְׁכּוֹר חַיִּים כָּמוֹנִי מִתְגּוֹלֵל בְּשִׁכְחָתוֹ.
לִפְעָמִים אֲנִי זוֹכֵר אוֹתָךְ בִּזְמַנִּים
שֶׁלֹּא שֵׁעַרְתִּי וּבִמְקוֹמוֹת שֶׁלֹּא נוֹעֲדוּ לְזִכָּרוֹן,
אֶלָּא לַחוֹלֵף וְלָעוֹבֵר שֶׁלֹּא נִשְׁאָר;
כְּמוֹ בִּנְמַל תְּעוּפָה כְּשֶׁהַנּוֹסְעִים הַמַּגִּיעִים
עוֹמְדִים עֲיֵפִים לְיַד הַסֶּרֶט הַנָּע וְהַמִּסְתּוֹבֵב
שֶׁמֵּבִיא אֶת מִזְוְדוֹתֵיהֶם וַחֲבִילוֹתֵיהֶם,
וְהֵם מְגַלִּים אֶת שֶׁלָּהֶם בִּקְרִיאוֹת שִׂמְחָה
כְּמוֹ בִּתְחִיַּת הַמֵּתִים וְיוֹצְאִים אֶל חַיֵּיהֶם.
וְיֵשׁ מִזְוָדָה אַחַת שֶׁחוֹזֶרֶת וְשָׁב נֶעֱלֶמֶת
וְשָׁב חוֹזֶרֶת, לְאַט לְאַט, בָּאוּלָם הַמִּתְרוֹקֵן,
וְשָׁב וְשָׁב הִיא עוֹבֶרֶת,
כָּךְ עוֹבֶרֶת דְּמוּתֵךְ הַשְּׁקֵטָה עַל פָּנַי,

כָּךְ אֲנִי זוֹכֵר אוֹתָךְ, עַד
שֶׁהַסֶּרֶט יַעֲמֹד מִלֶּכֶת. וְדֹמּוּ סֶלָה.

Yehuda Amichai, *Gam ha'egrof haya pa´am yad petuha ve'etsbaot* (Jerusalem and Tel Aviv: Schocken, 1989), pp. 70–71.

AND THE MIGRATION OF MY PARENTS

And the migration of my parents
Has not subsided in me. My blood goes on sloshing
Between my ribs, long after the vessel has come to rest.
And the migration of my parents has not subsided in me.
Winds of long time over stones. Earth
Forgets the steps of those who trod her.
Terrible fate. Patches of a conversation after midnight.
Win and lose. Night recalls and day forgets.
My eyes looked long into a vast desert
And were calmed a bit. A woman. Rules of a game
I was not taught. Laws of pain and burden.
My heart barely ekes out the bread
Of its daily love. My parents in their migration.
On Mother Earth, I am always an orphan.
Too young to die, too old to play.
The weary hewer and the empty quarry in one body.
Archaeology of the future, repositories
Of what was not. And the migration of my parents
Has not subsided in me. From bitter nations I have learned
Bitter tongues for my silence
Among these houses, always like ships.
And my veins and my sinews, a thicket
Of ropes I cannot unravel. And then
My death and an end to the migration of my parents.

Yehuda Amichai: A Life of Poetry, 1948–1994, edited and translated by Benjamin Harshav and Barbara Harshav (New York: HarperCollins, 1994), p. 51.

וַהֲגִירַת הוֹרַי

נַהֲגִירַת הוֹרַי לֹא נִרְגְּעָה בִּי.
דָּמִי מַמְשִׁיךְ עֲדַיִן לְשַׁקְשֵׁק בְּדַפְנוֹתַי
גַּם אַחַר שֶׁכְּבָר הֻנַּח הַכְּלִי עַל מְקוֹמוֹ.
וַהֲגִירַת הוֹרַי לֹא נִרְגְּעָה בִּי.
רוּחוֹת זְמַן רַב עַל אֲבָנִים.
הָאֲדָמָה שׁוֹכַחַת צַעֲדֵי דּוֹרְכִים בָּהּ.
גּוֹרָל נוֹרָא. קִטְעֵי שִׂיחָה אַחַר חֲצוֹת.
הֶשֵּׂג וּנְסִיגָה. לַיְלָה מַזְכִּיר וְיוֹם מַשְׁכִּיחַ.
עֵינַי שֶׁהִסְתַּכְּלוּ זְמַן רַב לְתוֹךְ מִדְבָּר גָּדוֹל
וְנִרְגְּעוּ מְעַט. אִשָּׁה אַחַת. כְּלָלֵי מִשְׂחָק
שֶׁלֹּא הִסְבִּירוּ לִי הֵיטֵב. חֻקֵּי כְּאֵב וָכֹבֶד.
עוֹד עַכְשָׁו לִבִּי, בְּקֹשִׁי יִשְׁתַּכֵּר
בְּלֶחֶם אַהֲבָתוֹ הַיּוֹמְיוֹמִית. הוֹרַי בְּמוֹ הֲגִירָתָם.
עַל אֵם הַדֶּרֶךְ, בָּהּ אֲנִי תָּמִיד יָתוֹם בְּלִי אֵם,
צָעִיר מִדַּי בִּשְׁבִיל לָמוּת, זָקֵן מִדַּי לַמִּשְׂחָקִים.
וַעֲיֵפוּת חוֹצֵב וְרֵיקָנוּת הַמַּחֲצָבָה בְּגוּף אֶחָד.
אַרְכֵאוֹלוֹגְיָה שֶׁל עָתִיד, בָּתֵּי נְכוֹת
שֶׁל מַה שֶּׁלֹּא הָיָה. וַהֲגִירַת הוֹרַי
לֹא נִרְגְּעָה בִּי, וּמֵעַמִּים מָרִים לָמַדְתִּי
שָׂפוֹת מָרוֹת לְמַעַן שְׁתִיקָתִי
בֵּין הַבָּתִּים, אֲשֶׁר דּוֹמִים לָאֳנִיּוֹת תָּמִיד.
וּכְבָר עוֹרְקַי וְגַם גִּידֵי כִּסְבַּךְ
שֶׁל חֲבָלִים שֶׁלֹּא אַתִּיר. וְאַחַר כָּךְ
מוֹתִי וְסוֹף לַהֲגִירַת הוֹרַי.

Yehuda Amichai, *Shirim: 1948–1962* (Jerusalem and Tel Aviv: Schocken, [1963] 2002), p. 221.

I WANT TO DIE IN MY OWN BED

All night the army came up from Gilgal
To get to the killing field, and that's all.
In the ground, warp and woof, lay the dead.
I want to die in my own bed.

Like slits in a tank, their eyes were uncanny,
I'm always the few and they are the many.
I must answer. They can interrogate my head.
But I want to die in my own bed.

The sun stood still in Gibeon. Forever so, it's willing
To illuminate those waging battle and killing.
I may not see my wife when her blood is shed,
But I want to die in my own bed.

Samson, his strength in his long black hair,
My hair they sheared off when they made me a hero
Perforce, and taught me to charge ahead.
I want to die in my own bed.

I saw you could live and furnish with grace
Even a lion's maw, if you've got no other place.
I don't even mind to die alone, to be dead,
But I want to die in my own bed.

Yehuda Amichai: A Life of Poetry, 1948–1994, edited and translated by Benjamin Harshav and Barbara Harshav (New York: HarperCollins, 1994), p. 37.

אֲנִי רוֹצֶה לָמוּת עַל מִטָּתִי

כָּל הַלַּיְלָה עָלָה צָבָא מִן הַגִּלְגָּל
לְהַגִּיעַ עַד שְׂדֵה הַקֶּטֶל וְעַד בִּכְלָל.
הַמֵּתִים בָּאֲדָמָה שָׁכְבוּ בָּעֶרֶב וּבַשֶּׁתִי.
אֲנִי רוֹצֶה לָמוּת עַל מִטָּתִי.

עֵינֵיהֶם הָיוּ צָרוֹת כְּבַטָּנָק הָאֶשְׁנַבִּים,
אֲנִי תָּמִיד מְעַטִּים וְהֵם רַבִּים.
אֲנִי מֻכְרָח לַעֲנוֹת. הֵם יְכוֹלִים לַחְקֹר אוֹתִי.
אֲבָל אֲנִי רוֹצֶה לָמוּת עַל מִטָּתִי.

שֶׁמֶשׁ דֹּם בְּגִבְעוֹן. הוּא מוּכָן לַעֲמֹד נֶצַח.
בִּשְׁבִיל לְהָאִיר לְעוֹרְכֵי קְרָב וָרֶצַח,
אוּלַי לֹא אֶרְאֶה כְּשֶׁיַּהַרְגוּ אֶת אִשְׁתִּי,
אֲבָל אֲנִי רוֹצֶה לָמוּת עַל מִטָּתִי.

שִׁמְשׁוֹן, גְּבוּרָתוֹ בְּשֵׂעָר אָרֹךְ וְשָׁחוֹר,
אֶת שֶׁלִּי גָּזְזוּ כְּשֶׁעֲשׂוּנִי לִגְבּוֹר
חוֹבָה וְלִמְּדוּנִי לִדְרֹךְ אֶת קַשְׁתִּי.
אֲנִי רוֹצֶה לָמוּת עַל מִטָּתִי.

רָאִיתִי כִּי אֶפְשָׁר לָגוּר וּלְהִסְתַּדֵּר
וּלְרַהֵט גַּם לֹעַ אַרְיֵה, אִם אֵין מָקוֹם אַחֵר.
כְּבָר לֹא אִכְפַּת לִי לָמוּת בִּיחִידוּתִי,
אֲבָל אֲנִי רוֹצֶה לָמוּת עַל מִטָּתִי.

Yehuda Amichai, Shirim: 1948–1962 (Jerusalem and Tel Aviv: Schocken, [1963]2002), p. 118.

NOT LIKE A CYPRESS

Not like a cypress,
Not all at once, not all of me,
But like grass, in a thousand shoots,
Wary and green,
To be hidden like lots of children in a game
And one seeker.
And not like the only man,
The son of Kish, many found him
And made him king.
But like rain in many spots
From many clouds, to shudder, to be drunk
By many mouths, to be breathed
Like air a whole year
And strewn like blossoms in the spring.

Not the sharp ringing,
Waking the doctor on duty,
But rapping, on many windows,
In side entrances,
With many jittery heartbeats.

Then, the quiet exit, like smoke
Without fanfare, a resigning minister,
Children tired of play,
A stone in its last somersaults
After a steep slope, where the plain
Of the great concession begins. From it,
Like accepted prayers,
Rises dust in a myriad of grains.

Yehuda Amichai, *A Life of Poetry*, 1948–1994, edited and translated by Benjamin Harshav and Barbara Harshav (New York: HarperCollins, 1994), p. 35.

לֹא כַּבְּרוֹשׁ

לֹא כַּבְּרוֹשׁ,
לֹא בְּבַת אַחַת, לֹא כֻּלִּי,
אֶלָּא כַּדֶּשֶׁא, בְּאַלְפֵי יְצִיאוֹת זְהִירוֹת-יְרֻקּוֹת,
לִהְיוֹת מֻסְתָּר כְּהַרְבֵּה יְלָדִים בַּמִּשְׂחָק
וְאֶחָד מְחַפֵּשׂ.

וְלֹא כַּגֶּבֶר הַיָּחִיד,
כְּבֶן-קִישׁ, שֶׁמְּצָאוּהוּ רַבִּים
וְעָשׂוּ אוֹתוֹ לְמֶלֶךְ.
אֶלָּא כַּגֶּשֶׁם בְּהַרְבֵּה מְקוֹמוֹת
מֵעֲנָנִים רַבִּים, לְהִתְחַלְחֵל, לִהְיוֹת שְׁתוּי
פִּיּוֹת רַבִּים, לִהְיוֹת נָשׁוּם
כָּאֲוִיר בַּשָּׁנָה וּמְפֻזָּר כִּפְרִיחָה בָּאָבִיב.

לֹא הַצִּלְצוּל הַחַד, הַמְּעוֹרֵר
בְּשַׁעַר הָרוֹפֵא הַתּוֹרָן,
אֶלָּא בִּדְפִיקוֹת, בְּהַרְבֵּה אֶשְׁנַבִּים
בִּכְנִיסוֹת צְדָדִיּוֹת, בְּהַרְבֵּה דְּפִיקוֹת לֵב.

וְאַחַר-כָּךְ הַיְצִיאָה הַשְּׁקֵטָה, כְּעָשָׁן
בְּלִי תְּרוּעָה, שַׂר מִתְפַּטֵּר,
יְלָדִים עֲיֵפִים מִמִּשְׂחָק,
אֶבֶן בַּגִּלְגּוּלִים הָאַחֲרוֹנִים
לְאַחַר הַמּוֹרָד הַתָּלוּל, בַּמָּקוֹם שֶׁמַּתְחִיל
מִישׁוֹר הַוִּתּוּר הַגָּדוֹל, אֲשֶׁר מִמֶּנּוּ,
כַּתְּפִלּוֹת הַמִּתְקַבְּלוֹת,
עוֹלֶה וְאָבָק בְּהַרְבֵּה רִבּוֹא גַּרְגִּירִים.

Yehuda Amichai, Shirim: 1948–1962 (Jerusalem and Tel Aviv: Schocken, [1963] 2002), p. 98.

ELEGY ON AN ABANDONED VILLAGE

1

The wine of August was spilled on the face of the girl, but
the destruction was sober. Thick wooden beams stuck out
from the life of forgotten people; and a distant love
hurled itself, echoing like thunder, into the ravine.
And slowly the valleys rose to the mountain, in the midday   5
hours, and we were almost sad. And like some stranger
in a strange city, who reads in a book of addresses and names,
I stand and choose a hotel, temporary: here.

2

The enormous snow was set down far away. Sometimes
I must use my love as the only way to describe it,   10
and must hire the wind to demonstrate the wailing of women.
It's hard for stones that roll from season to season
to remember the dreamers and the whisperers in the grass,
who fell in their love. And like a man who keeps shaking
his wrist when his watch stops: Who is shaking us? Who?   15

3

The wind brought voices from far away, like an infant
in her arms. The wind never stops. There, standing,
are the power-plants that discovered our weakness when
we needed to appear strong, needed to make
a decision in the dark, without a mirror or a light.   20

Thoughts have dropped and fly parallel to the ground, like birds.
And beside the sea: picnickers sit among friends.
Their money was brought from far away; their portrait is seen
on crumpling paper. In their laughter: blossoming clouds.
Our heart beats in the footsteps that watchmen take, back and forth.   25
And if someone should love us, surely the distant snow
will realize it, a long time before we do.

4

The rest is not simply silence. The rest is a screech.
Like a car shifting gears on a dangerous uphill road.
Have you listened closely enough to the calls of the children   30
at play in the ruined houses, when their voices stop
short, as they reach the ceiling, out of habit, and later
burst up to the sky? Oh night without a Jerusalem,
oh children in the ruins, who will never again be birds,
oh passing time, when newspapers that have yellowed already   35
interest you again: like a document. And the face of last year's
woman lights up in the memory of a distant man.
But the wind keeps forgetting. Because it is always there.

Should I wait here for God's voice, or for the scream of a train
between the hard-pressing hills? Look, children and birds   40
were closed and opened, each into song and muteness.
Or girls on their long road: look as again they turn into
fig trees; how wonderful they are for love. And the thunder
of sparrows as they rise from the garbage; see what is written
on stones. You weren't the one who wrote it. And yet   45
it is always your handwriting. Stay for a while, in the narrow
place between earth and its short god. Listen as the tin
gradually matures in its rust, and the voice of alleys
changes too late: not till death has arrived.

For only in the half-destroyed do we understand   50
the blue that covers the inside of rooms, like doctors
who learn by the bodies gaping in front of them. But we
will never know how blood behaves when it's inside,
within the whole body, when the heart shines into it, from
far away, in its dark path. And girls are still   55
hidden among the fresh laundry hanging in the air
that also will turn into rain among the mountains
sent to scout and uncover the nakedness of the land;
and uncovered it; and stayed in the valleys, forever.

The Selected Poetry of Yehuda Amichai, translated by Chana Bloch and Stephen Mitchell (Berkeley and Los Angeles: University of California Press, 1996), pp. 42–43.

אֶלֶגְיָה עַל כְּפָר נָטוּשׁ

[א]

יַיִן תַּמּוּזִים נִשְׁפַּךְ עַל פְּנֵי הַנַּעֲרָה,
אֲבָל הַהֶרֶס הָיָה מְפֻכָּח. קוֹרוֹת עֵץ בָּלְטוּ
מִתּוֹךְ קוֹרוֹת בְּנֵי אָדָם נִשְׁכָּחִים; וְאַהֲבָה רְחוֹקָה
הֵטִילָה עַצְמָהּ, כְּרַעַם, לְתוֹךְ הַבִּקְעָה.
וּלְאַטָּם הִתְרוֹמְמוּ הָעֲמָקִים אֶל הָהָר
בִּשְׁעוֹת הַצָּהֳרַיִם וְכִמְעַט עֲגַמְנוּ. וּכְזָר
בְּעִיר זָרָה, הַקּוֹרֵא בְּסֵפֶר כְּתֹבוֹת וְשֵׁמוֹת,
אֲנִי עוֹמֵד וּבוֹחֵר לִי מָלוֹן אַרְעִי: כָּאן.

[ב]

הַשֶּׁלֶג הַגָּדוֹל הִנֵּה הַרְחֵק. לְעִתִּים אֲנִי
חַיָּב לְהִשְׁתַּמֵּשׁ בְּאַהֲבָתִי כְּדֵי לְתָאֵר אוֹתוֹ,
וְלִשְׁכֹּר אֶת הָרוּחַ כְּדֵי לְהַדְגִּים יְלֵל נָשִׁים.
קָשֶׁה עַל אֲבָנִים הַמִּתְגַּלְגְּלוֹת מֵעוֹנָה לְעוֹנָה
לִזְכֹּר אֶת הַחוֹלְמִים וְאֶת הַמְרַשְׁרְשִׁים בָּעֵשֶׂב,
אֲשֶׁר נָפְלוּ בְּאַהֲבָתָם. וּכְאָדָם הַמְנַעֲנֵעַ
אֶת יָדוֹ כְּשֶׁשְּׁעוֹנוֹ עָמַד: מִי מְנַעֲנֵעַ אוֹתָנוּ, מִי?

[ג]

הָרוּחַ הֵבִיאָה קוֹלוֹת מֵרָחוֹק, כְּתִינוֹק
בִּזְרוֹעוֹתֶיהָ. לֹא נִפְסֶקֶת הָרוּחַ. וְעוֹמְדוֹת
תַּחֲנוֹת הַכֹּחַ אֲשֶׁר גִּלּוּ אֶת חֻלְשָׁתֵנוּ
כְּשֶׁהָיִינוּ צְרִיכִים לְהַרְאוֹת חֲזָקִים
וּלְהַחֲלִיט בַּחֹשֶׁךְ, בְּלִי מַרְאֶה נָאוֹר.

מַחֲשָׁבוֹת הַנְּמִיכוּ עוּף בְּמַקְבִּיל לָאֲדָמָה, כְּצִפֳּרִים.
וּלְיַד הַיָּם, יָשְׁבוּ אוֹכְלִים בֵּין יְדִידֵיהֶם.
כַּסְפָּם מֵרָחוֹק הוּבָא וּדְיוֹקַן פְּנֵיהֶם נִרְאָה
עַל נְיָר מִתְקַמֵּט. בִּצְחוֹקָם פָּרְחוּ עֲנָנִים.
וּבְצַעֲדֵי שׁוֹמְרִים, הָלוֹךְ נָשׁוֹב, לָנוּ הַלֵּב.
וְאִם אוֹהֵב אוֹתָנוּ מִישֶׁהוּ, יָדַע זֹאת,
הַשֶּׁלֶג הָרָחוֹק, זְמַן רַב לְפָנֵינוּ.

הַיֵּתֶר אֵינוֹ שְׁתִיקָה. הַיֵּתֶר צְעָקָה.
כְּמְכוֹנִית בַּעֲלִיָּה הַמְּסֻכֶּנֶת, הַמַּחֲלִיפָה הִלּוּךְ.
הַאִם הֶאֱזַנְתָּ דַּיֶּךְ לִקְרִיאַת הַטַּף
בְּמִשְׂחָקָם, בְּחֻרְבוֹת הַבָּתִּים, כְּשֶׁקּוֹלוֹתֵיהֶם
נֶעֱצָרִים בְּגֹבַהּ הַתִּקְרָה, מִתּוֹךְ הֶרְגֵּל, וְאַחַר כָּךְ
יִפְרְצוּ לַשָּׁמַיִם? הוֹי לַיְלָה בְּלִי יְרוּשָׁלַיִם,
הוֹי יְלָדִים שֶׁלְּעוֹלָם לֹא יִהְיוּ שׁוּב לְצִפֳּרִים,
הוֹי זְמַן שֶׁעוֹבֵר, כְּשֶׁעִתּוֹנִים, שֶׁכְּבָר הִצְהִיבוּ, שׁוּב
מְעַנְיְנִים אוֹתְךָ. אַחֶרֶת: כְּמִסְמָךְ, כִּתְעוּדָה,
וּפְנֵי הָאִשָּׁה שֶׁל אֶשְׁתָּקַד יִהְיוּ חֲשׁוּבִים בְּזִכְרוֹן אָדָם רָחוֹק.
אַךְ הָרוּחַ תָּמִיד שׁוֹכַחַת, כִּי הִיא נִמְצֵאת תָּמִיד.

הַאִם כָּאן אֲחַכֶּה לְקוֹל הָאֱלֹהִים, אוֹ לְצַעֲקַת
הָרַכֶּבֶת בְּמוֹעֲקָתָהּ, בֵּין הַגְּבָעוֹת הַלּוֹחֲצוֹת אוֹתָהּ?
רְאֵה, יְלָדִים וְצִפֳּרִים נִסְגְּרוּ וְנִפְתְּחוּ, חֲלִיפוֹת, לְשִׁיר וּלְאֵלֶם.
רְאֵה נְעָרוֹת בְּדַרְכָּן הָאֲרֻכָּה, שֶׁבָּהּ הֵן נֶהְפָּכוֹת
שׁוּב לַעֲצֵי תְּאֵנָה; הֵן נִפְלָאוֹת לְאַהֲבָה. שְׁמַע
אֶת רַעַם לַהֲקַת הַזַּרְזִירִים הַמִּתְרוֹמְמִים מִן הָאַשְׁפָּה,
רְאֵה אֶת הַכָּתוּב עַל אֲבָנִים. לֹא אַתָּה כְּתַבְתָּ. וּבְכָל זֹאת
כְּתַב יָדְךָ הוּא תָּמִיד. שְׁהֵה מְעַט בַּמָּקוֹם הַצַּר בֵּין
הָאֲדָמָה וֵאלֹהֶיהָ הַנְּמוּכִים. שְׁמַע אֶת הַפַּח הַמִּתְבַּגֵּר
לְאַט בַּחֲלוּדָה וְאֶת קוֹל הַסִּמְטָאוֹת הַמִּתְחַלֵּף
בְּאֵחוּר וְרַק אַחַר הַמָּוֶת.

כִּי רַק בְּחֶרֶב לְמֶחֱצָה נָבִין אֶת
תְּכֵלֶת פְּנִים הַחֲדָרִים, כְּרוֹפְאִים
הַלּוֹמְדִים לְפִי הַגּוּפוֹת הַפְּעוּרוֹת לִפְנֵיהֶם,
אַךְ לְעוֹלָם לֹא נֵדַע אֵיךְ הַדָּם מִתְנַהֵג,
כְּשֶׁהוּא בִּפְנִים, בַּשֵּׁלֶם, כְּשֶׁהַלֵּב מֵאִיר אוֹתוֹ
מֵרָחוֹק בְּדַרְכּוֹ הָאֲפֵלָה, וַעֲדַיִן נְעָרוֹת
מִסְתָּרוֹת בֵּין הַכְּבָסִים הַתְּלוּיִים בָּאֲוִיר
שֶׁגַּם הוּא יֵהָפֵךְ לְגֶשֶׁם בֵּין שְׁלוּחוֹת
הֶהָרִים אֲשֶׁר נִשְׁלְחוּ לָרֶגֶל וּלְגַלּוֹת אֶת עֶרְוַת
הָאָרֶץ, וְגָלוּ וְנִשְׁאֲרוּ לָעַד בַּעֲמָקִים.

Yehuda Amichai, Shirim: 1948–1962 (Jerusalem and Tel Aviv: Schocken, [1963] 2002),
pp. 363–65.

Appendix B

MAP OF WUERZBURG

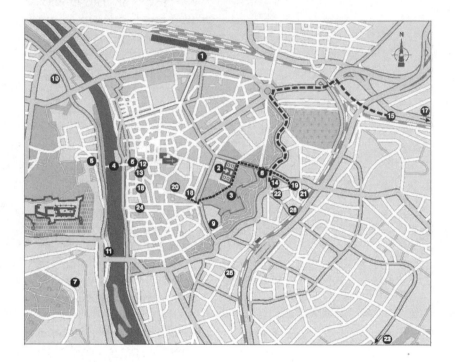

LEGEND:

Public Buildings:
1. Main train station and Kilian's fountain
2. Residenz (the palace)
3. The Hofgarten
4. The old Main Bridge
5. Vierroehren Fountain
6. First Memorial for Baron Zobel
7. Kaeppele
8. Statue of Valentin Becker

Stops on the Narrator's Journey:
9. Courthouse
10. Castle
11. Rollschuhplatz
12. Butcher shop, Domstrasse 4
13. Passageway and the Café Cabinet
14. Platz'scher Garden
15. Cargo train station

Former Jewish Buildings:
16. Synagogue complex and school, Domerschulstrasse 21
17. Road to the Jewish cemetery
18. Amichai's birthplace, Augustinerstrasse 9
19. Amichai's former apartment on Alleestrasse 11
20. Samuel and Friedrich Pfeuffer's store, Domerschulstrasse 13
21. Ruth Hanover's apartment, Alleestrasse 20
22. Lore Kleemann's apartment, Alleestrasse 4
23. The road to Gut Keesburg
24. Ricka Goldbach's and Henrietta's apartment
25. Samuel Pfeuffer's apartment, Friedenstrasse 35
26. Jewish old-age home
   ▬▬▬▬ Road of the deportation, April 25, 1942
   -------- Amichai's road to school

Source: Christian Leo, *Zwischen Erinnern und Vergessen: Jehuda Amichais Roman "Nicht von jetzt, nicht von hier" im philosophischen und literarischen Kontext* (Between remembering and forgetting: Yehuda Amichai's novel *Not of This Time, Not of This Place*, in the philosophical and literary context) (Wuerzburg: Koenigshausen und Neumann, 2004), 258. Reproduced by permission of Christian Leo and Winfried Weber, Geographisches Institut, Wuerzburg.

Notes

1. INTRODUCTION (PP. 1–24)

1. Yehuda Amichai, "The Rustle of History's Wings, as They Said Then," *The Great Tranquility: Questions and Answers*, trans. Glenda Abramson and Tudor Parfitt (New York: Sheep Meadow Press, 1997), 22 (subsequently, GT). Originally published as *Shalva gedola: she'elot uteshuvot* (Tel Aviv: Schocken, 1980). This poem will subsequently be cited as "History's Wings."

2. Yehuda Amichai Papers. General Collection, Beinecke Rare Book and Manuscript Library, Yale University, New Haven, Conn. (subsequently, Amichai papers / Beinecke). There were 34 boxes in the precatalogued archive with consecutively numbered files in each box. References to these materials cite the uncatalogued box number and file number.

3. Yehuda Amichai, *Akhshav uvayamim ha'aherim* (Now and in Other Days) (Tel Aviv: Likrat Press, 1955).

4. Yehuda Amichai's letters to Ruth Z. (August 31, 1947–April 11, 1948) will be housed at Hayisre'elim harishonim (First Israelis Archive), Heksherim: The Research Center for Jewish and Israeli Literature and Culture, Ben-Gurion University of the Negev. References cite the number of the letter (as given by Amichai) and the date. Letters to Ruth Z., #6, September 9, 1947; #8, September 14, 1947; #21, October 14–15, 1947. In these letters, Amichai discusses using the letters as an archive to record their love affair.

5. Ruth Z., conversation with author, May 2003; "History's Wings"; Boaz Cohen, "Don't Call Me a National Poet" (interview with Amichai), *Yedi'ot Aharonot*, September 24, 2000; Corinna Benning, interview with Amichai, Bavarian radio station BR Alpha, May 4, 1998. Full interview in Christian Leo, *Zwischen Erinnern und Vergessen: Jehuda Amichais Roman "Nicht von jetzt, nicht von hier" im philosophischen und literarischen Kontext* (Wuerzburg, Germany: Koenigshausen und Neumann, 2004), 247–57 (subsequently, *Between Remembering and Forgetting*).

6. Ruth Z., conversations with author, July 13, 2004, and December 13, 2004.

7. "History's Wings."

8. Yehuda Amichai, "A Meeting with My Father," GT, 7.

9. Cohen, "Don't Call Me a National Poet."

10. Yehudit Tzvik, ed., "Dates and Turning Points in Amichai's Life," in *Yehuda Amichai: mivhar ma'amare bikoret al yetsirato* (Yehuda Amichai: A Selection of Critical Essays on His Writings) (Tel Aviv: Hakibbutz Hameuchad, 1988), 237–39.

11. Amichai papers / Beinecke, box 10, file 150. Proof that Amichai took part in supplying the dates in the monograph are handwritten drafts (in both Hebrew and English) of the biography and the list of dates that are found in the monograph.

12. Yehuda Amichai, "Other Evenings," *Gilyonot* 25, no. 12 (1951): 350.

13. Glenda Abramson's translation is included in Gershon Shaked, "Amichai and the Likrat Group: The Early Amichai and His Literary Reference Group," in *The Experienced Soul*, ed. Glenda Abramson (Boulder, Colo.: Westview Press, 1997), 93–120.

14. Yehuda Amichai, *Shirim: 1948–1962* (Poems: 1948–1962) (Tel Aviv: Schocken, 1963) (subsequently, *Poems: 1948–1962*). All page references are to the 2002 edition. English translations for most of these poems appear in *The Selected Poetry of Yehuda Amichai*, trans. Chana Bloch and Stephen Mitchell (Berkeley and Los Angeles: University of California Press, 1996) (subsequently, SP) and in *Yehuda Amichai: A Life of Poetry 1948–1994*, ed. and trans. Benjamin Harshav and Barbara Harshav (New York: HarperCollins, 1994) (subsequently, LOP). If no references to the English translations are cited, it is because there are no English translations for that poem.

15. Glenda Abramson, *The Writing of Yehuda Amichai: A Thematic Approach* (Albany: SUNY Press, 1989), 13–18.

16. Nili Scharf Gold, "Images in Transformation in the Recent Poetry of Yehuda Amichai," *Prooftexts* 4 (1984): 141–52. This idea was subsequently developed by Gold in "Text of Deceit" (Ph.D. diss., Jewish Theological Seminary of America, 1990), 249–332; *Lo kabrosh: gilgule imagim vetavniyot beshirat Yehuda Amichai* (Not Like a Cypress: Transformations of Images and Structures in the Poetry of Yehuda Amichai) (Tel Aviv and Jerusalem: Schocken, 1994), 117–75; and "And the Vows Are Not Vows: On Amichai's Later Poetry," *Siman Kri'a*, Tel Aviv University, no. 22 (1991): 361–78.

17. "What Did I Learn in the Wars," LOP, 411.

18. Dahlia Karpel, "Hoping for the Nobel Prize" (interview with Amichai), *Ha'ir*, November 3, 1989: 23–24, 89; Dan Omer, "In This Burning Country, Words Must Serve as Shade" (series of interviews with Amichai), *Proza*, no. 25 (July 1978): 4–11; Aryeh Arad, "Bells Announcing Bad Tidings: The Poet Yehuda Amichai Tells of His Childhood in Southern Germany," *Bamahane* (n.d. [most likely the 1960s]): 18–19, 39.

19. Karpel, "Hoping for the Nobel Prize," 23.

20. John R. Schwabacher and Susan Wolfe, *Remembering* (New York: iUniverse, 2003), 3.

21. Norbert Hellmann, interview with author, December 16, 2004.

22. Official list of the texts printed in the German *Volksschulbuecher* during the beginning of the 1930s. Amtsblatt des Bayerischen Staatsministerium fuer Unterricht und Kultus (Bavarian Ministry of Education) (no. 4, 755), 12–13. For the similarity to the Jewish school curriculum, see Joseph Walk, *Juedische Schule und Erziehung im Dritten Reich* (Frankfurt on Main: Hain Verlag, 1991), 80 f; 85–7; 145–48; and Roland Flade, *Die Wuerzburger Juden* (Wuerzburg, Germany: Stuertz Verlag, 1987), 286 f.

23. Theodor Wilhelm, *Paedagogik der Gegenwart*, Auflage 4 (Stuttgart: Kroener Verlag, 1967); Wolfgang Scheibe, *Die Reformpaedagogische Bewegung 1900–1932: Eine einfuehrende Darstellung*. Auflage 9 (Weinheim Basel: 1984). Collectively, the curriculum was called *Heimatkundlicher Sachunterricht*.

24. Omer, "In This Burning Country," 4; Arad, "Bells Announcing Bad Tidings," 18.

25. Leo, *Between Remembering and Forgetting*, 101; Rosa Grimm, interview with author, October 2004; Claudia Schulke, "Spurensuche und lyrisches Ich,'" *Frankfurter Allgemeiner Zeitung*, February 23, 1992.

26. Letters to Ruth Z., #85, March 7, 1948; #51, December 17, 1947. In both letters, Amichai cites Rilke's assertion that artists must draw upon their childhood to support his own belief in the artistic role of childhood.

27. Gershon Shaked was one exception to this rule, but as he was focused primarily on prose, he examined the novel's ties to the artist's childhood without emphasizing the absence of that childhood in the poetry. See Gershon Shaked, *Gal hadash basiporet ha'ivrit* (A New Wave in Hebrew Fiction) (Tel Aviv: Sifriyat Po'alim, 1971), 89–124.

28. "Hebrew literature" refers to works written in Hebrew before and after the establishment of the State of Israel in 1948; "Israeli literature" refers to works written in Israel after 1948.

29. Boaz Arpaly, "On the Political Significance of Amichai's Poetry," in Abramson, ed., *The Experienced Soul*, 27–50. Arpaly's name is spelled differently in the two sources cited in this book. I defer to the spelling of each source.

30. Shaked, "Amichai and the Likrat Group," 93.

31. Lea Goldberg, "'Ad barzel'; On Yehuda Amichai: Upon Receiving the Shlonsky Prize," *Al Hamishmar*, July 26, 1957; as quoted in ibid., 104–5.

32. Dan Tseleka, *Encyclopedia Judaica* vol. 2 (Jerusalem: Keter, 1971), 838.

33. LOP, "Now When the Water Presses Hard," / "I Want to Die in My Own Bed," 21, 37.

34. Yehuda Amichai, "Through Two Points, Only One Straight Line Can Pass," SP, 13.

35. Ibid., 10.

36. Arpaly, "On the Political Significance," 34–36.

37. Amichai received the prize in 1982. The judges' decision is quoted in full in Beni Tzifer, "Two Scales, Major and Minor, Gilboa and Amichai," *Ha'aretz*, November 13, 1981.

38. Ted Hughes, as quoted by the Institute for the Translation of Hebrew Literature, at http://www.ithl.org.il/amichai (accessed February 15, 2007).

39. Eyal Meged, "Towards the End You Become Simpler," *Yedi'ot Aharonot*, November 8, 1985; Esther Fuchs, "I Am a Man Who Writes Poems" (interview with Amichai, Austin, Texas, March 22, 1982) in *Encounters with Israeli Authors* (Marblehead, Mass.: Micah Publications, 1982), 86–92, 89; Arad, "Bells Announcing Bad Tidings," 19.

40. Yoram Bronowsky, obituary for Yehuda Amichai, *Ha'aretz*, September 22, 2000; Mel Gussow, "Yehuda Amichai, Poet Who Turned Israel's Experience into Verse, Dies at 76," *New York Times*, September 23, 2000.

41. "Poem #32," LOP, 279.

42. Yehuda Amichai, "Autobiography 1952," *Likrat* 2 (August 1952): 13.

43. LOP, 7.

44. "Poem #32," LOP, 279.

45. Gershon Shaked, *Hasiporet ha'ivrit 1880–1980* (Hebrew Narrative Fiction: 1880–1980), vol. 4 (Tel Aviv and Jerusalem: Hakibbutz Hameuchad and Keter, 1988), 15–16 (subsequently, *Hebrew Narrative Fiction*).

46. Ibid., vol. 3, 235.

47. Ibid., vol. 4, 72.

48. Abramson, *The Writing of Yehuda Amichai*, 17.

49. Amichai papers / Beinecke, box 19, file 274, notebook from November 30, 1965, "Autobiography" (unpublished Hebrew poem).

50. Shaked, *Hebrew Narrative Fiction*, vol. 4, 71–76.

51. LOP, 411.

52. *Poems: 1948–1962*, 201.

53. Ibid., 99.

54. This translation combines the translation in LOP, 4, and Arieh Sachs's translation in *Modern Poetry in Translation*, no. 1, ed. Ted Hughes and Daniel Weissbort (London: Cape Goliard Press, 1965), 1–3.

55. Yehuda Amichai, interview with author, June 23, 1996.

56. Amichai papers / Beinecke, box 1, file 15. In this book, the spelling follows the new standard German spelling, using a *ue* instead of the customary umlaut. In the archival fragment, Amichai used the traditional spelling. When referring to the fragment, I will use Amichai's spelling.

57. Leon Wieseltier, "Yehuda Amichai: Posthumous Fragments," *New York Times*, November 21, 2004.

58. Yehuda Amichai, "Generations in the Land" (text of a speech given at the *Agudat hasofrim* [author's guild] conference), Tel Aviv, *Lamerhav*, May 3, 1968.

59. Baruch Kurzweil, "Autobiographic Poetry in the Great Desert," *Ha'aretz*, July 12, 1963, 10.

60. Yotam Re'uveni, "Yehuda Amichai" (interview with Amichai), *Yedi'ot Aharonot*, May 1985; Omer, "In This Burning Country," 7.

61. Re'uveni, "Yehuda Amichai."

62. Michael Miro, "Writing is the Product of Wonderful Laziness" (interview with Amichai), *Pi Ha'aton*, March 19, 1978.

63. Yehuda Amichai, "To Live Reality," *Ha'aretz*, November 30, 1973.

64. Arad, "Bells Announcing Bad Tidings," 18; Norbert Hellmann, interview with author, December 16, 2004.

65. Zehava Mendelssohn, interview with Amichai in the *Jerusalem Post Magazine*, February 12, 1971, 12; Amichai, interview with author, June 23, 1996.

66. Yehuda A[michai]. Holocaust Testimony (HVT-2679), interview conducted by Geoffrey Hartman and Benjamin Harshav, November 3, 1994, Fortunoff Video Archive for Holocaust Testimonies, Yale University Library; Benny Morris, "Power of Imagination," *Jerusalem Post, 40th Independence Day Magazine*, April 20, 1988, 24.

67. Yehuda A[michai]. Holocaust Testimony.

68. Benning interview in Leo, *Between Remembering and Forgetting*, 247.

69. Gold, "And the Vows Are Not Vows," 361–78, 363.

70. "A Poet," *Poems: 1948–1962*, 146: "... he would only write in the meantime / until he finds what he really wants to do." These lines imply that he did not want or intend to become a poet. "Consecration of a Prophet in an Army Camp," in *Poems: 1948–1962*, 92; see also Meged, "Towards the End You Become Simpler"; Fuchs, "I Am a Man Who Writes Poems," 89; Arad, "Bells Announcing Bad Tidings," 19.

71. Yehuda Amichai, *Gam ha'egrof haya pa'am yad petuha ve'etsba'ot* (Even the Fist Was Once an Open Palm and Fingers) (Tel Aviv: Schocken, 1989), 70.

72. Ibid., 70; LOP, 411.

73. LOP, 411.

74. Yehuda Amichai, *Patu'ah, sagur, patu'ah* (Open Closed Open) (Tel Aviv: Schocken, 1998).

75. Meged, "Towards the End You Become Simpler."

76. Letters to Ruth Z., #31, November 7, 1947; #46, December 7, 1947; #53, December 21, 1947.

77. Letter to Ruth Z., #82, February 28, 1948.

78. Rainer Maria Rilke, *Die Weise von Liebe und Tod des Cornets Christoph Rilke*, trans. Alfred Perles (1899; London: Turret Books, 1987).

2. CHILDHOOD IN WUERZBURG (PP. 26–46)

1. "Israelischer Autor mit Erinnerungen an Wuerzburg," *Volksblatt*, Office for Public Relations (Amt fuer Offentlichkeit und Statistik), press release dated August 5, 1991. In interviews with the German media, especially later in his life, Amichai spoke at length about his memories of Wuerzburg, its landscapes, and the strong bond he felt with it. He tended to camouflage this connection when talking to the Israeli media.

2. Egon Johannes Greipl, ed., *Fenster zur Vergangenheit (Photographs of Old Wuerzburg 1860–1925)* from the photo archive of the Office of Bavarian Landmarks (Munich: Bayerisches Landesamt fuer Denkmalpflege, 2004), 81, picture 39 (subsequently, *Photographs of Old Wuerzburg*). See also Christian Leo, *Zwischen Erinnern und Vergessen: Jehuda Amichais Roman "Nicht von jetzt, nicht von hier" im philosophischen und literarischen Kontext* (Wuerzburg, Germany: Koenigshausen und Neumann, 2004), 150–51 (subsequently, *Between Remembering and Forgetting*).

3. Greipl, *Photographs of Old Wuerzburg*, 47, 49.

4. Zvi Avneri, *Encyclopedia Judaica*, vol. 16 (Jerusalem: Keter Publishing, 1974), s.v. "Wuerzburg," 675–76.

5. Erich Hubala, Otto Mayer, and Wolf Christian von der Muelbe, *Die Residenz zu Wuerzburg* (Wuerzburg, Germany: Edition Popp, 1984), 13.

6. Erich Bachmann, Burkard von Roda, and Werner Helmberger, *Residenz und Hofgarten Wuerzburg*, Auflage 13 (Munich: Bayerische Verw., 2001), 10–37.

7. Avneri, *Encyclopedia Judaica*, "Wuerzburg."

8. Karlheinz Mueller, interviews with author, July 2001; Karlheinz Mueller, *Die Wuerzburger Judengemeinde im Mittelalter* (Wuerzburg, Germany: Freunde Mainfränkischer Kunst und Geschichte, 2004), 125–37. During the demolition of a monastery's wall in 1987, Mueller discovered fragments of Jewish tombstones from before the fourteenth century. Over one thousand tombstones were reconstructed.

9. Roland Flade, *Die Wuerzburger Juden* (Wuerzburg, Germany: Stuertz Verlag, 1987), 143–58 (subsequently, *The Jews of Wuerzburg*).

10. John R. Schwabacher and Susan Wolfe, *Remembering* (New York: Universe, 2003), 5.

11. Henry Eschwege, interview with author, February 23, 2005. For firsthand recollections of Wuerzburg's Jewish community, I interviewed the following people who grew up there: Ludwig Bravman, interviewed July 14, 2005; Elizabeth Cecchetti (formerly Ruth Schwabacher), November 1, 2002, and December 18, 2002, plus letter, March 29, 2004; Mordechai Einsbacher, December 10, 2004; Henry (formerly Hans) Eschwege, February 1, 2005, February 23, 2005; Norbert Hellmann, December 16, 2004, series of interviews July 7–31, 2005; Ruth Kobliner (née Katzmann), letters: September 23, 2002, and September 24, 2002, telephone interviews: October 4, 2002, October 29, 2002, November 10, 2002; Otto Schlame, November 17, 2002; Bill (formerly Wolfgang) Schwabacher, July 12, 2002, October 24, 2004, letter: October 6, 2004. These interviews and letters are subsequently cited using only the interviewee's surname and the interview date.

12. Hans Steidle, *Jakob Stoll und die Israelitische Lehrerbildungsanstalt: Eine Spurensuche Israelitische Kultusgemeinde Wuerzburg* (Wuerzburg, Germany: Koenigshausen und Neumann, 2003). The Israelitische Lehrerbildungsanstalt (ILBA) in Wuerzburg was the regional Jewish teacher's college. It had a strictly Orthodox orientation and trained cantors and elementary school teachers.

13. Christoph Daxelmueller and Roland Flade, *Ruth hat auf einer schwarzen Floete gespielt: Geschichte, Alltag und Kultur der Juden in Wuerzburg* (Wuerzburg, Germany: Echter Verlag GmbH, 2005) 28, 30, 32 (subsequently, *Ruth Played on a Black Flute*); Flade, *The Jews of Wuerzburg*, 172.

14. Flade, *The Jews of Wuerzburg*, 170.

15. Ibid., 173.

16. Ibid., 187.

17. Ibid., 90.

18. Norbert Hellmann, "Jewish Life in Wuerzburg (pre–World War II)," *Mitteilungen* (Rosh Hashanah 5755 [1995]): 25–30.

19. Hellmann, December 16, 2004.

20. Kobliner, October 4, 2002; Eschwege, February 1, 2005.

21. Hellmann, "Jewish Life in Wuerzburg," 27. *Nusach* means the style of a prayer service, usually either Ashkenaz or Sepharad.

22. Hellmann, December 16, 2004.

23. Hellmann, "Jewish Life in Wuerzburg," 25.

24. Georg Rentner, *Wesenszuege und Wandlungen des literarischen Kanons in den deutschen Volksschulbuechern*, ed. Joachim S. Hohmann (Frankfurt on Main: 1993), 124–26; Wolfgang Hegele, *Literaturunterricht und literarisches Leben in Deutschland (1850–1990)* (Wuerzburg, Germany: Historische Darstellung-Systematische Erklaerung, 1996), 34–39.

25. Flade, *The Jews of Wuerzburg*, 195–96; Daxelmueller and Flade, *Ruth Played on a Black Flute*, 57.

26. Archives of the Jewish community of Wuerzburg, old files number WR 576-79 (subsequently cited as Archives of the Jewish Community).

27. The biblical description of Yehuda as a lion cub, "*gur arye Yehuda,*" is the source of the association. Gersfeld Jews used the Weyhers cemetery, 20 kilometers away. When the author visited it in October 2004, she saw many Wahlhaus tombstones; a Yehuda Wahlhaus who died in the nineteenth century might have been Yehuda Pfeuffer's namesake.

28. From Yehuda Amichai's speech upon receiving the Kulturpreis (cultural prize) in Wuerzburg, June 22, 1981, as quoted in *Main Post*, August 5, 1991, and in Roland Flade, "Reliving Childhood at Saint Kilian's Festival," *Allgemeine Juedische Wochenzeitung* (Bonn), no. 35, August 29, 1991. (The speech is subsequently cited as "Kulturpreis speech.") See also the photograph in Werner Dettelbacher, *Damals in Wuerzburg: Bilddokumente aus der Zeit von 1914–1945* (Wuerzburg, Germany: Steurz, 1971), 132.

29. Yehuda Amichai, "When I Was a Child," in Shirim: 1948–1962 (Poems: 1948–1962) (Tel Aviv: Schocken, 1963), 11 (subsequently, *Poems: 1948–1962*). Page references are to the 2002 Hebrew edition. The English translation for this poem can be found in *The Selected Poetry of Yehuda Amichai*, trans. Chana Bloch and Stephen Mitchell (Berkeley and Los Angeles: University of California Press, 1996), 6 (subsequently, SP). SP translates *hof* (shore) as "seashore." If references to the English translations are not cited, it is because no published English translations are available.

30. Hans Steidle, "Rueckkehr an einen Ort, an den man nicht zurueckkehren kann," in *Ein kleines Geburtstags-praesent aus Wuerzburg: Festgabe fuer Jehuda Amichai zum 75 Geburtstag*, ed. Hans Steidle (Wuerzburg, Germany: Verlag der Leonhard-Frank-Gesellschaft, 1999), 24 (subsequently, *A Small Birthday Present from Wuerzburg*); Leo, *Between Remembering and Forgetting*, 81

31. Rosa Grimm, series of interviews with author, October 1–4, 2004; Corinna Benning, interview with Yehuda Amichai, May 4, 1998, on Bavarian radio station BR Alpha. The full transcript of the interview appears in Leo, *Between Remembering and Forgetting*, 247–57.

32. Yehuda Amichai, "Throw Pillows," in *Even a Fist Was Once an Open Palm with Fingers*, ed. and trans. Benjamin and Barbara Harshav (New York: HarperCollins, 1991), 70.

33. Housing Registry in the City Archive of Wuerzburg, Augustinerstrassse 8, November 8, 1920, and August 18, 1920.

34. Aryeh Arad, "Bells Announcing Bad Tidings: The poet Yehuda Amichai Tells of His Childhood in Southern Germany" (interview with Amichai), *Bamahane* (N.d. [most likely the 1960s]).

35. Angela Sey, "Interview," interview with Amichai, *Das Aktuelle*, 1992, 17; Greipl, *Photographs of Old Wuerzburg*, 133; author's visit to Wuerzburg, October 3, 2004. *Vierroehren* means "four pipes."

36. Elmar Hahn and Joseph Kern, *Wuerzburg* (Wuerzburg, Germany: Elmar Habn, 1999), 52–53.

37. Flade, "Reliving Childhood at Saint Kilian's Festival"; Hans Steidle, ed., *A Small Birthday Present from Wuerzburg*, 24; Werner Dettelbacher, "Die Geschichte des Ludwig Pfeuffer," in Steidle, ed., *A Small Birthday Present from Wuerzburg*, 9.

38. Yehuda Amichai, "Lekha dodi," in *Pa'amonim verakavot: mahazot vetaskitim* (Bells and Trains: Plays and Skits), (Tel Aviv: Schocken, 1992), 171–89 (subsequently, *Bells and Trains*).

39. Yehuda Amichai, "Yehuda Amichai," in *Mein Judentum*, ed. Hans Jürgen Schultz (Stuttgart: Kreuz, 1978), 20–35 (subsequently, "Yehuda Amichai").

40. Alvin Kass, *Encyclopedia Judaica*, vol. 15, 1974, s.v. "Wimpel." It is made from the cloth laid under the baby during circumcision. The inscription on it states the most important stations and values of a Jewish life; Eschwege, February 23, 2004. Cantor Eschwege's humorous watercolor illustrations include a boy and a girl underneath a marriage canopy, a Torah scroll, etc.

41. Yehuda Amichai, "The Times My Father Died," in *Baru'ah hanora'a hazot* (In That Terrible Wind) (Tel Aviv: Schocken, 1961), 132–40 (subsequently, "The Times My Father Died"). English translation available in *The World Is A Room and Other Stories by Yehuda Amichai*, trans. Yosef Schachter (Philadelphia: Jewish Publication Society of America, 1984), 185–97. Yehuda Amichai, *Lo me'akhshav lo mikan* (Not of This Time, Not of This Place) (Tel Aviv: Schocken, 1963).

42. Author's visits to Wuerzburg, 2001 and 2004; Amichai, Kulturpreis speech; Arad, "Bells Announcing Bad Tidings," 18.

43. Yehuda Amichai's letters to Ruth Z. (August 31, 1947–April 11, 1948) will be housed at Hayisre'elim harishonim (First Israelis Archive), Heksherim: The Research Center for Jewish and Israeli Literature and Culture, Ben-Gurion University of the Negev. References cite the number of the letter (as given by Amichai) and the date. Letters to Ruth Z., #39, November 23, 1947; #93, undated (letter #92 was dated March 25, 1948, letter #94, April 1).

44. Yehuda Amichai Papers. General Collection. Beinecke Rare Book and Manuscript Library, Yale University, New Haven, Conn. (subsequently, Amichai papers / Beinecke), box 14, file 205, "A Private Space: Yehuda Amichai, a poet" from *Sof Shavu'a*. There were 34 boxes in the precatalogued archive, with consecutively numbered files in each box; references to these materials cite the uncatalogued box number and file number. Cecchetti,

December 18, 2002; Eschwege, February 1 and February 23, 2004; Bravman, July 14, 2005. Yehuda Amichai, *Katholisches Sonntagsblatt*, no. 31, August 2, 1981. A shortened version of this speech is reprinted in Amichai, "Yehuda Amichai," 29.

45. Amichai, "When I Was a Child," *Poems 1948–1962*, 11; SP, 6.

46. Yehuda Amichai, "My Father," *Akhshav uvayamim ha'aherim* (Now and in the Other Days), (Tel Aviv: Likrat Press, 1955), 32.

47. Amichai, "Letter of Recommendation," in *Me'ahore kol ze mistater osher gadol* (Behind All This There is Great Happiness), (Tel Aviv: Schocken, 1976), 41; SP, 101.

48. Dan Omer, "In This Burning Country, Words Must Serve as Shade" (series of interviews with Amichai), *Proza*, no. 25 (July 1978): 4; Amichai papers / Beinecke, box 19, file 277, August 1978–1979; box 19, file 279, notebook 1965–1966.

49. Hellmann, December 16, 2004.

50. Wuerzburg Housing Registry. Records show the Pfeuffers moving in in 1920 and leaving in 1928.

51. Archives of the Jewish Community; Steidle, *A Small Birthday Present from Wuerzburg*, 24.

52. Kobliner, October 4, 2002.

53. Steidle, *A Small Birthday Present from Wuerzburg*, 22.

54. Benning interview, in Leo, *Between Remembering and Forgetting*, 247.

55. Amichai papers / Beinecke, box 4, blue notebook from 1970.

56. Author's visit to Wuerzburg, October 2004.

57. Yehuda A[michai]. Holocaust Testimony (HVT-2679), interview conducted by Geoffrey Hartman and Benjamin Harshav, November 3, 1994, Fortunoff Video Archive for Holocaust Testimonies, Yale University Library.

58. Arad, "Bells Announcing Bad Tidings," 19; Einsbacher, interview with the author, December 10, 2004.

59. Yehuda A[michai]. Holocaust Testimony.

60. "Yehuda and Rachel had an exceptional relationship as children." Kobliner, October 4, 2002.

61. Amichai papers / Beinecke, box 31, folder 385, typed draft of *Every Man Is Born a Poet* (without publication details), 4; box 12; folder 178, draft of an interview with Yehuda Amichai by Doron Weber.

62. Rahel Hollander-Steingart, "In My Heart Is a Museum" (interview with Amichai), *Jerusalem Post, Rosh Hashanah Supplement*, September 28, 1981, 5; Amichai papers / Beinecke, box 12, folder 178, draft of interview with Weber, 7.

63. Amichai, "Uncle David's Photograph," *Poems 1948–1962*, 134; SP, 16.

64. Archives of the Jewish Community.

65. Walter Stumpf, interview with author, October 3, 2004; Kobliner, November 2002; Mr. Wieber, interview with author, October 3, 2004. According to Kobliner, 37 Jewish families were called Wahlhaus.

66. Archives of the Jewish Community. Two dates are given for their marriage. It is possible that July 12, 1920 (Wuerzburg Housing Registry; City Archives), was the official state marriage, while the Jewish ceremony was held on May 13.

67. Amichai papers / Beinecke, box 12, folder 178, draft of interview with Weber, 10; see also box 19, file 278, September 1974 to January 1975.

68. Kobliner, October 4, 2002.

69. Archives of the Jewish Community.

70. Yehuda A[michai]. Holocaust Testimony; Amichai, "Yehuda Amichai," 22–23; Amichai papers / Beinecke, box 12, folder 178, draft of interview with Weber, 7; Omer, "In This Burning Country," 4.

71. Amichai papers / Beinecke, box 31, folder 385, draft of *Every Man Is Born a Poet*, 4.

72. Archives of the Jewish Community. The records show Friedrich Pfeuffer living at Neubaustrasse 14 in May 1906 and his absence during the war; Omer, "In This Burning Country," 4; Yehuda A[michai]. Holocaust Testimony.

73. Amichai papers / Beinecke, box 19, file 278, 1966, "Spoletto" notebook. Amichai refers to this in similar language in a note to himself.

74. Amichai, Kulturpreis speech.

75. Yehuda A[michai], Holocaust Testimony; Yehuda Amichai, interview with author, 1996; Einsbacher, December 19, 2004; Kobliner, October 4, 2002. This incident was retold by most of the interviewees, demonstrating the impact that Friedrich's "joke" had on the community.

76. Yehuda A[michai]. Holocaust Testimony.

77. Amichai, "Yehuda Amichai," 29; Aloma Halter, "Poems, Prayers and Psalms," interview with Amichai in *Contact* (July 26, 1991): 11–12; Ram Evron, interview with Amichai for Israeli Television, 1998.

78. Zehava Mendelssohn, interview with Amichai, *Jerusalem Post Magazine*, February 12, 1971, 12; Kobliner, October 29, 2002; Amichai papers / Beinecke, box 19, file 278, 1966 notebook.

79. Hollander-Steingart, "In My Heart Is a Museum," 5.

80. Amichai, "Yehuda Amichai," 22.

81. Amichai papers / Beinecke, box 31, folder 385, draft of *Every Man Is Born a Poet*.

82. Amichai, "Yehuda Amichai," 25.

83. Arad, "Bells Announcing Bad Tidings," 18; Yehuda A[michai]. Holocaust Testimony; Omer, "In This Burning Country," 4.

84. For information about each member of the community, see Reiner Straetz, *Biographisches Handbuch Wuerzburger Juden 1900–1945* (Wuerzburg, Germany: Verlag Ferdinand Schoeningh, 1989).

85. Shraga Har-Gil, *Alte Liebe Rostet Nie* (Wuerzburg, Germany: Koenigshausen & Neumann, 2004), 56–64. Ehrenhard Skiera, *Reformpaedagogik in Geschichte und Gegenwart: Eine kritische Einfuehrung* (Munich: Wien, 2003), 195–98; Eduard Spranger, *Pestalozzis Denkformen*

(Heidelberg: Quelle und Meyer Verlag, 1959), 35–80; Juergen Zinnecker, "The Problem of Generations: About Karl Mannheim's Canonical Texts," in *Generationswechsel und historischer Wandel*, ed. Andreas Schulz and Gundula Grebner, Historische Zeitschrift, Beiheft 36 (Munich: R. Oldenbourg, 2003), 35–39ff.; Amichai, Kulturpreis speech.

86. Daxelmueller and Flade, *Ruth Played on a Black Flute*, 37; blood libels are accusations that Jews use human blood, especially blood of Christian children, in religious rituals.

87. Amichai, "Yehuda Amichai," 28.

88. Dettelbacher, *Damals in Wuerzburg*, 113. On November 19, 1930, the audience attending a show by the renowned Hebrew-speaking theater troupe Habima was attacked by a mob incited by a local Nazi, shouting, "*Jude verrecke*" (Die with a lot of suffering, Jew). There are conflicting reports as to whether or not the police intervened. Daxelmueller and Flade, *Ruth Played on a Black Flute*, 37; Flade, *The Jews of Wuerzburg*, 250; *Damals in Wuerzburg*, 87.

89. Cecchetti, December 18, 2002.

90. Amichai papers / Beinecke, box 14, file 205.

91. Bravman, July 14, 2005; Schwabacher and Wolfe, *Remembering*, 8.

92. A copy of that photograph appears on the cover of Hans Steidle, ed., *A Small Birthday Present from Wuerzburg*.

93. Letter to Ruth Z., #46, December 7, 1947; Schwabacher, October 2004; Cecchetti, December 18, 2002.

94. Leo, *Between Remembering and Forgetting*, 31, 129, 258; Flade, *The Jews of Wuerzburg*, 355; Daxelmueller and Flade, *Ruth Played on a Black Flute*, 86. The route that they took to school was similar to that of the Jews of Wuerzburg during the third deportation (April 25, 1942).

95. Schwabacher and Wolfe, *Remembering*, 3. The Ring Garten is a circle of gardens that surrounded the old city of Wuerzburg; it was created from the old moat, which was filled in and planted with flowers and trees.

96. The school year started May 1, 1930, and ended March 28, 1931. The Jewish Volksschule began one week after Easter, in accordance with the new Prussian schedule adopted by Bavaria. Werner Dettelbacher, "Jugendjahre in der Sanderau und im Frauenland," in *Meine Jugend in Wuerzburg*, ed. Roland Flade (Wuerzburg, Germany: Mainpresse Zeitungsverlags Gesellschaft, 2000), 99; Theodor Wilhelm, "Der reformpaedagogische Impuls: Bildungspolitik, Schulreform, Bildungsreform am Beginn der Zwanziger Jahre," in *"Neue Erziehung"-"Neue Menschen": Ansaetze zur Erziehungs- und Bildungsreform in Deutschland zwischen Kaiserreich und Diktatur*, ed. Ulrich Herrmann (Basel: Weinheim, 1987), 178, p.180ff.; Photograph (1935–1936) courtesy of Elizabeth Cecchetti. She is sitting on the middle bench in a plaid dress with a white collar.

97. Leo, *Between Remembering and Forgetting*, 258; Hellmann, July 7, 2005.

98. Hellmann, July 7, 2005.

99. Ibid.; Schwabacher, July 12, 2002.

100. Hellmann, July 7, 2005. There is no archival material regarding this curriculum, as the school was completely destroyed. It is hard to know what religious knowledge Amichai gained in Israel and what in Wuerzburg.

101. "I definitely did not learn modern Hebrew in school," Bravman, July 14, 2005. "The study was a translation, word for word, not even sentence by sentence. . . . The instruction of modern Hebrew became a part of the curriculum only in the mid-thirties when going to Palestine became an escape from the Nazis." Eschwege, February 1, 2005. Other classmates confirmed this: Schwabacher, July 12, 2002; Hellmann, December 16, 2004; Cecchetti, December 18, 2002.

102. Hellmann, December 16, 2004.

103. Cecchetti, December 18, 2002; Schwabacher, July 12, 2002.

104. Amtsblatt des Bayerischen Staatsministerium fuer Unterricht und Kultus (Nr. IV 755), 12–13 (henceforth, Bavarian Ministry of Education). For the similarity between the Jewish and Bavarian school curricula, see Joseph Walk, *Juedische Schule und Erziehung im Dritten Reich* (Frankfurt on Main: Hain Verlag, 19910, 8off., 85–87, 145–48ff.; and Flade, *The Jews of Wuerzburg*, 286ff.

105. Bavarian Ministry of Education, May 24, 1924: Prussian edict for a new concept of reading books. Wolfgang Scheibe, *Die Reformpaedagogische Bewegung 1900–1932: Eine einfuehrende Darstellung* (Basel: Weinheim, 1994 [1969]), 273–77. Wilhelm, "Der reformpaedagogische Impuls."

106. Collectively, the curriculum was called *Heimatkundlicher Sachunterricht*. Theodor Wilhelm, *Paedagogik der Gegenwart* Auflage 4 (Stuttgart: 1967); Scheibe, *Die Reformpaedagogische Bewegung 1900–1932*. The following are textbooks, published by Oldenbourg Verlag Muencher (Munich): Hans Stieglitz, et al., eds., *Lesebuch fuer den 2. und 3. Schuelerjahrgang katholischer Volkshauptschulen Bayerns* (1927); Wilhelm Ledermann, et al., eds., *Lesebuch fuer den 4. und 5. Schuelerjahrgang katholischer Volkshauptschulen Bayerns*, Auflage 4. (1930 [1927]); Joseph Prestel, et al., eds., *Lesebuch fuer den 6. und 7. Schuelerjahrgang katholischer Volkshauptschulen Bayerns* (1927).

107. See the following, published by Stuertz Verlag (Wuerzburg), edited by Markus Koch: *Deutsche Singfibel fuer das 1, und 2. Schuljahr der Grundschule: Ministeriell genehmigt, 5, unveraenderte Auflage* (1930 [1927]); *Singbuechlein fuer den 3, und 4, Schuelerjahrgang der Grundschule: Ministeriell genehmigt 2, unveraenderte Auflage* (1927); *Singbuechlein fuer den 5, bis 8. Schuelerjahrgang der Grundschule: Ministeriell genehmigt* (1927).

108. Amichai often wrote about them in his letters to Ruth Z; for example, letter #19, October 10, 1947.

109. Letters to Ruth Z., #5, September 7, 1947; #52; December 19, 1947; #68, January 25, 1948; #86, March 10, 1948; #37, November 18, 1947; #43; November 29, 1947.

110. Ruth Z., interview with author, August 29, 2004.

111. The original Brothers Grimm rhyme is in the German translation of Amichai's novel, *Nicht von jetzt, nicht von hier*, trans. Ruth Achlama (Zurich: Pendo Verlag AG, 1988 [1992]), 122.

112. Arad, "Bells Announcing Bad Tidings," 19.

113. Lederman, et al., *Lesebuch fuer den 4 und 5.*

114. Amichai, interview with author, June 23, 1996.

115. Schwabacher, July 12, 2002; Schlame, November 2002; Arad, "Bells Announcing Bad Tidings," 18; Cecchetti, March 29, 2004; Bravman, July 14, 2005; Omer, "In This Burning Country," 4; Kobliner, October 4, 2002.

116. Letter to Ruth Z., #53, December 21, 1947.

117. Amichai papers / Beinecke, box 19, file 278, March 7, 1987.

118. Simon Berlinger, "ILBA—Wuerzburg: Rueckblick eines Absolventen," in *"Denn das Sterben des Menschen hoert nie auf . . .": Aspekte juedischen Lebens in Vergangenheit und Gegenwart*, ed. Ulrich Wagner (Wuerzburg: Schriften des Stadtarchivs Wuerzburg. Heft 11, 1997), 64; Hellmann, December 16, 2004.

119. Hollander-Steingart, "In My Heart is a Museum," 5; Hellmann, December 16, 2004; Arad, "Bells Announcing Bad Tidings."

120. Eschwege, February 23, 2004. Jafet and Levandowsky are renowned composers of Jewish cantorial music.

121. Amichai, *Lekha Dodi*, in *Bells and Trains: Plays and Skits.*

122. Arad, "Bells Announcing Bad Tidings," 19.

123. Letter to Ruth Z., #46, December 7, 1947; Eschwege, February 1, 2005.

124. Hellmann, December 16, 2004; Eschwege, February 1, 2005.

125. Flade, *The Jews of Wuerzburg*, 195–96; Skiera, *Reformpaedagogik in Geschichte und Gegenwart*, 68–76. Esra was a German-Jewish organization that supported Jewish agricultural settlement in Erez Yisrael.

126. Brith Halutzim Datiyim means Association of Religious Pioneers.Edith Raim, "Verfolgung und Exil der Juedischen Familie Hanover aus Wuerzburg," in *Mainfraenkisches Jahrbuch fuer Geschichte und Kunst*, no. 56 (Wuerzburg: Freunde Maintraenkischer Kunst and Geschichte E.V., 2004), 317–37 (subsequently cited as "Wandering and Exile").

127. Hellmann, December 16, 2004.

128. He also knew Veitshoechheim, the baroque summer castle of the prince-bishops, with one of the last European rococo gardens. Amichai, *Katholisches Sonntagsblatt*.

129. Letter to Ruth Z., #22, October 16, 1947.

130. Amichai, "Yehuda Amichai," 24.

131. Schlame, November 2002; Hellmann, "Jewish Life in Wuerzburg," 26.

132. Amichai, interview with author, June 23, 1996. Amichai remembered the inner rhythm of the rabbi's German speeches and the music of his sentences.

133. Amichai, "Yehuda Amichai," 26.

134. Yehuda A[michai]. Holocaust Testimony. For artistic descriptions of the wine harvest, see Leonhard Frank, *Die Raeuberbande* (Bibliothek des 20. Jahrhunderts herausgegeben von Walter Jens und Marcel Reich-Ranicki) (Stuttgart and Munich: Nymphenburger

Verlagshandlung, 1975), 7; Heribert Schenk, *Das Frankenweinbrevier* (Wuerzburg, Germany: Pius Halbig, 1959).

135. Amichai papers / Beinecke, box 1, file 15; box 19, file 277, loose paper inside a dark brown notebook.

136. Amichai papers / Beinecke, box 19, file 277, January 9, 1966.

137. "The Travels of Benjamin the Last, of Tudela," in *Akhshav bara'ash: shirim 1963–1968* (Now in the Storm: Poems 1963–1968), (Tel Aviv: Schocken, [1968] 1975), 97–139 (subsequently, *Now in the Storm*). Translated into English in Yehuda Amichai, *Yehuda Amichai: A Life of Poetry 1948–1994*, ed. and trans. Benjamin Harshav and Barbara Harshav (New York: HarperCollins, 1994), 160 (subsequently, LOP).

138. Schwabacher, July 12, 2002; Schlame, November 2002.

139. Amichai papers / Beinecke, box 4, file 65, red pad without a date.

140. Yehuda Amichai, "The Times My Father Died," 132–33; Amichai, *The World Is a Room*, 185.

141. The memorial prayer, *Yizkor*, is recited on the last day of Passover, Shavu'ot, Shmini Azeret, and Yom Kippur. Most children must leave, as they usually have both parents, except those who have to "remember" their dead parent; Amichai, "Yehuda Amichai," 25. Arad, "Bells Announcing Bad Tidings," 19.

142. Included in the evening prayer of Yom Kippur.

143. Letter to Ruth Z., #11, September 24, 1947.

144. Schlame, November 2002.

145. Amichai, "Yehuda Amichai," 25.

146. Ibid.; Hellmann, December 16, 2004; Einsbacher, December 10, 2004.

147. Yehuda Amichai, "Exodus." This short story first appeared in *Lamerhav, Masa* under the title "On Haggadah and Exodus," April 4, 1958, 7. It was later collected in *Baru'ah hanora'a hazot* (In That Terrible Wind), 247–55.

148. Amichai, "Yehuda Amichai," 25.

149. Omer, "In This Burning Country," 4.

150. Letter to Ruth Z., #46, December 7, 1947.

151. Arad, "Bells Announcing Bad Tidings," 19; Letter to Ruth Z. #19, October 10, 1947.

152. The statue, called "Jesus am Oelburg," was built in 1732.

153. Omer, "In This Burning Country," 4.

154. Kobliner, November 2002; Schlame, November 2002; Einsbacher, December 10, 2004.

155. Dahlia Karpel, "Hoping for the Nobel Prize" (interview with Amichai), *Ha'ir*, November 3, 1989; letter to Ruth Z., #46, December 7, 1947; Omer, "In This Burning Country," 4; Arad, "Bells Announcing Bad Tidings," 19.

156. Raim, "Wandering and Exile," 317; Daxelmueller and Flade, *Ruth Played on a Black Flute*, 66. There is now an inscription for Little Ruth on Klara Hanover's tombstone in Wuerzburg.

157. Raim, "Wandering and Exile," 19; Straetz, *Biographisches Handbuch Wuerzburger Juden*; Kobliner, November 2002.

158. Daxelmueller and Flade, *Ruth Played on a Black Flute*, 37.

159. Dettelbacher, *Damals in Wuerzburg*, 114. The inscription was "One nation, one life, one will, 1914–1933." War veterans and Nazi party veterans participated; Jews were excluded.

160. Ibid., 117. The police warned the editor that the Nazis would take over the newspaper. On April 20, 1934 (Hitler's birthday), the editor was arrested and there was a spontaneous attack on the newspaper.

161. Ibid., 113, 115–16.

162. Arad, "Bells Announcing Bad Tidings," 18. As Amichai described it, "To this day, I'm afraid of churches. I have in regard to them a feeling of terrible stress. I always feel a feeling of all Jews that the sound of a church bell brings bad tidings always."

163. Archives of the Jewish Community; Claudia Schulke, "Spurensuche und lyrisches Ich," *Frankfurter Allgemeiner Zeitung*, February 23, 1992.

164. Eschwege, February 1, 2005.

165. Archives of the Jewish Community; Schulke, "Spurensuche und lyrisches Ich."

166. Hellmann, December 16, 2004.

167. Arad, "Bells Announcing Bad Tidings," 18.

168. Amichai papers / Beinecke, box 12, folder 178, draft of interview with Weber, 7; Arad, "Bells Announcing Bad Tidings," 18; Schulke, "Spurensuche und lyrisches Ich." In his interview with Arad, Amichai wanted to show that he did not suffer much from the Nazis; in this version, he said that his father convinced the SS that he lost the pin. However, in his interview with Schulke, Amichai said that the SS broke the door down to arrest his father after they heard that he threw the pin in the garbage.

169. Amichai, "The Times My Father Died," 136; Amichai, *The World Is a Room*, 191.

170. The unofficial boycott was on Purim, March 11, 1933. Daxelmueller and Flade, *Ruth Played on a Black Flute*, 71.

171. Amichai papers / Beinecke, box 12, folder 178, draft of interview with Weber, 8.

172. Schwabacher, July 12, 2002; Cecchetti, December 18, 2002.

173. Kobliner, October 4, 2002; Schlame, November 2002; Eschwege, February 1, 2004; Bravman, July 14, 2005; Einsbacher, December 10, 2004.

174. Arad, "Bells Announcing Bad Tidings," 19.

175. Amichai, interview with author, June 23, 1996.

176. Report of actions against professional Jews (doctors, lawyers and merchants) [from the state archive, these reports were sent to Munich every 3 months], no. 537; Regierungspraesidium von Unterfranken und Aschaffenburg an das Staatsministerium des Innern: Monatsbericht fuer April 1935, 1.

177. Daxelmueller and Flade, *Ruth Played on a Black Flute*, 75.

178. Schwabacher, July 12, 2002.

179. Cecchetti, December 18, 2002; Schlame, November 2002.

180. "I remember one incident, perhaps because I was little and I thought my brother would protect me. We used to go to school and there was a green area and we walked in the middle of it. . . . [A] few children started chasing us. . . . They were big, they were Nazis with swastikas and a ribbon on the shirt, and I was very scared. After that, my father took us to school." Cecchetti, December 18, 2002.

181. Amichai, "Yehuda Amichai," 28. Amichai, Kulturpreis speech. In Bavaria, a church decoration called *Saujuden* showed Jews nursing from the udders of a sow; the motif is from the fifteenth or sixteenth century. As pigs are considered dirty, no one drinks their milk. Nazis built their antisemitism on this kind of historical Christian hostility.

182. Laura R. Eschwege, "A Once in a Lifetime Trip," *Jewish Press*, March 7, 1980; Yehuda A[michai]. Holocaust Testimony.

183. Schwabacher, July 12, 2002.

184. Arad, "Bells Announcing Bad Tidings," 18.

185. Cecchetti, December 18, 2002; Steidle, *A Small Birthday Present from Wuerzburg*, 10; Leo, *Between Remembering and Forgetting*, 133.

186. See the second part of chapter 3 for the full discussion of Little Ruth's fate.

187. Yehuda A[michai]. Holocaust Testimony. "They brought two Jews from the village who were beaten to death by Nazi hooligans . . . not even organized SS. . . . [T]hat was one of the reasons that [my father] packed up."

188. Amichai papers / Beinecke, box 4, file 60, seminar paper on medieval poet Samuel Hanagid submitted to Professor Schirman, 1951, 33.

189. Arad, "Bells Announcing Bad Tidings," 18; Amichai papers / Beinecke, box 12, folder 178, draft of interview with Weber, 8; Judy Cooper-Weill, "A Day in the life of Yehuda Amichai," *Newsview*, January 23–29, 1985, 32.

190. Kobliner, October 4, 2002.

191. Daniel Efron, *Encyclopedia Judaica*, vol. 16, 1974, s.v. "white paper." The immigration certificate they obtained was the Arab-supported British "white paper" that limited Jewish immigration to Palestine.

192. Schulke, "Spurensuche und lyrisches Ich"; Amichai papers / Beinecke, box 12, folder 178, draft of interview with Weber, 8.

193. Sources vary on the emigration dates of members of the Pfeuffer family. Archives of the Jewish Community show that Samuel and Friedrich Pfeuffer emigrated to Palestine on July 23, 1936. The Giebelstadt archives state that Erich and Siegfried Pfeuffer emigrated on June 18, 1936 (Petah Tikva, Schapiro St. 28).

194. Schulke, "Spurensuche und lyrisches Ich"; Grimm, interview with author, October 2004; Leo, *Between Remembering and Forgetting*, 101.

195. Daxelmueller and Flade, *Ruth Played on a Black Flute*, 81.

196. Ibid., 39.

197. Avneri, *Encyclopedia Judaica*, s.v. "Wuerzburg"; Flade, *The Jews of Wuerzburg*, 358; Straetz, *Biographisches Handbuch Wuerzburger Juden*.

198. Yehuda Amichai, "Through Two Points Only One Straight Line Can Pass," in *Poems: 1948–1962*, 90. In SP, 13, this line is translated as, "and inside, voices talked of future war."

3. THE MURKY MIRROR OF WUERZBURG IN AMICHAI'S WORK (PP. 47–100)

1. Glenda Abramson, *The Writing of Yehuda Amichai: A Thematic Approach* (Albany: SUNY Press, 1989), 17.

2. Dan Omer, "In This Burning Country, Words Must Serve as Shade" (series of interviews with Amichai), *Proza*, no. 25 (July 1978): 8.

3. Yehuda Amichai, *Lo me'akhshav lo mikan* (Not of This Time, Not of This Place), (Tel Aviv: Schocken, 1963) (subsequently, *Not of This Time*). Translated by Shlomo Katz as *Not of This Time, Not of This Place* (New York: Harper and Row, 1968) (subsequently, Katz).

4. Yehuda Amichai, "Bells and Trains," in *Pa'amonim verakavot* (Bells and Trains: Plays and Skits), (Tel Aviv: Schocken, 1992), 7–30. Yehuda Amichai, "The Times My Father Died," "Exodus," and "Venice—Three Times." These stories appeared in newspapers and magazines in the late 1950s and are collected in Amichai, *Baru'ah hanora'a hazot* (In That Terrible Wind) (Tel Aviv: Schocken, [1965] 1985), 132–40, 247–55, 287–98 (subsequently, *In That Terrible Wind*). "The Times My Father Died" is translated into English in Amichai, *The World is a Room and Other Stories by Yehuda Amichai*, trans. Yosef Schachter (Philadelphia: Jewish Publication Society of America, 1984), 185–97.

5. Yehuda Amichai, "Masot Binyamin ha'aharon mitudela," in *Akhshav bara'ash: shirim 1963–1968* (Now in the storm: Poems 1963–1968), (Tel Aviv: Schocken, [1968] 1975), 97–139. Translated as "The Travels of Benjamin the Last, of Tudela," in *Yehuda Amichai: A Life of Poetry 1948–1994*, ed. and trans. Benjamin Harshav and Barbara Harshav (New York: HarperCollins, 1994), 160–88 (subsequently, LOP). Also translated as "Travels of the Last Benjamin of Tudela," in *The Selected Poetry of Yehuda Amichai*, trans. Chana Bloch and Stephen Mitchell (Berkeley and Los Angeles: University of California Press, 1996), 60–86 (subsequently, SP).

6. "The Travels of Benjamin the Last, of Tudela" is a combination of first- and second-person lyrical narrative and follows parallel sequences, one of immigration and growing up, the other of a heated extramarital love affair. Because of the late date of its publication (1968), it is beyond the scope of this study, although it will occasionally be mentioned if a particular analysis requires it.

7. This collection of nearly 100 love letters, which Amichai wrote from 1947 to 1948, is the earliest body of Amichai's writings found. The discovery of these letters is detailed in chapter 1. Yehuda Amichai's letters to Ruth Z. (August 31, 1947—April 11, 1948) will be housed at the Hayisre'elim harishonim (First Israelis Archive), Heksherim: The Research

Center for Jewish and Israeli Literature and Culture, Ben-Gurion University of the Negev. References cite the number of the letter (as given by Amichai) and the date.

8. Yehuda Amichai Papers. General Collection, Beinecke Rare Book and Manuscript Library, Yale University (subsequently, Amichai papers / Beinecke), box 9, file 135. There were 34 boxes in the precatalogued archive with consecutively numbered files in each box. References to these materials cite the uncatalogued box number and file number. Yehuda Amichai's speech upon receiving the Kulturpreis (cultural prize) in Wuerzburg, June 22, 1981, as quoted in *Main Post*, August 5, 1991, and in Roland Flade, "Reliving Childhood at Saint Kilian's Festival," *Allgemeine Juedische Wochenzeitung* no. 35, August 29, 1991 (subsequently, Kulturpreis speech).

9. Yehuda Amichai, "My Mother Baked the Whole World for Me," in *Shirim: 1948–1962* (Poems: 1948–1962) (Tel Aviv, Israel: Schocken, 2002 [1963]), 13 (subsequently, *Poems: 1948–1962*); "My Mother Baked the Whole World for Me," LOP, 4. English translations for most of the poems in *Poems: 1948–1962* appear in SP and LOP. When an English translation is not cited, this indicates that English translations are unavailable.

10. *Poems: 1948–1962*, 239; LOP, 53.

11. *Poems: 1948–1962*, 300.

12. Amichai papers / Beinecke, box 19, file 277, January 9, 1966.

13. *Poems: 1948–1962*, 11; "Grasses and masts stood at the seashore," SP, 6; "Grass and masts stood at the shore," LOP, 3. I am using a combination of both translations for maximal accuracy.

14. *Poems: 1948–1962*, 107.

15. Amichai papers / Beinecke, box 31, file 380, notebook entitled "Spoleto, 1967"; this line was translated posthumously and published as an undated fragment in Leon Wieseltier, "Yehuda Amichai: Posthumous Fragments," *New York Times*, November 21, 2004.

16. SP, 7.

17. Omer, "In This Burning Country," 4; Amichai papers / Beinecke, box 19, file 277, August 1978–1979; box 19, file 279, notebook 1965–1966.

18. *Poems: 1948–1962*, 31; SP, 6.

19. *Poems, 1948–1962*, 158; Yehuda Amichai, "A Girl Whose Name Is Sarah," in *More Love Poems* (Tel Aviv: Schocken, 1994), 23.

20. *Poems: 1948–1962*, 310.

21. Ibid., 240.

22. Amichai bases this line on a Talmudic idiom that suggests that a person's character is revealed by his drinking, his handling of money, and his expression of anger ("*adam nikar bekoso bekiso uveka'aso*").

23. *Poems: 1948–1962*, 241.

24. Yehuda Amichai, *Me'ahore kol ze mistater osher gadol* (Behind All This There Is Great Happiness) (Tel Aviv: Schocken, 1976), "Two Poems from Lekha Dodi," #1, 52, "Poems of the Land of Zion," #11, 11 (subsequently, *Behind All This*).

25. *Poems: 1948–1962*, 347–53, 353.

26. Closing the gates can be understood as closing the gate to the paradise of childhood (see Christian Leo, *Zwischen Erinnern und Vergessen: Jehuda Amichais Roman "Nicht von jetzt, nicht von hier" im philosophischen und literarischen Kontext* (Wuerzburg, Germany: Koenigshausen und Neumann, 2004) as well as closing the gates of heaven in the Yom Kippur prayer. For a further discussion on the metaphor of "closing the gate," see chapter 4.

27. Omer, "In This Burning Country," 6; Yotam Re'uveni, "Yehuda Amichai: This Is the Place," *Yedi'ot Aharonot*, May 1985, 19; Michael Miro, "Writing Is the Product of Wonderful Laziness" (interview with Amichai), *Pi Ha'aton*, March, 19, 1978; Yehuda Amichai, "To Live Reality," *Ha'aretz*, November 30, 1973.

28. See Amichai papers / Beinecke, box 4, file 64, notepad, February 1957–March 1957; box 4, folder 63, undated notepad Fav-O-Rite; box 19, folder 278, notebook from 1965.

29. Ibid., box 1, file 14, torn out piece of paper that, judging by its size, must have been from the period between 1954 and 1960.

30. Ibid., box 1, file 21, numbered, yellow, lined paper, 2.

31. *Poems: 1948–1962*, 366. Translated in SP as "The Elegy on the Lost Child" (43–47) and in LOP as "Elegy on the Lost Child" (72–76).

32. Amichai papers / Beinecke, box 4, file 64, small gray notebook, November-December 1957; box 4, file 65, notepad, December, 1957.

33. Letter to Ruth Z., #94, April 4, 1948.

34. In Amichai papers / Beinecke, box 1, file 21; on a piece of paper, Amichai wrote of a child disappearing because he had "run away" to his adult life.

35. Ibid., box 1, file 17.

36. Ibid., box 1, file 21, on a piece of paper.

37. Abramson, *The Writing of Yehuda Amichai*, 15. Glenda Abramson can be credited with combining the notion of the lost love with the idea of the actual lost child, Little Ruth, who never lived to adulthood.

38. Shimon Sandbank, *Shete berekhot baya'ar* (Two Pools in the Forest) (Israel: Hakibbutz Hameuchad, 1976), 207.

39. SP, 43, lines 2–3.

40. *Poems: 1948–1962*, 366, line 4; SP, 43, line 4.

41. SP, 43, lines 2–3.

42. Ibid., 44, lines 15–16.

43. See Boaz Arpali, *Haperahim veha'agartal* (The Flowers and the Urn: Amichai's Poetry, 1948–1968) (Tel Aviv: Hakibbutz Hameuchad, 1986), 201. Additionally, see note 37 in this chapter.

44. In Amichai's novel, the idea of "closing the doors" becomes a leitmotif. See the discussion in chapter 4.

45. *Poems: 1948–1962*, 367, line 29; SP, 44, lines 30–31.

46. *Poems: 1948–1962*, 368, line 58; SP, 45, line 58.

47. *Poems: 1948–1962*, 370, line 108; SP, 46, line 109.

48. *Poems: 1948–1962*, 371, line 133; SP, 47, line 135.

49. *Poems: 1948–1962*, 368, lines 53–54; SP, 45, lines 54–55.

50. *Poems: 1948–1962*, 369, line 78; SP, 45, line 78.

51. *Poems: 1948–1962*, 369, line 93; LOP, 74.

52. Amichai papers / Beinecke, box 4, file 64, in a cluster of papers inside a paper on which it says "1958–59."

53. Amichai papers / Beinecke, box 1, file 21, on numbered, yellow, lined paper, 2.

54. *Poems: 1948–1962*, 367, line 32; SP, 44, lines 33–35.

55. *Poems: 1948–1962*, 367, lines 32–33; SP, 44, lines 34–35.

56. *Poems: 1948–1962*, 369, line 82; SP, 45, lines 81–83.

57. For more on "burnt mouths," see discussion of "The Clouds Are the First To Die" later in this chapter.

58. Amichai papers / Beinecke, box 19, folder 278, light green notebook, 1966.

59. *Poems: 1948–1962*, 371, lines 138–39; SP, 47, lines 139–40.

60. *Poems: 1948–1962*, 370, lines 116–17; SP, 46, lines 119–20.

61. Amichai papers / Beinecke, box 4, file 64, small gray notebook, November–December 1957; box 4, file 65, notepad, December 1957.

62. Ibid., box 4, file 64, small gray notebook, November–December 1957.

63. *Poems 1948–1962*, 371, lines 139–40; SP, 47, lines 141–42.

64. *Poems 1948–1962*, 368, lines 66–67; SP, 45, lines, 66–68.

65. Amichai papers / Beinecke, box 4, file 64, small gray notebook, November–December 1957.

66. *Poems: 1948–1962*, 368, lines 66–67. This translation is a combination of LOP, 74, lines 75–76 ("the child hid, curled up / Among the stones for buildings of tomorrow") and SP, 45, lines 67–68 ("for the child bent over / and hid in the stones of tomorrow's houses").

67. Amichai papers / Beinecke, box 4, file 64, small gray notebook, November–December 1957.

68. Abramson, *The Writing of Yehuda Amichai*, 147.

69. Hans Steidle, "Rueckkehr an einen Ort, an den man nicht zurueckkehren kann," in *Ein kleines Geburtstagspraesent aus Wuerzburg: Festgabe fuer Jehuda Amichai zum 75 Geburtstag*, ed. Hans Steidle (Wuerzburg, Germany: Verlag der Leonhard Frank-Gesellschaft, 1999), 12–40 (subsequently, *A Small Birthday Present from Wuerzburg*).

70. When possible, translations from the original Hebrew novel follow Shlomo Katz's English translation, which is an abridged version and only contains approximately half of the material in the original. When there is no reference to the English translation, it indicates that English translations are unavailable for those particular lines.

71. Dan Miron, *Hapreda min ha'ani he'ani* (Taking Leave of the Impoverished Self: Ch. N. Bialik's Early Poetry, 1891–1901), (Tel Aviv: Open University, 1986).

72. Yehuda Amichai, "Return to the City of Childhood," *Bamahane*, January 5, 1962, 24, as quoted in Abramson, *The Writing of Yehuda Amichai*, 147.

73. See Hayim Nahman Bialik, "Ehad ehad uve'en ro'e" (One by One and Invisible), in *Hayim nahman Bialik: hashirim* (H. N. Bialik: Poems), ed. Avner Holtzman (Tel Aviv: Dvir, 2004), 423. Amichai's words are inspired by this poem.

74. *Not of This Time*, 586.

75. Abramson, *The Writing of Yehuda Amichai*, 152.

76. Amichai also wrote "The Travels of Benjamin the Last, of Tudela" during this period.

77. *Not of This Time*, 14; Katz, 7.

78. *Not of This Time*, 28.

79. Ibid., 53; Katz, 36.

80. *Not of This Time*, 23; Katz, 16.

81. *Not of This Time*, 30.

82. See Gershon Shaked, *Hasiporet ha'ivrit: 1880–1980* (Hebrew Narrative Fiction: 1880–1980), vol. 5 (Tel Aviv and Jerusalem: Hakibbutz Hameuchad and Keter, 1998), 19; and Shaked, *Gal hadash basiporet ha'ivrit* (New Wave in Hebrew Fiction), (Tel Aviv: Sifriat Poalim, 1971). Shaked suggested that the novel is an attempt to write about the fate of a generation that returns from war disappointed and is searching for an actualization of its individual personality.

83. This discussion deals exclusively with the German plot, which occupies approximately half the chapters.

84. *Not of This Time*, 53; Katz, 36.

85. *Not of This Time*, 58; Katz, 40.

86. *Not of This Time*, 489; Katz, 275.

87. This detail appears prominently in the radio skit "Bells and Trains," in *Pa'amonim verakavot*, 7–30.

88. *Not of This Time*, 97.

89. Ibid., 66; Katz, 48.

90. *Not of This Time*, 255–56; Katz, 154–55.

91. *Not of This Time*, 392; Katz, 233.

92. The clusters are: St. Augustine Street and its vicinity; Allee Street; the train tracks; the hospital and old-age home; his route to school; Jewish Wuerzburg and the area near the synagogue complex.

93. *Not of This Time*, 255–56; Katz, 154–55.

94. *Not of This Time*, 276.

95. Ibid., 216, 274, 517; Katz, 138.

96. *Not of This Time*, 544.

97. Archives of the Jewish community of Wuerzburg, old files number WR 576–79 (subsequently, Archives of the Jewish Community).

98. Leo, *Between Remembering and Forgetting*, 1–3, 15–18, 73–82.

99. *Not of This Time*, 107; Katz, 70.

100. *Not of This Time*, 98; Katz, 63.

101. Steidle, *A Small Birthday Present from Wuerzburg*, 12–40, 21–26.

102. *Not of This Time*, 298.

103. See chapter 2 for specific details of Amichai's boyhood, upon which the novel draws.

104. *Not of This Time*, 220, 311.

105. Ibid., 558–60; Katz, 294. The description of the actual visit to the Hofgarten appears only on page 558 out of the 619 pages of the Hebrew original.

106. See discussion of "Twenty New Quatrains" earlier in this chapter.

107. *Not of This Time*, 35, 37.

108. Ibid., 557; Katz, 295.

109. Leo, *Between Remembering and Forgetting*, 231–36.

110. *Not of This Time*, 369.

111. Ibid., 366.

112. In this ritual, the children of the community would lift the baby's cradle three times, chanting "*Hollekreisch, Hollekreisch, wie soll das Kind heissen*" ("What shall the name of this child be?") and then shout the given name. (Jewish Encyclopedia.com, s.v. "Holle Kreish," by Kaufman Kohler) http://www.jewishencyclopedia.com/view_friendly.jsp? artid=853 &letter=H (accessed February 15, 2007).

113. *Not of This Time*, 402; Katz, 241.

114. *Not of This Time*, 401; Katz, 240.

115. *Not of This Time*, 301.

116. Ibid., 335; Katz, 206.

117. *Not of This Time*, 400; Katz, 237.

118. *Not of This Time*, 365.

119. Ibid., 138; Katz, 90.

120. Yehuda A[michai]. Holocaust Testimony (HVT-2679), interview conducted by Geoffrey Hartman and Benjamin Harshav, November 3, 1994, Fortunoff Video Archive for Holocaust Testimonies, Yale University Library; Yehuda Amichai, "Yehuda Amichai," in *Mein Judentum*, ed. Hans Jürgen Schultz (Stuttgart: Kreuz, 1978), 20–35 (subsequently, "Yehuda Amichai").

121. Amichai papers/ Beinecke, box 19 (probably), file 286, notebook dated September–December 1990, 11 (December 11); letter to Ruth Z., #46, December 7, 1947.

122. Arye Arad, "Bells Announcing Bad Tidings: The Poet Yehuda Amichai Tells of His Childhood in Southern Germany" (interview with Amichai), *Bamahane* (N.d. [most likely the 1960s]), 19.

123. Omer, "In this Burning Country," 4, 7.

124. The novel's portrayal of Henrietta, one of Joel's "aunts," contrasts with that of Little Ruth. Although the Holocaust had a marked effect on Henrietta's life, Joel feels no guilt or remorse when they reunite.

125. Not of This Time, 127.

126. Ibid., 20; Katz, 13.

127. Not of This Time, 56; Katz, 39.

128. Not of This Time, 36; Katz, 24.

129. Not of This Time, 25; Katz, 18.

130. Not of This Time, 96; Katz, 61.

131. Not of This Time, 490; Katz, 276.

132. Not of This Time, 490.

133. Edith Raim, "Verfolgung und Exil der Juedischen Familie Hanover aus Wuerzburg," in *Mainfraenkisches Jahrbuch fuer Geschichte und Kunst*, no. 56 (Wuerzburg, Germany: Freunde Mainfraenkischer Kunst and Geschichte E.V., 2004), 317–37, 317–18; Ruth Kobliner, interview with author, September 23, 2002.

134. Not of This Time, 369; Katz, 220. For other descriptions of her, see Not of This Time, 98; Katz, 63; Not of This Time, 490; Katz, 276; and Not of This Time, 127; Katz, 82.

135. Kobliner, interview with the author, September 23, 2002; Otto Schlame, interview with the author, November 2002; Mordechai Einsbacher, interview with the author, December 10, 2004; Ludwig Bravman, interview with the author, July 14, 2005.

136. Not of This Time, 542, 185; Katz, 115.

137. Not of This Time, 98; Katz, 63

138. Not of This Time, 108, 541; Katz, 72.

139. Not of This Time, 128. See the discussion of Sonnet II, "Binyamina, 1948," in chapter 8 for the first literary metabolism of this memory.

140. Amichai papers / Beinecke, box 4, File 65, notepad marked "1958."

141. Letter to Ruth Z., #46, December 7, 1947; Amichai papers / Beinecke, box 19, file 286, notebook September–December 1990.

142. Letter to Ruth Z., #46, December 7, 1947.

143. Amichai papers / Beinecke, box 19 (probably), file 286, notebook September–December 1990.

144. Not of This Time, 299

145. Ibid., 370; Katz, 221.

146. Not of This Time, 399; Katz, 237–38.

147. Not of This Time, 565.

148. Ibid., 429; Katz, 256.

149. Not of This Time, 424; Katz, 252.

150. Not of This Time, 96; Katz, 61.

151. Not of This Time, 125; Katz, 81.

152. Not of This Time, 158.

153. Ibid., 176; Katz, 106–7.

154. *Not of This Time*, 459; Katz, 263.

155. *Not of This Time*, 369; Katz, 220.

156. Amichai papers / Beinecke, box 4, file 63, undated pad labeled "Fav-O-Rite for water color NY Chicago." *Not of This Time*, 96; Katz, 61. In the novel, Ruth skipped on one leg to the train after the Nazis had taken away her prosthetic leg and crutches.

157. Letter to Ruth Z. #2, September 3, 1947.

158. Yehuda Amichai, "A Pity. We Were Such a Good Invention," translated by Assia Gutmann in *Love Poems* (Tel Aviv: Shocken, 1977), 33.

159. The draft is in Amichai papers / Beinecke, box 19, folder 279, notebook from 1966, July 17, 1966.

160. *Not of This Time*, 430–32; Katz, 257–59.

161. *Not of This Time*, 432; Katz, 259.

162. *Not of This Time*, 232; Katz, 144.

163. *Not of This Time*, 432; Katz, 259.

164. *Not of This Time*, 232; Katz, 144.

165. *Not of This Time*, 85; Katz, 52.

166. *Not of This Time*, 125; Katz, 81.

167. *Not of This Time*, 126; Katz, 81.

168. Arad, "Bells Announcing Bad Tidings," 18; Yehuda A[michai]. Holocaust Testimony.

169. Omer, "In This Burning Country," 4.

170. *Not of This Time*, 182; Katz, 112.

171. *Not of This Time*, 182; Katz, 113.

172. *Not of This Time*, 438.

173. Ibid., 490.

174. Arnold Band alerted me to this connection.

175. *Not of This Time*, 232; Katz, 144.

176. *Not of This Time*, 233; Katz, 144. The English reads "After a while not even Ruth was allowed into the park." The word order has been changed to reflect the Hebrew better.

177. *Not of This Time*, 311.

178. Ibid., 557; Katz, 294.

179. *Not of This Time*, 558; Katz, 296.

180. *In That Terrible Wind*, 229.

181. Leo, *Between Remembering and Forgetting*, 98–100; Rosa Grimm, interview with author, October 2004. These Wuerzburgian Amichai scholars and enthusiasts questioned Amichai's motives for attributing Little Ruth's death to Wuerzburg.

182. "Hanukkah," *Poems: 1948–1962*, 303.

183. A spinning top that children play with on Hanukkah.

184. Amichai papers / Beinecke box 19 (probably), file 286, notebook September–December 1990.

185. Ibid., box 19, file 278, 1991.

186. *Not of This Time*, 496.

187. Letters to Ruth Z., #46, December 7, 1947; #45, December 5, 1947.

188. *Sich den Mund verbrennen* (to burn one's mouth / have a burnt mouth). This idiom also appears in "Poems for Rosh Hashanah," *Poems: 1948–1962*, 122, and "Elegy on the Lost Child," *Poems: 1948–1962*, 369.

189. Adolph Eichmann was head of the Department of Jewish Affairs in the Gestapo and was chief of operations in the deportation of three million Jews to extermination camps. He stood trial in Jerusalem from April 2 to August 14, 1961, and was executed on May 31, 1962.

190. The term "idiolect" refers to linguistic usages that characterize a specific work or corpus of an author. It signifies the personal, idiosyncratic, and exclusive vocabulary of the writer, because the usage and the meaning the author gives to the words in the context of the specific work is unique. See Michael Riffaterre, *Semiotics of Poetry* (Bloomington and London: Indiana University Press, 1978), 21, 23.

191. Amichai papers / Beinecke, box 12, File 172, hardcover notebook, 1997–1998. The words "Richard Strauss, 1864–1948" are written in Hebrew and the word "Metamorphoses" is written in Roman letters.

192. Claudia Schulke, "Spurensuche und lyrisches Ich," *Frankfurter Allgemeiner Zeitung*, February 23, 1992.

193. Amichai papers / Beinecke, file 63, pad that says "Fav-O-Rite for water color NY Chicago," note entitled "Trips to Germany, 1992," no date.

194. "The Clouds Are the First To Die," in *Poems: 1948–1962*, 128.

195. Quatrain 46 of "In a Right Angle," in *Poems: 1948–1962*, 184; SP, 29.

196. See, for example, Dan Pagis, "Footprints," in *Kol hashirim* (Collected Poems) (Jerusalem: Hakibbutz Hameuchad, 1991), 141, and other poems under the subtitle "Gilgul," 125–59.

197. Quatrain 46 of "In a Right Angle," in *Poems: 1948–1962*, 184; SP, 29. SP reads, "the girl in her fiery cloud."

198. Yehuda Amichai, *Velo al menat lizkor* (Not in Order to Remember) (Jerusalem: Schocken, 1978), 111–14; LOP, 220–21.

199. LOP, 220; Poem 6, the last poem in "Poems of the Hot Wind," was not translated

200. Nili Gold, *Lo kabrosh: gilgule imagim vetavniyot beshirat Yehuda Amichai* (Not Like a Cypress: Transformations of Images and Structures in the Poetry of Yehuda Amichai) (Tel Aviv: Schocken), 24, 62, 118–19.

201. Yehuda Amichai, *Shalva gedola: she'elot uteshuvot* (Tel Aviv: Schocken, 1980), 64 (subsequently, *Shalva gedola*), translated as *The Great Tranquility: Questions and Answers*, trans. Glenda Abramson and Tudor Parfitt (New York: Sheep Meadow Press, 1997), 43 (subsequently, GT); Little Ruth is also mentioned obliquely as "The girl from my childhood, they killed" in "Poems for Zion and Jerusalem," Poem 11 in *Behind All This*, 11.

202. "All These Make a Strange Dance Rhythm," in GT, 16. *Shalva gedola*, 31.

203. Steidle, *A Small Birthday Present from Wuerzburg*, 11.

204. *Shalva gedola*, 31; GT, 16.

205. Yehuda Amichai, *Gam ha'egrof haya pa'am yad petuha ve'etsba'ot* (Even the Fist Was Once an Open Palm and Fingers) (Tel Aviv: Schocken, 1989), 70; LOP, 431.

206. Kobliner, interview with author, October 4, 2002; Raim, "The Wandering and Exile," 319, 321, 26, 333.

207. Arad, "Bells Announcing Bad Tidings," 19, 39.

208. *Not of This Time*, 566; Katz 302–3.

209. *In that Terrible Wind*, 229.

210. Amichai papers / Beinecke, box 4, file 63, undated pad that says "Fav-O-Rite for water color NY Chicago."

211. *Not of This Time*, 58.

212. Ibid., 295; Katz, 179.

213. *Not of This Time*, 566; Katz, 302–3.

214. Arad, "Bells Announcing Bad Tidings," 39.

215. Amichai, *Gam haegrof*, 70; LOP, 431–32.

216. Harshav translated it as "Amen" to make it more readily understandable to the English reader.

4. HIDING BETWEEN THE LANGUAGES (PP. 101–50)

1. Yehuda Amichai Papers. General Collection, Beinecke Rare Book and Manuscript Library, Yale University (subsequently, Amichai papers / Beinecke). There were 34 boxes in the precatalogued archive with consecutively numbered files in each box. References to these materials cite the uncatalogued box number and file number.

2. Dan Omer, "In This Burning Country, Words Must Serve As Shade" (series of interviews with Amichai), *Proza*, no. 25 (July 1978): 4–5 (subsequently, "In this Burning Country").

3. Aryeh Arad, "Bells Announcing Bad Tidings: The Poet Yehuda Amichai Tells of His Childhood in Southern Germany," *Bamahane* (n.d. [most likely the 1960s]): 18 (subsequently, "Bells Announcing Bad Tidings").

4. Gershon Shaked, *Hasiporet ha'ivrit: 1880–1980* (Hebrew Narrative Fiction: 1880–1980), vol. 3 (Tel Aviv and Jerusalem, Israel: Hakibbutz Hameuchad and Keter, 1988), 81–89.

5. Amalia Kahana-Carmon, "She Writes Nicely, but Only about That Which Is Marginal," *Yedi'ot Aharonot*, January 25, 1988.

6. Nili Carmel-Flumin, "A Day of Hebrew Poetry in Washington" (interview with Amichai), *Yedi'ot Aharonot*, May 31, 1985, 22.

7. Yehuda Amichai, "To Live Reality," *Ha'aretz*, 1973.

8. The rhythms and fluctuations of a mother's voice and speech penetrate the nervous system of the fetus beginning in the fifth month of pregnancy, when the development

of the ear is complete. Thomas R. Verny, *The Secret Life of the Unborn Child* (New York: Summit Books, 1981). The otolaryngolist Alfred Tomatis was the first to argue, in *L'oreille et le langage* (1963), that the fetus hears. See Tomatis, *The Ear and Language* (Norval, Ontario, Canada: Moulin, 1996). See also Paul Madaule, *When Listening Comes Alive: A Guide to Effective Learning and Communication* (Norval, Ontario, Canada: Moulin, 1993). See Jacques Mehler, "Language in the Infant's Mind," *Philosophical Transactions: Biological Sciences* vol. 346 no. 1315 (October 29, 1994): 13–20. William P. Fifer and Christine Moon, "The Role of the Mother's Voice in the Organization of Brain Function in the New Born," *Acta Paediatrica*, suppl. 397 (June 1994): 86–93. For a psychoanalytic dimension of the corporeal experience of absorbing language, see: Jacqueline Amati-Mehler, Simona Argentieri, and Jorge Canestri, *The Babel of the Unconscious: Mother Tongue and Foreign Languages in the Psychoanalytic Dimension*, trans. Whitelaw Cucco (Madison, Conn.: International University Press, 1993). For Lacan's theories of the child's relationship with the "other," see Jacques Lacan, *Les écrits techniques de Freud* (1953–54), ed. Jacques-Alain Miller (Paris: Éditions de Seuil, 1975); translated into English by John Forrester as *Freud's Papers on Technique: 1953–1954* (New York: W. W. Norton, 1988). See also Jacques Lacan, *Le moi dans la théorie de Freud et dans la technique de la psychanalyse* (1954–55), ed. Jacques-Alain Miller (Paris: Éditions de Seuil, 1978); translated into English by Sylvana Tomaselli as *The Ego in Freud's Theory and the Technique of Psychoanalysis: 1954–1955* (New York: W. W. Norton, 1988).

9. Yehuda Amichai, "Yehuda Amichai," in *Mein Judentum*, ed. Hans Jürgen Schultz (Stuttgart: Kreuz, 1978), 22–35, 30 (subsequently, "Yehuda Amichai").

10. Yehuda Amichai, interview with author, June 23, 1996.

11. For a discussion of Amichai's visual and experiential memories, see chapters 3, 4, and 6.

12. Angela Sey, "Interview," interview with Amichai, *Das Aktuelle*, 1992, 17.

13. Amichai, "Yehuda Amichai," 22–35. Amichai wrote his article in German and translated his poems that appear in it into German by himself.

14. Yehuda Amichai, interview with author, June 23, 1996.

15. Arad, "Bells Announcing Bad Tidings," 18; Omer, "In This Burning Country," 4; Amichai, "Yehuda Amichai," 30; Rahel Hollander-Steingart, "In My Heart Is a Museum" (interview with Amichai), *Jerusalem Post*, Rosh Hashanah Supplement, September 28, 1981.

16. Yehuda Amichai, "Memories of Israel," *Diversion*, May 1988, 171–75, 320, 322,173–74; Yehuda Amichai, "A Language of the Heart," British Broadcasting Corporation, Radio 3, Talks and Documentaries Dept., prerecorded April 9, 1979, transmitted September 19, 1979; Haim Chertok, "A Conversation with Yehuda Amichai," *Jewish Frontier* (June/July 1985): 15; Amichai papers / Beinecke, box 31, folder 385, typed draft of *Every Man Is Born a Poet* without publication details; Yehuda Amichai, interview by Dahlia Karpel, "Hoping for the Nobel Prize," *Ha'ir*, November 3, 1989.

17. Henry Eschwege, interview with author, February 1, 2005; Norbert Hellmann, interview with author, December 16, 2004. Hellmann stated that even in Hebrew classes, German was the language of instruction.

18. Yehuda Amichai, "Agnon and I," *Ha'aretz*, January, 1978.

19. Yehuda Amichai, interview by David Montenegro, *The American Poetry Review* (November/December 1987): 15; Yehuda A[michai]. Holocaust Testimony (HVT-2679), interview conducted by Geoffrey Hartman and Benjamin Harshav, November 3, 1994, Fortunoff Video Archive for Holocaust Testimonies, Yale University Library (subsequently, Yehuda A[michai]. Holocaust Testimony).

20. Yehuda Amichai, "The Travels of Benjamin the Last, of Tudela," in *Yehuda Amichai: A Life of Poetry, 1948–1994*, ed. and trans. Benjamin Harshav and Barbara Harshav (New York: HarperCollins, 1994), 169, lines 325–36 (subsequently, LOP.)

21. See Nili Gold, "The Feminine in Amichai's Poetics," in *The Experienced Soul: Studies in Amichai*, ed. Glenda Abramson (Boulder, Colo.: Westview Press, 1997), 77–92.

22. The four years Amichai spent in the British army exposed him to English and indirectly probably strengthened his German.

23. Claudia Schulke, "Spurensuche und lyrisches Ich," *Frankfurter Allgemeiner Zeitung*, February 23, 1992; R. H.,"Auch die Erinnerung ist Gegenwart," *Koelner Stadt-Anzeiger*, September 25, 1992; Ruth Z., interview with author, May 2003.

24. Gerd Loschuetz, "Wie lange koennen Erinnerungen standhalten?" *Frankfurter Rundschau*, February 2, 1992.

25. Amichai papers / Beinecke, box 10, file 145, handwritten note, February 15, 1990.

26. Nili Gold, "Betrayal of the Mother Tongue in the Creation of National Identity," in *Ideology and Jewish Identity in Israeli and American Literature*, ed. Emily Miller Budick (Albany: SUNY Press), 235–58.

27. For a more exhaustive discussion of the letters, see chapters 7–11.

28. Omer, "In this Burning Country," 5.

29. Ruth Z., interviews with author, May 2003; August 29, 2004.

30. Both Amichai and Ruth knew English, but it was a mere third language. Amichai was versed in English poetry, quoting Shakespeare, Auden, and Eliot, yet none of the segments he quotes are about love.

31. Letter to Ruth Z., #20, October 12–13, 1947. Yehuda Amichai's letters to Ruth Z. (August 31, 1947–April 11, 1948) will be housed at Hayisre'elim harishonim (First Israelis Archive), Heksherim: The Research Center for Jewish and Israeli Literature and Culture, Ben-Gurion University of the Negev. References cite the number of the letter (as given by Amichai) and the date.

32. Letter to Ruth Z. #31, November 7, 1947.

33. Letter to Ruth Z., #10, September 1947.

34. Ibid., #78, February 18, 1948.

35. Ibid., #6, September 9, 1947.

36. Morgenstern was a favorite among German-speaking young poets at that time. Arnold Band recalls, for example, the leading poet Nathan Zach's infatuation with Morgenstern's romantic verse.

37. Letter to Ruth Z., #5, September 7, 1947.

38. Morgenstern best expressed Amichai's excruciating longing for his beloved. Amichai never sent his translation of "The Prayer of Separated Lovers" to Ruth, but three weeks later (in letter to Ruth Z., #12, September 25, 1947) he quoted his translation of another Morgenstern poem, and sent her yet another full poem in German six weeks later (in #31, November 7, 1947). The poem was "It Is Night," and its speaker describes yearning in vivid, physical terms: "my heart comes to you . . . [for] it can no longer bear to stay in me."

39. Letter to Ruth Z., #22, October 16, 1947.

40. Ibid.; Richard Hoffman, "Lullaby for Miriam," Annenberg Rare Book and Manuscript Library, University of Pennsylvania.

41. Ruth Z., interview with author, August 29, 2004; Ingrid Wiltmann, *Nur Ewigkeit ist kein Exil. Lebensgeschichten aus Israel. Mit einem Nachwort von Anat Feinberg* (Moehlin, Switzerland: Rauhreif, 1997), S. 90–98. Amichai's German boxing teacher, Horst Schade, like others of his generation, worshipped Rilke and taught this admiration to Amichai. Many of Amichai's age were introduced to Rilke by older mentors.

42. See Shimon Sandbank, "Amichai: The Playing and the Abundance," *Lamerhav*, June 3, 1969 (subsequently cited as "Amichai: The Playing and the Abundance"), reprinted in Yehudit Tzvik, ed., *Yehuda Amichai: mivhar ma'amare bikoret al yetsirato* (Yehuda Amichai: A Selection of Critical Essays on His Writings) (Tel Aviv: Hakibbutz Hameuchad, 1988), 105–14. Sandbank discusses a general German flavor in Amichai's poetry and its affiliation with Rilke, but this chapter focuses instead on Amichai's intimate connection to his linguistic sources. See also Shimon Sandbank, *Shete brekhot baya'ar* (Two Pools in the Forest) (Tel Aviv, Israel: Hakibbutz Hameuchad, 1976) (subsequently, *Two Pools in the Forest*); Nili Sadan-Lubenstein, "Imagistic Patterns in the Poetry of Amichai," *Iton 77* (October 1983).

43. Letter to Ruth Z., unnumbered letter 101, August 2, 1950. See chapter 11 for a full discussion of the roots of Amichai's affinity for Rilke.

44. Letter to Ruth Z., unnumbered letter 101, August 2, 1950.

45. Ibid., #51, December 17, 1947; ibid., #85, March 7, 1948; Rainer Maria Rilke, *Briefe an einen Jungen Dichter*, translated by M. D. Herter Norton as *Letters to a Young Poet* (New York: W. W. Norton, 1934).

46. Letter to Ruth Z., #42, November 28, 1947.

47. Sandbank, "Amichai: The Playing and the Abundance," 113.

48. Letter to Ruth Z., #42, November 28, 1947; Letter to Ruth Z., #8, September 14, 1947. The depiction of autumn in Hebrew poetry of that period (as in poems by Hayim Gouri and Nathan Alterman) often contrasts with the Israeli climate.

49. Ibid., #78, February 18, 1948.

50. Ibid., #60, January 7, 1948.

51. Ibid., #79, February 20, 1948.

52. Ibid., #63, January 14, 1948; Yehuda Amichai, "Bagina hatsiburit" (In the Public Garden), in *Shirim: 1948–1962* (Poems: 1948–1962) (Tel Aviv: Schocken, 2002 [1963]), 185–210. English translations for most of these poems appear in *The Selected Poetry of Yehuda Amichai*, trans. Chana Bloch and Stephen Mitchell (Berkeley and Los Angeles: University of California Press, 1996) (subsequently, SP), and in LOP. When references to an English translation are not cited, it is because English translations for that poem are unavailable. See chapter 9 for an extended discussion of the relationship between Rilke and "In the Public Garden."

53. Letter to Ruth Z., #68, January 25, 1948; Ibid., #19, October 10, 1947.

54. Official list of the texts printed in the German *Volksschulbuecher* during the beginning of the 1930s can be found in Amtsblatt des Bayerischen Staatsministerium fuer Unterricht und Kultus (no. 4, 755).

55. In letter to Ruth Z., #52, December 19, 1947, Amichai pondered the subject of parting, evoking Grimm's tales of separated brothers and sisters who lose their way in the forest. Amichai's imagination turned the Carmel groves in which he wanders into a thick, European forest filled with legendary magical creatures. He imagined Ruth in America as the one lost in the woods, being seduced by sorcerers and witches (letter to Ruth Z., #5, September 7, 1947); Ruth Z., interview with author, August 29, 2004.

56. Hans Christian Andersen wrote in Danish, but his stories were translated into German and were a part of the German curriculum. Amichai's associations with them would have been in the German translation. See Hans Stieglitz, Heinrich Weichser, Franz Weigl, and Johann Zinkl, eds., *Lesebuch fuer den 2 und 3. Schuelerjahrgang katholischer Volkshauptschulen Bayerns* (Munich: 1927); Wilhelm Ledermann, Hans Plecher, Franz Weigl, and Johann Zinkl, eds., *Lesebuch fuer den 4 und 5. Schuelerjahrgang katholischer Volkshauptschulen Bayerns. 4. Auflage* (Munich: 1930 [1927]); Dr. Joseph Prestel, Heinrich Weichser, Franz Weigl, and Johann Zinkl, eds., *Lesebuch fuer den 6 und 7. Schuelerjahrgang katholischer Volkshauptschulen Bayerns* (Munich: 1927).

57. Ruth Z., interview with author, May 2003.

58. Letters to Ruth Z., #19, October 10, 1947; #65, January 19, 1948; #86, March 10, 1948.

59. Ibid., #86, March 10, 1948.

60. Ibid., #37, November 18, 1947.

61. Ibid., #65, January 19, 1948.

62. Ibid., #43, November 29, 1947.

63. Markus Koch, ed., *Deutsche Singfibel fuer das 1. und 2. Schuljahr der Grundschule: Ministeriell genehmigt. 5. unveraenderte Auflage* (Wuerzburg, Germany: Stuertz Verlag, 1930 [1927]); Letter to Ruth Z., #91, March 21, 1948.

64. "Travels of the Last Benjamin of Tudela," SP, 82, lines 880–82.

65. "On the Road," *Poems: 1948–1962*, 233.

66. "Through Two Points, Only One Straight Line Can Pass," *Poems: 1948–1962*, 113; SP, 13.

67. "The Visit of the Queen of Sheba," Poem 4, *Poems: 1948–1962*, 168; SP, 24; "Last Night in the Boulevard," *Poems: 1948–1962*, 220; "The Tired People," *Poems, 1948–1962*, 225.

68. "Manners," *Poems: 1948–1962*, 316.

69. "The Poem of the Cyclamen," *Poems: 1948–1962*, 106.

70. "The Visit of the Queen of Sheba," Poem 4, *Poems: 1948–1962*, 168; SP, 24.

71. "In the Right Angle" #25, *Poems: 1948–1962*, 179; LOP, 43.

72. Letter to Ruth Z., #9, September 17, 1947.

73. Yehuda Amichai, interview with author, June 23, 1996.

74. Amichai papers / Beinecke, box 19, file 276, November 30, 1965; ibid., box 19, folder 279, notebook from 1965, on which it says "In a hotel in Jerusalem."

75. Amichai likely had additional notebooks or papers, which have since been lost, on which he wrote more complete drafts. As a result, many poems in the collection have no parallel drafts in the Beinecke Library.

76. Amichai papers / Beinecke, box 4, file 64, notepad from March 1959; ibid., box 4, folder 65, January 1958.

77. The "translation" metaphor has been applied to the psychoanalytic realm. According to Freud and other psychoanalysts, the psychoanalyst "translates" the subconscious into the various codes of normative language. The poet's work is not dissimilar: he delves into his subconscious and "translates" it into words. The language closest to the subconscious is the mother tongue. A poet who does not write in his mother tongue thus has a vast translating project. For Freud and the analyst's work in a multilingual context, see Jacqueline Amati-Mehler, "La langue exilée," *Revue française de psychanalyse* (March 1993): 917–25.

78. Amichai papers / Beinecke, box 4 folder 63, undated notepad Fav-O-Rite.

79. Ibid., box 1, file 17.

80. *Poems: 1948–1962*, 313; LOP, 61. I am grateful to Rabbi Thomas Klein for the elucidation of the Talmudic context of this poem.

81. This verse is part of the "Searching for Leaven" ritual, traditionally recited in Aramaic, not Hebrew.

82. Thanks to Rabbi Thomas Klein for his assistance in searching Talmudic and Rabbinic issues.

83. LOP, 61.

84. Amichai papers / Beinecke, box 4, file 63, March 1959; ibid., box 4, file 64, notepad from March 1959.

85. LOP, 61.

86. Yehuda Amichai, "I Write from Right to Left," *Moznayim*, 10, no. 33 (March 1960): 275.

87. Glenda Abramson, *The Writing of Yehuda Amichai: A Thematic Approach* (Albany: SUNY Press, 1989), 83–84.

88. Amichai, "I Write from Right to Left," 275.

89. Amichai papers / Beinecke, box 4, folder 65; small beige Block-Not notepad 104, April 1959.

90. Ibid., box 4, file 65, small orange notepad, spring 1956.

91. Ibid., box 4, file 65, small gray notepad marked "January 1958."

92. For example, the line "the flower holds my hand" first appears in German in Amichai papers / Beinecke, box 4, file 64, notepad from April 1957. It appears in Hebrew in ibid., box 4, file 64, in a notepad marked "July–August 1958," as part of a draft for "Summer or Its End." While the line did not make it into the published poem, it proves that Amichai translated his German lines for use in his Hebrew poetry.

93. *Sade* appears in the feminine in the Talmud, but sounds incorrect in modern Hebrew. Amichai's mistake may also stem from the fact that the plural form of the masculine noun *sade* is feminine.

94. "Of Three or Four in a Room" in *Poems: 1948-1962*, 97.

95. Ibid., 116.

96. LOP, 21; I slightly altered the translation made by Harshav to demonstrate the awkwardness of the original construction.

97. *Poems: 1948–1962*, 26; LOP, 12.

98. I have modified Harshav's translation to reflect the awkwardness in the Hebrew. The second quoted line is translated in Harshav as "Pour down."

99. *Poems: 1948–1962*, 114; LOP, 36.

100. Amichai papers / Beinecke, box 4, file 65, small orange notepad, spring 1956 (scrap #2).

101. Amichai also used German to draw images of beauty that are more romantic than much of his Hebrew verse. See ibid., box 4, file 64, small brown notebook, July 1959; ibid., box 4, file 62, notepad, May 1957; ibid., box 4, file 65, on an undated scrap of paper; ibid., box 4, folder 63; small orange notebook September 1958; ibid., box 4, file 64, small brown notebook, July 1959.

102. Sandbank, *Two Pools in the Forest*, 206, 245, fnn. 52 and 53.

103. *Poems: 1948–1962*, 357. This poem contains an additional Hebrew phrase with a German construction: "And the one that was loaned to your body, the blood. . . ."

104. To demonstrate how easily the original Hebrew is converted to a correct German construction, I am not using existing English translations for this discussion.

105. SP, 42. See chapter 12 for the full discussion of "Elegy on an Abandoned Village."

106. "From a Letter," *Poems: 1948–1962*, 232; "The Intention Was Different," *Poems: 1948–1962*, 300.

107. "From a Letter," *Poems: 1948–1962*, 232.

108. Amichai papers / Beinecke, box 19, file 277, 1967.

109. Ibid., box 19, file 277, dark green / brown (khaki) notebook, June 23, 1966.

110. "The Travels of the Last Benjamin of Tudela," SP, 60–86; 72, lines 530–31. Memories of his migration are incorporated into this epic, published in 1968; ibid., box 10, file 151. He wrote it during this time (drafts for "Tudela" in the archive are written on the back of Hanna Sokolov's old tests).

111. I saw the notebooks in the archive before it was catalogued and recommended that access to them be restricted because they contain very personal materials. My recommendation was accepted.

112. Amichai papers / Beinecke, box 19; folder 277, light blue notebook (summer 1967). An embodiment of Amichai's resorting to German to express loss never made it to the archive. According to Yehudit Silber, Amichai wrote a poem in German about Ruth Hanover and sent it to Rabbi Hanover, who was living in America. The poem has since been lost.

113. Ibid., box 19, folder 279, notebook from 1965, on which it says "In a hotel in Jerusalem."

114. Ibid., box 31, file 379, Batman notebook, 1966.

115. Ibid., box 19, file 276, November 30, 1965.

116. Ibid., box 31, file 13, folder 379, black marble notebook number 7 (1966).

117. Ibid., box 1, file 13, notebook from 1980, on a torn sheet in Hebrew. Neither the 1966 poem nor the 1980 poem are published.

118. Ibid., box 19, file 279, blue notebook from 1966; ibid., box 19, file 276, notebook from September 1974–January 1975. For Amichai's father in his poetry, see: Abramson, *The Writing of Yehuda Amichai*, 50–71.

119. Amichai papers / Beinecke, box 12; file 174, colorful notebook with red car on it (January–February 1977).

120. Yehuda Amichai, *Lo me'akhshav lo mikan* (Not of This Time, Not of This Place) (Tel Aviv: Schocken, 1963) (subsequently, *Not of This Time*). Translated as *Not of This Time, Not of This Place*, trans. Shlomo Katz (New York: Harper and Row, 1968) (subsequently, Katz). If there is no reference to the English translation, it is because there is no available English translation for the lines being cited. The often-transliterated German quoted in the original Hebrew is absent in the English version, thus preventing the English reader from being aware of the German layers of the text. The analysis here, therefore, will refer to both the Hebrew original and the English translation.

121. The only other work in which Amichai uses German is the skit "Class Meeting," in which a new immigrant in Jerusalem speaks two German words, *Kein Hebraisch*, in Yehuda Amichai, *Pa'amonim verakavot* (Bells and Trains) (Tel Aviv: Schocken, 1992), 236.

122. Yehuda Amichai, interview with author, June 23, 1996; Dan Miron, interview with author, summer 1997. Miron claimed that the original manuscript containing the German passages was lost.

123. *Not of This Time*, 66; Katz, 48. Another example of the comforting effects of German occurs in *Not of This Time*, 93; Katz, 59. Joel is ready to avenge the death of Little Ruth, but is disarmed when he hears the familiar names of German coins. He then realizes that he is no longer ready to fight.

124. *Not of This Time*, 397.

125. Ibid., 331.

126. The following textbooks were published by Oldenbourg Verlag Muencher (Munich): Hans Stieglitz, et al., eds., *Lesebuch fuer den 2. und 3. Schuelerjahrgang katholischer Volkshauptschulen Bayerns* (1927); Wilhelm Ledermann, et al., eds., *Lesebuch fuer den 4. und 5. Schuelerjahrgang katholischer Volkshauptschulen Bayerns. 4. Auflage* (1930 [1927]). These stories appear in their original German in the German translation of the novel, *Nicht von jetzt, nicht von hier*, trans. Ruth Achlama (Zurich: Pendo Verlag AG, 1998 [1992]). "Little Red Riding Hood" appears on p. 221, "Sleeping Beauty" on p. 352, and the quote *"Fuchs du hast die Gans gestohlen"* (fox, you stole the goose) on p. 270.

127. Norbert Hellmann, interview with author December 16, 2004; Ludwig Bravman, interview with author, July 14, 2005.

128. *Not of This Time*, 151; Katz, 94.

129. *Nicht von jetzt, nicht von hier*, 122. In Germany, *A Winter's Tale*, Heine also references these lines.

130. *Not of This Time*, 151; Katz, 94.

131. *Not of This Time*, 152; Katz, 95.

132. Amichai papers / Beinecke, box 4, file 65, small gray notepad (January 1958; Koh I Noor; Be quiet).

133. Joseph Prestel, et al., eds., *Lesebuch fuer den 6. und 7. Schuelerjahrgang katholischer Volkshauptschulen Bayerns* (Munich: Oldenbourg Verlag Muencher, 1927).

134. Heinrich Heine, "Der Heimkehr: 1823–1824," in *Buch der Lieder*, 1827. Translated as "Lorelei" in *Songs of Love and Grief: A Bilingual Anthology in the Verse Forms of the Original*, trans. Walter W. Arndt (Evanston, Ill.: Northwestern University Press, 1995), 40–41. "Lorelei" (or "The Lorelei") is the second untitled poem in "Der Heimkehr."

135. *Songs of Love and Grief*, 40–41.

136. *Not of This Time*, 422–3; Katz, 250.

137. This classical poem was an integral part of the curriculum in the German-Jewish elementary school.

138. *Not of This Time*, 422–3; Katz, 250; *Nicht von jetzt, nicht von hier*, 282.

139. *Not of This Time*, 57.

140. For example, *"Hexenschuss.* A witch hit me." *Not of This Time*, 312; Amichai's idiosyncratic etymological thinking is at play in the novel. The word *Hexenschuss* in common usage is a neck "ache." Amichai interprets it literally, "a witch hit me." (*Hexe* means "witch" in German; *Schuss* is a shot, as in gunshot).

141. Not of This Time, 462.

142. Ibid., 127.

143. Ibid., 266.

144. Not of This Time, 589. The Hebrew version translates all the different names of the places around Gersfeld into Hebrew; Katz, 317.

145. Not of This Time, 95.

146. Ibid., 99.

147. Ibid., 406.

148. Ibid., 127.

149. Ibid., 435, 512.

150. Ibid., 406.

151. Ibid., 267.

152. Ibid., 517.

153. Dan Miron, interview with author, summer 1997.

154. Not of This Time, 322; Likewise, the character of Leonora rests because "time does not call her." While this construction sounds strange in English or Hebrew, it stems from a German expression. Ibid., 497.

155. Lebkuchen are traditional German Christmas cookies similar to gingerbread, but in the Jewish museum in Berlin, one can still see a kosher Lebkuchen from the southern German town of Trier.

156. Not of This Time, 562; Katz, 299.

157. Amichai papers / Beinecke, box 1, file 16; ibid., box 19, file 284, notebook from January–June 1987.

158. Ibid., box 4, file 16, undated sheet of paper marked "IV."

159. Not of This Time, 86; Katz, 53.

160. Not of This Time, 148; Katz, 94.

161. Not of This Time, 567; Katz, 304; The song appears again in Not of This Time, 124, Katz 80.

162. Christian Leo, Zwischen Erinnern und Vergessen: Jehuda Amichais Roman "Nicht von jetzt, nicht von hier" im philosophischen und literarischen Kontext (Wuerzburg, Germany: Koenigshausen und Neumann, 2004), 115 (subsequently, Between Remembering and Forgetting). The phrase, "Muß i denn zum Staedtele hinaus" is in Nicht von jetzt, nicht von hier, 355.

163. Leo, Between Remembering and Forgetting, 149, fn. 76. According to Leo, the secondary character Mr. Greenbaum is modeled on Mr. Rosenbaum, a Wuerzburgian Holocaust survivor. After WWII, he worked in the Israeli Holocaust Museum Yad vashem, and showed Amichai this classified photograph.

164. Ibid. According to Leo, Wahler, a lawyer who worked at the Nuremberg trial, was originally from Wuerzburg and had left in a Kindertransport. He discovered the photographs of the Wuerzburg deportation, found his parents in them, and used them in the

trial. After the trial, the files disappeared before the Nazis pictured could be identified and resurfaced only in 2000. Wahler saved the originals; ("*Muss i denn . . .*" was written on the original photographs).

165. Author's visit to Wuerzburg, October 1, 2004; Leo, interview with author, September 2004; Leo, *Between Remembering and Forgetting*, 1, fn. 7. Amichai gave his translator a short version of the novel in Hebrew, and she corrected it, translated it, and sent it to Germany. Amichai then compared the two texts and corrected the translation.

166. The process of revealing the meaning of a text through its translation to the author's mother tongue is discussed in Gold, "Betrayal of the Mother Tongue," 246–47.

167. For example, at the end of the booklet published in Wuerzburg in honor of Amichai's seventy-fifth birthday, the editor wrote that there is no answer to why it became possible to kill the Jews of Wuerzburg, and ended with the German idiom "*Diese Tuer is nicht geschlossen* [this door is not closed]." Hans Steidle, ed., *Ein kleines Geburtstagspraesent aus Wuerzburg: Festgabe fuer Jehuda Amichai zum 75 Geburtstag* (Wuerzburg, Germany: Verlag der Leonhard Frank-Gesellschaft, 1999), 39.

168. *Not of This Time*, 54.

169. Amichai papers / Beinecke, box 1, file 15, on the back of stationary from Hotel Helmhaus, Zurich; ibid., box 19, file 284, January, 1987–June 1987; ibid., box 12, file 172, yellow notebook, November 1984–September 1985.

170. *Not of This Time*, 53.

171. Ibid., 184.

172. "'*Saujuden!*' (filthy Jews!);" ibid., 204. Amichai did not translate it correctly; ibid., 572.

173. Ibid., 126, 407.

174. Ibid., 106.

175. LOP, 428.

176. Yehuda Amichai, interview with author, June 23, 1996.

177. Amichai papers / Beinecke, box 12, file 172, notebook, November 1984–September 1985.

178. Ibid., box 12, file 172, notebook, November 1984–September 1985

179. Ibid., box 19, file 284, January 1987–June 1987; ibid., box 12, file 172, yellow notebook, November 1984–September 1985.

180. Ibid., box 19, file 284, notebook from January–June 1987.

181. Ibid., box 1, file 16, large, torn, white piece of paper.

182. Ibid., box 19, file 285, notebook from September 1991.

183. Ibid., box 20; folder 297; undated brown notebook.

184. Johann Wolfgang von Goethe, "Der Erlkoenig," in *The Poems of Goethe*, trans. E. A. Bowring (Boston: S. E. Cassino, 1882), 99.

185. Rosa Grimm, interview with author, March 2005; Joseph Prestel, et al., eds., *Lesebuch fuer den 6. und 7.*

186. SP, 60–86; 82, lines 921–24.

187. Yehuda Amichai, "A Journey in the Map of the Past," *Bamahane* #13, no. 18 (January 2, 1962): 11.

188. *Not of This Time*, 34.

189. Ibid., 563; Katz, 300.

190. *Not of This Time*, 567; Katz, 303.

191. Yehuda Amichai, interview with author, June 23, 1996.

192. Amichai papers / Beinecke, box 4, file 60, notebook that had the paper in it (submitted in his third, senior year), probably around 1954/1955, 30–31.

193. Yehuda Amichai, *The Great Tranquility: Questions and Answers*, trans. Glenda Abramson and Tudor Parfitt (New York: The Sheep Meadow Press, 1997), 7 (subsequently cited as GT). Originally published in *Shalva gedola: she'elot uteshuvot* (Tel Aviv: Schocken, 1980). The poem refers to a real meeting, which was recorded in Letter to Ruth Z., #21, October 14–15, 1947.

194. GT, 7.

195. In Letter to Ruth Z., #38, November 21, 1947, Amichai refers to a casualty in an ambush as the *akedah*.

196. Genesis 22:2.

197. Amichai papers / Beinecke, box 31, file 378, notebook 1965.

198. Ibid., box 20, file 297, no date.

199. This address also exists in the Bible in Elisha's call to Elija, who ascended to heaven. The repeated address is also a formula for a cry of lament, as in David's cry for Absalom: "My son, Absalom, my son, my son Absalom" (Samuel II 19:5).

200. Loschuetz, "Wie lange koennen Erinnerungen standhalten?"; Sey, interview with Amichai.

201. Schulke, "Spurensuche und lyrisches Ich."

5. GROWING UP IN PALESTINE (PP. 151–59)

1. Yehuda Amichai's letters to Ruth Z. (August 31, 1947–April 11, 1948) will be housed at Hayisre'elim harishonim (First Israelis Archive), Heksherim: The Research Center for Jewish and Israeli Literature and Culture, Ben-Gurion University of the Negev. References cite the number of the letter (as given by Amichai) and the date. Letter to Ruth Z., #48, December 9, 1947.

2. Amichai's recollections of this trip appeared first in 1963 and were republished in Yehuda Amichai, "Venice–Three Times," in *Baru'ah hanora'a hazot: sipurim* (In That Terrible Wind) (Tel Aviv: Schocken, [1965] 1985), 287–98 (subsequently, *In That Terrible Wind*).

3. Letter to Ruth Z., #3, September 5, 1947; Yehuda A[michai]. Holocaust Testimony (HVT-2679), interview conducted by Geoffrey Hartman and Benjamin Harshav, November 3, 1994, Fortunoff Video Archive for Holocaust Testimonies, Yale University Library (subsequently, Yehuda A[michai]. Holocaust Testimony.)

4. Yehuda Amichai, "Memories of Israel," *Diversion*, May 1988, 171–75, 320, 322.

5. Letter to Ruth Z., #8, September 14, 1947.

6. Amichai, "Memories of Israel," 174; Judy Cooper-Weill, "A Day in the Life of Yehuda Amichai," *Newsview*, January 23–29, 1985, 32.

7. Yehuda A[michai]. Holocaust Testimony.

8. Bea Stadtler, "The Story of an Israeli Soldier-Poet," *Cleveland Jewish News*, April 7, 1967, 23; Zehava Mendelssohn, interview with Amichai, *Jerusalem Post Magazine*, February 12, 1971, 12.

9. Mendelssohn, interview with Amichai.

10. Dan Omer, "In This Burning Country, Words Must Serve as Shade" (series of interviews with Amichai), *Proza*, no. 25 (July 1978): 4–5.

11. Amichai, "Memories of Israel," 320.

12. Benny Morris, "Power of Imagination," *Jerusalem Post, 40th Independence Day Magazine*, April 20, 1988, 24.

13. Amichai, "Memories of Israel," 320.

14. Yehuda A[michai]. Holocaust Testimony.

15. Amichai, "Memories of Israel," 175, 320; Roland Flade, *Die Wuerzburger Juden* (Wuerzburg, Germany: Stuertz Verlag, 1987), 302 (subsequently, *The Jews of Wuerzburg*).

16. Rahel Hollander-Steingart, "In My Heart Is a Museum" (interview with Amichai), *Jerusalem Post, Rosh Hashanah Supplement*, September 28, 1981, 5.

17. Yehuda Amichai, "Yehuda Amichai," in *Mein Judentum*, ed. Hans Jürgen Schultz (Stuttgart: Kreuz, 1978), 22–35 (subsequently, "Yehuda Amichai").

18. Yehuda Amichai, "Memories of Israel," 174; Yehuda A[michai]. Holocaust Testimony.

19. Flade, *The Jews of Wuerzburg*, 302.

20. Yehuda A[michai]. Holocaust Testimony; Amichai, "Yehuda Amichai," 29.

21. Amichai, "Yehuda Amichai," 29.

22. Flade, *The Jews of Wuerzburg*, 302–3; Amichai, "Yehuda Amichai," 30.

23. Yehuda Amichai, interview with author, June 23, 1996.

24. Yehuda A[michai]. Holocaust Testimony; Rochelle Furstenberg, "Poet Revolutionary" (interview with Yehuda Amichai), *Jerusalem Report*, December 1, 1994.

25. Yehuda Amichai Papers. General Collection, Beinecke Rare Book and Manuscript Library, Yale University (subsequently, Amichai papers/Beinecke), box 12, file 175, March 1981–September 1982 notebook. There were 34 boxes in the precatalogued archive with consecutively numbered files in each box. References to these materials cite the uncatalogued box number and file number.

26. Amichai, "Yehuda Amichai," 30; Omer, "In This Burning Country," 4.

27. Dan Ben-Amos, conversation with author, April 2006.

28. Ludwig Bravman, interview with author, July 14, 2005; Ya'akov Pfeuffer, interview with author, October 2002; Mordechai Einsbacher, interview with author, December 10, 2004; Norbert Hellmann, interview with author, December 16, 2004; Henry Eschwege, interview with author, February 1, 2005.

29. Yehuda A[michai]. Holocaust Testimony.

30. Hollander-Steingart, "In My Heart Is a Museum," 5.

31. Letter to Ruth Z., #7, September 11, 1947.

32. Amichai papers / Beinecke, box 20, file 298, hardcover, black notebook, July 1980–October 1980.

33. Amichai, "Yehuda Amichai," 31; Yehuda A[michai]. Holocaust Testimony.

34. Omer, "In This Burning Country," 4–5. Omer quotes a poem in which Amichai says, "In Petah Tikva . . . In my Childhood." Yehuda Amichai, Poem #27, Hazman (Tel Aviv: Schocken, 1977).

35. Amichai papers / Beinecke, box 31, folder 385, typed draft of Every Man Is Born a Poet, without publication details 4; Yehuda A[michai]. Holocaust Testimony.

36. Hayim Nagid, "I Think That This Land Is Paradise for Poets" (interview with Amichai), Ma'ariv, April 15, 1977.

37. Yehuda A[michai]. Holocaust Testimony.

38. Omer, "In This Burning Country," 7, 8.

39. Ruth Kobliner, interview with author, October 4, 2002; Furstenberg, "Poet Revolutionary."

40. Kobliner, interview with author, October 4, 2002.

41. Yehuda A[michai]. Holocaust Testimony.

42. Amichai, interview with author, June 23, 1996. Amichai named the rabbi in his novel after him.

43. Ibid. When Amichai did attend services, he went to the Yeshurun synagogue or to another synagogue in the neighborhood, Sha'arey Hessed.

44. Amichai papers / Beinecke, box 19, file 276, undated page.

45. Yehuda Amichai, "A Song of Lies on Sabbath Eve," in Shalva gedola: she'elot uteshuvot (Tel Aviv: Schocken, 1980), 69; translated as "Sabbath Lie," in Yehuda Amichai, The Great Tranquility: Questions and Answers, trans. Glenda Abramson and Tudor Parfitt (New York: Sheep Meadow Press, 1997), 47 (subsequently GT).

46. Edith Raim, "Verfolgung und Exil der Juedischen Familie Hanover aus Wuerzburg," in Mainfraenkisches Jahrbuch fuer Geschichte und Kunst, no. 56 (Wuerzburg, Germany: Freunde Mainfraenkischer Kunst and Geschichte E.V., 2004), 319–24 (subsequently, "The Wandering and Exile")

47. Aryeh Arad, "Bells Announcing Bad Tidings: The Poet Yehuda Amichai Tells of His Childhood in Southern Germany," (interview with Amichai), Bamahane (N.d. [most likely the 1960s]), 19, 39; Corinna Benning, interview with Yehuda Amichai, Bavarian radio station BR Alpha, May 4, 1998. For complete transcription, see Christian Leo, Zwischen Erinnern und Vergessen: Jehuda Amichais Roman "Nicht von jetzt, nicht von hier" im philosophischen und literarischen Kontext (Wuerzburg, Germany: Koenigshausen and Neumann, 2004), 247–57. See also chapter 3.

48. Chanoch Rinott, Encyclopedia Judaica, vol. 16, s.v. "Youth Aliyah" (Jerusalem: Keter, 1974, 861–65). Started in 1932, Youth Aliyah was a branch of the Zionist movement founded

for the purpose of rescuing Jewish children. It brought 5,000 children to Palestine before WWII; Kobliner, interview with October 4, 2002; Raim, "The Wandering and Exile," 319.

49. Raim, "The Wandering and Exile," 321, 326.

50. Ibid., 321.

51. Kobliner, interview with author, October 4, 2002.

52. Raim, "The Wandering and Exile," 321. A letter from Rosi to her father indicates that she knew about her father's arrest after Kristallnacht and that the Pfeuffers would have known of it as well.

53. Ibid, 322.

54. Amichai, "Memories of Israel," 320.

55. Yehuda A[michai]. Holocaust Testimony.

56. Dahlia Karpel, "Hoping for the Nobel Prize" (interview with Amichai), Ha'ir, November 3, 1989; Morris, "Power of Imagination," 22; Kobi Nisim, interview with Amichai, Al Hamishmar, June 5, 1992.

57. Kobliner, interview with author, October 4, 2002; Einsbacher, interview with author, December 10, 2004. One such Wuerzburgian was Mordechai Einsbacher, one of Amichai's classmates, who had survived the concentration camps.

58. Raim, "The Wandering and Exile," 333.

59. Ibid., 323–24.

60. Ibid., 321.

61. Ibid., 327.

62. Ibid., 321. According to the Gestapo file in the Wuerzburg archive, Ruth Hanover left for Holland on January 4, 1939, with the help of the Jewish Welfare Organization; Arad, "Bells Announcing Bad Tidings," 39.

63. Edgar Reichmann, "Yehuda Amichai talks to Edgar Reichmann," UNESCO Courier XLVII, no. 10, (October 1994), 7.

64. Omer, "In This Burning Country," 5; Furstenberg, "Poet Revolutionary."

65. Omer, "In This Burning Country," 5.

66. Alex Zehavi, "Poetry as Consolation" (interview with Amichai), Davar, May 7, 1976.

67. Yehuda Amichai, "Agnon and I," Ha'aretz, January, 1978.

68. Zehavi, "Poetry as Consolation."

69. Hollander-Steingart, "In My Heart Is a Museum," 5; Idit Klein, Judith Rosenbaum, and Tanya Schlam, "The Joy of the Struggle: A Talk with Yehuda Amichai," Urim V'Tumim #6, no. 2 (winter 1991): 28. (Urim V'Tumim is a student quarterly of Yale's Jewish community.)

70. Ram Evron, interview with Amichai for Israeli television, 1998.

71. Hollander-Steingart, "In My Heart Is a Museum," 5.

72. Ibid.; Yehuda A[michai]. Holocaust Testimony.

73. Esther Fuchs, "I Am a Man Who Writes Poems" (interview with Amichai conducted in Hebrew, Austin, Texas, March 22, 1982), in Encounters with Israeli Authors (Marblehead, Mass.: Micah, 1982), 86–92, 90.

74. Amichai, "Agnon and I."

75. Yehuda A[michai]. Holocaust Testimony; Yehuda Amichai, "A Language of the Heart," British Broadcasting Corporation, Radio 3, Talks and Documentaries Dept., prerecorded April 9, 1979, transmitted September 19, 1979.

76. Yehuda A[michai]. Holocaust Testimony.

77. Morris, "Power of Imagination," 22.

78. Amichai, "Yehuda Amichai," 31.

79. Omer, "In This Burning Country," 5.

80. Ibid.

81. Yehuda A[michai]. Holocaust Testimony.

82. Omer, "In This Burning Country," 5.

83. Amichai papers / Beinecke, box 6, folder 99.

84. Hollander-Steingart, "In My Heart Is a Museum," 5.

85. Yehuda A[michai]. Holocaust Testimony; Hollander-Steingart, "In My Heart Is a Museum," 5.

86. Mendelssohn, interview with Amichai, 12. Yehuda's art teacher was the great Israeli painter Ardon. German boxing champion Horst Schade, who was married to a Jew, taught Amichai boxing and poetry; Yehuda A[michai]. Holocaust Testimony; Ingrid Wiltmann, Nur Ewigkeit ist kein Exil: Lebensgeschichten aus Israel: Mit einem Nachwort von Anat Feinberg (Moehlin, Switzerland: Rausreif, 1997), 90–98.

87. Omer, "In This Burning Country," 5.

88. Ibid.; Yehuda A[michai]. Holocaust Testimony; Hollander-Steingart, "In My Heart Is a Museum," 5.

89. Yehuda A[michai]. Holocaust Testimony.

90. Ibid.; Yehuda Amichai, speech given at the creative writing workshop at the Poetry Society in New York City, 1996.

91. Omer, "In This Burning Country," 5.

92. Yehuda Amichai, "Class Reunion," in In That Terrible Wind, 7–48, 11.

93. Amichai, "Memories of Israel," 320.

94. Amichai, "Yehuda Amichai," 31.

95. Raim, "The Wandering and Exile," 333.

96. Yehuda A[michai]. Holocaust Testimony.

97. Amichai, "Memories of Israel," 320; Omer, "In This Burning Country," 5.

98. Omer, "In This Burning Country," 5; Hollander-Steingart, "In My Heart Is a Museum," 5.

99. Amichai, interview with Evron, 1998.

100. Interview with Amichai in Yedi'ot Aharonot, 1989.

101. Yehuda A[michai]. Holocaust Testimony; Omer, "In This Burning Country," 5; interview with Amichai in Yedi'ot Aharonot, 1989.

102. Yehuda Amichai, "Class Reunion," 25.

103. Omer, "In This Burning Country," 5.

104. Ibid.

105. Interview with Amichai in *Yedi'ot Aharonot*, 1989.

106. Amichai, "Agnon and I."

107. Interview with Yehuda Amichai in *Yedi'ot Aharonot*, 1989.

108. Yehuda A[michai]. Holocaust Testimony.

109. Omer, "In This Burning Country," 5; interview with Amichai in *Yedi'ot Aharonot*, 1989; Hollander-Steingart, "In My Heart Is a Museum," 5; Stadtler, "The Story of an Israeli Soldier-Poet," 23.

110. Yehuda A[michai]. Holocaust Testimony; interview in *Yedi'ot Aharonot*, 1989.

111. Stadtler, "The Story of an Israeli Soldier-Poet," 23.

112. Amichai, "Agnon and I."

113. Omer, "In This Burning Country," 5; Yehuda A[michai]. Holocaust Testimony.

114. Omer, "In This Burning Country," 5.

115. Amichai, "Agnon and I."

116. Yehuda A[michai]. Holocaust Testimony.

6. "AND THE MIGRATION OF MY PARENTS HAS NOT SUBSIDED IN ME" (PP. 160–78)

1. Chapter title is from Yehuda Amichai, "And the Migration of My Parents," *Shirim: 1948–1962* (Poems: 1948–1962) (Tel Aviv: Schocken, [1963] 1977), 191 (subsequently, *Poems: 1948–1962*). Translated in *Yehuda Amichai: A Life of Poetry 1948–1994*, ed. and trans. Benjamin Harshav and Barbara Harshav (New York: HarperCollins, 1994), 51 (subsequently, LOP). When references to a Hebrew text are made and no published English translations are cited, there are no English translations for the lines being discussed. This chapter draws on my article "And the Migration of My Parents Has Not Subsided in Me: Yehuda Amichai, *Middle Eastern Literatures: Incorporating EdebiYat*, vol. 8, no. 2 (July 2005), 171–75.

2. Yehuda Amichai Papers. General Collection, Beinecke Rare Book and Manuscript Library, Yale University, New Haven, Conn. (subsequently, Amichai papers / Beinecke), box 12; folder 178, draft of an interview with Yehuda Amichai by Doron Weber, 8. There were 34 boxes in the precatalogued archive with consecutively numbered files in each box. References to these materials cite the uncatalogued box number and file number.

3. Benny Morris, "Power of Imagination," *Jerusalem Post, 40th Independence Day Magazine*, April 20, 1988, 24; Rahel Hollander-Steingart, "In My Heart Is a Museum" (interview with Amichai), *Jerusalem Post, Rosh Hashanah Supplement*, September 28, 1981, 5.

4. The sources in which Amichai or others claim that he emigrated in 1936 generally date from the 1960s, and the ones in which he or others claim that it was 1935 were published later. Sources that say that he arrived in Israel in 1936 include Aryeh Arad, "Bells Announcing Bad Tidings: The Poet Yehuda Amichai Tells of His Childhood in Southern Germany" (interview with Amichai), *Bamahane* (n.d. [most likely the 1960s]); Dan Tsalka,

Encyclopedia Judaica, vol. 2 (Jerusalem: Keter Publishing, 1971), s.v. "Yehuda Amichai," 838; Dor ba'aretz [A Generation in the Land (An Anthology)] (Tel Aviv: 1958), 339. Sources that claim that he arrived in 1935 include Yehuda Amichai, "Yehuda Amichai," in Mein Judentum, ed. Hans Jürgen Schultz (Stuttgart: Kreuz, 1978); Haim Chertok, "A Conversation with Yehuda Amichai," Jewish Frontier, June / July 1985, 15; Judy Cooper-Weill, "A Day in the Life of Yehuda Amichai," Newsview, January 23–29, 1985, 32; Roland Flade, Die Wuerzburger Juden (Wuerzburg, Germany: Stuertz Verlag, 1987); Yehuda Amichai's speech upon receiving the Kulturpreis (cultural prize) in Wuerzburg, June 22, 1981, as quoted in Main Post, August 5, 1991, and in Roland Flade, "Reliving Childhood at Saint Kilian's Festival," Allgemeine Judische Wochenzeitung (Bonn), no. 35, August 29, 1991, 24; Werner Dettelbacher, "Die Geschichte des Ludwig Pfeuffer," in Ein kleines Geburtstagspraesent aus Wuerzburg, ed. Hans Steidle (Wuerzburg, Germany: Leonhard-Frank-Gesellschaft, 1999), 9; Amichai, interview with the author, June 1996; "Dates and Turning Points in Amichai's Life," in Yehuda Amichai: mivhar ma'amare bikoret al yetsirato, Yehudit Tzvik, ed. (Yehuda Amichai: A Selection of Critical Essays on His Writings) (Tel Aviv: Hakibutz Hameuchad, 1988). The only exception is an interview with Yehuda Amichai, Jerusalem Post, July 26, 1991, which, despite being a late interview, gives 1936 as the year of his immigration.

5. Dan Omer, "In This Burning Country, Words Must Serve as Shade" (series of interviews with Amichai), Proza, no. 25 (July 1978): 6.

6. Hollander-Steingart, "In My Heart Is a Museum," 5; Morris, "Power of Imagination," 24; Amichai papers / Beinecke, box 12, file 178, draft of interview with Amichai by Doron Weber.

7. Yehuda Amichai, "Venice–Three Times," in Baru'ah hanora'a hazot: sipurim (In That Terrible Wind) (Tel Aviv: Shocken, [1961] 1985), 287–98 (subsequently, In That Terrible Wind).

8. Immigration is one of the least-visited topics in Amichai's works. His second novel, Mi yitneni malon (Hotel in the Wilderness) (Tel Aviv: Bitan, 1971), is about being in exile. In describing Israelis in America and the alienation of the foreigner, it comes close to the subject, as well as by its affinity to the quasi-European weather and nature and Christian culture. Thus, it implicitly echoes the sentiments of immigrants.

9. Poems: 1948–1962, 213.

10. Yehuda Amichai, "Memories of Israel," Diversion, May 1988, 173–74.

11. Yehuda Amichai, "The Travels of Benjamin the Last, of Tudela," in Akhshav hara'ash (Now in the Storm: Poems 1963–1968) (Tel Aviv: Schocken, [1968] 1975) (subsequently, Now in the Storm), 97–139; LOP, 169–88. This autobiographical epic is unique in Amichai's oeuvre. It combines first- and second-person lyrical narratives, which unfold parallel narratives, one of immigration and growing up, the other of a heated, extramarital love affair with a divorce pending. Because of its later publication (1968), it is beyond the scope of this study. I consider it as a frame of reference, but not as an object of independent analysis.

12. The term "idiolect" refers to linguistic usages that characterize a specific work or a specific corpus of an author. It is the personal, idiosyncratic, and exclusive vocabulary of

the writer. Although the words exist in the language, the usage and meaning given to them in the context of an author's specific work are unique. See Michael Riffaterre, *Semiotics of Poetry* (Bloomington: Indiana University Press, 1978), 21, 23.

13. Quatrain 13 of the cycle "In a Right Angle," *Poems: 1948–1962*, 176. Translated into English in *The Selected Poetry of Yehuda Amichai*, trans. Chana Bloch and Stephen Mitchell (Berkeley and Los Angeles: University of California Press, 1996), 28 (subsequently, SP).

14. Yehuda Amichai's letters to Ruth Z. (August 31, 1947–April 11, 1948) will be housed at Hayisre'elim harishonim (First Israelis Archive), Heksherim: The Research Center for Jewish and Israeli Literature and Culture, Ben-Gurion University of the Negev. References cite the number of this letter (as given by Amichai) and the date. Letter to Ruth Z., #3, September 5, 1947.

15. Amichai papers / Beinecke, box 19, file 278 [or 279?], 1966 notebook, with cover inscribed, "Number Two," July 27, 1966. A similar association between ships and sadness is found in a poem entitled "Ein Schiff" in box 4, file 62, light blue notepad without a cover, no date.

16. *Poems: 1948–1962*, 164–73; SP, 21–27.

17. *Poems: 1948–1962*, 164–66; SP, 23. SP translates the third quoted line, "some temperate, some burning."

18. The trope of migrating birds is prevalent in the work of immigrant Israeli Hebrew poets. Amichai uses it sparingly but is clearly aware of that tradition. Especially relevant are Lea Goldberg's famous lines, "Perhaps only migrating birds know—/ . . . / the pain of two homelands." See the discussion in Dan Pagis, "The Pain of Two Homelands," in *Mihuts lashura* (Outside of the Line: Essays and Notes on Modern Hebrew Poetry), ed. Hanan Hever (Tel Aviv: Keshev Leshira, 2003), 84–95.

19. "Farewell," *Poems: 1948–1962*, 219; LOP 50; "Instructions for Her Voyage," *Poems: 1948–1962*, 239; LOP, 53; "A Man Near the Window," *Poems: 1948–1962*, 218; "A Last Night in the Boulevard," *Poems: 1948–1962*, 220; "Leaving," *Poems: 1948–1962*, 224; "The Time-Table," *Poems: 1948–1962*, 228; "A Room in the Hotel," *Poems: 1948–1962*, 229; "From a Letter," *Poems: 1948–1962*, 232.

20. "In a Right Angle," *Poems: 1948–1962*, 177,179, Amichai papers / Beinecke, box 1, file 15, on the back of stationery from Hotel Helmhaus, Zurich.

21. Ibid., box 31, folder 379, brown marble notebook, 1966, number 4. The same scrap speaks of travel and describes a meeting at Café Schraft in New York, so it was probably written during his trip to America.

22. Letter to Ruth Z., #3, September 5, 1947.

23. Ibid., #4, September 6, 1947.

24. *Poems: 1948–1962*, 219; SP, 31.

25. Letter to Ruth Z., #48, December 9, 1947.

26. *Poems: 1948–1962*, 226; SP, 32. SP translates the first quoted line: "Like two briefcases, we were interchanged for each other. . . ."

27. *Poems: 1948–1962*, 219; LOP, 50.

28. *Poems: 1948–1962*, 221; LOP, 51. The Harshavs' translation appears here with the following changes: line 8 in Harshav reads "Win and lose. Night recalls and day forgets." In line 11, the word "burden" is used instead of "gravity." In line 12, the words "even now" have been added. In line 13, the words "very own" have been added. Line 14 reads "On Mother Earth" instead of "On the crossroad, where. . . ." Line 16 reads "The weary hewer and the empty quarry in one body." In line 21, the words "which are" have been added.

29. Letter to Ruth Z., #1, August 31, 1947; Amichai papers / Beinecke, box 1, file 16, on three pieces of paper that are torn and burnt at their edges, found inside a separate bag inside file 16.

30. Shimon Sandbank, *Shete berekhot baya'ar* (Two Pools in the Forest) (Tel Aviv: Hakibbutz Hameuchad, 1976), 210, 212, 246.

31. Dan Miron, *Mul ha'ah hashotek* (Facing the Silent Brother: Essays on the Poetry on the War of Independence) (Jerusalem: Keter, 1992), 271–313.

32. Letter to Ruth Z., #18, October 8, 1947. Amichai also describes Ruth Z. as a boat in letter #33, November 11, 1947.

33. Yehuda Amichai, "You Pulled Me Like a Ship," *Likrat* 2, August 1952, 9.

34. Yehuda Amichai, "Little Song," in *Velo al menat lizkor* (Not to Remember) (Tel Aviv: Shocken, [1971] 1978), 129.

35. The vowels are the only difference between the two words; in Hebrew, vowels are indicated through vocalization marks underneath the letters and therefore, in the case of *oni / ani*, the resemblance is striking.

36. "Autobiography 1952" is a canonized poem. First published in *Likrat* 2 (August 1952): 13, it was later included in *Akhshav uvayamim ha'aherim* (Now and in the Other Days) (Tel Aviv: Likrat, 1955), 13; also reprinted in *Poems: 1948–1962*, 16; SP, 2.

37. "These Are Preparations for a Trip," *Now in the Storm*, 24; Amichai papers / Beinecke, box 31, file 379, 1966, black marble notebook no. 6.

38. A variation on the grouping of father, son, container/vessel, holy ark, and worry recurs in "Poem #10" in Yehuda Amichai, *Zeman* (Time) (Tel Aviv: Schocken, 1977), which describes the child sleeping in the holy ark of his father's worry. For a detailed discussion, see Nili Gold, *Lo kabrosh: gilgule imagim vetavniyot beshirat Yehuda Amichai* (Not Like a Cypress: Transformations of Images and Structures in the Poetry of Yehuda Amichai) (Tel Aviv and Jerusalem: Schocken, 1994), 164–74.

39. "Autobiography 1952," *Poems: 1948–1962*, 16; LOP, 7.

40. *Poems: 1948–1962*, 30; SP, 5.

41. "Farewell," *Poems: 1948–1962*, 219; LOP, 50.

42. Exodus 22:20.

43. *Now in the Storm*, 115, lines 446–47; SP, 71, lines 448–40.

44. *Now in the Storm*, 120, lines 563–64; SP, 74, lines 565–66.

45. *Now in the Storm*, lines 1038–39; SP, 86, lines 1044–46.

46. SP, 13. As noted in chapter 2, this could also relate to the parents' worried discussions in Palestine.

47. Amichai papers / Beinecke, box 4, file 60, notepad from November 1958.

48. See Nili Gold, "Betrayal of the Mother Tongue in the Creation of National Identity," in *Ideology and Jewish Identity in American and Israeli Literature*, ed. Emily Miller Buddick (Albany: SUNY-Albany Press, 2001), 278–302; 356–59.

49. Amichai papers / Beinecke, box 4, folder 63, small orange notebook, September 1958; a similar sentiment is found in ibid., box 4, file 64, in papers inscribed "1958–59."

50. For further discussion of this segment of "The Travels of Benjamin the Last, of Tudela," see chapter 4.

51. *Poems: 1948–1962*, 110–11, lines 335–44; LOP, 169, lines 325–34. See chapter 4 for further discussion of these lines.

52. *Poems: 1948–1962*, 30; SP, 5.

53. Genesis 22:13.

54. For the binding of Isaac in Israeli literature, see Ruth Kartun-Blum, *Profane Scriptures: Reflections on the Dialogue with the Bible in Modern Hebrew Literature* (Cincinnati, Ohio: Hebrew Union College Press, 1999).

55. "As for the World," *Poems: 1948–1962*, 213; LOP, 47.

56. "A Man near the Window," *Poems: 1948–1962*, 188.

57. "Such as Sorrow," *Poems: 1948–1962*, 226; SP, 32. SP translated the word tikim (bags) as "briefcases" and omitted the words "like a raincoat in the stations."

58. *Poems: 1948–1962*, 194.

59. Ibid., 215; LOP, 48.

60. *Poems: 1948–1962*, 215; LOP, 48.

61. Amichai papers / Beinecke, box 4, file 65, little gray notebook 112, September 1957.

62. Amichai papers / Beinecke, box 4, file 64, small orange notepad, spring 1956. A similar sentiment is voiced in box 4, file 63, pad that says "Fav-O-Rite for water color NY Chicago," n.d.

63. Amichai papers / Beinecke, box 4, file 63, pad that says "Fav-O-Rite for water color NY Chicago," n.d.

64. In that respect, this poem is similar to "Little Ruth." Both are the only poems in the entire corpus that carry the weight of a highly intense trauma. For a discussion of "Little Ruth," see chapter 3.

7. THE LOVE STORY (PP. 191–208)

1. The word "seminary" here does not denote any theological or religious affiliation or teaching.

2. Ruth Z., written communication with author, May 2003.

3. Background information for this chapter is drawn from the author's interviews and written communications with Ruth Z. These occurred on May 2003; August 22, October 22, and December 13, 2004; January 13 and December 14, 2005; and January 15, February 12, and March 9, 2006.

4. "A Meeting with My Father," in Yehuda Amichai, *Shalva gedola: she'elot uteshuvot* (Tel Aviv: Schocken, 1980), 8. Translated in *The Great Tranquility: Questions and Answers*, trans. Glenda Abramson and Tudor Parfitt (New York: Sheep Meadow Press, 1997), 7 (subsequently, GT).

5. The exception is the sonnet published in the military radio newspaper in 1944.

6. He later joined the Hagana and the Palmah. The Hagana was the largest Jewish underground defense organization, and the Palmah was its permanently mobilized strike force.

7. In passing, Amichai mentioned his relationship with Ruth Z. in two interviews. See Boaz Cohen, "Don't Call Me a National Poet," *Yedi'ot Aharonot*, September 24, 2000; and Dan Omer, "In This Burning Country, Words Must Serve as Shade" (series of interviews with Amichai), *Proza*, no. 25 (July 1978): 4–11; Corinna Benning, interview with Yehuda Amichai, May 4, 1998, on Bavarian radio station BR Alpha. A transcription of the full interview is found in Christian Leo, *Zwischen Erinnern und Vergessen: Jehuda Amichais Roman "Nicht von jetzt, nicht von hier" im philosophischen und literarischen Kontext* (Wuerzburg, Germany: Koenigshausen und Neumann, 2004), 247–57 (subsequently *Between Remembering and Forgetting*).

8. Shazar would become Israel's third president, 1963–1973.

9. Ruth's father left London in 1926, but because of her brother's young age, the rest of the family remained until 1927. The family traveled by boat to Alexandria and then by taxi to Kantara, where they embarked on a coal train for 17 hours to Lod, where her father picked them up on March 15, 1927.

10. Yehuda Amichai Papers. General Collection, Beinecke Rare Book and Manuscript Library, Yale University, New Haven, Conn. (subsequently, Amichai papers/Beinecke), box 19, file 278, "Three Times Ruth." There were 34 boxes in the precatalogued archive with consecutively numbered files in each box. References to these materials cite the uncatalogued box number and file number.

11. Yehuda Amichai's letters to Ruth Z. (August 31, 1947–April 11, 1948) will be housed at Ḥayisre'elim harishonim (First Israelis Archive), Heksherim: The Research Center for Jewish and Israeli Literature and Culture, Ben-Gurion University of the Negev. References cite the number of the letter (as given by Amichai) and the date. Letters to Ruth Z., #46, December 7, 1947; #45, December 5, 1947.

12. Ibid., #41, November 26, 1947. While Amichai's letter clearly describes this routine, Ruth Z. disputed that it occurred in her February 12, 2006, correspondence with the author.

13. Omer, "In This Burning Country," 6.

14. Letter to Ruth Z., unnumbered [98], April 11, 1948.

15. Ibid., #9, September 17, 1947, ibid., #15, October 2, 1947, ibid., #41, November 26, 1947. While Amichai specifically mentioned Café Atara and their regular table there, Ruth Z. disputed that they went there in her February 12, 2006, correspondence with the author.

16. Ibid., #72, February 4, 1948.

17. Ibid., #54, December 24, 1947. Kibbutznik is slang for a member of a kibbutz, a voluntary collective community, mainly agricultural, in which there is no private wealth.

18. Ibid., #69, January 28, 1948.

19. Ibid., #58, January 2, 1948; #69, January 28, 1948. This conversation would be echoed in an unpublished poem he sent her in a letter.

20. Ibid., #69, January 28, 1948.

21. Ibid., #32, November 9, 1947.

22. Ibid., #21, October 14–15, 1947.

23. Ibid., #80, February 23, 1948.

24. Ibid., #13, September 2[?], 1947, Erev Sukot. Amichai did not date this letter, but letter #12 is dated September 25 and letter #14 is dated September 30.

25. Yigal Lossin, *Pillar of Fire: The Rebirth of Israel—A Visual History*, trans. Zvi Ofer, ed. Carol S. Halberstadt (Jerusalem: Shikmona 1983), 451.

26. Ruth Z., interviews with author, July 13, 2004, and December 13, 2004; Omer, "In This Burning Country," 6.

27. Letter to Ruth Z., unnumbered [102], Tishrey (September/October) 1951.

28. Ibid., #3, September 5, 1947.

29. Ibid., #9, September 17, 1947.

30. Ibid., #82, February 28, 1948.

31. Ibid., #13, September 2[?], 1947, Erev Sukot. See footnote 24, above.

32. Ibid., #90, March 19, 1948. Ruth Z. disputed this account in her correspondence of February 12, 2006.

33. Ibid., #86, March 10, 1948; ibid., #90, March 19, 1948.

34. Ibid., #90, March 19, 1948. Dr. Joseph (Dov Yosef) later became the first finance minister of Israel and Yitzhak Ben-Zvi became Israel's second president.

35. See chapter 9 for an explication of the segment "Avraham and I and Ruth" from "In the Public Garden."

36. Yehuda Amichai, "Bagina hatsiburit" (In the Public Garden), in *Shirim: 1948–1962* (Poems: 1948–1962) (Tel Aviv: Schocken, 2002 [1963]), 185–210 (subsequently, *Poems: 1948–1962*). If an English translation is not cited, it is because English translations for that poem are unavailable.

37. Letter to Ruth Z., #86, March 10, 1948.

38. Ruth Z., interviews with author, July 13, 2004, and December 13, 2004. Ruth remembered spending only two weeks in Binyamina. In Omer, "In This Burning Country," 6, Amichai said it was three.

39. Brother of the well-known author Y. H. Brenner.

40. Ruth Z., interviews with author, July 13, 2004, and December 13, 2004; Omer, "In This Burning Country," 4–11; Cohen, "Don't Call Me a National Poet."

41. Letter to Ruth Z., #82, February 28, 1948.

42. Ibid., #72, February 4, 1948.

43. Cohen, "Don't Call Me a National Poet."

44. The *Irgun Tsvai Le'umi* (National Military Organization) was known in Hebrew by its acronym *Etzel*, and in English as the Irgun or IZL. It was dedicated to fighting the British and Arabs.

45. Cohen, "Don't Call Me a National Poet." This was the only time that Amichai ever mentioned Ruth by name or referred to Binyamina explicitly. While his account may give the impression that they shared a room, Ruth Z. clarified that they did not.

46. Letter to Ruth Z., #44, December 3, 1947. She was the widow of Mordechai ben Hillel Hakohen.

47. Ibid., #64, January 16, 1948.

48. Ibid., #23, October 18, 1947; ibid., #60, January 7, 1948.

49. Ibid., #9, September 17, 1947.

50. Ibid., #23, October 18, 1947.

51. Ibid., #20, October 12–13, 1947; #15, October 2, 1947.

52. Ibid., #48, December 9, 1947.

53. Ibid., #15, October 2, 1947.

54. Ibid., #62, January 12, 1948.

55. Nili Gold, "The 'Feminine' in Yehuda Amichai's Poetics," in *The Experienced Soul: Studies in Amichai*, ed. Glenda Abramson (Boulder, Colo.: Westview Press, 1997), 77–92. This side of his personality was evident at this early stage.

56. Letter to Ruth Z., #59, January 4, 1948.

57. Photograph in the possession of Ruth Z.

58. Ibid. See the discussion of the poem "Other Evenings" in chapter 1.

59. Letter to Ruth Z., #72, February 4, 1948. Tel el-Kadi is the Arab name. It is also known as Tel Dan.

60. The closeness between Yehuda and Ruth's brother-in-law survived time and his breakup with Ruth. In a play written fifteen years later, Amichai commemorated him by naming the protagonist after him.

61. Letter to Ruth Z., #48, December 9, 1947.

62. Ibid., #92, March 25, 1948.

63. Ibid., #48, December 9, 1947.

64. Photographs in the possession of Ruth Z.

65. Letter to Ruth Z., #48, December 9, 1947.

66. Ruth Z., interview with author, May 2003. Amichai stated that he was just "sick" of Jerusalem.

67. Cohen, "Don't Call Me a National Poet"; Yehuda Amichai, "The Rustle of History's Wings, as They Said Then," GT, 22; Benning interview, in Leo, *Between Remembering and Forgetting*, 247.

68. In the Hebrew alphabet, the symbol for P is the same as the one for F. When written without vowels, the common way of writing, *Pilpel* and *Falafel* look identical.

69. Letters to Ruth Z., #14, September 30, 1947; #15, October 2, 1947.

70. "And We Shall Not Get Excited," *Poems: 1948–1962*, 313; LOP, 61.

71. After the UN vote, Palestine was thrown out of the sterling block, which affected the assets of Ruth's parents, among others.

72. Letter to Ruth Z., #3, September 5, 1947.

73. Ibid., #8, September 14, 1947.

74. "In the Public Garden," *Poems: 1948–1962*, 210.

75. Letter to Ruth Z., #1, August 31, 1947; letter to Ruth Z., #72, February 4, 1948.

76. Ibid., #1, August 31, 1947.

77. Ibid., #49, December 11, 1947.

8. THE LITERARY LEGACY OF THE LOVE STORY (PP. 209–41)

1. Dan Omer, "In This Burning Country, Words Must Serve as Shade" (series of interviews with Amichai), *Proza*, no. 25 (July 1978): 4–11. The poem that Amichai published in a military journal in 1944 was also a love sonnet.

2. For detailed description of the love affair between Amichai and Ruth Z., see chapter 7. In this chapter, when biographical events are mentioned, Yehuda Amichai is called "Yehuda." When literary analysis is employed, he is called "Amichai."

3. It is possible that someone like Amichai's sister holds other unreleased correspondence or poetry, but this is the earliest that has come to light to date.

4. "Ahavnu kan" (We Loved Here) was first published in *Akhshav uvayamim ha'aherim* (Now and in the Other Days) (Tel Aviv: Likrat, 1955) (subsequently, *Now and in the Other Days*), 57–81. *Now and in the Other Days* was included in Amichai's canonic collection, *Shirim: 1948–1962* (*Poems: 1948–1962*) (Tel Aviv: Schocken, 1963) (subsequently, *Poems: 1948–1962*), 57–73; this sonnet cycle is subsequently cited as "We Loved Here." All citations of Hebrew poems in this chapter refer to that collection unless otherwise noted. Part of the cycle is translated as "We Loved Here" in *The Selected Poetry of Yehuda Amichai*, trans. Chana Bloch and Stephen Mitchell (Berkeley and Los Angeles: University of California Press, 1996), 8–9 (subsequently, SP), and in *Yehuda Amichai: A Life of Poetry 1948–1994*, ed. and trans. Benjamin Harshav and Barbara Harshav (New York: HarperCollins, 1994), 23–26 (subsequently, LOP). If no published English translations are cited, it is because there are no English translations for the lines being discussed.

5. See chapter 7. Boaz Cohen, "Don't Call Me a National Poet," *Yedi'ot Aharonot*, September 24, 2000.

6. A sonnet is a fourteen-line poem, with a defined rhyme scheme, meter, and structure. A Petrarchan sonnet is comprised of an octave (its first two, four-line stanzas) and a sestet (the last two, three-line stanzas).

7. Omer, "In This Burning Country," 5, 7.

8. Shimon Sandbank, *Shete berekhot baya'ar* (Two Pools in the Forest) (Tel Aviv: Hakibbutz Hameuchad, 1976) (subsequently, *Two Pools in the Forest*), chapter 8. Rilke often used the Petrarchan sonnet form, especially in the collection *New Poems*. Rilke's sonnet sequence *Sonette an Orpheus* (1923) was very influential.

9. See chapter 2.

10. In Sonnet I, *nu* appears nine times; in Sonnet II, four times; in Sonnet IV, eight times; in Sonnet V, seven times; in Sonnet VI, eleven times.

11. When Amichai was awarded the Israel Prize, one of the arguments that the judges made in his favor was that he changed the face of the pathos-laden Hebrew poetry of the 1940s and 1950s.

12. Line 14.

13. See the discussion of trains in chapter 3 for the early biographical memory that spurred this image.

14. Line 5.

15. *Poems: 1948–1962*, 37; SP, 7.

16. A semaphore is a signaling apparatus, using flags, lights, or mechanically moving arms, such as one used on a railroad.

17. "With a strong hand and an outstretched arm [*zero'a*]." Deuteronomy 4:34. Amichai used similar imagery in an undated poem entitled "On the Road to the Negev, 1948" that he sent Ruth after their relationship had ended, saying that she would never know what happened to him "after the green curve."

18. Lines 1, 5, and 7 of "Binyamina, 1947."

19. Line 8.

20. Most Hebrew verbs are comprised of three-letter root stems to which vowels, prefixes, and suffixes are added to create conjugations and other derivatives. For example, the verb root S.G.R. (closing) would become *eSGoR* to indicate "I will close" and *SaGaRnu* to indicate "we closed."

21. Line 2.

22. Line 5. The rhythm and atmosphere of this condensed chain of verbs is reminiscent of H. N. Bialik's long poem "Zohar" (Splendor), which Amichai undoubtedly knew.

23. See chapter 7.

24. Line 9.

25. In Hebrew, the verb with the root N.Sh.R. specifically indicates the falling of leaves, but Amichai used it here to describe tombstones.

26. Line 13.

27. Yehuda Amichai's letters to Ruth Z. (August 31, 1947–April 11, 1948) will be housed at Hayisre'elim harishonim (First Israelis Archive), Heksherim: The Research Center for Jewish and Israeli Literature and Culture, Ben-Gurion University of the Negev. References cite the number of the letter (as given by Amichai) and the date. Amichai explicitly suggested this artistic process in Letter to Ruth Z., #94, April 1, 1948.

28. Lines 2–3.

29. "When I Was a Child," Poems: 1948–1962, 11; SP, 6.

30. "When I Was a Child," Poems: 1948–1962, 11; LOP, 3.

31. Amichai, "God Has Pity on Kindergarten Children," Poems: 1948–1962, 15; LOP, 6.

32. Sonnet VI, line 7.

33. Rahel Bluwstein, Shirat Rahel (The Poetry of Rahel) (Tel Aviv: Davar, 1964), 58.

34. Nili Scharf Gold, Lo kabrosh: gilgule imagim vetavniyot beshirat Yehuda Amichai (Not Like a Cypress: Transformations of Images and Structures in the Poetry of Yehuda Amichai) (Tel Aviv and Jerusalem: Schocken, 1994), 189–90 (subsequently, NLC).

35. Amichai, "And the Migration of My Parents," in Poems: 1948–1962, 221; LOP, 51; lines 5–6.

36. Ibid., lines 5–6.

37. Sonnet VI, line 1.

38. See Boaz Arpali, Haperahim veha'agartal (The Flowers and the Urn: Amichai's Poetry 1948–1968) (Tel Aviv: Hakibbutz Hameuchad, 1986) (subsequently, The Flowers and the Urn); NLC, 31–68.

39. NLC, 220, 243–46.

40. "The Smell of Gasoline Ascends in My Nose," Poems: 1948–1962, 25; SP, 3.

41. "My Father," Poems: 1948–1962, 32.

42. Tuvia Ruebner, interview with author, May 1996. During those years, Amichai also became acquainted with Lea Goldberg, the master of the sonnet in modern Hebrew literature. There was a period when a few young poets in Jerusalem would gather at her house for poetry workshops.

43. Poems: 1948–1962, 57–73; SP, 8–9; LOP, 23–26.

44. Dan Miron, Facing the Silent Brother: Essays on the Poetry of the War of Independence (Jerusalem: Keter, 1992), 295–313.

45. Sandbank, Two Pools in the Forest, 245, fn. 54.

46. Omer, "In This Burning Country," 6. Amichai separated from Horn in the early 1960s.

47. For a discussion of the role of intertextuality, see Michael Riffaterre, Semiotics of Poetry (Bloomington: Indiana University Press, 1978), 63, 100, 124, 134. Following Riffaterre, I use the term "intratextuality" to describe the relationship between texts within the same literary corpus by the same author. Frequently, elements from Amichai's early works resurface in his later ones, yet sometimes an intratext is written later than the text and sheds light on it retroactively. This is the case with the phrase ahavnu kan.

48. They are stylistically consistent with the poems in Amichai's earliest published collection and his entire subsequent corpus.

49. The numbers refer to Amichai's original numbering of the "We Loved Here" sonnets.

50. *Poems 1948–1962*, 58; LOP, 23.

51. In German, as in English, the conjugation of the verb "to love" in the past first-person plural is more precise than in Hebrew: we loved, *wir liebten*; we have loved, *wir haben geliebt*; we had loved, *wir hatten geliebt*. Amichai's sensitivity to the disparity in the usage of tenses between European languages and Hebrew is explicitly expressed in his novel: "It was impossible to reconstruct those feelings. . . . Everything became absolute past-tense. Not like in the English language, that has in it possibilities of escape to past continuous and future continuous, and past inside past and past inside future. In the feeling of Joel, the past of a moment ago was similar to the past of thousands of years ago." Yehuda Amichai, *Lo me'akhshav lo mikan* (Not of This Time, Not of This Place) (Tel Aviv: Schocken, 1963), 598.

52. *Poems: 1948–1962*, 70–71.

53. *Poems: 1948–1962*, 68–69.

54. Ruth Z., interview with author, January 13, 2005.

55. See chapter 1; Yehuda Amichai, "The Rustle of History's Wings, as They Said Then," *The Great Tranquility: Questions and Answers*, trans. Glenda Abramson and Tudor Parfitt (New York: Sheep Meadow Press, 1997), 22 (subsequently, GT). Originally published as *Shalva gedola: she'elot uteshuvot* (Tel Aviv: Schocken, 1980).

56. The word used for "union" is "*yihud,*" which typically denotes the private time allotted to the couple after the wedding ceremony.

57. Ruth Z., interview with author, July 13, 2004, and December 13, 2004.

58. GT, 22.

59. Letters to Ruth Z., #81, February 25, 1948; #91, March 21, 1948.

60. Glenda Abramson's translation is included in Gershon Shaked, "Amichai and the Likrat Group: The Early Amichai and His Literary Reference Group," in *The Experienced Soul*, ed. Glenda Abramson (Boulder, Colo.: Westview Press, 1997), 105.

61. "To want" in Hebrew is devoid of the connotations with poverty found in English. The biblical verse "God is my shepherd, I shall not want" uses a different root in Hebrew (H.S.R.).

62. Abramson, "Amichai and the Likrat Group," 105, lines 4–8.

63. Letter to Ruth Z., unnumbered [98], April 11, 1948.

64. The third and last "Tiberias" sonnet from *Al Hamishmar* was not included in "Ahavnu kan" or in any of Amichai's published collections.

65. The image of letters without an address also appears in "In the Public Garden," the subject of chapter 9. This is not coincidental, for both works have strong ties to the affair and the time frame in which it occurred.

66. Letter to Ruth Z., #5, September 7, 1947.

67. Ibid., #33, November 11, 1947.

68. See Sonnet 1, *Poems: 1948–1962*, 70; SP, 8; LOP, 23.

69. Letter to Ruth Z., unnumbered letter [98], April 11, 1948.

70. *Poems: 1948–1962*, 65, 66.

71. Ibid., 65.

72. The tenor is the subject with which the vehicle of a metaphor is identified. The vehicle is the word or phrase that is applied to the tenor and gives the metaphor its figurative power. For example, in "your eyes are ravens," "eyes" are the tenor, "ravens" are the vehicle.

73. Although the linguistic correlations to "Binyamina, 1947" suggest otherwise, an alternate reading could be that the life-altering "event" was his wedding with Tamar or another highlight of their relationship.

74. Letters to Ruth Z., #65, January 19, 1948; #85, March 7, 1948.

75. Letter to Ruth Z., #82, February 28, 1948. Whichever love story is alluded to, the climactic event has already occurred in the past and has become tainted for the speaker of the poem. Sonnet 20 employs a similar wordplay with the word *koteret* when it says that "the two of us" are hiding "behind the giant lines in the *koteret*."

76. Instances of this use of color include "green curve" (Sonnet II); weeds, forest, and fields (Sonnet IV); grass (Sonnet V); tree, grass, orchards (Sonnet VI).

77. The role of the color green reaches mammoth proportions in a poem written to Ruth after the breakup, entitled "Poem from 1948."

78. The image of mastlike antennae on house roofs is reminiscent of a sonnet about alienation by Lea Goldberg, titled "Tel Aviv, 1935": "The masts on the house-roofs were then / Like the masts of Columbus' ship / and every crow . . . announced a different shore." Here, Goldberg expresses the alienation of immigrants by giving masts to their rootless homes. Stanley Burnshaw, T. Carmi, and Ezra Spicehandler, eds., *The Modern Hebrew Poem Itself* (Cambridge, Mass.: Harvard University Press, [1965] 1989), 130–13.

79. For a discussion of "ungrammaticality," see Riffaterre, *Semiotics of Poetry*, 164–65.

80. From the root *Ayin. Zayin. Bet.*, *la'azov* means "to leave." Therefore, the third line of the sonnet may be translated as "we abandoned everything," while the fourth line is, "like a suddenly abandoned room."

81. Most of the other sonnets in "Ahavnu kan" speak either in the first-person masculine singular, the third person, or the first-person plural; they only occasionally slip into a direct address to a feminine singular.

82. The time 5:45 a.m. is repeated in Amichai's later poems in connection with parting.

83. Ruth Z., interview with author, March 9, 2006.

84. The verb *lehavlig* (to restrain) is connected to the noun *havlaga* (restraint), which was the political term used to define the military policy of the Hagana in Palestine and meant "to hold back the impulse to retaliate," specifically in the face of violence. It therefore marks the period when the poem was composed or to which it refers: Amichai's relationship with Ruth Z., not the 1950s as Amichai said in Omer, "In This Burning Country," 6.

85. Chaim Nachman Bialik, "Im dimdumey hahama" (At Twilight), in Burnshaw, Carmi, and Spicehandler, eds., *The Modern Hebrew Poem Itself*, 28–30. Bialik (1873–1934) is considered the greatest classical poet of modern Hebrew poetry. The intertextual relationship between the two texts might be stronger than it first appears. Bialik's poem is also subversive—what begins as a romantic scene turns into an antiromantic statement against unrealistic dreams. "At Twilight" speaks of distant lands and of dreams that turn out to be destructive. Ruth's travel to a faraway land only to end their relationship might be likened to the outcome of Bialik's poem. Furthermore, the word *zahav* (gold) appears in both Bialik's poem and in Sonnet 14. It refers to the quality of the distant islands, but one may also see a connection to America, the land of gold. This is especially poignant when the lonely existence of the woman in Sonnet 14 is compared to a bank filled with gold.

86. While in Hebrew the forget-me-not flower is called the "remember me" flower, in German, as in English, it is called "forget-me-not" (*vergiss-mein-nicht*). The image of a "flower of forgetting" creates a clearer pun in German.

87. Letter to Ruth Z., #58, January 2, 1948.

88. Sweet grapes represent sexual maturity in the collection *Now and in the Other Days*. There, the implication is that the beloved will use her experiences with the speaker to mature sexually with someone else. In the "Poems for Tamar," which deal with requited love, the beloved's laughter is described as "round, grape laughter" in a poem that continues with a description of her body and ends with "everything was possible." See *Poems: 1948–1962*, 27–29; SP, 4.

89. Amichai expressed this feeling explicitly in his letter to Ruth Z. #58, January 2, 1948.

90. When considering the intertextual interpretation relating the sonnet to "At Twilight," the reference to "tall towers" parallels the "tall worlds" in Bialik's poem.

91. Amichai, "Bagina hatsiburit" (In the Public Garden) in *Poems: 1948–1962*, 185–210; subsequently, "In the Public Garden."

92. Letter to Ruth Z., #63, January 14, 1948; "In the Public Garden" segment entitled "Dry!" 206.

93. Letter to Ruth Z., #1, August 31, 1947.

94. Letters to Ruth Z., #2, September 3, 1947; #3, September 5, 1947; #12, September 25, 1947; #35, November 16, 1947; #49, December 11, 1947; #56, December 29, 1947; #63, January 14, 1948.

95. Ibid., #3, September 5, 1947.

96. Ibid., #2, September 3, 1947.

97. Ibid., #35, November 16, 1947.

98. Ibid., #12, September 25, 1947.

99. Ibid., #56, December 29, 1947.

100. Ibid., #63, January 14, 1948.

101. Ibid., #56, December 29, 1947.

102. The exact phrase that Amichai uses is "*Lo mikan*" (not from here). It is as though as long as the two were "*kan*" (here), they were in the state of "*ahavnu*" (love), but when she is near the distant water, or "*lo mikan*" (not from here), then the state of love is also no more.

103. Amichai, "Once More," in *More Love Poems* (Tel Aviv: Schocken, 1994), 78–79.

104. Letter to Ruth Z., #43, November 29, 1947.

105. Ibid., unnumbered [98], April 11, 1948.

9. LOVERS IN THE PUBLIC GARDEN (PP. 243–65)

1. Yehuda Amichai, *Bagina hatsiburit* (In the Public Garden) (Tel Aviv: Akhshav, 1959); Amichai, *Bemerhak shete tikvot: shirim* (Two Hopes Away: Poems) (Tel Aviv: Hakibbutz Hameuchad, 1958) (subsequently, *Two Hopes Away*); *Two Hopes Away* was later included in *Shirim: 1948–1962* (Poems: 1948–1962) (Tel Aviv: Schocken, 1963) (subsequently, *Poems: 1948–1962*). Citations of Hebrew poems refer to that collection unless otherwise noted. Gabriel Moked, "In the Public Garden," *Yedi'ot Aharonot*, September 18, 1959. Quoted in Yehudit Tzvik, ed., *Yehuda Amichai: mivhar ma'amare bikoret al yetsirato* (Yehuda Amichai: A Selection of Critical Essays on His Writings) (Tel Aviv: Hakibbutz Hameuchad, 1988), 19.

2. "In the Public Garden," *Poems: 1948–1962*, 185–210. When no published English translations are cited, it is because there are no English translations for the lines being discussed.

3. Individual poems later published as part of this cycle appeared in newspapers in March and April 1959.

4. Moked, "In the Public Garden."

5. Maxim Gilan, "The World of Desire of Yehuda Amicahi," *Lamerhav*, September 4, 1959. Quoted and summarized in Tzvik, *Yehuda Amichai*, 20.

6. Hilel Barzel, "The Existential Trend in Our Poetry," *Ha'aretz*, November 25, 1960; Y. Lichetenbaum, "About Young Poets," *Moznayim*, no. 10 (1960). Quoted and summarized in Tzvik, *Yehuda Amicahi*, 19–20.

7. Moked, "In the Public Garden."

8. Nathan Zach, "The Light Muse," *Davar*, August 28, 1959. Quoted and summarized in Tzvik, *Yehuda Amichai*, 20.

9. Boaz Arpali, *Haperahim veha'agartal* (The Flowers and the Urn) (Tel Aviv, Israel: Hakibbutz Hameuchad, 1986), 52–53.

10. Yehuda Amichai's letters to Ruth Z. (August 31, 1947–April 11, 1948) will be housed at Hayisre'elim harishonim (First Israelis Archive), Heksherim: The Research Center for Jewish and Israeli Literature and Culture, Ben-Gurion University of the Negev. References cite the number of the letter (as given by Amichai) and the date. Letter to Ruth Z., #23, October 18, 1947.

11. Gidon Katzenelson, "Only Now or Also Tomorrow," *Ha'aretz*, June 11, 1959. Quoted and summarized in Tzvik, *Yehuda Amichai*, 19; B. Y. Michli, "Notes in the Margins of Our Modern Literature," *Pri Ha'aretz*, 1966. Later included in Tzvik, *Yehuda Amichai*, 19.

12. Except for the poem that Amichai published in 1944 in the military newspaper *Ha-gilgal*. See chapter 5.

13. Letter to Ruth Z., #46, December 7, 1947.

14. Ibid.

15. Ruth Z., interview with author, January 13, 2005. This idea was inherited from a tradition in Amichai's family of writing celebratory rhymes for birthdays and other holidays.

16. Letter to Ruth Z., #63, January 14, 1948.

17. For the purpose of clarity, I have numbered the segments. My numbers appear in parentheses, in the body of the text after the title of each segment mentioned. In the endnotes, each segment is cited with its title, segment number, and page number. The sonnet cycle "We Loved Here" and two cycles of quatrains are the exceptions to the norm of autonomous poems in the first two volumes.

18. Letter to Ruth Z., #46, December 7, 1947.

19. "Dead Man Hanging" (17), 195; "The Death of the Butterfly" (21), 197; and "Who Am I?" (31), 202–3, among others.

20. "Public Lonely" (1), 187; and "Male Pompadour Flying" (6), 189; "Two Heads" (12), 192; "Dead Man Hanging" (17), 195; and "Night Butterfly" (20), 196–97.

21. "Avraham and I and Ruth" (22), 197–98; "The End" (2), 187; and "The Empty Lot" (11, 24), 191–92, 198.

22. "I Pass By" (5), 188; "Male Pompadour Flying" (6), 189.

23. "Wunderkind" (7), 189–90; and "My Son Is a Hero" (8), 190.

24. "Questionnaire" (15), 194; "Cross Out the Incorrect Answer" (16), 194–95; and "Cross Out the Inappropriate" (18), 195.

25. "Girl Being Photographed" (14), 193–94.

26. "What's Your Name What's His Name" (26), 199–200.

27. "Public Sleep" (30), 202.

28. "Night Butterfly" (20), 196–97; and "The Death of the Butterfly" (21), 197.

29. "The Cat Thinks" (23), 198.

30. "A Phone Rings" (29), 201.

31. "Conversation at Midnight" (34), 203–4.

32. Letter to Ruth Z., #78, February 18, 1948.

33. In another letter, Amichai saw himself in the role of God: he was "playing" the children in his class because "their strings are pure." He used the questions he asked while teaching as "hands playing the violins." Ibid., #60, January 7, 1948.

34. Ibid., #9, September 17, 1947.

35. Ibid., #34, November 13, 1947.

36. Shimon Sandbank, *Shete berekhot baya'ar* (Two Pools in the Forest) (Tel Aviv, Israel: Hakibbutz Hameuchad, 1976), 198, 207.

37. Letter to Ruth Z., #34, November 13, 1947.

38. Ruth Z., interview with author, December 14, 2005; letter to Ruth Z., #90, March 19, 1948.

39. Letter to Ruth Z., #90, March 19, 1948.

40. Ibid. See chapter 7.

41. While letter to Ruth Z., #90, March 19, 1948, says this specifically, Ruth denied it in a February 12, 2006, letter to the author.

42. Letter to Ruth Z., #90, March 19, 1948.

43. "Public Lonely" (1), 187; "Male Pompadour Flying" (6), 189; "Two Heads" (12), 192; "Dead Man Hanging" (17), 195; and "Night Butterfly" (20), 196–97.

44. Letter to Ruth Z., #28, October 30, 1947.

45. In addition to the birthday poem, ten segments can be linked to Ruth: "The End" (2), 187; "They Saw You, They Saw You" (3), 188; "The Empty Lot" (11, 24), 191–92, 198; Woman in a Dress of Sails" (19), 195–96; "Avraham and I and Ruth" (22), 197–98; "Who Am I?" (31), 202–3; "Conversation at Midnight" (34), 203–4; "Receive!" (40), 206; and "Last Conversation in a Whisper" (50), 210.

46. "The End" (2), 187.

47. Letter to Ruth Z., unnumbered [98], April 11, 1948.

48. "They Saw You, They Saw You" (3), 188.

49. "Woman in a Dress of Sails" (19), 195–96.

50. One mechanism of Amichai's camouflage is scrambling. In "In the Public Garden," the incriminating Ruth segments are separated from each other in a way that makes connecting the dots almost impossible.

51. "Who Am I?" (31), 202–3.

52. "Night Butterfly" (20), 196–97; and "The Death of the Butterfly" (21), 197.

53. Letter to Ruth Z., #33, November 11, 1947. For a full discussion of "Hada'aya," see chapter 11.

54. "A Conversation at Midnight" (34), 203–4.

55. Letter to Ruth Z., #97, April 7, 1948.

56. "The Empty Lot" (11, 24), 191–92, 198.

57. Letter to Ruth Z., #63, January 14, 1948.

58. Of the 50 segments, Segments 38–43, Segment 47, and Segment 50 are in the letter in part or in full.

59. "The Great Prayer" (38), 205.

60. Letter to Ruth Z., #13, September 2[?], 1947 (letter #12 is dated September 25, and letter #14 is dated September 30).

61. Poems: 1948–1962, 87; translated in The Selected Poetry of Yehuda Amichai, trans. Chana Bloch and Stephen Mitchell (Berkeley and Los Angeles: University of California Press, 1996), 10.

62. The image of extinguishing burning hands appears more elaborately in "We Loved Here." See chapter 8.

63. Letter to Ruth Z., #12, September 25, 1947.

64. Ibid., #10, September [?] 1947 (letter #9 is dated September 17, and letter #11 is dated September 24).

65. Ibid., #15, October 2, 1947.

66. Ibid., #5, September 7, 1947. Letters without an address reappear in "We Loved Her." See chapter 8.

67. Letter to Ruth Z., #81, February 25, 1948.

68. This is akin to the request that God "close the yearning ones" in "Dry!" (39), 205–6.

69. "Fold!" (41), 206.

70. Letter to Ruth Z., #9, September 17, 1947.

71. "Collect!" (42), 207.

72. "Give!" (47), 208–9.

73. Ruth Z., interview with author, December 14, 2005.

74. Letter to Ruth Z., #46, December 7, 1947.

75. T. S. Eliot, *The Waste Land*, in *The Complete Poems and Plays* (New York: Harcourt Brace, 1967), 37–55; 40.

76. Gershon Shaked, "Amichai and the Likrat Group: The Early Amichai and His Literary Reference Group," in *The Experienced Soul*, ed. Glenda Abramson (Boulder, Colo.: Westview Press, 1997), 111.

10. THE HAIFA LETTERS (PP. 268–89)

1. Boaz Arpaly, "On the Political Significance of Amichai's Poetry," in *The Experienced Soul*, ed. Glenda Abramson (Boulder, Colo.: Westview Press, 1997), 27–50; 45.

2. Yehuda Amichai, "Memories of Israel," *Diversion*, May 1988, 171–75, 320, 322; 173–74. He echoed this sentiment in: workshop on creative writing at the Poetry Society in New York City, October 1996; interview with Yehuda Amichai, *Jerusalem Post*, July 26, 1991; Yehuda A[michai]. Holocaust Testimony (HVT-2679), interview conducted by Geoffrey Hartman and Benjamin Harshav, November 3, 1994, Fortunoff Video Archive for Holocaust Testimonies, Yale University Library; Eyal Meged, "Towards the End You Become Simpler," *Yedi'ot Aharonot*, November 8, 1985; Michael Miro, "Writing is the Product of Wonderful Laziness" (interview with Yehuda Amichai), *Pi ha'aton*, March 19, 1978.

3. Two letters never arrived; two were, for some reason, not preserved. Ninety-two are in the collection.

4. During this period of the correspondence, Palestine under the British Mandate was also referred to as the Land of Israel. Here, I use these terms interchangeably.

5. Yehuda Amichai's letters to Ruth Z. (August 31, 1947–April 11, 1948) will be housed at Hayisre'elim harishonim (First Israelis Archive), Heksherim: The Research Center for Jewish and Israeli Literature and Culture, Ben-Gurion University of the Negev. References cite the number of the letter (as given by Amichai) and the date. In letter to Ruth Z., #85, March 7, 1948, for example, the setting sun "ignites" the dense clouds, turning them into

a "golden-red bonfire." In letter to Ruth Z., #6, September 9, 1947, he compares the "steaming boats" to pots in a busy "kitchen" and the setting sun to the "fire" under them.

6. Israel declared independence on May 14, 1948; the British Mandate officially ended at midnight, May 15.

7. "Yishuv" (literally, "settlement") refers to the body of Jewish residents in Palestine before the establishment of the State of Israel. It will be used here to refer to this population.

8. Letter to Ruth Z., #6, September 9, 1947.

9. Orah Hadas (née Haklay), interview with author, June 2, 2004.

10. Letters to Ruth Z., #57, December 31, 1947; #33, November 11, 1947.

11. Ibid., #2, September 3, 1947. Howard Morely Sachar, *The Course of Modern Jewish History* (New York: Dell, 1958), 473. On August 31, 1947, the UN Special Committee on Palestine proposed terminating the British Mandate and dividing Palestine into separate and sovereign Arab and Jewish states.

12. Letter to Ruth Z., #7, September 11, 1947.

13. Arthur Goldschmidt and Lawrence Davidson, *A Concise History of the Middle East* (Boulder, Colo.: Westview Press, 2006), 16. Letter to Ruth Z., #5, September 7, 1947.

14. Letter to Ruth Z., #5, September 7, 1947.

15. Ibid., #21, October 14–15, 1947.

16. Rina Ofek (née Reznikov), telephone interview with author, December 5, 2004.

17. Letter to Ruth Z., #11, September 24, 1947.

18. Ibid., #23, October 18, 1947.

19. Ibid., #40, November 24, 1947.

20. Ofek, telephone interview with author, December 5, 2004.

21. Ibid.

22. Hadas, interview with author, June 2, 2004.

23. Letter to Ruth Z., #42, November 28, 1947.

24. Ofek, telephone interview with author, December 5, 2004.

25. Letter to Ruth Z., #6, September 9, 1947.

26. Boaz Arpali, *Haperahim veha'agartal* (The Flowers and the Urn) (Tel Aviv: Hakibbutz Hameuchad, 1986), 13–49.

27. Letter to Ruth Z., #42, November 28, 1947.

28. Ibid., #33, November 11, 1947.

29. Ibid., #35, November 16, 1947.

30. Hadas, interview with author, June 2, 2004. Amichai knew Orah from the teachers' college. She was the daughter of the vice principal.

31. Letter to Ruth Z., #35, November 16, 1947.

32. Ibid.

33. Hadas, interview with author, June 2, 2004.

34. Letters to Ruth Z., #35, November 16, 1947; #36, November 18, 1947.

35. Amichai's literary elaboration on Hayim Goldman's funeral will be discussed in the next chapter.

36. Letter to Ruth Z., #36, November 18, 1947.

37. Ibid., #37, November 18. 1947. Amichai's impressions of the funeral filled two letters, written on the same day.

38. Ibid., #36, November 18, 1947.

39. Ibid., #38, November 21, 1947.

40. Ibid., #36, November 18, 1947.

41. Ibid., #38, November 21, 1947.

42. Ruth Kartun-Blum, *Profane Scriptures* (Cincinnati, Ohio: Hebrew Union College Press, 1999), 15–65.

43. Yehuda Amichai, "A Meeting with My Father," *The Great Tranquility: Questions and Answers*, trans. Glenda Abramson and Tudor Parfitt (New York: Sheep Meadow Press, 1997), 7 (subsequently, GT). Originally published as *Shalva gedola: she'elot uteshuvot* (Tel Aviv: Schocken, 1980), 8.

44. Letter to Ruth Z., #39, November 23, 1947.

45. Ibid., #42, November 28, 1947.

46. Ibid., #43, November 29, 1947.

47. The Arab revolt of 1936–1939 was an uprising by the Arabs in Palestine during the British Mandate.

48. Letter to Ruth Z., #44, December 3, 1947.

49. Ibid., #48, December 9, 1947.

50. Ibid., #45, December 5, 1947.

51. Ibid., #46, December 7, 1947. See chapters 2 and 3 for the discussion of the Hanukkah play.

52. Letter to Ruth Z., #45, December 5, 1947.

53. Ibid. #39, November 23, 1947.

54. Ibid., #60, January 7, 1948.

55. Ibid., #49, December 11, 1947.

56. Ibid., #50, December 14, 1947.

57. Ibid.

58. Ibid., #59, January 4, 1948.

59. Hadas, interview with author, June 2, 2004.

60. Letter to Ruth Z., #46, December 7, 1947.

61. Ibid., #55, December 25, 1947.

62. Ofek, telephone interview with author, December 5, 2004.

63. Letters to Ruth Z., #52, December 19, 1947; #53, December 21, 1947; #55, December 25, 1947.

64. Ibid., #55, December 25, 1947; Ofek, phone interview with author, December 5, 2004. Ofek remembered how the refugees hung ropes with army blankets between the families to provide some privacy.

65. Letter to Ruth Z., #53, December 21, 1947.

66. Letters to Ruth Z., #19, October 10, 1947; #24, October 20, 1947.

67. Ibid., #91, March 21, 1948.

68. Ibid., #56, December 29, 1947.

69. Letters to Ruth Z., #6, September 9, 1947; #81, February 25, 1948; ibid., unnumbered [101], August 2, 1950.

70. Ibid., #57, December 31, 1947.

71. Ibid., #60, January 7, 1948.

72. Letters to Ruth Z., #58, January 2, 1948; #74, February 8, 1948; #79, February 20, 1948. (This includes neither "In the Public Garden," which was written and completed on December 6, 1947, nor another segment of it that was probably written in November but sent in April. See chapter 9.) Hadas, interview with author, June 2, 2004. Orah noticed how his work was affected by the violence: "He saw himself as a poet and he wanted to be a poet. . . . The War of Independence affected him strongly. I saw that in the poems that he sent me. He wrote about the war."

73. Letter to Ruth Z., #58, January 2, 1948. Amichai first situated the idea of "chance and fate" in a violent context when he was affected by the killing of Hayim Goldman; see letter to Ruth Z., #36, November 18, 1947. As far as we know, he did not put this idea into a poem until January.

74. Ibid., #64, January 16, 1948.

75. Ibid., #62, January 12, 1948.

76. Yehuda Amichai, "Ani rotse lamut al mitati" (I Want to Die in My Bed), in *Shirim: 1948–1962* (Poems: 1948–1962) (Tel Aviv: Schocken, 2002 [1963]), 118 (subsequently, *Poems: 1948–1962*). Translated as "I Want to Die in My Own Bed," in *Yehuda Amichai: A Life of Poetry 1948–1994*, trans. and ed. Benjamin Harshav and Barbara Harshav (New York: HarperCollins, 1994), 37 (subsequently, LOP). Subsequent quotations of this poem are from this translation.

77. Letter to Ruth Z., #65, January 19, 1948.

78. This metaphor may have been inspired by T. S. Eliot's references to *Hamlet* in *The Waste Land* and "The Love Song of J. Alfred Prufrock." In the latter, the protagonist compares himself to Hamlet; it is parallel to the lengthy elaboration on the theme in Amichai's letter to Ruth Z., #65, January 19, 1948.

79. Letter to Ruth Z., #65, January 19, 1948.

80. These thirty-five soldiers, the *lamed-he*, who were killed in an attempt to bring aid to a beleaguered Gush Etzion, have become legendary heroes in the history of Israel's War of Independence.

81. Letter to Ruth Z., #65, January 19, 1948; Ruth Z., interview with author, January 13, 2005.

82. Abba Eban, *Abba Eban: An Autobiography* (New York: Random House, 1977), 103. On March 19, 1948, Warren Austin, the U.S. ambassador to the United Nations, suggested that the partition should be "temporarily" suspended. Sachar, *The Course of Modern Jewish History*, 476.

83. Letters to Ruth Z., #51, December 17, 1947; #75, February 11, 1948; #68, January 25, 1948; #70, January 30, 1948.

84. Letter to Ruth Z., #72, February 4, 1948.

85. Letters to Ruth Z., #58, January 2, 1948; #59, January 4, 1948; #64, January 16, 1948; #68, January 25, 1948; #72, February 4, 1948; #78, February 18, 1948.

86. Ibid., #73, February 6, 1948.

87. Ibid., #72, February 4, 1948.

88. Ibid., #78, February 18, 1948.

89. Ibid., #93, no date (letter #92 was from March, 25, 1948; letter #94 was from April 1).

90. Ibid., #74, February 8, 1948.

91. Ibid., #82, February 28, 1948.

92. Ibid., #81, February 25, 1948.

93. Ibid., #79, February 20, 1948; Amichai associates death and music in the story "Dicky's Death," in *Baru'ah hanora'a hazot: sipurim* (In That Terrible Wind) (Tel Aviv: Schocken, 1961), 256. Translated as "Dicky's Death," in *The World Is A Room and Other Stories by Yehuda Amichai*, trans. Yosef Schachter (Philadelphia: Jewish Publication Society of America, 1984), 111–12.

94. Letter to Ruth Z., #80, February 23, 1948.

95. Ibid., #81, February 25, 1948.

96. Letters to Ruth Z., #49, December 11, 1947; #60, January 7, 1948.

97. Ibid., #82, February 28, 1948.

98. Ibid., #88, March 14, 1948.

99. Letters to Ruth Z., #87, March 12, 1948; #88, March 14, 1948; #90, March 19, 1948.

100. Letters to Ruth Z., #94, April 1, 1948; #96, April 6, 1948.

101. Ibid., #88, March 14, 1948.

102. Letters to Ruth Z., #94, April 1, 1948; #96, April 6, 1948.

103. Ibid., #97, April 7, 1948.

104. Letters to Ruth Z., #70, January 30, 1948; #72, February 4, 1948.

105. Hadas, interview with author, June 2, 2004.

106. Letter to Ruth Z., #67, January 23, 1948.

107. Letters to Ruth Z., #68, January 25, 1948, #93, no date (letter #92 was dated March 25, 1948; letter #94 was dated April 1).

108. Ibid., #75, February 11, 1948.

109. Letters to Ruth Z., #72, February 4, 1948; #75, February 11, 1948; #79, February 20, 1948; #87, March 12, 1948.

110. Ibid., #75, February 11, 1948.

111. Letters to Ruth Z., #75, February 11, 1948; #79, February 20, 1948.

112. Ibid., #83, March 2, 1948.

113. Ibid., #84, March 5, 1948.

114. Letters to Ruth Z., #72, February 4, 1948; #87, March 12, 1948.

115. Ibid., #90, March 19, 1948.

116. Ibid., #93, no date (letter #92 was from March 25,1948; letter #94 was from April 1).

117. Ibid., #91, March 21, 1948.

118. Ibid., #93, no date (letter #92 was from March 25, 1948; letter #94 was from April 1).

119. In 1948, Passover began on April 24, but the Passover break usually starts earlier. Letter to Ruth Z., #93; no date (letter #92 was from March, 25, 1948; letter #94 was from April 1); Hadas, interview with author, June 2, 2004.

120. Letter to Ruth Z., unnumbered [98], April 11, 1948.

121. Yehuda Amichai, "The Rustle of History's Wings, As They Said Then," GT, 22. This poem closes with the lines, "And with the terrible wisdom of war they told me to carry / my first-aid bandage right over my heart / over the foolish heart that still loved her. . . ." The implication might be that despite his previous experience in war, his friends had to tell him to protect his heart.

122. Letter to Ruth Z., unnumbered [98], April 11, 1948.

123. Letters to Ruth Z., #61, January 9, 1948; #62, January 12, 1948.

124. Yehuda Amichai, Shirim: 1948–1962 (Poems: 1948–1962) (Tel Aviv: Schocken, 1963), 118.

125. Letter to Ruth Z., #44, December 3, 1947.

126. Letters to Ruth Z., #44, December 3, 1947; #49, December 11, 1947; #62, January 12, 1948; #78, February 18, 1948.

127. Ibid., #62, January 12, 1948.

128. Ibid., #49, December 11, 1947.

129. LOP, 37; see Nili Gold, "The 'Feminine' in Amichai's Poetics," in The Experienced Soul, ed. Glenda Abramson (Boulder, Colo.: Westview Press, 1997), 77–92.

130. Letter to Ruth Z., #65, January 19, 1948.

131. Letters to Ruth Z., #72, February 4, 1948; #79, February 20, 1948.

132. Ibid., #79, February 20, 1948.

133. Yehuda Amichai, "A Journey in the Map of the Past," Bamahane 13, no. 18, January 2, 1962, 10.

11. THE MAKING OF A NATIONAL POET (PP. 290–312)

1. Yehuda Amichai's letters to Ruth Z. (August 31, 1947–April 11, 1948) will be housed at the Hayisre'elim harishonim (First Israelis Archive), Heksherim: The Research Center for Jewish and Israeli Literature and Culture, Ben-Gurion University of the Negev. References cite the number of the letter (as given by Amichai) and the date. In letter to Ruth Z., unnumbered [101], August 2, 1950, Amichai expressed this sentiment explicitly.

2. Letter to Ruth Z., unnumbered [98], April 11, 1948.

3. Ibid., #9, September 17, 1947.

4. The letters to Ruth Z. that contain original poems are #3, September 5, 1947; #4, September 6, 1947; #7, September 11, 1947; #8, September 14, 1947; #9, September 17, 1947; #18, October 8, 1947; #27, October 27, 1947; #33, November 11, 1947; #52, December 19, 1947; #63, January 14, 1948; #74, February 8, 1948; #79, February 20, 1948; #86, March 10, 1948; and #97, April 7, 1948.

5. Six contain German poems in the original, and seven contain Amichai's translations. See chapter 4 for the discussion of German in the letters.

6. Letters to Ruth Z., #85, March 7, 1948; #82, February 28, 1948. See chapter 1 for a discussion of Amichai's rewriting of Rilke in the letters; see chapter 4 for Amichai's identification with Rilke, strengthened by Amichai's attachment to their shared mother tongue.

7. Letter to Ruth Z. #85, March 7, 1948.

8. Ibid., #82, February 28, 1948.

9. Other aspects of Rilke's influence are detailed in chapters 4, 8, 9, and 12.

10. Shimon Sandbank, in particular, established the literary connections between Rilke and Amichai in *Shete berekhot baya'ar* (Two Pools in the Forest) (Tel Aviv: Hakibbutz Hameuhad, 1976), 173, 202–4, 206–7 (subsequently, *Two Pools in the Forest*).

11. Ruth Z., interview with author, January 13, 2005; Orah Hadas (née Haklay), interview with author, June 2, 2004.

12. Letter to Ruth Z., #62, January 12, 1948.

13. Ibid., #67, January 23, 1948.

14. Ibid., # 91, March 21, 1948. Amichai referred to poetry again as his "road" in unnumbered letter to Ruth Z., # [98], April 11, 1948.

15. Ibid., #85, March 7, 1948; Rainer Maria Rilke, *Briefe an einen Jungen Dichter*, trans. M. D. Herter Norton as *Letters to a Young Poet* (New York: W. W. Norton, 1934).

16. Letter to Ruth Z., #85, March 7, 1948.

17. Ibid., #80, February 23, 1948.

18. Ibid., #85, March 7, 1948.

19. Ibid., #22, October 16, 1947.

20. Letters to Ruth Z., #33, November 11, 1947; #65, January 19, 1948.

21. Ibid., #65, January 19, 1948.

22. Ibid.

23. Ibid., #2, September 3, 1947.

24. Ibid., #56, December 29, 1947.

25. Proverbs 3:10 and Deuteronomy 28:7–8.

26. Letter to Ruth Z., #85, March 7, 1948.

27. Ibid., #7, September 11, 1947.

28. Ibid., #59, January 4, 1948.

29. Ibid., # 97, April 7, 1948.

30. Ibid., #85, March 7, 1948.

31. Letters to Ruth Z., #94, April 1, 1948; #59, January 4, 1948.

32. Ibid., #94, April 1, 1948.

33. Ibid., #33, November 11, 1947.

34. Ibid., #38, November 21, 1947.

35. Ibid., #9, September 17, 1947.

36. Ibid.

37. Ibid., #55, December 25, 1947.

38. Ibid., unnumbered [98], April 11, 1948.

39. Ibid., #25, October 22, 1947.

40. Letters to Ruth Z., #6, September 9, 1947; #25, October 22, 1947.

41. Ibid., #32, November 9, 1947.

42. Ibid., #14, September 30, 1947.

43. Ibid., #78, February 18, 1948.

44. Ibid., #23, October 18, 1947.

45. Ibid., #11, September 24, 1947.

46. Ibid., #42, November 28, 1947.

47. Ibid., #9, September 17, 1947.

48. Ibid., #20, October 12–13, 1947.

49. Ruth Z., interview with author, December 13, 2004. Herbert was a sculptor and a close friend of Amichai's whom they often visited in Jerusalem. Yehuda Amichai, "April 25" in "American Notes," *Moznayim* (November 1967): 22. Amichai wrote in the entry about him, "Herbert died. . . . [H]e was my close friend and from age eighteen to twenty-five, was like a spiritual father."

50. See the discussion of this event in chapter 10.

51. Letter to Ruth Z., #36, November 18, 1947.

52. It may be that T. S. Eliot's quotation from Ophelia's mad scene in *The Waste Land* further influenced Amichai's Shakespearean description of the funeral. T. S. Eliot, *The Waste Land*, in *The Complete Poems and-Plays* (New York: Harcourt Brace, 1967) (subsequently, *The Waste Land*), 37–55; 42, line 172: Eliot quotes Ophelia's parting words, "good night, ladies, good night, sweet ladies, good night, good night." William Shakespeare, *Hamlet*, ed. Ann Thompson and Neil Taylor, 3rd ed. (London: Arden Shakespeare, 2006), act 4, sc. 5, lines 77–78.

53. *Hamlet*, act 4, sc. 5.

54. Letter to Ruth Z., #37, November 18, 1947.

55. Yehuda Amichai, "A Meeting with My Father," in *Shalva gedola: she'elot uteshuvot* (Tel Aviv: Schocken, 1980), 8. Translated as *The Great Tranquility: Questions and Answers*, trans. Glenda Abramson and Tudor Parfitt (New York: Sheep Meadow Press, 1997), 7 (subsequently, GT). This sentiment is reflected in the letter to Ruth Z., #65, January 19, 1948.

56. Letters to Ruth Z., #6, September 9, 1947; #14, September 30, 1947; #32, November 9, 1947; #46, December 7, 1947.

57. Letters to Ruth Z., #6, September 9, 1947; #42, November 28, 1947. It is unclear what kind of publication *The Free Autobiography* was. A thorough search of the Jewish National and University Library (Jerusalem) yielded no results.

58. Ibid., #33, November 11, 1947.

59. Letters to Ruth Z., #6, September 9, 1947; #23, October 18, 1947; #25, October 22, 1947; #26, no date (letter #25 was from October 22 and letter #27 was from October 27).

60. Ibid., #25, October 22, 1947.

61. Ibid., #23, October 18, 1947.

62. Ibid., #33, November 11, 1947.

63. Ruth Z., interview with author, December 13, 2004.

64. Letter to Ruth Z., #33, November 11, 1947.

65. Letter to Ruth Z., #13, September 2[?], 1947, Erev Sukot.

66. Ruth Z., interview with author, January 13, 2005.

67. Letter to Ruth Z., #81, February 25, 1948.

68. Ibid., #24, October 20, 1947.

69. Boaz Arpali, *Haperahim veha'agartal* (The Flowers and the Urn) (Tel Aviv: Hakibbutz Hameuchad, 1986), 13–49 (subsequently, *The Flowers and the Urn*).

70. In the impoverished Palestine of the late 1940s, there were poor people who would carry secondhand goods on their backs and sell them on the street. They were called by the Yiddish word "*Alte Sachen*" (old things). Amichai refers to this occupation in "Hada'aya." See letters to Ruth Z., #31, November 7, 1947; #33, November 11, 1947; #36, November 18, 1947. Notably, the protagonist of the novel Amichai published in 1963 is also an archeologist.

71. This image echoes Eliot's phrase, the "photographic delineation of low life," from T. S. Eliot, "Philip Massinger," *The Sacred Wood: Essays on Poetry and Criticism* (London: Methune, 1920), para. 20.

72. See the following two poems for examples of quoted conversations in Amichai's published works: Yehuda Amichai, "On the Day My Daughter Was Born No One Died," GT, 27; Yehuda Amichai, "As at Funerals," *Yehuda Amichai: A Life of Poetry 1948–1994*, trans. and ed. Benjamin Harshav and Barbara Harshav (New York: HarperCollins, 1994), 373 (subsequently, LOP). Letters to Ruth Z., #25, October 22, 1947; #30, November 4, 1947.

73. See letters to Ruth Z., #8, September 14, 1947; #18, October 8, 1947; #27, October 27, 1947; #33, November 11, 1947; #63, January 14, 1948.

74. See letters to Ruth Z., #8, September 14, 1947; #18, October 8, 1947; #27, October 27, 1947; #33, November 11, 1947; #46, December 7, 1947; #79, February 20, 1948; #81, February 25, 1948.

75. Ibid., #33, November 11, 1947.

76. Ibid., #42, November 28, 1947.

77. Ibid., #46, December 7, 1947.

78. Ibid., #33, November 11, 1947.

79. Ibid., #63, January 14, 1948.

80. Ibid., #85, March 7, 1948.

81. Ibid., #7, September 11, 1947.

82. Ibid., #27, October 27, 1947.

83. Ibid., #5, September 7, 1947.

84. Ibid., #6, September 9, 1947.

85. Ibid., #79, February 20, 1948.

86. Letters to Ruth Z., #9, September 17, 1947; #46, December 7, 1947; #79, February 20, 1948.

87. Sandbank, *Two Pools in the Forest*, 173. Years later, Shimon Sandbank noted in his analysis of the connection between Amichai and Rilke, "[T]he only poets who truly affect a poet are close to him. . . ."

88. Shimon Sandbank, "Amichai: The Playing and the Abundance," *Lamerhav*, June 3, 1969, reprinted in Yehudit Tzvik, ed., *Yehuda Amichai: mivhar ma'amare bikoret al yetsirato* (Yehuda Amichai: A Selection of Critical Essays on his Writings) (Tel Aviv: Hakibutz Hameuhad, 1988), 105–14. Sandbank aptly observed, "There are countless lines in Amichai that reflect almost in an undefinable way, the language, the thematics, the details and the images of Rilke."

89. Rainer Maria Rilke, *Das Buch der Bilder*, translated as *The Book of Images*, trans. Edward Snow (New York: North Point Press, 1991), ix–xvi.

90. Letter to Ruth Z., #31, November 7, 1947.

91. Ibid., #4, September 6, 1947.

92. Ibid., #8, September 14, 1947.

93. Ibid., #18, October 8, 1947.

94. Ibid.

95. Ibid., #14, September 30, 1947.

96. Ibid., #31, November 7, 1947.

97. Letter to Ruth Z., #6, September 9, 1947. For poetry as photography and etching, see letter to Ruth Z., #50, December 14, 1947.

98. Ibid., #1, August 31, 1947.

99. Ibid., #12, September 25, 1947.

100. Ibid., #70, January 30, 1948.

101. Ibid., #34, November 13, 1947. The subject of the "day" occupies Hebrew poetry of the period of the War of Independence. While other poets see "the day" as a redemptive historical occurrence, Amichai speaks of the exact opposite: the day as the everyday.

102. Ibid., #46, December 7, 1947.

103. Ibid., #9, September 17, 1947.

104. Ibid., #88, March 14, 1948.

105. Ibid., #92, March 25, 1948.

106. Eliot, *The Waste Land*, 40, lines 225–30.

107. Letter to Ruth Z., #92; March 25, 1948.

108. Eliot, *The Waste Land*, 40, lines 255–56.

109. Gershon Shaked, "Amichai and the Likrat Group: The Early Amichai and His Literary Reference Group," in *The Experienced Soul*, ed. Glenda Abramson (Boulder, Colo.: Westview Press, 1997), 110–12. See the discussion in the conclusion of chapter 9.

110. Eliot, *The Waste Land*, 40, lines 111–20.

111. Yehuda Amichai, "In the Public Garden," in *Shirim: 1948–1962* (Poems: 1948–1962) (Tel Aviv: Schocken, 2002 [1963]), 185–210 (subsequently, *Poems: 1948–1962*).

112. See chapter 4 for a discussion of the "spring earth" in Amichai. The concept of spring earth derives from Amichai's German background, but it is probably also inspired by Eliot.

113. Letter to Ruth Z., #88, March 14, 1948.

114. *Poems: 1948–1962* includes the poems that were first published in the 1955, 1958, and 1959 volumes, as well as poems first published in the 1962 collection.

115. "Lo kabrosh," *Poems: 1948–1962*, 98; translated as "Not Like a Cypress," in *The Selected Poetry of Yehuda Amichai*, trans. Chana Bloch and Stephen Mitchell (Berkeley and Los Angeles: University of California Press, 1996) , 42, (subsequently, SP), and LOP, 35.

116. "I Want to Die in My Own Bed," *Poems: 1948–1962*, 118; LOP, 37. See chapter 10 for discussion of this poem.

117. Sigmund Freud, "On Femininity," in *New Introductory Lectures on Psycho-Analysis* (1933a [1932]), standard ed., vol. 22, 112–35; Hélène Cixous, as quoted in Toril Moi, *Sexual / Textual Politics: Feminist Literary Theory* (London and New York: Methuen, 1985), 104.

118. Letter to Ruth Z., #33, November 11, 1947. He uses similar imagery in letter to Ruth Z., #58, January 2, 1948.

119. SP, 12.

120. Eliot, *The Waste Land*, 38, line 19.

121. Letter to Ruth Z., #88, March 14, 1948.

122. SP, 12.

123. Letter to Ruth Z., #33, November 11, 1947.

124. See Nili Gold, "The 'Feminine' in Amichai's Poetics," in Abramson, ed., *The Experienced Soul*, 77–92.

125. Hélène Cixous, *Three Steps on the Ladder of Writing*, trans. Sarah Cornell and Susan Seller (New York: Columbia University Press, 1993), 104, 118.

126. Gold, "The 'Feminine' in Amichai's Poetics," 84–85.

127. LOP, 35: "Then, the quiet exit, like smoke / Without fanfare." The Hebrew word translated as "fanfare" is *teru'a*, a word reserved almost exclusively for the ceremonial blast of the ram's horn (shofar), the biblical sign of heightened events, especially war.

128. Letter to Ruth Z., #65, January 19, 1948.

129. Ibid., #34, November 13, 1947.

130. Ibid.

131. Ibid., #28, October 30, 1947. These words also appear in Amichai's poem "In the Public Garden."

132. Ibid., #62, January 12, 1948.

133. LOP, 35.

134. Letter to Ruth Z., #65, January 19, 1948.

12. CONCLUSION (PP. 313–22)

1. Quoted by Jess Row in "Haitian Fathers," *New York Times Book Review*, September 9, 2007, 10.

2. Yehuda Amichai, "Elegy on an Abandoned Village," in *Shirim: 1948–1962* (Poems: 1948–1962) (Tel Aviv: Schocken, 2002 [1963]), 363 (subsequently, *Poems: 1948–1962*). Translated as "Elegy on an Abandoned Village," in *The Selected Poetry of Yehuda Amichai*, trans. Chana Bloch and Stephen Mitchell (Berkeley and Los Angeles: University of California Press, 1996), 42 (subsequently, SP).

3. Yehuda Amichai, "Poems on an Abandoned Village," *Yocheni* 1, (1961): 14–16.

4. See chapter 4 for a parallel reading of Amichai's German hometown in this poem.

5. Dahlia Karpel, "Hoping for the Nobel Prize" (interview with Amichai), *Ha'ir*, November 3, 1989.

6. Yehuda Amichai's letters to Ruth Z. (August 31, 1947–April 11, 1948) will be housed at the Hayisre'elim harishonim (First Israelis Archive), Heksherim: The Research Center for Jewish and Israeli Literature and Culture, Ben-Gurion University of the Negev. References cite the number of the letter (as given by Amichai) and the date. Letter to Ruth Z., #60, January 7, 1948.

7. Letters to Ruth Z., #55, December 25th, 1947; #56, December 29, 1947; #57, December 31, 1947; #60, January 7, 1948.

8. Roughly until the 1980s, most kibbutz children lived in a communal "children's house" with furniture and bathrooms built for children. Parents would come to put their children into bed at night.

9. "Two Poems about the First Battles," *Poems 1948–1962*, 23. In the autobiographical essay he wrote in *Bamahane*, Amichai wrote that this poem was written about a stop in the moshav named "kefar Warburg" in 1948. Based on the letters, there must have been more than one stop in a kindergarten.

10. Letter to Ruth Z., #56, December 29, 1947.

11. "Elegy on an Abandoned Village," SP, 43, lines 47–48.

12. Letters to Ruth Z., #57, December 31, 1947; #60, January 7, 1948. William Shakespeare, *Hamlet*, ed. Ann Thompson and Neil Taylor, 3rd ed. (London: Arden Shakespeare, 2006), act 5, sc. 2. Andrea Siegel, unpublished lecture (Boston: Association for Jewish Studies, December, 2001); she identified Amichai's allusion to Shakespeare's line in "Elegy on an Abandoned Village" without the benefit of the letters.

13. Letters to Ruth Z., #36, November 18, 1947; #37, November 18, 1947.

14. Another difference in Amichai's translation: the word "rest" appears in "Elegy" as "*yeter*," which has connotations of "surplus" or "excess." In both letters, "rest" is translated as "*she'ar*," which means "remainder" or "remnant."

15. SP, 42, line 28. The translation above differs from Bloch and Mitchell's in the following ways: Bloch and Mitchell added the word "simply" to the first line; and they translate *tse'aka* as "screech" instead of "scream."

16. Letter to Ruth Z., #56, December 29, 1947.

17. SP, 42, line 9.

18. Letter to Ruth Z., #86, March 10, 1948.

19. Ibid., #58, January 2, 1948.

20. Ruth Z., interviews with author, July 13, 2004, and December 13, 2004; Omer, "In This Burning Country Words Must Serve as Shade," (series of interviews with Amichai), *Proza*, no. 25 (July 1978), 6. See chapters 7 and 8.

21. SP, 42, line 11.

22. Ibid., line 16.

23. Yehuda Amichai Papers. General Collection, Beinecke Rare Book and Manuscript Library, Yale University (subsequently, Amichai papers / Beinecke), box 4, file 65, little gray notebook 112, September 1957. There were 34 boxes in the precatalogued archive with consecutively numbered files in each box. References to these materials cite the uncatalogued box number and file number.

24. Ibid., box 4, file 65, little gray notebook 112, September 1957.

25. For a discussion of the connection between word and thing (also of the word "wind"), see: Nili Gold, "Betrayal of the Mother Tongue in the Creation of National Identity," in *Ideology and Jewish Identity in Israeli and American Literature*, ed. Emily Miller Budick (Albany: SUNY Press, 2001), 235–58.

26. "Elegy on an Abandoned Village," *Poems: 1948–1962*, 363, lines 2–3; SP, 42, lines 2–3.

27. SP, lines 39–40. I added the words "in its stress" to Bloch and Mitchell's translation.

28. *Poems: 1948–1962*, 363, lines 39–40; SP, 43, lines 39–40.

29. Amichai papers / Beinecke, box 4, file 62; notepad, May 1957; ibid., box 4, file 63, gray notebook, April 1957.

30. SP, 42, lines 6–8.

31. SP, 42, line 6.

32. Amichai papers / Beinecke, box 4, file 63, gray notebook, April 1957.

33. *Poems: 1948–1962*, 191. Translated in *Yehuda Amichai: A Life of Poetry 1948–1994*, ed. and trans. Benjamin and Barbara Harshav (New York: HarperCollins, 1994), 51.

Select Bibliography

YEHUDA AMICHAI: PUBLISHED WORKS

(*This bibliography lists only those works by Amichai that are referenced in this study.*)

Akhshav bara'ash: shirim 1963–1968 (Now in the Storm: Poems 1963–1968). Tel Aviv: Schocken, 1975.

Akhshav uvayamim ha'aherim (Now and in Other Days). Tel Aviv: Likrat Press, 1955.

"Agnon and I." *Ha'aretz*, February 10, 1978.

"April 25." In "American Notes," *Moznayim* 6, no. 25 (November 1967): 13–24.

"Autobiography 1952." *Likrat* 2 (August 1952): 13.

Bagina hatsiburit (In the Public Garden). Tel Aviv: Akhshav, 1959.

Baru'ah hanora'a hazot: sipurim (In That Terrible Wind). Tel Aviv: Schocken, 1985 [1961].

Bemerhak shete tikvot: shirim (Two Hopes Away: Poems). Tel Aviv: Hakibbutz Hameuchad, 1958.

Gam ha'egrof haya pa'am yad petuha ve'etsba'ot (Even the Fist Was Once an Open Palm and Fingers). Tel Aviv: Schocken, 1989.

"Generations in the Land." *Lamerhav*, May 3, 1968.

"I Write from Right to Left." *Moznayim* 33, no. 10 (March 1960): 275.

"A Journey in the Map of the Past." *Bamahane* 13, no. 18, January 2, 1962, 10–11.

Katholisches Sonntagsblatt, no. 31, August 1981, 2.

"A Language of the Heart." British Broadcasting Corporation, Radio 3, Talks and Documentaries Department. Recorded April 9, 1979. Broadcast September 19, 1979.

Lo me'akhshav lo mikan (Not of This Time, Not of This Place). Tel Aviv: Schocken, 1963.

Me'ahore kol ze mistater osher gadol (Behind All This There Is Great Happiness). Tel Aviv: Schocken, 1976.

"Memories of Israel." *Diversion*, May 1988: 171–75, 320, 322.

Mi yitneni malon (Hotel in the Wilderness). Tel Aviv: Bitan, 1971.

More Love Poems. Bilingual edition; various translators. Tel Aviv: Schocken, 1994.

"Other Evenings." *Gilyonot* 25, no. 12 (1951): 350.

Pu'amonim verakavot. mahazot vetaskitim (Bells and Trains. Plays and Skits). Tel Aviv. Schocken, 1992.

Patu'ah, sagur, patu'ah (Open Closed Open). Tel Aviv: Schocken, 1998.

(Poems of Tiberias.) *Al Hamishmar*, July 1, 1949.

(Poems on an Abandoned Village.) *Yocheni* 1 (1961): 14–16.

(Return to the City of Childhood.) *Bamahane*, January 5, 1962. Quoted in Abramson, *The Writing of Yehuda Amichai*, 147.

Shalva gedola: she'elot uteshuvot (The Great Tranquility: Questions and Answers). Tel Aviv: Schocken, 1980.

Shirim: 1948–1962 (Poems: 1948–1962). Tel Aviv: Schocken, [1963] 2002.

Speech upon receiving the Kulturpreis (cultural prize) in Wuerzburg, June 22, 1981. Quoted in Main Post, August 5, 1991, and in Roland Flade, "Reliving Childhood at Saint Kilian's Festival," Allgemeine Judische Wochenzeitung, no. 35 (August 29, 1991): 24.

"To Live Reality." Ha'aretz, November 30, 1973.

Velo al menat lizkor (Not to Remember). Tel Aviv: Schocken, [1971] 1978.

"Yehuda Amichai." In Schultz, Mein Judentum, 20–35.

(You Pulled Me Like a Ship.) Likrat 2 (August 1952): 9.

Zeman (Time). Tel Aviv: Schocken, 1977.

YEHUDA AMICHAI: TRANSLATED WORKS

(This bibliography lists only translations that are referenced in this study.)

The Great Tranquility: Questions and Answers. Translated by Glenda Abramson and Tudor Parfitt. New York: Sheep Meadow Press, 1997.

Love Poems. Various translators. Tel Aviv: Schocken, 1977.

Nicht von jetzt, nicht von hier. Translated by Ruth Achlama. Zurich: Pendo Verlag AG, 1998.

Not of This Time, Not of This Place. Translated by Shlomo Katz. New York: Harper and Row, 1968.

Open Closed Open. Translated by Chana Bloch and Chana Kronfeld. New York: Harcourt, 2000.

The Selected Poetry of Yehuda Amichai. Translated by Chana Bloch and Stephen Mitchell. Berkeley and Los Angeles: University of California Press, 1996.

The World Is a Room and Other Stories by Yehuda Amichai. Translated by Yosef Schachter. Philadelphia: Jewish Publication Society of America, 1984.

Yehuda Amichai: A Life of Poetry, 1948–1994. Edited and translated by Benjamin Harshav and Barbara Harshav. New York: HarperCollins, 1994.

ARCHIVAL SOURCES

A[michai], Yehuda. Holocaust Testimony (HVT-2679). Interview conducted by Geoffrey Hartman and Benjamin Harshav, November 3, 1994. Fortunoff Video Archive for Holocaust Testimonies, Yale University Library, New Haven, Conn.

Amichai, Yehuda. Letters to Ruth Z., 1947–1948. Will be housed at Hayisre'elim harishonim (First Israelis Archive), Heksherim: The Research Center for Jewish and Israeli Literature and Culture, Ben-Gurion University of the Negev.

Dokumentationszentrum fuer juedische Geschichte und Kultur Wuerzburg (Documentation Center for Jewish History and Culture, Wuerzburg).

Gemeindearchiv Giebelstadt (Community Archive of Giebelstadt).

Staatsarchiv Wuerzburg (State Archive of Wuerzburg).

Stadarchiv Wuerzburg (City Archive of Wuerzburg).

Yehuda Amichai Papers. General Collection, Beinecke Rare Book and Manuscript Library, Yale University, New Haven, Conn.

SECONDARY SOURCES

Abramson, Glenda, ed. *The Experienced Soul*. Boulder, Colo.: Westview Press, 1997.

Abramson, Glenda. *The Writing of Yehuda Amichai: A Thematic Approach*. Albany: SUNY Press, 1989.

Amati-Mehler, Jacqueline. "La langue exilée." *Revue française de psychanalyse* (March 1993): 917–25.

Amati-Mehler, Jacqueline, Simona Argentieri, and Jorge Canestri. *The Babel of the Unconscious: Mother Tongue and Foreign Languages in the Psychoanalytic Dimension*. Translated by Whitelaw Cucco. Madison, Conn.: International University Press, 1993.

Arad, Aryeh. "Bells Announcing Bad Tidings: The Poet Yehuda Amichai Tells of His Childhood in Southern Germany." *Bamahane* (n.d. [mid-1960s?]): 18–19, 39.

Arpali, Boaz. *Haperahim veha'agartal* (The Flowers and the Urn: Amichai's Poetry 1948–1968). Tel Aviv: Hakibbutz Hameuchad, 1986.

Arpaly, Boaz [Boaz Arpali]. "On the Political Significance of Amichai's Poetry." In Abramson, ed., *The Experienced Soul*, 27–50.

Bachmann, Erich, Burkard von Roda, and Werner Helmberger. *Residenz und Hofgarten Wuerzburg*. 13th ed. Munich: Bayerische Verw., 2001.

Barzel, Hillel. "The Existential Trend in Our Poetry." *Ha'aretz*, November 25, 1960.

Benning, Corinna. Interview with Amichai. Bavarian Radio Station BR Alpha, May 4, 1998. Transcribed in Leo, *Zwischen Erinnern und Vergessen*, 247–57.

Berlinger, Simon. "ILBA—Wuerzburg: Rueckblick eines Absolventen." In *"Denn das Sterben des Menschen hoert nie auf . . .": Aspekte juedischen Lebens in Vergangenheit und Gegenwart*, edited by Ulrich Wagner, 45–72. Wuerzburg, Germany: Schriften des Stadtarchivs Wuerzburg. Heft 11, 1997.

Bialik, Chaim Nachman. "Im dimdumey hahama" (At Twilight). In Burnshaw, Carmi, and Spicehandler, eds., *The Modern Hebrew Poem Itself*, 28–30.

Bialik, Hayim Nahman (Chaim Nachman Bialik). *Hashirim* (The Poems). Edited by Avner Holtzman. Tel Aviv: Dvir, 2004.

Bluwstein, Rahel. *Shirat Rahel* (The Poetry of Rahel). Tel Aviv: Davar, 1964.

Bronowsky, Yoram. Obituary of Yehuda Amichai. *Ha'aretz*, September 22, 2000.

Burnshaw, Stanley, T. Carmi, and Ezra Spicehandler, eds. *The Modern Hebrew Poem Itself*. Cambridge, Mass.: Harvard University Press, 1989.

Carmel-Flumin, Nili. "A Day of Hebrew Poetry in Washington." Interview with Amichai. *Yedi'ot Aharonot*, May 31, 1985.

Chertok, Haim. "A Conversation with Yehuda Amichai." *Jewish Frontier* (June / July 1985): 15.

Cixous, Hélène. *Three Steps on the Ladder of Writing*. Translated by Sarah Cornell and Susan
    Seller. New York: Columbia University Press, 1993.
Cohen, Boaz. "Don't Call Me a National Poet." Interview with Amichai. *Yedi'ot Aharonot*,
    September 24, 2000.
Cooper-Weill, Judy. "A Day in the Life of Yehuda Amichai." *Newsview*, January 23–29, 1985.
Daxelmueller, Christoph, and Roland Flade. *Ruth hat auf einer schwarzen Floete gespielt:*
    Geschichte, Alltag und Kultur der Juden in Wuerzburg. Wuerzburg, Germany: Echter Verlag,
    2005.
Dettelbacher, Werner. *Damals in Wuerzburg: Bildokumente aus der Zeit von 1914–1945*.
    Wuerzburg, Germany: Stuertz Verlag, 1971.
———. "Die Geschichte des Ludwig Pfeuffer." In Steidle, *Ein kleines Geburtstagspraesent aus*
    Wuerzburg, 9–11.
———. "Jugendjahre in der Sanderau und im Frauenland." In Flade, *Meine Jugend in*
    Wuerzburg, 99–124.
Eban, Abba. *Abba Eban: An Autobiography*. New York: Random House, 1977.
Eliot, T. S. *The Sacred Wood: Essays on Poetry and Criticism*. London: Methuen, 1920.
———. *The Waste Land*. In *The Complete Poems and Plays*, 37–55. New York: Harcourt Brace,
    1967.
Eschwege, Laura R. "A Once in a Lifetime Trip." *Jewish Press*, March 7, 1980.
Evron, Ram. Interview with Amichai. Israeli Television, 1998.
Fifer, William P., and Christine Moon. "The Role of the Mother's Voice in the
    Organization of Brain Function in the Newborn." *Acta Paediatrica* supplement, no. 397
    (June 1994): 86–93.
Flade, Roland. *Die Wuerzburger Juden*. Wuerzburg, Germany: Stuertz Verlag, 1987.
Flade, Roland, ed. *Meine Jugend in Wuerzburg*. Wuerzburg, Germany: Mainpresse
    Zeitungsverlags Gesellschaft, 2000.
Frank, Leonhard. *Die Raeuberbande*. Stuttgart, Germany: Walter Jens und Marcel Reich-
    Ranicki, 1975.
Freud, Sigmund. "On Femininity." In *New Introductory Lectures on Psycho-Analysis* (1933a
    [1932]). Standard ed., vol. 22, chap. 33, 112–35.
Fuchs, Esther. "I Am a Man Who Writes Poems." Interview with Amichai. In *Encounters*
    with Israeli Authors, edited by Fuchs, 86–92. Marblehead, Mass.: Micah, 1982.
Furstenberg, Rochelle. "Poet Revolutionary." *Jerusalem Report*, December 1, 1994, 42–47.
Gilan, Maxim. "The World of Desire of Yehuda Amichai." *Lamerhav*, September 4, 1959.
    Quoted and summarized in Tzvik, *Yehuda Amichai*, 20.
Gold, Nili Scharf. "And the Vows Are Not Vows: On Amichai's Later Poetry." *Siman Kri'a*,
    Tel Aviv University, no. 22 (1991): 361–378.
———. "And the Migration of My Parents Has Not Subsided in Me: Yehuda Amichai." In
    Middle Eastern Literatures: Incorporating EdebiYat 8, no. 2 (July 2005), 171–85.

———. "Betrayal of the Mother Tongue in the Creation of National Identity." In *Ideology and Jewish Identity in Israeli and American Literature*, edited by Emily Miller Budick, 235–58. Albany: SUNY Press, 2001.

———. "The 'Feminine' in Amichai's Poetics." In Abramson, *The Experienced Soul*, 77–92.

———. "Images in Transformation in the Recent Poetry of Yehuda Amichai." *Prooftexts* 4 (1984): 141–52.

———. *Lo kabrosh: gilgule imagim vetavniyot beshirat Yehuda Amichai* (Not Like a Cypress: Transformations of Images and Structures in the Poetry of Yehuda Amichai). Tel Aviv: Schocken, 1994.

———. *Transformation of Images and Structures in the Poetry of Yehuda Amichai*. PhD diss., Jewish Theological Seminary of America, 1990.

Goldberg, Lea. "'Ad barzel': On Yehuda Amichai; Upon Receiving the Shlonsky Prize." *Al Hamishmar*, July 26, 1957. Quoted in Shaked, "Amichai and the Likrat Group," 104–5.

———. "Tel Aviv, 1935." In Burnshaw, Carmi, and Spicehandler, eds., *The Modern Hebrew Poem Itself*, 130–31.

Goldschmidt, Arthur, and Lawrence Davidson. *A Concise History of the Middle East*. Boulder, Colo.: Westview Press, 2006.

Greipl, Egon Johannes, ed. *Fenster zur Vergangenheit*. Munich: Bayerisches Landesamt fuer Denkmalpflege, 2004.

Gussow, Mel. "Yehuda Amichai, Poet Who Turned Israel's Experience into Verse, Dies at 76." *New York Times*, September 23, 2000.

Hahn, Elmar, and Joseph Kern. *Wuerzburg*. Wuerzburg, Germany: Elmar Habn, 1999.

Halter, Aloma. "Poems, Prayers and Psalms." Interview with Amichai. *Contact* (July 26, 1991): 11–12.

Har-Gil, Shraga. *Alte Liebe Rostet Nie*. Wuerzburg, Germany: Koenigshausen and Neumann, 2004.

Hegele, Wolfgang. *Literaturunterricht und literarisches Leben in Deutschland (1850–1990)*. Wuerzburg, Germany: Historische Darstellung–Systematische Erklaerung, 1996.

Heine, Heinrich. "Der Heimkehr: 1823–1824." Translated by Walter W. Arndt as "Lorelei" in *Songs of Love and Grief: A Bilingual Anthology in the Verse Forms of the Original*, 40–41. Evanston, Ill.: Northwestern University Press, 1995.

Hellmann, Norbert. "Jewish Life in Wuerzburg (Pre–World War II)." *Mitteilungen* (Rosh Hashono 5755 [1995]): 25–30.

Hoffman, Richard. "Lullaby for Miriam." Annenberg Rare Book and Manuscript Library, University of Pennsylvania, Philadelphia.

Hollander-Steingart, Rahel. "In My Heart Is a Museum." Interview with Amichai. *Jerusalem Post, Rosh Hashanah Supplement*, September 28, 1981.

Hubala, Erich, Otto Mayer, and Wolf Christian von der Muelbe. *Die Residenz zu Wuerzburg*. Wuerzburg, Germany: Edition Popp, 1984.

Hughes, Ted, and Daniel Weissbort, eds. *Modern Poetry in Translation*, no. 1. London: Cape Goliard, 1965.

"Interview with Yehuda Amichai." *Jerusalem Post*, July 26, 1991.

"Israelischer Autor mit Erinnerung an Wurzburg." *Voklksblatt*, August 5, 1991.

Kahana-Carmon, Amalia. "She Writes Nicely, But Only about That Which Is Marginal." *Yedi'ot Aharonot*, January 25, 1988.

Karpel, Dahlia. "Hoping for the Nobel Prize." Interview with Amichai. *Ha'ir*, November 3, 1989.

Kartun-Blum, Ruth. *Profane Scriptures: Reflections on the Dialogue with the Bible in Modern Hebrew Literature*. Cincinnati, Ohio: Hebrew Union College Press, 1999.

Katzenelson, Gidon. "Only Now or Also Tomorrow." *Ha'aretz*, June 11, 1959. Quoted and summarized in Tzvik, *Yehuda Amichai*, 19.

Klein, Idit, Judith Rosenbaum, and Tanya Schlam. "The Joy of the Struggle: A Talk with Yehuda Amichai." *Urim vetumim: A Student Quarterly of Yale's Jewish Community* 6, no. 2 (winter 1991): 28.

Kurzweil, Baruch. "Autobiographic Poetry in the Great Desert." *Ha'aretz*, July 12, 1963.

Lacan, Jacques. *Le moi dans la théorie de Freud et dans la technique de la psychoanalyse (1954–55)*. Edited by Jacques-Alain Miller. Paris: Éditions de Seuil, 1978. Translated by Sylvana Tomaselli as *The Ego in Freud's Theory and the Technique of Psycholanalysis: 1954–1955*. New York: W. W. Norton, 1988.

———. *Les écrits techniques de Freud (1953–54)*. Edited by Jacques-Alain Miller. Paris: Éditions de Seuil, 1975. Translated by John Forrester as *Freud's Papers on Technique: 1953–1954*. New York: W. W. Norton, 1988.

Leo, Christian. *Zwischen Erinnern und Vergessen: Jehuda Amichais Roman "Nicht von jetzt, nicht von hier" im philosophischen und literarischen Kontext*. Wuerzburg, Germany: Koenigshausen und Neumann, 2004.

Lichtenbaum, Y. Unsigned review of "Bagina hatsiburit" (In the Public Garden), by Amichai. *Haboker*, August 14, 1959. Quoted and summarized in Tzvik, *Yehuda Amichai*, 19–20.

Loschuetz, Gerd. "Wie lange koennen Erinnerungen standhalten?" *Frankfurter Rundschau*, February 2, 1992.

Lossin, Yigal. *Pillar of Fire*. Edited by Carol S. Halberstadt. Translated by Zvi Ofer. Jerusalem: Shikmona, 1983.

Madaule, Paul. *When Listening Comes Alive: A Guide to Effective Learning and Communication*. Norval, Ontario, Canada: Moulin, 1993.

Meged, Eyal. "Towards the End You Become Simpler." *Yedi'ot Aharonot*, November 8, 1985.

Mehler, Jacques. "Language in the Infant's Mind." *Philosophical Transactions of the Royal Society of London* 346, no. 1315 (1994): 13–20.

Mendelssohn, Zehava. Interview with Amichai. *Jerusalem Post Magazine*, February 12, 1971.

Michali, B. Y. *Pri ha'aretz* (Fruit of the Land). Tel Aviv: Agudat Hasofrim and Masada, 1966.

Miro, Michael. "Writing Is the Product of Wonderful Laziness." Interview with Amichai. *Pi Ha'aton*, March 19, 1978.

Miron, Dan. *Hapreda min ha'ani he'ani* (Taking Leave of the Impoverished Self: Ch. N. Bialik's Early Poetry 1891–1901). Tel Aviv: Open University, 1986.

———. *Mul ha'ah hashotek* (Facing the Silent Brother: Essays on the Poetry of the War of Independence). Jerusalem: Keter, 1992.

Moi, Toril. *Sexual / Textual Politics: Feminist Literary Theory*. London: Methuen, 1985.

Moked, Gabriel. "In the Public Garden." *Yedi'ot Aharonot*, September 18, 1959. Quoted in Tzvik, *Yehuda Amichai*, 19.

Montenegro, David. Interview with Amichai. *American Poetry Review* (November / December 1987).

Morris, Benny. "Power of Imagination." *Jerusalem Post, 40th Independence Day Magazine*, April 20, 1988.

Müller, Karlheinz. *Die Wuerzburger Judengemeinde im Mittelalter*. Wuerzburg, Germany: Freunde Mainfränkischer Kunst und Geschichte, 2004.

Nagid, Hayim. "I Think That This Land Is Paradise for Poets." Interview with Amichai. *Ma'ariv*, April 15, 1977.

Nisim, Kobi. Interview with Amichai. *Al Hamishmar*, June 5, 1992.

Omer, Dan. "In This Burning Country, Words Must Serve as Shade." Series of interviews with Amichai. *Proza*, no. 25 (July 1978): 4–11.

Pagis, Dan. *Kol hashirim* (Collected Poems). Jerusalem: Hakibbutz Hameuchad and Mosad Bialik, 1991.

———. "The Pain of Two Homelands." In *Mihuts lashura* (Outside of the Line: Essays and Notes on Modern Hebrew Poetry), edited by Hanan Hever, 84–95. Tel Aviv: Keshev Leshira, 2003.

R. H. "Auch die Erinnerung ist Gegenwart." *Koelner Stadt-Anzeiger*, September 25, 1992.

Raim, Edith. "Verfolgung und Exil der Juedischen Familie Hanover aus Wuerzburg." *Mainfraenkisches Jahrbuch fuer Geschichte und Kunst*, no. 56. Wuerzburg, Germany: Freunde Mainfraenkischer Kunst and Geschichte E.V., 2004, 317–37.

Reichmann, Edgar. "Yehuda Amichai Talks to Edgar Reichmann." *Unesco Courier* 47, no. 10 (October 1994): 5–7.

Re'uveni, Yotam. "Yehuda Amichai: This Is the Place." Interview with Amichai. *Yedi'ot Aharonot*, May 1985.

Rentner, Georg. *Wesenszuege und Wandlungen des literarischen Kanons in den deutschen Volksschulbuechern*. Frankfurt on Main: Hrsg. und eingeletet von Joachim S. Hohmann, 1993.

Riffaterre, Michael. *Semiotics of Poetry*. Bloomington: Indiana University Press, 1978.

Rilke, Rainer Maria. *The Book of Images*. Translated by Edward Snow. New York: North Point Press, 1991.

———. *The Lay of Love and Death of Coronet Christopher Rilke*. Translated by Alfred Perles. 1899. Reprint, London: Turret Books, 1987.

———. *Letters to a Young Poet*. Translated by M. D. Herter Norton. New York: W. W. Norton, 1934.

Sachar, Howard Morely. *The Course of Modern Jewish History*. New York: Dell, 1958.

Sadan-Lubenstein, Nili. "Imagistic Patterns in the Poetry of Amichai." *Iton 77* (September 1983; October 1983): 89–99.

Sandbank, Shimon. "Amichai: The Playing and the Abundance." *Lamerhav*, June 3, 1969. Reprinted in Tzvik, *Yehuda Amichai*, 105–14.

———. *Shete berekhot baya'ar* (Two Pools in the Forest). Tel Aviv: Hakibbutz Hameuchad, 1976.

Scheibe, Wolfgang. *Die Reformpaedagogische Bewegung 1900–1932: Eine einfuehrende Darstellung*. 9th ed. Basel: Weinheim, 1994.

Schulke, Claudia. "Spurensuche und lyrisches Ich." *Frankfurter Allgemeiner Zeitung*, February 23, 1992.

Schultz, Hans Jürgen, ed. *Mein Judentum*. Stuttgart: Kreuz, 1978.

Schwabacher, John R., and Susan Wolfe. *Remembering*. New York: iUniverse, 2003.

Sey, Angela. Interview with Amichai. *Das Aktuelle* (1992): 17.

Shaked, Gershon. "Amichai and the Likrat Group: The Early Amichai and His Literary Reference Group." In Abramson, *The Experienced Soul*, 93–20.

———. *Gal hadash basiporet ha'ivrit* (A New Wave in Hebrew Fiction). Tel Aviv: Sifriyat Po'alim, 1971.

———. *Hasiporet ha'ivrit 1880–1980* (Hebrew Narrative Fiction: 1880–1980). Vol. 4. Tel Aviv and Jerusalem: Hakibbutz Hameuchad and Keter, 1988.

Shakespeare, William. *Hamlet*. Edited by Ann Thompson and Neil Taylor. 3rd ed. London: Arden Shakespeare, 2006.

Shamir, Moshe, Shlomo Tanay, and Azriel U'chmani, eds. *Dor ba'aretz* (A Generation in the Land). Tel Aviv: Sifriyat Po'alim, 1958.

Siegel, Andrea. Lecture presented at the annual meeting of the Association for Jewish Studies, Boston, Mass., December 16, 2001.

Skiera, Ehrenhard. *Reformpaedagogik in Geschichte und Gegenwart: Eine kritische Einfuehrung*. Munich: Wien, 2003.

Spranger, Eduard. *Pestalozzis Denkformen*. Heidelberg: Quelle und Meyer Verlag, 1959.

Stadtler, Bea. "The Story of an Israeli Soldier-Poet." *The Cleveland Jewish News*, April 7, 1967.

Steidle, Hans, ed. *Ein kleines Geburtstagspraesent aus Wuerzburg: Festgabe fuer Jehuda Amichai zum 75 Geburtstag*. Wuerzburg, Germany: Verlag der Leonhard Frank-Gesellschaft, 1999.

Steidle, Hans. *Jakob Stoll und die Israelitische Lehrerbildungsanstalt: Eine Spurensuche Israelitische Kultusgemeinde Wuerzburg*. Wuerzburg, Germany: Koenigshausen und Neumann, 2003.

———. "Rueckkehr an einen Ort, an den man nicht zurueckkehren kann." In Steidle, ed., *Ein kleines Geburtstagspraesent aus Wuerzburg*, 12–40.

Straetz, Reiner. *Biographisches Handbuch Wuerzburger Juden 1900–1945.* Wuerzburg, Germany: Verlag Ferdinand Schoeningh, 1989.

Tomatis, Alfred. *L'oreille et le Langage.* Norval, Ontario, Canada: Moulin, 1996.

Tzifer, Beni. "Two Scales, Major and Minor, Gilboa and Amichai." *Ha'aretz*, November 13, 1981.

Tzvik, Yehudit. "Dates and Turning Points in Amichai's Life." In Tzvik, *Yehuda Amichai*, 237–39.

Tzvik, Yehudit, ed. *Yehuda Amichai: mivhar ma'amare bikoret al yetsirato* (Yehuda Amichai: A Selection of Critical Essays on His Writings). Tel Aviv: Hakibbutz Hameuchad, 1988.

Verny, Thomas R. *The Secret Life of the Unborn Child.* New York: Summit Books, 1981.

Walk, Joseph. *Juedische Schule und Erziehung im Dritten Reich.* Frankfurt on Main: Hain Verlag, 1991.

Wieseltier, Leon. "Yehuda Amichai: Posthumous Fragments." *New York Times*, November 21, 2004.

Wilhelm, Theodor. "Der reformpaedagogische Impuls: Bildungspolitik, Schulreform, Bildungsreform am Beginn der Zwanziger Jahre." In *"Neue Erziehung"–"Neue Menschen" Ansaetze zur Erziehungs*, edited by Ulrich Herrmann, 177–99. Basel: Weinheim, 1987.

———. *Paedagogik der Gegenwart.* 4th ed. Stuttgart: Kroener Verlag, 1967.

Wiltmann, Ingrid. *Nur Ewigkeit ist kein Exil: Lebensgeschichten aus Israel; Mit einem Nachwort von Anat Feinberg.* Moehlin, Switzerland: Rausreif, 1997.

Wolfgang von Goethe, Johann. *The Poems of Goethe.* Translated by E. A. Bowring. Boston: S. E. Cassino, 1882.

Zach, Nathan. "The Light Muse." *Davar*, August 28, 1959.

Zehavi, Alex. "Poetry as Consolation." Interview with Amichai. *Davar*, May 7, 1976.

Index

"Elegy on an Abandoned Village" (Amichai), 126, 314–22, 346–49, 423n14

"Elegy on the Lost Child" (Amichai), 56–62, 326–35

Eliot, T. S.: and Amichai's exposure to modern poetry, 159; influence on "In the Public Garden," 263–64, 306; influence on "Not Like a Cypress," 308–309; letters to Ruth Z. and development of Amichai as poet, 292, 419n71, 421n112; and reality as mosaic, 304–307; and references to *Hamlet*, 414n78, 418n52

emotional role, of German language, 127–30, 132–33, 142–43, 150, 386n123

"Empty Lot, The" (Amichai), 254–55

environment. *See* landscape; nature

eroticism, of "In the Public Garden," 244, 253–54. *See also* sexual imagery

Eschwege, Henry, 73

Eschwege, Ruben Moses, 28

Europe, references to cities and history of, 52–53. *See also* Germany

Even the Fist Was Once an Open Palm and Fingers (Amichai 1989), 22

"Farewell" (Amichai), 164, 165, 170

father: in *Not of This Time, Not of This Place*, 131–32; and poetic imagery, 149; portrayal of in "Ibn Gabirol," 51–52; relationship with, 130. *See also* "A Meeting with My Father"; Pfeuffer, Friedrich Moritz; "The Times My Father Died"

fire, and imagery in "We Loved Here," 237, 238

"First Love" (Amichai), 99

"First Snow" (Amichai), 129–30

folktales and folksongs, 37, 113, 133–34, 140–41. *See also* Andersen, Hans Christian; *Grimm Brothers Collection of Folktales*

fragmentation: and influence of T. S. Eliot, 306; and style of "In the Public Garden," 244, 246

"From Chance to Fate" (Amichai), 279

"From a Letter" (Amichai), 126–27

"From the Poems of Tiberias" (Amichai), 227

gardens. *See* Hofgarten; "In the Public Garden"

gates: and childhood memories of Wuerzburg, 35, 53–54, 185; images of in *Not of This Time, Not of This Place*, 70–71, 87; and metaphor of closing, 141, 371n26

genres: and "Binyamina, 1947" sonnets, 210, 218–19; and "In the Public Garden" as innovation, 246, 265; and strategy of camouflage, 48, 62; and use of German language, 106

"Geometry Exercises" (Amichai), 129

German language: and education as child, 37; and "Elegy on an Abandoned Village," 319–20, 321; and "Elegy on the Lost Child," 60–62; and love affair with Ruth Z., 194; and notes to self, 55; and reinterpretation of poetry, 16–18, 24; and strategies of camouflage, 101–50; and use of past tense, 405n51. *See also* translation

Germany: and antisemitism before World War II, 27, 35, 368n181; childhood and landscape of southern, 34; and education during Weimar Republic, 38; and landscape imagery, 116; Zeitgeist of in 1930s, 174. *See* Gersfeld; Holocaust; Nazis; Wuerzburg

Gersfeld, Germany, 28, 32, 34, 217, 359n27

Gerusalemme (ship), 151

Geula School (Haifa), 271–72, 276, 278, 284

Gilan, Maxim, 243, 245

holidays (Jewish), and Amichai's childhood in Germany, 40–41. See also *bikkurim*; Hanukkah; "Hanukkah"; Yom Kippur

Holle Kreisch (German Jewish folk tradition), 72, 374n112

Holocaust: allusions to in "Elegy on the Lost Child," 59–60; Little Ruth as symbol of, 93–94, 97; references to in *Not to Remember*, 95; references to in *Not of This Time, Not of This Place*, 62, 67, 68, 76, 88, 91, 98, 375n124

homeland, and German language, 58

Horn, Tamar (first wife), 220, 227, 241, 406n73, 407n88

Hughes, Ted, 10

"Ibn Gabirol" (Amichai), 51–52

identity: and Amichai as adolescent, 102; Amichai's development of national, 267–68, 269; conflict of in "Elegy on the Lost Child," 61; and Israeli landscape in Amichai's poetry, 54–55; Zionist ideology and Israeli national, 12, 13. *See also* self

imagery. *See* alienation; body; father; music; semaphore; sexual imagery; travel; visual imagery

immigration: and British administration of Palestine during 1930s, 102, 368n191; depictions of experience, 105, 160–78, 385n110, 395n8; and "Elegy on an Abandoned Village," 322; and image of birds, 396n18; and linguistic struggle in modern Hebrew literature, 102–103, 116–17; of Pfeuffer family to Palestine, 7, 45–46, 151–52; question about date of Amichai's, 21, 368n193, 394–95n4

individual, emphasis on voice of in poetry, 9

"In the Public Garden" (Amichai): and camouflage, 242, 410n50; and development as poet, 276, 297; and images of everyday life, 304; influence of T. S. Eliot on, 263–64, 306; and letters to Ruth Z., 291; and love affair with Ruth Z., 237, 243–66, 405n65; public response to, 200; Rilke's "Love Song" and image of violin in, 112–113, 301; and U.N. decision on partition of Palestine, 207–208

"In a Right Angle" (Amichai), 95

"Instructions for Her Voyage" (Amichai), 49

"In Yemin Moshe" (Amichai), 51, 54

Irgun (military organization), 198, 201, 401n44

Israel: and Amichai's self-portrayal, 10–14, 106, 192; and Amichai's transformation into patriot during 1947-1948 in Haifa, 267–89; and Declaration of Independence, 240, 277; and images of landscape in Amichai's works, 109–10, 116; and view of Amichai as quintessential Israeli, 10–11. *See also* Haifa; immigration; Jerusalem; Palestine; War of Independence; Zionism

Israeli literature: Amichai's influence on, 7, 265; use of term, 355n28. *See also* Hebrew literature

Israel Prize, 10, 403n11

"It Has Been a While since They Asked" (Amichai), 14

"I Want to Die in My Own Bed" (Amichai), 286–88, 308, 310, 342–43

"I Write from Right to Left" (Amichai), 121–22

Jerusalem: and adolescence, 154; and love affair with Ruth Z., 197–98; and references to childhood, 50, 51;

Jerusalem (continued)
    references to in Poems: 1948–1962, 55;
    and setting of "In the Public Garden,"
    248–49. See also Israel
Jewish community: and Memorbuch, 137; of
    Wuerzburg, 27, 46, 71–74, 320, 358n8,
    387n164. See also Judaism
Judaism, and Amichai's adolescence in Pal-
    estine, 156. See also havdalah; holidays;
    Jewish community; prayer; synagogue

Kafka, Franz, 157
Katzmann, Ernestina, 42
Katzmann, Ruth (cousin), 34, 39, 42,
    155, 183
Kehila Kedosha (holy congregation), 71–72
kibbutz, 204–205, 316–17, 422n8
Kleemann, Lore, 36, 133, 134, 135
Kleine Nitze (Wuerzburg), 30
Kristallnacht, 95

landscape: allusions to European in Poems:
    1948–1962, 54, 56, 58; and allusions to
    Jerusalem in "In Yemin Moshe," 51; in
    "Binyamina, 1947" sonnets, 212; and
    Israeli identity, 54–55; and use of Ger-
    man language, 109–10, 116; in "We
    Loved Here" sonnets, 235–36. See also
    nature; water
language. See German language; Hebrew
    language; past tense; translation
Lasker-Schueler, Elsa, 154, 157
Lehmann, Max, 42
"Lekha Dodi" (Amichai), 38
Leo, Christian, 62–63, 81, 387–88n163–65
letters, between Amichai and Ruth Z: and
    association between travel and parting,
    164; author's discovery of, 2, 4, 369n7;
    and "Binyamina, 1947" sonnets, 209–19;
    "In the Public Garden" and prose of,

245, 247–66; and making of Amichai
    as poet, 290–312; and references to
    childhood, 49, 56, 82, 90; as record of
    love affair, 192; and reinterpretation
    of poetry, 23–24, 314, 316; and strategy
    of camouflage, 20, 22; and transforma-
    tion of Amichai from immigrant child
    into Israeli patriot, 267–89; and use of
    German language, 107–16, 194; and
    "We Loved Here" sonnets, 219, 226,
    227–28, 242
literary sketches, letters to Ruth Z. as, 291,
    294–97
"Little Match Girl, The" (Andersen), 37,
    114
"Little Mermaid" (Andersen), 81–82
Little Ruth. See Hanover, Ruth
"Little Ruth" (Amichai), 96–100, 170, 336–
    39, 398n64
loneliness, as theme in poetry, 111, 128–29
"Lorelei, The" (Heine), 135–36, 137
love: association between language and ro-
    mantic, 118–19; and memory in "Elegy
    on the Lost Child," 57–58, 371n37. See
    also love affair
love affair, between Amichai and Ruth Z.:
    chronology of, 2–5, 191–208; descrip-
    tions of in "Binyamina, 1947" and "We
    Loved Here" sonnets, 209–42; impact
    of on poetry, 8; and publication of "In
    the Public Garden," 243–66
"Love Song" (Rilke), 111–12, 247–48
"Lullaby for Miriam" (Beer-Hofmann),
    109–10

Ma'aleh High School (Jerusalem), 157
Mas, Danny, 114, 280
masculine/feminine dichotomy, in "Not
    Like a Cypress," 308–10
May, Karl, 42, 152

"Meeting with My Father, A" (Amichai), 148–49, 297

Meltzer, Feival, 157

memory: and love in "Elegy on the Lost Child," 57–58; and *Memorbuch* in Jewish community, 137; and use of German language, 129

"Metamorphoses" (Amichai), 93

military. *See* army; War of Independence

Miron, Dan, 63, 131, 138, 167, 385n122

modernism, and influence of T. S. Eliot on Amichai, 305

Moked, Gabriel, 243

Morgenstern, Christian, 108–109, 302, 381n36, 381n38

mosaic, and view of reality, 304–307

motivation: for concealment of past, 47; for linguistic conversion of immigrants, 105

Moznayim (literary journal), 121

mundane, introduction of into Hebrew literature by Amichai, 211–12, 221–22, 304

music: and childhood, 38, 68, 69; and imagery "In the Public Garden," 112–13, 247, 248, 301; and imagery in *Not of This Time*, 93, 377n191; love of classical, 301–302; and writings on violence and war, 282

name: and childhood in Germany, 26, 28; and immigration to Israel, 101–102, 151; Ruth Z. choice of Hebrew, 2–3, 205–206; and strategy of camouflage, 21

narrative, and letters to Ruth Z, 115, 294–97

nationalism, in "I Want to Die in My Bed," 286–88

national poet, Amichai's status as, 8. *See also* Israel

nature: and imagery in "Binyamina, 1947" sonnets, 213; and language in "First Snow," 129. *See also* landscape

Nazis, and childhood in Germany, 13, 42–46, 85–86, 367n168, 368n180–81, 368n187

Netsah Israel School (Petah Tikva), 153

"New Hebrews," image of, 102

"Not Like a Cypress" (Amichai), 307–12, 344–45

Not to Remember (Amichai 1971), 95

Not of This Time, Not of This Place (Amichai 1963): autobiographical references in, 45, 48, 62–100; critical literature on, 8; and emigration, 160–61; and German language, 131–45, 386n123, 386n140; Little Ruth as protagonist of, 20; revenge plot of, 45, 64–65, 84, 132

Now and in Other Days (Amichai 1955), 50, 219, 243, 407n88

Now in the Storm: Poems 1963–1968 (Amichai), 161

"Now, When the Water Presses Hard" (Amichai), 123

Ofek, Rina Reznikov, 270–71, 272, 278, 414n64

"On the Day You Left" (Amichai), 303

"On Every High Hill" (Amichai), 122–23

"On the Road to the Negev, 1948" (Amichai), 403n17

Open Closed Open (Amichai 1998), 23

organizations. *See* Hagana; Irgun; Palmah; youth organizations

"Other Evenings" (Amichai), 4, 265

Palestine: and adolescence of Amichai, 151–59; British policy on immigration to, 198, 368n191; emigration of Pfeuffer family to, 7, 45–46; and immigrant refugees during 1930s, 102; United Nations Special Committee and partition of, 207, 275;